The Three-Tiered Approach to the Study of Collective Bargaining and Industrial Relations

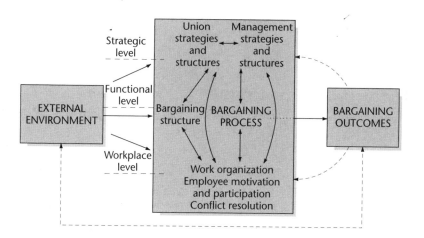

An Introduction to Collective Bargaining and Industrial Relations

An Introduction to Collective Bargaining and Industrial Relations

Fourth Edition

Harry C. Katz
Cornell University

Thomas A. Kochan
Massachusetts Institute of Technology

Alexander J. S. Colvin
Pennsylvania State University

McGraw-Hill
Irwin

Boston   Burr Ridge, IL   Dubuque, IA   New York   San Francisco   St. Louis
Bangkok   Bogotá   Caracas   Kuala Lumpur   Lisbon   London   Madrid   Mexico City
Milan   Montreal   New Delhi   Santiago   Seoul   Singapore   Sydney   Taipei   Toronto

McGraw-Hill
Irwin

AN INTRODUCTION TO COLLECTIVE BARGAINING & INDUSTRIAL RELATIONS

Published by McGraw-Hill/Irwin, a business unit of The McGraw-Hill Companies, Inc., 1221 Avenue of the Americas, New York, NY, 10020. Copyright © 2008 by The McGraw-Hill Companies, Inc. All rights reserved. No part of this publication may be reproduced or distributed in any form or by any means, or stored in a database or retrieval system, without the prior written consent of The McGraw-Hill Companies, Inc., including, but not limited to, in any network or other electronic storage or transmission, or broadcast for distance learning.

Some ancillaries, including electronic and print components, may not be available to customers outside the United States.

This book is printed on acid-free paper.

1 2 3 4 5 6 7 8 9 0 DOC/DOC 0 9 8 7

ISBN 978-0-07-313715-5
MHID 0-07-313715-4

Editorial director: *Brent Gordon*
Executive editor: *John Weimeister*
Managing developmental editor: *Laura Hurst Spell*
Editorial assistant: *Heather Darr*
Editorial assistant: *Sara Knox Hunter*
Associate marketing manager: *Kelly Odom*
Project manager: *Dana M. Pauley*
Production supervisor: *Gina Hangos*
Lead designer: *Matthew Baldwin*
Senior media project manager: *Susan Lombardi*
Cover design: *Studio Montage, St. Louis, MO*
Typeface: *10/12 Times New Roman*
Compositor: *Laserwords Private Limited*
Printer: *R. R. Donnelley*

Library of Congress Cataloging-in-Publication Data

Katz, Harry Charles, 1951-
    An introduction to collective bargaining and industrial relations / Harry C. Katz,
Thomas A. Kochan, Alexander J. S. Colvin.—4th ed.
        p. cm.
    Includes index.
    Includes bibliographical references and index.
    ISBN-13: 978-0-07-313715-5 (alk. paper)
    ISBN-10: 0-07-313715-4 (alk. paper)
    1. Collective bargaining. 2. Industrial relations. I. kochan, Thomas A.
II. Colvin, Alexander James. III. Title.
HD6971.5.K38 2008
331.89—dc22
                                                                2007013506

www.mhhe.com

To our many teachers

About the Authors

Harry C. Katz is the Dean and Jack Sheinkman Professor of Collective Bargaining at Cornell University's School of Industrial and Labor Relations (ILR). His major publications include: *Converging Divergences: Worldwide Changes in Employment Systems* (with Owen Darbishire), 2000, *Telecommunications: Restructuring Work and Employment Relations Worldwide*, 1997; and *Shifting Gears: Changing Labor Relations in the U.S. Automobile Industry,* 1985. Professor Katz received his Ph.D. in Economics from the University of California at Berkeley in 1977.

Thomas A. Kochan is the George M. Bunker Professor of Management at MIT's Sloan School of Management. Kochan is a past president of the Industrial Relations Research Association (IRRA). In 1996, he received the Heneman Career Achievement Award. From 1993 to 1995 he served on the Clinton Administration's Commission on the Future of Worker/Management Relations, which investigated methods to improve the productivity and global competitiveness of the American workplace. His recent publications include: *After Lean Production: Evolving Employment Practices in the World Auto Industry,* 1997; *Employment Relations in a Changing World Economy,* 1995; and *The Mutual Gains Enterprise,* 1994. Professor Kochan received his Ph.D. in Industrial Relations from the University of Wisconsin in 1973.

Alexander J. S. Colvin is Associate Professor, Labor Studies and Industrial Relations, Pennsylvania State University. He received his Ph.D. in Industrial and Labor Relations from Cornell University in 1999 and his LL.B. from the University of Toronto Faculty of Law in 1992. His current research includes examination of the impact of restructuring in the telecommunications industry on the work organization and employment conditions of employees and managers. Dr. Colvin received the Annual Industrial Relations Research Association Best Dissertation Award for "Citizens and Citadels: Dispute Resolution and the Governance of Employment Relations" for 2000. He also received the John Dunlop Young Scholar Award from the Labor and Employment Relations Association in 2003.

Professors Katz and Kochan (with Robert McKersie) are the co-authors of *The Transformation of American Industrial Relations,* which was awarded the Terry Book Award in 1988 as the most significant contribution to the field of management by the Academy of Management.

Preface

This book provides an introduction to collective bargaining and industrial relations. It is appropriate for students and industrial relations professionals including unionists, managers, and neutrals. The strength of this text lies in its logical coherence and its comprehensive coverage of contemporary developments.

Key Features

The key features of the text include the following:

- A three-tiered strategic choice framework guides the text in a unified manner (presented in Chapter 1).
- A thorough grounding in labor history (Chapter 2) and labor law (Chapter 3) assist students in learning the basics.
- Boldface key terms in text and an end-of-book glossary define the terms.
- Related Web sites are provided at the end of the chapters.
- The influence of business and union strategies is examined in Chapters 5 and 6 with numerous contemporary illustrations.
- The processes of contract negotiation (Chapters 8 and 9) and contract administration (Chapter 11) are considered, with frequent comparisons with nonunion practices and developments. Four grievance arbitration cases covering a range of current issues are offered in Appendix C.
- Thorough analysis of participatory processes and their relationship to collective bargaining are made in Chapter 12.
- The special aspects of collective bargaining in the public sector are spotlighted in Chapter 13.
- A separate chapter on comparative and international issues (Chapter 14) culminates the frequent comparisons made throughout the text. Chapter 14 includes discussion of Japanese, German, Polish, and Korean industrial relations developments; the emergence of a single EU market; the pressures created by multinational corporations; and recent international workers' rights disputes and campaigns.
- Two mock collective bargaining exercises, one in the private sector (involving blue-collar workers) and one in the public sector (involving police officers), are included in Appendixes A and B. Support material is available online at www.mhhe.com/Katz4e that allows students to engage in contract costing and financial forecasting with the private sector bargaining exercise.
- An *Instructor's Resource CD*, which includes an extensive Instructor's Manual, Test Bank, PowerPoint presentation, and Transparency Masters.

Central Themes and Text Organization

The text follows a three-tiered strategic-choice framework. We introduce the reader to collective bargaining by simultaneously moving across and downward through the three tiers of industrial relations activity. We move across the framework by examining how environmental forces shape collective bargaining, then turn to the process of collective bargaining, and continue moving across the framework by analyzing bargaining outcomes. As the discourse moves from the environment to the bargaining process and then to bargaining outcomes, it follows in the tradition of John Dunlop's seminal work, *Industrial Relations Systems.*

The text also moves downward through the three-tiered framework by examining how business and union strategies constrain the process and outcomes of collective bargaining. After considering strategic issues we analyze the middle tier of bargaining, where contract negotiation and administration are so important. Further down we examine workplace issues such as the organization of work and communication procedures. Harry Katz and Tom Kochan (along with Robert McKersie) originally developed this three-tiered framework in our book, *The Transformation of American Industrial Relations,* 2d edition (Ithaca: ILR Press, 1994).

By examining the influence of business and union strategies on industrial relations, this book provides a broader focus than most other introductory texts. Yet, we feel the student must understand the influence of Wall Street, production strategies, union choices, and other strategic forces to accurately comprehend how collective bargaining works in the modern economy. A separate chapter examining participatory processes and their connections to collective bargaining (Chapter 12) is the result of our concern for workplace issues. Worker and union participation programs have become a central part of many labor–management relationships, particularly in the manufacturing sector. Students and professionals must study this development to adequately prepare for the realities they will experience in the industrial relations world.

Our writing on participation is heavily influenced by the findings of our own field research. Nonetheless, in contrast to the *Transformation* book, this text is less prescriptive or predictive. Our goal in this text is to convey the challenges and issues posed by the new participatory processes. We hope that critics of these programs will learn as much from our discussion of these issues as will supporters of the programs.

The focus in this book also is broadened by our concern for international developments. We highlight international comparisons and pressures through examples throughout the text and focus on these issues in a separate chapter (Chapter 14). International events and emergence of a vibrant international workers' rights movement are some of the most exciting developments of the day. Readers should understand the central roles that industrial relations problems and labor unions play in these events.

Extensive coverage of developments in the nonunion sector also distinguishes this book from others. The nonunion sector is important in its own right given the decline in U.S. union membership. Furthermore, analysis of the nonunion sector contributes to an understanding of the pressures and changes occurring within the union sector.

The public sector has increased in importance as unionization has declined in the private sector. We examine the special features of the public sector in Chapter 13.

Our broad focus helps the reader gain a full understanding of collective bargaining. We present numerous illustrations throughout the text, some of which are highlighted as cases.

Knowledge of labor history and labor law help ground the reader in the workings of American collective bargaining. These topics are covered early in the book (Chapters 2 and 3).

Students also can expand their understanding of collective bargaining through the two mock bargaining exercises provided in the appendixes. The first of these exercises involves a fictitious private sector manufacturing firm, "D. G. Barnhouse." Full instructions for this exercise and recommendations gained from our own classroom experience are provided in the *Instructor's Manual*. Student material is available online at www.mhhe.com/Katz4e. This material allows the student (even those with no previous computer experience) to cost Barnhouse contract settlement terms and forecast the financial and employment implications of alternative settlements. We have used this material in our classes and highly recommend it.

The second mock bargaining exercise, provided in Appendix B, involves the police of "Queen City." This exercise gives students a feel for the role that political and urban pressures exert in public sector bargaining.

The four grievance arbitration cases in Appendix C illustrate a range of contemporary developments and enable students to test their skills as third parties.

Instructor's Resource CD

The IRCD includes an Instructor's Manual, Test Bank, PowerPoint, Transparency Masters, and Computerized Test Bank. In addition to suggestions about how to use the mock bargaining exercises and supplementary material for those exercises, the Instructor's Manual includes answers to the end-of-chapter discussion questions, chapter outlines, lecture outlines, and a listing of recommended supplementary films (and videos) and the companies that sell those materials. In our teaching of introductory collective bargaining, we have found that the mock bargaining exercises and films help convey how bargaining really works. We would appreciate hearing your reaction to the text and these materials.

Many of these instructor resources, as well as self-grading student quizzes, are also available through the book's Online Learning Center at www.mhhe.com/katz4e.

Acknowledgments

A number of people assisted in the development of this book and we are deeply grateful to all of them. Ben Whipple developed the remarkably simple contract-costing program available for use with the D. G. Barnhouse mock bargaining exercise. Able research assistance was provided by Dan Zinn, Anne Vanden Boom, and Evan Fried. The staff of Mcgraw-Hill/Irwin, Heather Darr, improved this book in many ways.

We are also thankful for the expert guidance of the following manuscript reviewers: Monica Bielski, University of Arkansas at Little Rock; Joan M. Chapdelaine, Salve Regina University; William Recker, Northern Kentucky University; Barbara Sacks, Webster University.

This book is dedicated to our many teachers. It was they who generated the spark that led us into the field of industrial relations, a field we continue to find stimulating and rewarding. We hope this book can generate similar sparks for the reader.

Harry C. Katz

Thomas A. Kochan

Alexander J. S. Colvin

Contents in Brief

Contents

Part 1

Introduction

1

A Framework for Analyzing Collective Bargaining and Industrial Relations

Whether we are at work or at leisure, we are affected by the conditions under which we work and the rewards we receive for working. Work plays such a central role in our lives and in society that the study of relations between employee and employer cannot be ignored.

This book traces how labor and management, acting either as individuals or as groups, have shaped and continue to shape the employment relationship. Employment is analyzed through the perspective of **industrial relations,** which is the interdisciplinary field of study that concentrates on individual workers, groups of workers and their unions and associations, employers and their organizations, and the environment in which these parties interact.

Industrial relations differs from other disciplines that study work because of its focus on labor and trade unions and on the process of collective bargaining. Thus this book describes how collective bargaining works and helps explain, for example, why it may lead to high wages in one situation and to low wages in another.

The study of industrial relations focuses on the key participants involved in the process, the role of industrial conflict, and the performance of collective bargaining. This chapter defines these various aspects of industrial relations and describes how this book analyzes them.

The Participants

The key participants (or parties) involved in the process of industrial relations are management, labor, and government.[1]

Management

The term **management** refers to those individuals or groups who are responsible for promoting the goals of employers and their organizations. In fact, management encompasses at least three groups: (1) owners and shareholders of an organization, (2) top executives and line managers, and (3) industrial relations and human resource staff professionals who specialize in managing relations with employees and unions. Management plays key roles in negotiating and implementing a firm's industrial relations policies and practices.

Labor

The term **labor** encompasses both employees and the unions that represent them. Employees are at the center of industrial relations. Employees influence whether the firms that employ them achieve their objectives, and employees shape the growth and demands of unions.

Government

The term **government** encompasses (1) the local, state, and federal political processes; (2) the government agencies responsible for passing and enforcing public policies that affect industrial relations; and (3) the government as a representative of the public interest. Government policy shapes how industrial relations proceed by regulating, for example, how workers form unions and what rights unions may have.

Assumptions about Labor and Conflict

More Than Just a Commodity

One of the most important assumptions guiding the study of industrial relations is the view that labor is more than a commodity, more than a marketable resource. For instance, because workers often acquire skills that are of special value to one firm and not to another, the possibilities for them to earn as much "in the labor market" as they can at their existing employer are limited. In addition, changing jobs often costs workers a lot: moving locations can be expensive and can also entail large personal and emotional costs. For these reasons and others, labor is not as freely exchanged in the open, competitive market as are other, nonhuman, market goods.

Furthermore, labor is more than a set of human resources to be allocated to serve the goals of the firm. Instead, employees are also members of families and communities. These broader responsibilities influence employees' behaviors and intersect with their work roles.

A Multiple Interest Perspective

Because employees bring their own aspirations to the workplace, industrial relations must be concerned with how the policies that govern employment relations, and the work itself, affect workers and their interests, as well as the interests of the firm and the larger society. Thus, industrial relations takes a **multiple interest** perspective on the study of collective bargaining and industrial relations.

The Inherent Nature of Conflict

A critical assumption underlying analysis of industrial relations is that there is an inherent conflict of interest between employees and employers. That conflict arises out of the clash of economic interests between workers seeking high pay and job security and employers pursuing profits. *Thus, conflict is not viewed as pathological.* Although conflict is a natural element of employment relations, society does have a legitimate interest in limiting the intensity of conflicts over work.

Common as Well as Conflicting Interests

There are also a number of common interests between employers and their employees. Both firms and their workforces can benefit, for example, from increases in productivity through higher wages and higher profits.

At the workplace there is no single best objective that satisfies all the parties. *The essence of an effective employment relationship is one in which the parties both successfully resolve issues that arise from their conflicting interests and successfully pursue joint gains.*

Collective bargaining is only one of a variety of mechanisms for resolving conflicts and pursuing common interests at the workplace. In fact, collective bargaining competes with these alternative employment systems. Not all employees, for example, perceive deep conflicts with their employers or want to join unions. In dealing with their employers, some workers prefer individual over collective actions. Others exercise the option of *exit* (quitting a job) when dissatisfied with employment conditions rather than choosing to *voice* their concerns, either individually or collectively.[2]

One of the roles for public policy is therefore not to require unionization and collective bargaining for all workers, but to provide a fair opportunity for workers to choose whether collective bargaining is the means they prefer to resolve conflicts and to pursue common interests with their employer.

Trade-Offs among Conflicting Goals

Since many of the goals of the major actors—workers and their unions, employers, and the public or the government—conflict, it is not possible to specify a single overriding measure of the effectiveness of collective bargaining. Focusing on any single goal would destroy the effectiveness of collective bargaining as an instrument for accommodating the multiple interests of workers and employers in a democratic society.

Unions could not survive or effectively represent their members, for example, if employers were completely free to suppress or avoid unionization. Likewise, employers could not compete effectively in global or domestic markets if collective bargaining constantly produced wages or other conditions of employment that increased costs above what the market would bear.

The Three Levels of Industrial Relations Activity

This book uses a three-tiered approach to analyze the operation of industrial relations.[3] (Exhibit 1–1 provides the framework for this approach.) First we consider the environmental contexts of collective bargaining; then we look at the operation and outcomes of the bargaining system.

The top tier of industrial relations, the **strategic level,** includes the strategies and structures that exert long-run influences on collective bargaining. At this level we might compare the implications for collective bargaining of a business strategy that emphasizes product quality and innovation against a business strategy that seeks to minimize labor costs.

EXHIBIT 1–1
Conceptual
Framework
for the Study
of Collective
Bargaining

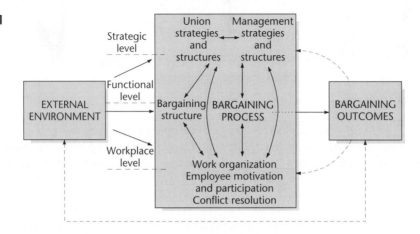

The middle tier of industrial relations activity, the **functional level,** or collective bargaining level, involves the process and outcomes of contract negotiations. Discussions of strikes, bargaining power, and wage determination feature prominently here.

The bottom tier of industrial relations activity, the **workplace level,** involves those activities through which workers, their supervisors, and their union representatives administer the labor contract and relate to one another on a daily basis. At the workplace level adjustment to changing circumstances and new problems occurs regularly. A typical question at this level, for example, is how the introduction of employee participation programs has changed the day-to-day life of workers and supervisors.

It is through the joint effects of the environment and the actions of the parties within this three-tiered structure that collective bargaining either meets the goals of the parties and the public or comes up short.

The Institutional Perspective

The perspective that guides our analysis of industrial relations was first developed by institutional economists at the University of Wisconsin. John R. Commons (1862–1945), the person who most deserves the title of "father of U.S. industrial relations," identified the essence of institutional economics as "a shift from commodities, individuals, and exchanges to transactions and working rules of collective action."[4] Commons and his fellow institutionalists placed great value on negotiations and on compromise among the divergent interests of labor, management, and the public.

The institutionalists in the United States were heavily influenced in their thinking by Sidney and Beatrice Webb, two British economists and social reformists, who were members of the Fabian socialist society. They viewed trade unions as a means of representing the interests of workers through the strategies of *mutual insurance, collective bargaining, and legal enactment.*[5]

In following the Webbs, the institutionalists rejected the arguments of Karl Marx. Marx argued that the pain of the exploitation and alienation inflicted on workers by the

If the capitalist refuses to accept the workman's terms, he will, no doubt, suffer some inconvenience as an employer. To fulfill his orders, he will have to "speed up" some of his machinery, or insist on his people working longer hours. Failing these expedients he may have to delay the delivery of his goods, and may even find his profits, at the end of the year fractionally less than before. But, meanwhile, he goes on eating and drinking, his wife and family go on living, just as before. His physical comfort is not affected: he can afford to wait until the labourer comes back in a humble frame of mind. And that is just what the labourer must presently do. For he, meanwhile, has lost his day. His very subsistence depends on his promptly coming to an agreement. If he stands out, he has no money to meet his weekly rent, or to buy food for his family. If he is obstinate, consumption of his little hoard, or the pawning of his furniture, may put off the catastrophe; but sooner or later slow starvation forces him to come to terms. And since success in the higgling of the market is largely determined by the relative eagerness of the parties to come to terms—especially if this eagerness cannot be hidden—it is now agreed, even on this ground alone, "that manual labourers as a class are at a disadvantage in bargaining."

Source: Mrs. Sidney Webb, ed., *The Case for Factory Acts* (London: Grant Richards, 1901), pp. 8–9.

capitalistic system would eventually lead to the revolutionary overthrow of the system. He believed that workers would eventually develop a class consciousness that would pave the way for revolution and the ultimate solution to their problems—a Marxian economic and social system. Marx supported trade unions in their struggles for higher wages, but he believed they should simultaneously pursue the overthrow of the capitalistic system.

There were, however, some interesting similarities in the views of Commons, Marx, and the Webbs. Like Marx and the Webbs, Commons and other institutional economists rejected the view of labor as a commodity, for two fundamental reasons. First, the institutionalists saw work as being too central to the interests and welfare of individual workers, their families, and their communities to be treated simply as just another factor of production.[6]

Second, the institutionalists echoed the Webbs and the Marxist theorists by arguing that under conditions of "free competition" most individual workers deal with the employer from a position of unequal bargaining power. That is, in the vast majority of employment situations, the workings of the market tilt the balance of power in favor of the employer. The selection from Beatrice Webb's classic essay on the economics of factory legislation in Britain, shown in Box 1–1, amply illustrates this argument.

The institutionalists concluded that labor required protection from the workings of the competitive market and that unions could materially improve the conditions of the worker. This led them to advocate two basic labor policies: legislation to protect the rights of workers to join unions; and legislation on such workplace issues as safety and health, child labor, minimum wages, unemployment and workers' compensation, and social security.[7] Thus, in addition to making scholarly contributions, the institutionalists served as early advocates of the legislative reforms that became the centerpiece of the New Deal labor policy.

The Performance of Collective Bargaining

The performance of collective bargaining can be assessed by looking at how well it serves the goals of the parties involved and the public.

Labor's Goals

To see if collective bargaining is meeting labor's goals we can examine wages, benefits, safety conditions, and employee job satisfaction. A number of union–management efforts now seek to improve the quality of working life and employment security. Because many of these joint processes have expanded beyond the traditional agenda of collective bargaining, their success or failure in serving workers' interests must also be assessed.

Management's Goals

Management is concerned with the effects of collective bargaining on labor costs, productivity, profits, product quality, and the degree of managerial control. Management also has goals for various personnel concerns, such as employee turnover, motivation, and performance. All of these indicate the extent to which collective bargaining aids or hinders employers' quests for competitiveness in the product market.

Management, particularly in the United States, historically has not been very sympathetic to collective bargaining. The vast majority of U.S. employers have resisted unionization of their employees and have often been only reluctant participants in collective bargaining. Managers tend to evaluate the performance of collective bargaining by comparing it with the nonunion alternatives.

The growing sophistication of human resource management strategies and the increasing competitive pressures from nonunion sectors have led more and more corporate managers to scrutinize the performance of their labor relations functions. Most top executives are trying to integrate their labor relations strategies with their business strategies. For example, firms in the steel, auto, aerospace, and apparel industries have worked with unions to modify labor relations practices in order to make new investments in plant and equipment pay off.

The Public's Goals

Identifying the goals of collective bargaining for the public and the government is a more difficult task. Government labor policy requires the maintenance of industrial peace and union democracy. In addition, the government is concerned about the effects of collective bargaining on inflation and unemployment and on working conditions, such as safety and health, equal employment opportunity, and income security.

A free labor movement is important to any political democracy. So it is also necessary to assess whether public policies and private actions are producing a bargaining system that strengthens democracy at the workplace and in the society at large.

Since less than one-fifth of the U.S. labor force is now represented by trade unions, the regulation of employment conditions involves more than just collective bargaining. In some instances public policies preempt collective bargaining by creating alternative means through which labor-management issues are addressed, such as through government regulation of pensions.

The Plan of the Book

The chapters that follow analyze industrial relations by simultaneously moving across and downward through Exhibit 1–1. The framework in Exhibit 1–1 is broader and more dynamic than most models of collective bargaining. In particular, it emphasizes the range of choices management, labor, and government policymakers have in responding to environmental changes (such as increased competition or changes in technology), rather than in treating technology or competitive pressures solely as overriding constraints.

The following discussion provides a more elaborate description of the terms used in Exhibit 1–1. This material also sketches out in more detail the topics included in each chapter and their connections as the book moves across and downward through Exhibit 1–1. The reader may wish to return to this material from time to time as a review strategy to put the individual topics and chapters in perspective.

The Environment

The external environment sets the context for collective bargaining and strongly influences the bargaining process and bargaining outcomes. The **external environment** includes five key dimensions: the economic environment (micro and macro), law and public policy, the demographic context, social attitudes, and the technological context. The laws and public policies that regulate collective bargaining are a key aspect of the environment and are outlined in Chapter 3. Chapter 4 describes how each component of the environment influences the process and the outcomes of bargaining.

The environment often transmits its effects through the exercise of **bargaining power.** For example, a law that grants employees the right to strike is important because it facilitates the emergence of collective bargaining and thereby alters the balance of power between labor and management. The ensuing shift in the balance of power is particularly noteworthy to the extent that it leads to different employment conditions (such as higher wages) than would otherwise exist. In this way something in the external environment (a law) affects the frequency of bargaining (the bargaining process) and wage levels (a bargaining outcome).

Similarly, the economic features of product and labor markets affect the behavior of labor and management and the outcomes of collective bargaining. Workers and unions, for example, have more bargaining leverage and are able to win higher wages during contract negotiations when it is easier for striking workers to find temporary or alternative employment. Thus, an aspect of the macroeconomy (the unemployment rate) influences workers' bargaining power and bargaining outcomes (the wage settlement).

Do the provisions of typical collective bargaining contracts adequately address the needs of women in the work force, of youths, and of the elderly? Is the government enforcing the existing labor laws? These questions concern additional interactions between the external environment (in the first case, the demographic context; in the second case, the public policy context) and collective bargaining.

As the book traces how the various components of the environment affect the bargaining process and bargaining outcomes, the discussion moves across the middle tier of the framework outlined in Exhibit 1–1. At the same time it is important to be aware of how the strategies and structures of labor and management both shape the middle tier of industrial relations activity and exert impacts at the workplace. Thus, as the text moves across the framework the analysis also simultaneously moves downward through our three-tiered framework. The framework starts at the top by first considering the role played by labor and management strategies and structures.

The Strategic (Top) Tier

At the top tier of industrial relations activity are the strategies and structures that guide the long-run direction of U.S. industrial relations.

Management's Strategies and Structures

The strategies and structures of management are critically important in shaping the evolution of industrial relations. For instance, is a given company's top management content to work with its union(s) over the long run, or is it fundamentally committed to devoting its resources to nonunion pursuits and operations?

Chapter 5 analyzes the various strategic options available to managers, including the growing availability and sophistication of nonunion alternatives to collective bargaining. What leads management to aggressively seek to avoid unions in one case, whereas in another situation management is content to negotiate with the unions that represent its employees and to focus on improving the existing collective bargaining relationship? To help us understand what motivates management, Chapter 5 contrasts the key features of some of the nonunion employment systems with those of both traditional union practices (the *New Deal system*) and the participatory practices that have recently emerged in a number of unionized settings.

While management strategies are important, so are the various structures that management uses to organize itself for industrial relations. The second part of Chapter 5 considers how management organizes its industrial relations staffs.

Labor's Strategies and Structures

Labor's strategies and structures also exert a critical influence on the course of industrial relations. The various aspects of labor's strategic issues are addressed in Chapter 6. For example, is a given union leadership committed to maintaining a distanced and adversarial posture in negotiations, or is it interested in exchanging new forms of flexible work organization for greater control over the design of the production process? In addition, should the labor movement focus on political action or seek to improve employment conditions through collective bargaining? These are but two of the strategic issues that face the labor movement.

The labor movement, like management, also structures itself in its efforts to shape industrial relations. Chapter 6 describes the organizational structure of the American labor movement and delineates the division in the responsibilities of the American Federation of Labor–Congress of Industrial Organizations (AFL-CIO), national unions, and local unions.

A key strategic issue, perhaps the single most important issue, for the labor movement today is the extent of the work force that belongs to a union. Concerns about union organizing led to changes in the leadership and strategic direction of the AFL-CIO and the emergence of a rival Change to Win labor federation that are reviewed in this chapter. To understand the context for these changes in the strategic approach of the labor movement, Chapter 6 traces current union membership figures and some of the trends. This chapter also explains why union membership as a fraction of the work force has declined so substantially in the United States.

The emphasis in this book on the strategic level of industrial relations activity contrasts with most traditional treatments of unions and employers. The traditional approach focuses on a narrow concept of the internal management structure for labor relations or on union wage objectives and internal politics. Today an understanding of the links between business and union strategies and collective bargaining is needed to interpret or to participate in the bargaining process.

The Functional (Middle) Tier

The middle tier of activity within a bargaining relationship encompasses the heart and soul of the bargaining process. This tier is the arena in which the process of contract negotiations takes place. It is here also that the terms and conditions of the labor agreement (the outcomes of bargaining) are established and periodically modified.

Union Organizing and Bargaining Structure

The formation of unions and workers' expression of interest in union representation precedes negotiations and the determination of bargaining outcomes. In the United States unions establish their right to represent workers in defined **bargaining units** through the vote of prospective members in a **representation election.** Thus, the first stage in our discussion of the process of bargaining (in Chapter 7) is consideration of how representation elections are held and the laws that regulate the conduct of those elections.

Unions have not fared very well in the representation elections held in the United States, particularly since the early 1970s. Thus an analysis of union organizing must consider some of the tactics management has been using to such great success and some of the recent steps taken by unions to increase their membership.

A critical factor that shapes the form and often the outcomes of organizing is the structure of the bargaining unit, the second major topic addressed in Chapter 7. **Bargaining structure** refers to the scope of employees and employers covered or in some way affected by the terms of a labor agreement. For example, are a number of different employers covered by a single collective bargaining agreement? Does a given company bargain with one union or with many? Does a given union represent workers with diverse or with homogeneous skills?

The structure of bargaining in the United States is highly decentralized: the U.S. Bureau of Labor Statistics estimates (no exact census has ever been attempted) that somewhere between 170,000 and 190,000 separate collective bargaining agreements currently exist in this country. This figure may overstate the actual degree of decentralization of bargaining, however. An informal process known as **pattern bargaining** often operates to tie separate agreements together, so that a change in one leads to similar changes in others within the same firm, region, or industry. For instance, the United Auto Workers union, which represents workers in both the auto parts and the auto assembly sectors, regularly has tried to extend the contract improvements it won in the assembly plants of the major manufacturers to the parts-producing plants owned by other companies.

Chapter 7 explores how the strength of pattern bargaining and other aspects of bargaining structures change over time. This analysis demonstrates the important links between bargaining structure and other concepts in the framework.

The Negotiations Process

At the heart of union–management relations is the negotiation of collective bargaining agreements, the topic that is the focus of Chapter 8. If a union wins the right to represent a group of workers, the next phase in the bargaining process involves the union's (and workers') efforts to negotiate a favorable collective bargaining agreement. The **negotiations process** is a complicated affair, involving tactics, strategies, and counterstrategies by both labor and management. Given the mixed-motive nature of collective bargaining, the parties are often torn in negotiations between their distributive and integrative impulses. In this chapter we examine efforts adopted by some parties in recent years to maximize the joint gains in bargaining through a so-called **interest-based bargaining** approach. What makes the subject of negotiations particularly challenging is its dynamic nature.

Analysis of the process of negotiations considers the following sort of questions:

1. How can the dynamics of the negotiations process be described and explained?
2. What causes strikes to occur in some negotiations and not in others and to vary in frequency and intensity over time and across industries?
3. What role do union and business strategies play in shaping the negotiations process?
4. How can the parties increase the joint gains that could benefit both labor and management?

Chapter 8 examines the complete cycle of negotiations, starting with the presentation of opening offers and demands and proceeding through the signing of the final agreement.

Impasse Resolution

When labor and management reach an impasse in contract negotiations, a variety of techniques can be (and have been) used to settle the dispute. Chapter 9 assesses various **impasse resolution** techniques. This chapter examines the frequency of their use and some of the strengths and weaknesses of each.

Bargaining Outcomes

The bargaining process is important in its own right, but it is particularly relevant for its effects on workers' employment conditions, as analyzed in Chapter 10. Employment conditions are the most important **bargaining outcomes** that are shaped by collective bargaining.

Most, but not all, of the outcomes of the negotiations process are codified in the collective bargaining agreement. Exhibit 1–2 shows the range of the terms and conditions of employment that are covered in many labor contracts. This list illustrates that most of the agreements address, at the very least, the following sets of issues: (1) wage and fringe benefit levels, payment systems, and administration; (2) job and income security; (3) physical working conditions; (4) selected personnel management and plant operation practices; and (5) union and management rights and responsibilities.

Nonetheless, the scope and content of bargaining agreements in the United States vary widely. Yet, because contract provisions define the rights and obligations of each of the parties, they furnish a starting point for assessing how well the interests of workers, employers, unions, and society are faring at the workplace.

Recently, a number of companies and unions have moved to simplify the rules contained in their agreements as part of their efforts to lower costs and to increase flexibility in managing human resources. The chapter addresses both the historical growth in the complexity of bargaining agreements and the more recent efforts to streamline some of the work rule provisions.

EXHIBIT 1–2
Typical Provisions in Collective Bargaining Agreements

Source: Adapted from Joseph W. Bloch, "Union Contracts— A New Series of Studies," *Monthly Labor Review* 87 (October 1964), pp. 1184–85.

Establishment and Administration of the Agreement

Bargaining unit and plant supplements
Contract duration and reopening and renegotiation provisions
Union security and the checkoff
Special bargaining committees
Grievance procedures
Arbitration and mediation
Strikes and lockouts
Contract enforcement

Wage Determination and Administration

Rate structure and wage differentials
Incentive and bonus plans
Production standards and time studies
Job classification and job evaluation
Individual wage adjustments
General wage adjustments during the contract period

Job or Income Security

Hiring and transfer arrangements
Employment and income guarantees
Reporting and call-in pay
Supplemental unemployment benefit plans
Regulation of overtime, shift work, etc.
Reduction of hours to forestall layoffs
Layoff procedures, seniority, recall
Worksharing in lieu of layoff
Attrition arrangements
Promotion practices
Training and retraining
Relocation allowances
Severance pay and layoff benefit plans
Special funds and study committees

Functions, Rights, and Responsibilities

Management rights clauses
Plant removal

Subcontracting
Union activities on company time and premises
Union–management cooperation
Regulation of technological change
Advance notice and consultation

Plant Operations

Work and shop rules
Rest periods and other in-plant time allowances
Safety and health
Plant committees
Hours of work and premium pay practices
Shift operations
Hazardous work
Discipline and discharge

Paid and Unpaid Leave

Vacations and holidays
Sick leave
Funeral and personal leave
Military leave and jury duty

Employee Benefit Plans

Health and insurance plans
Pension plans
Profit-sharing, stock purchase, and thrift plans
Bonus plans

Special Groups

Apprentices and learners
Handicapped and older workers
Women
Veterans
Union representatives
Nondiscrimination clauses

The Workplace (Bottom) Tier

The management of conflict and the delivery of due process are only two of several key activities that occur on a continuous basis at the workplace level of industrial relations activity. Other activities involve the motivation, participation, and supervision of individual workers and the structuring of work into jobs, groups, or teams. Should work be organized into highly fragmented jobs or, rather, placed in team systems of work organization? What does a shift to a team system imply for union leaders and the operation of the grievance system? These questions illustrate the issues being raised by the recent changes that have been occurring at the workplace level.

Administration of the Bargaining Agreement

Much of the workplace interaction between labor and management in unionized settings in the United States focuses on administration of the collective bargaining agreement. At the centerpiece of contract administration are the grievance and arbitration procedures analyzed in Chapter 11. Some analysts view grievance arbitration as the most significant innovation of the U.S. industrial relations system.

Grievance and arbitration procedures have been affected by the growth of external laws governing health and safety, equal employment opportunity, and other matters that influence the rights of individuals and add to the responsibilities of both unions and employers. Chapter 11 considers how these external laws also influence the workplace.

Participatory Processes

The negotiation and administration of a collective bargaining agreement have traditionally provided a way for employees to participate in decisions that shape their work lives and employment conditions. There has been much effort to go beyond these procedures and to directly involve employees in making decisions. Chapter 12 analyzes the variety of participatory processes that have emerged. The text also assesses forms of work organization, including team systems and quality circles, that have become part of labor and management's efforts to improve productivity and product quality.

Participatory processes have sprung up at strategic levels as well as at the workplace level. The options range from forms of employee ownership, to labor-management committees, to union representation on corporate boards, to the workplace processes discussed above.

Special Topics

Chapters 13 and 14 address selected topics that complete our understanding of collective bargaining in the modern economy.

Public Sector Collective Bargaining

The rules and procedures in public sector collective bargaining, examined in Chapter 13, differ from those used in the private sector in the United States. The public sector employs a wide diversity of employees, including public school teachers, municipal police and firefighters, and the office staffs of city, state, and federal governments. Public employees are not covered by the National Labor Relations Act (NLRA). This chapter considers the extent to which the theories presented in earlier parts of the book carry over to the public sector.

International and Comparative Industrial Relations

These days the industrial relations developments that are occurring around the world warrant the special attention they are given in Chapter 14. The labor movement has been at the forefront of the sweeping political changes that occurred in the formerly Communist bloc and in newly industrialized countries such as Korea. In these countries the labor movement is as much concerned with political change as it is with the determination of work conditions on the factory floor.

International trade and competitiveness have moved to the forefront of economic policy in the United States. In particular, there is much discussion about whether globalization has fundamentally increased management's power and advantage. Concern about globalization, for example, has spurred various international workers' rights initiatives. Chapter 14 reviews the effects of globalization and provides examples of recent international workers' rights disputes and campaigns. Chapter 14 also reviews in detail the industrial practices in Japan and Germany. These two countries are informative because their practices are so different from those in the United States and because the performance of these economies has been relatively strong. Examination of industrial relations in other countries provides insight into American practice.

Labor Policy

Chapter 15 returns to a primary focus on issues in the United States. This concluding chapter assesses broad public and social policies and their effects on industrial relations. In the face of all the changes emerging in U.S. collective bargaining, this chapter also considers the various policy options and the merits and implications of the alternative policies.

Summary

The expansion of participatory processes and the diffusion of team forms of work organization are some of the many changes that have been occurring in industrial relations in recent years. Yet these are only a few among many critical changes that have emerged. In the face of the wide-ranging changes that have come to industrial relations and collective bargaining, many of the earlier textbooks addressing those subjects have become out of date. For some analysts collective bargaining in recent years was noteworthy because of the modest wage increases or heightened concern for employment security that characterized collective bargaining in these years. For others, it was the continuing decline in private sector union representation that was so unusual. And for some other analysts it was the heightened pressures of globalization or new union organizing strategies that were most important. To us, each of these and other events were noteworthy, but it is even more important to understand how the various changes and events *fit together as a shift in the nature and form of industrial relations.*

We believe there has been a fundamental transformation in American industrial relations that includes shifts in the focus of activity from the middle level to both the strategic and the workplace levels. Concern over employment security, union decline, and participation programs and other events in the United States can all be understood as parts of this transformation.

We developed the model of industrial relations presented in Exhibit 1–1 in our efforts to comprehend the scope of the changes that are under way. We believe these changes in collective bargaining should be viewed as neither a fluke nor a special case but, rather, as an illustration of the dynamics of industrial relations.

One cannot gain an understanding of recent developments or the workings of industrial relations without a sense of history. Chapter 2 provides a historical perspective on the evolution of industrial relations in the United States. This chapter highlights some of the key events and turning points in that history as it provides a perspective on the wide-ranging changes that have been occurring in collective bargaining in the United States.

Discussion Questions

1. Name the actors, generally and specifically, who are involved in the collective bargaining process.

2. Exhibit 1–1 is essential in understanding how this book is arranged and proceeds in its analysis of collective bargaining. Describe this figure and how it pertains to the study of collective bargaining.

3. One of the fundamental aims of collective bargaining is the reduction of conflict between employees and employers. What are some basic assumptions about labor and conflict in this book?

4. What are some of the ways in which we judge the effectiveness of collective bargaining, with respect to the different actors involved in the process?

Related Web Sites

General index of union Web sites:
http://www.access.digex.net/~umwu/unions.html

Union sources and links:
http://garnet.berkeley.edu:3333/labor/index.html
http://www.uniteunion.org

Federal Web locator:
http://www.vcilp.org/Fed-Agency/fedwebloc.html#search

Cornell University's School of Industrial and Labor Relations:
http://www.ilr.cornell.edu/gernal_ilr_info/aboutilr.html

General collective bargaining Web sites:
http://claims.ubc.ca/collective/december/default.htm

Centers for the Study of Labor Relations:
http://www.nlma.org/lbr-link.htm

Suggested Readings

Dunlop, John T. *Industrial Relations Systems* (New York: Holt, 1958).

Kaufman, Bruce. *The Origins and Evolution of the Field of Industrial Relations* (Ithaca, New York: ILR Press, 1993).

Kochan, Thomas A., Harry C. Katz, and Robert B. McKersie. *The Transformation of American Industrial Relations,* 2d ed. (Ithaca, New York: ILR Press, 1994).

Webb, Sidney, and Beatrice Webb. *Industrial Democracy* (London: Longmans, Green and Co., 1920).

End Notes

1. See John T. Dunlop, *Industrial Relations Systems* (New York: Holt, 1958).

2. See Albert O. Hirschman, *Exit, Voice, and Loyalty: Responses to Declines in Firms, Organizations, and States* (Cambridge: Harvard University Press, 1970).

3. For a summary of the theoretical and empirical research on which this model is based, see Thomas A. Kochan, Harry C. Katz, and Robert B. McKersie, *The Transformation of American Industrial Relations,* 2d ed. (Ithaca, New York: ILR Press, 1994).

4. John R. Commons, *Institutional Economics: Its Place in the Political Economy* (New York: Macmillan, 1934), p. 162.

5. Sidney and Beatrice Webb, *Industrial Democracy* (London: Longmans, Green and Co., 1920).

6. Commons, *Institutional Economics,* p. 559.

7. For a discussion of the policies advocated by the early institutionalists and ultimately passed in the wave of New Deal legislation, see Joseph P. Goldberg, Eileen Ahern, William Haber, and Rudolph A. Oswald, *Federal Policies and Worker Status since the Thirties* (Madison, WI: Industrial Relations Research Association, 1977).

Chapter 2

The Historical Evolution of the U.S. Industrial Relations System

Collective bargaining is one means for organized groups of workers and their employers to resolve their conflicting interests. It is by no means, however, the only way to conduct industrial relations. Indeed, in the long history of industrial society, collective bargaining is only a recent arrival. Moreover, collective bargaining has had to adapt to changing times and changing values.

This chapter examines the evolution of industrial relations in the United States. Throughout American labor history there has been much violence and substantial hardships on the participants. At the same time, there was much ingenuity as economic expansion transformed a nation of immigrants into the world's leading industrial power. The history that follows highlights the individuals who played key roles in that transformation.

The timeline provided in Exhibit 2–1 lists the key events in the evolution of U.S. industrial relations. In this chapter, we begin our discussion of the nature and consequences of these events.

The Colonial and Preindustrial Era

From the beginning of colonial times to the Revolutionary War, employment relationships were dominated by the master-servant principles inherited from British common law. Many early settlers gained their passage to the United States by becoming **indentured servants** to a shipowner. Under this arrangement, on arrival at a colonial port, the ships' captain sold the servant to an employer for a certain number of years (not to exceed seven). Many of these indentured servants were individuals seeking to escape their past problems or those forced to leave their home country. One observer described them as follows:

> Among those who repair to Bristol from all parts to be transported for servants to his Majesty's plantations beyond seas, some are husbands that have forsaken wives, others wives who have forsaken their husbands; some are children and apprentices run way from their parents and masters, often-times unwary and credulous persons have been tempted on board by

EXHIBIT 2–1
U.S. Industrial Relations Timeline

1794:	Shoemakers form first American union in Philadelphia.
1806:	Shoemakers' case holds that unions are 'criminal conspiracies'.
Early 1800s:	Utopians active, led by Horace Greely.
1842:	*Commonwealth* v. *Hunt* decision holds unions are not conspiracies per se.
1860s:	Secret society of the Molly Maguires active.
1869:	Knights of Labor founded.
1870–80s:	Knights of Labor period of success, later fade away.
1886:	American Federation of Labor founded, led by Gompers until 1924.
1886:	Haymarket affair, police kill union protestors.
1892:	Homestead strike, Carnegie breaks steel union.
1893:	Pullman strike, company defeats railway union.
1908:	Danbury Hatters case, union members fined for secondary boycott.
1914:	Clayton Act, unsuccessful attempt to reverse Danbury Hatters case.
1917–18:	U.S. in WWI, tight labor markets help unions, but Wobblies (IWW) repressed.
1920s:	Open shop movement leads to union decline.
1930s:	Union resurgence, Great Depression, New Deal, Industrial unionism.
1932:	Norris LaGuardia Act bans labor injunctions, yellow-dog contracts.
1933:	National Industrial Recovery Act passed, but unconstitutional.
1935:	Wagner Act (NLRA) protects the right to organize.
1935:	AFL and CIO split.
1937:	NLRA held constitutional in *NLRB* v. *Jones & Laughlin*.
1941–45:	U.S. in WWII, War Labor Board regulates industrial relations.
1946:	Postwar strike wave, highest strikes and union membership (35.5 percent).
1947:	New Republican congress passes the Taft-Hartley Act.
1950s:	'Heyday' of American unions, over 30 percent unionization.
1955:	AFL and CIO merge to form AFL-CIO.
1959:	Union corruption concerns lead to Landrum-Griffin Act.
1960–70s:	Public sector workers get right to organize.
1980–90s:	Major union membership decline.
1981–83:	Recession costs union jobs, especially in autos and steel.
1980s:	Permanent replacement workers used in PATCO & Phelps-Dodge strikes.
1990s:	UAW defeated in Caterpillar strike.
1995:	John Sweeney elected President of AFL-CIO on reform ticket.
2005:	Union membership at 12.5 percent; AFL-CIO and Change-to-Win split.

men-stealers, and many that have been pursued by hue-and-cry for robberies, burglaries, or breaking prison, do thereby escape the prosecution of law and justice.[1]

The Dominance of Agriculture

Colonial employers were eager for the arrival of these workers given the general shortage of labor for their farms and plantations. From 1609, when the first slaves were imported into Virginia, until 1808, when the slave trade was outlawed, indentured servants were supplemented by slaves brought from Africa and the East Indies. In this period agriculture was dominant and included large plantations in the south, farms in Quaker Pennsylvania, and family plots in Puritan New England.

Coinciding with these rural farming-based economies were a growing number of artisan services and manufactures—shopkeepers, toolmakers, and blacksmiths. One historian described the origins of the small business entrepreneurs as follows:

> A large proportion of the most successful manufacturers in the United States consists of persons who were journeymen, and in a few instances were foreman, in the work-shops and manufactories of Europe; who having been skillful, sober, frugal, and having thus saved a little money, have set up for themselves with great advantage in the United States.[2]

A Shortage of Skilled Labor

When a shortage of skilled labor appeared in the 13 colonies, colonial leaders lobbied to have more skilled workers delivered to their shores to help take advantage of the opportunities for development. Captain John Smith of Jamestown put it this way:

> When you send again, I entreat you rather send but thirty carpenters, husbandmen, gardeners, fishermen, blacksmiths, masons, and digger up of trees' roots, well provided, than a thousand such as we have.[3]

Colonial employers complained that the shortage of skilled labor forced them to pay "excessive rates." One historian estimated that wages for skilled labor were 30 to 100 percent higher than those paid to comparable workers in England.[4] In response, employers and communities often lured skilled workers away from each other. This, in turn, led the Massachusetts Bay Colony and other colonial governmental authorities to try to regulate competition by putting an upper limit on wages. These early efforts at government regulation of the labor market generally failed in the face of the strong and growing demand for skilled labor.

Labor Force Diversity

From the beginning, our labor force was highly diverse—consisting of indentured servants, slaves, immigrants, well-paid skilled artisans, and small shopkeepers and farmers—both male and female and of all skin colors. This diversity became a hallmark of the American labor force and reduced the development of a class consciousness that helped unions develop in Europe. The American workforce diversity, coupled with expanding opportunities, led to little interest in collective organization in the preindustrial days of the 18th century.

Early Unionism

The development of unionism in the colonies was closely intertwined with the development of industry and the industrial revolution. Not all workers were able to easily adjust their work habits to fit the stringent time and disciplinary requirements of industrial work. Managers in the early mills and factories of New England had to impose strong discipline and extensive socialization on immigrants and other first-generation factory workers to make them adapt to the new work system.[5] Box 2–1 excerpts a disciplinary code imposed by a New England employer in the early 1800s. It illustrates the lengths some employers went to in their effort to maintain work discipline.

Box 2–1

GENERAL REGULATIONS
To Be Observed by Persons Employed by The
LAWRENCE MANUFACTURING COMPANY

1st. All persons in the employ of the Company, are required to attend assiduously to their various duties, or labor, during working hours; are expected to be fully competent, or to aspire to the utmost efficiency in the work or business they may engage to perform, and to evince on all occasions, in their deportment and conversation, a laudable regard for temperance, virtue, and their moral and social obligations; and in which the Agent will endeavor to set a proper example. No person can be employed by the Company, whose known habits are or shall be dissolute, indolent, dishonest, or intemperate, or who habitually absent themselves from public worship, and violate the Sabbath, or who may be addicted to gambling of any kind.

2d. All kinds of ardent spirit will be excluded from the Company's ground, except it be prescribed for medicine, or for washes, and external applications. Every kind of gambling and card playing, is totally prohibited within the limits of the Company's ground and Board house.

3d. Smoking cannot be permitted in the Mills, or other buildings, or yards, and should not be carelessly indulged in the Board Houses and streets. . . .

Lowell, Massachusetts, 21 May 1833.

Source: William Cahn, *A Pictorial History of American Labor* (New York: Crown Publisher, 1972), p. 49.

One reason employers had to go to such great lengths to maintain work discipline was because working conditions were harsh. Box 2–2 describes the working conditions in a southern cotton mill at the turn of the 19th century.

The First Trade Unions

The first groups of workers to challenge employers by joining together and demanding improved wages were skilled craftsmen. Most authorities cite the Federal Society of Journeymen Cordwainers, the union of Philadelphia shoemakers organized in 1794, as the first modern trade union in the United States.[6] The shoemakers were joined by printers, carpenters, and other artisans in New York and a few other large cities.

Generally these unions started when workers jointly agreed on a new wage for their work and laid down their tools if employers resisted the new rate. In other cases, unions were spurred after employers posted wage cuts. Collective bargaining as we know it today did not really occur in the colonial period. Either the unilateral demands of one side were met and work continued, or employers replaced the strikers with workers willing to do the job for the wages they offered. In response, local unions began to coordinate their efforts.

Why Workers Formed Unions

What led workers during the process of industrialization to turn to unions to press their interests? John Commons (see Chapter 1) studied the formation of the earliest American unions in the shoe industry. He argued that unionism was a response to the competitive pressures (he labeled them **competitive menaces**) workers faced as a result of the expansion of the market. The competitive menaces led to lower cost competition (from "bad wares"), lower wages, and worsening employment conditions.

The increased competitive pressures were themselves products of the expansion of markets under way in the economy caused by innovations in transportation. As markets expanded, the unity of production found in the position of the master shoemaker gave way to a division in work responsibilities as first journeymen and then assembly workers were

The cotton mill village was like one big white family closed off to the external world. Rows and rows of white clapboard houses lined dirt roads leading to the mill, while the mill owner lived some distance away in a mansion.

Workers, mostly women and children, labored sixteen hours a day for wages that were just enough to pay rent on their mill houses and their bills at the general store. Mill workers survived primarily on food grown in their own gardens. Mill owners not only encouraged child labor, they insisted upon it. Some mill villages provided schools, but most did not, and the majority of this first generation of mill workers grew up illiterate. The church was usually built on land owned by the mill which also provided its financial support. Thus sermons frequently followed the theme of hard work, deprivation, and suffering as the path to salvation.

Source: Victoria Byerly, *Hard Times Cotton Mill Girls: Personal Histories of Womanhood and Poverty in the South* (Ithaca, NY: ILR Press, 1986), p. 12.

used to make shoes. On the technological side there was a shift from hand tools to power machinery and the assembly line.

Although a social transformation was simultaneously occurring along with the increased competitive pressures, Commons argued that workers and early unions did not react against the work relations or the technology per se. Commons concluded that unions were a reaction to the ensuing deterioration in wages and working conditions. Thus, in Commons's view, workers turned to unions as a device to improve their lot and not as a mechanism to alter the social relations of production or to gain "control" of the production process.[7]

Early Court Reaction to Unionism

Employment relationships during the early years of industrialization in this country were governed solely by the common-law traditions carried over from Great Britain. Neither any constitutional provision nor any state or federal statutes explicitly addressed the rights of workers or the obligations of employers. It was left to the courts to develop their own prescriptions of the rights and responsibilities of the parties to employment contracts.[8]

Common-law rule generally translated into few enforceable contractual or implied rights for individual employees. Most courts, in fact, were outright hostile toward collective action by labor organizations.

The Conspiracy Doctrine

The actions of the shoemakers' union led to a famous trial in 1806 and a court decision that dominated rulings until the 1840s. A group of journeymen shoemakers (cordwainers) in Philadelphia joined together in 1804 and refused to work with people who were not members of their association. The shoemakers also won an increase in their wage rate. The employer of the shoemakers went to court to counteract the workers' and union's actions. A jury then convicted and fined the shoemakers on the grounds that they had formed an illegal **criminal conspiracy** through their union. The jury argued that the shoemakers' union was illegal on its own terms and had unjustly injured shoemakers who were not part of the union. Box 2–3 describes the Philadelphia shoemakers' case in more detail.

State and local courts in many jurisdictions followed the lead provided by this case. The courts found unions to be criminal conspiracies that impinged on industrial workers' "freedom" to contract with an employer. The courts issued decisions that limited the

In 1798, the Federal Society of Journeymen Cordwainers managed to boost the wages for making shoes to nearly $1 a pair. The journeymen shoemakers struck again in the fall of 1804, and gained an increase in wages to $2.75 for making a pair of cossack boots, regardless of how they were sold. But after Christmas, when retail orders dropped off, the employers paid a quarter less for "order work" boots (wholesale) and a quarter more for "bespoke" (retail) boots. This wage reduction led to a strike in 1805 when the journeymen demanded a flat price of $3 on both wholesale and retail work. The employers won the strike, and then turned to the courts.

A trial took place in the Philadelphia mayor's court. The jury was made up of merchants and craftsmen: two innkeepers, a merchant, three grocers, a hatter, a tobacconist, a watchmaker, a tailor, a tavernkeeper, and a bottler. A shoemaker called as one of the jurors was disqualified because of his occupation.

The prosecution (the employers) charged that the shoemakers (the defendants), "not being content to work and labour . . . at the usual prices and" had attempted "unjustly and oppressively to increase and augment the prices . . . and unjustly to exact and procure great sums of money for their work and labour." The shoemakers were said to have "unlawfully, perniciously, and deceitfully" formed an organization that governed members and other journeymen through "unlawful and arbitrary bye laws, rules and orders."

Said the prosecutors, "Our position is that no man is at liberty to combine, conspire, confederate, and unlawfully agree to regulate the whole body of workmen in the city." These charges were brought under the rubric of English common law concerning criminal conspiracy.

The defense argued that any assembly could be judged unlawful under the prosecution's interpretation of conspiracy law. Said one defense lawyer, "A country dance would be criminal, a cotillion unlawful, even a minuet a conspiracy; and nothing but a horn pipe or a solo would be stepped with impunity!"

When the arguments were all in, the jury deliberated for one evening and returned a verdict of guilty. Each of the defendants was ordered to pay $8—about a week's pay—plus the costs of trial, and to "stand committed until the fines were paid."

Source: From Gloria Stevenson, "Cordwainers Put Their Soles into Bargaining," in *200 Years of American Worklife* (Washington, DC: U.S. Department of Labor, 1977), pp. 29–31.

ability of workers to unionize or, once unionized, to use strikes, boycotts, or other forms of economic pressure.

The courts reflected the conservative, laissez faire economic and political culture of the country. Private property was to be protected; combinations of economic power, including combinations of labor power, were to be limited, and individual (not collective) freedom to contract was to be preserved. All these principles worked against workers' efforts to build strong and durable unions.

Pre-Civil War Organizing Efforts

Political Initiatives

The combined effects of the criminal conspiracy doctrine and the economic depression that followed the end of the War of 1812 led to the disappearance of most of the early unions. Then around 1820, as the political and voting rights of male, white taxpayers gradually expanded, workers began to form **workingmen's political parties.** The two largest workingmen's parties were found in Philadelphia and New York. These parties were short-lived and generally disintegrated over internal disputes about which candidate to support in the election of 1832, which put Andrew Jackson in the White House.

The failure of the workingmen's parties to put together an effective political coalition to advance labor's interests was only the first in a long sequence of similar failed political efforts by labor parties over the course of U.S. history.

Labor's Economic Advances

Labor was making significant economic strides during these years, however. In the textile mills of New England workers successfully agitated for limitations on the use of child labor. The practice of working from "can't see to can't see" (sun-up to sun-down) was first ended by skilled workers in New York, and gradually the 10-hour day became the accepted norm in surrounding industries. Later, Andrew Jackson's brand of people's democracy brought a recognition of the need for a public education system to provide the labor force needed for the expanding economy.[9]

The 1830s also brought the rise and fall of the first effort to create a National Trades Union. By this time, manufacturing was beginning to grow in New England, and various small unions of skilled artisans had been formed. The goal of the National Trades Union, like the umbrella organizations that followed in later years, was to bring separate unions together to promote the interests of all workers. The National Trades Union met in annual conventions three times in New York between 1832 and 1837 and then collapsed in the depression of 1837.[10]

By the 1840s the great wave of immigrants from Europe was in full force. The skilled and highly disciplined northern European carpenters, mechanics, and farmers were joined by the poorer and less skilled Irish who, along with the slaves in the south, continued to expand the ethnic and religious diversity in the labor force. Some immigrants, such as the Jews from Russia and Poland who settled in tight communities in New York and several other large cities, carried a tradition of union organizing with them to the United States from Europe. In general, however, the ethnic diversity and competition among workers of different ethnic and skill levels made collective organization difficult.

The Utopian Movements

During the mid and late 1800s a number of new approaches to collective organization based on various utopian principles were put forward. The **utopians** proposed the creation of communities of citizens, workers, and managers who would work and advance together. Their aim was to avoid the divisive and dehumanizing effects of the factory system.

Box 2–4 summarizes the ideas of Horace Greeley, one of the most famous utopian thinkers. The utopians' vision must have sounded like an attractive alternative to workers in the nation's first factories, and these ideas gained a strong following. However, the diversity in the working class, the lure of rising real wages, and the opportunities to move west limited the appeal of the utopian cause.

The Means-Ends Doctrine: Commonwealth v. Hunt

Unions were helped by a shift in the courts' interpretations of the criminal conspiracy doctrine in the 1840s. The most famous decision came in 1842 in *Commonwealth* v. *Hunt.* In settling that case Judge Shaw concluded that unions per se were not illegal conspiracies. Judge Shaw argued that the court had to examine how unions pursued their goals.

Courts had to assess whether unions had abused their power or had violated the constitutional rights of workers or private property holders in taking any given action. Thus, a **means-ends doctrine** emerged in court decisions.[11] By the late 1800s judges had

Among the most effective utopian reformers was Horace Greeley, the editor of the *New York Tribune*.

"The earth, the air, the waters, the sunshine, with their natural products, were divinely intended . . . for the enjoyment of the whole human family," stated Greeley. "But as society is now organized, this is not, and cannot be done. . . ."

"The right of owning land is one thing," Greeley said. "The right to own thousands and even millions of acres of land is another. I condemn the system of land monopoly."

Greeley's voice, loud and shrill, was one of many being raised for the cause of "elevating the masses." As Emerson said: "Greeley does the thinking for the whole west." And, indeed, the words of Bayard Taylor, the writer, were accurate when he said: "The *Tribune* comes next to the Bible all through the west."

Perhaps of all Greeley's many directives to his readers, the one most remembered was "Young man, go west and grow up with the nation."

The fact that there were available lands in the west theoretically permitted a method of escape for the industrial workers. Some working men and women did go west to escape from industrial work.

Source: William Cahn, *A Pictorial History of American Labor,* 3rd printing (New York: Crown Publishers, 1976), pp. 71–72.

---

generally turned from restricting unions' right to exist to issuing injunctions that limited the ability of unions to strike, picket, or boycott employers. This shift in the courts helped unions, but it did not eliminate the many barriers that impeded their expansion.

The Yellow-Dog Contract

One way unions continued to be limited was through the employers' use of the common law in their dealings with employees. Employers in this period could require employees to sign a **yellow-dog contract,** a type of loyalty oath, that stated the employee would neither join nor participate in the activities of a union. Since courts would enforce these contracts as a condition of employment, employees could be fired if they later became involved with a union. Yellow-dog contracts also provided the basis for legal action against union organizers on the grounds that they were interfering with a contractual relationship.

The Labor Wars

From 1860 through the first decade of the 20th century there was a series of bitter and sometimes violent struggles between workers and their employers. Some of these struggles remained local and concerned only groups of workers and a single employer, while others spread to include workers across the country.

The nation's coal fields were the site for some of the most violent disputes. Worker rebellions in coal were often triggered when mine owners unilaterally cut wages, in some cases by as much as a third.

The Molly Maguires

A secret association of militant Irish miners formed the **Molly Maguires** in 1862 to help striking mine workers resist wage cuts. The conspiracy lasted more than 10 years, when the Maguires were eventually infiltrated by a spy from the Pinkerton Detective Agency who had been hired by employers. The Pinkerton agent developed evidence (later judged by most historians to be of dubious validity) that was used to convict and execute 10 members of the Molly Maguires for murder.

During the late 1800s and early 1900s, when gunfire and bloodshed often accompanied workers' attempts to form unions, a sweet-faced old woman known only as Mother Jones tramped over most of the country's coalfields to encourage miners to organize and strike.

Mother Jones looked like a kindly grandmother. A mere 5 feet tall and weighing less than 100 pounds, she generally wore a genteel, lacetrimmed, black dress and a Victorian bonnet. But while Mother Jones appeared gentle, her words and actions were as hard as the life in the mines.

In 1917–18, 87-year-old Mother Jones told a group of striking West Virginia miners, "You goddamned cowards are losing this strike because you haven't got the guts to go out there and fight and win it. Why the hell don't you take your high-power rifles and blow the goddamned scabs out of the mines?"

The miners loved Mother Jones; mine owners, police, and many less radical union leaders looked forward to her death. She was arrested and jailed several times, once for allegedly conspiring to commit murder, stealing a machine gun, and attempting to blow up a train with dynamite. When she died at the age of 100, the priest who delivered her eulogy said, "Sometimes she used methods that made the righteous grieve. . . . but her faults were the excesses of her courage, her love of justice, the love in her mother's heart."

Source: From Gloria Stevenson, "That's No Lady, That's Mother Jones," in *200 Years of American Worklife* (Washington, DC: U.S. Department of Labor, 1977), pp. 104–8.

The battles between the Molly Maguires and employers in the mining industry were only one example of the violent wave of strikes that occurred in the last third of the 19th century. Strikes in the railroad, steel, meat-packing, and other growing manufacturing industries often erupted into violent clashes between strikers, strikebreakers, local police, and, in some cases, private security forces.

The hardships experienced by workers of this era produced a number of militant supporters who urged labor to fight back. One of the most colorful was a woman who became known as "Mother Jones." (See Box 2–5.)

The Haymarket Affair

A major outburst of violence occurred in Chicago in 1886 in events that came to be known as the **Haymarket affair.**[12] Tensions had been building in Chicago after an employer initiated lockout of workers at the McCormick Harvester Works plant on the outskirts of the city. At one point a fight broke out between strikebreakers who had crossed a picket line and the locked out workers. Police arrived to quell the fight and started shooting, killing four.

A rally was called and 4,000 people gathered the following evening at Haymarket Square in Chicago to protest the shootings. After a peaceful meeting police arrived, and then a bomb went off. The police proceeded to open fire on the crowd, killing 10 and wounding another 50.

Eight anarchists were subsequently charged with the bombing and convicted, although no evidence was ever presented that linked these men to the actual bombing. Four of the men were hanged, one committed suicide, and the others served prison sentences that were later commuted by the governor of Illinois.

The Homestead Strike

Another illustration of the forces that confronted early American unionism comes from the **Homestead strike** directed against the Carnegie Steel Company in 1892. The Homestead mill had a long-standing wage agreement with the Amalgamated Association of Iron, Steel, and Tin Workers. Then Andrew Carnegie purchased the Homestead mills in 1889 and placed Henry Clay Frick in charge.[13]

In February 1892 Frick and the Amalgamated reached an impasse in their negotiations over a new contract after Frick demanded steep reductions in wages. The workers struck. Frick proceeded to erect barbed-wire fences around the plant, hired 300 Pinkerton (private security) guards, and began to hire strikebreakers. As the Pinkertons were being moved up the Ohio river to guard the plant, they were confronted by striking steelworkers. A battle followed in which a dozen men were killed on each side, and the Pinkertons were driven off.

The strike then spread to other mills, and so did the violence. The strike dragged on for months. With their personal and union coffers wiped out, the steelworkers eventually conceded and went back to work as nonunion workers. The Amalgamated was shattered as a union, and steel unionism was eliminated from many of the steel mills in the Pittsburgh area.

The Pullman Strike

Led by Eugene V. Debs in the early 1890s, the American Railway Union instigated a series of industrial actions against the railroad companies and the wage cuts they were demanding.[14] At one point the union had a membership of 150,000 workers. But then came the **Pullman strike.**

The employees of the Pullman Palace Car Company lived in a company-run town in Pullman, Illinois. They paid their food, utility, and tax bills to the company. In the depression year of 1893, the company cut workers' wages by 22 percent without any reduction in rents and other services; so employees asked for a wage increase. However, the company proceeded to fire some of the workers who tried to restore the wage cuts through negotiation. Pullman workers then appealed to the American Railway Union for help, and a sympathetic work stoppage ensued on railroads across the country.

As the strike spread, a court injunction was issued on the grounds that striking railway workers were impeding the delivery of mail and interstate commerce. President Grover Cleveland sent in federal troops to enforce the order. Violence followed, including the burning of freight cars and other railway equipment.

Debs, who had been indicted for conspiracy in restraint of commerce, appealed to other trade unions to strike in support of the railway workers. Debs's appeal met with little support, and, facing a growing number of state and federal troops, the strikers returned to work defeated. Debs (see Box 2–6) went to jail but eventually emerged as the leading American socialist of his time.

The Need for National Unions

As transportation networks expanded across the country, workers were confronted by employers who could transfer goods and work across state borders. Up against these factors, local strikes and union action had limited power. The need for national labor organizations became ever more clear, and a number of national trade unions were formed.

The early national unions, such as the American Railway Workers, saw their membership fluctuate along with movements in the national economy.[15] When times were good, membership expanded and union powers increased. When the economy went into one of the severe recessions that marked early American industrialization, union membership waned as organized workers lost the power to press their demands.

The Knights of Labor

In 1869 the **Knights of Labor** emerged as one of the most important early national labor movements in the United States. The group was part fraternal society and part union. The Knights organized workers on a city-by-city basis across crafts. The philosophy espoused by the Knights proclaimed that all workers had common interests, regardless of skill or occupation.

The constitution of the Knights declared that the ultimate aim of the organization was the establishment of cooperative institutions. After this was accomplished, the Knights believed labor and capital could then live harmoniously together. To promote these objectives, the Knights favored organization, education, and cooperation.[16] With regard to trade union activities, the Knights advocated the substitution of arbitration for strikes. The Knights also favored such policies as the establishment of an eight-hour work day, legislative regulation of health and safety conditions, prohibition of child labor, and government ownership of railroads, telegraphs, and telephones. The Knights was a reformist organization seeking trade union and legislation action to limit the excesses of industrial society.

Terence Powderly (see Box 2–7) became head of the Knights in 1879 and had as his ultimate objective the establishment of producers' cooperatives. He felt that strikes and other union activities were destructive and incapable of bringing about the necessary political reforms. He favored negotiation and arbitration.

Splits eventually emerged within the leadership of the Knights concerning the extent to which the organization would devote its attention to trade unionism versus political activity. Many of the rank and file members of the Knights, in contrast to Powderly, favored the use of strikes and boycotts to achieve higher wages.

Membership in the Knights of Labor fluctuated greatly along with the national economy and the fortunes of local branches, peaking in 1886 at around 700,000.[17] Yet, by the late 1880s, the influence of the Knights was waning. The organization suffered from the bad publicity surrounding the violence that had emerged in the coal fields, at Homestead, and

"The working women and men of America, yes and of the world, have reason to hold in grateful appreciation the memory of . . . heroic women who struggle for freedom of opportunity for all," stated Terence V.

Powderly, who was the Knights of Labor's most influential leader.

Source: William Cahn, *A Pictorial History of American Labor* (New York: Crown Publishers, 1977), pp. 115–20.

at Pullman. The Knights also suffered greatly from the publicity following events that occurred at Haymarket Square in Chicago in 1886.

The Industrial Workers of the World

The **Industrial Workers of the World (IWW)** provided workers with a radical alternative. The platform of the IWW was to organize labor into industrial unions that would take direct and vigorous action to improve working conditions (see Box 2–8). The IWW also favored the creation of an independent political party to work for the overthrow of capitalism and to establish instead a "co-operative commonwealth."[18] The membership of the IWW came largely from miners and lumber workers.

The IWW developed a reputation of a violence-prone band of misfits who were solely concerned with the overthrow of American institutions. Yet, while the strikes of the IWW were often raucous and sometimes turned violent, much of the violence was initiated by local authorities and vigilante groups, and IWW members were themselves often the victims of the violence.[19]

Although the platform of the IWW focused on the overthrow of capitalism, at its height the IWW led a series of strikes that focused on improvements in wages and working conditions. The IWW was never able to attain a large membership. The IWW suffered from a poor image and a tension between its bold political goals and the more practical objectives favored by much of its membership.

When World War I began, "Big Bill" (William D.) Haywood and other leaders of the IWW opposed U.S. involvement and favored neither side in the conflict on the grounds that only capitalists would benefit from the war. Haywood and other IWW activists were eventually tried for sedition, and the IWW faded from the scene.

Injunctions and Antitrust Rulings

Unions faced additional difficulties in the early 1900s when the courts began to find that union actions were a violation of **antitrust legislation.** Federal antitrust legislation had passed Congress in an attempt to protect against the power acquired by expanding business combinations.

The Sherman Antitrust Act

The **Sherman Antitrust Act** of 1890 declared illegal every contract, combination, or conspiracy that restrained trade across state boundaries. The act did not refer directly to unions because Congress had business trusts and monopolies in mind and not unions when passing the law. Nevertheless, courts began to apply the Sherman Antitrust Act to unions.

The most celebrated antitrust case against a union (the **Danbury Hatters case**) occurred in 1908. The United Hatters of America had called for a consumer boycott against the D. E. Loewe Company in an effort to gain union recognition. The union then went

The working class and the employing class have nothing in common. There can be no peace so long as hunger and want are found among millions of working people and the few, who make up the employing class, have all the good things of life.

Between these two classes a struggle must go on until the workers of the world organize as a class, take possession of the earth and the machinery of production, and abolish the wage system.

We find that the centering of the management of industries into fewer and fewer hands makes the trade unions unable to cope with the ever growing power of the employing class. The trade unions foster a state of affairs which allows one set of workers to be pitted against another set of workers in the same industry, thereby helping defeat one another in wage wars. Moreover, the trade unions aid the employing class to mislead the workers into the belief that the working class have interests in common with their employers.

These conditions can be changed and the interest of the working class upheld only by an organization formed in such a way that all its members in any one industry, or in all industries if necessary, cease work whenever a strike or lockout is on in any department thereof, thus making an injury to one an injury to all.

Instead of the conservative motto, "A fair day's wage for a fair day's work," we must inscribe on our banner the revolutionary watchword, "Abolition of the wage system."

It is the historic mission of the working class to do away with capitalism. The army of production must be organized, not only for the every-day struggle with capitalists, but also to carry on production when capitalism shall have been overthrown. By organizing industrially we are forming the structure of the new society within the shell of the old.

Source: Paul F. Brissenden, *The I.W.W.: A Study of American Syndicalism,* 2d ed. (NY: Columbia University Press, 1920), pp. 351–52.

a step further and called for boycotts against other firms doing business with Loewe, a tactic known as a **secondary boycott.** The secondary boycott was directed at retailers, wholesalers, and customers and proved to be successful. Loewe and Company then went to court.

The U.S. Supreme Court eventually heard the case and ruled that unions were covered under the Sherman Antitrust Act. Specifically, the court directed the United Hatters to pay $250,000 in treble damages to the company.

The Clayton Act

Unions campaigned aggressively against the use of court injunctions and succeeded in gaining passage of the **Clayton Act** in 1914. The act declared that "the labor of a human being is not a commodity or article of commerce." Labor thought this language would lead to the end of labor injunctions. Yet courts interpreted the act narrowly, and unions continued to face judges who issued injunctions that limited the ability of unions to strike, picket, or boycott employers.

The Norris-LaGuardia Act

It was not until passage of the **Norris-LaGuardia Act** in 1932 that clear language outlawing the use of injunctions in most labor disputes was signed into law. The Norris-LaGuardia Act also outlawed yellow-dog contracts. Other provisions of the Norris-LaGuardia Act endorsed workers' rights to strike and to take other collective actions in their self-interest. These provisions foreshadowed the more comprehensive endorsement of collective bargaining that was to come with the passage of the National Labor Relations Act in 1935.

Samuel Gompers was proud of being a "practical" man. He believed in applying sound business practices to the union movement. He was not a theorist, but was convinced of the importance to labor of fighting for immediate aims. Once asked the objectives of the A.F.L., he reportedly answered with one word: "More."

The A.F.L. under Gompers avoided politics in the usual sense. "No party politics, be they democratic, republican, populist, socialist or any other, shall have a place in the Federation," said Gompers. But the A.F.L. did play an important role, under pressure from its members, in helping win social and labor legislation, nationally and in the states. Gompers was skeptical of some legislative proposals supported by liberal leaders, even opposing as a socialist trend government health, unemployment insurance, and old-age pensions. Gompers believed labor's gains should be won largely by collective bargaining. But he did lend the A.F.L. influence, which was considerable, for or against numerous other legislative efforts.

Source: William Cahn, *A Pictorial History of American Labor* (New York: Crown Publishers, 1976), pp. 205–7.

The Norris-LaGuardia Act lacked enforcement procedures. Thus, union recognition and collective bargaining remained a voluntary process between labor and management.

The Rise of the AFL

It was the **American Federation of Labor (AFL),** founded in 1886, that overcame the opposition of employers and the courts to build a membership able to survive the ups and downs of business cycles. The AFL was led by the former cigar maker Samuel Gompers (see Box 2–9) for all but one year between 1886 and his death in 1924.

Business Unionism

The AFL espoused a **business unionism** philosophy. This philosophy was well expressed by Gompers when he said that "the trades unions pure and simple are the organizations of the wage workers to secure their present material and practical improvement and to achieve their final emancipation."[20] Business unionism cut a compromise between the reformist Knights of Labor and the radical IWW.

The AFL was in favor of political action through which labor would help its friends and punish its opponents, but it eschewed any permanent political alliances or long-term political objectives. The AFL strategy was to promote the organization of workers into unions that had **exclusive jurisdiction** (where only one union represented a designated group of workers). The AFL strove to use collective bargaining to achieve improved wages and working conditions.

The AFL was (and is) a federation of national unions. It does not negotiate collective bargaining agreements but, rather, acts as the representative of national unions in political activities and political lobbying. The AFL also provides assistance to national unions in their union-organizing activities.

Craft Focus

One of the guiding principles of the AFL was that workers should be organized into separate **craft unions.** For this, each trade—such as carpenters, printers, machinists, and the skilled trades within large manufacturing firms—was to organize workers engaged in these occupations, regardless of the industry or firm in which the workers were employed.

The Evolution of Management in Industrial Relations

A full understanding of industrial relations history requires an equally well grounded understanding of the evolution of managerial practices. There is a growing school of thought among historians that it is American management, more than American unions, that makes U.S. labor history and contemporary industrial relations practices unique.[21] At the heart of this uniqueness lie two interrelated features of American management—the desire for autonomy from government or any other institution that might limit management's prerogatives and a deep-seated opposition to unions.

The Origins of Factory Management

Over the course of the 1800s a continual expansion of potential markets for manufactured goods was made possible by the growth of the railroad, telephone, and telegraph industries. This increase in markets led employers to adopt the factory system and mass production technologies (the assembly line). Through the factory system employers gained from economies of scale and low production costs.

"If a man is dissatisfied, it is his privilege to quit." This oft-quoted statement of a steel industry executive during the McKees Rocks, Pennsylvania, strike in 1909 captures the prevailing philosophy of U.S. employers and their response to worker unrest in the years before World War I. Company executives asserted their rights as owners to treat labor as a commodity and to oppose challenges to their authority by unions.

The Drive System

To manage the expanding factories, employers initially gave substantial power to line foremen, who were considered the **drive system** of management.[22] Hiring, firing, and general supervision of labor were all controlled by these foremen.[23] The arbitrary and often discriminatory treatment of workers by foremen created extremely high turnover rates among both unskilled and skilled workers. One estimate, for example, put turnover in auto plants before 1913 at 370 percent per year!

The costs of high turnover did not, however, go unnoticed by some managers. In 1913, for example, Henry Ford decided to introduce the $5 a day wage for his employees in an effort to lower employee turnover and to improve the performance of his auto assembly lines.

Around World War I the combination of tight labor markets, government pressure for wartime production, and a rising threat of unionization led a number of large firms to establish the professional personnel departments that are described in the next section. But the drive system continued to dominate the workplace in the majority of smaller establishments. And, regardless of whether foremen or personnel managers administered personnel policies, one managerial value held constant: unions capable of directly challenging management authority were to be avoided.

Scientific Management

The first important step toward establishing a professional personnel management function within the firm came with the introduction of **scientific management.** Although the ideas behind the scientific management movement can be traced as far back as the mid-1800s, Frederick Taylor's promotion of this movement in the first two decades of the 20th century was critical. Scientific management blended economic incentives and industrial engineering techniques to produce the "one best way" for organizing work. By tying the individual worker's wages to output, it was assumed, the interests of the worker—economic rewards—and the interests of the firm—productivity—could be made compatible.

Box 2–10 describes how scientific management principles were applied on Henry Ford's assembly line. Management's function was to design the jobs and to supervise and compensate the workforce so as to eliminate conflicts of interest between workers and the employer. Industrial engineering principles (such as time-and-motion studies) and incentive wages were employed to this end.

Scientific management stood in direct contradiction to the beliefs held by those who advocated collective bargaining. Instead of seeing conflicts of interest as an inherent part of the employment relationship, advocates of scientific management argued that appropriate task designs and wage systems could eliminate the sources of conflict between workers and employers. Because the optimal work system was to be determined through "scientific" engineering studies, there was no role for bargaining and therefore no need for union representation.

One lasting effect of scientific management was its advocacy of industrial engineering principles and a narrow division of labor in organizing work. This form of job design and work organization gradually became the standard in the mass-production industries, and unions inherited this form when they expanded their membership in the mass-production industries (such as auto, steel, and textiles) in the 1930s.

Welfare Capitalism, Human Relations, and the American Plan

By 1920 another competing method of management gained popularity. The **human relations movement** (or **welfare capitalism**) stressed the social significance of work and work groups. Human relations theory predicted that satisfied workers would achieve higher productivity. The scientific management and human relations schools both believed that by following their principles employers could eliminate conflict with workers, thereby eliminating workers' need for union representation.

As the basic tenets of human relations gained influence over the 1920s, personnel departments gradually expanded in scope and influence. The departments centralized and standardized many of the functions that had previously been controlled by foremen. Hiring, firing, discipline, promotion, and compensation policies were developed and administered by the personnel staff. Foremen, in turn, were trained to follow these policies.

Management's Response to Unionism in the 1920s

Coinciding with the growth of progressive personnel policies during and after World War I was an aggressive **open shop movement.** This movement sought to discourage unionization through company-controlled independent unions and the expansion of pension, welfare, and profit-sharing programs. By the mid-1920s, these progressive personnel programs were commonplace among the very largest firms in manufacturing and service industries.[24]

Production efficiency in the final assembly of cars rose, but the soaring demand for Ford's Model T, introduced in 1908, rose even faster. Ford still had to rely on skilled mechanics to perform the complicated tasks in the Piquette plant—such as filing and fitting together the parts for transmissions and engines. These workers were not protected by union work rules, but their monopoly of mechanical skills and their crucial role in the production process enabled them to work at their own pace. Even the less-skilled assembly workers had some control over their work pace. As they pushed their bins from car to car, they could slow down to rest or to speak a word with their workmates. Beyond a certain point, supervisors simply could not force the men to adopt a faster gait or completely abandon their occasional socializing.

To gain greater control over the production process, Ford began to lay plans for a new plant in the rural village of Highland Park. It would be, he announced, the biggest automobile plant in the world, employing new production methods that would revolutionize the auto industry.

Ford was not alone in seeking ways to spur production and lower labor costs. Factory owners had been mechanizing and deskilling certain kinds of production for many years, but after 1900, the nation's larger corporations attempted to do so on a broader, more systematic basis. The principles of this new "scientific management" were most vigorously espoused by Frederick Taylor, a former steel mill supervisor who became, after 1903, the nation's leading consultant on "productivity"—or worker output.

Like Ford, Taylor complained that in most workplaces—whether union or nonunion—"The shop [is] really run by the workmen and not by the bosses. The workmen together carefully plan . . . just how fast each job should be done." Taylor's solution was simple: "All possible brainwork should be removed from the shop and centered in the planning or laying-out department." Management, in short, should redesign every job and divide it into dozens of simple, repetitive tasks performed by unskilled laborers or semi-skilled machine tenders. Skilled workers with their relatively high pay would no longer have to be tolerated in such large numbers. With deskilling, most craftsmen would be replaced, in Taylor's words, "by men of smaller attainments, who are therefore cheaper than those required under the old system."

When Taylor came to Detroit in 1909 and spoke to executives at Packard, Henry Ford was already planning to make his new Highland Park plant (dubbed the "Crystal Palace" because of its many windows) a model of "scientific management." Between 1910 and 1913, he put his ideas into practice by standardizing parts production and developing the auto industry's first moving assembly line. Where before entire engines had been built by a single mechanic with a few helpers, now the engine blocks were pulled past a line of over 100 workers. Each worker performed a specialized task as the engine (or its parts) moved past: one would ream bearings, one every seven seconds, all day long; the next would file bearings, one every 14 seconds, all day long; and the next would put bearings on camshafts, one every 10 seconds, all day long.

H. L. Arnold, writing of Ford in 1916, concluded that the company "desires and prefers machine operators who have nothing to unlearn, who have no theories of correct surface speeds for metal finishing, and who will do what they are told, over and over again, from bell-time to bell-time.

Source: Quoted from Steve Babson, *Working Detroit* (New York: Adama Books, 1984), pp. 29–31.

With the growth of progressive personnel policies came a corresponding growth in suppressive anti-union practices, such as industrial espionage, blacklisting of union members or supporters, strikebreaking, and use of private police forces to disband picket lines. Company-controlled unions were set up in a number of chemical, oil, and other large firms.

The combination of progressive and suppressive policies to avoid unions was highly successful. Union membership fell from 5.8 million members in 1921 to fewer than 2 million members in 1931.

The Rise of Industrial Unionism

As the organization of production moved from small shops to large-scale mass production, the vast array of semiskilled and unskilled production workers were left without a basis for organizing. Furthermore, the AFL's emphasis on craft organizing made it difficult to counter the power of large-scale industrial corporations. For example, in 1919 a strike against the steel industry was called by 24 different unions with jurisdiction over different craft groups. The strike ultimately failed in part because of the inability of these unions to coordinate their efforts.

As a result, by the early 1920s a number of union leaders and socialists were urging the formation of new **industrial unions** that would organize all production and maintenance workers in a given industry, regardless of their skill level or craft. Since this approach to organizing would cut into the jurisdictions of many established craft unions, it was opposed vigorously by Gompers, by his successor as president of the AFL, William Green, and by other AFL union presidents.

The CIO Challenge to the AFL

The debate between the advocates of AFL craft unions and the advocates of industrial unionism came to a head at the AFL convention in 1935. At this convention John L. Lewis, president of the United Mine Workers and a leading spokesman for industrial unionism (see Box 2–11), lost a crucial vote on the issue of granting charters to industrial unions in the auto and rubber industries. A fight ensued, and Lewis landed a punch on the nose of "Big Bill" Hutcheson, president of the Carpenters' Union. Lewis and his supporters then stormed out of the convention and established the Committee for Industrial Organization as a rival federation to the AFL. Later this group changed its name to the **Congress of Industrial Organizations (CIO).**

The member unions in the CIO enlisted a large number of socialists as union organizers and, in general, projected a more militant image in collective bargaining than did many of the AFL unions. At the same time, the CIO and the AFL shared a commitment to the use of collective bargaining as the central means of achieving economic gains for their members.

The National Industrial Recovery Act

The great depression and its staggering unemployment raised doubts in the work force's mind about management's true commitment to progressive personnel policies. Labor unrest was rising, both in its frequency and its intensity. Encouraged by the passage of the **National Industrial Recovery Act (NIRA)** in 1933, Section 7(a) of which declared the rights of employees to self-organize, workers began organizing in greater numbers and strikes increased. By 1934 union membership and strike activity had returned to the levels reached in the years immediately after World War I.[25]

But in 1935 the Supreme Court ruled the NIRA unconstitutional. The stage was set for a crucial public policy debate, the ultimate outcome of which was the **New Deal** industrial relations system.

No labor leader played a more important or colorful role in history from the 1930s to the 1950s than John L. Lewis. His skill in capturing the changed political climate of the Roosevelt administration is illustrated by the following handbill used in organizing coal miners in the 1930s.

> The United States Government Has Said LABOR MUST ORGANIZE. . . . Forget about injunctions, yellow dog contracts, blacklists, and the fear of dismissal. The employers cannot and will not dare to go to the Government for privileges if it can be shown that they have denied the right of organization to their employees. ALL WORKERS ARE FULLY PROTECTED IF THEY DESIRE TO JOIN A UNION.

Organize John L. Lewis did—5 million American workers into industrial unions in the major mass production industries of the nation in about 4 years.

. . .

Lewis was the son of a Welsh immigrant coal miner. He went to work in the coal mines at 14 and his quick mind, strong personality, and gift for oratory soon won him election to Illinois union posts. In 1920 Lewis became president of the United Mine Workers of America. From that time until his death in 1960 he pursued the course of organizing the unorganized and representing workers in collective bargaining and political affairs with the vigor and style that is nicely captured in the following excerpt from one of his speeches:

> I have never faltered or failed to present the cause or plead the case of the mine workers of this country. I have pleaded your case from the pulpit and the public platform; in joint conferences with the operators of this country; before the bar of state legislatures; in the councils of the President's cabinet; and in the public press of this nation—not in the quavering tones of a feeble mendicant asking alms, but in the thundering voice of the captain of a mighty host, demanding the rights to which free men are entitled.

Source: Quoted from B. Kimball Baker, "The Great Depression," in *200 Years of American Worklife* (Washington, DC: U.S. Department of Labor, 1977), pp. 142, 150.

The New Deal Labor Policy

The election of Franklin D. Roosevelt as President in 1932, and the economic and social crises caused by the great depression (described in Box 2–12), gave rise to a new era in federal labor policy. Roosevelt introduced a series of new governmental programs designed to bolster citizens' purchasing power and to assist workers and the poor to cope with their economic hardships. The new programs included unemployment insurance, job creation, social security, and the minimum wage. Roosevelt's program became known as the New Deal.

The National Labor Relations Act

A critical part of the New Deal agenda was enactment of a new labor policy. The cornerstone of the new national labor policy was the **National Labor Relations Act (NLRA)** of 1935, also known as the Wagner Act after its chief legislative sponsor, Senator Robert F. Wagner of New York. The NLRA was important because it explicitly encouraged collective bargaining. The NLRA gave employees the right to organize themselves into unions, set standards for union elections, and specified unfair labor practices of employers.

John L. Lewis and his CIO colleagues quickly capitalized on this changing environment by, among other things, imploring workers to join unions with slogans such as "The

People perceived the Great Depression in different ways. Some looked at it dramatically, as did British economist John Maynard Keynes when he compared the situation in Europe and on the American continent to the Dark Ages. Others looked at it simply, like the 14-year-old Appalachian boy in Chicago who said, "See, I never heard that word 'depression' before. They would all just say 'hard times' to me."

The bare facts of the situation are eloquent enough. By early 1933 unemployment had increased to about 13 million—about 25 percent of the labor force. A third of these people were between the ages of 16 and 24. Hourly wages were down 60 percent. Industrial output was down by about half. On the farm, income was off by two-thirds, tenancy had doubled. One of every 4 farms was being foreclosed, and 500,000 farm families were living at the starvation level. A million transients were on the road, including 200,000 young people.

Unemployed autoworkers marched on the closed River Rouge Ford plant in Dearborn, Michigan, and four of them were shot by notorious "security guard" Harry Bennett and his thugs.

Former professionals and skilled tradespeople demonstrated potato papers and patent medicines in store windows and sold apples on street corners to the tune of a popular song, "Brother Can You Spare a Dime?" which reflected the desperate times.

A huge band of jobless veterans encamped in Washington and were routed in a needless show of military force which involved future war heroes named MacArthur, Eisenhower, and Patton.

Source: Quoted from B. Kimball Baker, "The Great Depression," in *200 Years of American Worklife* (Washington, DC: U.S. Department of Labor, 1977), pp. 140–41.

President Wants You To Organize!" (See also Box 2–11.) It was in this new environment that the autoworkers in Detroit and the rubber workers in Akron refused to leave their plants and staged successful **sit-down strikes,** through which they gained collective bargaining contracts. Unrest and worker militancy convinced many employers in the steel industry and others that unions and collective bargaining were to stay.

The Roots of the NLRA in American Practice and Experience

The NLRA did not constitute a completely new or untried way for resolving labor and management conflicts. Instead, the act embodied many of the principles and practices that had demonstrated their fit with American political values and with the practices of many unions and companies. The railroad, clothing, and other industries, for example, had developed ongoing relationships in the years before the depression.

The new law also codified many of the policies that had been recommended and pursued by the national War Labor Board (regulating wages and prices) in World War I and the National Labor Board that had been established under the now-defunct NIRA. The law also endorsed the pragmatic form of collective bargaining that had been promoted by the AFL.

Nonetheless, the law was not passed without vocal and vociferous opposition from employer groups. It was not until the NLRA was ruled constitutional by the Supreme Court in 1937, in the *NLRA* v. *Jones & Laughlin* case,[26] that most firms began to accept the inevitability of collective bargaining.

Indeed, it was not the law alone that produced the transition to what we will refer to as the **New Deal industrial relations system.** Instead, this turning point in industrial relations was brought about by the confluence of (1) a shift in political power that accompanied the depression and the election of the Roosevelt administration, which created the support needed to enact legislation in favor of worker and union rights to bargain; (2) a shift in the strategy of the labor movement away from the craft union and voluntarist model of the AFL under Gompers to the industrial unionism model of organizing and representing workers promulgated by the CIO; and (3) the passage of a law that provided a stable foundation for collective bargaining.

This was indeed a unique confluence of events. The events surrounding passage of the NLRA were unique because, as labor historian Irving Bernstein has argued, the NLRA was passed at "the most favorable possible moment," when political support for improving the economic conditions of the nation's workers was at its historic high-water mark.[27]

The New Deal industrial relations system is examined below using the three-tiered model of the strategic, middle, and workplace levels of industrial relations practices.

The Middle Level: Collective Bargaining as the Cornerstone

The enactment of the NLRA signaled the choice of the middle tier of activity as the preferred forum for labor and management jointly to address and to resolve their differences. Once a majority of workers indicated that they wanted to be represented by a union, management was required by law to negotiate with that union over wages, hours, and working conditions.

It was hoped the NLRA would foster industrial peace. Peace would be encouraged, first, by replacing what had often been violent conflicts over union recognition with orderly election procedures and, second, by lending a degree of permanence to the union's right to represent the employees. Employers could no longer unilaterally terminate their recognition of a union during recessions.

The Strategic Level: Management Acts and the Union Reacts

Management rights to make strategic business decisions were left intact by the NLRA. As collective bargaining evolved, the principle "management acts and the workers react" became its key doctrine.[28]

Leaving strategic business decisions to management fit not only management's desire for control over the key decisions on resource allocation in the firm, but also the business unionism philosophy of the labor movement. Even the supporters of industrial unionism held to the view that unions should not seek to participate directly in managerial decision making or to gain control of private enterprise. Instead, unions sought to preserve their independence through the maintenance of a clear separation between union and management duties.

The American labor movement had a moderate agenda for political and social reform. Labor had no ultimate political goal of overthrowing the capitalist system but, rather, sought to improve workers' living standards gradually. Thus, at the strategic level, the New Deal system coincided with the values held by many in the ranks of the labor movement, as well as those held by management and the American public.

The Workplace Level: Job Control Unionism

The arrival of established rules for collective bargaining did not produce a revolutionary new system for organizing work. The principles of scientific management had spread in industry as many employers became convinced of the need to rationalize the structure of jobs and the methods of pay. What collective bargaining did do was to codify many of the existing work systems within the labor contract.[29]

The writing of labor contracts met the needs of both management and labor. Labor reaped greater uniformity and fairness in workplace administration and thereby overcame much of the arbitrary power previously exercised by foremen. Management, in turn, achieved the work force stability necessary to take advantage of growing market opportunities. Government policymakers came to value the industrial peace this system provided during World War II, and they actively promoted this system.

The Post–World War II Evolution of the New Deal System

The New Deal system gradually diffused throughout the United States as union membership expanded from 3.5 million in 1934 to 17 million, or approximately 35 percent of the nonagricultural labor force, by the mid-1950s. Although the 1950s proved to mark the peak of union penetration in the private sector economy, the New Deal principles continue to shape collective bargaining to the present day. Within this long evolution, however, several distinct stages of development can be identified.

The 1940s: Institutionalization of Basic Principles

The exigencies of World War II demanded that labor and management maximize production of the goods needed to support the war, while avoiding both strikes and wage and price inflation. To help achieve these objectives, the Roosevelt administration established the national **War Labor Board (WLB)** in January 1942. The WLB was a tripartite agency, composed of neutrals who chaired boards of inquiry that included representatives of labor and management. Although the agency lacked any legal enforcement power, the tripartite structure, the national commitment to the war effort, and the implicit threat of more direct legislative intervention gave the "recommendations" of the agency considerable influence. From 1942 to 1945 the WLB succeeded in helping settle over 20,000 labor-management disputes.[30]

In carrying out this role, the board also used its offices to promote wider acceptance of collective bargaining. In fact, many of the actual contracts the board wrote remained in effect, with minor changes, throughout the postwar era.

In addition to its substantive role in helping gain acceptance of collective bargaining, the WLB served as a training group for many of the leading mediators, arbitrators, and government advisors who would later shape the evolution of collective bargaining in the decades that followed the war. Those professionals shared a deep commitment to a type of collective bargaining that involved little direct government intervention. George W. Taylor, chairman of the WLB and a leading teacher and neutral after the war, described his and his colleagues' views as follows:

> One conclusion invariably emerges whenever and wherever "the labor problem" is subjected to impartial analysis. It is: collective bargaining must be preserved and strengthened as the bulwark of industrial relations in a democracy. This is just another way of saying that organized labor and management should settle their own differences by understanding, compromises, and agreement without government interference. A rare unanimity of opinion exists about the soundness of collective bargaining as the most appropriate means for establishing conditions of employment.[31]

After the war ended and the WLB was disbanded, a surge of strikes overtook the nation, as illustrated in Box 2–13. The strikes were in part spurred by labor's efforts to gain wage

With the end of the war, the expected strike wave began. . . . Forty-three thousand oil workers struck in twenty states on September 16th (1945). Two hundred thousand coal miners struck September 21st. . . . Forty-four thousand Northwest lumber workers struck, seventy thousand Midwest truck drivers, forty thousand machinists in San Francisco and Oakland. East Coast longshoremen struck for nineteen days, flat glass workers for 102 days, and New England textile workers for 133 days. . . .

When G.M. failed to respond to a union offer to have all issues settled by arbitration if the company would open its books for public examination, 225,000 workers struck on November 21st. . . . On January 15th, 1946, 174,000 electrical workers struck. Next day 93,000 meatpackers walked out. On January 21st, 750,000 steelworkers struck, the largest strike in United States history. At the height of these and 250 lesser disputes, 1,600,000 workers were on strike. On April 1st, 340,000 soft-coal miners struck. . . . The first six months of 1946 marked what the U.S. Bureau of Labor Statistics called the "most concentrated period of labor-management strife in the country's history," with 2,970,000 workers involved in strikes starting in this period.

Source: Jeremy Brecher, *Strike!* (San Francisco: Straight Arrow Books, 1972), pp. 227–28.

increases that had been forgone during the war. In 1946 more production time was lost because of strikes than in any year before or since.

The strike wave, along with a general swing toward a more conservative political climate and a switch to Republican control of the Congress, contributed to the passage of the Labor Management Relations Act, known as the Taft-Hartley Act, in 1947. The act's amendments to the NLRA strengthened management's power at the bargaining table by limiting the union's rights to boycott the employer and by establishing a detailed set of rules that governed the union's obligation to bargain. It also designated the rights of the government to intervene in strikes that constituted national emergencies.

All of those changes reflected a shift in the public's view. The postwar strike wave had led many in the public to conclude that unions were too powerful.

Given this turn in the political environment, employers might have attempted, as in previous periods of labor history, to break from their union relationships. Collective bargaining had become sufficiently entrenched, however, and unions were viewed as sufficiently strong that a rebalancing of labor-management power occurred instead.

Throughout the 1940s management in the larger unionized firms had taken steps to professionalize their industrial relations staffs. The postwar strike wave further elevated the importance of trained professionals who could help stabilize labor-management relations by establishing formal procedures for negotiating and administering labor contracts. As the large firms adapted to collective bargaining, they served as examples for smaller organizations.[32] Thus, the rise of powerful unions had produced a managerial response to professionalize labor-management relations.

Unions, too, faced and made a number of key strategic choices in the 1940s that had an important bearing on the shape of collective bargaining in subsequent years. In the immediate postwar years conflicts emerged inside unions over the role of Communists in the labor movement. The net results of these battles were that the CIO expelled a number of Communist-dominated unions (such as the United Electrical Workers) and that some individual unions (such as the United Auto Workers) purged Communist party members from leadership positions.

The 1946 round of bargaining in the auto industry illustrates the choices union leaders made that were to affect the long-term development of collective bargaining. During the 1946 Auto Workers' strike against General Motors, Walter Reuther, head of the General Motors department of the union, called on GM to open its financial records to the union. Reuther proposed limiting the UAW wage demands in return for a pledge by GM not to raise prices. If those demands had been accepted, it would have transformed collective bargaining by expanding union influence over to strategic management issues. But as a result of his demands, Reuther came under heavy criticism from Philip Murray, president of the CIO. Murray urged Reuther to accept the more conventional steel industry wage pattern and to stay out of the managerial decision-making process in order to maintain labor's independence from management. Reuther eventually dropped his proposal and negotiated a conventional wage settlement.

The labor movement broadly chose not to press for inroads into managerial prerogatives and instead focused on improving wages and gradually expanding the scope of issues covered under the contract. Unions chose to follow the practices encouraged by the early administrators of the Wagner Act and nurtured by the members of the War Labor Board.

The 1950s: A Return to Hard Bargaining

By the 1950s few differences remained in the bargaining agendas or organizing strategies of the AFL and CIO unions. As a result, these two federations merged in 1955 to become the AFL-CIO. The merger allowed the member unions to focus their energies more directly on expanding the wage and benefit gains introduced in collective bargaining in the 1940s.

The early years of the 1950s saw collective bargaining spread throughout the major firms and unions in key sectors of the economy including steel, coal, rubber, meat packing, and transportation. The **scope of bargaining** also continued to expand and take up such topics as supplementary unemployment benefits, pensions, severance payments for workers dislocated by technological change or plant closings, and a variety of other fringe benefits and working conditions.[33]

But near the end of the decade a harder line in collective bargaining appeared as firms sought to limit any further expansion of the scope of bargaining or the influence of unions. The most visible example of this was General Electric's policy, which came to be known as **Boulwarism** after Lemuel Boulware, the architect of the policy and GE's vice president of industrial relations.[34] Boulwarism was a management strategy for regaining the initiative in bargaining. GE polled workers to determine their needs and then made one "firm and final" offer in negotiations. This offer reflected the financial condition of the firm and the results of the worker surveys. Boulwarism was eventually ruled by the courts to be a violation of the bargaining requirements in the NLRA. Boulwarism illustrates the aggressive position that had spread in management circles, however. By 1959, for example, at U.S. Steel a 116-day strike occurred over management's right to change work rules. Similar strikes broke out in the late 1950s in the railroad, airline, electrical products, and other industries.

Management's tougher stance paralleled a decline in labor's public image and political influence. In the late 1950s a series of congressional hearings highlighted corruption within the Teamsters and other unions. The culmination of the congressional debates over internal union affairs was the passage of the Labor-Management Reporting and Disclosure Act (Landrum-Griffin Act) as an amendment to the NLRA. As spelled out in more detail in the next chapter, Landrum-Griffin established reporting and disclosure requirements for union finances, specified the rights of individual union members, and regulated how union leaders could represent their members' interests.

Nonetheless, although many firms adopted a hard line in bargaining, collective bargaining continued in many sectors of the American economy in the 1950s. Only a few firms began to experiment with an alternative—a new form of nonunion human resource management. It was not until the turbulent 1960s that the latter spread.

The 1960s: Rank-and-File Unrest

The 1960s were marked by strong economic growth as well as social and political upheavals. These upheavals included the civil rights movement, urban riots, and wide-scale protests over continued expansion of the Vietnamese war. The economic growth and environment of protest fed employee militance at the workplace. This was exemplified by a growing number of contract demands, wildcat strikes during the term of the contract, and rank-and-file rejections of contracts negotiated by their union leaders.[35] At the same time, unions were beginning to reap success in organizing large numbers of public sector workers.

The 1960s were years of great challenge to management and union leaders alike. In the private sector the parties struggled to cope with pent-up pressures and conflicts at the workplace and in local unions. In the public sector labor and management searched for principles to guide the extension of collective bargaining to this new terrain.

Meanwhile, stimulated by governmental research and development expenditures to support the effort to catch up with the Soviet Union in the space race, the demand for white-collar, technical, and managerial employees expanded rapidly. What later came to be known as the high technology industries were born and flourished.

These forces had two effects on collective bargaining. First, the power of personnel and human resource management professionals grew as they were charged with satisfying the needs of the expanding highly skilled employees. The role of human resource professionals was further expanded by passage of new government regulations that covered the workplace, such as equal employment opportunity laws. Second, the high-technology organizations developed novel human resource strategies and policies. Unions found it very difficult to organize the expanding high-tech firms.

As a result of these and other pressures, the late 1950s and early 1960s marked a turning point for union membership levels in the private sector. From the early 1950s to today growth in union membership has not kept pace with increases in the size of the labor force.

The 1970s: Stability and Atrophy

The 1970s may go down in American labor history as one of the least distinguished in the history of collective bargaining. As the economic pressures to change collective bargaining intensified, labor and management continued to follow the patterns of behavior that had developed in the earlier years. Management became preoccupied with holding the line against any further union gains in bargaining. And labor leaders seemed to push no further than preserving the gains they or their predecessors had achieved in collective bargaining in previous decades.

Interest in issues such as productivity improvement and the quality of working life began to surface in labor-management discussions. But little more than isolated and limited experimentation in collective bargaining resulted.

Government policymakers as well were stymied. A political stalemate emerged between labor and management, evidenced by the failure of Congress and a Democratic President to pass labor law reforms in 1978.[36] No party—labor, management, or governmental—successfully initiated any bold advance in bargaining practice, yet each seemed quite effective in constraining the actions of the others. Despite pressures from mounting foreign competition and domestic nonunion competition, union workers' wages grew more rapidly throughout the 1970s than did nonunion wages.

During the 1970s industrial relations professionals continued to emphasize the goals of labor peace and stability, while pressures for change continued to mount. As a result, they became more defensive and isolated from other managers within many corporations, and their influence with top executives began gradually to erode. It was not until a dramatic shift in the environment took place in the early 1980s, however, that these mounting pressures suddenly propelled the parties into an era of fundamental change in collective bargaining.

The 1980s: Experimentation and Change

The election of Ronald Reagan as President reflected a strong conservative shift in the political climate of the country. This shift was vividly illustrated early in Reagan's administration when he fired and permanently replaced air traffic controllers (members of the Professional Air Traffic Controller Union, PATCO) who had gone out on strike in August 1981.

PATCO had been engaging in an illegal strike over the terms of a new collective bargaining contract. Although the President's actions were directed at employees of the federal government, those actions sent a strong message to employers that the labor movement had lost not only much of its political power but also the public's support. The firing of striking controllers and the demise of PATCO solidified the resolve of employers to seize the initiative in collective bargaining.

The deep economic recession of 1981–83 further mobilized many employers to sidestep or even abolish collective bargaining. The rise in the value of the U.S. dollar against foreign currencies further reduced the competitiveness of U.S. producers that operated in foreign markets. Massive layoffs in key, highly unionized sectors resulted, reaching deep into union ranks and thereby cutting off the unions' primary source of bargaining power. Plant closings and mass layoffs spread to the point that some analysts argued that a deindustrialization of America was underway. Thus began the era of **concessionary bargaining** that entailed unions agreeing to wage cuts or freezes or in other ways giving back to employers previous gains. Union concessions along with other factors led to particularly difficult times for poorly educated workers, and this contributed to a growing inequality in the income distribution.

The rate of decline in union membership not only continued during the 1980s, it accelerated. By 1985 the labor movement publicly acknowledged the depth of its membership crisis and called on its leaders to consider a variety of new strategies.[37]

At the same time, new forms of employee participation and new concepts of how to organize work appeared in some workplaces. Thus, on the one hand unions were negotiating concessionary agreements and losing members. On the other hand, some of the concessionary contracts included gains by providing employees with employment security or direct participation in business decisions. Employers were taking things away from unions while at the same time offering unions some of the very things they had always wanted. By the late 1980s better times appeared in some manufacturing industries, such as autos and aerospace, and elements of traditional collective bargaining including pattern bargaining began to reappear.

Although these contradictory pressures did not hit all bargaining relationships with equal force, their cumulative effects posed fundamental challenges to the basic principles that underlaid the New Deal industrial relations system. There were changes occurring at all three levels of the traditional bargaining system.

At the workplace level unions were challenged by new forms of worker and union participation and by more direct communication between workers and management. At the middle level of industrial relations, unions were making major concessions to their traditional wage settlements and **work rules** (such as fewer job classifications). Meanwhile, substantial strategic level changes were also occurring that often involved greater union involvement in strategic business issues.

The nature and extent of these changes varied considerably across the range of bargaining relationships in different industries and firms. By no means were they universal, and they may not prove to be lasting features of collective bargaining. But the new practices were in use in enough bargaining relationships to lead many American managers and unionists to discuss whether these new practices were superior to traditional collective bargaining.

Thus, the 1980s proved to be a critical period of experimentation and new strategic choices for management, labor, and government decision makers. All three of these actors now had to decide which of the new ideas deserved to be encouraged and which of the traditional practices should be preserved.

The 1990s: Income and Collective Bargaining Polarization

Even though the economy experienced an extremely strong recovery which started in the early 1990s, there was growing polarization in collective bargaining and in the labor market experiences of American employees. In the early 1990s, corporate downsizing and reengineering led to layoffs and insecurity, particularly among middle managers and white collar employees that bore an uncharacteristicly large share of the brunt of these initiatives. Income bifurcation continued in the face of large rewards to those employees who were highly educated (and particularly large rewards to top corporate management), while poorly educated workers fared very badly as new technologies and heightened international competition spurred industrial changes.

Unions everywhere became concerned about employment security, a concern that helped spur the negotiation of modest pay increases, which in turn helped produce low rates of inflation and unemployment in this period. Meanwhile, labor-management relations also became more polarized. At some firms unions and management deepened a participatory style of interaction that included team forms of work organization and union involvement in business issues. On the other side stood highly conflictual relationships, as at the Caterpillar Corporation, where bitter strikes involved the use of permanent striker replacements and union decertification.

The nonunion sector continued to grow in the private sector as management aggressively resisted union organization and took advantage of new technologies and relatively lax enforcement of the nation's labor laws to shift work within or outside the country, or relied on outsourcing or "contingent labor" to meet competitive pressures and union organizing efforts. Unions struggled to battle back with a renewed emphasis on organizing and with new leaders at the head of the AFL-CIO.

2000 to the Present: Challenges of the New Millennium

Recent economic pressures have spurred a substantial increase in the amount and nature of the variation in employment practices in the United States. Some of the increased variation has been spurred by a decline in unionization and the differences that exist between the union and nonunion sectors. Perhaps most striking is the fact that even within the union and nonunion sectors variation has been increasing through the spread of a diverse array of employment practices.

In the late 1990s and at the start of the new millennium, hyper-mobility appeared in the labor market for computer programmers and related professional employees as employees relatively easily moved across firms, in part to take advantage of attractive stock option offers. Highly skilled employees gained substantial individual bargaining power in this period and this led to significant increases in their earnings. Given the continuing presence of a large low-wage sector in the U.S. labor market, these pressures led to further income bifurcation. Yet, when the high-tech bubble burst in mid-2000, the extent and attractiveness of interfirm mobility declined sharply.

Faced with a growing nonunion sector, the American labor movement increased the intensity of its efforts to revitalize. Union organizers increasingly were being elected to leadership positions (including the presidency in some cases) in national unions. National unions and the AFL-CIO began to spend significant monies on organizing, and innovative organizing tactics, including efforts to organize on a community or regional basis, spread. Debates within the labor movement led some national unions to withdraw from the AFL-CIO and create a rival union confederation, the Change to Win coalition. Some unions began to make greater use of a triangular agenda linking organizing, politics, and collective bargaining. Overall, while some unions found innovative ways to gain bargaining leverage, other unions struggled in the face of declining bargaining power.

Wide variation has appeared in the tenor of recent U.S. collective bargaining. In some firms heightened conflict has appeared, while in some others extensive partnerships have been forged. While some workers suffered greatly as management took advantage of power provided through nonunion growth and globalization, in some other firms unions used innovative bargaining or traditional strike leverage to make gains.

The expansion of international trade and the accelerated expansion of multinational corporations extended markets internationally and challenged the international labor movement to forge cross-national unionism. While a number of American unions took steps in this direction, their efforts faced persistent barriers. Meanwhile, a variety of organizations and activities seeking to protect international labor rights were spurred by concerns about the effects of globalization. These activities included antisweatshop campaigns on university campuses and "fair" trade initiatives.

Debates on the virtues of the market-driven U.S. economic system shifted with the bursting of the dot com bubble and were also strongly affected by the emergence of corporate financial scandals involving Enron, Worldcom, and other major U.S. corporations in 2002. Criticisms surfaced concerning whether the market and financially oriented U.S. economic system gave too much authority to corporate owners and top executives and provided too limited a role to representatives of the public and employees.

Summary

The history of collective bargaining traced in this chapter reveals that developments in collective bargaining cannot always be accurately predicted by extrapolating from existing patterns of behavior. Incremental changes in the status quo did provide a good prediction for the relatively stable years of the 1950s and the 1970s. But events in the 1920s did not anticipate the arrival of industrial unionism and the enactment of the New Deal model in the 1930s. Furthermore, status quo bargaining in the 1970s was followed by the fundamental changes to the New Deal system from the early 1980s on. Then in the new millennium a rival union confederation emerged promoting aggressive organizing and bargaining strategies.

The lesson is clear. Relations between labor and management are highly dynamic and adapt over time to changes in the environment and the wants of the participants.

It is also clear that collective bargaining gained acceptance in American society only recently and then only as part of a larger set of economic and social reforms. Furthermore, management and labor attitudes toward unions continued to shift over the last 40 years in response, in part, to shifts in environmental pressures. To understand the operation of collective bargaining, it is necessary to explore how forces in the environment interact with the strategies and structures of labor and management.

American labor history reveals the critical influence of labor law and public policy on the evolution of collective bargaining. Chapter 3 focuses on the evolution of American labor law, and Chapter 4 examines other environmental influences on industrial relations.

Discussion Questions

1. Briefly explain why workers joined unions, according to Commons.
2. Discuss the legal reaction toward unionization before the NLRA (1935).
3. Contrast the drive system and scientific management.
4. Identify the different national unions that emerged in the United States in the 19th century and contrast their basic goals.
5. What was the impact of the NLRA after it was held constitutional?
6. Outline the key eras that appeared in American collective bargaining after World War II.

Related Web Sites

American Federation of Labor–Congress of Industrial Organizations (AFL-CIO):
http://www.aflcio.org/home.htm
http://www.aflcio.org/sweeny.htm

United Automobile Workers (UAW):
http://www.uaw.org/history/index.html

General Motors (GM):
http://www.gm.com/about/info/news/ message.html
http://www.gm.com/about/info/ overview/history/index.html

Industrial Workers of the World (IWW):
http://www.iww.org/qanda/s1.html

Boeing:
http://www.boeing.com

International Association of Mechanics (IAM):
http://iamaw.org/special/interest_ resources.htm

United Food and Commerical Workers (UFCW):
http://ufcw.org/home.html
http://ufcwlocal951.com/collective_ bargaining.html

Hormel:
http://www.hormel.com

Suggested Readings

Brody, Davis. *Workers in Industrial America: Essays on the Twentieth Century Struggle* (New York: Cambridge University Press, 1982).

Harris, Howell. *The Right to Manage* (Madison: University of Wisconsin Press, 1983).

Jacoby, Sanford M. *Employing Bureaucracy* (New York: Columbia University Press, 1985).

Lens, Sidney. *The Labor Wars: From the Molly Maguires to the Sit-Downs* (Garden City, NY: Doubleday, 1973).

Rayback, Joseph G. *A History of American Labor* (New York: Macmillan, 1966).

Salvatore, Nick, ed. *Seventy Years of Life and Labor: An Autobiography of Samuel Gompers* (Ithaca, NY: ILR Press, Cornell University, 1984).

End Notes

1. Quoted from Henry Pelling, *American Labor* (Chicago: University of Chicago Press, 1960), p. 4.
2. Ibid., p. 12.
3. Thomas Brooks, *Toil and Trouble* (Chicago: University of Chicago Press, 1971), p. 2.
4. Ibid., p. 4.
5. Herbert Gutman, *Work, Culture, and Society in Industrializing America* (New York: Alfred A. Knopf, 1975).
6. Neil W. Chamberlain and James W. Kuhn, *Collective Bargaining,* 3d ed. (New York: McGraw-Hill, 1986), pp. 6–8.
7. John R. Commons, "American Shoemakers, 1648–1895," *Labor and Administration* (New York: Macmillan Co., 1913), pp. 210–64. On this issue Marxist theories and the institutionalist view of what early unions and workers wanted differed deeply. The Marxists claimed that unionism entailed an effort by workers to regain control over the production process. The institutionalists argued that workers and unions were primarily oriented (at least in the United States) toward improving workers' income and work conditions.
8. Sanford M. Jacoby, "The Duration of Indefinite Employment Contracts in the United States and England: An Historical Analysis," *Comparative Labor Law* 5 (Winter 1982): 85–128.
9. For a thorough historical analysis of labor developments during this period, see Joseph G. Rayback, *A History of American Labor* (New York: The Free Press, 1966), pp. 75–92.
10. Brooks, *Toil and Trouble,* p. 28.
11. For a good concise summary of the *Commonwealth* v. *Hunt* case and other legal doctrines in American labor history, see William B. Gould, *A Primer on American Labor Law* (Cambridge, MA: MIT Press, 1986).
12. Rayback, *A History of American Labor,* pp. 166–68.
13. Ibid., pp. 196–97.
14. Rayback, *A History of American Labor,* pp. 200–207.
15. Lloyd Ulman, *The Rise of the National Trade Union* (Cambridge, MA: Harvard University Press, 1958).
16. Rayback, *A History of American Labor,* pp. 142–65.
17. Ibid., p. 162.
18. Ibid., pp. 238–49.
19. Ibid., p. 248.
20. Nick Salvatore, ed., *Samuel Gompers, Seventy Years of Life and Labor: An Autobiography* (Ithaca, NY: ILR Press, 1984).
21. Sanford Jacoby, ed., *Masters to Managers* (New York: Columbia University Press, 1990).
22. For a good discussion of the drive system and other aspects of American management, see Sanford Jacoby, ed., *Masters to Managers.*
23. In 1890 there were an estimated 90,000 foremen in American industry. By 1900 their numbers grew to 360,000. Robert

Reich, *The Next American Frontier* (New York: Bantam, 1983).

24. Progressive personnel policies did not diffuse to many small firms or to industries such as railroads and mining. See Sanford M. Jacoby, *Employing Bureaucracy* (New York: Columbia University Press, 1985).

25. Ibid., p. 224.

26. *NLRA* v. *Jones & Laughlin Steel Corp.,* 301 U.S. 1 (1937).

27. Irving Bernstein, *The Lean Years* (New York: Houghton Mifflin, 1972).

28. For a discussion of the origins of this principle, see Robert F. Hoxie, *Trade Unionism in the United States* (New York: Appleton and Company, 1920).

29. Jacoby, *Employing Bureaucracy,* pp. 243–53.

30. See War Labor Board, *Termination Report of the War Labor Board* (Washington, DC: GPO, 1946).

31. George W. Taylor, *Government Regulation of Industrial Relations* (New York: Prentice Hall, 1948), p. 1.

32. James N. Baron, Frank R. Dobbin, and P. Devereaux Jennings, "War and Peace: The Evolution of Modern Personnel Administration in U.S. Industry," *American Journal of Sociology* 92 (September 1986): 350–84.

33. For a description of these provisions, see the U.S. Department of Labor, Bureau of Labor Statistics series of publications called "Characteristics of Major Collective Bargaining Agreements" (Washington, DC: Bureau of Labor Statistics, 1979). See also "Basic Patterns in Union Contracts" (Washington, DC: Bureau of National Affairs, 1984).

34. Herbert N. Northrup, *Boulwarism* (Ann Arbor: Graduate School of Business, University of Michigan, 1964).

35. William E. Simkin, "Refusal to Ratify Contracts," in *Trade Union Government and Administration,* ed. Joel Seidman (New York: Praeger, 1970), pp. 107–48.

36. D. Quinn Mills, "Flawed Victory in Labor Law Reform," *Harvard Business Review* 52 (May–June 1979): 99–102.

37. AFL-CIO Committee on the Evolution of Work, "The Changing Situation of Workers and Unions," (Washington, DC: AFL-CIO, February 1985).

Chapter 3

The Legal Regulation of Unions and Collective Bargaining

This chapter begins to move horizontally across the three-tiered framework by examining the legal regulation of industrial relations in the United States. Federal and state law is a key part of the environment that influences the collective bargaining process and bargaining outcomes (see Exhibit 1–1, the functional level). To understand how collective bargaining works, then, requires familiarity with labor law. This chapter describes the development of labor law in the United States and the major laws and administrative agencies that currently shape the conduct of collective bargaining.

The Conspiracy Doctrine

The major developments in U.S. labor policy are outlined in Exhibit 3–1. In the United States the earliest public policy statements about the legality of union formation and activity appeared in the decisions of state courts. From 1800 to 1890 the state courts relied on interpretations derived from British common law to regulate the conduct of unions and employers. The first landmark case among these decisions was the 1806 Philadelphia **Cordwainers' case** in which the court ruled that efforts by unions or other combinations of workers to raise wages were intrinsically illegal. In other words, unions were viewed as a form of criminal conspiracy.

The conspiracy doctrine changed after the 1842 Massachusetts decision in *Commonwealth* v. *Hunt* in which the court attempted to distinguish between legal and illegal means for achieving unions' ends. The court ruled that unions had a right to exist, but they were prohibited from using coercive pressures to achieve their goals.

Throughout the 1800s the courts viewed unions with hostility and suspicion. They had trouble fitting the idea of unions and collective activity into a constitutional system and a political ideology that emphasized individual action and freedom of contract, property

EXHIBIT 3–1
Overview of Major Developments in U.S. Labor Policy

Date	Event	Description
1806	*Cordwainers'* case	A combination of workers seeking a wage increase is a criminal conspiracy.
1842	*Commonwealth* v. *Hunt*	Unions are lawful. Combinations of workers are allowed as long as lawful means are used to gain lawful ends. Courts still hostile to unions.
1890	Sherman Antitrust Act	"Every combination . . . or conspiracy in restraint of trade or commerce among the several states . . . is hereby declared to be illegal." Used by employers seeking injunctions for union activity.
1894	*Debs* case	A famous use of the injunction. Eugene Debs jailed for refusing to obey a court back-to-work order in the American Railway Union strike.
1906	*Danbury Hatters* case	Union boycott of goods in violation of the Sherman Act. Union is assessed triple damages.
1912	Lloyd-LaFollette Act	Public employees are allowed to request raises from Congress. Postal workers may organize, but not strike.
1914	Clayton Act	"Labor is not a commodity," but courts continue to find union acts illegal.
1926	Railway Labor Act	Railway workers are allowed to organize and bargain collectively. National Mediation Board added in 1934.
1932	Norris-LaGuardia Act	Federal courts are severely restricted in issuing injunctions against unions; yellow-dog contracts "shall not be enforceable."
1933	National Industrial Recovery Act (NIRA)	Workers are extended the "right to organize and bargain collectively through representatives of their own choosing . . . free from interference, restraint, or coercion of employers" [Sec. 7(a)].
1935	*Shechter Poultry* case	Supreme Court decision: NIRA is held unconstitutional.
1935	National Labor Relations Act (NLRA), or the Wagner Act	Establishes organizing rights, unfair (employer) labor practices, and the National Labor Relations Board (NLRB).
1935	Social Security Act	Includes OASDHI (old age, survivors, disability, and health insurance and OAA (old age assistance).
1937	*NLRB* v. *Jones & Laughlin*	NLRA ruled constitutional by the Supreme Court.
1938	Fair Labor Standards Act	Regulates wages and hours. Stipulates overtime pay and minimum wage requirements.
1947	Taft-Hartley Act	Amends the NLRA. Adds unfair union labor practices [Sec. 8(b)].
1959	Landrum-Griffin Act	Establishes a bill of rights for union members. Requires financial disclosing by unions. Lists guidelines for trusteeships and elections.
1962	Executive Order 10988	Encourages public sector bargaining. Requires maintenance of management rights. Orders added by Nixon in 1970 (Executive Order 11491). Followed by passage of state laws giving employees of local and state governments the right to bargain.

(continued)

EXHIBIT 3–1
(*continued*)

Date	Event	Description
1962	Wage-price policies	Establish guideposts in 1962–66; set controls in 1971–73; set guidelines in 1978–79.
1964	Civil Rights Act, Title VII	Unlawful for employer or union to discriminate on the basis of race, color, religion, gender, or national origin.
1967	Mandatory Retirement Act	"Age Discrimination in Employment Act"; outlaws mandatory retirement rules for workers up to age 70.
1970	Occupational Safety and Health Act (OSHA)	Establishes standards for on-the-job safety and health and the Occupational Safety and Health Administration.
1972	Supplementary Security Income Act	Effective January 1, 1974. Replaces OAA of the 1935 Social Security Act.
1974	Employee Retirement Income Security Act (ERISA)	Establishes minimum standards for private pension plans.
1978	Civil Service Reform Act	Establishes the Federal Labor Relations Authority (FLRA). Oversees and regulates labor relations in the federal government.
1989	Worker Adjustment and Retraining Notification Act	Requires employers to provide advance notice to employees affected by a plant closing or mass layoff.
1990	Americans with Disabilities Act (ADA)	Unlawful for an employer to discriminate against a qualified individual with a disability. Requires reasonable accommodations to be made to allow an individual with any mental or physical impairment to apply for or sustain an employment opportunity.
1991	Civil Rights Act Amendments	Title VII amended to reverse a number of the conservative court decisions made in the 1980s and to allow for compensatory and punitive damages.
1993	Family and Medical Leave Act (FMLA)	Requires employers with 50 or more employees to grant up to 12 weeks of unpaid leave per year to employees who are unable to perform their job duties because of a serious health condition, having a child, or who need to care for ill family members.

rights, and laissez faire capitalism. As a result, the ability of workers to engage in collective action in pursuit of their goals was severely limited. In addition, the statutory void meant that legal challenges to union action largely were confined to local or state courts; there was little or no federal involvement in labor relations during this time.

The Sherman Antitrust Act

When federal laws were applied to unions, unions initially fared poorly. With application of the federal Sherman Antitrust Act, for example, unions found themselves being treated like any other commodity or factor of production. That is, the courts viewed unions as labor market monopolies to be limited, as were other combinations or conspiracies that aimed to restrict free trade in product markets.

In the 1800s and early 1900s, whether through implementation of the conspiracy doctrine or the Sherman Antitrust Act, courts also used injunctions to discourage strikes and other forms of union pressure against employers. With an injunction a court rules illegal a union action, such as a strike, and imposes penalties, such as jail, on individuals who defy court orders. In many ways injunctions were more punishing than were other court actions. For one thing, employers could gain injunctions against union actions more quickly.

An additional tool for employers to weaken unions was the willingness of the courts to enforce what were known as "yellow-dog contracts." Under a yellow-dog contract, a prospective employee agreed that he or she would not join a union while working for the employer. If the prospective employee refused to sign the yellow-dog contract, the employer would not offer a job. Courts went so far as to order injunctions against unions that sought to recruit as members employees who had signed yellow-dog contracts, on the principle that this was an illegal interference with contract.

The Clayton Act

Unions and union supporters lobbied hard for an end to labor injunctions. Finally, in 1914 the Clayton Act was passed. Unions hoped it would lead to an end to labor injunctions through the language the act contained, which distinguished labor from other commodities. Yet, union hopes were not satisfied as federal courts subsequently interpreted the Clayton Act narrowly and state courts continued to issue injunctions against union actions. Meaningful protection of union activities came only with the passage of federal legislation that granted unions the rights to exist and to strike.

Legislation Granting Rights to Collective Bargaining

Legal and public policy opposition to the formation of unions began to erode in the early 20th century. First, the Lloyd-LaFollette Act of 1912 gave postal employees the right to organize. Then, during World War I, the War Labor Board adopted a policy statement that supported the right of private-sector workers to organize into unions and to bargain collectively. The **Railway Labor Act,** passed in 1926, gave railway employees the right to organize and to bargain collectively.

All of these laws and policies represented pragmatic adjustments in response to union power and labor turmoil. The already existing postal service and railroad unions used their power to obtain favorable legislation. Similarly, wartime production needs made it crucial to avoid disruptive strikes. In response, employers during the First World War agreed not to break those unions that already existed, setting the stage for a greater acceptance of unionization in later decades.

The Railway Labor Act

The Railway Labor Act continues today to regulate the conduct of collective bargaining in the railroad industry, as well as the air transportation industry (which was added to the original act in 1936). Given the continuing role of the act, we discuss its terms and administration in detail in this section.

Spurred by previous labor strife in the railroad industry, President Calvin Coolidge had urged the railroad companies and unions to develop procedures that would bring about industrial stability. In 1926 Congress passed the Railway Labor Act, closely following proposals that had been recommended by labor and management in the industry.

The act specifies that employees have the right to organize unions without employer interference and to bargain collectively through representatives of their own choosing. Railroad employers are obligated by the law to negotiate with the freely selected collective bargaining representatives of their workers. The chief purpose of the law was to establish a variety of procedures to reduce conflict in the railroads.[1]

A Test of Constitutionality

Given the previous resistance to collective bargaining and unionism expressed by the courts, the constitutionality of the Railway Labor Act was in question until a key ruling by the U.S. Supreme Court.

In the *Texas and New Orleans Railroad Company* v. *Brotherhood of Railway and Steamship Clerks* case of 1930, the company argued that the act impinged on its First and Fifth Amendment rights that gave the company control over the selection and discharge of employees. The Supreme Court rejected these arguments in that same year and went on to uphold the constitutionality of the Railway Labor Act. The Supreme Court stated that Congress had the right to become involved in labor relations in the railroad industry because of its interest in maintaining the flow of interstate commerce. The Court held that promotion of collective bargaining was of the "highest public interest," for such a procedure would prevent "the interruption of interstate commerce by labor disputes and strikes."[2] For the first time, the U.S. Supreme Court had recognized the authority of government to protect the right of workers to organize into unions and to collectively bargain.

Administration of the Act

In 1934 the Railway Labor Act was amended by Congress. A **National Mediation Board** was established and empowered to assist the collective bargaining process. The board, which still exists, is authorized to conduct elections to determine which union the employees desire for collective bargaining purposes. The union that receives the majority of votes is certified as the lawful representative of the employees. The board is also authorized to mediate disputes that arise between railway unions and companies during the negotiation of collective bargaining agreements.

With the critical role of the airline industry in contemporary travel and high levels of unionization in the industry, resolving collective bargaining disputes involving airlines and their unions is an important task in the modern economy. In recent years, the National Mediation Board has played a critical role in helping avert strikes and lockouts involving a number of major airlines that could have led to significant disruptions in air travel for large parts of the country.

The Norris-LaGuardia Act : *Federal anti-injunction Act*

The endorsement of collective bargaining provided in the Railway Labor Act was path breaking, but its effects on labor and management in the broad economy were limited by the fact that the act initially applied only to the railroad industry. Through the Norris-LaGuardia Act passed in 1932, Congress provided an even stronger endorsement of collective bargaining.

The Norris-LaGuardia Act allows private sector employees "full freedom of association, self-organization, and designation of representatives of (their) own choosing, to negotiate the terms and conditions of employment." The greatest practical impact of the act arose from the restraints it imposed on the issuance of labor injunctions. This earned the act its frequent alternative name of the "Federal Anti-injunction Act." Nevertheless, as mentioned in the discussion of antitrust acts above, state courts continued to issue frequent labor injunctions.

Congress justified the Norris-LaGuardia Act by pointing to the need for collective bargaining in modern society. Sections of the act state that, under prevailing economic conditions, the unorganized worker is at a disadvantage when confronted by the power held by large modern corporations. To redress this imbalance, the act endorsed collective bargaining and limited the power of the courts to intervene in labor disputes. To understand how Congress came to endorse collective bargaining, it is important to recognize that the Norris-LaGuardia Act was being debated (and passed) at a time when the U.S. economy was already in the midst of the great depression.

It is noteworthy that the Norris-LaGuardia Act did not grant to unions any new legal rights; it merely allowed them greater freedom to act by reducing interference from the courts.

The National Industrial Recovery Act

allowed to form groups.
minimum wages

After the election of Franklin Roosevelt as President of the United States, the federal government took a number of steps to promote industrial recovery from the depression. A key part of the federal government's plan to promote recovery was contained in the National Industrial Recovery Act (NIRA), which passed in 1933. The law provided that business people across various industries could form groups and pass codes, a system of principles and rules, that would stipulate business plans and regulate prices. The hope was that collusion between businesses and the regulation of production and prices would stimulate output and the economy. Congress stipulated that each of these business codes would include a minimum wage for the workers covered by the code. Promoters of this feature of the act argued that higher minimum wages would increase the purchasing power of workers and thereby stimulate the economy.

Promotion of Collective Bargaining

The most significant clause in the NIRA for unions was Section 7(a), which provided legal protection for the right of workers to bargain collectively. As with minimum wages, the rationale for the promotion of collective bargaining was that it would elevate worker purchasing power and thereby stimulate the national economy and help bring the country out of the depression.

Section 7(a) contained two key principles: (1) that employees have the "right to organize and bargain collectively through representatives of their own choosing, and shall be free from interference, restraint, or coercion" from employers in the exercise of those rights; and (2) that no employee can be required as a condition of employment to join a company-dominated union.[3]

Supreme Court Ruling

The NIRA had important symbolic effects, but its direct effects were limited because it was ruled unconstitutional in 1935 by the Supreme Court. The Court held that the law illegally delegated power to the Congress and exceeded Congress's authority to regulate interstate commerce. Nevertheless, from 1933 (when the NIRA was passed) until 1935 (when it was struck down) union membership increased from 2.9 to 3.9 million.

The National Labor Relations Act

The most significant boost for unionism in the private sector of the U.S. economy came with passage of the National Labor Relations Act (NLRA) in 1935. The NLRA made unions and union activity (including strikes) legal in the private sector and did much more as well.

EXHIBIT 3–2

The Major Features of the National Labor Relations Act, as Amended

Section	Provisions
National Labor Relations Act (NLRA; Wagner Act) 1935	
1	*Findings and policy:* An endorsement of collective bargaining, worker self-organization, and selection of representatives.
2	*Definitions:* Of employer, employee, labor organization, unfair labor practice.
3–6	*National Labor Relations Board:* Its establishment, authority, funding, and structure.
7	*Rights of employees:* Includes rights to self-organize and select representatives for bargaining.
8	*Unfair (employer) labor practices:* Prohibits interference with employee's Section 7 rights.
9	*Representatives and elections:* Majority's selection is exclusive bargaining representative. Board can define appropriate unit, certify employee representative.
10	*Prevention of unfair labor practices:* Board can issue cease and desist orders, take "affirmative action, including reinstatement of employees with or without back pay."
11–12	*Investigatory powers:* The NLRB can issue subpoenas, examine witnesses, etc. Refusal to obey may result in court contempt proceedings.
13–16	*Limitations:* Act does not limit the right to strike.
Labor-Management Relations Act (LMRA; Taft-Hartley Act) 1947 (amendments to NLRA)	
2	*Definitions:* Added supervisor, professional employee, agent.
3	*National Labor Relations Board:* Expanded from three to five members.
7	*Rights of employees:* Required to refrain from activities listed in section 7.
8	*Unfair labor practices:* Creates 8(b), Unfair Labor Organization Labor Practices.
9	*Representatives and elections:* Separate standards for professional employees, craft groups, guards. Expanded and defined election procedure.
Title II	*Conciliation of labor disputes:* In industries affecting commerce; national emergencies.
Sec. 301	*Suits by and against labor organizations.*
Labor-Management Reporting and Disclosure Act (LMRDA; Landrum-Griffin Act) 1959 (amendments to LMRA)	
Title I	*Bill of rights of members of labor organizations:* Includes freedom of speech and assembly, protection from dues increase without vote, and improper disciplinary action.
Title II	*Reporting by labor organizations:* Provides for reporting of officers' names, provisions for members' rights, annual financial statements.
Title III	*Trusteeships:* Defines reasons for trusteeships; provides for reports on all trusteeships.
Title IV	*Elections:* Guarantees regular local and national (and/or international) elections by secret ballot of all members in good standing.
Title V	*Safeguards for labor organizations:* Officials' Fiduciary Responsibility, requires bonding for all individuals who handle funds or property.

As stated in its preamble, the purpose of the NLRA is to promote the orderly and peaceful recognition of unions and the use of collective bargaining as a means for establishing the terms and conditions of employment.

The NLRA was later amended. The Taft-Hartley amendments of 1947 added a list of unfair labor practices for unions and turned the NLRA into a detailed and comprehensive code of conduct for collective bargaining; the Landrum-Griffin amendments of 1959 added provisions that governed internal union affairs and sought to define the rights of union members vis-à-vis their union organizations and leaders. The provisions of these acts are summarized in Exhibit 3–2.

The importance of the NLRA can be conveyed through the following exercise. Before you began taking this course, how many of you knew that our current federal labor law not only says unions are legal but actually states a preference for collective bargaining? Given the active employer resistance to unions that prevails in our economy and the low esteem with which many in the public view unions, we would guess that this would be a surprise, if not a shock, to most Americans. We return to this inconsistency between the language of the NLRA and current attitudes later in this chapter and elsewhere in this book. For now, we only note it as a strange irony of U.S. public policy and practice.

Key Provisions of the NLRA

Since the NLRA is the most important law regulating industrial relations, we describe its key provisions in some detail here. Our description takes into account the Taft-Hartley and Landrum-Griffin amendments to the NLRA.

Section 1

The motivation for the NLRA is provided in Section 1. Congress states that actions by employers who deny employees the right to organize and who refuse to accept collective bargaining lead to labor strife and are harmful to the nation because these actions lead to the disruption of commerce. Congress goes on to conclude that, in the absence of collective bargaining rights, employees are at a power disadvantage relative to employers and this is harmful to the economy because it depresses worker purchasing power. Congress declares that it is the policy of the United States to encourage the practice of collective bargaining.

Section 2

Section 2 defines the terms used in the act. The most important definitions relate to the terms *employer, employee, supervisor,* and *professional.*

An **employer** includes "any person acting in the interest of an employer." Employers excluded from the act's coverage include federal, state, or local governments or any organizations owned by these agencies; companies subject to the Railway Labor Act; and union representatives when acting as bargaining agents.

Employees covered by the NLRA "include any employee." It is important to recognize that the protections are not limited to union members or union represented employees; they apply to union and nonunion employees alike. Individuals whose work has ceased due to a labor dispute or to an unfair labor practice are still covered by the act. Employees continue to receive protection from the act after they leave an organization until they obtain "any other regular and substantially equivalent position." However, individuals employed as agricultural laborers, as independent contractors, or by a spouse or parent; those in domestic service; and those covered by the Railway Labor Act are excluded from coverage by the act.

A **supervisor** is defined as any individual who has authority to "hire, transfer, suspend, layoff, recall, promote, discharge, assign, reward, or discipline other employees" if the exercise of the above authority "requires the use of independent judgment." Supervisors are excluded from coverage by the act.

A **professional employee** is any employee engaged in work "predominantly intellectual and varied in character . . . involving the consistent exercise of discretion and judgment." Separate rules apply to how professional employees may be grouped with nonprofessional employees for bargaining purposes.[4]

Section 3

Section 3 establishes the **National Labor Relations Board (NLRB).** The board consists of five members appointed by the President and confirmed by the Senate. Members on the NLRB serve five-year terms. The NLRB can delegate authority to determine representation and election questions to its regional directors. The NLRB also has a general counsel who has the responsibility to investigate unfair labor practice charges and issue complaints.

Section 7

Section 7 grants to employees "the right to self-organization" and the right to "bargain collectively through representatives of their own choosing, or to engage in other concerted activities for the purpose of collective bargaining." Unions were thereby granted the right to picket and strike.

An employer may not discriminate against workers because they have participated in a strike. The employer, however, may hire either temporary or permanent replacements for striking workers. Striking workers who are permanently replaced can lose their jobs, even if the strikers offer to return to work, although such a striker has a right to recall if future openings appear at the workplace.[5]

Employers may **lock out** employees over mandatory subjects of bargaining. Thus, after bargaining in good faith with a union, an employer may lock out to force the union to agree to the employer's terms, even though the workers are content to accept present conditions and to continue bargaining.[6]

A strike that is part of a secondary boycott is illegal. Suppose a union has a labor dispute with an employer (called the *primary employer* because the dispute is primarily between this employer and the union). A way for the union to increase the pressure on this primary employer is to use union power against other employers (*secondary employers*). For instance, a union in dispute with a manufacturing company may want to exercise leverage against the employer by extending a strike to a company that supplies parts to the manufacturing company. The NLRA does not allow any such *secondary boycott.*[7]

Section 8

Section 8 also outlines unfair labor practices that can be committed by either employers or unions. These are actions that constitute violations of the rights specified in other parts of the act.

A. **Unfair Labor Practices by Employers:** An employer may not interfere with or coerce employees in the exercise of their Section 7 rights (Section 8(a)(1) of the act). The employer may not dominate or interfere with labor organizations or contribute financial or other support to these organizations (Section 8(a)(2) of the act).

Employers also are forbidden from discriminating against individuals based on their views toward or activities in unions (Section 8(a)(3) of the act). Thus, an employer cannot intimidate a union by firing union activists or choose not to promote individuals because they are active supporters of a union. The act does allow employers and unions to negotiate collective bargaining agreements that require union membership as a condition of the continuation of employment (a *union shop* clause).[8] The Supreme Court subsequently limited this section of the act to only allow employees to be required to pay dues to the union, not to be required to be actual members of the union (a *dues* or *agency shop*).[9]

B. **Unfair Labor Practices by Unions:** Unions cannot coerce employees in the exercise of their Section 7 rights. Unions cannot cause an employer to discriminate against employees who have been denied union membership except if such a denial was due to a failure to pay dues.

Section 8 requires the employer (Section 8(a)(5) of the act) and the union (Section 8(b)(3) of the act) to bargain collectively with each other in good faith. **Bargaining in good faith** means that the employer and the representative of the employees "meet at reasonable times and confer in good faith with respect to wages, hours, and other terms and conditions of employment." This has been interpreted to disallow behavior that shows that management or labor have no intention of coming to resolution and the making of long laundry lists of items to negotiate on but have no bearing on the parties' real positions. The duty to bargain does not require either side to agree to a proposal or to make concessions.

Wages, hours, and conditions of employment are thus **mandatory subjects of bargaining.** If either side chooses to bargain over one of these issues, the other side is obligated to continue talks. In NLRB and court decisions, mandatory bargaining has been defined for those subjects that directly affect the employment relationship. There also are **permissible subjects of bargaining,** such as corporate advertising policy. Both sides can either refuse to bargain or voluntarily choose to bargain over a permissible subject. Economic weapons, such as striking or picketing, cannot be used to force agreement to proposals on a permissible subject. **Illegal subjects of bargaining** are topics that may not be lawfully included in a labor contract, such as a closed shop clause or a racially discriminatory clause. A closed shop provides that individuals must be a member of the union in order to be eligible for hire.

Under Section 8, unions are also not allowed to engage in or encourage individuals to strike or to refuse to handle goods in cases when the object is one of the following:

1. Forcing an employer or self-employed person to join any labor or employer organization.
2. Forcing an employer to bargain with a labor organization that is not a duly certified labor organization.
3. Forcing an employer to assign work to employees unless the NLRB has ordered the employer to do so.

These unfair labor practice provisions prohibit **recognition strikes,** which were a common organizing tactic of unions in the 1930s and earlier decades. In a recognition strike, workers supporting the union go on strike until the employer agrees to recognize the union as the representative of the workers. Unions are also prohibited from requiring employees to pay excessive union membership fees; requiring an employer to pay for services that are not performed; or to engage in picketing to seek employer recognition of the union, unless a representation petition if filed with the NLRB within 30 days of the start of picketing.

Section 8 also outlaws hot cargo clauses except in the construction and apparel industries. A **hot cargo clause** requires that employees not handle particular goods. Such clauses had been common in the trucking industry where they prevented drivers from handling goods manufactured by a nonunion firm.

Section 9 provides that union representatives are selected by the majority of employees in a unit designated for such purposes (by the NLRB). A victorious union wins exclusive representation rights. This means that only one union gains the right to negotiate contracts for a designated bargaining unit. The act goes on to specify guidelines regarding how the appropriate bargaining unit is determined (we discuss this in Chapter 6).

Section 10

If the NLRB finds that an unfair labor practice has occurred, it is empowered to issue cease-and-desist orders and to order back pay to injured employees. The NLRB must petition a court of appeals for enforcement of its orders.

National Emergency Disputes

Title II of the NLRA includes procedures to be applied when a strike has caused a **national emergency dispute.** To avoid such cases the act creates the **Federal Mediation and Conciliation Service (FMCS)** and gives it the task of mediating labor disputes so as to assist the free flow of commerce.

When national emergencies arise out of labor disputes, a board of inquiry may be appointed by the President to conduct hearings and make recommendations for settling the dispute. The President can ask the attorney general to seek an injunction against the strike or lockout that is precipitating the national emergency. If an injunction is ordered, an 80-day cooling-off period follows. A court injunction requires the two sides to work under the terms of the previously expired contract while holding further negotiations supervised by a federal mediator. After 60 days, if no agreement has been reached, federal fact-finders issue a report on the dispute. After that the National Labor Relations Board has 15 days to poll employees to see if a majority would accept management's final offer and another five days to count union votes. If the union membership rejects the offer, the union is free to strike. The President can forward recommendations for a settlement to the U.S. Congress who can then impose a settlement, but this authority rarely has been exercised.

Administration of the NLRA

The NLRB, a five-member board with a general counsel and 50 regional boards and staffs, administers the NLRA. The key functions of the NLRB are to supervise and conduct representation elections and to adjudicate charges of unfair labor practices.

Such charges start with a complaint filed by an employee, employer, or union with a regional NLRB office. The charge is investigated by the NLRB, and, if it is warranted, a hearing is conducted before an administrative law judge who makes a recommendation to the NLRB. The NLRB then can issue cease-and-desist orders or dismiss the case.

Throughout the process the NLRB and its agents try to find a settlement to the charge. Suppose a union charges that organizers from its supporters were being harassed and threatened by their supervisors during a union election campaign. After investigating the charge, the NLRB might recommend as a settlement that the employer stop this action and post a notice promising not to continue the practice. Needless to say, the employer in this case might reject the proposed settlement, and the procedure would proceed.

After hearing the recommendation of the administrative judge, the NLRB has the power to award back pay to injured employees, but the NLRB cannot assess punitive damages.

Furthermore, the board must turn to the courts to enforce its orders, and aggrieved parties can appeal NLRB decisions to the Federal Circuit Court of Appeals.

The Taft-Hartley Act

By the end of World War II labor unions had grown in strength and membership. The strike wave that occurred after the war stimulated hostility toward unions. Congress responded by passing the **Labor–Management Relations Act** (often referred to as the **Taft-Hartley amendments**) in 1947. The primary purpose of the act was to shift the balance of power more toward management and grant individuals more rights in their dealing with labor unions. The major provisions of the act include the following:

1. Section 7 was modified to protect employees' rights not to engage in union activities.
2. A list of unfair labor practices that could be committed by unions was added to Section 8 (see above).
3. Workers were allowed to decertify their unions. A majority of unionized workers thus can vote to get rid of union representation.
4. Unions were prohibited from engaging in representation strikes to try to pressure the employer to accept union representation. (Representation strikes had been a major union organizing tactic in the 1930s.)
5. Employers were allowed to make anti-union statements during union organizing campaigns as long as they did not include threats of reprisals or promises of benefits.
6. Supervisors were excluded from the coverage of the NLRA.
7. Closed shops (in which union membership is required before an individual can be hired) were outlawed.
8. States were allowed to pass laws outlawing the union shop (right to work laws).[10]
9. Procedures for national emergency disputes were added.

The Taft-Hartley amendments excluded supervisors in the private sector from coverage under the NLRA. Section 2(11) of the amendments defines a supervisor as an employee

> having authority in the interest of the employer, to hire, transfer, suspend, layoff, recall, promote, discharge, assign, reward, or discipline other employees, or responsibly to direct them, or to adjust their grievances, or effectively to recommend such action, if . . . such authority is not a merely routine or clerical nature, but requires the use of independent judgment.

Thus, a supervisor is defined in terms of the duties the employee performs and the power the employee has to make key personnel management decisions or to exercise independent judgment.[11]

Although the law does not prevent supervisors from forming unions, it also does not provide any legal protection for such activity.

The Taft-Hartley exclusion of supervisors rested on the argument that if supervisors unionized, they would become less loyal to management and less committed to the goals of their employer. Plainly, some of the opposition to supervisory bargaining reflects a belief that management deserves a set of loyal representatives of its own interests. The actual legislative rationale for this policy, however, rested on assumptions about the responsibilities supervisors had at the time Taft-Hartley was enacted.

Two questions are immediately obvious. First, are the roles and powers of today's supervisors still the same as they were assumed to be in 1947? Second, would the negative organizational consequences hypothesized by the congressional majority in 1947 actually result if supervisors were given the same collective bargaining rights as other workers?

These questions have recently become the focal point of a debate over the rights of college faculty members to unionize and to bargain. In a test case decided in 1980 the Supreme Court ruled that the faculty at New York City's Yeshiva University had managerial responsibilities and therefore excluded them from coverage under the NLRA.[12] The Court reasoned that because the faculty members were involved in hiring, promotion, course assignment, and a variety of other managerial decisions that affected wages, hours, and working conditions, they fit the definition of supervisor embodied in the law. Thus, Yeshiva had no legal obligation to recognize a union of faculty members, and collective bargaining with faculty members in this university, as well as in several others, ended. Although many observers have criticized the logic of the Yeshiva ruling, and although the NLRB has subsequently found faculty members at several other universities to be eligible for coverage under the law, the debate over this question has intensified.

Nurses are another group that has been subject of intense debates concerning potential supervisory status. Although the core of nurses' professional work consists of caring for patients, some nurses who possess advanced training, for example, registered nurses (RNs), are frequently given additional authority to direct the work of nursing assistants and others with more limited training. The critical question becomes whether this leadership role in directing as well as performing patient care functions puts these nurses into a supervisory position and hence ineligible for the protections of the NLRA.

The Landrum-Griffin Act

The **Labor–Management Reporting and Disclosure Act** of 1959, commonly referred to as the **Landrum-Griffin amendments,** is primarily concerned with the internal practices of unions. The major purpose of these amendments to the NLRA is to protect union members from improper union conduct.[13] The law also is directed at eliminating arrangements between unions and employers that deprive union members of proper union representation.

Landrum-Griffin passed Congress in the aftermath of a series of well-publicized hearings on union corruption that were conducted by the McClellan Anti-Racketeering Committee in Congress. Much of the Committee's attention focused on the activities of the International Brotherhood of Teamsters and led to the expulsion of the Teamsters union from the AFL-CIO.[14]

Union Members' Bill of Rights

The Landrum-Griffin amendments include a "bill of rights" section for union members. Rights are stipulated for nomination of candidates for union office, voting in elections, attendance at membership meetings, and participation in the business transactions of unions. The act also regulates union dues and fees and affirms the right of any union member to sue the organization. The act provides that no union member may be fined, suspended, or otherwise disciplined by the union except for the nonpayment of dues, unless the member has been granted procedural safeguards.

The Regulation of Union Finances and Administration

Landrum-Griffin requires every labor organization to report its financial and administrative practices regularly to the **U.S. Department of Labor (DOL).** Information on the financial affairs of the union must be made available to union members.

The act makes union officers responsible for proper use of union funds. Union members are granted the right to sue union officers for relief on the grounds that officers have violated their financial obligations.

In addition, Landrum-Griffin regulates internal union elections. The act establishes requirements for the frequency of elections and regulates nomination, campaign rules, and election procedures.

The act also oversees how a union can regulate its local unions. The law specifically directs how and when local unions can be put into trusteeships. A trusteeship is a procedure by which the parent union (often the national offices of a union) suspends the autonomy of a local union. Typically, local unions are put into trusteeship if the parent organization feels there have been violations of the union's constitution or irregularities in the administration of the local union. Congress added these requirements after hearing reports of the misuse of trusteeships by certain national unions.

Landrum-Griffin imposes on unions requirements and obligations that go far beyond those imposed on corporations and other organizations. As a result, the internal operation and affairs of unions are under special scrutiny, and unions do not have the independence granted other private organizations.

The Value of Collective Bargaining

With passage of the NLRA, the U.S. federal government became committed to the promotion of collective bargaining. Since this commitment is so central to American labor law, it is useful to examine the rationale for this commitment in some detail.

The Contribution to Political Democracy

Collective bargaining involves the right to negotiate a labor agreement without direct interference from the government or other outside forces. The political rationale for collective bargaining can be stated simply: the right to form unions and carry out strikes is an essential component of political democracy. Walter Oberer and Kurt Hanslowe stated this premise succinctly:

> One way of defining a free society may indeed be: a society the members of which are free to assert their individual interests collectively.[15]

One of the most famous and important examples of this function of an independent labor movement was the role of the Solidarity trade union in Poland in opposing the communist regime in that country during the 1970s and 1980s. The development of this independent labor union and its opposition to the communist government played a central role in leading to the demise of communist rule in Poland and throughout the rest of Eastern Europe.

The Need for the Right to Strike

Since the freedom to enter a contract also requires the freedom to reject a contract offer, the right to negotiate and the right to strike are closely related. Milton Konvitz stated this well in an article that explored the philosophical bases for the right to strike:

Without the power to affect the course of events, a person or a group lacks the responsibility to reach decisions. Power is the source of responsibility. Without the right to strike, unions will lack the foundation for voluntary negotiation and agreement. If a free labor agreement—free collective bargaining in a free enterprise system—is in the public interest, so is the right to strike, which makes the free labor agreement possible.[16]

Additional Justifications for Collective Bargaining

Three additional justifications have been offered by industrial relations scholars for promoting and protecting collective bargaining. First, it is often argued that employees and employers have a better understanding of their needs, priorities, and problems than do outsiders. This suggests that more effective solutions to problems, or compromises that are more workable and acceptable to the parties, will be found in a bargaining process than where third parties constrain the participants from pursuing their own interests. Second, and perhaps more important, the parties may lose the capability to resolve their own problems once they begin to rely on outsiders for resolving their differences. The notion here is that effective problem resolution is a dynamic process that requires continual contact between the parties in dispute. Third, there is good reason to believe that when employees feel as though they have a say in the determination of their working conditions, morale is raised and often productivity is increased.

Yet we must be careful not to view the rights to form unions and to strike as unconditional. The exercise of these rights can, of course, conflict with other objectives of the larger society, including the public's interest in industrial peace and social stability. At times these objectives come into conflict.

Even though society has an interest in limiting conflicts that create social costs and social inconvenience, at the same time, the mere existence of public inconvenience is not in and of itself sufficient grounds to limit labor and management's right to negotiate and labor's right to engage in a strike if they cannot agree.

Given the important roles the negotiations process and the strike play in a collective bargaining system, on the one hand, and the potentially harmful impact a strike may exert on the public, on the other, it is not surprising that industrial relations scholars and the public often disagree on how well the process is performing. Archibald Cox, for example, once described the negotiations process as the "ideal of informed persuasion" because of the effective way the strike threat forces negotiators to face reality and make compromises.[17]

A Criticism of Unrestrained Collective Bargaining

Compare Cox's view with the following of Abe Raskin, longtime labor reporter and editor for *The New York Times:*

> The more ludicrous the whole performance of [collective bargaining] becomes, the more insistently learned scholars explain why it all makes sense and why any community action to protect itself by substituting reasons for the unrestrained exercise of force in settling labor disputes represents a stab in the back toward Nathan Hale, Paul Revere, and all the other apostles of American liberty.
>
> It is past time to arise and proclaim that the Emperor has no clothes. It is my conviction that, when all the people have to suffer because of the willfulness or ineptitude of economic power blocks, it is an affirmation—not a denial—of democracy to provide effective government machinery for breaking deadlocks.

The question, in my estimation, is not whether to do it but simply how. I see no reason why in this institution alone, of all the facets of our society, we should exalt the right to make war as the hallmark of industrial civilization when we seek to exorcise it everywhere else, even in the global relations of sovereign powers.[18]

Thus, while the traditional supporters of the institution of collective bargaining seek to place walls around the process to promote and protect collective bargaining, others argue for greater governmental intervention to resolve disputes before strikes impose those costs on the public.

Public Sector Labor Law

The NLRA covers private sector employment relationships. Since passage of the NLRA, 41 states have passed collective bargaining legislation that governs employees of state and local governments. In addition, collective bargaining rights were extended to federal employees through Executive Order 10988 in 1962. The Civil Service Reform Act of 1978 established a new Federal Labor Relations Authority (FLRA) to oversee and regulate the conduct of collective bargaining in the federal sector. A few states have extended bargaining rights to farm workers. Most of these state laws are modeled after the principles set forth in the NLRA, but they differ considerably in the procedures specified for implementing the principles.

An estimated three-quarters of the civilian workforce—or about 103 million of the approximate 135 million people in the labor force as of February 2001—had some form of collective bargaining rights from federal, state, or local statutes, according to the federal Government Accounting Office (http://www.gao.gov/new.items/d02835.pdf). Among the 115 million private sector workers, about 78 percent had bargaining rights, mostly from coverage under the NLRA. The largest groups of the 32 million civilian workers without collective bargaining rights under any law, either federal or state were an estimated 8.5 million independent contractors; 5.5 million employees of certain small businesses; 10.2 million supervisory/managerial employees (including 8.6 million first-line supervisors); 6.9 million federal, state and local government workers; 532,000 domestic workers; and 357,000 agricultural workers.

Employment at Will

A central focus in collective bargaining is the negotiation and administration of procedures that provide employees with due process. **Due process** in the union sector comes in part through contract negotiations and the grievance procedures, topics examined later in Chapters 8 and 11. To understand the contribution of unionism to due process it is necessary to examine what takes place where unions are absent.

In the absence of a collective bargaining agreement, U.S. courts have applied a common law doctrine called employment at will.[19] The **employment-at-will doctrine** stipulates that the employee and employer are free to end the employment relationship at any time, for any reason, and without liability, provided that the termination does not violate any statutory provisions. Application of this doctrine leads to the result that, in the absence of some sort of complaint procedure, nonunion employees have no recourse if they are discharged unless statutory or constitutional provisions are violated by the action.

It is important to understand that the employment-at-will doctrine means that an employer can fire an employee for an unfair or bad reason without legal liability. So, for example, an employee could be fired for poor performance when in fact the employee's performance was exemplary or an employee could be fired arbitrarily for the color of shirt he or she wore to work that day. In either case, the employer can fire the employee without notice, without giving any severance pay, and the employee has no legal recourse. A survey testing people's knowledge of employment found that most American employees wrongly believe that the law is that they can only be fired for just cause, that is, for a good reason.[20] Although this is incorrect, this false belief may shape employee attitudes and behavior in the workplace and diminish public pressure for changes in the law.

The Scope of the Doctrine

The employment-at-will doctrine is a default rule. This means that the parties are free to modify it through a contract if they so choose. They can do so by specifying in the employment contract that termination of employment only be for just cause or that employment shall last for a specified period of time. Most individual employees lack the bargaining power to negotiate such a contract and employers are rarely willing to offer one. Indeed, employers are often careful to include in any employment contract or handbook a statement that it is in no way intended to modify or alter the employment-at-will rule. However, there are three categories of employees that are usually not subject to employment-at-will.

The first category of employees who have contracts that modify the employment-at-will doctrine is that of unionized employees. The vast majority of unions negotiate clauses in their collective bargaining agreements stating that employees can only be dismissed for just cause.

Individual employees may also negotiate just cause or specified term of employment clauses in their individual employment contracts, but they must have sufficient bargaining power to get the employer to agree to this. For example, CEOs and other high level executives commonly negotiate provisions in their contracts for compensation if they are terminated without just cause.

The third category of employees outside the employment-at-will doctrine is public sector employees covered by civil service and other public employee statutes that often contain specific rules about when and how these employees can be fired.

Exceptions Created by State Courts

In recent decades a number of state courts have modified application of the employment-at-will doctrine. Whereas labor law is covered by federal statutes, the states have primary authority over individual employment law. As a result, each state has its own employment law. Although they follow the same general principles, some are more favorable to employees than others. California, for example, is often considered to be the state where the courts are most favorable to employees.

State courts have awarded compensation to discharged employees based on three general categories of exceptions to the employment-at-will doctrine: implied contracts; public policy; and the covenant of good faith and fair dealing.

1. When an employer's written policies or oral statements constitute an implied contract, providing employment security. A contract can also be implied by actions taken by the employer. The **implied contract** can serve to limit the employee's discharge to just cause, namely, to cases where the employer has legitimate business reasons for the discharge. For example, where an employer had induced a prospective employee to move across the country to take up a new position based on promises of job security, this was held by a court to have created an implied contract requiring just cause for discharge.[21]

A related concept is the idea that an employee handbook could constitute a contract modifying the employment-at-will doctrine. In a number of state court cases from the 1970s on, the courts found that employee handbooks could be contracts modifying employment at will. However, courts have also held that many handbooks are simply aspiration statements by employers, not binding contracts. In addition, after the initial wave of handbook cases, employers began to include waivers specifically stating that the handbook was not a contract and that it did not modify employment at will. The courts have generally accepted these waivers so long as they are prominent and clearly written. The result is that most employee handbooks are not considered contracts, even though employees may wrongly view them this way.

2. When an employee is fired for refusing to violate a **public policy,** commonly one reflected in a statute. Employees cannot be terminated for exposing or refusing to participate in employer conduct that violates statutory policy. For example, the firing of an employee for cooperating with a police investigation into criminal wrongdoing into a coworker was found by an Illinois court to violate public policy.[22] In this case the court reasoned that there is no right to terminate a contract for an unlawful reason or a purpose that contravenes public policy. Such a privilege would encourage lawlessness, which the law is designed to prevent. Although the public policy exception may sound broad, the courts have generally limited its application to situations where the dismissal is undermining a public policy clearly established in the state's constitution, statutes, or regulations. For example, a claim based on the public policy exception was rejected by the Pennsylvania Supreme Court where the employee had made complaints about the safety of a chemical in the workplace where a *federal*, but not a *state*, statute supported the finding that this was an unsafe chemical.[23]

3. In a smaller number of states, the courts have recognized the existence in employment contracts of a **covenant of good faith and fair dealing.** An application of this covenant is the idea that the employer cannot cheat the employee out of the benefits of their employment. For example, a Massachusetts court held that where a long-serving sales employee was fired shortly before he was due to collect a large bonus for sales he had made, this violated the covenant of good faith and fair dealing.[24] However, courts in only 13 states have currently accepted this covenant as being part of their state's employment law. Even where it has been accepted, finding that the covenant has been violated usually involves some showing of deception or other nefarious action by the employer, rather than simply a bad or unfair decision.

Although the three exceptions to the employment-at-will doctrine provide some important legal protections for employees, each exception has substantial limitations and only applies to a limited, specific category of dismissals. Thus, even with recent court modifications, nonunion employees have relatively few grounds to redress discharge. This is why allegations of insufficient due process arise frequently in union organizing drives.

Employment Standards Laws

Society also has seen fit to regulate certain employment conditions more directly than it does collective bargaining. In the United States, these employment standards laws set certain minimum standards for employment and establish a basic social safety net for workers. As compared to other countries, however, the United States tends to have relatively little direct regulation of employment conditions (what is called **substantive regulation**). In Western Europe, for instance, national laws directly set minimum wages and working conditions more extensively than do their counterpart regulations in the United States. (See Chapter 14 for examples.)

Employment standards laws in the United States have been passed at both the state and federal levels. These employment standards generally apply to all employees, whether represented by unions or not. Indeed, many of these employment standards laws were enacted partly as a result of political support for them from the labor movement. Employment standards laws provide a minimum set of standards for employment conditions that unions can then improve on through collective bargaining.

Workers Compensation   Workers compensation statutes were some of the earliest employment laws, enacted by many states in the early 20th century.[25] Workers compensation laws provide for a type of basic no-fault insurance to compensate workers for injuries suffered on the job. Under workers compensation laws employees automatically receive compensation if they can show they were injured on the job, whether or not the employer was at fault. In return, employers cannot be sued by employees who have been injured on the job; this was a substantial benefit for employers who were concerned over the costs of injured worker lawsuits. The system is financed by workers compensation premiums paid by employers. All states have now adopted some form of workers compensation system.

Social Security Act of 1935   In the Social Security system established by this statute, employees and employers pay premiums into Social Security while they are working. Once the employee retires, he or she is then paid a standard benefit that provides for a basic income level during retirement. Although Social Security was designed to be supplemented by private pension plans and individual employee savings, it was a remarkably successful program in reducing the formerly endemic poverty among older Americans. The Act led to the development of 65 as the standard retirement age, since this was the age that workers were initially able to receive Social Security benefits. (This age has now been raised to 67 for workers born in 1960 or thereafter.) The Social Security Act also funds disability benefits and unemployment compensation benefits through a system of grants to support unemployment insurance programs run by the states.

Fair Labor Standards Act   The Fair Labor Standards Act (FLSA) passed by Congress in 1938, regulates a number of minimum conditions of employment. It provides for a minimum wage, which is periodically updated by Congress. It establishes a minimum age of employment (16 for most jobs, 18 for hazardous jobs, and 14 for certain jobs such as newspaper delivery). It also provides for overtime pay: an employer must pay one-and-a-half times ordinary wages for the employee for any hours worked over 40 hours in the same week. Employees not covered by these wage and hours rules, mostly managers and professionals paid by salary, are called **exempt employees,** and as a result are not entitled to overtime pay under the FLSA. Although the overtime pay requirement was designed to limit hours worked by individual employees and established the idea of the standard 40 hour work week, the FLSA does not set any maximum on the hours worked in a day or week by employees.

Occupational Safety and Health Act The Occupational Safety and Health Act (OSHA) passed in 1970 sets minimum standards for safety and health in the workplace. Extensive regulations enacted under the authority of OSHA establish specific rules about safe practices in the workplace, maximum levels of exposure to dangerous substances and other occupational safety and health issues. The act is administered by the Occupation Safety and Health Administration, part of the U.S. Department of Labor, whose inspectors are authorized to inspect workplaces and investigate claims of rule violations and dangerous practices. Research has found that enforcement of OSHA rules tends to be more active in unionized workplaces.[26]

Employee Retirement Income Security Act The Employee Retirement Income Security Act (ERISA) passed in 1974 was designed to regulate the operation of pension and other employee benefit plans. It establishes minimum standards for the operation of private pension plans so as to avoid problems that could lead to the misuse and/or squandering of pension funds that employees are relying on for retirement income.[27] A weakness of ERISA is that while it regulates the operation of private pension plans, it does not require an employer to provide a pension plan for its employees or indicate how generous any plan that is established will be. In addition to pension plans, ERISA also regulates the operation of **welfare plans,** which include employer provided health insurance plans.

Worker Adjustment and Retraining Notification Act The Worker Adjustment and Retraining Notification (WARN) Act passed in 1988 was designed to reduce the impact of plant closings and mass layoffs on workers by providing for advanced notice of layoffs and enhanced retraining opportunities. The WARN Act provides that an employer with 100 or more employees who dismisses 50 or more of these employees during a 30-day period must provide written notice to the employees at least 60 days in advance of the impending layoff. If the employer fails to provide this advanced notice, it can be liable for the corresponding amount of lost wages. The WARN Act was a response to growing public concerns over layoffs in many traditional manufacturing industries in the 1980s. A more recent wave of WARN Act–based litigation occurred in response to the mass layoffs and downsizing in the wake of the collapse of the dot-com boom of the late 1990s.[28]

Family and Medical Leave Act Passed in 1993, the Family and Medical Leave Act (FMLA) requires that employers with 50 or more employees grant up to 12 weeks of unpaid leave to employees per year. The act covers those who are unable to perform their job duties because of a serious health condition, having a child, or a need to care for ill family members. The FMLA was enacted with the hope of facilitating for working parents a balance between the demands of the workplace and those of the family.

The FMLA is the most recent major piece of employment standards legislation enacted at the federal level. After periods of expansion in the 1930s and 1960s–early 1970s, enactment of new employment standards laws has slowed in recent decades. In the late 1970s and 1980s U.S. public policy changed to a less interventionist style as policy returned to an emphasis on competitive markets at the micro and macro levels of the economy. Important developments at the micro level include deregulation of the transportation and telecommunications industries. The most recent innovations in employment standards laws have come at the state level. For example, in 2002, California became the first state to enact a law providing for paid family and medical leave, financed through the state's unemployment compensation system.[29] Under this law, employees receive 55 percent of their usual wages for up to six weeks of paid leave to care for a newborn, a newly adopted child, or an ill family member. In the absence of federal government action on employment issues of public concern, we may continue to see initiatives such as this being developed by individual states.

Employment Discrimination Law

Employment discrimination laws are part of the more general set of civil rights laws enacted to prevent racial, gender, religious, and other types of discrimination in society. Legal prohibitions against discrimination in employment are based on a series of statutes enacted from the 1960s onwards. As with employment standards laws, employment discrimination laws apply to unionized and nonunion employees alike. Unions themselves can also be liable if they engage in discriminatory practices, for example, by discriminating based on race or gender in admission to a union-run apprenticeship program.

The key statute for employment discrimination law is **Title VII of the Civil Rights Act of 1964.** Title VII prohibits discrimination in employment on the grounds of "race, color, religion, sex, or national origin." Note that Title VII prohibits discrimination based on any of these grounds, not just discrimination against minority groups. So a majority group white employee or a male employee can equally file a claim under Title VII if he believes he was discriminated against; these are often referred to as reverse discrimination lawsuits.

There are two different types of employment discrimination prohibited by Title VII: disparate treatment and disparate impact. In **disparate treatment** claims, the employee argues that he or she was treated differently because of his or her race, color, religion, sex, or national origin. So an employee who wasn't hired or was fired because of his or her race would be arguing the employer engaged in disparate treatment based on race. Workplace sexual harassment is a type of disparate treatment based on sex and is prohibited by Title VII. Illegal sexual harassment in the workplace can involve either **quid pro quo claims,** where the employee is subject to demands for sexual favors in return for promotions or other benefits or based on threats, or **hostile environment** claims, where the employee is subject to sexually related comments or conduct that are so severe and pervasive as to alter the terms and conditions of employment. Sexual harassment claims can be especially difficult for unions to deal with as both the alleged harasser and victim may be represented by the union.

In **disparate impact** claims, the employee or group or employees argues that the employer has a policy that, while it may appear neutral, in practice excludes a group of employees covered by one of the prohibited grounds. For example, if an employer has a minimum height requirement for a job, then this will tend to exclude a disproportionate number of women from the job. If the employer cannot justify this minimum height requirement as being job related and consistent with **business necessity,** then the requirement will be held to have an illegal disparate impact based on sex.

Subsequent employment discrimination laws have covered other grounds of discrimination. The **Age Discrimination in Employment Act** (ADEA) of 1967 prohibited discrimination against older workers over the age of 40. Unlike Title VII, the ADEA does not prohibit reverse discrimination, so an employee cannot make a claim concerning discrimination based on his or her youth and in any event is not covered by the ADEA if under the age of 40. The **Pregnancy Discrimination Act** of 1978 amended Title VII to define discrimination based on pregnancy as a type of sex discrimination; this reversed a previous Supreme Court case that had held pregnancy discrimination was not sex discrimination. The **Americans with Disabilities Act** (ADA) passed in 1990 prohibits discrimination based on disabilities. The ADA also establishes a positive duty on employers to provide reasonable accommodations to employees with disabilities who are otherwise qualified to do their jobs.

The **Civil Rights Act of 1991** amended Title VII to reverse a series of conservative Supreme Court decisions in the 1980s that were viewed by Congress as having weakened the Act. The Civil Rights Act of 1991 for the first time provided for jury trials in Title VII cases. The 1991 law also allows compensatory damages for victims of discrimination if they suffer emotional distress, mental anguish, and other nonpecuniary losses in addition to lost wages. Punitive damages may be recovered as well if the employer acted with malice and reckless indifference to the law. Under the 1991 law, protected groups can more easily show disparate impact; the law instructs that employers show that hiring practices are related to the job in question and consistent with business necessity. The law also provides that employers bear the burden of justifying practices that cause adverse impact. Overall, the Civil Rights Act of 1991 strengthened the enforceability of Title VII and caused employers to take more preventative steps to avoid discrimination suits.

Filing Employment Discrimination Complaints

To begin a legal claim for employment discrimination under the federal statutes, an employee must first file a complaint with the Equal Employment Opportunity Commission (EEOC). The EEOC will investigate the complaint and, if merited, attempt to conciliate between the employee and employer so as to encourage a mutually acceptable resolution. After this administrative process is complete, the EEOC will issue a finding of cause or no cause. Whatever finding it makes, the EEOC will also issue the employee with a "right to sue" letter indicating that the employee has completed the required administrative process and is free to proceed to court with the claim if he or she wishes. The employee can then litigate the claim of employment discrimination claim through the courts. Note that the employee is able to bring a lawsuit arguing that he or she has been subject to employment discrimination even though the EEOC may have issued a "no cause" finding; the employee is still entitled to his or her day in court.

In a small number of cases, the EEOC will file suit in court against the employer on behalf of the employee. Given the limited resources of the EEOC, this only occurs in a minority of cases (usually 1–2 percent of all cases) where there are particularly important issues involved or large numbers of employees potentially affected. In the vast majority of cases, if the employee wishes to proceed with a lawsuit, he or she must retain an attorney privately to handle the case. Most attorneys who represent employees as plaintiffs in cases do so on a contingency fee basis, where the attorney receives nothing if the employee loses the case and a percentage (typically 30–40 percent) of any damages awarded if the employee is successful.

The Growth of Employment Litigation and Its Outcomes

Recent years have seen growing concerns over rising levels of employment litigation and large, unpredictable damage awards made by juries. Levels of employment litigation

EXHIBIT 3–3
**Employment
Discrimination
Charges,
Settlements
and Cases
Filed**

Year	Total Charges Filed with EEOC	Monetary Benefits by EEOC ($ million)	Total Cases Filed in Federal District Courts by Private Parties[†]
1980	59,328	$ 20.94	
1981	56,228	16.22	
1982	54,145	33.53	
1983	70,252	40.29	
1984	71,197	38.83	
1985	72,002	54.18	
1986	68,882	46.39	
1987	65,844	24.79	9,140
1988	63,778	55.61	9,055
1989	59,411	35.39	8,937
1990	62,135	19.28	8,459
1991	63,898	10.79	8,371
1992	72,302[*]	71.10	11,318
1993	87,942	36.40	10,787
1994	91,189	39.60	12,833
1995	87,529	18.90	15,705
1996	77,990	50.80	19,381
1997	80,680	114.70	21,492
1998	79,591	95.50	23,606
1999	77,444	98.40	23,721
2000	79,896	49.80	22,553
2001	80,840	51.20	
2002	84,442	52.80	
2003	81,293	148.70	
2004	79,432	168.10	
2005	75,428	107.70	

[*]The EEOC began enforcing the Americans with Disabilities Act on July 26, 1992; from 1993–2005, 15–20,000 charges were filed under the ADA annually.

[†]Figures in this column are based on Federal Judicial Center data assembled by Professors Theodore Eisenberg and Kevin M. Clermont: http://teddy.law.cornell.edu:8090.

increased from the 1960s onward with the passage of new employment discrimination and employment standards statutes. Additional impetus to the growth of employment litigation came in the 1970s and 1980s from the development by state courts of exceptions to the doctrine of employment at will.

Evidence is less clear that there has been a continued expansion of employment litigation in recent years. Exhibit 3–3 lists annual numbers of employment discrimination complaints filed with the Equal Employment Opportunity Commission from 1981 to the present, as well as the rate of complaints adjusted by population. Although annual numbers of complaints are substantial, there has been relatively little change in them over the past quarter-century. However, data from 1987 to 2000 indicate that there was a substantial rise in the number of employment discrimination lawsuits filed in federal courts over that period, from 8,937 cases in 1987 to 22,553 cases in 2000. This growth in the number of cases filed may reflect the greater damages available in discrimination lawsuits after the passage of the

1991 Civil Rights Act. The availability of punitive damages and compensatory damages for pain and suffering would have increased the incentive for pursuing a claim of employment discrimination through the courts and facilitated the financing of cases by plaintiff attorneys through contingency fee arrangements.

What about the outcomes of litigation? A study of employment discrimination verdicts in the federal courts from 1994 to 2000 found that the median (typical) award was $110,000 and the mean (average) award was $301,000.[30] The much higher mean award amount compared to the median reflects the influence of a relatively small number of large awards of over a million dollars. Although these awards are not typical, they tend to receive greater attention and likely influence perceptions of a threat to companies from litigation by employees.

Seniority and Equal Employment Opportunity Policy Goals

Seniority provisions in collective bargaining often regulate which worker will be laid off and who is eligible for a promotion. Seniority provisions operate on the principle of the worker with the most seniority, that is, who has been in the job the longest, being the first for eligibility for promotion and last to be laid off. By protecting the interests of more senior existing employees, who often are predominantly older, white, and male, seniority systems may come into conflict with the goals of employment discrimination law. The use of seniority in recent years has been restricted in order to attain equal employment objectives.

In the past, seniority had served in some cases to discriminate against minorities and women by establishing segregated seniority units or progression ladders. Some firms had set up departmentwide seniority units that systematically excluded blacks, women, and other minority groups such as Latinos and Asians from the most desirable jobs and progression ladders. Blacks and Latinos, for example, may have been hired only as laborers, while whites were hired into higher paying jobs in the maintenance department. Where this occurred, or where firms refused to hire minority or female workers at all, the effects of past discriminatory acts were perpetuated by the use of seniority criteria for either competitive- or benefit-status purposes.

Policy Goals

Satisfaction of **equal employment opportunity** goals has led courts (1) to ensure that present practices and seniority rules do not discriminate against any individuals or groups, (2) to avoid perpetuating the effects of past discrimination, and (3) to protect the interests of nonminority workers who are not responsible for the past discrimination but who may have indirectly benefited from it.

Key Court Decisions on Seniority Systems

In 1977 the Supreme Court ruled that job-based or departmental seniority units are legal as long as there is no intent to discriminate. Prior to this interpretation the majority of lower federal courts had declared seniority systems illegal if they perpetuated the effects of past discrimination. This decision indicated a movement toward the application of stricter standards to be applied to claims of discrimination not only in the realm of seniority systems but in almost every facet of work-life.

Apart from the traditional judicial ruling, some federal agencies have negotiated a number of "consent decrees" to settle civil rights class suits involving departmental seniority units that exclude minority workers from the most desirable jobs. One such decree was in the steel industry: its effects were to change the seniority system from departmentwide to plantwide units. The change also provided a system of transfer rights to minority workers who had been discriminated against under the old system.

A consent decree cannot be treated as binding on persons who are not parties to the proceedings in which it was negotiated.[31] Therefore, individuals adversely affected by a consent decree can challenge the decree in a later case. Seniority systems may not, however, be altered by a court for the benefit of workers who were not themselves victims of discrimination. Section 703(h) of the Civil Rights Act establishes seniority systems as exceptions to Title VII liability. In effect, "it is not unlawful for an employer to apply different standards of compensation, or different terms, conditions, or privileges of employment pursuant to a bona fide seniority system . . . provided that such differences are not the result of the intention to discriminate because of race, color, religion, sex, or national origin." Therefore, an employer may follow an existing seniority system when making layoffs, even if the effect is disproportionately adverse to recently hired blacks and women, as long as the seniority system is bona fide.[32] "A bona fide system means one that was created for legitimate purpose, rather than for the purpose of discrimination."[33]

Similar issues regarding the role of seniority rights have arisen in the application of the Americans with Disabilities Act of 1990. The Act states that an individual with a disability should be reasonably accommodated to perform the essential functions of a job, including reassignment. However, as in discrimination cases, the courts have ruled that the individual cannot be reassigned if another employee has seniority rights to the position under a bona fide seniority system. The courts have deemed that seniority provisions in collective bargaining agreements are bona fide systems and the courts have adopted a "per se rule" that an accommodation for a handicapped employee that would compel an employer to violate a collective bargaining agreement is unreasonable in all cases.[34]

Policy Goals and Key Court Decisions on Affirmative Action

The term **affirmative action** was first introduced in Executive Order 10925 signed by President Kennedy in 1961. The concept provides an opportunity for employers and unions to voluntarily modify their employment practices and introduce affirmative actions in order to remedy the effects of past discrimination. While Title VII does not require affirmative actions to be taken, it does require nondiscrimination in hiring, pay, and promotion. Many businesses have found that affirmative action programs help to assure compliance with this standard.

Affirmative action can be viewed in two realms. The first is in the federal setting. This stems from an executive order signed by President Johnson in 1965, requiring federal contractors to have goals and timetables for hiring that are representative of the national labor market. The second is in public and private firms that have been required to develop affirmative action hiring and promotion goals and timetables by individual court decisions.[35]

Throughout the 1960s and early 1970s the Supreme Court's civil rights rulings expanded the legal avenues available to women and minorities in battling discrimination, both past and present, in the workplace. However, beginning in the late 1970s the Court made a conservative shift in its dealings with affirmative action issues. This trend culminated with the Court's 1995 ruling in *Adarand* v. *Pena*.[36] This 5–4 ruling, dealing with federal affirmative action programs, held that race-based preference programs are constitutional *only* in response to quantifiable evidence of discrimination against an affected party. In other words, there is to be no across-the-board entitlement, among all members of a minority group, to government preference based solely upon historic discrimination. This decision has been viewed by some as a major obstacle to the ability of federal programs to award benefits based on race or sex.

The burden of proving discrimination at all times remains with the plaintiff. Statistical disparities alone are insufficient to prove discrimination. The plaintiff(s) must demonstrate that the discriminatory practice was not relevant to the defendant's business needs and that the adverse impact resulted from a particular employment practice. The burden then shifts to the employer to prove that there is a legitimate business necessity for the practice. The employer may also rebut the charge of discrimination by showing by the preponderance of the evidence that the same action would have been taken if there had not been any discrimination.[37]

The Court has made it clear that to succeed in a discrimination suit, or to legally implement an affirmative action program, parties must adhere to strict standards. An affirmative action is permissible *only* under the following conditions:

A. There is a "manifest imbalance" in the composition of the workforce.
B. The plan is "narrowly tailored" and designed to eliminate the imbalance in such a way that does not "unnecessarily trammel" the legitimate expectations of other workers.
C. Race or sex are not the sole determinants in making any employment selection decision. The courts frown on employment selections based solely upon these criteria. The employer must consider other pertinent factors such as experience and qualification.
D. The preferences terminate once balance in the job category has been achieved.[38]

An example of the effects of the Court's revised view of affirmative action can be seen in a training program to which the company and the union agreed to admit more minorities than would have been eligible under the previous seniority rules.[39] The Supreme Court has adopted a "strict scrutiny" standard in determining whether an affirmative action plan is valid. A plan is valid only if there is a "compelling interest" for implementing the plan. In addition, the plan must be "narrowly tailored" to achieve its objectives.[40] The government must identify and document the existing discrimination suffered by the particular groups in the labor force and develop programs that are specifically designed to remedy that discrimination. In effect, governments can implement affirmative action programs only if they can prove specific acts of discrimination by a specific agency or institution.

Recently, the circuit courts have required more evidence for an affirmative action plan to pass the "strict scrutiny" standard, such as persuasive statistical data and anecdotal evidence to establish past discrimination of a particular group. Generally, the statistical evidence must show that the affirmative action plan is a "modest solution" to a history of discrimination that caused a significant underrepresentation of minorities to a particular job.[41] The courts have also identified a "narrowly tailored" plan as one that will only affect the specific underrepresented group and will have a minimal impact on the hiring or promotion of other groups. In analyzing race conscious remedial effects of past discrimination, the courts consider four factors: (1) the necessity for the relief and efficacy of alternative remedies; (2) the flexibility and duration of the relief; (3) the relationship between the numerical goals and the relevant labor market; and (4) the impact of the relief on the rights of third parties.[42]

Important Administrative Agencies

This chapter has focused on the legal regulation of collective bargaining and unions. The administration of these regulations, critical to the functioning of collective bargaining, is in the hands of a variety of administrative agencies. Summarized below are the key activities of the most important administrative agencies operating in the labor area.

1. *National Labor Relations Board (NLRB):* Administers the National Labor Relations Act including the Taft-Hartley and Landrum-Griffin amendments. Key activities include designating bargaining units, conducting representation elections, and investigating and adjudicating unfair labor practice charges. The NLRB includes national and regional boards.

2. *U.S. Department of Labor (DOL):* Serves as the advisor to the President on labor issues. Conducts research and collects data on labor matters. Oversees the administration of a variety of regulations concerning equal employment opportunity, health and safety, and internal union affairs. Maintains a large staff in Washington, D.C., and regional offices.

3. *Federal Mediation and Conciliation Service (FMCS):* Offers mediation services to labor and management in their collective bargaining activities.

4. *National Mediation Board:* Administers the Railway Labor Act. Oversees union representation and provides mediation services to the parties during impasses.

5. *State and local agencies:* A variety of agencies regulate the conduct of public sector bargaining. Some of the agencies provide mediation services to parties engaged in collective bargaining in both the private and public sectors. Agencies also oversee the administration of state regulations dealing with employment conditions.

6. *Equal Employment Opportunity Commission (EEOC):* Responsible for investigating and conciliating claims of employment discrimination based on federal antidiscrimination statutes.

Summary

Labor laws are an important part of the environment that influences the conduct of collective bargaining. How workers join unions, the process of negotiations, the right to strike, and the scope of collective bargaining are all shaped by labor laws.

The National Labor Relations Act is the key labor law that governs collective bargaining in the private sector in the United States. The NLRA, passed in 1935, gives unions the right to strike, provides unions with exclusive jurisdiction, establishes representation election procedures, defines unfair labor practices, and in many other ways regulates collective bargaining. The National Labor Relations Board administers the NLRA, including the conduct of representation elections. A number of other administrative agencies also are involved in collective bargaining, including the Federal Mediation and Conciliation Service and the U.S. Department of Labor.

Significant issues addressed by the Taft-Hartley amendments to the NLRA, added in 1947, include union unfair labor practices, secondary boycotts, and representation limits on supervisors. The Landrum-Griffin amendments to the NLRA, passed in 1959, regulate union internal finances and governance.

Before passage of the NLRA, courts had restricted worker and union rights by applying conspiracy doctrines and injunctions. In the early 1900s a variety of laws, including the Clayton Act, the Norris-LaGuardia Act, and the Railway Labor Act, brought piecemeal changes to the regulation of collective bargaining. The NLRA established a comprehensive foundation for worker and union rights.

Separate state laws regulate public sector bargaining. As described in Chapter 13, the presence and scope of these laws vary greatly across states. Bargaining in the airline and railroad industry is regulated by the Railway Labor Act.

Frequently throughout the rest of this text reference is made to one of these labor laws as we discuss how collective bargaining works. Yet the influence of the law is often felt in combination with some other aspect of the environment. The next chapter examines how these other environmental factors shape collective bargaining.

Discussion Questions

1. How was the NLRA different from any previous labor law in the United States?

2. Describe what the NLRA requires regarding bargaining in good faith. How would you tell if labor and management in a particular negotiation actually were bargaining in good faith?

3. U.S. labor law is often said to put heavy emphasis on the procedural regulation of collective bargaining and to involve relatively little regulation of substantive bargaining outcomes. In what sense is this true?

4. Discuss whether collective bargaining in the railroads and airlines should be regulated with labor laws that differ from the laws that apply to other private sector employees.

5. Do you think employment-at-will is fair and effective? Why or why not?

6. Describe what employment discrimination laws prohibit.

Related Web Sites

General labor law materials:
http://www.law.cornell.edu/topics/labor.htm

Index of labor law acts and associations:
http://ibewlocal58.org/laborlaw.htm

National Labor Relations Act and National Labor Relations Board:
http://www.laborwatch.com/nlra_ulm_pdf.htm

Suggested Readings

Cox, Archibald. *The Law and National Labor Policy* (Los Angeles: Institute of Industrial Relations, University of California, 1960).

Feldacker, Bruce S. *Labor Guide to Labor Law,* 4th ed. (Upper Saddle River, NJ: Prentice Hall, 2000).

Gold, Michael Evan. *An Introduction to Labor Law,* 2nd ed. (Ithaca, NY: ILR Press, 1998).

Morris, Charles, editor. *American Labor Policy* (Washington, DC: Bureau of National Affairs, 1988).

End Notes

1. Benjamin J. Taylor and Fred Whitney, *Labor Relations Law,* 5th ed. (Englewood Cliffs, NJ: Prentice Hall, 1987), pp. 146–149.

2. Ibid., p. 147.

3. Ibid., p. 151.

4. Section 9(b) of the Taft-Hartley amendments to the NLRA prohibits the NLRB from including professional employees in a bargaining unit with nonprofessional employees unless the professional employees favor such a move with a majority vote. The formation of bargaining units is discussed in Chapter 7.

5. See Michael Evan Gold, *An Introduction to Labor Law* (Ithaca, NY: ILR Press, 1989), pp. 44–45.

6. Ibid., p. 45.

7. Ibid., p. 48.

8. The Taft-Hartley amendments, as discussed in the following section, allow states to ban union shop clauses.

9. *NLRB* v. *General Motors Corp.,* 373 U.S. 734 (1963).

10. Twenty states currently have right to work laws that ban the union shop.

11. Charles J. Morris, ed., *The Developing Labor Law* (Washington, DC: Bureau of National Affairs, 1971), p. 204.

12. *NLRB* v. *Yeshiva University,* 444 U.S. 672 (1980).

13. Taylor and Whitney, *Labor Relations Law,* pp. 584–621.

14. In 1989 the Teamsters Union reaffiliated with the AFL-CIO, but subsequently disaffiliated again in 2006.

15. Walter Oberer and Kurt Hanslowe, *Labor Law: Collective Bargaining in a Free Society* (St. Paul, MN: West Publishing, 1972), p. 42.

16. Milton R. Konvitz, "An Empirical Theory of the Labor Movement: W. Stanley Jevons," *Philosophical Review* 62 (January 1948): 75.

17. Archibald Cox, "The Duty to Bargain in Good Faith," *Harvard Law Review* 71 (1958): 1409.

18. A. H. Raskin, "Collective Bargaining and the Public Interest," in *Challenges to Collective Bargaining,* ed. Lloyd Ulman (Englewood Cliffs, NJ: Prentice Hall, 1967), p. 156.

19. Sanford M. Jacoby, "The Duration of Indefinite Employment Contracts in the United States and England: An Historical Analysis," *Comparative Labor Law* 5 (Winter 1982): 85–128.

20. Pauline T. Kim, "Bargaining with Imperfect Information: A Study of Worker Perceptions of Legal Protections in an At-Will World," *Cornell Law Review* 83 (1997): 105–156.

21. *Torosyan* v. *Boehringer Ingelheim Pharmaceuticals, Inc.,* 662 A.2d 89 (Conn. 1995).

22. *Palmateer* v. *International Harvester Company,* 85 Ill.2d 124 (1981).

23. *McLaughlin* v. *Gastrointestinal Associates,* 561 Pa. 307 (2000).

24. *Fortune* v. *National Cash Register Co.,* 364 N.E.2d 1251 (Mass. 1977).

25. Terry Thomason, Timothy P. Schmidle, and John F. Burton, Jr., *Workers Compensation: Benefits, Costs, and Safety under Alternative Insurance Arrangements* (Kalamazoo, MI: W.E. Upjohn Institute for Employment Research, 2001).

26. David Weil, "Enforcing OSHA: The Role of Labor Unions," *Industrial Relations,* 30(1) (Winter 1991), pp. 20–36.

27. Dallis L. Salisbury, "The State of Private Pensions," in *The Future of the Social Safety Net: Social Insurance and Employee Benefits,* eds. Sheldon Friedman and David C. Jacobs (Champaign, IL: Industrial Relations Research Association, 2001), Ch. 6.

28. Diane E. Lewis, "An Old-Economy Law on Layoffs Applies for Downsizing Dot-Coms," *Boston Globe,* February 19, 2001, p. A1.

29. "California Becomes First State to Authorize Paid Family Leave," *Daily Labor Report,* September 24, 2002, p. AA-1.

30. Theodore Eisenberg and Margo Schlanger, "The Reliability of the Administrative Office of the U.S. Courts Database: An Initial Empirical Analysis," *Notre Dame Law Review* 78 (August, 2003): 1455–1496.

31. *Martin* v. *Wilkes,* 487 U.S. 1204 (1990).

32. *Firefighters' Local Union 1784* v. *Stotts,* 467 U.S. 561 (1984).

33. *Eckles* v. *Consol Rail Corp.,* 94 F.3d 1041, 7th Circ., 1996.

34. *Willis* v. *Maritime Assoc.,* 244 F.3d 675, 5th Circ., 1998.

35. "Don't Give Up On Affirmative Action," *The Washington Post,* February 17, 1995, p. EO3.

36. 515 US 200 (1995).

37. *Price Waterhouse* v. *Hopkins,* 485 U.S. 933 (1990).

38. *United Steel Workers of America* v. *Weber,* 443 U.S. 193 (1979).

39. Ibid.

40. *City of Richmond* v. *J.A. Croson Co.,* 484 U.S. 1058 (1990).

41. *Majeski* v. *City of Chicago,* 218 F.3d 819, 7th Circ., 2000.

42. *Dallas Fire Fighters Assoc.* v. *City of Dallas,* 159 F.3d 438, 5th Circ., 1998.

Chapter 4

The Role of the Environment

This chapter moves horizontally across the three-tiered framework by examining how the environment influences the bargaining process and bargaining outcomes at the functional level. The discussion focuses on five key aspects of the environment: the economic, public policy, demographic, social, and technological contexts of the bargaining relationship.

The environment is most important through its effects on the bargaining power held by labor and management, which determines bargaining outcomes. A union, for example, will be better able to gain a high wage and other favorable contract terms when the union has relatively high bargaining power. It is often something in the environment that determines whether a union has a lot of bargaining power in one situation and little power in another. Thus we start this chapter with a discussion of how the environment influences bargaining power and the bargaining process. For instance, the text traces how a low unemployment rate (an aspect of the economic environment) strengthens workers' ability to hold out on strike and thereby gives a union greater bargaining power.

The role of environmental factors is well illustrated by events in recent years as labor and management were forced to respond to heightened international competition and continuing corporate restructuring. To understand how the environment affected collective bargaining in recent years and in other periods a conceptual framework is needed.

A Conceptual Framework to Analyze the Environment

This book uses as a framework an extension of the model proposed by John Dunlop. Dunlop classified the industrial relations environment into three main influences: (1) the **economic context,** (2) the **technological context,** and (3) the **locus of power** in the larger society.[1] This book also considers the influence of the **social context** and the **demographic context.** The underlying theme is that labor and management can influence the environment and the environment also influences them.

On the one hand, the external environment provides both incentives and constraints to labor and management in their efforts to meet their bargaining goals; thus it is important to consider how the environment shapes the power of the bargaining parties. On the other hand, the parties to collective bargaining also seek to mold their environment to better serve their needs; thus environmental influences are not entirely outside human control.

For example, since the 1920s, many textile, apparel, and other small, soft-goods employers have migrated from the northeast to the south, partly (if not primarily) to take advantage of a more favorable economic environment (such as lower labor costs).

More recently, many U.S. manufacturing firms have opened production facilities overseas or established joint ventures with foreign producers, thereby helping to create an economic environment of sluggish employment growth in their industries. In this way these firms have directly shaped the economic environment for collective bargaining.

The involved parties' ability to influence their environment is even more pronounced in the case of public policy because, quite simply, organized labor and management are the prime lobbyists influencing the public policies that regulate their own behavior. Consequently, in the long run the environment is to some extent influenced by the bargaining parties. Only in the short run should the environment be viewed as external and relatively fixed.

Bargaining Power

The environment is particularly influential through the effects it exerts on the bargaining power held by labor and management. Two aspects of **bargaining power** come into play, the total power and relative power of labor and management. **Total power** concerns the total profits (or economic rents) that are available to labor and management. The greater is the total power, the more profit (or economic rents) that are available for labor and management to divide up. Both labor and management prefer situations with greater total power. **Relative power** has to do with the relative strength of labor and management, in other words, the ability of either side to gain a larger share of a given amount of profit. In contrast to total power, with regard to relative power the interests of labor and management conflict.

The Determinants of the Total Power of Labor and Management

The total power of labor management is heavily influenced by two factors—the degree of competition facing the employer and the state of the economy. The degree of competition is affected by the amount of competition the employer faces from both domestic and international competitors. Firms that face few competitors and thereby exert market power earn greater profits (and economic rents) and thus, have more resources for labor and management to divide up. In the most concentrated of industries, a firm will be a monopoly and earn monopoly profits. In this case the total power of labor and management is at its maximum and bargaining is made easier by the fact that both high wages and high profits can be funded out of the firm's monopoly profits.

The state of the economy influences total power by affecting the level of demand (i.e., sales) and profits. The interests of labor and management with regard to total power are in common as both sides prefer less competition and a strong economy.

The Determinants of the Relative Bargaining Power of Labor and Management

The relative bargaining power enjoyed by a union is heavily influenced by the union's and its members' abilities to withdraw their labor, usually (though not always) through a strike. Workers are more likely to win higher wages and other gains the more they are willing and able to sustain a strike. Moreover, strikes, once undertaken, are more likely to succeed the greater the costs of the strike to the employer. Thus, the employer's relative bargaining power is heavily influenced by their ability to withstand a strike. The simplest measure of relative bargaining power is the amount of strike leverage each party holds.

Workers can also withdraw their labor through more informal actions, such as "working to rule" (following rules strictly rather than pursuing effective work practices), the "blue flu" (large-scale worker absenteeism), and other means of slowing production. The discussion that follows focuses on the effects of strikes that entail workers who fully withdraw their labor. Nevertheless, many of the points raised carry over to less extreme forms of labor withdrawal.

How Strike Leverage Influences Relative Bargaining Power

The relative degree to which workers and the employer are willing and able to sustain a strike is their **strike leverage.** More specifically, to measure each party's strike leverage, one needs to know what costs a strike would impose on each party and what alternative income sources there are available to each party to offset any income losses induced by a strike. The discussions of the environmental contexts that follow help us understand what determines strike leverage.

The Economic Context

Economic factors critically influence both total and relative bargaining power. Economic factors can be separated into those that are macrolevel (economywide) and those that are microlevel (relevant only to a specific bargaining relationship).

Microeconomic Influences on Total Bargaining Power

Microeconomic factors influence the total bargaining power of a particular employer or union through the effects competitive conditions exert on a firm. The greater the market power of a firm (i.e., the less competition it faces in the markets in which it competes) the greater will be the profits earned by the firm. With greater profits, there are more resources for the parties to divide based on their relative power. A firm's market power is affected by the degree of domestic and international competition faced by the firm. With regard to total power, labor and management have common interests with both sides preferring that the firm possess market power (this is true if other factors are held constant, in particular, factors that affect the relative power of labor and management). The existence of these potential common interests explains why unions sometimes join with the management of a firm and push for government regulations that enhance the market power of a firm. For example, in 2001 (and at other times) the USW joined with a number of steel companies to lobby the U.S. federal government to restrict and impose higher tariffs on the importation of foreign steel.

EXHIBIT 4–1
Determinants of Management's Strike Leverage

Microeconomic Influences on Relative Bargaining Power

Microeconomic factors influence the relative bargaining power of labor and management through effects on the parties' strike leverage and the elasticity of demand for labor (the wage–employment trade-off).

Management's Strike Leverage

The more an employer is willing and able to sustain a strike, the more likely the workforce will be to settle a strike before attaining all the union's goals. Employee strike leverage derives from the strike's influence on firm profits. The greater the profits lost by the firm, the more ready the firm will be to give in to labor's demands. During a strike a firm's profits are, in turn, shaped by a strike's effects on production and sales. Exhibit 4–1 diagrams the principal determinants of an employer's strike leverage: workers' ability to harm production, sales, and profits; and management's ability to find alternative means to maintain production, sales, and profits.

> *The effects of a strike on production:* Once a strike has begun, the first indicator of workers' bargaining power is the degree to which the strike has impaired production and/or service. Workers who succeed in actually halting production because there are no readily available labor substitutes—supervisors, employees in or from another plant, strikebreakers, or automated equipment—have substantial strike leverage and bargaining power. In other words, these workers are essential to the production process. Craft workers, who are typically very difficult to replace because of their skills, often have significant strike leverage. For example, the high skill levels of electricians and repair machinists help explain why they earn so much more than production workers in the auto, steel, and textile industries.
>
> *The effects of a strike on sales:* The power of a striking work group is tempered, however, if the halt in production does not lead to a reduction in sales. Employers can sever, or at least weaken, the link between production and sales if inventories are high or if alternative production sites can be used to produce what normally would be produced at the struck site. Whether alternative production is available is influenced by the bargaining structure (are the other sites covered by the same union or contract) and by the extent to which other workers at other sites join or support the strike.
>
> *The effects of a strike on profits:* Finally, even if production and sales are stopped by a strike, the firm may not necessarily witness a serious decline in profits. For

example, firms with relatively high ongoing capital or interest expenses have a harder time withstanding a loss of income caused by a strike. This helps explain why construction workers, who can temporarily halt costly construction projects, have so much bargaining power. In contrast, firms facing a strike that also shuts down all the competitors' operations have an easier time withstanding strikes because their lost sales and profits may be largely postponed rather than permanently forgone. Firms that have substantial savings or alternative income sources (such as from other lines of business) can more easily absorb the costs of a strike. Later sections of this chapter discuss how the recent growth in employers' nonunion operations has improved their strike leverage through this channel.

The Union's Strike Leverage

Consider the other side—the union's strike leverage. A union's strike leverage is determined by the ability and willingness of the workforce to stay out on strike. The longer workers are willing and able to stay on strike, the greater the bargaining power held by the union representing those workers and the more likely they are to win favorable employment terms from an employer, other factors held constant.

Alternative sources of worker income: Workers' willingness to stay out on strike is heavily influenced by the degree to which alternative sources of income are available to the striking work force. Obviously, workers in unions that offer ample strike benefits can better afford to stay out on strike than can those in other unions. Likewise, when striking workers can more readily find temporary or part-time work that supplements any union strike benefits or when they have accumulated substantial savings or assets, workers are more able to sustain a strike action.

Worker solidarity: Another set of factors that influence worker strike leverage beyond the microeconomic environment is the attitude of union members. Workers' feelings of solidarity with one another influence whether picket lines will be honored, and any pent-up frustrations will influence workers' willingness to stay out on strike. In brief, strikes are highly emotional undertakings, and they depend on numerous factors, not simply the microeconomic environment.

The Wage-Employment Trade-off

Strike leverage determines whether workers are able to press for a higher wage settlement or other more advantageous contractual provisions. But higher wages often bring cuts in employment, and thus unions may, in some cases, choose not to raise wages as much as they could. This is called the **wage-employment trade-off.**

The key point is that there are employment effects from wage increases as well as direct wage gains. Unions sometimes moderate their wage demands given these employment effects. For example, unionized apparel workers received only modest wage increases in their collective bargaining agreements in recent years, in part because they feared that any higher wage payments would cause apparel firms to more aggressively shift production offshore or to outsource production domestically to nonunion plants or firms than they would otherwise. This trade-off between wages and employment is therefore another important microeconomic influence on bargaining power and outcomes.

Marshall's Four Basic Conditions

Unions are more likely to consider the employment effects that result from a wage increase when these effects are greater. Why a wage increase leads to large reductions in employment in one situation and to only small reductions in employment in another is explained by **Marshall's Conditions.**

In his seminal analysis of labor and management relative bargaining power, Alfred Marshall argued that unions are most powerful when the **demand for labor** is highly **inelastic**—that is, when increases in wages will not result in significant reductions in employment in the unionized sector.[2] Marshall further proposed four basic conditions under which the demand for union labor would be inelastic: (1) when labor cannot be easily replaced in the production process by other workers or machines; (2) when the demand for the final product is price inelastic (that is, demand is not sensitive to changes in the price of the product); (3) when the supply of nonlabor factors of production is price inelastic; and (4) when the ratio of labor costs to total costs is small.[3] Let us address each of these conditions in turn.

> *The difficulty of replacing workers:* The first condition, the degree to which *workers are difficult to replace,* depends on the production technology. The more difficult it is to replace workers with machines or other workers, the less apt the workers will be to fear their displacement.
>
> Unions can try to limit the ease with which management can introduce new technology by raising the costs of substituting other factors of production for union labor, but they face a dilemma in that strategy. Collectively bargained constraints on technological change may keep unions from losing employment, but slowing that rate of technological change may also constrain the rate of productivity growth, limiting the long-run potential for wage increases.
>
> *The demand for the product:* Workers face less of an employment decline from raising wages if the demand for the product produced by these workers is not sensitive to the price of the product. This sensitivity (what economists call the *elasticity of product demand*) is a second key condition identified by Marshall. This condition is somewhat different from the other three in that it is influenced by consumer preferences and not by the actions of either the firm or the union. The elasticity of product demand depends on the willingness of consumers to substitute other products.
>
> A modern-day illustration of this principle is the threat to union power raised by foreign imports that become more attractive to domestic consumers as wages and prices in the domestic unionized economy rise. The auto, apparel, steel, and electrical appliance industries are all recent cases in point.
>
> Unions do try to influence consumer actions through "Buy Union" campaigns. Box 4–1 illustrates two different approaches to such campaigns. The ad on the right tells readers of the union newsletter where to find labels that identify whether various products are union made. The ad on the left is trying to discourage readers from purchasing a product the union claims is being produced by nonunion labor.
>
> *The supply of other inputs:* Marshall's third condition is the responsiveness of the price of other inputs in the production process to the demand for those inputs (what economists call the *elasticity of supply of other factors of production*). When an employer turns to alternative inputs to economize on union labor, unions will be more

able to push up wages (with less fear of employment cutbacks) if the price of other inputs rises a lot as their use increases. Thus, the more inelastic the supply curve for alternative inputs is, the greater is union power. Whereas Marshall's first condition concerns the degree to which it is *technologically feasible* to substitute machines or other factors of production for unionized labor, his third condition concerns the costs to the firm of increasing its use of alternative factors.

Labor's share of total costs: Marshall's fourth condition is that unions are more powerful when labor costs represent only a small proportion of total costs. This condition has often been restated as *the importance of being unimportant.* An employer is less likely to resist union pressure if a given wage increase affects only a very small proportion of the total cost of the product. Thus, a small craft unit, such as the skilled maintenance employees in a plant, is often less likely to meet management resistance to its wage demands than would a broad bargaining unit that represents all production and maintenance employees.[4]

Bargaining in the public sector demonstrates the difficulties unions experience when labor costs represent a large proportion of total production costs. Labor costs for local government often run between 60 and 70 percent of the budget, and in some jurisdictions occupations such as fire fighters run as high as 90 percent of the budget. When local government officials seek to control total budget costs, they take a very hard line in collective bargaining because the wages and salaries of public employees represent their largest controllable cost.

Do Unions and Workers Care about the Wage-Employment Trade-off?

All of the Marshallian conditions are based on the assumption that workers and unions are concerned about the employment effects of wage increases. If union members are willing to accept a slow rate of growth in employment or a decline in the number of union jobs as a trade-off for higher wages, the sources of power discussed above are less important.

Perhaps the classic example of a union that ignored the employment effects resulting from wage increases was the United Mine Workers of America (UMW) in the 1940s. UMW President John L. Lewis demanded high wage increases while giving employers a free hand to invest in labor-saving technology. The result was that, though mine workers' wages increased, employment in the industry declined sharply throughout the 1940s and into the 1950s.[5] Despite this decline, the union's leaders did not soften their demands for higher wages.

The industrial relations community has long engaged in a heated debate over the role the wage-employment trade-off actually plays in collective bargaining. Arthur Ross argued that political factors rather than employment consequences shape union wage policy. Ross also claimed that workers' wage demands are heavily influenced by their making comparisons with the wages of other workers or unions (by "orbits of coercive comparisons"), a practice that gives union leaders some leeway in defining their wage goals.[6]

John Dunlop had a very different view of union wage policy, claiming that unions do consider the employment consequences of their wage demands and that they may even try to maximize the employer's payroll.[7]

Concessionary bargaining from the 1980s on offered evidence that unions and workers do consider the employment effects of higher wages, particularly when they might lead to a plant closing. Yet, as Ross asserted, political factors played an important role in shaping whether and to what extent employment was a concern in wage bargaining. Workers' willingness to accept concessions and what they won in exchange for those concessions was affected by a host of factors, including business and union strategies.

Macroeconomic Influences on Total and Relative Bargaining Power

Economists refer to unemployment and the growth in national product or productivity as macroeconomic factors. The overall state of the economy affects bargaining power through a variety of channels. A firm is likely to be earning higher profits (greater total power) when the economy is strong and demand is growing. Holding relative bargaining power constant, both sides prefer periods of economic growth as these can sustain high wages and profits.

With regard to relative bargaining power, a union's strike leverage depends in part on the availability of jobs—both for the striking workers and for their spouses or other family members who might help support the strikers. The higher the unemployment rate, the less likely striking workers or family members will be to find substitute employment and the more likely the family members normally employed will be on layoff. Thus, during the upswing of a business cycle (as the unemployment rate declines), unions generally gain strike leverage. Conversely, the relative power of unions declines during periods of rising unemployment. The factors at work here include those discussed earlier regarding striking workers' needs for alternative income sources and employers' vulnerability to strikes when product demand is high. During periods of slack demand employers may, in fact, welcome a strike because they can then lower their inventories and use the strike as a substitute for layoffs.

Wage Flexibility over the Business Cycle

The connection between macroeconomic conditions and bargaining power is supported by evidence that the rate of wage increases in the economy responds to the business cycle. Wages rise more quickly in times of a growing economy, and they increase more slowly (or fall) in times of sluggish macroeconomic activity.

Nevertheless, declines in product demand and increases in unemployment have been shown to have a weaker downward effect on collectively bargained wage increases than on wage increases in the nonunion sector.[8] Unions tend to aggressively resist wage cutting, making it harder for union employers than for nonunion employers to cut wages or to moderate the pace of wage increases during recessionary periods. The fact that union wage rates are often set in multiyear agreements (labor contracts in trucking and the auto industry, for example, have traditionally been three years in duration) makes union wages less responsive than nonunion wages to changing economic conditions.

Exhibit 4–2 traces a number of the key macroeconomic variables in the United States. Many later sections of this book discuss U.S. economic trends, and the reader may find it useful to refer back to this chart. This book also frequently discusses how industrial relations behavior influences the economy's performance.

The Effects of Collective Bargaining on Macroeconomic Performance

The analysis of the macroeconomics of collective bargaining cannot close without identifying how bargaining outcomes in turn affect the economy itself. Bargaining outcomes not only illustrate the success of the macroeconomic policies designed to curb inflation and unemployment, but they also add a dynamic component of feedback to our framework. Bargaining outcomes influence the economic context for future collective bargaining negotiations and set the cycle of events in motion again.

The effects of collective bargaining settlements on the economy are complex and hotly debated by economists. There is much debate, for example, surrounding whether unions are the cause of inflation.

Do Unions Cause Inflation?

For union wage increases to lead directly to inflation, the union–nonunion wage differential would have to be ever widening. Although this differential did widen during the

EXHIBIT 4–2
Macroeconomic
Data for the
United States,
1965–2004

Year	Inflation Rate[a] (%)	Unemployment Rate[b] (%)	Wage Increase in Major Collective Bargaining Settlements[c] (%)	Productivity Increase (Output per Worker Hour)[d] (%)	Unit Labor Cost Increase[e] (%)	Policy[f]
1965	1.6	4.5	3.8	3.4	.4	Guideposts
1966	2.9	3.8	4.8	3.2	2.5	Guideposts
1967	3.1	3.8	5.6	.1	3.9	Jawboning
1968	4.2	3.6	7.4	2.8	4.4	None
1969	5.5	3.5	9.2	−.5	6.5	None
1970	5.7	4.9	11.9	−.1	5.8	None
1971	4.4	5.9	11.7	3.4	2.3	Controls
1972	3.2	5.6	7.3	3.6	3.1	Controls
1973	6.2	4.9	5.8	2.8	4.9	Controls
1974	11.0	5.6	9.8	−3.0	11.4	Decontrol
1975	9.1	8.5	10.2	1.3	7.2	None
1976	5.8	7.7	8.4	3.4	5.0	None
1977	6.5	7.1	7.8	1.0	6.4	None
1978	7.6	6.1	7.6	1.0	7.4	Guidelines
1979	11.3	5.8	7.4	−1.0	10.0	Guidelines
1980	13.5	7.1	9.5	−1.3	11.0	Guidelines
1981	10.3	7.6	9.8	1.0	8.3	None
1982	6.2	9.7	3.8	−1.7	8.2	None
1983	3.2	9.6	2.6	5.5	−.3	None
1984	4.3	7.5	2.4	2.7	2.3	None
1985	3.6	7.2	2.3	1.4	3.0	None
1986	1.9	7.0	1.2	2.0	2.1	None
1987	3.6	6.2	2.2	.8	3.1	None
1988	4.1	5.5	2.5	1.3	3.3	None
1989	4.8	5.3	4.0	1.3	1.8	None
1990	5.4	5.6	4.0	.6	4.1	None
1991	4.2	6.8	3.6	.8	3.3	None
1992	3.0	7.5	2.7	4.5	1.1	None
1993	3.0	6.9	2.3	1.0	1.5	None
1994	2.6	6.1	2.0	1.5	.6	None
1995	2.8	5.6	2.3	.4	1.6	None
1996	3.0	5.4	3.0	2.0	.8	None
1997	2.3	4.9	3.0	2.4	1.3	None
1998	1.6	4.5	3	2.7	3.2	None
1999	2.2	4.2	3.2	3.2	1.8	None
2000	3.4	4	3.8	2.0	4.2	None
2001	2.8	4.8	4.2	1.0	1.4	None
2002	1.6	5.8	3.9	3.8	−.4	None
2003	2.3	6.0	3.1	3.4	.1	None
2004	2.7	5.5	3.2	3.4	1.1	None

[a] The data are from U.S. Department of Commerce, *Statistical Abstract of the U.S.*, various years.
[b] The data are taken from the *Handbook of U.S. Labor Statistics*, Bernam Press U.S. Data Book Series, various years.
[c] The figures represent wage adjustments in all private sector industries for the first year of a contract. Data for 1996 and later are from the *Source Book on Collective Bargaining: Wages, Benefits and Other Contract Issues*, BNA Plus Publications, BLS, various years.
[d] The data are from, the *Handbook of U.S. Labor Statistics*, various years. The figures represent the output per hour of all workers in the nonfarm business sector.
[e] The data are from the *Handbook of Labor Statistics*, various years.
[f] See text for descriptions of these terms.

1970s, it then narrowed in the 1980s and 1990s, and, in any case, it has historically not been continuously increasing. Thus, even though union workers receive higher wages than do their nonunion counterparts, this earnings differential does not apparently produce inflation.

Furthermore, since unions represent less than 10 percent of the labor force, an increase in union wages will not be very inflationary unless union wage increases spill over to nonunion wages. Whether they do spill over to the nonunion sector has been widely debated, but there is little empirical evidence of this effect at an aggregate level.

A more significant way in which unions might cause the inflation rate to rise is through the slower response of union wages than nonunion wages to changing economic conditions. A number of studies have shown that wages in the unionized sector (or in highly unionized industries) respond less to increases in unemployment than do wages in the nonunion sector.[9] Thus, traditional strategies for reducing the rate of inflation by increasing the rate of unemployment and thereby holding down wage increases may be less effective for union wages than for nonunion wages.

The Political Influence of Unions on the Macroeconomy

Some observers have argued that all of these direct economic effects of unions on wages are less important in the overall wage-price inflationary spiral than are the political lobbying efforts of unions. For example, a wage-price spiral would continue only if the government pursues expansionary **monetary** or **fiscal policies,** or both. An **expansionary policy** encourages enough economic growth and allows the reemployment of any workers displaced by inflationary wage increases. Although the labor movement is certainly not the only lobbying group that supports expansionary monetary and fiscal policies, its support is a critical supplement to its more decentralized strategies to achieve individual wage and benefit agreements. Without an adequate rate of expansion and economic growth, collectively bargained wage increases would exert a greater toll on the employment opportunities of unionized members of the labor force.

The labor movement also supports a wide range of other economic and social policies that supplement its collective bargaining efforts. Again, it has been argued that many of these policies lead to a greater inflationary pressure than do the individually bargained wage increases. Some observers suggest, for example, that the union movement's support of full-employment policies, minimum-wage legislation, and various income-transfer policies such as unemployment compensation, workers' compensation, and social security all adds to the inflationary pressures in the economy.

Yet the effects of these policies on the economy as a whole are very unclear. Some economists claim that full-employment policies actually reduce inflationary pressures by promoting training and labor-market mobility and thereby expanding the available work force. And even if these policies were shown to contribute to inflationary pressures, it may be that these pressures are well worth the benefits provided by the policies.

Together macroeconomic and microeconomic forces act as one major set of determinants of the process and outcomes of collective bargaining. The factors described in the remainder of this chapter either supplement the economic forces or serve as the mechanisms through which the economic forces are translated into actual results in the collective bargaining system.

The Legal and Public Policy Context

Law and public policy influence the legal standing of unions, unions' bargaining power, and employment conditions. This section describes specifically how the law exerts these effects.

The Legality of Unionism and Union Activity

Public policy determines how easy it is for unions to form and sustain themselves. Imagine what would happen in a country where unionism was deemed to be illegal and workers were sent to jail if they tried to form unions or to carry out strikes. One would expect that under such a public policy there would be few unions and little activity carried out by organized representatives of workers. What would be the long-term consequences of such policies, and would this regime be sustainable?

With unions and union activity outlawed one would expect workers to exert little countervailing influence to other powerful social forces. Experiences in the eastern European countries such as Poland, however, reveals the social conflict that can result under such a system. In Poland, the union, Solidarity, led a challenge to the Communist government, and unions were later active in the overthrow of governments in other eastern European and in the former Soviet Union countries. Unionism has thus come to promote more than just the improvement of the working conditions of Polish workers. Events there and in other parts of the former Communist bloc remind us of the role that unions can play as a democratic force in society.

Banning unions is one extreme. Legally requiring union membership is potentially the other extreme role that public policy may play. There is no democratic government that has chosen to follow this course. Rather, public policies toward unionism in the United States and other democratic countries have taken a middle course between the extremes of banning and requiring unionism. There exists sizable variation across democratic countries in the regulations concerning which and how workers can join unions. In every country there also has been significant change in the regulations for unions over time.

The NLRA's Effects on Bargaining Power

The NLRA and state statutes governing public or agricultural employees in the United States do more than just give unions the right to exist. These acts exert sizable effects on the process and outcomes of collective bargaining through their regulation of the actions by workers, unions, and employers in the course of collective bargaining. For example, the NLRA grants unions the right to strike and obligates employers to bargain in good faith. Without these rights the bargaining power of unions might be severely weakened.

The NLRA influences the bargaining power of workers and employers in a multitude of ways, and many of those effects are through subtle channels. For instance, as discussed in Chapter 3, the Taft-Hartley amendments to the original NLRA made it illegal for supervisors to join unions representing production workers.[10] By taking away the protection of the law, the passage of this amendment led to the demise of the numerous foreman unions that had formed. For those foreman unions the amendments had a clear effect.

The Effects of Direct Regulation of Employment Conditions

Society also has seen fit to regulate certain employment conditions more directly than it does collective bargaining. In the United States federal regulations cover overtime hours (their limits and pay), unemployment insurance, pensions, and a host of other issues. These regulations are clearly important to the extent they set employment terms. They also are important through their indirect effects on bargaining power. For instance, the fact that workers in some states can collect unemployment insurance while they are on strike makes those workers more able to sustain strike action and increases their bargaining power, if everything else is the same.[11] Unions in the United States and other countries support legislated minimum wages and minimum standards for other employment conditions. In 1996, unions in the United States lobbied successfully for an increase in the minimum wage.

An Illustration of Government Employment Regulation: Pensions

An example of how government has influenced employment conditions is found in the area of pensions. The **Employee Retirement Income Security Act (ERISA)** of 1974 has had profound effects on pensions. The act (1) specifies minimum standards for vesting of pension contributions, (2) requires more detailed reporting and disclosure of information about the plan to both employees and the government, (3) requires all future liabilities be fully funded on an annual basis and all past unfunded liabilities be amortized over a number of years, and (4) establishes an insurance protection program for workers affected by plan terminations. The costs of the termination insurance are met by a tax on existing plans.

The major policy problem created by ERISA lies in the potential liabilities to the government from the termination of major multiemployer plans. See Box 4–2 for an account of how the Pension Benefit Guarantee Corporation (empowered under ERISA to insure pension plans) acquired enormous liabilities as a result of the bankruptcy of the LTV Corporation. Controversy also surrounds the changes being made to pension plans at IBM and other companies (see Box 4–3). These and similar cases have added to the controversy surrounding ERISA.

Overall, ERISA is a good example of both the speed by which changes can be achieved through direct governmental regulation and the complex problems that result when the federal government attempts to establish uniform practices and standards in an area that previously was characterized by diversity.

The Shift to Less Government Intervention

From the late 1970s on, U.S. public policy changed to a less interventionist style as policy returned to an emphasis on competitive markets at the micro- and macrolevels of the economy. Important developments at the microlevel included **deregulation** of the transportation and telecommunications industries.

Although deregulation was not motivated by labor policy concerns, it has had sizable effects on the process and outcomes of collective bargaining. Unions have trouble keeping wages out of competition and maintaining their penetration of any industry in the face of entry by new competitors. This has been well illustrated by the trucking industry since passage of the Motor Carrier Act of 1980, which reduced the regulation of industry pricing, and entry by the Interstate Commerce Commission. In the airline industry deregulation in 1978 spurred the growth of nonunion carriers and concessionary bargaining in the unionized airlines. In the telecommunications industry deregulation has led to both a growth in the share of telecommunications markets that are served by nonunion companies such as WorldCom and the breakup of a national bargaining structure in the former Bell Telephone System.

President Bush's support for free trade in recent years sparked heated debates over trade policy as the nation faced large trade deficits and a loss of employment in those industries

The Pension Benefit Guarantee Corporation (PBGC) is a government agency that serves as statutory trustee for LTV Corporation's terminated pension plans. On June 18, 1990, the Supreme Court ruled that PBGC's decision to restore LTV's pension plans was consistent with the Employee Retirement Income Security Act (ERISA). The court reasoned that PBGC has broad authority to restore terminated pension plans to employers who negotiate "follow-on" pension plans that supplement the benefits paid by the PBGC.

After accumulating $2.3 million in unfunded liabilities under its three pension plans, LTV Corporation filed for bankruptcy under Chapter 11 (in July 1986.) As a result, LTV notified PBGC, which insured $2.1 billion of the company's unfunded pension liability, that it was unable to continue complete funding of its pension plans. Consequently, in January 1987, PBGC terminated LTV's pension plans and began paying benefits (though lower than those had the plan not been terminated) to LTV plan participants.

The decrease in benefits resulted in a United Steelworkers suit against LTV. In response, LTV negotiated a follow-on plan, that made up the benefit difference the participants lost as a result of the plan termination. Therefore, the follow-on plan put retirees in exactly the same position as had the pension plans not been terminated.

Section 4047 of ERISA empowers the PBGC to restore a pension plan when restoration furthers the interests of Title VII and ERISA. Based on its determination that a dramatic economic upturn in the steel industry had reduced the risk of large unfunded liabilities, the PBGC (in August 1987) decided to restore LTV's pension plans under ERISA. However, when the PBGC attempted to enforce the restoration order, a New York District Court ruled that PBGC's decision was arbitrary and capricious because of its reliance on the follow-on plan and insufficient evidence of LTV's financial improvement.

However, the Supreme Court reversed this decision in ruling that the PBGC is not required to consider federal labor and bankruptcy laws in returning a previously terminated pension plan to a private employer in bankruptcy proceedings.

Health care and life insurance benefits for the retirees of the LTV Steel Corporation ended March 31, 2002, when its $85 million trust fund ran out. This surprised company executives who had expected the Pension Benefit Guarantee Corporation to become a trustee of the company's defined pension benefit plans. After the trust ran out retirees over the age of 65 were forced to turn to Medicare to cover their health coverage. But retirees under the age of 65 must pay to extend their health care coverage under the Consolidated Omnibus Budget Reconciliation Act (COBRA). However, neither COBRA nor Medicare fully covers the health care expenses of retirees. Medicare requires significant out-of-pocket expenses, and the average cost of family coverage under COBRA is $600 per month.

Meanwhile, the USW continues to lobby Congress for legislation that would create a federal trust fund to cover the "legacy costs" of pension and health benefits for approximately 600,000 retired steelworkers. Opponents to this legislation argue that the steel industry has been supported by the government for too long and should not receive additional special government aid.

Sources: *Daily Labor Report* (Washington, DC: Bureau of National Affairs): various issues from January 5, 1989, to June 19, 1990, and "LTV Retirees to Lose Health Benefits; USW Calls for Trusts to Cover Legacy Costs." *Daily Labor Report,* 38, February 26, 2002: A–8.

most threatened by foreign competition and imports. The increasing internationalization of the U.S. economy and globalization has also raised questions whether the labor law framework adopted in the 1930s is still appropriate.

The Labor Movement's Criticism of the NLRA

A questioning of the value of the NLRA has arisen from union leaders' frustrations with declining union membership and new organizing difficulties. Labor leaders (and others) argue that NLRA decisions and representation elections now come about only after

On July 31 2003, the U.S. District Court for the Southern District of Illinois ruled against IBM in a lawsuit claiming that changes in the company's pension plan violated the ban of age discrimination by the Employee Retirement Income Security Act (ERISA). This case questioned the legality of so-called cash balance pension plans and, as such, it had the potential to affect millions of workers across the country.

The dispute over age discrimination began in 1995 when IBM first amended its pension plan by adopting a "pension credit formula" (PCF). Using this formula, employees would earn a specific number of "base points" per year, depending on their age: Using these points, a formula would then calculate and establish an employee's monthly retirement at age 65. However, under the PCF, an employee earning a yearly salary of $60,000, who began working at IBM at age 50 and retired at 65, would amass $1,922 less in pension benefits per year than an employee earning the same annual salary who began working at IBM at age 35 and retired at 50. Therefore, the district court concluded that this formula decreased benefits on account of age by reducing the rate of growth for older workers.

The lawsuit also cited a second amendment to the benefits plan that was said to have contributed to age discrimination. In 1999, IBM, looking to reduce pension costs, again modified its pension benefit plan by implementing what is known as a "cash balance plan." Historically, this type of system could potentially decrease the pension of an older worker by up to 50 percent or more. In the case of IBM, it was proposed that 5 percent of an employee's pay be deposited into an account every year, into which interest would accumulate over time. This, however, effectively brings about less growth in benefits over time to older workers than it does younger workers, as the deposits inherently have less time to mature.

In September of 2004, IBM agreed to pay upwards of $1.5 billion and replaced the cash balance plan from 1999 with a more traditional defined contribution plan to settle the dispute. However, during this time, IBM filed an appeal to the U.S. Court of Appeals for the Seventh Circuit and, on August 7, 2006, IBM was exonerated from the charges as the appeals court overruled the previous decision.

Contrary to what the federal district court claimed in its 2003 ruling, the Appeals Court held that the employees who filed suit against IBM failed to take into account the time value of money. In order for age discrimination to be demonstrated, the court found that one must show that the underlying reason for discrimination is in fact age. Although less money will accrue over the course of an older worker's career due to the changes made by IBM, the court concluded that this effect is simply something naturally correlated with age and not something that discriminates based on it.

Sources: "Court Finds IBM's Benefit Formula Violated ERISA's Age Discrimination Ban," 08/04/03. *Daily Labor Report*, August 4, 2003: AA-1; "WSJ: IBM Pension Plan Changes are Ruled Discriminatory," 07/31/03. *Communication Workers of America*, July 31, 2003; "Seventh Circuit Rules IBM's Plan Didn't Discriminate Against Older Workers," 08/08/06. *Daily Labor Report*, August 8, 2006: AA-1.

enormous delays—caused in part by the lack of commitment to the original purposes of the NLRA. The delays are also alleged to be the result of employer practices, such as the filing of numerous challenges and requests for postponement, which only serve to thwart the original intent of the NLRA for timely and fair elections. Overall, these critics argue that NLRB enforcement procedures operate to the advantage of management and against the original purposes of the law.

Labor leaders blame their lack of success in organizing on weaknesses in the NLRA and stepped-up union-avoidance tactics on the part of management. And so they now debate whether unions and workers would be better served by major changes in the NLRA or by its complete elimination.[12] Adding complexity to this debate is the fact that, in some cases, U.S. unions clearly have benefited from the NLRA and its administration by the NLRB.

In May of 1999, the International Union of Electronic Workers filed charges against Quadrtech Corp., a jewelry manufacturer, because the company moved its manufacturing operation from Gardena, California, to Tijuana, Mexico, one day after the union's win in a representation election at the company. The NLRB agreed with the union and issued an unfair labor practices complaint because the company refused to bargain in good faith over the effects of the relocation decision. A judge of the U.S. District Court for California ordered Quadrtech to settle the unfair labor practice charges with the NLRB. The NLRB and Quadrtech reached a formal settlement that ordered the company to cease and desist laying off union workers and subcontracting or relocating work in retaliation for union activities. Quadrtech also agreed to cease refusing to bargain with the union over mandatory subjects of bargaining, such as layoffs or relocating work, and interfering with the employees' exercise of their Section 7 NLRA rights. The settlement also required Quadrtech to restore union work to the Gardena plant, along with all equipment that had been relocated to Tijuana. The company had to reinstate and pay back pay to all workers who were laid off during the relocation. Finally, Quadrtech agreed to post a notice stating that it would not threaten or retaliate against its workers because they chose union representation.

Source: "Unfair Labor Practices: Quadrtech Agrees to Settle with NLRB, Scrap Move to Mexico, Bargain in Good Faith," *Daily Labor Report,* 241, December 14, 2000: A–7.

For example, Box 4–4 describes how one company was forced to cancel plans to move its manufacturing operations from California to Mexico after the NLRB upheld an unfair labor practice complaint brought by the union that represents workers in the plant.

The Demographic Context

The changing nature of the labor force has also caused many to question whether collective bargaining is obsolete. It is therefore important to examine the nature of those changes and to explore their implications for collective bargaining.

Changes in the demographic characteristics of workers or jobs will influence the needs and expectations of workers. These, in turn, may affect the individual's interest in union membership or willingness to stay out on strike.

Labor Force Trends

Since World War II the U.S. labor force has grown at an unprecedented rate, largely as a result of the postwar baby boom. The labor force then began to grow more slowly in the 1990s than it had in the previous 20 years as fewer baby boomers entered the labor force but, rather, traveled through it. In fact, a slowdown in the growth of the labor force began in the late 1970s as the last of the boomers entered the labor force.

As the trend continues, the median age of the labor force will change accordingly. The median age peaked in 1960 at 40.5 and remained relatively constant until the first of the baby boomers entered the labor force in 1970, at which time it declined significantly. The median age was 39.0 in 1970 and had fallen to 34.8 by 1982. By 2008, one out of every six workers in the American labor force will be over the age of 55 and by 2020 that number will increase to one out of every five workers. As a result, the median age will again rise, reaching a new high of 40.7.[13]

These general patterns mean that over the course of this decade unions and employers will be faced with an aging work force as the baby boom cohort moves through its prime working years. As this happens workers will be in sharp competition for jobs at the higher levels of careers and occupations. Workers may become frustrated if their aspiration for upward mobility is not attainable. This could produce workplace conflicts and a heightened demand for employee participation and voice and, possibly, for union representation.

Over the longer run, the problems of an aging population will become increasingly important, and the ratio of those not in the labor force to those in the labor force will increase—posing difficult problems indeed for all the actors in the industrial relations system.

Women in the Labor Force

The growing number of working women is one of the most significant labor force developments. In 1972 one-half of all women participated in the labor force; in 2005, 72.6 percent of women between the ages of 25 and 54 worked.[14] The employment-population ratio for adult women reached record highs in 2000 at 60.3 percent. The general trend can largely be explained by women's changing marital status, educational attainment, and career expectations.

One component of the trend has been the increased participation in the labor force of women with young children. Women have been taking less time off from work for child rearing. By 2000, the percentage of working women with children reached 72.3 percent, and from 2000–2005 this number remained steady at just around 70.5 percent.[15]

Consequently, working mothers have begun to challenge employers and unions to meet their social needs. They pose a particular challenge because the propensity to work has been greater among the more highly educated women. Between 1975 and 2004, the labor force participation rate for female college graduates ages 25–64 receiving at least a bachelors degree rose from 61 to 82.5 percent. Women were increasingly gaining access to managerial and professional jobs. In fact, in 2004, over one-third of women in the labor force were working in these two fields.[16] Although most of the remaining employment gains for women was in lower paying sales and administrative support jobs, for every woman who found a job in one of these occupations, two found a job in managerial and professional specialty occupations. Thus, in addition to being a growing component of the labor force, women may well become a vocal component. Their increasing numbers and their increasing education, militancy, and consciousness of women's issues may pressure employers and unions to change their postures toward female workers. Finally, women may present a new focal point for union-organizing campaigns.

Educational Attainment

The educational attainment of workers has increased over the last 30 years. In 1990 the median number of years of school completed for all workers was 13, or just slightly beyond a high school degree.[17] (It was 12.4 in 1970.) In 1970, 63.9 percent of all workers had graduated from high school and 12.9 percent had graduated from college. In 2005, only 9.6 percent of the civilian workforce had less than a high school diploma, while 32.8 percent were college graduates.[18] The workforce is becoming more educated, and this trend is probably strongly influenced by the fact that the advantages of a college education are becoming more apparent. The income differential between college educated and high school educated

EXHIBIT 4–3
The relative Size of Industrial Sectors in the United States*

Source: *Handbook of U.S. Labor Statistics,* Bernam Press U.S. Data Book Series, ninth edition, 2006, pp. 181–82.

Year	All Service-Producing	All Goods-Producing	Manufacturing Only	Government Only
1919	52.6%	47.4%	39.4%	9.9%
1920	53.3	46.7	39.0	9.5
1930	59.3	40.7	32.5	10.7
1940	59.1	40.9	33.9	11.6
1950	59.1	40.9	33.7	13.3
1960	62.3	37.6	31.0	15.4
1970	66.7	33.3	27.3	17.7
1980	71.6	28.4	22.4	18.0
1990	77.2	22.8	17.4	16.7
1995	79.3	20.7	15.8	16.5
2000	80.5	19.5	14.0	15.7
2001	81.9	18.1	12.5	16.0
2002	82.7	17.3	11.7	16.5
2003	83.2	16.8	11.2	16.6
2004	83.4	16.6	10.9	16.4

*The percentages represent workers as a percentage of the total nonagricultural labor force.

workers grows every year. Median weekly earnings for workers with a college degree rose 13.2 percent between 2003 and 2006, to $1019, while earnings for workers with a high school diploma increased only by 6.9 percent in the same years, to $592.

There is, however, an important caveat to consider in projecting the overall "quality" of the labor force. High rates of teenage unemployment (13.1 percent for 16- to 19-year olds in 2005), high dropout rates from high schools (8.3 percent of white youth and 9.7 percent of black youth were high school dropouts in 2003), and the poor quality of education offered in urban and, particularly, in poor urban areas all suggest that a large number of new entrants in the labor force over the next decade will have little work experience, few skills, and a low potential for adapting to the rigors of organizational life.[19] Teenagers who grow up in areas with few or no jobs, high rates of crime, and poor schools will pose significant challenges to managers and union leaders of the future. Past experience has shown that it is difficult indeed for employers to reverse the effects of these liabilities.

These two separate educational patterns pose different but equally challenging problems to future managers and union leaders. The more highly educated workers may be less tolerant of authority, seek more involvement on their jobs, and demand more career development opportunities, while the educationally disadvantaged will require more remedial training to mold them into more literate, trainable, and motivated participants in the labor force.

Occupational and Industry Trends

As the supply characteristics of the U.S. labor force have been changing, so has the occupational and industry demand for labor. The most obvious trends in the occupational distribution since 1960 have been the growth of the white-collar sector and the decline of the blue-collar sector. Over half of the labor force is now classified as white-collar; in 1960 that proportion was 43 percent. As Exhibit 4–3 shows, as of 2004 the percentage of the labor force employed in service-producing jobs, the **service sector,** was 83.4 percent, whereas the percentage employed in goods-producing jobs was only 16.6 percent. The Bureau of Labor Statistics predicts that health services, business services, social services, engineering and management will grow at a rate of more than two times faster than the economy as a whole from 2004–2014.[20]

These major shifts in industry demand over the last 30 years have profound implications for collective bargaining. The portion of the labor force employed in manufacturing jobs, the traditional stronghold of unions, has declined significantly. Furthermore, manufacturing industries have been migrating from the northeast and north central regions of the country to the south and southwest. There has been a sizable movement of jobs away from the most unionized industries and regions to industries and areas where unions have traditionally been less successful in organizing workers.

There has also been a significant increase in the share of employment in **part-time** jobs. In 2005, 17.6 percent of employees worked part time. Of these, 89 percent (15.7 percentage points of the 17.6 percent) voluntarily chose part-time work, while 11 percent (1.9 percentage points) were working part-time jobs because they could not find full-time work.[21]

As part-time work has grown, so has the number of jobs being performed at home. **Home-based work** has grown in rank, partly in response to advances in information technologies that make it possible to perform production tasks at home while in communication with a business or businesses out of the home. This is especially true of several data-processing occupations. Both part-time workers and home-based workers are difficult to reach with union-organizing drives.

The Internet has revolutionized the workplace; meetings can now be held online and telecommuting allows employees to work at home and still remain in contact with their employers. Certain employees greatly benefit from this new technology such as parents with small children and the disabled. However, these home-based workers pose challenges for the labor movement given how hard it is to organize them.

In recent years many businesses also increasingly have turned to employment agencies or temporary help agencies to help them respond to seasonal and other fluctuations in demand through the hiring of temporary workers ("temps"). Although temporary workers give companies more flexibility, these employees typically receive few or no fringe benefits, low wages, and no job security even if they work full-time hours. Although temporary workers are often disgruntled, unions find them extremely difficult to organize.

Is the U.S. Economy Deindustrializing?

The increase in the number of service and part-time jobs has spurred an intense debate. Barry Bluestone and Bennett Harrison claim that the growth in these jobs signals a decline in the manufacturing base of the U.S. economy (they call the process **deindustrialization**). They further argue that these shifts in job composition go hand-in-hand with increasing inequality in the income distribution. The better-paying jobs such as skilled trades, steel, and auto production jobs, they claim, are disappearing and are being replaced by lower-paying service jobs.[22] The spread of corporate downsizing led Bennett Harrison to conclude that American corporations are becoming "lean and mean." These developments may have contributed to the growing income inequality that occurred in the United States from 1980 on.

On the other side of the debate stand analysts such as Robert Lawrence who hold that the growth in the number of service and part-time jobs has been a response to the availability and desires of workers who want and are skilled for those jobs.[23] These observers see this as a sign of health in the U.S. economy and compare the job growth in the United States over the last 30 years to the sluggish employment growth in Europe over the same period.[24] There is a middle position in this debate, as well, with some disclaiming any deindustrialization but at the same time pointing to many persistent problems in the U.S. labor market.[25]

This debate subsumes a disagreement over both what the facts are and how the facts should be interpreted. Yet the debate is crucial to the future of the labor market because the issues at stake are of enormous importance. For if one decides that the labor market is relatively healthy, there is little reason to seek government policies to alter the outcomes in that labor market, and vice versa. Furthermore, any answer to the question whether deindustrialization or income inequality is taking place will affect government policy toward collective bargaining and many other labor market institutions.

The shift to greater service sector, part-time, and home-based employment has two indisputable implications for collective bargaining and union organizing. First, since part-time workers have looser attachments to a single employer than others (they are often only temporarily employed), union organizing among them is more difficult and probably requires nontraditional techniques. It is not surprising that the labor movement has vigorously opposed the growth of temporary and home-based work. It is unlikely, however, that labor's opposition will have any effect on the growth occurring in these types of employment relationships. Thus, to organize these workers, unions will need to develop policies and strategies that are tailored to their particular needs. One strategy that has been discussed within labor's ranks is to provide associate member status or individual forms of representation to these workers.[26] Other solutions may be developed outside the United States since the growth in temporary, part-time, and home-based work is a problem confronting labor movements all over the globe.

Second, the ease of replacing striking service workers makes it difficult for unions to acquire bargaining leverage through the strike. Several unions that represent service workers have been experimenting with strategies to broaden support for their demands within community groups such as churches. Service unions also have been experimenting with working to rule and other strategies that can exercise leverage against employers while not involving strike action.

Demographic Profile of Union Members

The average union member is more apt to be working in industries, occupations, and regions in which the demand for labor is either declining or growing at a slower pace than elsewhere in the economy. In addition, women, whose labor force participation is increasing rapidly, are underrepresented in the unionized sector.

There are many challenges posed for unions by these developments. The traditional constituency of unions—male, blue-collar, manufacturing, mining, construction, and transportation workers living in the northeast or north central regions—is declining in significance. Current union members are on average older and less well educated than the new entrants to the labor force. Unions may have difficulty adjusting to the demands of a younger, more vocal constituency.

Demographic Challenges for Unions

Demographic diversity can affect union policies. Once they join unions, people tend to try to shape union policies to reflect their own preferences. This process of political representation becomes troublesome to unions if members' views change rapidly. The very purpose of a union is to pursue the common goals of its members through the exercise of collective power. Thus, the more rapid the demography changes and the more heterogeneous the union constituency becomes, the greater the potential for internal conflict and the more difficulty the union will have in trying to establish bargaining priorities.

New union members sometimes have a difficult time creating an effective political base. This is a problem that sometimes confronts newly hired, younger workers as they try to influence the existing, often older, union leadership. Note the same problem faces women, racial and ethnic minorities, or any other new groups that move into union jobs. Until they can establish an effective political base and exert pressure on existing union leaders, their particular needs are not likely to be given as high a priority as they might desire.

In short, the demographic context of collective bargaining influences union membership, the attitudes union members have toward their jobs, and the skills workers bring to the job. If unions are unsuccessful at organizing the new workforce, their membership will decline even further. If unions do succeed at organizing the new workers, they will face pressures for change—both within their own organizations and at the bargaining table. In any event, it is clear that any analysis of collective bargaining must account for the demography of the labor force.

The Social Context

What is the image of the union movement in the eyes of the American public? Is the society supportive of or hostile to unions? These are aspects of the social context that can affect industrial relations.

Polls that include questions about unions reveal fluctuations over time in the public's image of unions. Gallup polls, for example, show a decline in the share of the population that "approves" of labor unions from 71 percent in 1965 to 55 percent in 1981. However, public support for unions has improved in recent years. The percentage of the public that approves of labor unions, according to the Gallup Poll, increased to 65 percent in 1999 and stood at 58 percent in 2005 (for the latter figure see Box 4–5). When asked where their sympathies have been in recent labor disputes, more of the public was sympathetic to unions (52 percent) than to companies (34 percent,) as shown in Box 4–5.

Responses to other questions regularly asked in the Gallup and other polls reveals that the level of public confidence in organized labor (and big business) are consistently and substantially lower than those of the military, church and religion, the Supreme Court, and public schools. Yet, the public does not feel particularly threatened by "Big labor" as compared to "Big government" or "Big business," (see Box 4–5).

These responses are not unusual. Analysis of a wide range of poll data shows that the public and union members hold complex attitudes toward unions. For example, polls consistently have shown that the American public holds union leaders in low esteem. But, although skeptical of union leaders, the American public has continued to express strong approval of the functions unions perform in representing worker interests. Polls show, for example, that a majority of the population approve of unions in general and believe in the right of workers to join unions of their own choosing.[27] Thus, the majority of Americans apparently accept the legitimacy of unions as a means for protecting the economic and job-related interests of workers.

Public attitudes toward unions expressed in recent Gallup polls are:

1. Do you approve or disapprove of labor unions?

   58% Approve

   33% Disapprove

   9% No opinion

2. In the labor disputes of the last two or three years, have your sympathies, in general, been with unions or companies?

   52% Unions

   34% Companies

   6% Neither

   3% Both

   5% No opinion

3. In your opinion, which of the following will be the biggest threat to the country in the future—big business, big labor, or big government?

   27% Big business

   8% Big labor

   61% Big government

   4% No opinion

Sources: Data for Questions 1 and 2 are from Gallup polls conducted in August 2005. Data for Question 3 are from a Gallup poll conducted in December 2005. Daniel B. Cornfield, "Shifts in Public Approval of Labor Unions in the United States, 1936–1999," The Gallup Organization, http://www.gallup.com/poll/gs990902.asp.

American workers also seem to have a **dual image of trade unions.** On the one hand, the majority of workers see unions as big, powerful institutions in society that exert significant control over political decision making and elected officials, as well as over employers and union members. The majority also take a skeptical view of union leaders' personal motivations. On the other hand, an equally large majority of workers see unions as being helpful or instrumental in improving the working lives of their members. Evidently, then, most U.S. workers are skeptical of the political activities of trade unions but accepting of their collective bargaining activities.

The Technological Context

Technological change had a major role in workers' early efforts to look to unions as a way to alter their employment conditions. It also is clear that our economy is in the midst of ongoing technological changes that will have huge effects on future employment conditions. Yet, in the face of this agreement, many people still disagree over how and why technology influenced early unionization and what current technological changes imply for the future of industrial relations.

The Historical Debate over the Influence of Technology: Commons versus Marx

Both Karl Marx and John R. Commons believed that workers were spurred to join unions by technological change, the shift from craft systems of production to the hiring of wage labor, and the rise of the modern factory system. But they disagreed sharply over exactly why changes in technology and the organization of work had that effect.

To Marx the critical event in industrialization was the chasm that capitalist methods of production opened up between workers and the owners of the means of production. That chasm, according to Marx, would inevitably result in a worsening of working conditions, a profit crisis, and the emergence of a revolutionary class consciousness among workers. Followers of Marx went on to argue that it was the loss of control that workers experienced as a result of the shift in production methods and ownership that led them to form unions. To those observers collective bargaining was, and is, a continuing battle between workers and managers over control of the production process. Harry Braverman built on this argument and claimed that technological change typically leads to a lowering of the skills required in jobs **(deskilling)** as part of this battle for control.[28]

Commons, on the other hand, observed that the shift in production methods was itself a product of an expansion of the market brought about by urbanization and new transportation methods. To Commons, as the market expanded and the ownership of production changed, workers came up against a host of competitive menaces such as prison or child labor. Workers then turned to unions to protect themselves and to improve their standard of living. Commons and his students, such as Selig Perlman, argued that unions and workers sought income and job security rather than control of the production process.[29] Thus, although Marx and Commons differed sharply over the interpretation of unions' objectives, both saw the rise of capitalism as the spur to unionization.

To Clark Kerr, John Dunlop, Frederick Harbison, and Charles Myers it was the process of **industrialization** and not capitalism per se that brought forth the changes in the relationship between workers and employers that, in turn, led to unionization.[30] They argued that modern technology produced a need for rules to govern relations between workers and employers. Collective bargaining and contractually negotiated rules were a logical way to formalize and structure the rules required in modern industry. Given this framework, specific technological changes are important within collective bargaining because they result in changes in the relative bargaining power held by management or labor. In this regard, the industrialization thesis is closer to Commons than to Marx.

The Influence of Microelectronic Technology on Skill Levels

The recent expansion in the use of microelectronic technology has reignited the debate over the effects of technological change. To some this technology can open the way to less hierarchical, higher skilled work and further growth in real incomes. To others the new technology is being used to wrestle control away from the work force and to deskill workers now just as it allegedly was in the past.[31] These latter observers see little evidence of a shift away from the hierarchical forms of work organization. In fact, these modern proponents of the deskilling thesis argue that much of the concessionary bargaining from the 1980s on illustrated management efforts to increase the pace of work and use new technology to weaken workers' bargaining leverage and skills. The deskilling thesis proponents also predict that new technology will lead to significant employment displacement and unemployment.

A number of behavioral scientists believe that new technologies serve to "unfreeze" existing practices and open up a variety of options for reconfiguring the organization of work, career ladders, compensation criteria, and other aspects of the employment relationship.[32] According to this view there is no single effect of technology on skills or worker power; rather, its effects depend on the choices made by decision makers and the way the new technology is implemented.

The High-Tech Paradox

The growing presence of Japanese manufacturing plants in the United States has produced some important new thinking about the concept of technology, its relationship to industrial relations practices, and its effects on economic performance. Part of the interest in Japanese manufacturing practices was fueled by what we call the **high-tech paradox:** evidence that America's highest technology plants are not our most productive. Instead, experience in the auto industry has demonstrated that the highest productivity and the best product quality in the industry are being achieved in those plants that effectively integrate new technologies and manufacturing practices with innovative human resource and industrial relations practices.

Evidence on this point includes case study comparisons of the relatively low-tech New United Motors Manufacturing Incorporated (NUMMI), a joint-venture GM-Toyota plant in California, with several other U.S. plants that had invested in the highest robotics, information processing, and materials handling technologies available. To the surprise of many industry and academic experts, NUMMI's productivity and quality record surpassed the performance achieved in these high-tech facilities.[33] The consensus explanation that emerged from these comparisons was that NUMMI did a better job of training, motivating, and involving the work force in the process of continuous improvement, and that they combined this human resource strategy with flexible work systems and advanced manufacturing practices such as just-in-time inventory control and statistical process quality controls.[34]

What emerged from this and other evidence was a hypothesis that it was the "integration" of new industrial relations and manufacturing practices that was the key to productivity and quality improvement and not just new technology alone. Evidence of this integration hypothesis also came from comparisons of the productivity and quality of an international sample of automobile assembly plants scattered around the world.[35] The integration of technology with solid human resources and industrial relations innovations is so important because it allows, as two analysts of the Japanese manufacturing practices put it, workers to "give wisdom to the new machines."[36]

Recent Environmental Pressures on Collective Bargaining

In the face of the strong economic growth experienced in the United States in the 1990s, a few unions, such as the autoworkers and airline pilots, were able to achieve solid collective bargaining gains. Nevertheless, a number of changes in the environment placed unions at a distinct disadvantage with regard to their bargaining leverage with management. Corporate restructuring and the availability of outsourcing and nonunion alternatives continue to put pressure on unions and increasing globalization heightened those pressures. The bursting of the dot.com bubble in the spring of 2000 and the retrenchment that followed a wave of corporate financial scandals in 2002 also strained the U.S. economy and weakened union leverage.

Pressure from Nonunion Competition

Unions face competition particularly from the growing numbers of domestic nonunion firms. In industries such as construction, trucking, textiles, and mining the share of nonunion production had risen substantially. Furthermore, even in traditional strongholds of unionism such as steel and autos, nonunion firms were entering the industry. Nonunion competition became an even greater threat as employers became more willing and able during strikes to shift production to nonunion sites. As a result, unions became less able to take wages out of competition, and, as predicted by our earlier theoretical discussion, their bargaining power declined significantly.

Heightened International Competition

The growing penetration of imports in several key manufacturing industries and the large trade deficit, carried the issue of the international economy straight to collective bargaining agendas. Foreign workers had become a major competitive threat to organized labor in the United States because it is very difficult for unions to take wages out of competition when goods and investments move easily across national and international borders. Perhaps the growth of the multinational companies is the modern-day equivalent of the competitive menaces faced by the Philadelphia shoemakers described so well by Commons.

Union Image Problems

Economic pressures were only part of the story, however. The labor movement encountered a public that was often skeptical of the value of unions and worker solidarity. Strikers often found their picket lines crossed by fellow workers and less support for strikes in the broader community. When unions sought recourse through the NLRB or the courts to block such management practices as the movement of operations to other sites or the abrogation of collective bargaining contracts during bankruptcy reorganization, they received little help.

Signs of Innovation in the Labor Movement

The economy, public policy, ideology, and demography had all taken a turn that would hamper the efforts of organized labor. And yet, in the face of all these environmental pressures, the union movement was exhibiting some signs of innovation and adaptation. There has been a broadening of the bargaining agenda and increased union involvement in managerial decision making. Moreover, the labor movement began to engage in serious soul-searching, which culminated in the first contested election for the presidency of the AFL-CIO and the election of John Sweeney in 1995. Sweeney ran on a platform that sought to shift the focus in union activity and expenditures toward union organizing. A variety of union revitalization measures then spread.

Summary

This chapter examines how the environment influences the bargaining process. The five key aspects of the environment are economic, public policy, demographic, social, and technological factors.

Important economic factors include those that operate at the firm level (called the microeconomic influences) and the state of the labor market and the overall economy (called the macroeconomic influences). The economic environment is most important through the effects it exerts on the bargaining power held by labor and management. Bargaining power is heavily influenced by strike leverage and the extent to which an increase in wages leads to a decline in employment (called the wage-employment trade-off).

Public policy shapes the rights of the parties and the procedures used in collective bargaining. There has long been a strong preference in the United States for labor laws that give employees, unions, and management the right to directly shape employment terms with limited interference from the government. The most important labor law in the United States is the National Labor Relations Act and its amendments. There also are substantive laws that directly influence particular employment conditions, such as pensions and equal employment opportunity rights, although we have relatively less substantive employment regulation by the government than do other countries.

Major demographic issues include the increased labor force participation of women that has occurred after World War II. The labor force is becoming more diverse and unions face a challenge in altering their policies to increase their appeal to the new workers, many of whom work in the service sector.

The public continues to express support for the general purposes served by unions. When asked about union leaders or the willingness to join unions, however, the public's attitudes toward unions turn less favorable.

Technology influences employment levels and bargaining leverage. In recent years there has been much debate over how technology is affecting worker skill levels. On the shop floor labor relations play an important role in shaping how well new technology is implemented. There is much recent evidence that the best-performing plants in the United States are those that successfully integrate human resource and technological improvements.

How well collective bargaining serves the interests of labor and management often depends on its ability to adapt to changes in the environment. Economic pressures on the U.S. collective bargaining system have steadily grown along with the expansion in international trade. There are also pressures from the other key environmental dimensions. To help build a better understanding of how collective bargaining could respond to these environmental challenges, the next chapter examines how collective bargaining works.

Discussion Questions

1. Define bargaining power and strike leverage.

2. Several microeconomic factors play a part in both a union's and an employer's strike leverage. Briefly describe some of these factors.

3. Describe some of the ways the National Labor Relations Act influences the bargaining power of labor and management.

4. Briefly discuss some of the recent demographic trends in the workforce.

5. Is the labor law framework that was adopted in the 1930s still appropriate?

6. What changes in the industrial environment placed unions at a disadvantage in the 1990s?

Related Web Sites

United Mine Workers (UMW):
http://www.access.digex.net

LTV Corporation & Pension Benefit Guarantee Corporation:
http://www.pbgc.gov/coal.htp

Suggested Readings

Blauner, Robert. *Alienation and Freedom* (Chicago: University of Chicago Press, 1964).

Ehrenberg, Ronald G. and Robert S. Smith. *Modern Labor Economics,* 8th ed., (Reading, MA: Addison-Wesley, 2003).

Harrison, Bennett. *Lean and Mean: The Changing Landscape of Corporate Power in the Age of Flexibility* (New York: Basic Books, 1994).

Osterman, Paul. *Securing Prosperity: The American Labor Market—How It*

Has Changed and What to Do about It (Princeton: Princeton University Press, 1999).

Weber, Arnold R., and Daniel J.B. Mitchell. *The Pay Board's Progress* (Washington, DC: Brookings Institution, 1978).

End Notes

1. John T. Dunlop, *Industrial Relations Systems* (New York: Holt and Company, 1958).

2. Elasticity of demand refers to the slope of the demand curve for labor. The more inelastic is demand, the more vertical the demand curve and the less responsive is the demand for labor to any change in the price of labor. A perfectly elastic demand curve would be horizontal. Alfred Marshall, *Principles of Economics,* 8th ed. (New York: Macmillan, 1920), pp. 383–86.

3. Others have pointed out that for a low labor cost ratio to act as a source of power, as Marshall hypothesized, the elasticity of demand for the final product must be greater than the elasticity of substitution of nonlabor inputs in the production process. See Richard B. Freeman, *Labor Economics,* 2d ed. (Englewood Cliffs, NJ: Prentice Hall, 1979), pp. 67–71.

4. Note, a small bargaining unit can be affected by employers that consider the "spillover" effects of a settlement negotiated with one small unit on the rest of the firm's work force.

5. Even if the union had tried to influence employment levels, it might not have been successful in the face of technological change in the industry.

6. Arthur M. Ross, *Trade Union Wage Policy* (Berkeley: University of California Press, 1948).

7. John T. Dunlop, *Wage Determination under Trade Unions* (New York: Macmillan, 1944).

8. Daniel J. B. Mitchell, *Unions, Wages, and Inflation* (Washington, DC: Brookings Institution, 1980), pp. 113–62.

9. See, for example, Farrell E. Bloch and Mark S. Kuskin, "Wage Determination in the Union and Nonunion Sector," *Industrial and Labor Relations Review 31* (January 1978): 183–92.

10. The Taft-Hartley amendments do allow management to voluntarily bargain with a union representing supervisors. Such bargaining is extremely rare.

11. The effects of public policies on strike leverage are discussed in Robert Hutchens et al., *Strikes and Subsidies: The Influence of Government on Strike Activity* (Kalamazoo, MI: W. E. UpJohn Institute, 1989).

12. In "AFL-CIO Will Oppose Collyer Nomination as Board Counsel," *Daily Labor Report* 9 (May 1984): A–4.

13. "Forum Cites Aging Workforce, 'Skills Gap' as Long-Term Challenges for United States," *Daily Labor Report,* July 6, 2004: A-3.

14. "Employment and Earnings" (Washington DC: US-Department of Labor Statistics), January 2006, Table A-13.

15. www.bls.gov/news.release/pdf/famee.pdf

16. www.bls.gov/cps/wlf-table8-2005.pdf

17. "Educating America: An Investment for Our Future," Report by the Council of Economic Advisors and the U.S. Department of Labor, (Washington, DC: GPO, 1995), chart D.

18. *Statistical Abstract of the United States, 2001,* 21st edition (Washington, D.C.: U.S. Department of Commerce, 2001), Table 571.

19. *Statistical Abstract of the United States,* 2006, 125th edition (Washington DC: U.S. Department of Commerce, 2006), Table 259.

20. "2004–14 Employment Projections," December 7, 2005. www.bls.gov/emp

21. "Employment and Earnings" (Washington DC: U.S. Bureau of Labor Statistics), January 2006, Table A-18.

22. Barry Bluestone and Bennett Harrison, *The Deindustrialization of America* (New York: Basic Books, 1982).

23. Robert Z. Lawrence, *Can America Compete?* (Washington, DC: Brookings Institution, 1985).

24. See, for example, Neal Rosenthal, "The Shrinking Middle Class: Myth or Reality," *Monthly Labor Review,* March 1985, pp. 3–10.

25. See, for example, Paul Osterman, *Employment Futures* (New York: Oxford University Press, 1988).

26. AFL-CIO Committee on the Evolution of Work, "The Changing Situation of Workers and Their Unions" (Washington, DC: AFL-CIO, February 1985).

27. Daniel B. Cornfield, "Shifts in Public Approval of Labor Unions in the United States, 1936–1999," The Gallup Organization, http://www.gallup.com/poll/gs990902.asp.

28. Harry Braverman, *Labor and Monopoly Capital* (New York: Monthly Review Press, 1984).

29. Selig Perlman, *A Theory of the Labor Movement* (Philadelphia: Porcupine Press, 1979 reprint of 1928 edition).

30. Clark Kerr, John T. Dunlop, Frederick Harbison, and Charles A. Myers, *Industrialism and Industrial Man* (Cambridge, MA: Harvard University Press, 1960).

31. David F. Noble, *Forces of Production* (New York: Oxford University Press, 1986); Harley Shaiken, *Work Transformed* (New York: Holt, Rinehart & Winston, 1984).

32. Richard Walton, "Work Innovations in the United States," *Harvard Business Review* 57 (July/August 1979): 88–98; Barry Wilkinson, *The Shopfloor Politics of New Technology* (London: Heinemann Educational Books, 1983); Stephen Barley, "Technology, Power, and the Social Organization of Work," *Research in the Sociology of Organizations,* ed. Samuel B. Bacharach and Nancy DiTomaso (Greenwich, CT: JAI Press, 1990).

33. John F. Krafcik, "World Class Manufacturing: An International Comparison of Automobile Assembly Plant Performance," *Sloan Management Review,* 30 (1988): 41–52.

34. Haruo Shimada and John Paul MacDuffie, "Industrial Relations and Humanware: Japanese Investments in Automobile Manufacturing in the United States," Sloan School of Management Working Paper (Cambridge, MA: MIT, 1986).

35. John Paul MacDuffie and John F. Krafcik, "Flexible Production Systems and Manufacturing Performance," in *Transforming Organizations,* ed. Thomas A. Kochan and Michael Useem (New York: Oxford University Press, 1996).

36. Shimada and MacDuffie, "Industrial Relations and Humanware."

Part 2

The Strategic Level of Industrial Relations and Structures for Collective Bargaining

Chapter 5

Management Strategies and Structures for Collective Bargaining

Chapters 5 and 6 start the movement downward in our framework by considering how the strategies of both management and unions shape the course of industrial relations. Management is considered first because in recent years management has been the main initiator of change in industrial relations. It is management, for example, that has increased the growth of nonunion practices and pressured unionized workplaces for contractual changes that improve efficiency, quality, or customer service. This chapter examines the strategic choices exercised by management and the structures management commonly uses to engage in collective bargaining. The text examines why and how management has pursued various industrial relations options.

Some of our attention will again focus on the role of the environment. For instance, heightened international competition is one environmental pressure that has played a critical role in shaping management's strategic actions. At the same time, management retains a high degree of choice in deciding industrial relations policies. Tracing managerial strategies in this chapter requires consideration of both the union and nonunion industrial relations systems that stand as alternatives before management.

Where unions exist, one of management's key tasks is to bargain and to administer contracts with those unions. So, although it is necessary to assess management's broad industrial relations strategies, this chapter also reviews how management practically prepares and structures itself to participate in the collective bargaining process.

Management's Strategic Choices—Theoretical Considerations

Management makes strategic choices in the design of personnel policies and through responses to employees' desires and expectations, including their demands for union representation. Management also makes strategic choices about its business plans, choices that are sometimes heavily based on consideration of the linkages between human resources and **business strategies.**

107

If the employees become unionized, management will attempt to use its bargaining power to shape collective bargaining processes and outcomes within the context of its bilateral relationship with the union. Although an employer's need to negotiate with union representatives will add various constraints to its strategic options in unionized settings, the employer's preferences for personnel policies are still heavily influenced by business strategies. Managers may have to make decisions regarding, for example, whether to continue investing in a given product line, whether to try to operate nonunion establishments to produce a given product, or whether to supply a product by relying more heavily on the outsourcing of parts of its value chain to another plant or firm. These decisions all influence management's bargaining leverage in any part of the firm covered by a labor contract.

Alternative Industrial Relations Systems

In the contemporary scene, management is constrained to choose among a handful of alternative industrial relations system types, or patterns. Each of these six patterns, described in Exhibit 5–1, has key personnel policies. Although it is clearly an oversimplification to try to fit every firm into one of these six patterns, this categorization scheme can help clarify the choices commonly made by management.

Nonunion Industrial Relations Patterns

Within the nonunion sector there is wide diversity in industrial relations practices. In broad terms nonunion industrial relations systems exhibit three basic patterns.[1] The common element across the three nonunion patterns is that management policy is influenced by management's desire to stay nonunion. At the same time, management policy also is guided by the firm's desire to pursue company objectives that may have very little to do with union status. Personnel practices are influenced, for example, by firm productivity and product quality goals. Note that these patterns are only ideal types, so some firms may contain elements of one or more patterns.

The Paternalistic Pattern

In the **paternalistic pattern** of industrial relations, personnel policies tend to be informally administered, and their administration involves substantial discretion by operating managers. A paternalistic firm might, for example, offer no formal leave and sickness policies, and its supervisors would grant paid leaves on a case-by-case basis. Supervisors and other managers in these firms similarly exercise a high degree of discretion over other discipline and pay policies. The employment conditions of employees in these firms differ substantially across work groups, plants, and firms.

This pattern is common among small retail stores, such as grocery stores and gas stations, most start-up firms and small manufacturing plants.[2] Managers in firms following this pattern like the discretion they gain through informal policies. Often these firms are family owned or operated with family members personally directing personnel policies. Family owners dislike losing control over decisions and particularly fear the reduction of control that would occur if unions represented employees. Union avoidance is often a prime policy objective in the firms that follow the paternalistic pattern.

EXHIBIT 5–1
Union and Nonunion Industrial Relations Patterns

	Nonunion			Union		
	Paternalistic	Bureaucratic	Human Resource Management	Conflict	New Deal	Participatory
Policy / Rules	Informal	Formal / Rule bound	Flexible	Inflexible	Formal	Flexible
Management style	Managerial discretion	Written policies	Strong corporate culture	Aggressive	Adversarial	Involvement
Complaint procedure	None		Ombudsman	Excessive delays	Grievance system	Continuous problem solving
Work organization	Low skill	Detailed classifications	Teams	Detailed classifications	Detailed classifications	Teams
Pay procedure	Piece rates	Job evaluation	Pay-for-knowledge and contingent pay	Standard rates	Standard rates	Pay-for-knowledge and contingent pay
Job security	Temporary work	Cyclical insecurity	Career development	Unstable	Seniority-based layoffs	Employment security
Worker-manager relations	Hierarchical and personal	Hierarchical	Individual	Combative	Arms-length	Overlapping roles

highly standardized, written-out [handwritten]

The Bureaucratic Pattern

Larger firms find the diversity in personnel practices common to paternalistic firms too unsettling and costly. In their efforts to achieve economies of scale, larger firms find it advantageous to standardize and bureaucratize personnel policies, thereby creating a **bureaucratic pattern** of personnel administration. These firms have also come to realize that variation in policies can spur unionization if some employees believe other employees elsewhere in the firm are benefiting from more favorable policies.

The bureaucratic pattern is characterized by highly formalized procedures, such as clear (and typically written) policies on pay, leaves, promotion, and discipline. Firms that follow the bureaucratic pattern also make use of highly detailed and formalized job classifications and use job evaluation schemes to determine pay levels and job duties. Examples of firms that follow this pattern include most of the large, nonunion corporations that expanded in the post–World War II period.

The Human Resource Management Pattern

- influence strong company culture.
- ties interests w/company [handwritten]

As an outgrowth of their efforts to increase flexibility and cost competitiveness while maintaining their nonunion status, a number of firms began to adopt a new pattern of personnel policies in the 1970s.[3] This **human resource management** (HRM) **pattern**, like the bureaucratic pattern, relies on formal policies, but the nature of those policies is different from that traditionally found in nonunion firms. The HRM pattern includes policies such as **team forms of work organization, skill- or knowledge-based pay,** and elaborate communication and complaint procedures. Up until the late 1980s many HRM pattern firms also practiced **employment stabilization,** and rarely made use of layoffs. This changed dramatically when downsizing became commonplace and both the white and blue collar employees were subjected to involuntary termination or voluntary severance programs were used to reduce employment levels. HRM firms continued to subsidize employee training and career development but warned employees that their individual career development might require employer transitions and not just job changes within the firm. In effect, employers were forcing employees to take on more of the risk and instability associated with the modern economy.

Like the firms that follow the other nonunion patterns, the HRM firms vigilantly try to avoid unionization. Where they differ from the other nonunion firms is in the extent to which they consider union avoidance questions in decisions such as where to locate a new plant or store. Union avoidance issues also influence how these firms design other personnel policies, such as complaint and communication policies. In their efforts at union avoidance, as in so many of their personnel policies, the HRM firms try to coordinate their various policies. The HRM firms also are noteworthy for the extensive measures they take in trying to induce employees to identify their interests with the long-term interests of the firm. Those measures include publishing company newsletters, offering salaries to all employees, and nurturing strong corporate cultures. To enhance work practice flexibility and communication with employees, some companies use employee committees. The NLRA forbids company-dominated unions, and as a result, companies need to avoid using employee committees for this purpose (see Box 12–7).

Among the best-known examples of mature companies that continue to apply some or all of these practices successfully are Hewlett-Packard, IBM, Sun Microsystems, Procter & Gamble, Delta Airlines, Eastman Kodak, Intel, Motorola, DuPont, and Michelin Tire.[4] Two companies that have been relatively successful using these strategies in more competitive environments and with less-skilled workforces are Marriott Hotels and Sears Roebuck.[5]

The Role of Business Strategy in Shaping Nonunion Patterns

A number of factors influence which of these patterns are followed by nonunion firms. Management values and strategies play an important role. For instance, many of the HRM firms had strong founding executives who helped initiate strong corporate cultures.[6]

Business strategy also makes a difference. The HRM pattern seems to provide the advantage of more flexible and adaptable work organization through the use of team systems and skill-based pay.[7] These characteristics are particularly attractive to firms with rapidly changing technologies and markets. Thus, it is no surprise that many firms in high-technology industries follow the HRM pattern.

Steel minimills illustrate how business strategy is linked to personnel practices. Among nonunion minimills those producing a wide variety of products ("market" mills) and those concentrating on high-quality products tend to follow the sophisticated HRM pattern, while those pursuing a low-cost and high-volume product strategy tend to follow a variant of the bureaucratic pattern.[8]

In sum, companies with sophisticated personnel systems are most likely to be those that enjoy an environment of growth, high profits, large-scale operations, and employees with sufficient skills to warrant large investments in human resource management. Furthermore, they must have highly trained personnel staffs to effectively monitor employee attitudes and the personnel practices of other firms.

Union Patterns of Industrial Relations

In firms where at least some of the employees are unionized industrial relations policies also follow distinct patterns. There are currently three dominant union patterns.

The New Deal Pattern

The form of collective bargaining in the United States that dominated until the 1980s (and continues in a number of unionized firms) is the **New Deal pattern** characterized by highly detailed and formal contracts. This pattern includes grievance arbitration, seniority-based layoff procedures, numerous and detailed **job classifications,** and the standardization of pay.

The advantages to this pattern are that it is very good at providing stable labor relations. Some of that stability derives from the formal channels (such as the grievance procedure) through which problems can be addressed. These procedures are attractive to employees because they provide due process (see Chapters 3 and 11).

A subsequent section of this chapter examines the diversity that can exist even across plants that all follow this New Deal pattern. Nevertheless, firms that follow the New Deal pattern are clearly distinguished from the unionized firms that follow the other two patterns of collective bargaining: the conflict pattern and the participatory pattern.

The Conflict Pattern

Under the **conflict pattern** labor and management are engaged in a serious struggle over their basic rights. Often the issue in dispute is whether there will be union representation. The conflict pattern typically involves prolonged strikes. In some cases employees resort to sabotage or absenteeism to express their anger against employers in such a relationship.

Conflict imposes high costs on the firm through lost output or low productivity and costs on employees in the form of lost earnings. Because of the high costs to both parties of engaging in intense conflict, the conflict pattern tends not to be stable. The conflict pattern arises most often when a firm is trying to move from a union to a nonunion pattern or, sometimes, when a union tries to unionize a nonunion firm.

Caterpillar Corporation and the union (UAW) representing its employees were caught in a cycle of conflicts throughout the 1990s. Box 5–1 describes these events. A conflict pattern emerged at Caterpillar even though the company and the UAW had maintained relatively amicable and stable relations for many years prior to the 1990s, and the UAW in the 1990s had good relations with many of the other employers it negotiated with including. John Deere, Caterpillar's most direct domestic competitor.

Major league baseball also has followed the conflict pattern. Negotiation of a new contract between baseball owners and the Major League Players Association have either nearly or actually involved a strike or lockout in each of the eight contract negotiations that occurred between the 1970s and 2002 (see Box 8–5).

The Participatory Pattern direct movement of workers

A number of contemporary firms and unions have developed a **participatory pattern** of industrial relations, characterized by contingent compensation systems (linking firm or work group pay to economic performance), team forms of work organization, employment security programs, and more direct involvement by workers and unions in business decision making.

The participatory pattern tries to create mechanisms through which workers can directly solve production and personnel problems. Quality circle or team meetings are used to facilitate direct discussions between supervisors and workers in many firms. In these firms workers also are called on to become involved in business decisions such as scrap control or issues concerning how best to implement new technology. Not all organizations that set out to create greater participation by employees, however, end up with more employee participation. There are a number of reasons for these failures, including supervisor or employee resistance to change. This pattern is discussed more fully in Chapter 12. Southwest Airlines stands out in the U.S. airline industry for being successful in following this pattern from its founding in the 1970s to today.[9]

Management Attitudes toward Unionization

What influences whether management follows a union or a nonunion pattern? In part, the decision is a function of management's attitudes toward unionization. Much of U.S. labor history is a documentation of bloody organizing struggles and attempts by management to reduce the incentive for employees to join unions. Although the level of bloodshed has declined and the strategies used to oppose unionization have become more subtle over the years, management's vigorous opposition to unions continues to be very strong.

Douglas Brown and Charles Myers aptly described the sentiments of perhaps the majority of U.S. management executives in an article written in the mid-1950s:

> It may well be true that if American management, upon retiring for the night, were assured that by the next morning the unions with which they dealt would have disappeared, more management people than not would experience the happiest sleep of their lives.[10]

Based in Peoria, Illinois, Caterpillar is the state's largest manufacturer and the world's leading builder of heavy equipment. Fourteen thousand of its workers are represented by the United Auto Workers (UAW). The first major strike involving the two sides began in November 1991, after the UAW had won a contract with John Deere & Co. and proposed identical terms for Caterpillar. The company refused to agree to a pattern bargaining model, which prompted a host of wildcat strikes. Caterpillar in turn, instituted a lockout, contending that it was in a strong position to operate with temporary, white-collar, and retired workers. Misperceiving the company's ability to operate, all 14,000 members walked out in February 1992.

Caterpillar had faced nine strikes between 1948 and 1992 all short, with minor repercussions. Against this backdrop, the union believed that the February 1992 walkout would be settled quickly. This time the company countered with threats of permanent replacement. When workers strike over economic contractual issues, employers can use permanent replacements. Employers have been increasingly turning to this strategy since the mid-1980s. Following this trend, Caterpillar started advertising for workers shortly after the strike began. Not willing to lose their jobs over pattern bargaining, workers returned in the spring of 1992.

Without a contract and unhappy with the course of events, the UAW then launched an "in-plant campaign," relying on "slowdown" tactics. The company imposed strict disciplinary actions in response, which led to a second strike in June 1994. During this strike Caterpillar could not threaten permanent replacement because the UAW called this strike over the 101 unfair labor practice charges pending against the company with the NLRB. Caterpillar, however, continued to operate successfully.

Factors such as "doublesourcing," continuing to produce in other countries for exporting, a widening gap between high paying and low paying jobs, and technological advancement inside the plant calling for fewer workers, allowed Caterpillar to turn record-breaking profits. By December 1995, the workers had rejected the company's counteroffer, but the UAW urged them to return to work. With workers angry, confused, and still without a contract, the strike ended in December 1995.

Employees then worked under the unilaterally imposed terms instituted after the 1992 strike. Press reports suggested that they were not satisfied and felt as if they were in a "prison labor camp." Caterpillar implemented rules prohibiting the "display of unbusiness-like decorations and language," including posters, banners and picket signs. Many felt that the company's rules were too broad and aimed specifically at referrals to the labor dispute. Many employees chose to retire rather than risk the chance of suspension or dismissal.

In May of 1997, the UAW and Caterpillar agreed to meet with a federal mediator and a tentative agreement was reached in February of 1998. However, 58 percent of the membership voted against ratification. The two sides returned to the bargaining table and negotiated an identical contract with one major difference; in the new contract, all workers terminated for union activities would be reinstated whereas the previous proposal allowed for reinstatement of only 110 of the 160 discharged workers. The terminations pertaining to the other 50 individuals would have been arbitrated. On March 22, 1998, Caterpillar employees ratified a six-year contract effective from March 23, 1998, to April 1, 2004. The new contract was supported by 54 percent of members who voted.

Negotiations began again in December of 2003. Right at the start it was obvious that difficulties were going to ensue. With an inability to come to an agreement, the two sides agreed to extend the old contract through April 25, 2004. The UAW announced that it had authorized a strike should it be needed. As a result, Caterpillar proposed another offer, but on April 25 it was rejected by the membership at the suggestion of union leaders. In response, rather than reverting to the tactics that led to the six-and-a-half-year battle in the previous decade, the UAW urged its membership not to strike but rather to remain on the job until a contract was settled.

Over the next eight months, Caterpillar employees would go on to reject two more offers by management and remain at work under the old contract terms without a strike. Finally, on December 16, 2004, over a year after negotiations for the new contract began, Caterpillar and the UAW announced they had reached

(continued)

an agreement that the UAW was willing to recommend to its membership for ratification. Nearly a month later, membership voted to approve the new contract.

The six-year contract, which will expire on March 1, 2011, seemed to be a compromise that accomplished many of the goals of both Caterpillar and the UAW. The UAW was able to secure most benefits for current workers, while Caterpillar succeeded in gaining health care reductions and other compensation cost reductions. Most of the gains Caterpillar will make will come at the expense of new hires, who, instead of the old starting salary of $22.59 an hour, will receive $15.75 per hour. However, as opposed to current employees, who will not see a raise in base pay over the course of the contract, new hires will be granted a 2 percent increase in 2008. Moreover, consistent with the trend of many companies today, employees will begin paying 10 percent of their health insurance premiums, and that will rise to 20 percent during the life of the contract.

The most recent contract negotiations at Caterpillar include issues that are at the forefront of many collective negotiations, including health care cost containment. While things appear to be settled for a while at Caterpillar, only time will tell if this signals a new working relationship between management and labor at Caterpillar or whether hostilities resurface on the shop floor or in the 2011 contract renegotiation.

Sources: Various articles taken from *Daily Labor Report, Chicago Tribune, New York Times,* and *The Wall Street Journal,* 1991–2006.

Yet, even given the tenacious hold of this sentiment, some firms place a lower priority on remaining nonunion than others. Some employers have been pragmatic enough to recognize that in their situation either it is impossible to avoid unionization or the costs of attempting to avoid unions outweigh the potential benefits. These employers tend to be less aggressive in resisting unions. Thus, the intensity of employers' resistance to unionization, as well as the strategies they use to remain nonunion, has varied across firms and over time. Two union avoidance strategies stand out.

The Historical Evolution of Two Union Avoidance Strategies

As early as the 1920s two different strategies were used by employers to avoid unions: the direct union suppression approach (actively resisting any organizing drives); and the indirect union substitution approach (removing the incentives for unionization). Why do some firms use the first strategy while others try the second?

The strategies used to avoid unionization are to some extent a function of the firm's financial resources. If a firm can afford the specialized personnel and employee relations staffs necessary to implement the strategy, it will use the union substitution approach. Those firms unable to absorb the expenses associated with the substitution approach tend to oppose unions by using the direct suppression strategies.

Environmental factors also influence whether and how management responds to the threat of being unionized. Factors that tend to lead management to a suppression strategy include the presence of a hostile political environment toward unions; employment of low-wage workers who have few labor market alternatives; an abundant supply of alternative workers; low recruitment costs; and a low-profit, highly competitive industry.

Peer Review Complaint Procedures as a Union Substitution Device

As discussed more fully in Chapter 11, in recent years a number of firms have instituted peer review complaint procedures as part of a union substitution strategy.[11] This form of nonunion employee representation has significant advantages for management as a union substitution device, because peer review panels can be designed to avoid the danger of violation of section 8(a)(2) of the National Labor Relations Act, which renders illegal some other forms of nonunion employee representation established and dominated by employers. In its decision in *Keeler Brass,* 317 N.L.R.B. 1110 (1995), the National Labor Relations Board held that peer review type panels did not violate section 8(a)(2) so long as the panels simply issued final decisions on employee grievances and did not attempt to "deal with" management by negotiating how grievances were to be resolved. The ability of peer review panels to function legally within the confines of the general legislative prohibition on non-union employee representation plans creates a strong institutional incentive for employers to adopt this form of employee involvement in dispute resolution to help forestall threats of unionization.

Increased Union Suppression

There is some evidence suggesting that the use of union suppression tactics has increased in the past 40 years. For instance, the number of employees illegally discharged by employers during organizing campaigns, as determined by the NLRB, increased tenfold from 1960 to 1975 and remained at a relatively high level in recent years.[12] NLRB case records show that in recent years about one in twenty workers who vote to unionize are illegally fired for trying to organize. Thus, management's use of suppressive tactics against union activists is not merely an artifact of pre-New Deal labor history but a significant feature of contemporary industrial relations.

At the same time, some firms continue to reduce employee incentives to unionize through the substitution strategy. Many workers reluctantly turn to unionization only after they have exhausted all other means to influence employer policies. Many firms try to use human resource policies to meet employee needs before workers become frustrated enough to turn to a union. Although many firms that institute sophisticated human resource policies do so for business reasons and not solely to avoid unions, the effect of these policies is to lessen the incentive to unionize.

Many firms now have some parts of their business unionized while other parts operate on a nonunion basis. Since the early 1970s there has been substantial growth in the fraction of the establishments operating nonunion in those firms that have both union and nonunion operations and a substantial increase in the desire of management to remain as nonunion as possible.[13]

The Influence of Union Structure on Management's Unionization Policies

Another factor that influences whether a union avoidance strategy will be used by a firm is the degree of centralization in how bargaining occurs in a firm. Those firms that deal with a single union across the whole company are less likely than others to resist unions vigorously in any newly opened facilities. In these bargaining relationships the dominant union has the leverage needed to engage top management decision makers at the strategic level of the firm—the level where the basic decision is made on whether to resist or to recognize a union. If a union cannot reach this level of managerial decision making, the firm can more easily adopt a union avoidance strategy.

General Motors Tries and Then Abandons a Southern Strategy

The history of the United Auto Workers (UAW) and General Motors (GM) illustrates this point. In the late 1970s, GM agreed to UAW demands and ended its **southern strategy** (opening nonunion plants in the south and resisting union-organizing attempts). In return for GM neutrality the UAW agreed to continue union commitment to quality-of-working-life and other workplace innovations in the existing union facilities. Since it represented production workers across GM plants, the UAW had the foresight and the strength to induce GM to accept this bargain.

The Expansion of Double-Breasting

On the other hand, in some industries where unions lacked this strength, after becoming dissatisfied with their union contracts the companies were able to open either new, non-union operations or operations organized by different unions. The construction industry is an example of the former strategy. A number of large, traditionally union contractors have developed what has been described as a **double-breasted strategy**—that is, the running of separate union and nonunion divisions. In a typical double-breasted construction firm, commercial business is performed by unionized employees while residential construction projects are carried out by unorganized employees of the firm.

Firms in the bituminous coal industry are examples of the latter strategy. A number of operators that have opened new mines in recent years have strongly resisted organizing drives by the United Mine Workers (UMW) even though they have contracts with the union in their other mines. In addition, some firms that have opened surface (strip) mines in the west have strongly opposed organizing efforts by the UMW and have managed either to remain non-union or to be organized by the Union of Operating Engineers (UOE) instead of the UMW. Because of this opposition, the UMW bargained for and won a provision in its collective bargaining agreements designed to organize new mines. The provision gives laid-off UMW members preferential hiring rights in new mines opened by UMW-organized companies.

Both the construction and the mining examples suggest that the performance of the existing union–management relationship will influence the intensity of opposition by highly unionized companies to the extension of organization to new operations. It also appears that the greater the difference between labor costs in union and nonunion firms in an industry, the more aggressively management will oppose any new union organizing.

The Influence of Attitudes Held by Top Executives

A firm's opposition to unionization is also influenced by another factor that is difficult to measure—namely, the philosophy of the top corporate executives. It is these individuals who make the ultimate decisions on how hard a line to pursue against unions. Although their decisions are based in part on the potential economic costs and benefits of avoiding unionization, they are also based on the executives' personal views of unions.

The contrast between U.S. employers and some of their European counterparts is evident, and it is often argued that European employers are less anti-union than their American counterparts. While there are no good conclusive tests of this, it is interesting to note that western German employers did not oppose extending their labor legislation, including the use of works councils and codetermination, to eastern Germany as part of the employment laws that would govern establishments after unification. German employers seem to take this extension for granted.

Overview of the Trends in Management Policies toward Unionization

Overall, management's recent choices of the industrial relations patterns described in Exhibit 5–1 are as follows:

1. In the majority of nonunion or weakly unionized firms, avoiding unions is a top priority.
2. Highly organized firms tend to be less strongly opposed to unionization of new worksites, provided their economic and labor relations experiences with their present unions have been relatively favorable.
3. Firms of all types are strongly opposed to organization of white-collar employees, regardless of the firm's experiences with unions that represent their blue-collar workers.

Management Structures for Collective Bargaining

[handwritten margin notes: 3 characteristics /) size of labor relations staff /) centralization n decision-making n LR issues /) specialization n decision making]

This section considers how management structures itself to engage in collective bargaining. This remains an important consideration for firms that have at least part of their work force represented by unions.

There are three basic characteristics of management's collective bargaining structure: the size of the labor relations staff in relation to the number of employees in the organization, the degree of centralization in decision making on labor relations issues, and the degree of specialization in decision making on labor relations. The latter concerns the extent to which decision-making power is placed in the hands of the labor relations staff instead of in the hands of the operating, or line, managers.

The term **labor relations staff** refers to staff with responsibility for handling union-organizing attempts, negotiations, **contract administration,** and litigation with regard to union activity. The term does not refer to personnel staff who handle, for example, recruitment, staffing, equal employment opportunity, safety and health, and wage and salary administration. Most firms now integrate personnel and labor relations activities within a broad human resource management unit.

The management staff must first formulate industrial relations strategies.[14] Once basic strategic decisions are made, they must be implemented on a day-to-day basis. Management must allocate responsibility for decisions in a manner that allows the organization to adapt to new pressures from its environment. In short, management must develop a structure that enables the firm to bargain effectively and to manage its day-to-day relationship with the union.

When a firm's business strategy changes, there should be corresponding changes in management structure. This has been happening in recent years. As firms have shifted to business strategies that include tight cost controls, power has shifted from labor relations staff to line managers and human resource specialists.

Data from a number of surveys reveal the following common management industrial relations structures.[15]

The Size of the Labor Relations Staff

A majority of surveyed corporations have labor relations staff at the plant, division, and corporate headquarters levels. Nevertheless, the number of staff members employed by these corporations in relation to the number of unionized employees varies greatly. In the 601 firms that responded in one survey, there were an average of 13.4 labor relations professionals employed. The most common staffing level was one labor relations professional for each 200 to 400 union members, but there was much variation in staff levels across firms. Larger industrial relations staffs exist in those firms where unions are more able to impose significant costs on the firm.

Centralization in Decision Making

In general, there is a high degree of centralization of the responsibility for labor relations policy inside firms. Most firms place primary responsibility for developing overall union policy at the corporate level, either in the hands of the top labor relations executive or in the hands of the chief executive officer.

In the majority of firms, the corporate labor relations executive also has primary responsibility for the following functions: developing union avoidance activities, responding to union-organizing campaigns, conducting contract negotiations or advising negotiators, drawing up the final contract language, costing union proposals, and doing the general background research for bargaining. Only the administration of the contract and general trouble-shooting activities tend to be decentralized to the division or the establishment level.

The top level of the corporation also plays a very active role in reviewing and approving major policy decisions on bargaining. In most firms the top executive of the corporation has to at least review and approve key decisions. In a number of firms the chief executive even has primary responsibility for the crucial decisions establishing the limits of discretion for the management negotiators, determining the issues over which the firm should take a strike, and approving the final package.

In companies or industries in severe financial distress, chief executives take on more direct roles in shaping labor relations policies and often become directly involved in communicating with the work force or in negotiating concession agreements. This has been the case in the airline industry in recent years, especially in the difficult environment that followed the September 11, 2001, terrorist attacks. The CEOs of United Airlines and U.S Airways, for example, were the chief spokesmen for their companies as they communicated to their employees and to the government agency to which they applied for loan guarantees as part of their restructuring efforts. At American Airlines, CEO Donald Carty even set up a telephone and e-mail message system inviting employees to suggest ways the company might improve operations and return to profitability.

Specialization of the Labor Relations Function

There is evidence that power has shifted downward within management structures in recent years. Labor relations specialists have been losing power to line managers and, to a somewhat lesser degree, to human resource specialists. The main reason for this is that firms now have less need for the traditional expertise of the labor relations specialist—that of achieving stability, labor peace, and predictability. Rather, firms want expertise in union avoidance, cost control, and flexibility in work rules, and achieving these goals requires making changes in workplace practices.

This does not mean, however, that labor relations specialists are no longer necessary. Indeed, case studies reveal that lower-level labor relations managers secretly delight in the "mistakes" some of the line managers and human resource management specialists make as they take greater control over critical labor relations decisions. In one large firm a career labor relations manager related to us the story of how the new vice president of labor relations who was transferred from another functional area had to call in the "old hands" to find out how the contract ratification procedures worked.

As a result of their continuing needs for technical expertise, most firms continue to depend on teams of labor relations specialists to conduct negotiations and implement policies and agreements. But a number of major firms have established strategic planning groups for labor relations, and others have used cross-functional teams to develop new bargaining proposals.

The careers of labor relations professionals are changing dramatically and thus pose new educational and training requirements. The industrial relations professionals of the future will need the following:

1. Business, analytical, and planning skills.

2. Expertise in both traditional labor relations activities and personnel or human resource management activities.

3. A thorough understanding of operating management issues.

4. An ability to work as a member of a multidisciplinary team in implementing labor relations strategies and policies.

5. Skills in managing innovative labor-management **organizational change** efforts.

6. Expertise in Web-based communications and service delivery.

Corporate Restructuring and Governance

Throughout the past decade corporations increasingly moved toward a "core competency" business model. Those functions deemed central to the core business processes of the firm remained inside the firm's boundaries; other functions were increasingly outsourced to other firms. This trend affected industrial relations in two ways. First, and most importantly, many firms outsourced their manufacturing operations, and this often had the effect of reducing the number of unionized employees. Companies such as Lucent Technologies (formerly part of AT&T) illustrate this pattern. When Lucent was spun off from AT&T in 1994 it had approximately 90,000 employees of which just under 50,000 were union members. By the end of the decade Lucent had not only declined in size as it lost market share and the overall telecommunications market declined, it had also sold off most of its manufacturing operations in order to focus more directly on research and development of new technologies and on its service-oriented business units. By 2002 less than 20 percent of Lucent's workforce was unionized. An important part of what industrial relations professionals in firms like Lucent therefore do involves negotiating the issues involved in transferring employees and contractual rights and coordinating the flow of people and work across firm boundaries.

The second effect of recent corporate restructuring has been to outsource many of the human resource services heretofore provided in house. Training, benefits management, payroll, and other routine employee services have been outsourced by many companies. This reduces the career advancement opportunities for human resource professionals, including those serving in the industrial relations function. As a result, industrial relations professionals now spend an increasing amount of their time negotiating and coordinating employment practices with specialized (outside) human resource service providers.

The crisis in corporate confidence that emerged in the wake of the visible accounting and executive compensation scandals in recent years cast a shadow on all of the management profession, including those in labor relations. Whether the corporate reforms designed to better protect investors are also extended so as to strengthen worker rights and voice in corporate governance is uncertain. What is more likely is that these issues will surface more directly at the bargaining table and in union–management relations more generally in the years ahead. Thus, management labor relations professionals will need to be well educated in understanding how corporate governance works in the United States and perhaps in other countries where workers have stronger legal rights to information, consultation, and representation in corporate governance.

Summary

Historically, management has accepted the general value that unions provide to American society, yet aggressively avoided the expansion of unionism. Although most managers accept in the abstract the principle that unions have a legitimate role to play in a democratic society, in practice managers continue to act on the belief that unions are either unnecessary or undesirable within their own organization.

Yet management also continues to be as pragmatic as ever. If the costs of union avoidance are too high—that is, if unions are too powerful to avoid—management will work with union leaders to develop the strategies needed to be competitive. Many firms have been able to pursue two strategies simultaneously: They avoid further unionization in one location in the firm, while they cooperate with the existing union at another. It remains to be seen if management will continue to enjoy such discretion and power in the years ahead.

Firms generally follow either a paternalistic, bureaucratic, human resource, conflict, New Deal, or participatory industrial relations pattern. For each of these patterns there is a set of basic personnel policies. Which of these patterns a firm prefers to follow is, in part, shaped by the firm's business strategy.

Where some of its employees are unionized, management turns to its industrial relations staff to represent its interests in collective bargaining. These staffs vary in their size, centralization, and specification.

Given the changing nature of the corporation and that the scope of what work is performed within corporate boundaries and what is outsourced to specialized firms is changing, the nature of the labor relations task is changing. It is shifting from one focused primarily on interactions with unions to one that requires considerable cross-firm as well as union–management negotiations, coordination, and administration. Moreover, current debates over corporate governance may portend future changes in the knowledge base, skills, and activities of labor relations professionals.

Management makes a number of strategic choices in its relations with unions.

These choices include decisions regarding how aggressively to resist the expansion of union representation and how to relate to any unions that represent employees in a firm. Management's strategic industrial relations choices appear to be influenced by the business strategy pursued by the firm. Management's strategic choices also are strongly influenced by the strategies chosen by unions. If the respective union that management must bargain with prefers a confrontational approach, for example, it is unlikely that management would then choose to promote a participatory pattern of industrial relations. The next chapter considers union strategy and structure.

Discussion Questions

1. Briefly describe the nonunion industrial relations patterns found in Exhibit 5–1.
2. Describe the union patterns of industrial relations found in Exhibit 5–1.
3. Contrast the primary two union avoidance strategies used by management.
4. Describe the three key aspects of management industrial relations staff structure.
5. What tactics did the Caterpillar Corporation use in its dispute with the UAW? What factors gave Caterpillar management bargaining leverage?

Related Web Sites

IBM:
http://www.ibm.com

Delta Airlines:
http://www.delta-air.com/gateway/about/index.html

Eastman Kodak:
http://www.kodak.com/aboutKodak/aboutKodak.shtml

Motorola:
http://www.mot.com/General/inside.html

DuPont:
http://www.dupont.com/Corp/gbl-company/index.html

Michelin Tire:
http://www.michelin.com/us/eng/home.htm

Marriott Hotels:
http://www.marriotthotels.com

Sears Roebuck:
http://www.sears.com/company/pubaff/pubaff.htm

Caterpillar Corp.:
http://www.cat.com/about/index.htm

Union of Operating Engineers (UOE):
http://www.iuoe.org/index.html

John Deere & Co.:
http://www.deere.com
http://www.deere.com/news/teampower98.htm

American Airlines:
http://www.aa.com

Suggested Readings

Bendix, Reinhard. *Work and Authority in Industry* (New York: John Wiley, 1956).
Chandler, Alfred D., Jr. *Strategy and Structure* (New York: Anchor Books, 1966).
Foulkes, Fred. *Personnel Policies of Large Nonunion Companies* (Englewood Cliffs, NJ: Prentice Hall, 1980).
Harris, Howell. *The Right to Manage* (Madison: University of Wisconsin Press, 1982).
Jacoby, Sanford. *Modern Manors* (Princeton: Princeton University Press, 1997).
Milkovich, George T., and Jerry Newman. *Compensation,* 7th ed. (Boston: McGraw-Hill, 2002).
Slichter, Sumner, James J. Healy, and E. Robert Livernash. *The Impact of Collective Bargaining on Management* (Washington, DC: Brookings Institution, 1960).

End Notes

1. Topologies of industrial relations patterns with some similarities to this scheme are provided in Richard C. Edwards, *Contested Terrain* (New York: Basic Books, 1979) and in Alan Fox, *Beyond Contract: Work, Power and Trust Relations* (London: Faber and Faber, 1974).

2. See Peter Doeringer, "Internal Labor Markets and Paternalism in Rural Areas," in *Internal Labor Markets,* ed. Paul Osterman (Cambridge, MA: MIT Press, 1984).

3. This sophisticated human resource management pattern developed in a few nonunion firms in the 1950s and had roots in earlier corporate policies of the 1920s (often labeled welfare capitalism; see Chapter 2).

4. Delta Airlines is not a pure case of this nonunion pattern because its pilots are unionized.

5. For a history of the personnel policies followed by Sears, see Sanford M. Jacoby, *Modern Manors* (Princeton: Princeton University Press, 1997).

6. For evidence on the role of the founding executives, see Fred Foulkes, *Personnel Policies in Large Nonunion Companies* (Englewood Cliffs, NJ: Prentice Hall, 1980).

7. Thomas A. Kochan, Robert B. McKersie, and John Chalykoff, "The Effects of Corporate Strategy and Workplace Innovations on Union Representation," *Industrial and Labor Relations Review* 39 (July 1986): 487–501.

8. Jeffrey B. Arthur and Suzanne Konzelmann Smith, "The Transformation of Industrial Relations in the American Steel Industry, in *Contemporary Collective Bargaining in the Private Sector,* ed. Paula Voos (Ithaca: ILR Press, 1994).

9. For a history of how Southwest Airlines' labor policies fit with the company's business strategy and contributed to its success over the years, see Jody Hoffer Gittell, *The Southwest Way* (New York: McGraw-Hill, 2002).

10. Douglas V. Brown and Charles A. Myers, "The Changing Industrial Relations Philosophy of American Management," in *Proceedings of the Ninth Annual Winter Meetings of the Industrial Relations Research Association* (Madison, WI: IRRA, 1957), p. 92.

11. This section draws heavily from Alexander Colvin, "Citizens and Citadels: Dispute Resolution Procedures in the Nonunion Workplace," *Industrial Relations,* forthcoming.

12. Richard B. Freeman and James L. Medoff, *What Do Unions Do?* (New York: Basic Books, 1984), p. 232.

13. Compare the 1977 Conference Board survey described in Audrey Freedman, *Managing Labor Relations: Organization, Objectives, and Results* (New York: Conference Board, 1979) with the 1983 survey in Audrey Freedman, *A New Look in Wage Bargaining* (New York: Conference Board, 1985).

14. Alfred D. Chandler, Jr., *Strategy and Structure* (New York: Anchor Books, 1966), p. 15.

15. The observations in the discussions that follow are derived from the Conference Board survey described in Freedman, 1983 and 1985.

Chapter 6

Union Strategies and Structures for Representing Workers

Unions design critical strategies just as management does. Yet, the scope of union decisions is somewhat wider because unions must decide to what extent they seek to promote worker interests through political channels versus collective bargaining. Unions must decide whether and how they will pursue political and legislative issues and determine the appropriate mix of federal, state, and local political or legislative activity. At the same time, all unions participate in collective bargaining to some degree; thus strategic choices must be made about how to represent workers' interests through bargaining and through daily activities at the workplace. For example, unions must decide how much of their resources and energy to devote to organizing new members and how they will structure their internal organization to represent their members.

Unions also make strategic decisions on the form of collective bargaining and other representational activities they will pursue. In recent years these questions have come to have renewed significance—even among well-established unions—as leaders recognize that current strategies have not been successful in reversing the long-term decline in union membership. Among other things unions are now beginning to consider is whether to develop alternative models for representing and serving workers in relations with individual employers, when these workers move across employers, and perhaps even when they move in and out of the paid labor force as their family and life circumstances evolve over time.

No question is more central to unions than membership. The lifeblood of unions and the source of their bargaining power are their members. This chapter traces union membership trends and also considers the various theories explaining the ups and downs that have occurred in union membership in the United States and other countries throughout history.

Unions and Politics

The U.S. labor movement historically has devoted the bulk of its efforts to collective bargaining as opposed to political action. In general, American unions have followed a business unionism approach, as described in Chapter 2. Adhering to this philosophy, unions

123

tend to avoid identifying with any overarching political ideology and instead focus on improving members' conditions of employment through collective bargaining. This is certainly evident when we compare U.S. labor to political unionists in other countries.

In the United States political system there is no sizable labor party, as there is in a number of European countries. Furthermore, with few exceptions, U.S. unions have not identified themselves with a socialist political platform, another characteristic that is common among many European labor movements. But, these observations notwithstanding, researchers continue to debate how fully business unionism is an appropriate characterization of U.S. labor movement history, and contemporary unionists also continue to debate the proper role of unions in U.S. politics.

American Unions Do Have a Political Agenda

U.S. unions have historically played an important role as supporters of numerous welfare programs such as social security, medicare, child development, and related services for working families in general, and for low income families in particular. They also were strong supporters of the 1964 Civil Rights Act.

Unions also have been ardent and, again, successful supporters of federal legislation to protect and improve employment conditions. Here the list of federal programs includes the minimum wage, the Occupational Safety and Health Act, the **Davis-Bacon procedures,** Family and Medical Leave Act, and various pension regulations. AFL-CIO unions play an active role in the debates that surround federal legislation through the activities of the federation's **Committee on Political Education (COPE).**[1] Unions also remain an effective force in mobilizing voters in the United States.

U.S. unions are also active in state and local politics, both in the preparation of legislation and in the election of government officials. A number of state AFL-CIO and COPE organizations, community groups tied to unions, and local unions are very active in state and local affairs.

Labor's Voice in National and Corporate Affairs

In recent years the AFL-CIO has increased the resources devoted to assisting candidates for President and Congress who support its position on labor, trade, and other economic and social policies. While this often has meant that the labor movement is allied with the Democratic Presidential candidate, from time to time Republican members of Congress with strong labor voting records also receive assistance from labor unions in their states.

When John Sweeney became President of the AFL-CIO in 1995, he created a new Department of Corporate Affairs with the task of identifying strategies for convincing corporate behavior to become more responsive to worker interests regardless of whether or not a firm engages in collective bargaining. This department works with other shareholder activists to monitor and influence corporate behavior, executive compensation trends, and other corporate practices. Sometimes the department takes a more active approach. For example, in 2002 it went to court following the accounting scandal and bankruptcy at Enron Corporation to get the company's former employees moved from the bottom to the top of the list of creditors in claims against the company. Another unit within this department focuses on building community-industry coalitions to promote workplace innovations and reforms. This unit was very active in coordinating local union and employer efforts to aid workers and families who suffered human and job losses in New York City following the terrorist attacks on the World Trade Center.

Labor's Role in Coalition Politics

Recent years have seen a marked increase in efforts by the labor movement to build or join coalitions with other groups supporting changes in legislation or corporate behavior. A prime example of legislative coalition building is seen in the various "Living Wage" campaigns that have produced community-level ordinances in over 50 U.S. cities requiring companies that do business with local governments to pay workers wages above those required by federal or state minimums. To pass these laws unions have worked in coalition with local religious, ethnic, welfare, and family-centered interest groups. At an international level, labor has joined with various student groups and nongovernmental organizations (NGOs) in developing countries to oppose the use of child labor and other violations of human rights. Increasingly, therefore, labor's role in politics goes well beyond formal relationships with national political parties to focus on more informal issue-oriented coalitions and political campaigns.

Current Debates in Unions over the Appropriate Role of Politics   *some unionists want to shift to political action*

The debate over the role of politics continues among the ranks of the U.S. labor movement. Some unionists have recently called for a reorientation of labor's strategy away from its traditional emphasis on collective bargaining and toward political action as the preferred means to labor's ends. An independent labor party was created in 1995, but to date it has attracted few members and had limited political influence.

Labor's role in political affairs likely will take on even greater importance in the future, not as a movement supporting a separate political party, but as a builder and participant in coalition politics. These growing roles reflect the view of AFL-CIO leaders that they must represent working people not just as employees, but also as shareholders with significant pension investments in corporate equities and as citizens.

Union Growth and Membership Characteristics

union membership has steadily declined

A central strategic question that faces any individual union and the labor movement as a whole is how much to focus their resources on the attraction and retention of new members. Before exploring the factors that influence the growth of the labor movement, this chapter examines current patterns and recent trends in union membership. The data reveal a long-term decline in union membership and illuminate some of the organizing and representational problems confronted by unions in the United States.

Union Membership Figures: The Loci of Membership

Exhibit 6–1 plots union membership as a percentage of the nonagricultural labor force over the years 1930 to 2006. As shown in the exhibit, union membership peaked in the mid-1940s at around 35 percent. By 1960 membership had declined to 31 percent of the nonagricultural labor force and by 2006 it had declined even further to 12.0 percent.

1940s – 35, 2006 – 12

EXHIBIT 6–1
Union
Membership
as a Percentage
of the Non-
agricultural
Labor Force,
1930–2002

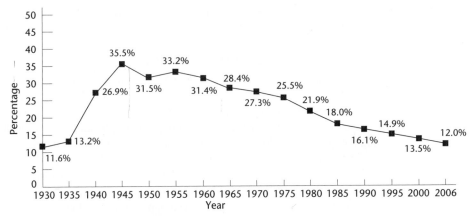

Note: The 1985, 1990, 1995, and 2006 figures are the percentage of employed wage and salary workers in all industries, private and public, who were union members. In 1980, this figure was 23.0 percent.

Sources: Thomas A. Kochan, Harry C. Katz, and Robert B. McKersie, *The Transformation of American Industrial Relations,* p. 31. The 1985 figure is from "Employment and Earnings," February 1987. The 1990 figure is from "News Bulletin," Bureau of Labor Statistics (Washington, DC, February 6, 1991), USDL 91–34, p. 1. The 1995 figure is from "News Bulletin," Bureau of Labor Statistics (Washington, DC, January 31, 1997), USDL 97–27, p. 1. The 2006 figure is from "Union Membership Rate, Dropped in 2006 to 12 Percent," *Daily Labor Report* 17, January 26, 2007.

Union density (also called *union penetration*) levels vary substantially across industries, occupations, regions, and worker skill categories. The data reviewed below analyze how union membership varies across these dimensions.

Some regions of the United States exhibit high rates of unionization, whereas other regions have very low union membership. In 2006, New York and Hawaii had the highest union densities in the nation, with, respectively, 24.4 and 24.7 percent of their labor forces organized.[2] At the other end of the spectrum were North and South Carolina with union densities of 3.3 percent.

By Industrial Sector

These overall figures, however, mask major differences in union membership trends across industrial sectors. Exhibit 6–2 reports union membership data by industrial sector from 1930 to 2006. Although the percentage of manufacturing employees unionized declined from 42.4 percent in 1953 to 13.0 percent in 2006, the percentage of government employees in labor unions rose over the same period from 11.6 to 36.2 percent. Thus, the explosion of unions in government employment during the 1960s and 1970s stands in stark contrast to the decline in manufacturing unionization.

Unionization in the **service sector** followed a different pattern. As Exhibit 6–2 shows, the percentage of service workers unionized rose from 9.5 percent in 1953 to 13.9 percent in 1975 but then fell to 3.1 percent in 2006.

By Occupation

Union membership also varies by occupation. Exhibit 6–3 presents estimates of the percentage of employees in major occupational groups that were members of trade unions in 2006. Within blue-collar ranks the highest levels of organization were among craft workers

EXHIBIT 6–2
Union Membership by Industrial Sector, 1930–2006[*]

Year	Manufacturing	Government	Services
1930	7.8%	8.5%	2.3%
1935	16.4	9.0	2.6
1940	30.5	10.7	5.7
1947	40.5	12.0	9.0
1953	42.4	11.6	9.5
1966	37.4	26.0	n.a.
1970	38.7	31.9	7.8
1975	36.0	39.5	13.9
1980	32.3	35.0	11.6
1983	27.8	36.7	7.7
1986	24.0	36.0	6.3
1990	20.6	36.5	5.7
1996	17.2	37.6	5.7
2000	14.8	37.5	5.6
2006	11.7	36.2	3.1

[*]The figures represent the percentage of workers in each industrial sector who were members of a union.

Sources: Figures through 1980 are from Leo Troy and Neil Sheflin, *Union Sourcebook* (West Orange, NJ: Industrial Relations Data and Information Services, 1981). Data for 1983–1986 are from the U.S. Department of Labor, Bureau of Labor Statistics, *Employment and Earnings* (Washington, DC: GPO, January 1985 and January 1987). 1990 data are from "News Bulletin," U.S. Department of Labor, Bureau of Labor Statistics (Washington, DC, February 6, 1991), USDL 91–34, table 2. Data for 2006 are from the BLS Web site: www.bls.gov/news.release/union2.nr0.htm

EXHIBIT 6–3
Union Membership by Occupation, 2006[*]

Source: "Union Members (Annual)" U.S. Department of Labor, BLS, www.bls.gov/news.release/pdf/union2.pdf

Occupational Classification	Percent Unionized
White-collar workers	
Executive, administrative, and managerial	4.9%
Professional	17.7
Sales occupations	3.1
Service occupations	11.4
Blue-collar workers	
Craft workers	15.8
Production	15.5
Farming, forestry, and fishing	3.5

[*]The figures represent the percentage of workers in each occupation who were members of a union.

(15.8 percent were organized) and the semiskilled occupations (15.5 percent of production workers were organized). teachers unionize often

Among white-collar workers professional occupations were the most organized, at 17.7 percent, in 2006. Many of the unionized workers in those occupations were in the public sector, such as public school teachers. Service workers were less organized (11.4 percent).[3] Only 4.9 percent of executive, administrative, and managerial employees and 3.1 percent of sales workers were organized. Although unions still have not penetrated very deeply into the white-collar occupations, white-collar unionists are accounting for an increasing

With doctors struggling to cope with the sweeping changes brought by managed care, associations representing most of the nation's podiatrists in 1996 formed the first nationwide labor union for doctors and affiliated with the AFL-CIO. The union organizers said they would negotiate traditional labor agreements when a group of podiatrists work as salaried employees of a hospital or government agency. But for the majority of their members, who historically have been treated as independent contractors, the union will engage in bargaining with managed care organizations. For members that are independent practitioners the union would provide a range of services such as political lobbying, but not engage in collective bargaining. By May 1997 the union had 7,000 members and expected to grow rapidly.

In a related development, in June 1997, The Committee of Interns and Residents, which represents 9,000 doctors-in-training, announced the organization's affiliation with the Service Employees International Union (SEIU). Of the 475,000 health care workers the SEIU currently represents, about 6,000 are doctors, mostly in the public sector.

In September of 1999, the American Medical Association (AMA) developed a resource center to help physicians form local collective bargaining units. Five board members from the AMA were assigned to oversee the development of the program, the Physicians for Responsible Negotiation (PRN). The goal of the PRN as outlined in its constitution does not reflect that of traditional labor organizations as it does not urge physicians to strike nor actively recruit members or petition the NLRB for recognition. Rather, the AMA seeks to offer its members an organizational structure and outside legal help for local groups of physicians to form collective bargaining units. PRN's underlying principles are quality care, patients' rights, and no strikes or other actions that could compromise patient care.

Although PRN has been successful in representing private sector physicians and continues to organize in the public sector, a recent Supreme Court decision is expected to drastically undercut unionization efforts among private sector physicians. In *NLRB* v. *Kentucky River Community Care, Inc.*, the court refused to enforce a board decision that six registered nurses were not supervisors because they did not exercise independent judgment. The court said that the NLRB's test for deciding whether a worker exercises independent judgment is inconsistent with the National Labor Relations Act. This holding, which is likely to lead to subsequent reevaluation of many decisions issued by the NLRB since 1994, found that health care professionals who exercise "ordinary professional or technical judgment" in directing less-skilled employees exercise "independent judgment." Therefore health care professionals are considered supervisors, as defined by the NLRA, and cannot join unions. According to PRN, the effect of the court's decision is a major setback for collective bargaining in the private sector because it reopens the question of which doctors are supervisors and which are not. The NLRB will now have to reevaluate and possibly disallow many recently formed collective bargaining units and this will decrease the number of physicians who have the right to organize. AMA Trustee Donald Palmisano said that even if the decision removes collective bargaining as an option for physicians, "the AMA will evaluate alternative strategies to ensure that these physicians have a legitimate voice in the decisions affecting patient care and their ability to practice quality medicine."

Sources: Steven Greenhouse, "Podiatrists to Form Nationwide Union; A Reply to H.M.O.'s," *New York Times,* October 25, 1996, p. A–1 and B–3; "CIR Announces Affiliation with SEIU; Groups Earmark $1.4 Million for Organizing," *Daily Labor Report,* June 9, 1997, No. 110, p. D–7; "AMA Begins Formation of Body to Help Physicians Form Local Bargaining Units." *Daily Labor Report* 177, September 14, 1999: A–3; and "High Court Ruling Causes PRN to End Organizing Effort for Private Sector Doctors." *Daily Labor Report* 111, June 8, 2001: A–6.

percentage of all union and association members. An interesting recent development (described in Box 6–1) is growing unionization among doctors as they face a loss of independence and fiscal pressures from the shift to HMOs.

By Demographic Group

Union membership levels also vary by demographic characteristics. In 2006, 13.0 percent of all men and 10.9 percent of all women were members of unions.[4] The number of female unionists as a percentage of all union members has been rising: women made up 39.6

EXHIBIT 6–4
Membership in Individual Unions, Selected Years

Source: Data from Courtney D. Gifford, *Directory of U.S. Labor Organizations, 2005 Edition* (Washington, DC: Bureau of National Affairs, June 2006), p. 3.

Union	Number of Members (in thousands)					
	1939	1960	1979	1983	2000	2004
National Education Association (NEA)	0	0	1,594	1,444	2,530	2,679
Service Employees (SEIU)	62	269	597	644	1,374	1,603
Food and Commercial Workers (UFCW)	66	364	892	1,203	1,380	1,359
State, County, and Municipal (AFSCME)	27	195	942	955	1,300	1,350
Teamsters	442	1,481	1,975	1,616	1,402	1,328
Teachers (AFT)	32	56	452	457	707	816
Laborers	158	443	537	461	818	744
Electrical Workers (BEW)	136	690	922	869	728	683
Machinists (IAM)	178	687	735	540	731	627
Auto Workers (UAW)	165	1,136	1,520	1,026	672	625
Communications (CWA)	71	269	523	578	500	557
Carpenters and Joiners	215	757	727	678	534	523
Steelworkers (USM)	225	945	1,205	694	612	512
Clothing and Textile (UNITE)	240	273	316	251	220	440[*]
Operating Engineers	58	282	452	436	379	391
Plumbers	61	261	338	329	307	325
Paperworkers	0	0	269	234	311	263
Postal Workers	0	0	263	226	316	239
Hotel and Restaurant	221	435	398	344	249	n.a.
Musicians (AFM)	127	260	274	219	105	n.a.

[*]Now UNITE-HERE.

percent of all union members.[5] Black workers are more likely to be members of unions than are whites. Bureau of Labor Statistics figures for 2006 indicate that 14.5 percent of all black workers were union members, as compared to 11.7 percent of all white workers.[6] Hispanics, however, have the lowest unionization rate at 9.8 percent.

Membership in the Large Unions

A majority of members are concentrated in a few of the large unions. Exhibit 6–4 shows that in 2004 the five largest unions in the country were the National Education Association (NEA); the Service Employees International Union (SEIU); the United Food and Commercial Workers Union (UFCW); the American Federation of State, County, and Municipal Employees (AFSME); and the International Brotherhood of Teamsters. The fastest growing unions in the country since 1970 (where growth did not occur through merger) have been public sector unions.

Recent Union Membership Declines

By 2006 union membership among the total nonfarm labor force had fallen to 12.0 percent from its 1945 peak of 35.5 percent. Union membership as a percentage of the work force declined particularly rapidly after 1977 (when it stood at 23.8 percent). This resulted because the most highly unionized industries were hit hardest by the effects of periodic recessions, by the declining competitiveness of U.S. manufactured goods on world markets, and by the economic and organizational restructuring under way within these industries.

public sector expand

private sector decline

As shown in Exhibit 6–4, from 1979 to 1983 alone the Steelworkers lost 511,000 members, the UAW lost 494,000 members, and the Machinists lost 195,000 members. While public sector union membership did expand in the early 1990s for a number of unions, as shown in Exhibit 6–4, many unions focused on the private sector saw their membership decline further in the 1990s, even when the economy expanded.[7]

Although these numbers demonstrate the large magnitude of the decline in unionization, they conceal an even more important characteristic of recent unionization patterns. Over the 1960s and 1970s a significant nonunion sector emerged in many industries, and this sector has continued to grow since then. This decline has been most surprising in industries that have historically been viewed as strongholds of unionism such as mining, construction, and trucking.

In the Coal Industry

In underground bituminous coal mining the nonunion sector has grown from virtually nothing to more than 50 percent of the industry. Major companies are now operating completely nonunion mines, often in the heart of United Mine Workers territory, such as Kentucky and West Virginia.

In the Construction Industry

In construction nonunion shops have begun to arise even among large commercial operations. During the 1950s and 1960s open-shop construction companies had moved into residential and light commercial construction, but unionized companies continued to dominate the important, heavy construction sector. Starting in the 1970s, however, the situation changed; increasingly, major office buildings and large industrial sites are being built by nonunion labor. Nonunion operations now are a majority of all construction work.

In the Trucking Industry

Over-the-road (intercity) trucking presents a similar picture. Since its deregulation in 1980 the industry has experienced a sharp transformation. Shortly after deregulation many large, unionized carriers went into bankruptcy and were replaced by smaller, independent, and generally nonunion companies. In time, many of the smaller firms also failed, so that by 1990 the largest three unionized carriers had increased their dominance and market share as a consequence of deregulation. Meanwhile, a variety of small and largely nonunion carriers had carved out specialized niches in the remaining parts of the market.

In the Telecommunications Industry

As the industry's technology shifted to wireless communications, and deregulation opened long-distance service to new entrants, companies and divisions of the former Bell System firms were established on a nonunion basis. As a result union membership in telecommunications declined from 55.5 percent in 1983 (predivestiture of AT&T) to 24.3 percent in 2001.

In Particular Companies

At the company level, data from a number of highly visible firms further illustrate this general trend. In the early 1960s General Electric had 30 to 40 nonunion plants, but by 1990 that number had roughly doubled as a result of the corporate restructuring and the opening of new, nonunion plants. Companies such as Monsanto and 3M have seen a drop in the representation rate for their production and maintenance workers—from approximately 80 to 40 percent or less. Similarly, some of the major companies in the auto parts industry, such as Dana, Bendix (now a part of Allied Signal), and Eaton, have developed sizable nonunion sectors.

American unions have faced serious declines in the share of the work force they represent since the early 1950s. What explains this decline? The next section considers in general terms the factors that influence union growth as general theories can help guide our analysis of recent U.S. experience.

Models of Union Growth

Two types of factors influence union growth. On the one hand, union growth is influenced by the state of the economy, which can be categorized as a cyclical factor. In addition, there are a host of historical, political, and social factors that have influenced unions' organizing success. These factors are often labeled as structural factors.

The Cyclical Factor   *economy & union membership positively correlated*

John R. Commons was one of the first to note that unions grew during economic prosperity and declined during economic downturns.[8] In the latter half of the 19th century union membership and the numbers of national unions rose and fell in sync with changes in the business cycle throughout that period.[9] Commons posited that as labor markets tightened during an upturn in the economy, workers became more aggressive in pursuing their goals, while employers became less resistant to collective efforts by their employees. Tighter labor markets gave workers more bargaining power and thereby increased the payoffs to unionization. With the higher profit rates that accompany prosperity, employers had more to lose during strikes and unionization drives, and therefore employers had fewer incentives to resist unionization. *employees could gain more employers could lose more during strikes*

This business cycle movement in union membership appears in other places and times. Analysis of union growth in the United States and in other countries reveals a persistent positive correlation between union membership and the strength of the economy.[10]

The Structural Factors   *union growth developed in spurts*
The Historical and Legal Influences

Although the **business cycle** clearly affects union growth, it is important to note that much of the growth in U.S. labor unions took place in only a few significant spurts. As Exhibit 6–1 shows, unionism flourished during the late 1930s and the early and mid-1940s. Public sector unionism also grew in a spurt, starting in the early 1960s. Evidence that cyclical factors are not the only influences on union growth comes from the fact that union growth did not rebound after 1992 even though these were years of economic expansion.

Events during the great depression and the two world wars illustrate that the most dramatic increases in union growth have come during times of major social upheavals. Analysts argue that the political climate of the 1930s and later the social upheavals caused by the wartime economy provided workers with strong motivation to turn to unions.

significant events : war, depression, politics

The Influence of Laws and Public Policy favorable political climate & laws

Union growth and decline also appear to be affected by the legal environment and public policy. It was not the effects of the great depression, but the encouragement to collective bargaining given by the NLRA that led to increases in unionization in the late 1930s and 1940s.

Union membership is low in states that have **right-to-work laws,** and this is another illustration of how public policy can influence union growth. These laws make it illegal to require employees to join unions as a condition of employment (such laws exist in 22 states).

Another illustration of how public policy affects union growth is the growth of public sector unions in the 1960s and 1970s. This growth occurred after many states passed legislation that protects the rights of public employees to unionize and to bargain collectively. Unfortunately, it is not entirely clear which was the cause and which the effect in those public sector developments.

On the one hand, union membership has grown fastest in states that passed legislation granting public employee unions the right to collective bargaining. On the other hand, an already favorable political climate, the existence of a strong potential for organizing, and, in some cases, the beginnings of union organization in the public sector all contributed to the passage of the state laws in the first place and may be the real major causes of union growth. Thus, it is probably safest to conclude that in the public sector the passage of legislation is both partially a cause and partially an effect of union growth.[11] This simultaneous or reciprocal causality in the relationship between public sector unionization and legislation plagues other efforts to sort out the independent effects of public policy variables on union growth in general (and on many other aspects of collective bargaining as well).

In summary, union growth in the United States and in other countries is affected by cyclical economic factors and by a number of structural factors. The latter include public policies and major historical and social events.

Explanations for Recent Union Declines

American unions have experienced a sizable decline in the share of the work force organized after the mid-1940s. Furthermore, from the 1980s on, unions in the United States were losing members in numerical (absolute) terms, and the decline in the percentage of the work force in unions accelerated. What explains these events? Do the general theories discussed above apply, or are special explanations needed?

The next section builds on a scheme offered first by Jack Fiorito and Cheryl Maranto to account for the decline that has occurred in American union membership.[12] They identify six categories of factors that have contributed to this decline. We then add a seventh.

Factor 1: Structural Changes in the Economy and the Labor Force   nature & location

Unions have had difficulty gaining new members in part due to changes that have occurred in the nature and location of jobs. Unions historically have had the greatest success in organizing urban jobs in the east, west coast, and north-central regions of the country. Yet jobs have been moving away from these regions. Unions also have had the greatest success

EXHIBIT 6–5
Employee
Perceptions of
Management's
Likely Response
to Union
Organizing

Source: Richard B.
Freeman and Joel
Rogers, *What Do
Workers Want?* (Ithaca:
Cornell University
Press, 1999).

How Might Your Management Respond to a Union Drive?			
	Nonunion	Union	Had an Organizing Drive
Welcome union	3%	12%	5%
Oppose through information	51	34	43
Threatening or harrassing union	15	28	23
Do nothing	19	14	24

Note: These responses are from a sample of private-sector employees.

with middle-aged males in blue-collar occupations. Again, the trends have worked against unions with the expansion of service and white-collar jobs, and young and female workers. Statistical tests suggest that roughly 40 percent of the decline in union membership (as a percentage of the workforce) that occurred in the previous 30 years can be explained by region, industry, and occupational characteristics.[13]

It is important to note that union declines in particular regions or occupations were not independent of management or union actions. The shift in employment to the south in part reflected management's decision to take advantage of the region's labor costs—lower than those prevailing in the more highly unionized north—and managers' beliefs that the social and political climate of the south reduced employers' vulnerability to unionization. Similarly, while employment opportunities were shifting to the service sector, unions did not follow suit by reallocating their organizing resources to take advantage of that shift.

Factor 2: Union Avoidance through Employer Election Campaign Practices *sophisticated tactics*

There is also evidence that many employers increased their resistance to unions and that, specifically, management became very sophisticated in the tactics employed during election campaigns. Management's tactics include the use of consultants, direct discussion with employees, speeches by executives of the firm during election campaigns, and in some cases, threats. Management's resistance to unions during election campaigns appears to have contributed to low union win rates in campaign elections.[14]

Employees certainly seem to feel that managers strongly oppose unionization and will go to great lengths to defeat a union organizing drive. Exhibit 6–5 reports survey evidence gathered by Professors Richard Freeman and Joel Rogers that asked employees in nonunion and union workplaces how they feel their management would respond to a union organizing drive. The survey evidence reveals that employees believe their managers would adopt aggressive measures to avoid unionization.

Factor 3: Employer Substitution through Personnel Practices *HR*

Management does not always wait until an organizing election to try to convince its employees that unions are unnecessary. Management can adopt sophisticated personnel practices that serve to substitute, at least in part, for union representation. In particular, the human resource industrial relations pattern (described in Chapter 5) has as one of its chief objectives avoidance of union representation. One key way the personnel practices differ from the election campaign practices discussed above is their long-run nature. It is useful also to keep in mind that management may have a number of reasons for using these personnel practices, including the fact that these practices can contribute to the firm's performance and adaptability.

Factor 4: Government Substitution

The government, at both the federal and state levels, since the late 1960s in particular, has become more directly involved in shaping employment conditions. Governmental influence on the substantive conditions of employment comes in part through regulations for equal employment opportunity, health and safety, and pension rights and funding. It is possible that by passing this legislation the government has weakened the need for unions by, in effect, giving the work force many of the things that unions provide.

Does the increasing role played by governments in the regulation of employment conditions actually sizably restrain union growth? Union substitution does not seem consistent with the success unions have had in a number of countries in Europe and Scandinavia with even more active governments (often Social Democratic governments) and strong and growing unions. Perhaps union substitution has had more significant effects in the United States.

Factor 5: American Worker Ideology

Some historians argue that the American work force possesses an ideology that leads workers away from unionism. The claim is that the particular American culture of individualism and the absence of class or aristocratic traditions lead to a weak union appeal.

Seymour Martin Lipset, for example, contrasted American and Canadian ideologies and claimed that these explain the relatively higher union membership in Canada. Unions are stronger in Canada even though there are many similarities in the economic conditions in the two countries. Lipset argued that U.S. citizens are individualistic (and hence not attracted to unions) whereas Canadians are culturally attracted to unions and other "communal" organizations. In Lipset's view, it was the union growth that occurred during the great depression in the United States that was the exceptional event and not the decline that U.S. unions experienced after the mid-1940s.[15]

Yet, just as there is much debate as to whether business unionism is (or ever was) an appropriate characterization of the American labor movement, there is debate as to whether the ideology possessed by workers in the United States is so different from that held by workers in other countries.

Moreover, opinion poll data indicate that attitudes of the public toward unions are quite similar in Canada and the United States and have moved in the same direction over the postwar period.[16] This too casts doubt on the claim that worker or public ideology explains the differences in union growth rates in the two countries.

It also is debatable whether it is appropriate to speak as if worker ideology emerges independent of management actions or the strategies used by the labor movement. Maybe American workers would have reacted differently, for example, if management was less resistant to unions or if unions offered a different set of policies.

Factor 6: Internal Union Affairs and Actions

Unions may bear some of the blame for their organizing difficulties and decline. One argument along these lines is that American unions have suffered from corruption and sluggish adaptation to changing times. Analysts also point to all the poor publicity generated by the charges of corruption that historically plagued the Teamsters union or the longshoring unions as part of the source of the low image the public holds of unions.

Others have argued that unions have done poorly in representation elections because they have not devoted enough resources to organizing. A number of critics have argued that labor no longer approaches the task of organizing new workers with the same enthusiasm or commitment as that which characterized the organizing drives of the 1930s.[17]

An analysis of overall trends in union election activity since 1950 shows that the number of elections held, the number of workers voting in those elections, and the unions' win rate in the elections held all declined.[18] As a result of these declines, the annual percentage of eligible workers in the labor force that became newly organized fell dramatically. The rate of new union organizing now produces only a fraction of the number of new union members needed just to offset the number of workers who are leaving unions when they leave the labor force.

To summarize, there are a number of potential explanations of the decline that has occurred in the percentage of the American labor force that belongs to a union. It may also be the case that the best explanation is a combination of some of the factors described above.

Factor 7: Limitations of the Standard Organizing and Representation Model

There may also be inherent limitations built into the traditional approaches unions use to recruit and retain members. Under American labor law, unions need to convince 50 percent of workers in a potential bargaining unit to join a union before it gains representation for any one worker. To do so the majority of workers need to be deeply dissatisfied with their employer and/or their working conditions and see unions as "instrumental" or effective means for improving their conditions. Moreover, once organized, an individual worker only remains as a union member as long as he or she stays with an employer that is under a collective bargaining contract.

These features of labor law and union organizing require considerable union resources to organize workers. And membership turnover is a particular problem. Survey data indicate that there are approximately twice as many former union members as there are current members. This means many individuals move in and out of union status at different points in the working lives. One researcher estimates that unions need to recruit five workers to gain one net new union member.[19]

We will explore the implications of this organizing model and alternatives to it in more depth in the next chapter. For now, it is sufficient to add it to the list of factors that account for the long-term decline in union membership and representation.

Union Structures for Collective Bargaining

For a union to pursue its goals effectively in the collective bargaining process it must have an appropriate structure. The structure of a union not only is important to its success in collective bargaining, but it also directs the internal distribution of power and influence among union decision makers. The next section describes the governance and activities of the AFL-CIO, of national unions, and of local unions.

The AFL-CIO
[handwritten: Federation, promotes political objectives]

The **AFL-CIO,** a federation of national unions, is the major labor federation in the United States. The primary roles of the AFL-CIO are to promote the political objectives of the labor movement and to assist the component unions in their collective bargaining activities. The AFL-CIO promotes the political objectives of unions through political lobbying and disseminating information to union members about political events and elections. With the election of President John Sweeney in 1995, the AFL-CIO shifted to more aggressively promote union organizing.

The federation has no formal authority over the collective bargaining activities of its member national unions and only rarely becomes directly involved in them. In recent years, however, the Building and Construction Trades Department and the Metal Trades Department of the AFL-CIO have played a more active and direct role in collective bargaining in selected construction projects and in the federal sector, respectively. From time to time, the Federation helps unions build new coalitions to bargain with a major employer. The Coalition of Kaiser Permanente Unions described in Box 6–2 is a current example. More generally, the staff departments of the federation offer extensive research and technical support to individual unions or to groups of unions experiencing common problems. In addition, competing unions turn to the federation to arbitrate their jurisdictional disputes.

The supreme governing body of the AFL-CIO is the biennial national convention. The chief officer of the federation is its president, and the most influential policymaking body is the Executive Council. The president has traditionally been the major source of power in the federation—with significant influence over the Executive Council and the membership—because the president has the authority to interpret the constitution between meetings of the Executive Council and manages the federation staff.

The Structure of National Unions

The **national union** is the key body and the center of power within most trade unions in the United States. National unions often are actively involved in the negotiation of collective bargaining agreements. The national unions also sanction and provide assistance to their member local unions.

[handwritten: (trade)   (industry)]

Craft versus Industrial Union Structure

It is important to understand how union jurisdiction influences how national unions perform their functions. Union jurisdiction determines the range of workers who can be legitimately organized by the union. Two of the most prevalent alternative union forms are craft or industrial unionism. A **craft union's** jurisdiction is limited to workers in a specific trade (such as painters, electricians, or carpenters) or profession (for example, teachers, nurses, pilots, baseball players, and fire fighters). An **industrial union's** jurisdiction typically encompasses all workers in a firm (such as, steel, autos, and coal mining).

The early U.S. unions were craft unions organized within local labor markets. From its formation in 1886 the AFL firmly adhered to the craft union principle as the cornerstone for organizing skilled workers. But as labor markets and product markets broadened with transportation improvements and the growth of mass production industries, the need to expand union jurisdictions became evident. Markets began to cross state lines, and unskilled workers

[handwritten: expanded w/ transportation & mass production]

In 1995 a crisis was building in the relationship between Kaiser Permanente Health and Hospital Corporation (KP) and the 26 local and 8 international unions that represent KP workers. Union members and leaders were frustrated with the number of layoffs, demands for wage concessions, strikes, and tensions that increasing competition in health care had produced in relations with KP. The largest single national union at KP, the Service Employees International Union (SEIU), began to convene its local unions with KP union members to discuss strategy. "This was contrary to how we wanted to build relationships and build the industry," recalled Margaret Peisert, then an SEIU researcher and now assistant director of the Coalition of Kaiser Permanente Unions.

SEIU then turned to the Industrial Union Department (IUD) at the AFL-CIO and asked its staff to call a meeting of all the unions representing workers at KP. KP nurses, represented by the American Federation of Teachers, joined the SEIU in this request. The IUD had many years of experience in coordinating bargaining efforts, and so Peter diCicco, then President of the IUD, welcomed setting up a meeting to address the critical problems at Kaiser. Peter diCicco describes how they got started:

> We took our normal approach. We called an initial meeting of all principal unions. More than 100 people attended. We knew from experience that we had to get all the unions on board with a clear strategy for how to deal with Kaiser. It became evident, given the negative attitude of the public toward strikes in health care, we had to consider other options—and so we began looking at other means to achieve bargaining strength—corporate campaigns and such. I went to the international unions for a supplemental budget to fund the corporate campaign. They accepted the supplemental budget and we staffed up and started the corporate campaign—a successful one. For example, we found a very negative quality report on KP from one region and began making it public to demonstrate we were ready to move in this direction if we didn't see a change in Kaiser's behavior.

> But it became clear to us if we unleashed lots of these data we would lose control of all this. The government might step in and we would all lose. So I went to the international union presidents and told them these guys (Kaiser) are not the worst of employers we deal with, and we might do permanent damage to them and to our 75,000 union members if we mount an all-out corporate campaign or use the information we amassed for short-term advantage or leverage. Was there an alternative? Perhaps we could use our bargaining strength at the table or offer the option of a partnership approach with Kaiser.

> We had John Sweeney, who at that time was President of the SEIU (later to become President of the AFL-CIO), make an overture to David Lawrence, (then KP's CEO) and that started the process. It took Kaiser six months to consider the idea. The Board of Directors discussed it at length. Fortunately, the former chair of Northwest Natural Gas was on the board and he had a very positive experience with a labor-management partnership in his company. After consulting with him and other board members, Lawrence came back to Sweeney and said, 'Let's explore this idea.'

The result was the formation of union coalition that went on to negotiate together (see Box 7–11 for a description of these negotiations) to achieve the first nationwide agreement covering all KP union members and to build the largest labor-management partnership ever constructed in the United States.

Note: A corporate campaign of the sort mentioned by diCiccio is a coordinated research and public disclosure initiative undertaken by unions to bring public attention to a company in an effort to change the company's labor relations practices.

Source: Thomas A. Kochan, Susan Eaton, and Robert B. McKersie, "The Kaiser Permanente Union Management Partnership: The First Five Years," unpublished manuscript, MIT Sloan School of Management, 2002.

became a significant part of the labor force, raising serious challenges to the appropriateness of the narrow, craft-based organizations.

In 1935 advocates of industrial unionism, led by John L. Lewis, president of the United Mine Workers, split with the craft union advocates in the AFL and formed what became in

1937 the Congress of Industrial Organizations (CIO). As the large industrial unions grew, corporations and markets continued to expand, and centralized bargaining became more popular—all of which helped to establish the national union as the central, or most power-ful, structure in most industrial unions.

The Governance of National Unions

National unions typically are governed by a constitution and bylaws. Commonly there are annual or biennial conventions held by the national union in which officers are elected, rules and bylaws are modified, and policies are debated. The local unions that are branches of the national union send delegates to the national union convention, often with the number of delegates determined by the number of members in the local union.

National unions have elected officers that frequently include a president, secretary-treasurer, vice presidents (each of which might oversee certain of the covered membership in various companies or industries), and an executive board. The national union also com-monly includes an administrative staff that is appointed by the president.

The staff of a national union implements policies in areas such as organizing, contract negotiation, grievance administration, health and safety, strike and welfare fund adminis-tration, and research. One important task performed by these staffs is communicating with organizations that are external to the union, such as other national unions, offices of the AFL-CIO, or governmental agencies. Another responsibility of the national union staff is to provide advice and assistance to the local unions within the national union.

The Local Union   *not always affliated w/ national union*

For most unionized workers the most extensive interaction they have with the union that represents them is through their contact with and involvement in a **local union.** The individual employee can participate in local union meetings and vote in the elections that determine local union officers. It is the local union that is involved in the initial processing of a grievance and the direction of any strike or picketing activities.

If a local union is not linked to any national union (as is the case in some small manufac-turing companies), the local union negotiates a collective bargaining agreement on its own. More typically, however, a local union is a branch of a national union and is thus governed by the constitution or bylaws of a national union. In addition to this formal connection, there is typically extensive contact between local and national union officers, especially during contract negotiations or contract administration.

The Division between Local and National Union Responsibilities

In most industrial unionized settings, such as the steel, auto, textile, and mining industries, the unionized employee is covered by both a local contract and a contract that is negotiated at the company level. The local union negotiates the local contract, whereas the national union negotiates the company or industry contract.

When there are both local and higher level (company or industry) collective bargaining agreements, each agreement covers different subjects. The local contract (which might cover either a single plant or all the plants in a company) usually includes issues such as the work rules for job requirements and seniority rights and the wage rates paid for spe-cific jobs. The company or national contract addresses matters such as the scheduled wage increase over the term of the contract and fringe benefits, and it sets out procedures for the grievance process.

nationals assists locals

The national union usually assists the local union during negotiation of the local collective bargaining agreement. The national union might provide an expert in negotiations who advises the local union during negotiations; in some instances the national union representative directs the union side in local negotiations. Or, the research staff of the national union may be involved by providing background information (about other wage settlements in the industry or economic trends) or technical assistance to the local union.

The local and national union staffs often have regular contact during the term of a labor agreement. National staff might provide, for example, technical assistance to a local union as it develops or implements health and safety or employee assistance programs. The national and local unions often coordinate their efforts during a union organizing drive. In addition, as discussed further in Chapter 11, in many unions it is the national union that decides whether an unresolved grievance is pressed to arbitration.

The Governance of Local Unions

The local union typically includes a number of elected executive officers, including a president and a secretary-treasurer. Industrial unions frequently also have bargaining chairs and bargaining committees that lead the local union in contractual negotiations. In the construction industry and some other local unions a business agent directs the local contractual negotiations, handles grievances, and in other ways operates as the chief administrative officer of the local union.

Local unions are funded out of the dues paid by unionized employees. In large and well-funded unions the executive officers of the local union will be paid full- or part-time to carry out union duties. In many locals the union president is the only full-time paid position, and other officers carry out union-related duties part-time and perform their normal jobs at other times.

Union officers are involved in formulating the strategic direction of the local union, but for the average worker the most important person who represents the union is the **shop steward.** In a typical union, the steward provides union services at the shop floor level to 10 to 20 workers. It is the steward that becomes involved most quickly if a grievance or other dispute arises between a worker and a supervisor. Furthermore, workers often hear about union events or programs from their steward.

Political Life inside Local Unions

Local union officers and stewards are chosen for their positions through elections. Many local unions elect officers for two- or three-year terms. Local union elections are frequently highly contested, with a large number of candidates running for positions. There is rarely anything similar to a formal political party in local unions, although there are often slates (groups) of candidates who join together informally during their campaigns for union office.

Union Democracy

How extensive is the amount of democracy inside national and local unions? Although it is difficult to generalize, given the wide diversity that exists within unions, overall, there is much **union democracy.** Union officers are elected regularly through democratic election processes. Compared to the way the executives in corporations are chosen, the election of union officers is clearly more democratic.

There tends to be greater stability in national union officer elections than in local union officer elections. The presidents of many national unions, for example, are often reelected to serve for a number of terms. Some of the important and colorful figures in U.S. labor history were national union presidents, such as John L. Lewis (in the United Mine Workers) and Walter Reuther (in the United Auto Workers) who were elected for a number of terms.

In most unions there are regular debates over the strategic direction and positions the union should take in contractual negotiations with management, another sign of healthy democratic processes. There are rarely formal political parties inside unions like the national political parties that exist in the United States. Instead, debates and coalitions tend to be formed around specific issues and events.

Recently, for example, there has been active debate inside unions over whether unions should cooperate more extensively with management. Sometimes this debate is triggered by management's requests for changes in work rules that can lead to improvements in plant productivity. Critics of the cooperative approach argue that the union might unnecessarily give up gains that had taken years to win or might lose the capability to defend workers' interests.

Union Corruption

There are some instances of corruption inside unions. For many years, for example, there have been allegations that officers in the Teamsters union were linked to organized crime. Box 6–3 discusses the racketeering charges brought against the Teamsters by the Justice Department and how they were settled.

One can also point to particular local unions in which corrupt practices or corrupt leaders exist as evidence that unions do not maintain purely democratic institutions. Nevertheless, there is evidence of lively debates inside unions and the democratic selection of nearly all union officers.

The Election of John Sweeney and the Reorientation of the AFL-CIO

Debates over the future of unions and the role of the AFL-CIO led to the first contested election for the presidency of the AFL-CIO upon the retirement of the long-standing previous president, Lane Kirkland. In October 1995, John Sweeney, formerly president of the SEIU, was elected on a platform that emphasized the need for aggressive union organizing and redirection in the role of the AFL-CIO.

Subsequently, with Sweeney as President, the AFL-CIO issued a new mission statement (see Exhibit 6–6) and launched a number of new initiatives including:

1. The creation of a new Organizing Department in the AFL-CIO with an initial $10 million annual budget. The AFL-CIO encouraged national unions to make organizing a priority and provided strategic research and other assistance to organizing efforts.

2. $40 million issue-oriented campaigns directed at electing a more labor-sympathetic Congress in the 1996, 1998, and 2000 elections. One aspect of this initiative, the spurring of enhanced member mobilization, showed impressive signs of success. While in 1992, 19 percent of voters were from union households; by 2000 this had increased to 26 percent.[20]

Racketeering Charges against the Teamsters Union and the Cycle of Reforms   Box 6–3

Scandals and reform cycles have been a part of the history of the Teamsters Union. Since the 1930s there have been charges that a number of the officers of the Teamsters union were linked to organized crime. Five of the presidents who have led the Teamsters union since the 1930s have been indicted for criminal charges. Three of those presidents went to prison, and a number of union officers and challengers to the union leadership were killed under suspicious circumstances.

In the 1980s the Justice Department of the U.S. government brought a racketeering case against the union. The U.S. Attorney's complaint, filed in federal court against the union, claimed that there were at least 200 Teamsters' officials with proved or alleged connections to organized crime. The Justice Department and the Teamsters Union settled the racketeering case out of court in 1989. In the settlement the union (with 1.6 million members) agreed to have national union officers directly elected by member voting in 1991. This replaced the traditional election of national union officers by local union leaders. The settlement also appointed a number of individuals designated by the Justice Department to temporarily oversee the financial operation of the national union and to take over the direction of some of the local branches of the union.

Surprisingly, Ron Carey, formerly the head of the UPS section of the Teamsters, was elected President of the Teamsters Union in the 1991 supervised election along with a slate of other reform candidates. Notably, Carey had received support from Teamsters for a Democratic Union (TDU), and there were high hopes after his election that the Teamsters could put their scandal-plagued legacy behind them.

Carey went on to defeat James Hoffa, Jr., by a narrow margin in a 1996 election to retain the Presidency of the Teamsters Union, but then scandal returned to the union when charges surfaced concerning the fund-raising activities used by Carey's administration during the 1996 election. The U.S. District Court, still overseeing

the union, ordered a rerun of the 1996 election and then disqualified Carey from participating in the rerun. Subsequently, Carey was barred from the union for alleged complicity in the illegal financing of his (and President Clinton's) 1996 reelection campaigns.

In November 1998, after campaigning that he would restore the strength the union had when his father had been president, James Hoffa, Jr., won the court-ordered rerun and assumed the presidency of the Teamsters Union. James Hoffa Jr. assumed the presidency in March of 1998, pledging to get the federal government out of the union's internal affairs. He initiated an anticorruption initiative known as Project RISE (respect, integrity, strength, ethics) to establish a code of conduct for its members. A key component of Project RISE is an assessment of any links to organized crime. Edward H. Stien, a former assistant U.S. attorney hired by the Teamsters to oversee Project RISE, expects that by working with the government to pursue ongoing investigations, the union will prove its capacity to govern itself.

However, tensions do still periodically surface between the Teamsters and the federal government over the continuing implementation of the 1989 consent agreement. In June 2002, Hoffa proposed a package of constitutional amendments, such as a one-member, one-vote principle and direct election of international officers by the membership. Hoffa hopes that clean international officer elections in fall 2002, as well as union constitutional reforms and Project RISE, will lead to the ending of court and federal oversight of the Teamster's internal affairs.

Sources: "1991 International Officers Election," in *Daily Labor Report* (Washington, D.C.: Bureau of National Affairs), June 12, 1990, p. A–16; "Decision of Kenneth Conboy to Disqualify IBT President Ron Carey," *Daily Labor Report,* November 18, 1997, pp. D–1–32; and "IBT Negotiating with Justice Department for End to 12-Year Government Oversight." *Daily Labor Report 95,* May 16, 2001: A–10.

3. Union Summer, started in 1996, placed college student interns in the field to assist union organizing and political activities.

4. A new Center for Strategic Campaigns was created in the AFL-CIO to help spur and coordinate corporate campaigns. Campaigns of this sort are described in the next chapter.

EXHIBIT 6–6
The New Mission Statement of the AFL-CIO

THE MISSION OF THE AFL-CIO is to improve the lives of working families—to bring economic justice to the workplace and social justice to our nation. To accomplish this mission we will build and change the American labor movement.

We will build a broad movement of American workers by organizing workers into unions. We will recruit and train the next generation of organizers, mass the resources needed to organize and create the strategies to win organizing campaigns and union contracts. We will create a broad understanding of the need to organize among our members, our leadership and among unorganized workers. We will lead the labor movement in these efforts.

We will build a strong political voice for workers in our nation. We will fight for an agenda for working families at all levels of government. We will empower state federations. We will build a broad progressive coalition that speaks out for social and economic justice. We will create a political force within the labor movement that will empower workers and speak forcefully on the public issues that affect our lives.

We will change our unions to provide a new voice to workers in a changing economy. We will speak for working people in the global economy, in the industries in which we are employed, in the firms where we work, and on the job everyday. We will transform the role of the union from an organization that focuses on a member's contract to one that gives workers a say in all the decisions that affect our working lives—from capital investments, to the quality of our products and services, to how we organize our work.

We will change our labor movement by creating a new voice for workers in our communities. We will make the voices of working families heard across our nation and in our neighborhoods. We will create vibrant community labor councils that reach out to workers at the local level. We will strengthen the ties of labor to our allies. We will speak out in effective and creative ways on behalf of all working Americans.

MISSION AND GOALS
OF THE AFL-CIO

5. The creation of a Field Mobilization Department AFL-CIO that invigorated Central Labor Councils (multiunion local bodies of the AFL-CIO) and used these councils to assist union organizing and community political activities.

Although there was much enthusiasm among union activists for these new initiatives, there also were some workers and established union leaders that disagreed with one or more of these tactics. In March 2001, the Carpenter's Union withdrew from the AFL-CIO over disagreements about the pace and nature of change inside the labor movement (see Box 6–4).

The AFL-CIO continues to update and revise its agenda. In late 2001, the federation adopted a new program focused on linking political activities with organizing and member mobilization. This new program was supported by an increase in the federation's per capita tax and, like other tax increases, was the subject of debate (see Box 6–5). It remains to be seen how much change in the actions of national and local unions actually occurs as a consequence of the new AFL-CIO initiatives and whether the withdrawal of the Carpenter's Union is followed by further dissension in the AFL-CIO.

In March of 2001, the general executive board of United Brotherhood of Carpenters (UBC) voted unanimously to withdraw from the AFL-CIO. Carpenters president Douglas McCarron said the decision was caused by disagreements over organizing and spending policies. He criticized the AFL-CIO for continuing to operate under archaic rules and procedures and for not addressing fundamental changes at the workplace. McCarron said his "obligation was to working carpenters, not to an institutional structure, and we made the changes that needed to be made." McCarron said he hoped that the AFL-CIO could resolve its internal conflicts so the two organizations could continue to have an open relationship.

AFL-CIO President John Sweeney expressed great disappointment over the decision. According to Sweeney, "Today's unions need to be unified to provide a strong voice for Carpenters members, other union members, and all working families, who face serious and challenging issues." Similarly, Edward Sullivan, president of the AFL-CIO's Building and Construction Trades Department (BCTD) stated that labor should remain united to face obstacles in the next few years, such as "a hostile administration and possibly a hostile Congress."

The UBC's withdrawal from the AFL-CIO has had an enormous financial impact on the BCTD, which relied on the Carpenters' Union as its single largest payer of per capita tax among its 15 affiliated unions. The BCTD and the AFL-CIO both had accused the UBC of deliberately paying per capita tax on fewer members than it has for several years. In February of 2000, an arrangement was approved by the federation's finance committee to bring per capita payments back to a more accurate level by adding 20,000 members per month. However, after the UBC's decision to disaffiliate, the federation's executive council unanimously supported a position to seek full repayment of the per capita tax due. The UBC has not yet responded to the demand. However, McCarron frequently expressed his disapproval of the tax payments before the withdrawal decision, even stating that they do "little more than support an organized bureaucracy in Washington that provides no direct benefits for his members."

McCarron stated that the disaffiliation is the right move for his union. He believes that unions do not need a federation to unite and promote the interests of workers. He wants the Carpenters' Union to work with moderate Republicans, as well as Democrats, and believes that now it will have flexibility to do so. Also, now that it is free from jurisdictional issues with other craft unions, in McCarron's words, the UCB can organize "the industry as it is today, not the way it was 25 years ago."

In late 2002, reports circulated regarding talks being held between the Carpenters Union and the AFL-CIO concerning possible UCB re-affiliation with the AFL-CIO's Building and Construction Trades Department.

Source: "AFL-CIO: Carpenters Unions Withdraws from the AFL-CIO, Citing Disagreement over Internal Policies," *Daily Labor Report* 62, March 30, 2001: AA–1.

A Servicing versus Organizing Model of Unionism

[handwritten annotation: Should there be movement away from servicing model to organizing model?]

As the share of the American work force represented by unions continued to decline, a debate surfaced within the labor movement regarding whether unions needed to shift away from their traditional *servicing model* of representation to an *organizing model*. The traditional servicing model is said to focus extensively on contract negotiations and contract administration, and the provision of various services to union members. In this approach the collective bargaining carried out by national and local unions was supplemented by AFL-CIO political lobbying. Relatively modest resources are directed in this approach to union organizing, and in the servicing model union member militance plays a critical role in strike actions but not in daily union affairs.

An organizing model of unionism, in contrast, focuses a substantial share of unions' activity and resources on organizing. Furthermore, this approach seeks to involve union

In May of 2002, the AFL-CIO executive board approved an increase of 4 cents per member per month in the per capita tax paid to the federation through July 2005. The increase is expected to raise an additional $7 million a year for political programs. According to President John Sweeney, the money will be spent on education and member mobilization, not candidates and political parties. The move was motivated by a 10-point program the federation adopted in its December convention. The program aims to link politics to organizing and mobilizing members through a series of initiatives. Member mobilization will take place around a "working families" agenda created in February of 2002. The agenda calls for creating and maintaining good jobs, rebuilding America with long-term investment, preserving retirement security, advocating universal health care, holding corporations accountable, and endorsing labor law reform to facilitate the organization of workers.

Only two unions voted against the tax increase, the International Brotherhood of Teamsters and the International Association of Machinists. Although IBT President James Hoffa said he shares the federation's goal of electing a majority in Congress that represents working families, the Teamsters want more participation in the selection of candidates to support and how political money will be spent. Hoffa also wants more accountability from candidates because politicians are known for "taking our money and then voting against us." Hoffa also is critical of the fact that the federation supports many more Democrats than Republicans. IAM President Thomas

Buffenbarger also expressed frustration at the limited return the federation and the labor movement had received from its prior political donations. However, unlike Hoffa, Buffenbarger blames the federation's loss of power on a Republican president and majority in Congress. He believes the labor movement needs to rebuild the Democratic Party by getting low-level party loyalists elected to state-level political positions and then move those individuals on to higher government positions over the years.

In response, Sweeney said the program "is not about money to candidates. It's about improving the lives of working families by elevating the issues most important to them—and then holding every candidate and every elected official accountable on those issues." Since many member unions want input on how the AFL-CIO spends its money, federation officials plan to spend time with the AFL-CIO political committee and bring recommendations to the federation's executive council (comprised of a number of national union presidents). Also, the AFL-CIO plans to have input from its affiliates in each budget cycle regarding how best to spend political monies. Steve Rosenthal, the federation's political director, said that the federation supports the Teamsters' strategy to support pro-worker Republicans and that the federation continues to aggressively search for Republican candidates to support.

Source: "AFL-CIO Executive Board Approves Per Capita Tax Increase for Political Programs." *Daily Labor Report* 100, May 5, 2002: AA-1.

members actively in the organizing process and in the internal operation of the union. Union member *mobilization* thus is used to spur *external* and *internal* organizing. How many unions actually adopt an organizing strategy and whether this will lead to sizable increases in union membership remains to be seen.

Union Mergers

One of the key ways a national union can alter its governance structure and form is through a **union merger** with another union. One goal of the AFL-CIO merger in 1955 was to promote greater rationalization of union structures through mergers and consolidation of member unions.[21] Indeed, George Meany and Walter Reuther, then leaders of the AFL and CIO, respectively, expected the original 135 unions in the new federation to be reduced to approximately 50. The number of unions in the AFL-CIO now stands at 69.[22]

[handwritten: union mergers leads to economics of scale, reduced competition]

The advantage of a merger for unions is the administrative benefits that accrue from greater economies of scale and the organizing and bargaining benefits from reduced inter-union competition and rivalry. Small unions that lack the financial resources and professional expertise needed to adequately service union members can be absorbed into larger, more richly endowed organizations. Reducing competition among unions in the same industry or occupation can free up resources previously used in fighting with each other to improve collective bargaining or political efforts. And, finally, unions whose traditional occupational or craft jurisdictions have eroded can concentrate on helping their members adjust to the changing environment by protecting their job security and expending less of their effort on ensuring the institutional survival of the union.

Critics of merger activity, on the other hand, posit that mergers do not necessarily reflect the rational consolidation of outmoded union jurisdictions. Instead, they say, some mergers are simply opportunistic or expansionist in nature and arise out of union leaders' desires for greater memberships, larger treasuries, more stable jobs for themselves, and increased status and power within the labor movement. Critics also question whether mergers increase unions' administrative or collective bargaining effectiveness. They stress the negative consequences of large-scale unions for membership control and union democracy.[23]

In the face of the drops in membership, a number of unions entered financial crises and drastically cut back the size of their staffs in recent years. Thus, just as the workers in declining industries were facing layoffs, so were a number of union staff members.

In response to financial and other pressures in recent years a number of unions pursued mergers (see Box 6–6). Some small unions responded by merging in an effort to regain bargaining strength and staff economies through the creation of a larger union. Other mergers involved larger unions such as the ILGWU and ACTWU, which merged in 1995 to form UNITE. Merger activity on the part of unions representing government workers previously had enabled several of the nation's largest unions, such as AFSCME and the SEIU, to grow when the organized sector of the U.S. work force was declining.

Changes in technology, along with the rising administrative costs of running an effective union, are likely to continue the pressure for union mergers. At the same time, however, the political problems associated with merging two or more autonomous, and often rival, organizations into one body (with, obviously, only one president) will continue to limit the rate of mergers. Critical questions that must be addressed are: Do mergers produce the improved administrative and bargaining service they promise? Do they enhance unions' and their members' abilities to adapt to technological change? And do those benefits result without also yielding losses in union membership control and internal union democracy? These are questions worthy of attention.

Unions as Networks *[handwritten: new nature of jobs]*

The increased mobility that characterizes workers' careers today, and perhaps even more tomorrow, has led some to suggest that a new conception of unions is needed. Unions may need to serve as networking agents for workers as they move through their careers and across the various jobs, and even as they move in and out of the paid labor force over the different stages of their family life. This conception reflects the data mentioned above that suggest many workers encounter unions at some point in their working lives, but do not retain their membership.

Unions continue to merge for a number of reasons, usually to increase their bargaining power and influence. Alan Barnes, secretary-treasurer of Paper, Allied-Industrial, Chemical and Energy Workers International Union Local 4367, said union mergers create a greater availability of resources and programs related to health and safety, organizing and research, and organization. PACE was created in 1999 following the merger of the Oil, Chemical and Atomic workers and the United Paperworkers International Union. Johnny Rodriguez, vice president of the United Food and Commercial Workers, said the advantage of mergers far exceed the growing pains. In May of 1999, the Textile Processors, Service Trades, Health Care, Professional and Technical International Union, a small independent union that represents 13,000 laundry, nursing home, and textile processing workers, merged with the UFCW. Rodriguez commented that he hopes to continue increasing membership through mergers because they "amplify and multiply your resources for the purpose of collective bargaining, organizing and community involvement" as well as "multiply your manpower, finances, and who you know in your community and political arena." James Hoffa, president of the Teamsters, vowed to expand the union through mergers during his presidency as well.

He just finalized an agreement to include the 50,000-member Brotherhood of Locomotive Engineers in the Teamsters Union.

Although the National Education Association and the American Federation of Teachers, the two largest organizations that represent teachers, have been expected to merge for years, no official merger has occurred. However, in July of 2001, the two entered into a partnership agreement that would provide a framework for additional cooperation between the two teachers' unions. The agreement created a joint council composed of 15 representatives of each organization. The council will include the eleven members of the AFT Executive Committee and the nine members of the NEA Executive Committee. It will decide which partnership activities the two organizations will participate in, such as holding conferences on topics of common interest and coordinating legal and legislative action.

Sources: "Union Mergers Give Workers Stronger Voice, Union Leaders Tell Labor-Management Forum," *Daily Labor Report* 65, April 4, 2000: C–1; "Hoffa Vows to Grow Union through Organizing, Mergers," *Daily Labor Report* 58, March 26, 2002: A–9; and "NEA Approves Partnership Agreement Providing for More Cooperation with AFT," *Daily Labor Report* 130, July 9, 2001: A–9.

Moreover, other data suggest that workers form their views of unions at an early age. If they are not recruited to join unions early in their careers, it is difficult to gain their interest in joining later on. This would require unions to view their role as full-service labor market institutions that provide representational services through collective bargaining where a majority of workers have voted for exclusive representation and individual services such as access to lifelong learning, information on job opportunities, and portable fringe benefit and pension coverage when majority status for bargaining purposes has not been obtained. It would also require significant changes in union structures. Unions would need stronger community or regional structures to support mobility and continuous service to individual members.

Whether or not this alternative view of unions gains momentum, it is clear that some strategy that goes beyond simply putting more resources into the traditional strategies and structures for organizing and representing workers will be needed if there is to be a significant reversal and revival of American unions.

Division in the AFL-CIO and the Formation of the "Change to Win Coalition"

With declining union membership rates has come divisions within the labor movement about how best to rebuild union strength. In 1995 John Sweeney was elected as president of the AFL-CIO on a reform platform challenging the existing direction and leadership of the AFL-CIO. A decade later, a new group of union leaders in turn emerged to challenge the Sweeney administration leadership of the AFL-CIO and propose a new direction for the labor movement. In 2001, the Carpenter's Union had withdrawn from the AFL-CIO over disagreements about the pace and nature of change inside the labor movement. By 2004, a number of major unions began issuing calls for changes in the AFL-CIO to devote greater resources to organizing and to encourage the merger of smaller unions to form larger, more powerful unions.[24]

During 2005, conflicts over the future direction of the AFL-CIO came to a head. In May 2005, four major unions, the SEIU, UNITE HERE, the Teamsters (IBT), and the Laborers' (ILIU), issued a joint proposal for reforms of the AFL-CIO. These reform proposals focused on three main areas. First, they argued that greater resources needed to be devoted to organizing activity. To encourage this, they proposed that half of the dues paid to the AFL-CIO by any unions that were active in organizing be rebated. Second, they argued that many existing unions were too small to devote adequate efforts to organizing. The reforms proposed designating "lead unions" for organizing particular industries, crafts, or employers and encouraging the merger of smaller unions to form larger unions. Third, they argued that the AFL-CIO was devoting too much of its political activities to getting candidates of one political party, the Democrats, elected. Instead labor's political efforts should be focused on building the labor movement and worker power, including supporting pro-labor Republican or third party candidates.[25]

The executive committee of the AFL-CIO rejected the proposed reforms and instead adopted a counterproposal offered by President Sweeney. Among the objections to the proposed reforms were concerns that shifting resources away from political activities and toward organizing would undermine the ability to get more pro-labor candidates elected; and pushing for merger of smaller unions would deny workers freedom of choice in representation.

In June 2005, the four dissenting unions, along with the United Food and Commercial Workers (UFCW), announced the formation of a new organization, to be called the "Change to Win Coalition" (CTW).[26] At the beginning of the July 2005 convention of the AFL-CIO (which ironically was supposed to be a celebration of the 50th anniversary of the formation of the federation by the merger of the formerly competing AFL and CIO), both the SEIU and Teamsters announced they were leaving the AFL-CIO, soon to be joined by the other members of the CTW Coalition.[27] In September 2005, the founding convention of the CTW Coalition was held in St. Louis, Missouri, signaling that for the first time in a half-century there were now two different major labor federations in the United States. In addition to its initial five members, the CTW Coalition was also joined by the Carpenters Union and the United Farm Workers. Together the seven unions in the CTW Coalition represent some six million workers, compared to the nearly nine million workers represented by unions still members of the AFL-CIO. Andy Stern, the president of the SEIU who is profiled in Box 6–7, emerged as one of the key leaders involved in the CTW Coalition.

Supporters of the CTW Coalition argue that with the decline in unionization levels in the country, a new, more dynamic and innovative union movement is needed and that the existing AFL-CIO federation was unable to provide this. By contrast, critics of the split have argued that dividing the labor movement into two competing federations will undermine the strength and unity of the movement. Some supporters of the existing AFL-CIO leadership have argued that the split is really a dispute about leadership and control of the labor movement. Much noted has been the split between John Sweeney, who was president of SEIU

The student has become the teacher, the son has become the father, the old has become the new—in more ways than one. Reminiscent of John L. Lewis and the CIO, Andy Stern, president of the Service Employees International Union, challenged John Sweeney and the AFL-CIO's reign when he became one of the founders of the Change to Win Coalition. But how did Stern come to be in such a position?

Born in West Orange, New Jersey, Stern began his career with the SEIU following his graduation from the University of Pennsylvania as a state service worker. It wasn't long until he became the president of the local branch, and two years after that, at age 29, Stern became the youngest person ever to be elected onto the SEIU's Executive Board. It was from there that he would begin to make his mark on the union world.

In 1984, then SEIU president John Sweeney took Stern to Washington to head a national organizing campaign. Stern ended up remaining by his side until 1995 when Sweeney asked for Stern's help in leading his campaign to take over the presidency of the AFL-CIO. After Sweeney won the election, an interim president was put into place within the SEIU until formal elections could be held. Soon after, fearing the strength and charisma Stern possessed, the interim president hastily fired him. Not willing to be beaten, Stern rushed back onto the scene and won the election, becoming the president of the international union in 1996. For the next eight years, Stern provided astonishing results, running the union and organizing 600,000 workers in the process—the same number of workers it took Sweeney nearly twice that time to organize. However, in 2002, a devastating event took place in Stern's personal life that challenged his ability to continue with his work.

Born with hypotonia, an unusually low muscle tone, Stern's daughter, Cassie, was feeble throughout childhood. In 2002, following surgery to correct scoliosis, Stern awoke to find his daughter frozen in her bed, breathless. After desperately trying to resuscitate her and get her to a nearby hospital, Cassie fell into a coma and died a few days later. Following this, Stern was unsure if he could continue with his life's work and even walked out of a few union meetings to clear his head.

One day, however, Stern was hit hard with the feeling that, although he could not save his daughter's life, he could do something about the millions of workers in poverty and oppression on the streets of America. With this philosophy, Stern went to John Sweeney and the ALF-CIO with his proposals for a more successful strategy. One of his largest qualms dealt with the fact that the federation was simply spread too thin. With 60 unions under the AFL-CIO, more than 50 of them average fewer than 60,000 members—hardly enough weight to influence industrywide organizing. Therefore, as opposed to the ALF-CIO's structure that included many different and competing unions in the same industry or sector, he wished to have only one or two giant unions representing all the workers there. Additionally, Stern claimed that the federation spent too much of its budget on political alliances and not nearly enough on member recruitment. To lay support to this claim, Stern cited his own successes, which had been brought about largely from direct member recruitment.

Although John Sweeney was sympathetic to Stern's vision and realized the need for change, there was not much modification within the AFL-CIO. As a result, in 2004, Stern, the SEIU, and three other unions formed the New Unity Partnership, aimed at industry-based organizing campaigns and new member recruitment. Practically on the day of the 50th anniversary of the AFL-CIO, Stern gave union heads a choice: either there be dramatic changes immediately, or Stern, the more than one-million members of the SEIU behind him, and other large unions (including the Teamsters) were going to walk. When little was done, in 2005, the NUP became the Change to Win Coalition, eventually taking in four other unions by 2006 and seceding from the AFL-CIO, with Stern at the helm.

Today, Stern is described by his critics as arrogant, overconfident, and even dictatorial. These people see his strides at changing the face of labor as an attempt to gain power rather than a way of truly making a difference. His supporters, however, see him in a different light. Sporting the color purple, the symbol of the SEIU, in nearly everything he does, Stern has gained the trust and admiration of countless followers. He, unlike most union bosses, takes part in even the most mundane of details during an organizing campaign and appears to live a modest life.

(continued)

But will Stern's tactics pay off for labor? Will his new way of organizing actually reverse the decreasing trend of the labor movement? Only time will tell, but one thing's for sure: The years to come are going to be an important period for the labor movement.

Sources: "Stern Criticizes AFL-CIO on Immigration Bill; Says Unions' Decline Led to Rise in Lawsuits," 3/20/06. *Daily Labor Report,* March 20, 2006: C-3; "Stern Outlines How He Would Change Labor Movement to Boost Organizing," 6/23/04. *Daily Labor Report,* June 23, 2004: C-1; "Can This Man Save Labor?" 9/13/04. *BusinessWeek,* September 13, 2004, p. 80; "Sweeping changes will save unions, says Stern, who knows turmoil," 2/27/05. *The Philadelphia Inquirer.* "Love, Labor Loss: A Child's Death Stirred Andrew Stern to Challenge Himself—and Unionism," 1/3/06. *The Washington Post.*

before assuming the leadership of the AFL-CIO, and Andy Stern, the most prominent leader of the CTW Coalition, who took over as president of SEIU following Sweeney in 1995.

One major concern following the split was that the two federations would compete with each other and be unable to work together on issues of common interest to unions. However, the initial experience has been that the two organizations are able to work together in some areas. In January 2006, the SEIU and AFSCME, leading national unions in the CTW and AFL-CIO camps respectively, launched a joint TV ad campaign opposing proposed cuts in government health care spending. AFSCME also signed agreements with UNITE HERE and the UFCW (both CTW) not to interfere with each other's existing collective bargaining relations, for example, by trying to get workers to switch their affiliation between unions in a "raid." In May 2006, CTW and the AFL-CIO announced the formation of a joint Coordinated Committee for Political Action. In addition, they announced support for involvement of locals of CTW unions in the state federations and central labor councils of the AFL-CIO. Taken together, these developments suggest that the acrimony and animosity involved in the split between the two union federations can be overcome where the unions can identify their common interests.

What are the implications of this recent dramatic split in the labor movement? For the labor movement, a danger is that its voice in the political realm will be weakened by being divided. This is a concern that has been strongly articulated by critics of the split among unions that have stayed within the AFL-CIO. As United Steelworkers President Leo Gerard commented at the time of the split, "Today is a tragic day because those who left the house of labor are weakening our house, and shame on them."[28] At the same time, there have been competing union federations at earlier points in American history. Indeed, the most dramatic growth in union membership occurred during the period from 1935 to 1955 when the labor movement was split into competing AFL and CIO federations. The initial Change to Win Coalition Statement issued in June 2005 harkened back to precisely that experience in invoking the historical example of the formation of the Committees for Industrial Organization in the 1930s to organize the new mass production industries of the time. Whether the CTW will be able to fulfill a similar role in the future and also whether there may be some future equivalent of the 1950s merger of the competing AFL and CIO are important issues that remain to be determined.

Summary

The union membership figures reported at the beginning of this chapter highlight one of the central challenges that face unions today. Unions' share of the U.S. labor force declined substantially since the early 1950s, a decline even more alarming given the inroads nonunion firms have achieved in many industries that were once bastions of union organization. Contributing to this decline have been innovative human resource and union avoidance policies adopted by some nonunion firms, structural shifts in the economy and labor force, the effects of heightened international competition and trade, and unions' past unproductive and, in some cases, only feeble efforts to counteract these developments.

Yet the outlook for the labor movement is not completely gloomy. The benefits of the human resource innovations that serve as a partial alternative to unionization have diffused to only a limited number of U.S. workers. And many workers lack the long-term attachment to an employment relationship necessary to make the new human resource management models work. These include the growing numbers of temporary, part-time, or flexible-contract employees and the growing numbers of professionals who hold a greater attachment to their occupation than to their employer. These workers may serve as a fertile ground for new approaches to recruiting and retaining union members.

At the same time, although some workers remain suspicious of union leaders and labor institutions, many appear to be attracted to a representational system that addresses workplace and strategic issues when those issues have a direct influence on their employment security and working conditions. These unmet needs for workplace and strategic representation have led unions and the AFL-CIO to begin to rethink some of their basic strategies and a rival, Change to Win, labor federation split off from the AFL-CIO. But whether lasting and deep changes in unions' organizing and representational strategies follow and whether these changes are linked to a new union political strategy remain to be seen.

Collective bargaining is the most central activity carried out by unions in the United States, given the business unionist focus in the American labor movement. At the same time, American unions are active in political and community affairs. The national unions participate in activities that include bargaining, political lobbying, and organizing drives, and they oversee the operation of member local unions.

Unions rely heavily on the participation of their members to elect officers and form their policies and strategies. With few exceptions, there is much democracy in the internal operation of American unions. Democracy is evident in the wide-ranging debates now occurring in unions over how they should respond to membership declines and environmental pressures.

Discussion Questions

1. What is the basic union philosophy in the United States? Discuss some of the debates surrounding this philosophy.

2. Various demographic features or characteristics, such as type of occupation, physical location, and other demographic trends, play a large role in union membership. Describe some of these characteristics or features.

3. The text gives seven possible explanations for the recent decline in union membership. Briefly discuss these possible reasons.

4. The structure of a national union is extremely important in its ability to negotiate successful contracts with employers. Discuss the role union jurisdiction plays in this structure.

5. Since the merger of the AFL-CIO many unions have merged and consolidated their memberships and structures. What are some of the arguments the proponents use in defending this practice? What are some of the arguments against this practice?

6. Describe the initiatives launched by the AFL-CIO under President John Sweeney's leadership and why some union leaders felt the need to create another federation, Change to Win, even in the face of these initiatives.

7. Do you think the split between the AFL-CIO and Change to Win (CTW) will strengthen or weaken the labor movement?

Related Web Sites

International Brotherhood of Teamsters:
http://www.teamster.org

American Federation of State, County, and Municipal Employees (AFSCME):
http://www.afscme.org

Service Employees Union (SEIU):
http://www.seiu.org/seiutop.html

3M:
http://www.mmm.com/profile/looking/index.html

Allied Signal:
http://www.alliedsignal.com

Bureau of Labor Statistics:
http://www.bls.gov

Carpenters Union:
http://www.carpenters.org

Suggested Readings

Barbash, Jack. *American Unions: Structure, Government and Politics* (New York: Random House, 1967).

Hurd, Richard. "Contesting the Dinosaur Image—The Labor Movement's Search for a Future," in *Industrial Relations at the Dawn of a New Millennium,* ed. M. Neufeld and J. McKelvery (Ithaca: NYSSILR, Cornell University, 1998).

Sayles, Leonard R., and George Strauss. *The Local Union* (New York: Harcourt, Brace and World, 1967).

Ulman, Lloyd. *The Rise of the National Trade Union* (Cambridge, MA: Harvard University Press, 1958).

End Notes

1. COPE is funded by voluntary contributions. Its activities include voter registration, efforts to encourage union members and supporters to vote, and the circulation of information on political matters and pending legislation.

2. http://stats.bls.gov/news.release/union2.nr0.htm

3. The figures for unionism in the service sector reported in Exhibits 6–2 and 6–3 may appear inconsistent, but they are not. The tables utilize different definitions of "service" work. Exhibit 6–2 reports unionism by industrial sector, whereas Exhibit 6–3 reports unionism by occupation.

4. http://stats.bls.gov/news.release/union2.nr0.htm

5. Ibid.

6. Ibid.

7. See Gary N. Chaison and Dileep G. Dhavale, "A Note on the Severity of the Decline in Union Organizing," *Industrial and Labor Relations Review* 23, no. 4 (April 1990): 366–73.

8. John R. Commons, *A Documentary History of American Industrial Society,* Vol. 5 (Cleveland: Arthur H. Clark, 1911), p. 19.

9. Lloyd Ulman, *The Rise of the National Trade Union* (Cambridge, MA: Harvard University Press, 1958), pp. 4–6.

10. See Orley Ashenfelter and John H. Pencavel, "American Trade Union Growth, 1900–1960," *Quarterly Journal of Economics* 83 (August 1969): 434–48.

11. Richard B. Freeman, "Unionism Comes to the Public Sector," *Journal of Economic Literature* 24 (March 1986): 42-86; Gregory Saltzman, "Bargaining Laws as a Cause and Consequence of Teacher Unionism," *Industrial and Labor Relations Review* 38, no. 2 (April 1985): 335–51.

12. Jack Fiorito and Cheryl L. Maranto, "The Contemporary Decline of Union Strength," *Contemporary Policy Issues,* n. 3 (July 1987): 12–27.

13. Henry S. Farber, "The Extent of Unionization in the United States," *Challenges and Choices Facing American Labor,* ed. Thomas A. Kochan (Cambridge, MA: MIT Press, 1985), pp. 15–43.

14. Common management campaign election tactics are discussed more fully in the next chapter.

15. Seymour Martin Lipset, "North American Labor Movements: A Comparative Perspective," in *Unions in Transition,* ed. Seymour Martin Lipset (San Francisco: ICS Press, 1986), pp. 421–52.

16. Peter G. Bruce, "Political Parties and Labor Legislation in Canada and the U.S.," *Industrial Relations* 28 (Spring 1989): 115–41.

17. See Paula Voos, "Union Organizing: Costs and Benefits," *Industrial and Labor Relations Review* 36 (July 1983): 576–91.

18. Richard B. Freeman, "Why Are Unions Faring So Poorly in NLRB Representation Elections?" in *Challenges and Choices Facing American Labor,* pp. 45–64; William

T. Dickens and Jonathan S. Leonard, "Accounting for the Decline in Union Membership, 1950–1980," *Industrial and Labor Relations Review* 38 (April 1985): 323–34.

19. Jelle Visser, "Why Fewer Workers Join Unions in Europe," *British Journal of Industrial Relations,* 40 (September 2002): 403–430.

20. Richard W. Hurd, "Contesting the Dinosaur Image—The U.S. Labor Movement's Search for a Future," *Transfer* 7 (Autumn 2001): 463.

21. For a comprehensive assessment of union mergers see Gary N. Chaison, *When Unions Merge* (Lexington, MA: D.C. Heath, 1986).

22. Courtney D. Gifford, *Directory of U.S. Labor Organizations, 2001 Edition* (Washington, DC: Bureau of National Affairs, 2001).

23. For a critical view of union mergers, see George W. Brooks and Sara Gamm, "The Causes and Effects of Union Mergers," report to the U.S. Department of Labor (September 1976).

24. "Stern Outlines How He Would Change Labor Movement to Boost Organizing," *Daily Labor Report* 120, June 23, 2004: C-1.

25. "Four Unions Offer Joint Reform Plan for AFL-CIO, Call for New Leadership," *Daily Labor Report* 94, May 17, 2005: C-1.

26. "Five Unions Form Coalition to Pressure AFL-CIO Leadership, Push for Change," *Daily Labor Report* 115, June 16, 2005: AA-1.

27. "SEIU, IBT Disaffiliate from AFL-CIO, Announce Plan to Set Up New Federation," *Daily Labor Report* 142, July 26, 2005: AA-1.

28. Ibid.

Part 3

The Functional Level of Industrial Relations

Chapter 7

Union Organizing and Bargaining Structures

Chapters 7, 8, 9, and 10 examine the middle (functional) level of industrial relations activity. The focus in this chapter is on the election process that creates, or organizes labor into, new unions and the bargaining structures that determine which employees are covered by a collective bargaining contract.

In some ways the representation election is the most important step in collective bargaining. If unorganized workers vote not to be represented by a union, for instance, collective bargaining cannot proceed. On the other hand, positive expression of worker interest in such an election opens the way for subsequent bargaining.

Various environmental factors shape the parties' power and preferences in the organizing process. The law, for example, plays a prominent role in union organizing drives and representation elections. Environmental factors also exert an important influence on the determination of the formal bargaining structures through which a union and management engage in bargaining. Strike leverage and the economic environment, for example, are prominent not only in their effects on organizing success but also in shaping the parties' preferences for particular bargaining structures.

Union Organizing

unions need to win election before having a bargaining representative.

Negotiations cannot take place until a bargaining representative has been duly certified as the exclusive representative of the employees. Normally, this requires that a union win a representation election (although an employer may voluntarily recognize a union if the union can demonstrate that it represents a majority of the employees involved).[1] The events and regulations that surround representation elections are described below.

The Organizing Process

30% for election to take place.

The key steps in the organizing and representation election process are described in Box 7–1. Note that before the NLRB will schedule an election, at least 30 percent of the election unit must have signed an **authorization card** indicating they would like an election to be held. Box 7–2 is a copy of an actual informational flyer and union authorization card used in

1. Interested employees seek out a union to learn their rights and gain help in organizing, or a union seeks out a group of employees in order to explain their rights and explore their interest in organizing.

2. The union builds support for organizing among the employees and solicits their signatures on authorization cards.

3. When sufficient cards are signed to indicate substantial employee support, the union asks for recognition as the bargaining agent for the employees. If at least 30 percent of the employees have signed cards, the union can petition for an NLRB certification election. If over 50 percent of the employees have signed cards, the union can ask the employer for recognition, or, if this is refused and serious unfair labor practices are committed by the employer, the union can ask the NLRB for certification. If the employer does not voluntarily recognize the union, either party can petition for an NLRB certification election to determine whether the union has majority support.

4. The NLRB investigates to determine whether an election should be held. The board considers the issues of whether it has jurisdiction, whether there is sufficient interest among the workers, and whether there is already a bargaining agent or there had been an election within the past 12 months. Most importantly, the NLRB determines the appropriate bargaining unit.

5. If the NLRB finds that the conditions for an election have been met, it orders that one be held. Procedures of varying formality are used, depending on the level of disagreement between the parties. Expedited procedures can be used if the union has engaged in organizational or recognitional picketing.

6. With the election date set, campaigning on both sides intensifies. Restrictions apply to both union and management behavior during this period, in an attempt to maintain "laboratory conditions," that is, to allow the workers to make free, uncoerced choices.

7. Representatives of the NLRB conduct a secret-ballot election. An individual's right to vote can be challenged by the union, by management, or by the NLRB. If there are more than two choices on the ballot and no option receives a majority vote, a runoff election will be held between the two choices that received the most votes.

8. If the union wins the election, then, following any objections or appeals, the NLRB certifies the union as the exclusive bargaining agent for the employees. The employer has the obligation to begin negotiating a first contract. If the employer wins the election, there can be no further election for 12 months.

a recent organizing campaign. To understand how the organizing process works, it is useful to step back and first ask why an individual might seek union representation.

Why Workers Might Want Union Representation

Evidence shows that for workers to express a preference for unionizing they must (1) be deeply dissatisfied with their current job and employment conditions, (2) believe that unionization can be helpful in improving those job conditions, and (3) be willing to overcome the generally negative stereotype of unions held by the population as a whole.

Workers might turn to unions because of their concerns with employment conditions or because they are unsatisfied with the process by which decisions are made at their workplace. Thus, workers might, for example, vote in favor of the union in the hope that subsequent contractual negotiations will improve wages. Or, a worker might be angered by a recent managerial decision, such as a layoff or a disappointing performance appraisal. In these cases the worker might turn to the union with the hope that the union will either

Yes, I am ready to join with other workers to win good family wage
jobs and a better future for workers in the Puget Sound.

Signing a card is just the first step. Building union power takes everyone getting
involved. Here's what you can do.

☑ Attend a union meeting.
☑ Ask other workers to sign a card.
☑ Pass out information about our union campaign.
☑ Stand up for our rights to organize.

Call Teamsters Local 174 for more information.

Detach and return card to the driver who gave it to you or mail in to Union.

Authorization Card for Union Representation

I will join with other workers to build a better future. I hereby authorize Teamsters
Local 174 to act as my exclusive bargaining agent and to represent me in
negotiations with my Employer for wages, hours and working conditions.

PRINT NAME   SOCIAL SECURITY #

PRINT ADDRESS   CITY   ZIP

PHONE   OWNER-OPERATOR or DRIVER

PRINT EMPLOYER'S NAME   LICENSE #

SIGNATURE   DATE

This card distributed by: (Print Name): _____

---

improve future management decisions or, at a minimum, give employees greater voice in
the process by which future decisions are made.

Evidence on employee motives for voting in favor of union representation is provided in
a survey by Richard Freeman and Joel Rogers reported in Exhibit 7–1. The survey evidence
shows that a very significant factor in employees' decision to unionize is their confidence
and trust in management and employees' feelings as to whether they are being treated fairly
by management.

Union Campaign Practices

Unions commonly rely on organizers to rally employee support during election campaigns.
These organizers often include paid full-time staff from existing unions who travel from
campaign to campaign. The union also often enlists some of the existing workforce to

EXHIBIT 7–1
**Employee
Motives for
Voting to
Unionize**

Source: Survey
evidence reported in
Richard B. Freeman
and Joel Rogers,
*What Do Workers
Want?* (Ithaca: Cornell
University Press,
1999).

Nonunion employees are more likely to say they would vote for a union when they also say that:

1. Relations between employees and management are bad.
2. They do not trust management.
3. They believe management shows little concern for employees.
4. They dislike their job.
5. They are dissatisfied with their influence and the workplace.
6. They believe management is unwilling to share power.

assist as organizers. Organizers and union supporters use a variety of mechanisms to try to promote a pro-union message. Group meetings are often held after work hours in a local church or community meeting room. Or, union supporters who have the opportunity to move around the plant (often these are craft workers) might spread the message during work hours.[2]

Management's Campaign Practices

Management is rarely a passive observer in the election process. Management often tries to design personnel and other corporate policies far in advance of any representation election to dissuade employees from favoring union representation. It is useful to review these tactics because they can be as important to the election outcome as the tactics management might carry out during an election campaign.

Common strategies used by management before the onset of organizing campaigns to reduce the incentives to unionize include most, if not all, of the following:

1. Wages and fringe benefits equal to or greater than those paid comparable workers in the local labor market.
2. A high rate of investment per worker in such employee programs as training and career development.
3. Extensive efforts to stabilize employment and avoid layoffs as much as possible.
4. Advanced systems of organizational communications and information sharing.
5. Informal mechanisms for, or encouragement of, participation in decision making about the way work is to be performed.
6. Development of a psychological climate that fosters and rewards organizational loyalty and commitment.
7. Rational wage and salary administration, performance appraisal, and promotion systems that reward merit but also recognize seniority.
8. A nonunion grievance procedure (usually without binding arbitration).
9. Location of new production or service facilities in rural areas or areas only sparsely unionized.

Management does not always have the will or foresight to put all the above policies in place. And even where some of them are in place, election campaigns can arise.

If faced with a representation election, management typically will adopt a number of tactics in an effort to convince employees to vote against union representation. Management

Although the NLRB rarely exercises its authority to order management to recognize a union, this does sometimes happen in the face of egregious employer violations of the nation's labor laws. A case occurred at a Nevada casino hotel, The Flamingo Hilton. The starting point was an organizing campaign run in 1993 by the United Steelworkers. Employees voted in 1993 by 495 to 389 against union representation after a bitter campaign. The Steelworkers then challenged the election vote claiming that Flamingo management had committed a number of unfair labor practices in the campaign. In August 1997, the NLRB set aside the election and ordered Flamingo management to recognize and bargain with the union.

The NLRB issued the bargaining order because, among other things, it found that Flamingo management had unlawfully screened job applicants based on their views toward unionization before and after the 1993 election.

The Board also found that Hilton executives were actively involved in an "unlawful campaign against the union." The list of unfair labor practices Flamingo was found to have committed include changing its health policy before the union election; increasing employee wages before the election and telling employees that the pay raise would be lost if the union won; implementing a complaint resolution procedure on election eve; soliciting employee complaints and implying that matters would be resolved if the union was defeated; and prohibiting employees from talking to one another about the union and interrogating employees coercively about their union sentiments.

Source: "NLRB: Labor Board Affirms Bargaining Order for Steelworkers Local at Flamingo Hotel," *Daily Labor Report,* August 11, 1997, 154, p. D–7.

---

will call meetings with employees (these might be individual or group) to explain its case. Under the NLRA management is allowed to hold these meetings on company time and in company facilities (the law allows so-called captive audience speeches up to 24 hours before the vote).[3] During such a meeting a management spokesperson (such as the company president) might remind the employees of the direct costs of union membership (dues) or the potential losses in income employees could withstand during any strikes that ensue.

no threat or promises, but predictions allowed

During the election campaign employers are not allowed by the NLRA to threaten to punish workers if they join or vote for a union. The NLRA also forbids employers from making promises to workers that might encourage them to reject the union. But an employer may make a prediction about the future if the prediction is based on fact. So an employer may say workers could be laid off if the union wins the election and successfully negotiates for a 50-cent raise—provided the employer has the evidence that a 50-cent raise would lead to layoffs.[4]

The NLRA empowers the NLRB to recognize and bargain with a union if it finds that an employer has committed egregious violations of the labor law during a representation campaign. Although the NLRB rarely issues bargaining orders, Box 7–3 describes a recent case where the Board did so.

It is now common for firms to hire consultants or law firms to either shape or directly carry out management's campaign. The materials in Box 7–4 depict some of the campaign literature issued by the union and management involved in the same organizing election. Imagine that you were an employee involved in this campaign and you received this literature. Would this material sway your decision to vote for or against union representation? Box 7–5 is a sample of the actual ballot used in a recent union representation election.

An Example of Management's Campaign Literature

Dear Fellow Employee:

Think about the election which will be held here at the plant on April 21. It is extremely important that we consider some very important things. What has our company done for you over the years? We provide jobs and a job today, particularly a steady one, is not as easy to get and hold on to as it was at one time. You know and I know that your company pays good wages and provides good fringe benefits such as paid holidays, paid vacations, pension plan, and a group hospital and life insurance plan. Also, NEVER FORGET THE CHRISTMAS BONUS EACH YEAR AND THE AMOUNT OF THE BONUS. Yes, your Company was interested in you long before the union organizers came along with their bill for union dues, assessments, per capita tax, and all these other names the union boys have for getting money out of the paychecks of employees.

Who are these outside union organizers and why are they here? They live off money collected by the Union from members, and they don't sell anything--except wild promises which they cannot guarantee. Now they have the nerve to ask you to help pay their expenses and their salaries. If this Union should win this election--though I know you will not allow this to happen as you have rejected this same bunch many times in the past years--one of the first things the Union would want is a "dues checkoff." This would mean that if you authorized it, union dues would be deducted from your paycheck and paid directly to the union. Yes, the Union wants to make sure they get their hook in you and keep it in you. Has the Union told you that this is what they will ask for? What about all the rules and regulations of this Union? There are two Union constitutions involved and they total over 95 pages. Were you given a copy of these rules and regulations by the Union organizers when they came to your home at night?

Talk this election over with your family. This is important to all of you. Remember--the Union did not give you your job and has never paid your wages and never will--the only thing a Union can truly guarantee is that Union members will have to pay the Union money--each and every month!

VOTE NO--MEANING NO UNION!

Sincerely,

John Smith
President

Strength.

That's what it takes to build a Union.
That's always what it takes to do what's right.

On Friday, just two days from now, we have a chance to show our strength.

*—It takes **strength** to talk seriously about the real issues: Insurance, 9-Day Rule, Seniority, Holidays, Funeral Pay, Favoritism, Respect on the Job.*

*—It takes **strength** to answer the tough questions.*

*—It takes **strength** to build an organization to make better lives for ourselves and our families.*

*—It even takes **strength** to sit there and listen to Mr. Smith's speeches knowing he refuses a fair, open, public debate.*

But we've done it. And we're proud of it!

We're strong. We're United. We're going to win!

For Our Families. For Our Future.

VOTE ☑ YES!

UNITED STATES OF AMERICA
National Labor Relations Board

SAMPLE

OFFICIAL SECRET BALLOT
For Certain Employees of
Delavan Industries, Inc.
Blasdell & West Seneca, NY

Do you wish to be represented for purposes of collective bargaining by

UNITED AUTOMOBILE, AEROSPACE & AGRICULTURAL IMPLEMENT WORKERS OF AMERICA, UAW?

MARK AN "X" IN THE SQUARE OF YOUR CHOICE

YES	NO
☐	☐

DO NOT SIGN THIS BALLOT. Fold and drop in ballot box.
If you spoil this ballot return it to the Board Agent for a new one.

The Election Unit

The election unit serves as the basis for the bargaining unit. The **election unit** is the group of employees that the NLRB (or the appropriate state agency with jurisdiction over the employees involved) determines is covered under the appropriate statute and is eligible to vote in the representation election.

Two main decisions must be made to define the appropriate election unit. First, the range of employees to be included must be decided. This may involve choosing between a craft election unit structure (covering only workers in a single occupation) and an industrial election unit structure (for example, all the blue-collar production and maintenance workers within a plant) and between employees at one plant or location and employees at multiple plants or job sites. Second, the issue of who functions as a supervisor or manager must be decided because, since the passage in 1947 of the Taft-Hartley amendments to the National Labor Relations Act, supervisors have been excluded from coverage of the act.

The Scope of the Unit—The NLRB's Criteria

Since the composition of the electorate can influence the outcome of the election, the scope of the election unit is often a hotly contested issue. Quite simply, the union typically will seek an election unit that maximizes its ability to win the election, and the employer will seek a unit that minimizes the union's chances of winning. The NLRA states that the fundamental objective in choosing an election unit should be to ensure that employees have "the full freedom in exercising the rights guaranteed by this act."

The NLRB and the state and local boards normally consider the following general criteria in deciding on the appropriate election unit:

1. The community of interests among the employees.
2. The potential effects of alternative units on stability in the labor-management relationship.
3. The need to provide sufficient freedom of choice to professional and skilled employees.
4. The history of bargaining or the employer's decision-making structure.

This fourth criterion is useful in resolving disputes between the parties over whether certain employees should be excluded because they perform supervisory or managerial functions.

Whether craft workers are put into the same election unit as production workers in the same plant (or company) is a difficult part of the election unit determination process. Although Section 9(b)(2) of the Taft-Hartley Act was designed to limit the NLRB's ability to put craft workers into industrial election units, the board has consistently rejected petitions to exclude craft workers from the large industrial units. Indeed, the board has argued that the interdependence between craft workers and production workers warrants a single comprehensive unit.[5]

The NLRB has been somewhat more willing to grant professional employees a separate bargaining unit. Section 9(b) of Taft-Hartley prohibits the NLRB from including professional employees in a bargaining unit with nonprofessional employees unless the professionals decide by a majority vote to be included in a larger, more comprehensive unit.

Election Unit Determination in Hospitals

The spread of bargaining to hospitals and the public sector has raised a number of questions about appropriate election units. Hospitals, for example, exhibit a wide range of fine distinctions among various professional and quasi-professional employees and vast differences in the nature of the tasks each group performs. The NLRB was asked to determine whether these various employees should be put into common election units when unions sought to organize various hospitals in the 1970s and 1980s. Should registered nurses, practical nurses, and nurses' aides all be included in a single unit, for example, or should they be separated into three distinct units for the purposes of a representation election? Should nurses be in the same election unit as hospital office or laboratory staffs?

The NLRB resolved these questions initially by establishing separate units for each of the following: registered nurses and laboratory specialists; business office and clerical employees; and service and maintenance employees. Later decisions of the NLRB, however, favored fewer and broader units. In 1990 the NLRB again reversed itself and decided to favor narrow units. Hospital employers then appealed this decision to the federal courts, where the debate continues.

Union Organizing Success Rates

In 2005, labor unions won 61.5 percent (1,302 out of 2,117) of the representation elections conducted.[6] This figure declined steadily after 1964, when unions won 61 percent of all the representation elections held, but has risen steadily since 1996. In 2005, unions organized some 63,700 workers through NLRB elections, down from 84,000 in the previous year. In 2004, unions won 63 percent of elections held for units of less than 50 employees,

EXHIBIT 7–2
Nonunion Employees' Desire for Unionization

If an election were held today to decide whether employees like you should be represented by a union, would you vote for the union or against it?		
	Public Sector	**Private Sector**
For the union	39%	32%
Against it	48	55

Source: Richard B. Freeman and Joel Rogers, *What Do Workers Want?* (Ithaca: Cornell University Press, 1999).

compared to a win rate of only 46.7 percent for units with more than 500 employees.[7] In large, multiplant companies unions have had trouble even securing enough signed authorization cards to certify to the board that an election should be held.[8]

Union involvement in representation elections and win rates in those elections vary much by union. The Teamsters are the most active union in representation elections by participating in 555 representation elections in 2005, accounting for more than one-fourth of all NLRB representation elections. The union involved in the second highest number of representation elections was the SEIU with 196 elections in 2005. The Laborers was the most successful of all unions in representation elections, winning 72.1 percent of NLRB elections in which it participated. The SEIU ranked second, winning 69.4 percent of its elections.

At the same time, the low level of recent union organizing success and the fact that less than 14 percent of the work force is now unionized should not be taken to mean that only a small fraction of the American work force desire union representation.[9] Exhibit 7–2 reports recent survey evidence compiled by Professors Richard Freeman and Joel Rogers showing that a sizable number of nonunion employees actually desire union representation. If you combine the 32 percent of nonunion private sector employees who desire union representation with the 90 percent of already unionized employees who want to maintain their union representation (as reported in Exhibit 7–3), then Freeman and Rogers calculate that 44 percent of the private sector work force desire union representation.

The number of public sector employees who desire union representation is even larger, as shown in Exhibit 7–2. This leads Freeman and Rogers to conclude that there is a sizable "representation gap" in the United States, given the difference between the large percentage of employees expressing a desire for union representation and the low percentage of employees currently represented.

In response to declining unionization American unions have adopted new organizing strategies (described later in this chapter). One aspect of the new organizing approaches of American unions is intensified efforts to organize professional employees and as Box 7–6 describes this includes organizing campaigns among university graduate assistants.

[handwritten: 44% private desire representation]

EXHIBIT 7–3
Union Members' Desire for a Continuation of Their Union Representation

If a new election were held today to decide whether to keep the union, would you vote to keep it or get rid of it?		
	Public Sector	**Private Sector**
Keep the union	83%	90%
Get rid of the union	13	8

Note: These responses are from a sample of unionized employees.
Source: Richard B. Freeman and Joel Rogers, *What Do Workers Want?* (Ithaca: Cornell University Press, 1999).

The Unionization of University Graduate Students   Box 7–6

The new century has seen a surge in organizing campaigns aimed at professional employees including university graduate students. According to Paul Almeida, president of the Department of Professional Employees at the AFL-CIO, universities are acting like companies when they seek only to "maintain the bottom line . . ."

The first successful unionization of university graduate assistants occurred at the University of Wisconsin in 1969. Collective bargaining, regulated by state public sector statutes, spread to other public universities over the next three decades, including the SUNY system in New York and the UC system in California. From 1999 to the spring of 2002, 32 additional public universities recognized graduate student bargaining agents. While the formation of graduate student union is somewhat of an anomaly, because unions traditionally arise in situations where workers have a long-term attachment to a firm, it was encouraged by the following factors. From 1970 to 2000, the median total years between the granting of baccalaureate and doctoral degrees increased by 1.5, while the fraction of PhDs finding employment declined substantially. This lengthening of the time it took students to earn a degree and the smaller and more distant payoffs contributed to a lack of economic security among graduate students and thus made them more susceptible to unionization.

In late 2000, the National Labor Relations Board extended the right to unionize to graduate teaching assistants at private universities. In the aftermath of this decision in January of 2002, New York University (NYU) and the United Auto Workers (UAW) reached the first collective bargaining agreement between a private university and its graduate teaching and research assistants. The NYU-UAW four-year agreement raised stipends for many graduate students by nearly 40 percent. The University also agreed to pay the full cost of health care benefits. In return, NYU retained control over academic decisions, such as which courses graduate students will teach and how many students will be in their classes. A no-strike provision was also included in the contract.

Efforts to organize graduate students have spread to other private universities such as Harvard, Columbia, and Cornell. Disgruntled graduate students accused university officials of exploiting them as cheap labor to compensate for a lack of tenured professors. At Columbia University administrators opposed the union on the grounds that the standard of higher education and the collegial relationship between students and faculty

advisors were at risk. In April 2002, Columbia filed an appeal with the NLRB, asking it to overrule the NYU decision because graduate students who teach as part of their academic training receive financial aid and thus should not be viewed as normal employees. A judgment in this case could take months.

Graduate student organizing at universities contributed to an expansion of unionization among professional occupations to the point that in 2002, 23 percent of all professional employees were unionized.

In July 2004 in a case involving graduate assistants at Brown University, the NLRB reversed its previous decision from the 2000 New York University case and held that graduate assistants are predominantly students not employees, resulting in their not having the right to engage in collective bargaining under federal labor law. This decision does not affect the right of graduate assistants at public universities to engage in collective bargaining under state labor laws, but it does remove the protections of labor law for graduate assistant unions seeking to organize at private universities. The decision also casts doubt over whether medical residents, interns and similar groups are also covered by federal labor law.

Although lack of coverage by federal labor law does not mean that existing collective bargaining relationships are automatically ended or contracts voided, it does assist employers in taking steps to terminate collective bargaining. For example, following the NLRB decision in the Brown University case, New York University decided to terminate collecting bargaining and end its recognition of the union representing its graduate assistants upon the termination of its initial collective bargaining agreement on August 31, 2005. After New York University's refusal to bargain a second contract, the graduate assistants union launched a strike in November 2005 to pressure the university to recognize the union and return to the bargaining table. Although the strike continued until the end of the 2005–06 academic year, the union did not succeed in pressuring the university to reverse its position and collective bargaining has not resumed at NYU.

Source: "NYU Becomes First Private University to Reach Pact with Graduate Assistants." *Daily Labor Report* 22, February 2, 2001:A-2. "NLRB 3-2 Reverses NYU, Won't Allow University Graduate Assistants to Organize." *Daily Labor Report* 136, July 16, 2004: AA-1; and "NYU Graduate Assistants Return to Jobs as Academic Year Begins." *Daily Labor Report* 175, September 11, 2006: A-6.

Even if a union wins a majority vote in a representation election, this does not ensure that a first contract will be negotiated. The NLRA requires that employers (and the union) bargain in good faith, but the law does not require that the parties reach agreement. In fact, first contracts are won in roughly only two-thirds of newly designated units.

Does the Election Campaign Influence How Workers Vote?

Research has shown that workers tend to become less inclined to vote for union representation if the election is delayed.[10] Studies also show that illegal employer behavior during the election campaign (a signal of aggressive employer opposition to bargaining) further reduces the probability that a first contract will be settled.[11] Evidence also shows that firms with previously poor worker-supervisor relations and low wages are more likely to commit unfair labor practice violations during election campaigns.[12]

There is controversial evidence over the extent to which election campaigns actually affect how individuals vote in representation elections. In the 1970s, for example, Julius Getman, Stephen Goldberg, and Jeanne Herman studied more than 30 election campaigns and concluded that illegal campaign tactics by either employers or unions had little effect on individual voting or on election outcomes.[13] They therefore argued that the NLRB should expend less effort in regulating campaign conduct (specifically, by investigating the accuracy of campaign statements, promises of benefits, or threats by either party).[14] Reanalysis of the Getman data and other studies of NLRB elections, however, shows that employer strategies both before and during election processes do significantly reduce the probability that a union will win an election.[15] Moreover, it also appears that employer opposition significantly reduces the chances that a union that wins a representation election will be successful in negotiating a first contract.[16]

Union Decertification

Unions gain members through winning union representation elections; they lose members through **decertification elections.** The 1947 Taft-Hartley amendments to the NLRA prescribed election procedures for decertifying a union.

The decertification elections held since Taft-Hartley have been far fewer than the representation elections, but in recent years their number has been increasing, and unions have been losing an increasing percentage of these contests. The first year after passage of Taft-Hartley, for example, witnessed 97 decertification elections, or only 3 percent of the 3,822 representation elections held that year. That percentage held steady throughout the 1950s and 1960s but began creeping upward in the 1970s. In 2005, there were 331 decertification elections. Unions retained representation rights in 33.5 percent of these decertification elections.[17]

Although decertification elections have increased, most union members appear to be satisfied by their unions and union leaders. A recent survey finds that union members are generally very satisfied with their personal experiences with the unions at their workplaces as revealed in the responses reported in Exhibit 7–4. Also, the survey data in Exhibit 7–3 show that 90 percent of union members would vote to keep their union if given the chance to directly vote on the issue.

The Debate Over Labor Law Reform

Unions' low win rate in representation elections has led to much debate over whether the endorsement of collective bargaining that is provided in the NLRA is being fulfilled.

EXHIBIT 7–4
Union
Members'
Satisfaction
with Their
Unions

How would you describe your personal experience with the union or employee organization at your workplace?		
	Public Sector	**Private Sector**
Very good	24%	26%
Good	40	45
Bad	6	5
Very bad	2	2
Neither good nor bad	26	22

Note: These responses are from a sample of unionized employees.
Source: Richard B. Freeman and Joel Rogers, *What Do Workers Want?* (Ithaca: Cornell University Press, 1999).

Remember, the original objective of the law was to ensure that employees are able to exercise free choice regarding union representation, untrammeled by false promises or information, threats of reprisals or promises of benefits, or misuse of economic power by the employer or the union.[18] To carry out this objective, the NLRB (and most state labor boards) attempted to establish **laboratory conditions** for the election process. The notion was that workers should be free to judge whether they wanted union representation in an environment free of coercion and misinformation.

Advocates of **labor law reform** often argue that penalties imposed on employers who commit unlawful behavior during an election campaign are too weak. Furthermore, they claim that the procedures for remedying unfair labor practices and or holding representation elections are too protracted. It is also argued that too often employers merely move or close operations as part of union avoidance strategies. The case of La Conexion, described in Box 7–7, illustrates many of these employer tactics and suggests why the labor movement is so frustrated with current procedures.

The last major congressional debate over labor law reform occurred in 1977 and 1978. Labor law reform bills introduced then would have imposed harsher penalties on labor law violators, required stricter time limits on the election process, and provided stronger remedies for victims of unfair labor practices. The bills were not passed (one bill passed the House of Representatives, but died in a filibuster in the Senate in 1978). In 1991, Congress debated labor law amendments that would limit employers' ability to hire permanent replacements during a strike. Then in 1994, a presidential commission, the so-called **Dunlop Commission,** recommended a number of changes in labor laws and the application of existing laws to overcome delays and other tactics employers have been using to oppose union organizing. These will be discussed in more detail in Chapter 15. But in the end, the Dunlop Commission's recommendations were ignored. As a result, the debate continues over the performance of the nation's labor policies.

Box 7–8 summarizes a number of the recommendations that have been made by advocates of labor law reform with little success. In the absence of legal reforms, many unionists and analysts suggest that aggressive employer union avoidance has become more common in recent years. This has led union activists to turn to increased union organizing efforts and to turn to nontraditional union organizing tactics.

In November 1997 the U.S. Court of Appeals for the District of Columbia Circuit reversed a ruling of the NLRB and found that Sprint had sound business reasons for closing its La Conexion Familiar facility. The closing had occurred three and a half years earlier, in July 1994, eight days before a scheduled representation election that was to be held among the facilities 177 Spanish-speaking workforce.

In August 1995, in response to an appeal by the Communications Workers of America, the union that had been leading the organizing drive at La Conexion, an NLRB administrative law judge found that the company had engaged in an extensive anti-union campaign replete with threats to close, but he declined to provide a remedy. In December 1995, the NLRB concluded that Sprint was guilty of "widespread misconduct, demonstrating a general disregard for the employees' fundamental rights." The board told Sprint to cease and desist from "threatening employees with the closure of any of its facilities if the union comes in." The NLRB did not require that the facility be opened. Rather, the board had told Sprint to offer each employee reinstatement to a position in its existing operations that is substantially equivalent to the employees' former jobs. The board also ordered that back pay be calculated from the date of termination to the offer of reinstatement.

Sprint then appealed the NLRB's decision to the U.S. Court of Appeals, which reversed the board's decision. In overturning the NLRB the court said that an "enormous body of financial data and testimony" pointed to the conclusion that the facility was closed due to grim financial performance, not as an attempt to thwart a union drive in violation of the NLRA. At the same time, the court acknowledged that Sprint had conducted an "illegal anti-union campaign" in the spring of 1994 and had created a "false paper trail" to head off any future questions about whether the facility was closed in violation of the NLRA.

This case has international significance as it led to the first complaint filed against the United States under the auspices of the North American Free Trade Agreement's labor side accord.

Sources: "Sprint Lawfully Shut Down Division During Union Campaign, Court Rules," *Daily Labor Report,* November 26, 1997, no. 228, p. D–9; and "NLRB Orders Sprint to Rehire 177 Workers at La Conexion Familiar," *Daily Labor Report,* December 31, 1996, no. 250, p. D–5.

Nontraditional Union Organizing Tactics

Corporate Campaigns *public, financial, political pressure*

Given the great difficulties they have been faced with by using traditional election campaign tactics, several unions have adopted more aggressive **corporate campaigns** and other tactics designed to increase the chances of organizing new workers. Corporate campaigns involve a variety of union efforts to bring public, financial, or political pressures to bear on top management.

In its extensive corporate campaign against the J. P. Stevens Company in the late 1970s, for example, the Amalgamated Clothing and Textile Workers Union (ACTWU) waged a successful national boycott of Stevens products, threatened to withdraw the union pension funds from banks that had officers on Stevens' board, and, eventually, after almost a decade of effort, negotiated its first contract with the company in 1981. Similar efforts have been mounted in attempts to organize the operations of such firms as Beverly Nursing Homes.[19]

Most of the union corporate campaigns have been accompanied by strategies designed to influence the firm involved in the election indirectly by pressuring individuals or other

1. Provide unions with rights of access to employees for campaign purposes equal to the access enjoyed by employers.

2. Stop attempting to regulate statements by employers or unions made as part of election campaigns.

3. Speed up the enforcement of current rules governing elections, and strengthen the penalties imposed on violators of the law by:

   a. using court injunctions to stop and/or remedy serious violations of the law, such as discriminatory discharges during campaigns;

   b. reinstating employees quickly, in time to allow union supporters to return to employment *before* the campaign is over and the vote is held;

   c. allowing employees or the union to sue for civil damages in cases of an employer's willful violation of an employee's rights; and

   d. lifting the constraint on the amount of the settlement available to an employee in cases where employer conduct exhibits a consistent pattern of illegal behavior. (Under current law a court can only award a settlement equal to the wages lost by an employee since the time of discharge.)

4. Conduct speedy elections, with a very short time allowed for campaigning.

5. Strengthen the ability of a union to strike to achieve a first contract by eliminating the ability of an employer to permanently replace strikers and by allowing other workers to boycott the goods of an employer on strike.

6. Require arbitration of first contracts if an impasse occurs.

Sources: Paul C. Weiler, "Milestone or Millstone: The Wagner Act at Fifty," in *Arbitration 1985: Law and Practice,* ed. Walter J. Gershenfeld (Washington, DC: Bureau of National Affairs, 1986), pp. 37–67; and Charles J. Morris, *American Labor Policy: A Critical Appraisal of the National Labor Relations Act* (Washington, DC: Bureau of National Affairs, 1987).

firms that do business with or have interlocking directorates with the firm. These efforts attest to the unfairness labor leaders perceive and the frustrations they have experienced with the election process as it has been administered by the NLRB.

The Justice for Janitors Campaign

Since the late 1980s, the SEIU has led a campaign to organize janitors in a number of regions of the country using nontraditional tactics that in some cases seek to go outside the NLRA and NLRB procedures to gain union representation. This Justice for Janitors campaign tries to organize on a multiemployer (regional) basis and often avoids normal NLRB-style representation elections by inducing employers to voluntarily recognize the union. The janitors campaign often puts pressure on the primary employers that typically rely on subcontractors to provide janitorial services in their buildings, as at the Apple Corporation described in Box 7–9. The Justice for Janitors campaign also tries to use alliances with community groups such as churches to gain public support for union organizing efforts.

The AFL-CIO Organizing Institute and the AFL-CIO Organizing Department

The AFL-CIO admitted the difficulties unions confronted in organizing in the well-publicized Evolution of Work report in 1985. In 1989 the AFL-CIO implemented one of the recommendations of the report by creating a new **AFL-CIO Organizing Institute.** The

In 1985, the Service Employee International Union (SEIU) launched its "Justice for Janitors" campaign in response to a strike by cleaning workers at Mellon Bank in Pittsburgh. The nationwide campaign to organize cleaning service workers has targeted high profile companies who contract out their cleaning services to nonunion cleaning companies. The SEIU targeted the large firms that use these nonunion cleaning companies, rather than the nonunion employers directly, because the union claims that the large firms set the standard for wages in the industry by determining the amount of money paid to the contractors. The union claims that the nonunion cleaning companies experience frequent wage and hour violations, provide poor wages and benefits, and make heavy use of undocumented workers. The SEIU cites figures showing that nonunion cleaning workers receive an average salary of $12,000 a year and no health care benefits.

Apple Computers Co., Hewlett-Packard, Carr Real Estate, Toyota Motor Corp., and Mattel Toys are among the large companies targeted by the campaign. In its Justice for Janitors campaigns the SEIU has used tactics such as picketing, demonstrations, coalitions with commercial groups, and negative corporate publicity to put pressure on both the large firms and the nonunion cleaning companies. Toyota and Mattel were placed on the union's annual "North America's Top Trash" list of antiworker companies.

The SEIU's organizing efforts have been successful in bringing 35,000 new members into the union. In its efforts to unionize the 4,000 janitors working in Washington's downtown commercial area, for example, the SEIU targeted Carr Real Estate Services Inc., Washington, D.C.,'s largest developer. Organizers used noisy street demonstrations, picketing in front of office buildings and officials' houses, and the publicizing of real estate tax breaks afforded big developers by the city to draw negative attention to the firm for its contract with nonunion cleaning companies. Carr Real Estate then filed unfair labor practice charges with the NLRB. An agreement eventually was signed between the parties, but Carr remained an SEIU organizing target.

In the spring of 1997, SEIU president Andrew Stern publicly acknowledged that the noisy demonstrations, traffic tie-ups, and civil disobedience against Carr and other Washington, DC, employers had produced too much antagonism. He pledged to end the strikes and pickets as well as the involvement of third parties in the dispute. Stern also emphasized that while a shifting of tactics was necessary, the union's goal continues to be the achievement of decent working conditions for janitors.

In 2000, the SEIU negotiated new collective bargaining agreements for more than 100,000 janitors in two dozen cities. The aim of the negotiations was to close the wage gap between janitors in cities and suburbs and increase the number of full-time jobs. By the end of the year, the union represented 185,000 janitors, 6.5 percent of employees nationally in this sector. However, in 22 major cities, the union represents 65 percent or more of eligible workers. The SEIU says it aims to continue to organize the majority of the market in geographic areas, since the only way to win significant improvements in a contract is to create "industry standards." Many employers hesitate to concede to better working conditions if their competitors are not organized and can benefit from lower wage rates.

The SEIU targeted three locations in the northeast for organizing campaigns in 2001: northern New Jersey, the suburbs of Philadelphia, and the city of Baltimore. The campaigns have been successful in all three areas, increasing the SEIU membership by 9,000. The higher wage rates negotiated in all of the new contracts do not go into effect until the majority of the cleaning service industry in each geographic area is organized. Wage rates in each area are expected to increase from $6.50 or $7.00 to $9.00 or $9.50.

In 2002, the SEIU turned its focus to two new areas in the northeast, the suburbs of Washington, D.C., and Boston. The SEIU's goals include organizing the low-wage, largely unorganized markets in the southeast and southwest so that national unionized companies can compete against local unorganized cleaning firms and increasing the percentage of full-time jobs in the suburbs.

Overall, the "Justice for Janitors" campaign has used innovative tactics to overcome enormous odds and organize unskilled workers in an extremely competitive industry. However, the campaign will face even tougher odds as it attempts to organize in the South and will have to make use of innovative organizing and bargaining strategies.

Source: "100,000 Janitors Covered in the SEIU Pacts Bargained During the 2000 in Two Dozen Cities," *Daily Labor Report* 229, November 28, 2000: C-1.

AFL-CIO has long had a department of organization and field services. The Organizing Institute was unique through its exclusive focus on organizing and through the clinical programs used to train new organizers. After John Sweeney's election to the presidency of the AFL-CIO, as discussed in the previous chapter, a new Organizing Department in the AFL-CIO was given a sizable budget and the task of extending the sort of activities begun in the Organizing Institute. In addition to recruitment and training of new organizers, the Organizing Department also provides affiliated unions with strategic planning and analysis for organizing campaigns. The AFL-CIO's Union Summer program funded college interns on summer union organizing projects.

A Rank-and-File Organizing Approach

One of the purposes of the organizing initiatives underway in the AFL-CIO is to diffuse some of the successful organizing strategies used by affiliated unions. Unions such as the Union of Needletrades, Industrial, and Textile Employees (UNITE) and the Service Employees International Union (SEIU) have had above-average success in their organizing. The campaigns of these unions use young, well-educated organizers and involve both extensive direct communication with prospective members and links to community groups such as churches. This approach to organizing has been labeled a *rank-and-file* style and contrasts with more top-down, traditional organizing that relied on appointed organizers and formal communication strategies. Rank-and-file organizing also tries to modernize and broaden the issues around which employees are attracted to unions by addressing child care, equal pay, and other issues that are of concern to the current work force. Research conducted by Kate Bronfenbrenner suggests that this rank-and-file method of union organizing has been more successful than traditional methods in the private sector.[20]

It is still too early to tell if the AFL-CIO will be able to greatly increase the use of rank-and-file organizing and whether this will have a significant impact on union organizing success.

Representation Election Employer Neutrality

Collective bargaining language concerning union organizing has become increasingly common.[21] Often included in such language is the employer's agreement to remain neutral in the organizing process. In the CWA, UAW, and USWA agreements, for example, neutrality is defined as "neither helping nor hindering" the union's organizing effort, but the contracts do allow managers to communicate "facts" to workers, in some cases only in reponse to inquiries. A different approach, typical of HERE agreements, is language that makes clear that the employer will not communicate opposition to union representation.[22] In a few cases employers have gone so far as to agree to inform employees that management welcomes union representation.

Union leaders argue that management should provide unions the opportunity to benefit from new investments and represent employees in new establishments. In some cases management has agreed and has accepted unions in new establishments if the union demonstrates flexibility and a commitment to labor-management cooperation.

One of the key strategic choices facing management is whether to contest unionism during a representation election or to voluntarily recognize the union in return for a more cooperative union–management relationship. Recent experience suggests that the parties can create a more positive working relationship by avoiding campaign election hostility and thereby start the union–management relationship off on a good footing. Unions have pushed management in recent years to use card check recognition, discussed more fully below, that goes even further than neutrality in assisting union organizing.

Voluntary Recognition

The NLRA allows employers to voluntarily recognize a union. The law, of course, also allows employers to remain neutral during a representation election campaign. In the 1940s and 1950s it was not uncommon for employers to either adopt **voluntary recognition** or maintain **employer election neutrality** during election campaigns. Employers' voluntary recognition of a union or neutrality in representation elections have declined relative to their use in the 1940s and 1950s. Nonetheless, there are some important exceptions to this trend.

The Xerox Case

Xerox is one exception. The Xerox Corporation has a bargaining relationship with UNITE (originally Xerox negotiated with ACTWU before that union merged with the ILGWU to form UNITE) that dates back to the 1930s. Because Joseph Wilson, the company's founder, believed strongly in the value of a positive labor-management climate and relationship, the company has historically remained neutral or unopposed to UNITE's representing Xerox production and maintenance workers when the company opened new plants. (Yet it is still the union's responsibility to seek and achieve recognition, either through an election or by presenting management with evidence that a majority of the workers have signed cards authorizing the union to represent them.)

The Southwest Airlines Case

Southwest Airlines was first formed as a regional carrier located in Texas. Its founder and CEO until his retirement in 2002, Herb Kelleher, viewed cooperative and flexible relations with the workforce as a key competitive advantage for a service-oriented business. He did not oppose unionization at Southwest and today it stands as one of the most highly unionized airlines in the country. The strategy has paid off well for Southwest over the years. It has grown to become the sixth largest carrier in terms of numbers of employees, and from 1990 to the present has been the most consistently profitable airline in the industry, with the highest level of customer satisfaction. Part of Southwest's success has been attributed to flexible labor contracts, cooperative relationships, and the involvement and coordination achieved across its workforce.

The General Motors Case

The history of union recognition and its relationship to the existing bargaining units at General Motors Corporation is equally instructive. In the early 1970s GM opened a number of new, nonunion plants in the south and was successful in keeping them nonunion despite United Automobile Workers (UAW) efforts to organize them. But in its 1976 negotiations with the company, the UAW insisted that GM agree to remain neutral in future organizing efforts in the new plants, and the union prevailed. Then in 1979 the parties agreed to an accretion clause, which provided that any new plants opened that did work traditionally done by UAW members would automatically be included in the bargaining unit and represented by the union. The union achieved these provisions by making it clear to the company that the UAW could not continue to cooperate with GM in expanding quality of working life

On June 12, 2002, workers at three Johnson Controls Inc. auto parts plants in Louisiana, Missouri, and Oklahoma overwhelmingly approved first contracts. Workers at the three plants and a Northwood, Ohio, facility were part of a coordinated strike that disrupted production at General Motors and Chrysler assembly plants that make use of parts produced at the plants.

Prior to the strike, Johnson Controls had refused to recognize the UAW at the Northwood plant. Johnson Controls has now agreed to recognize the UAW at 26 facilities, including Northwood, where a majority of workers have signed union authorization cards. These 26 facilities employ 8,000. The facilities also would abide by a negotiated employer neutrality agreement in which the company agrees not to derail the union campaign. In addition, the company agreed to binding arbitration to settle first contracts at any of the 26 plants where a majority of workers favor union representation.

Source: "JCI Workers Ratify First UAW Contract; Wages Increased, Plant Closings Banned," *Daily Labor Report* 117, June 18, 2002: A-3.

and other joint activities in existing sites if the company was determined to fight the union over union representation rights in the new facilities.

In 1985 GM and the UAW took this process one step further by jointly planning the design of the labor-management relationship and the work system to be included in a new division of the corporation created to build small cars. The agreement governing this new Saturn Division raised serious objections from conservative, anti-union groups. They argued that the agreement violated the NLRA because it established union recognition before employees had been hired and therefore did not give the new employees an opportunity to vote for or against union representation. The NLRB rejected this argument and let the agreement stand on grounds that there was a sufficient connection between the Saturn operations and other unionized GM facilities. Many of the workers who went to work at Saturn had previously worked at other GM facilities. Many of them applied for work at Saturn after becoming unemployed when their home GM plant closed.

General Motors and Ford, for example, agreed to accept card check recognition within their operations and those of any subsidiaries in their 1999–2003 collective bargaining agreements with the UAW. These provisions are particularly important in the newly created parts subsidiaries of these companies, Delphi and Visteon, as some of these plants are unorganized, and the number of unorganized plants may grow in the future due to acquisitions of unorganized facilities. Notably, Chrysler did not agree to the UAW's request for card check recognition in its 1999–2003 contract, a particularly important issue for the UAW given its ongoing efforts to organize the Alabama assembly plant originally built by Daimler Benz and now a part of Daimler-Chrysler.

The UAW is now engaged in an aggressive effort to organize the "independent" auto parts sector. While at one point this sector was heavily unionized, from the early 1970s on it became heavily nonunion in the face of aggressive managerial opposition to unionization and the UAW's (and other unions') inability to win representation elections. In its ongoing campaign, the UAW is pressing firms to accept card check recognition or, at a minimum, representation election neutrality. Box 7–10 describes the UAW's recent success in using card check procedures to gain members and first contracts at Johnson Controls Incorporated.

A few of the large telecommunication firms that used to be a part of the Bell System in recent years have accepted voluntary card check recognition procedures. What makes these cases so interesting is the fact that the employers were willing to agree to these policies toward organizing because the unions that represent telecommunications employees, the CWA and the IBEW, agreed in exchange to support either mergers or other regulatory policies that management favored.[23] Events at Verizon and SBC are described in Box 7–11.

As discussed in Box 7–12, questions also arose about the legality of card check recognition.

Options for Union Renewal

The limited success achieved in reversing membership declines through conventional organizing strategies has led some inside and outside the labor movement to urge unions to experiments with alternative approaches to recruiting, organizing, and retaining workers. The renewal strategies being used by various unions include:

- Organizing without relying on NLRB election procedures. Some unions have used their leverage in collective bargaining to gain neutrality and card check recognition

Neutrality Agreements/Card Check: Is it Legal?　Box 7–12

The ability to issue neutrality agreements during organizing drives and the use of card checks to officially recognize a union as the representative of employees at a company, thereby eliminating the need to go through an NLRB-sanctioned election, has recently come under serious scrutiny.

During the late months of 2003 and the early months of 2004, a lawsuit was filed by three employees of Dana Corp., a company that specializes in the manufacturing of certain automobile parts. The suit claimed that Dana and the UAW engaged in pre-recognition bargaining and, by doing so, violated the National Labor Relations Act. Specifically, the employees claimed that the neutrality agreement between Dana and the UAW was comprised of specific "principles" that the UAW and Dana would officially negotiate on once the UAW won representation rights, and that Dana was unlawfully assisting the union and the union unlawfully accepting this assistance. As a result, the suit claimed that the Section 7 rights guaranteed to workers under the NLRA were being violated.

An administrative law judge (ALJ) ruled that the neutrality agreement signed by the UAW and Dana did not in fact constitute pre-recognition bargaining. Nevertheless, an appeal was filed with the Board, and in April 2006, the NLRB asked parties concerned with the ruling to file briefs stating their position. Many companies—including Cingular Wireless, Liz Claiborne, and General Motors—agreed with the original ruling and asked the Board to uphold the ALJ's decision. They argued that this form of union drive helps to foster an integrative, win–win relationship, and it is a solution to many problems in the workplace, ultimately benefiting all. Moreover, because the company and the union are working together, employees gain a truly unique ability to gauge whether or not they wish to authorize that union to speak for them. Instead of the typical "union promises of 'pie in the sky' improvements that do not take costs into account," the employees are able to see an accurate depiction of the union's principles and what it may gain for the workers.

On the other hand, there are also those who sided with the Dana employees and issued briefs asking the Board to overturn the ALJ's decision. Among those are seven Republican members of Congress and another group of employees from a separate company who claimed similar wrongdoings by their employer and the UAW. The Congressmen issued a statement in which they asserted, "Extending an extant contract on a yet to be validated employee majority in a separate unit undercuts the very purpose of the Act—to facilitate a process to initiate collective bargaining only after majority status has been demonstrated. And it ignores that the freedom of employees to choose a collective bargaining representative is for the purpose of having the chosen representative negotiate a contract according to the employees' interest."

It is clear that both sides pose valid arguments regarding the legality of neutrality/card check agreements between companies and unions. Which arguments do you agree with?

Source: "Parties Weigh in on NLRB Case Involving Neutrality Agreement Between Dana, UAW," 06/21/06. *Daily Labor Report,* June 21, 2006: C-1.

agreements in new or otherwise unorganized units of employers as discussed above and in Boxes 7–10 and 7–11.

- Use of corporate campaigns and political influence with government regulatory bodies to neutralize employer opposition in organizing campaigns. The United Steel workers and CWA have used this approach with particular effectiveness.[24] The SEIU successfully used innovative grassroots organizing and political lobbying to designate a public sector employer in the process of organizing 75,000 home health care workers in California (see Box 7–13).

- Building community coalitions to support organizing efforts. The best known and most successful example of this is the SEIU "Justice for Janitors" campaign noted above and described in Box 7–9 that gained bargaining recognition from office building owners and cleaning contractors in Los Angeles.

SEIU Organizes 75,000 in Breakthrough 12-Year-Long Drive in California

Box 7–13

Not since the 1940s has a union been so successful in a single organizing drive as the Service Employees International Union (SEIU) was in 1999 when it won the rights to represent nearly 75,000 home health care workers in Los Angeles County, California. The organizing drive took 12 years to complete. In 1988, when the organizing campaign began, home health care workers in Los Angeles were paid slightly less than four dollars an hour—the state minimum at the time—not even enough to raise them above the federal poverty line. Furthermore, although working 40 hours a week would have been necessary for a worker to allow for some sort of standard of living, most workers were unable to find enough work to fulfill even that simple necessity. In addition, because they were seen as independent contractors, these workers were not entitled to any form of medical coverage, sick leave, pension, or vacation.

The frustrating situation of the workers created a double-edged sword for the SEIU and its organizing strategy. On the one hand, home health care workers would surely be willing to join a union that would be able to promise them a way out of the devastating circumstances most of the workers were in. On the other hand, workers worked far apart from one another, they spoke many different languages, and the turnover rate was extremely high since they received no benefits and poor pay. Because of this fragmentation of the workforce, it would be highly difficult to educate employees in the need for unionization.

Even more debilitating was the fact that there was no technical "employer" that could be bargained with. Although home health care workers were paid by a state-funded agency, this agency lacked the power to bargain with a union. Moreover, while customers were able to hire and dismiss workers, they had no ability to bargain as they had no way of providing any of the requests (increased pay, benefits, etc.) that the workers needed.

Faced with these challenges the SEIU took a three-fold approach toward organizing the home health care workers of Los Angeles. First, and possibly most important-ly, they concentrated on grassroots organizing. They soon found that even though the fragmentation of the work-force did indeed present a problem locating the workers, once they were found, persuading them to join the union was possible. SEIU organizers used word-of-mouth and door-to-door canvassing to get their message out.

Second, the union needed to find a way of establishing an employer of record that would be able to collectively bargain with the union on all matters. As such, they attempted to influence policy changes within the state to allow for better care for the workers and thus better care for the elderly by allying with other groups to push the government into creating a public authority as employer of record. While Los Angeles County fiercely opposed this at first—as it believed unionization and higher wages would take money away from the budget—the SEIU was successful in launching an enormous campaign that placed substantial pressure on key politicians. This ultimately resulted in the creation of the Personal Assistance Service Council (PASC) in 1997 as the employer of record for home health care workers in Los Angeles.

The decade-long struggle to organize home health care workers finally paid off in 1999, when it was announced that through a mail-in ballot, the SEIU had won the right to represent the nearly 75,000 workers in Los Angeles. As a result, a five-year contract was signed with the PASC entitling these workers to certain benefits (such as medical coverage for workers working more than 112 hours in two consecutive months, dental coverage, and many training programs such as English and computer classes, immigration support, and educational opportunities) and increases in wages.

Sources: "Homecare Worker Organizing in California: An Analysis of a Successful Strategy," *Labor Studies Journal*, Spring 2002; Teresa Lingafelter, "OUR VOICE: A Participatory Action Research Project of SEIU Local 434B," UC Institute for Labor and Employment, February 2003; "Workers Win a Big One in Los Angeles," *LRA Online*, April 1999.

- Recruiting individuals as "associate members" even if it is not possible to obtain exclusive representation status or a collective bargaining agreement. Teachers' unions have used this approach for many years and more recently unions such as the CWA have used it to establish and support temporary workers at Microsoft and employees at IBM.

Other ideas being debated within the labor movement include finding ways to do more to *retain* members once they are organized, even as they move across jobs. This would require unions to provide a range of labor market and continuous education and training services to workers to support their movement from one job to another. Another idea has been to organize and provide services to members via the Internet. A third related idea is to target youth as potential members by providing career counseling and job finding services and access to portable fringe benefits. All these efforts reflect data showing that many workers move in and out of union status over the course of their careers. If workers could be recruited into unions at the start of their careers and provided with reasons to retain their membership as they move through their working years, both the recruitment and turnover problems could be addressed at the same time. There is likely to be considerable experimentation with these alternative strategies in the years ahead.

Expanding the Definition of Unions

A number of organizations provide some but not all of the functions of traditional unions. This too is an area of considerable experimentation. One such organization, Working Today, recruits independent contract professionals in the media and graphic arts industries in New York City. Working Today provides health benefits, networking opportunties, and related services focused on the needs of these highly mobile professionals who, because they are independent contractors and not employees, are not covered under the National Labor Relations Act. Another form of representation is found in the various "caucus" or "network" groups established within many companies to support African-American, women, gay-lesbian, or other identity groups. Many professional associations also represent their members through lobbying efforts and sometimes in more informal interactions with employers. Prime examples are the bar associations that lawyers join and branches of the American Medical Association and the more specialized doctor's groups springing up around the country to represent medical residents seeking to reduce their hours of work (see Box 6–1).

Very few of these groups have collective bargaining rights, but they do provide their members with services and in some cases a form of voice at their workplaces. Whether traditional conceptions of what is a union or whether members of these organizations should be counted as union members now or in the future are open questions.

Bargaining Structure

Once unionization occurs, whether through an election or some other procedure, then bargaining over a contract ensues. Bargaining structure refers to the scope of the employees and employers covered or affected by the bargaining agreement.

Labor and management do not necessarily bargain contracts that only cover election units. For example, the employees in the various work sites of one employer represented by a union may wish to join together to negotiate a common contract covering the whole company. In the auto, rubber, and other industries where industrial unions are present there are companywide collective bargaining agreements. In addition, employees represented by the same union in a number of companies may prefer to band together and try to negotiate a common contract covering all the companies. This occurs in the coal, construction, and trucking industries. Such company or industrywide bargaining may not develop if the employees (or unions) prefer to bargain in a more decentralized manner and thereby maintain plant-level or company-level bargaining.

Employee and union preferences are not the only determinants of the bargaining structure, however. Before we trace some of the determinants of bargaining structure, we need some definitions.

Definitions of Bargaining Structure

The **formal bargaining structure** is defined as the bargaining unit, or the negotiation unit—that is, the employees and employers who are legally bound by the terms of an agreement. The **informal bargaining structure** is defined as the employees or employers who are affected by the results of a negotiated settlement, through either pattern bargaining or some other nonbinding process.

The U.S. Bureau of Labor Statistics estimates that between 180,000 and 194,000 separate bargaining agreements currently exist in the United States. Many labor contracts in this country cover members of one local union at a single employment site.

The Decentralization of Bargaining Structure in the United States

In comparison to other countries, the United States has a highly **decentralized bargaining structure.** In many European countries, such as Germany and Sweden, many labor contracts cover entire industries or broad regions (see Chapter 14). In recent years, however, many European employers have been arguing for greater decentralization of bargaining to allow individual firms the latitude to adjust to their particular economic circumstances. Many U.S. employers are pressing for even further decentralization of the formal and informal structures of bargaining in this country as well.

Types of Bargaining Units

The two primary characteristics of a bargaining structure are (1) the scope of employee or union interests represented in the unit, which can be either narrow craft or broad industrial or multiskill, and (2) the scope of employer interests represented in the unit, which can be multiemployer (centralized), single-employer—multiplant, or single-employer—single plant (decentralized).

Exhibit 7–5 illustrates this classification of bargaining structures. The vertical axis of the figure depicts the breadth of employee interests. For instance, in a single-employer—multiplant environment, a narrow bargaining unit might include only those craft or professional employees within one occupational class. Police, fire fighters, railroad workers, teachers, and airline pilots are examples of occupations typically represented in bargaining for narrow craft units. At the other end of the spectrum are the broad bargaining units that might include all the production and skilled employees in a firm. Such industrial unions bargain contracts that cover broad employee units in the auto, steel, farm equipment, state government, and textile industries.

There are also intermediate cases in which more than one, but not all the various union-represented employees in a firm, bargain in the same unit. A manufacturing plant where a number of the craft workers bargain together would be such a case.

The horizontal axis of Exhibit 7–5 depicts the range, or the degree of centralization, of employer interests in the bargaining unit. A unit representing only one plant is an example

EXHIBIT 7–5
Types and Examples of Bargaining Structures

Employee Interests Covered	Employer Interests Covered		
	Multiemployer (Centralized)	**Single-employer— Multiplant**	**Single-employer— Single Plant (Decentralized)**
Craft (Narrow)	Construction trades Interstate trucking Longshoring Hospital association	Airline Teacher Police Firefighters Railroad	Craft union in small manufacturing plant Hospital
Industrial or Multiskill (Broad)	Coal mining (underground) Basic steel (pre-1986) Hotel association	Automobiles Steel (post-1986) Farm equipment State government Textile	Industrial union in small manufacturing plant

of the most decentralized bargaining unit. An example of this is where a union negotiates a contract for the electrical (or production) workers in one plant.

A highly **centralized bargaining structure** covers all the plants of a number of companies with the same collective bargaining agreement. Although multiemployer bargaining units are relatively rare in the United States, some do exist. In the trucking industry, for example, a number of over-the-road (intercity and interstate) trucking companies have for a number of years bargained a single contract (the National Master Freight Agreement) with the Teamsters union to cover their unionized drivers. The coal industry has long had a master agreement negotiated with the United Mine Workers that covers the unionized mine workers in the mines of a number of coal companies. These multiemployer units are also found in the construction, longshoring, hotel, and (in some cities) hospital industries. In all these cases an employer association represents management at the bargaining table. These centralized agreements might cover a number of different employers either within a given locality (such as all of the voluntary hospitals in New York City) or within an industry (such as those coal producers that are members of the Bituminous Coal Operators' Association). Professional sports teams and unions likewise have this type of "industrywide" structure with a management association representing the owners of the various teams.

The intermediate case along the employer centralization dimension is found when a single contract covers multiple work sites of one employer. The automobile, steel, farm equipment, textile industry, and many state governments use this intermediate bargaining structure. In these cases employers with more than one plant negotiate a single contract that covers employees in a number of plants as opposed to having a separate contract for each one. Typically, these company agreements are supplemented with local agreements that cover those working conditions specific to a given site.

Another intermediate employer case occurs in public school districts where commonly a single agreement covers all the unionized teachers across the various schools within the district. Police and fire fighters also commonly have one contract that covers the various stations or districts in a city.

Determinants of Bargaining Structures

The major forces that affect the degree of centralization in bargaining structures are bargaining leverage, public policies, and organizational factors. How each of these factors influences bargaining structure is examined below.

Bargaining Leverage

Unions can increase their bargaining leverage if they organize a large share of the product market. One of the primary mechanisms for ensuring that wages are taken out of competition is to expand the bargaining structure to correspond with the scope of the market. But to achieve a high degree of employer centralization in the bargaining structure, unions usually must first organize a large proportion of the **product market** and then successfully maintain union coverage over time—a tall order.

This process is well illustrated by John R. Commons's famous account of early unionism among Philadelphia shoemakers. Commons described how in the absence of broad and aggressive unionism shoemakers were harmfully affected by the expansion of the shoe market (the product market) that had come about in the early 1800s because of improved transportation.[25] As it became possible for nonunion shoemakers outside the Philadelphia area to transport their products into the Philadelphia market and sell them at a low price, the bargaining power of the unionized shoemakers in Philadelphia was weakened. It therefore became important for the Philadelphia shoemakers to organize their fellow shoemakers from the surrounding areas and to see them covered under the same wage agreement to equalize and raise the price of labor.

Unions representing construction workers, for example, have a strong incentive to equalize the wage costs among competitive bidders on the same product. Thus, in the construction industry unions prefer bargaining with the multiple employers who are involved in a specific construction project. For example, where builders across a city bid for the contract to build an office building, the union representing carpenters in that city will try to bargain in a structure that spans the contractors across the city.

Employers Prefer Centralized Bargaining Structures in Some Cases

It should not be inferred that unions always gain (and employers always lose) a tactical advantage in larger or more centralized bargaining structures. Employers in the local service industries (such as hotels, restaurants, laundries, and local truck haulers) have often found it to their advantage to form associations and to bargain in multiemployer units.

For instance, consolidating the bargaining function allows employers to avoid being whipsawed by local union leaders. Union **whipsawing** occurs when a union negotiates a bargain at one plant or company and then puts pressure on the next plant or company to equal or surpass the contract terms just negotiated at the first site. The unions in the airline industry were able to follow this whipsawing strategy until the late 1970s. By consolidating the bargaining structure, however, employers can sometimes reduce the possibility of such union whipsawing. (Employers can also whipsaw a union when they gain a power advantage.)

Centralized Bargaining Can Stabilize Competition

In some cases a centralized bargaining structure can serve employer interests by stabilizing competition. Employers in small firms in a highly competitive industry may find it to their *wage standardization takes pay out of competition*

advantage to bargain centrally with a union. This can reduce the union's ability to whipsaw the small firms. If a strike occurs, the centralized bargaining structure also ensures that no single employer can gain an advantage because all the firms are shut down simultaneously.

The case in which an employer gains from centralized bargaining is well illustrated by the apparel industry. Employers have come to depend on the stability the apparel unions historically provided to their highly competitive industry. Labor costs are a significant component of total costs to the many small firms in the industry, and unionized employers are receptive to the wage standardization imposed by the union. Wage standardization ensures that competition across firms does not depend on their ability to gain low labor costs. The union representing apparel workers likes the centralized employer bargaining structure as this structure helps the union take wages out of competition.

Public Policies

Another crucial determinant of bargaining unit structures is the structure of the election unit imposed by the NLRB in a representation election. If the NLRB certifies the proper election unit to be an industrial unit, for example, this precludes a craft bargaining structure.

greater centralization

The influence of the NLRB is well illustrated by events at General Electric. For a number of years throughout the 1960s, the unions representing General Electric (GE) workers attempted to engage in coalition bargaining but met with strong resistance from the company. **Coalition bargaining** would have meant that a number of the unions representing employees at GE would sit at the negotiating table even when the contract with only one union was under discussion. The NLRB decided to allow the unions to engage in this form of coalition bargaining with GE. Other influential board decisions have been made on whether the employer can withdraw from the multiemployer bargaining unit after having given proper notice before the start of negotiations or only after an impasse has been reached.

con

Some have argued that the NLRB has exhibited a strong preference for larger bargaining units and thus has aided in the trend toward greater centralization. George W. Brooks has been one of the most articulate critics of the board's preference for large production and maintenance bargaining units and against craft severance.[26] He argued that the preference for centralization reduced employees' free choice among alternative unions and made it impossible for individual members to effectively influence the direction of their unions. This, in turn, he believed, produced undemocratic and unresponsive unions.

Organizational Factors

The internal organizational characteristics of employers also have generated pressures to broaden the bargaining unit. In particular, the growth of large corporations and the centralization of managerial decision making have led unions to seek centralized bargaining structures. A fundamental principle underlying their efforts is that in many cases, unions will benefit if the structure of bargaining is coterminous with the level at which the critical management decisions are being made. That is, if management is making most industrial relations decisions at the company level, then the union would often prefer to have bargaining occur at this level as well.

Bargaining Structure in the Telephone Industry

The telephone industry illustrates how management's organizational structure has influenced bargaining structure. The gradual centralization of managerial decision-making power within AT&T that occurred from the 1940s through the 1970s led, first, to the merger of many of the independent unions of telephone workers into the Communications Workers of America (CWA), a national union, and, then, to the development of a centralized, nation-wide contract and bargaining structure.[27]

After World War II, AT&T centralized its industrial relations policy making in its corporate headquarters in New York. In the 1950s and 1960s, however, the CWA still bargained separately with each state affiliate of the Bell System. Consequently, throughout the 1960s the union sought to bring about a more centralized or national bargaining arrangement. Although CWA succeeded in negotiating a national contract in 1974, the breakup of the Bell System into regional telephone companies in 1984 forced a return to decentralized bargaining in the CWA's subsequent negotiations with the new regional telephone companies. But even after the breakup, since AT&T remained a company of national scope with a centralized management, bargaining involving AT&T employees remained centralized at the national level.

Bargaining Structure in the Trucking Industry

On the other hand, the trucking industry illustrates how management may attempt to counter union centralization with a centralization of managerial decision-making power. In the 1950s James R. Hoffa, president of the Teamsters, sought to improve the bargaining power of the union and to consolidate his own power within the union by centralizing the structure of bargaining for the over-the-road (intercity and interstate) truckers. As Hoffa's drive succeeded, employers created a national truckers' association to conduct negotiations and to centralize some of the trucking firms' decision making. Then, when the Teamsters lost market share to nonunion firms in the 1980s, a number of truck companies pulled out of the truckers' association and the bargaining structure in trucking started to decentralize.

Coordinated Bargaining

In settings where no single union dominates in representing a firm's employees, the AFL-CIO has attempted to coordinate bargaining. For many years this coordination function was carried out by the AFL-CIO's Industrial Union Department (IUD). At its peak the IUD coordinated some 80 such contracts with its affiliated unions. This department was closed in 2000 and since then coordination has been carried out by other AFL-CIO staff.

One of the last coordinated bargaining structures put together by the IUD is currently in place at Kaiser Permanente. The process used to create this structure and the innovative arrangements labor and management then created to negotiate a single organizationwide agreement are described in Box 7–14. We will return to a description of how negotiations were carried out in this structure in Chapter 8. The success of coordinated bargaining depends to a great degree on the ability and the willingness of the different unions to work together and to maintain the support of their **rank-and-file** members. Long-standing coordinated bargaining arrangements can be found in the electrical products, glass, and machinery industries and in a number of highly diversified conglomerates such as General Electric, Pittsburgh Plate Glass, and Textron.

The Influence of Diverse Labor and Management Interests

In order to participate in centralized bargaining local union officials or managers have to give up some of their independent authority and conform to centralized decisions and

After forming their partnership with Kaiser Permanente (KP), the coalition of eight international and 25 local unions faced the question of what structure to propose to negotiate in collective bargaining. In the past, each local had negotiated a separate agreement. Since the various local unions had gained experience working together in negotiating the initial partnership agreement, their inclination was to have the local unions negotiate together and create a single national agreement with supplements that dealt with specific local issues. But KP officials were strongly opposed to this, fearing that a single common contract deadline would greatly increase union bargaining power by threatening a systemwide work stoppage.

A joint task force was created to explore whether a new approach could be developed. The initial idea favored by the union coalition and proposed by the task force was to negotiate a single national master agreement. When this idea was first proposed to KP management in 1999, it was rejected. Two of management's concerns were that units located in labor market areas outside of California would be unable to pay higher "national" rates, and that negotiating a master agreement would create considerable vulnerability to a systemwide strike. Since existing local agreements had different expiration dates, management felt safeguarded from the possibility of a major strike across the existing system.

After considerable discussion of these issues, Facilitator John Stepp then worked with KP leaders, as well as with the union leadership, to fashion an alternative approach with various "gates" that the parties would move through before negotiating a national agreement. Either side could exit the process as it passed through these gates if they felt it was not moving in a constructive fashion.

One important "gate" was agreement in principle that local labor market rates would continue to govern. Another critical step involved training of potential participants who would be involved in national and local negotiations in the concepts and skills of Interest Based

Negotiations (IBN). Another key "gate" was that either party could pull out of the process at any point. (As it turned out, neither party found it necessary to exercise this option.) KP and the union coalition eventually agreed to a revised proposal that called for the following: extensive use of IBN problem-solving principles and the necessary training to prepare the parties for this very complicated process; a single integrated national negotiation that would allow local agreements to retain their respective deadlines (thereby addressing one of management's fears of a common expiration date); and a series of decentralized task forces that would focus on particular issues.

Seven bargaining task groups (BTGs) were established to address (1) wages, (2) benefits, (3) work-life balance, (4) performance and workforce development, (5) quality and service, (6) employee health and safety, and (7) work organization and innovation. Each group engaged in an interest-based process of joint study, problem solving, and negotiations. These task groups reported their recommendations to a centralized Common Issues Committee (CIC) co-chaired by union and management chief negotiators. In addition to negotiating a national agreement, new local agreements were to be bargained, even though most of the existing local agreements were not approaching their expiration dates. The CIC sorted through the recommendations of the BTGs and identified those that needed to be forwarded to local tables and those that applied uniformly across the system and therefore needed to be negotiated centrally by the CIC. In the end, over 400 union and management negotiators were trained in IBN and participated in these negotiations. An agreement was reached in nine months and was ratified by over 80 percent of the rank and file.

Source: Robert B. McKersie, Susan Eaton, and Thomas A. Kochan, "Interest Based Bargaining at Kaiser Permanente," unpublished manuscript, MIT Sloan School of Management, 2002.

leaders. Needless to say, local unionists and managers are not always anxious to limit their own authority even where it may lead to a greater good for the whole organization. Having to conform to the wishes of a centralized authority is less painful where there are common goals. Thus, another factor that influences the emergence of centralized bargaining structures is the extent of diversity in the objectives across local actors and the degree to which there are traditions that generate organizational loyalty.

For example, even though the wages and benefits of police and fire fighters are often similar, if not identical, there is very little joint police-fire fighter bargaining in U.S. municipalities. The rivalry between these two groups and their history of separate organizations has precluded formal coordinated or coalition bargaining in most cities. The major exceptions to this pattern occurred when cities experienced extreme financial crises.

Union leaders' opposition to consolidated bargaining units or to formal union mergers acts as an additional constraint on the centralization of negotiations. The reasons for this are very simple. Any consolidation of negotiating units or unions means that some leaders are going to lose influence, status, and perhaps even their jobs.

Resolving Different Issues at Different Bargaining Levels

It should be noted that even within centralized bargaining structures many issues are negotiated on a local basis. That is, in most cases the master agreement negotiated at the centralized level covers only broad issues, ones that are universal in scope, such as wage rates and fringe benefits. Issues that are either company- or plant-specific, such as safety and health conditions, seniority provisions, production standards, shift changes, and overtime distribution, are often left to more decentralized levels of the bargaining structure.

James W. Kuhn showed that the structure of bargaining extends even further down to the departmental or informal work group level, where individual supervisors and work groups often negotiate unwritten side agreements or in fact ignore certain provisions of the contract. He termed this activity **fractional bargaining.**[28] Indeed, one of the most important developments from the 1980s on has been the shift in bargaining down to lower levels.

Pattern Bargaining

Pattern bargaining is an informal means for spreading the terms and conditions of employment negotiated in one formal bargaining structure to another. It is an informal substitute for centralized bargaining aimed at taking wages out of competition.

Students of collective bargaining first began noticing the importance of pattern bargaining after World War II. The War Labor Board (WLB) had encouraged the development of pattern settlements, first, by attempting to fashion a national wage policy and, second, by making the comparison between proposed wage settlements and other industry, area, and national settlements a prime criterion for deciding wage disputes.

The WLB is not the only source of pattern bargaining, by any means. Even before centralized bargaining appeared, and in some cases before unions themselves, steel companies, among other concentrated industries, tended to adjust their wages in tandem by following the lead of a principal firm—in the case of steel, the U.S. Steel Corporation (now USX).[29] Once firms started following patterns in their pricing policies it was only natural that unions sought to create patterns in negotiated agreements covering these firms.

Patterns within a Firm

The employees working within the same firm typically are very aware of what other employees in the firm are receiving in the way of pay or fringe benefits and very jealous of any differentials that emerge. The presence of internal promotion (and other features of an internal labor market) within a firm serves to heighten such comparisons. In the face of internal firm comparisons pattern bargaining follows where there is more than one negotiation that affects employees of the same firm. This is most common across the blue-collar employees of the same firm, but can also occur where unions represent both blue- and white-collar employees.

At Boeing, for example, the International Association of Machinists (IAM) represent production workers and a professional engineering union, the Seattle Professional Engineers and Employees Association (SPEEA), represents engineers. Historically, the IAM negotiations would set a wage and benefit pattern that was generally followed in negotiations with SPEEA. In 2000, however, Boeing sought to introduce major changes in health insurance in negotiations with its engineers shortly after it dropped this same demand in the final hours of contract negotiations with the IAM. As a result, SPEEA members went on strike and this eventually convinced the company to drop its health insurance demands in the SPEEA negotiations as well. This case demonstrates vividly the importance that employee groups place on internal comparisons and their sense of equity.

Pattern Bargaining in Other Countries

From time to time economists who would like to see labor and management follow simple principles that link wage adjustments to macroeconomic trends look to Japan's **Spring Wage Offensive** as a model. During this annual bargaining process in Japan a tremendous amount of information sharing and discussion takes place among government, management, and labor leaders over economic trends and prospects for the coming year. Out of these discussions often emerges a general view of what the overall rate of wage increase should be for the next year. Then, individual companies and their unions "separately" negotiate increases that are consistent with this overall rate (see Chapter 14).

The extreme diversity and decentralization of union and nonunion workplaces across the United States make a version of Japanese practice impractical here. Yet over the years there have been periods when something that approaches an interindustry if not a national pattern has been visible in the United States.

Some interindustry pattern bargaining was evident, for example, in the major bargaining rounds of the decade after World War II. In the early 1960s authors of two separate studies divided the manufacturing sector into what were termed "key" and "nonkey" industries.[30] The key industries tended to be the highly unionized, more concentrated, heavy durable goods industries. The studies showed that wages in those key industries moved in identifiable cycles of bargaining in the postwar-to-1960 period.

The most recent studies of the strength of national pattern bargaining have concluded that, although wage interdependence continues to exist among unionized industries, interindustry wage imitation was not as strong after the 1970s as in the earlier bargaining rounds. Furthermore, it is unlikely that national pattern bargaining will appear in the foreseeable future given the diversity of union and nonunion wage-setting processes.

Intraindustry Pattern Bargaining

Perhaps the greatest extent of pattern bargaining in the United States is the intraindustry variety (across firms in the same industry). The maintenance of patterns in the labor agreements negotiated across firms in the same industry stabilizes competition over wages. The

The board of the Allied Pilots Association (APA) approved an agreement in October 1999 that resolved a long-running dispute over the merger of Reno Air into American Airlines operations. The agreement is based on a proposal made by a federal mediator.

The dispute between American Airlines and the pilots began late in 1998 when American Airlines acquired Reno Air. American wanted to phase Reno Air's 300 pilots into its operations after they received training on its aircraft, while the union wanted them added to the pilots' seniority list effective with the acquisition (there are 9,500 American pilots). The pilots protested the company's handling of the merger with a massive sickout over the President's Day holiday weekend that caused thousands of flights to be cancelled. A federal judge later held the union and its top leaders in contempt for failing to end the sickout and ordered them to pay American Airlines $45.5 million to compensate the carrier for losses.

As part of the agreement, the key question that had been driving the dispute, when American Airlines was contractually required to bring the smaller carriers' pilots to parity with pilots at American Airlines, will be settled by an arbitrator. The court's $45.5 million fine was not altered by the agreement.

The APA and American Airlines also agreed to a joint problem-solving protocol with an initial focus on developing a protocol for future mergers and acquisitions to avoid similar disputes. The protocol calls for training in joint problem solving and twice yearly mediated problem-solving sessions including top officials of the company and union. The union also agreed to work with management to develop an expedited process for clearing a backlog of grievances.

Sources: "Mediated Talks between American, Pilots Union Set to Resume Next Week," *Daily Labor Report* 155, August 12, 1999: A-8; and "Board of Pilots Union at American Authorizes Talks to Extend Contract," *Daily Labor Report* 211, November 2, 1999: A-8.

---

existence of dominant unions within an industry also facilitates the spread of such patterns from one employer to another. Examples of this form of pattern bargaining are found in the auto, aerospace, and airline industries.

Intraindustry pattern bargaining can have drawbacks. A number of problems result from overextending a pattern settlement to firms or to different parts of an industry that are unable to absorb its costs. Overextension is likely to reduce employment opportunities for the pattern-following employees, encourage the entrance of new competitors into the industry, and ultimately reduce the ability of the union to take wages out of competition—which was the original purpose of pattern bargaining.

How far to extend industry patterns has become a central point of debate in the airline industry as the major carriers seek to expand the role of their regional or feeder airlines that serve smaller communities. Pilots want to limit the growth of these feeder airlines because they typically pay lower wages and therefore pose threats to the job security of pilots employed at the large firms. At the same time, airlines that urgently need to lower their overall cost structures are looking for ways to expand their regional carriers or form alliances with independent regional carriers. Disputes about whether or not to extend an industry pattern has led to protracted negotiations and several strikes in the airline industry, such as the one at Reno Airlines described in Box 7–15.

In moderation, however, pattern bargaining serves an important set of functions in a collective bargaining system. It reduces the number of strikes, since it not only serves as a standard for the acceptability of a proposed wage settlement, but also helps to establish norms of equity among workers. And, like other forms of pattern bargaining, intraindustry patterns can help unions take wages out of competition where the pattern is supported by a union's ability to maintain union organizing.

The Trend toward Greater Decentralization

From the 1980s on a number of bargaining units underwent decentralization in their structure. The steel industry is an illustration. At the beginning of the 1970s the 10 largest steel companies negotiated as a group (although formally each company signed a separate contract). But by 1982 the number of companies that participated in the industry association had shrunk to eight; by 1986 the association had disbanded, and bargaining with the seven remaining firms began to take place on a company-by-company basis. Although the settlements that resulted after 1986 carried through many of the common features of the earlier ones, significant variations across the agreements were introduced: variations in wages, fringe benefits, profit sharing, work rules, and the extent of employee participation in management decision making.

Over the previous 20 years the number of firms in the coal and trucking industries declined substantially. Furthermore, there were major declines in the number of workers covered by multiemployer or industrywide contracts in these industries. In communications the national contract of the 1970s, which covered all Bell System employees, gave way to greater decentralization after AT&T's divestiture of the regional telephone companies in 1984.

Some of the decentralization in bargaining structures has been induced by public policies. By far the most significant effects of government policy on bargaining structures have come in recent years from the deregulation of product markets in trucking, airlines, and communications. In all of these cases, the effect of deregulation has been to open the industry to new entrants that start on a nonunion basis, pay wages and benefits below the unionized rates in the industry, and, in turn, put pressures on unionized firms to seek labor contract terms in ways that will meet the new competitors. As a result, firms in all three of these industries attempted to decentralize their bargaining structures.

As mentioned earlier, in trucking, before industry deregulation in 1980, the Teamsters had negotiated a national master freight agreement that covered over-the-road (intercity and interstate) truck drivers. Essentially all the major trucking companies that hauled freight between cities and states or across the country were covered by this single, national contract.

After deregulation, however, there was an influx of new, nonunion firms and small, independent contractors in the full-truckload portion of the industry. Furthermore, intense price competition emerged among the firms that remained highly unionized (essentially the "less than truckload" businesses that required large networks of terminals). The net result of these pressures was considerable decentralization in the bargaining structure. Several full-truckload companies broke out of the master freight structure and negotiated separate contracts with different wage payment and pension arrangements.

In the airline industry, deregulation first had the effect of weakening the pattern bargaining that previously characterized negotiations across American, United, Northwest, and other major airlines. Under increased competitive pressure in the 1980s, pattern following gave way to a more varied pattern of company-specific adjustments, including two-tiered wage agreements (that is, wage settlements that lower the starting pay rates of future hires), changes in hours worked, wage cuts, profit-sharing plans, and employee memberships on company boards of directors.[31] The variety in collective bargaining outcomes that followed included employee ownership of United Airlines.

In the 1990s, as most airlines returned to profitability, pressures for pattern bargaining reemerged and resulted in a number of lengthy delays in contract negotiations. The machinists at Northwest eventually replaced the IAM as their representative with the Aircraft Mechanics Fraternal Association (AMFA). This then added pressure on the IAM to match the settlements reached by its new rival at Northwest with similar increases at United and other carriers. Overall, debates over pattern bargaining, along with the financial ups and downs of the airline industry, were contributing factors to the increased delays experienced in negotiating agreements in this industry in recent years.

Some observers have argued that pattern bargaining lost much of its significance from the 1980s on. This may be an overstatement, but there is strong evidence of greater variability in recent collective bargaining settlements across and within industries and even among different locations within the same firm.[32] Moreover, the economic returns to unions from pattern bargaining seemed to decline after 1980.

Summary

This chapter discusses union organizing and bargaining structures. These two central issues emerge early on in the chronology of the bargaining process. Union organizing decides whether there will be bargaining in the first place, and then the parties' attention turns to the structure of bargaining.

An organizing campaign is initiated by union organizers, typically including some full-time paid organizers and shop floor employees. To receive authorization from the NLRB for a representation election the union needs to have 30 percent of the election unit sign authorization cards. Management typically launches a countercampaign in which it tries to convince employees not to vote for union representation. The NLRB regulates conduct during this organizing campaign including union access and management's use of captive audience speeches. There has been much debate in recent years over whether the NLRB has effectively maintained laboratory conditions in election campaigns.

The NLRB plays an important role in this process in decisions made about the appropriate election unit. The NLRB takes into account both the degree to which employees have common interests and the administrative concerns of management. There is much strategic interplay in this process as the union and management try to shape an election unit that increases the likelihood of victory in the eventual election.

The environment and bargaining power are important determinants of organizing outcomes. Power affects whether a union has enough muscle to win an election or to induce an employer to avoid an election and grant quick union recognition through automatic recognition procedures.

Unions have not fared particularly well in their organizing efforts over the last 30 years. Management has been aggressive in developing personnel policies that weaken the appeal of unions and in the conduct of countercampaigns against unionization. But unions have not been passive either, as they turned to corporate campaigns and other new organizing tactics.

Bargaining structure determines which unionized employees are covered by a collective bargaining agreement. The two key dimensions are the scope of employee interests covered—whether craft or industrial—and the degree of centralization in firm coverage—ranging from single-plant to multiple-company agreements.

Compared with other countries the United States continues as an example of relatively decentralized bargaining structures. From the 1980s on previously centralized bargaining structures in trucking, steel, coal, and many other industries either fragmented or collapsed.

To see the consequences of successful union organizing and the role played by the structure of bargaining requires a more elaborate account of the negotiation of the collective bargaining agreement. The next chapter turns to that issue.

Discussion Questions

1. Briefly describe the organizing process.
2. What are some common strategies used by management to keep unions out of the company?
3. Define what is meant by bargaining structures and discuss some of the determining factors of bargaining structures.
4. What is pattern bargaining and how does it affect informal bargaining structures?
5. Why has collective bargaining in a number of firms and industries in the United States become more decentralized in recent years?
6. Explain what is meant by a "representation gap."

Related Web Sites

International Ladies Garment Workers Union (ILGWU) & Union of Needletrades, Industrial and Textile Employees (UNITE):
http://www.ilr.cornell.edu/lib/ bookshelf/Hottopics/UNITE/ UNITE_Merger/KeyEvents_ILGWU.html

Xerox:
http://www.xerox.com

NYNEX-Bell Atlantic:
http://www.bellatlantic.com/about/ about.htm

AT&T:
http://www.att.com

Levi-Strauss:
http://www.levistrauss.com/index_ about.html

United Steel Workers of America (USWA):
http://www.uswa.org/overview. html

Justice for Janitors:
www.seiu.org/j4j

Graduate student organizing at Columbia University:
www.columbia.edu/cu/asas/ faculty.htm

Suggested Readings

Freeman, Richard B., and Joel Rogers. *What Do Workers Want?* (Ithaca: Cornell University Press, 1999).

Bronfenbrenner, Kate, Richard W. Hurd, and Ronald L. Seeber, eds. *Organizing to Win: New Research on Union Strategies* (Ithaca, New York: ILR Press, 1998).

Turner, Lowell, Harry C. Katz, and Richard W. Hurd, eds. *Rekindling the Movement: Labor's Quest for Relevance in the 21st Century* (Ithaca, New York: ILR Press, 2001).

End Notes

1. It is also possible for the NLRB to order an employer to bargain with a union as a remedy for a representation election that involves extensive unfair labor practices on the part of the employer. This sort of "bargaining order" has been issued infrequently by the NLRB.

2. The NLRB can eliminate this practice if it interferes with the operation of the business.

3. The employer is not required by law to give the union the opportunity to respond to a captive audience speech.

4. Michael Evan Gold, *An Introduction to Labor Law* (Ithaca, NY: ILR Press, 1989), p. 27.

5. See Mallenkrodt Chemical Works, 162 NLRB 387 (1966).

6. "Number of Union Elections, Win Rate by Labor Unions Both Decreased in 2005," *Daily Labor Report* 116, Washington, DC: Bureau of National Affairs, April 26, 2006: C-1.

7. "Number of Elections Decreased in 2004: Union Win Rate Increased for Eighth Year," *Daily Labor Report*, Washington, DC: Bureau of National Affairs, May 3, 2005: C-1.

8. Research also has shown that national union characteristics play a role in union success in certification elections. More specifically, unions with greater internal democracy, less centralized bargaining, lower strike activity, and larger size have greater success in organizing both blue- and white-collar workers than do other unions. See Cheryl L. Maranto and Jack Fiorito, "The Effect of Union Characteristics on the Outcome of NLRB Certification Elections," *Industrial and Labor Relations Review* 40 (January 1987): 225–40.

9. A 1997 survey by Seymour Martin Lipset and Noah Meltz found that 47 percent of nonunion workers expressed a desire to join a union. See Seymour Martin Lipset and Noah M. Meltz, "Canadian and American Attitudes toward Work and Institutions," *Perspectives on Work,* vol. 1, no. 3, 1998, 14–19.

10. Myron Roomkin and Hervey Juris, "Unions in the Traditional Sectors: Mid-Life Passage of the Labor Movement," in *Proceedings of the Thirtieth Annual Meeting,* December 28–39, 1977, ed. Barbara D. Dennis, (Madison, WI: Industrial Relations Research Association, 1978), pp. 212–22.

11. William N. Cooke, *Union Organizing and Public Policy: Failure to Secure First Contracts* (Kalamazoo, MI: W. E. UpJohn Institute for Employment Research, 1985).

12. Richard B. Freeman and Morris M. Kleiner, "Employer Behavior in the Face of Union Organizing Drives," *Industrial and Labor Relations Review* 43, no. 4 (April 1990): 351–65.

13. Julius G. Getman, Stephen B. Goldberg, and Jeanne B. Herman, *Union Representation Elections: Law and Reality* (New York: Russell Sage Foundation, 1976).

14. Instead, the authors proposed reforms that would deter employers' anti-union strategies carried out before the campaign. The Getman, Goldberg, and Herman study led to considerable debate and controversy, both in public policy circles and among researchers. A summary of the debate is in Stephen B. Goldberg, Julius G. Getman, and Jeanne M. Brett, "The Relationship between Free Choice and Labor Board Doctrine: Differing Empirical Approaches," *Northwestern University Law Review* 79 (1984): 721–35.

15. See William T. Dickens, "The Effect of Company Campaigns: Law and Reality Once Again," *Industrial and Labor Relations Review* 36 (July 1983): 560–75.

16. Cooke, *Union Organizing and Public Policy.*

17. "Number of Union Elections, Win Rate by Labor Unions Both Decreased in 2005." *Daily Labor Report,* op. cit.

18. Sewell Mfg. Co., 138 NLRB 66 (1962), pp. 69–70.

19. A listing of corporate campaigns and analysis of their success is provided in Paul Jarley and Cheryl Maranto, "Union Corporate Campaigns: An Assessment," *Industrial*

and Labor Relations Review 43, no. 5 (July 1990): 505–24.

20. Kate Bronfenbrenner, "The Role of Union Strategies in NLRB Certification Elections, *Industrial and Labor Relations Review* 50, no. 2 (January 1997): 195–212.

21. Adrienne E. Eaton and Jill Kriesky, "Union Organizing under Neutrality and Card Check Agreements," *Industrial and Labor Relations Review* 55 (October 2001): 42.

22. Ibid., p. 47.

23. Harry C. Katz, Rosemary Batt, and Jeffrey H. Keefe, "The Revitalization of the CWA: Integrating Collective Bargaining, Political Action, and Organizing," *Industrial and Labor Relations Review* 56 (July 2003).

24. Ibid.

25. John R. Commons, "American Shoemakers, 1648–1895: A Sketch of Industrial Evolution," *Quarterly Journal of Economics* 25 (November 1919), reprinted and revised in *A Documentary History of American Society,* vol. 3, ed. John R. Commons (New York: Russell and Russell, 1958), pp. 18–58.

26. George W. Brooks, "Stability versus Employee Free Choice," *Cornell Law Review* 61 (March 1976): 344–67.

27. Jeffrey Keefe and Rosemary Batt, "Telecommunications Services: Union-Management Relations in an Era of Industry Re-Consolidation," in P. Clark, J. Delaney, and A. Frost eds., *Collective Bargaining: Current Developments and Future Challenges* (Champaign, IL: Industrial Relations Research Association, 2003).

28. James W. Kuhn, *Bargaining and Grievance Settlements* (New York: Columbia University Press, 1962).

29. George Seltzer, "Pattern Bargaining and the United Steelworkers," *Journal of Political Economy* 59 (August 1951): 322.

30. Otto Eckstein and Thomas A. Wilson, "The Determination of Money Wages in American Industry," *Quarterly Journal of Economics* 75 (August 1962): 370–414, and John E. Maher, "The Wage Pattern in the United States," *Industrial and Labor Relations Review* 15 (October 1961): 1–20.

31. Peter Cappelli, "Competitive Pressures and Labor Relations in the Airline Industry," *Industrial Relations* 24 (1985): 316–38.

32. John W. Budd, "The Determinants and Extent of UAW Pattern Bargaining," *Industrial and Labor Relations Review* 45 (April 1992): 523–39; and Christopher L. Erickson, "A Re-Interpretation of Pattern Bargaining, *Industrial and Labor Relations Review* 49 (July 1996): 615–34.

Chapter 8

The Negotiations Process and Strikes

Chapters 8 and 9 examine the process by which unions and employers negotiate collective bargaining agreements, continuing the analysis of the middle (functional) level of industrial relations activity. This chapter explains the dynamics of negotiations and the factors that lead to strikes; the next chapter discusses impasse resolution.

Negotiations and strikes are the most visible parts of a collective bargaining system. Contract negotiations provide labor and management with a predetermined time to set or revise the terms of the agreement governing their relationship. The pressures of a contract deadline and perhaps of a strike threat focus attention and clarify how important each party feels about critical issues and the need to either alter or preserve current practices. Negotiations may, from time to time, produce the strikes that often provide headlines for popular press coverage of collective bargaining. But negotiations are not independent of activities that occur over time at either the workplace or the strategic levels of the bargaining relationship. The strategies and tactics used in negotiations are both likely to reflect the level of trust labor and management representatives have for each other at the outset of negotiations and the results of negotiations will in turn affect the trust that carries over to the relationship of the parties during the term of the agreement. Thus, negotiations offer labor and management a pivotal event that may reinforce or change their future relations.

As we will see, many of the parties to collective bargaining today are attempting to bring a new approach to negotiations, often labeled *interest-based* bargaining or *mutual-gains* bargaining.[1] The new approaches seek to move away from more traditional *positional* bargaining in an effort to increase the potential for problem solving in negotiations. Thus the negotiations process involves making choices over how to bargain as well as tactical decisions on how to carry out the approach taken to best represent the parties' separate and joint interests.

To examine the various components of the negotiations process, this chapter uses the framework developed by Richard Walton and Robert McKersie to compare and contrast these two approaches to negotiations.[2] The Walton and McKersie framework is particularly useful in identifying the wide variety of pressures and competing interests that bear on the negotiators and the negotiations process.

The Four Subprocesses of Negotiations

Although the Walton and McKersie framework was originally developed to describe and analyze the traditional positional approach to bargaining that was quite common in the 1950s and 1960s when they developed their framework, their work also served as the theoretical basis for interest-based techniques that were developed in the 1980s. So we will summarize their framework first and then discuss how the dynamics of bargaining varies depending on the approach taken. Walton and McKersie argued that there are four **subprocesses of bargaining** within the negotiation of any collective bargaining agreement. The four subprocesses are distributive bargaining, integrative bargaining, intraorganizational bargaining, and attitudinal structuring. Each subprocess and the interrelations between the various subprocesses are analyzed below.

Distributive Bargaining *strike leveraged elasticity of demand for labor*

Distributive bargaining involves those aspects of negotiations in which one side's gain is the other side's loss. Distributive bargaining is win-lose or zero-sum bargaining. With distributive issues or processes, what labor gains management gives up. Examples of issues that most often are distributive in nature include wage rates and fringe benefits. With respect to the wage rate, labor gains more income from a higher wage, while management gives up some profit to pay the higher wage.[3] Similarly, workers lose when a fringe benefit (e.g., paid vacation time) is reduced, while management gains higher profits with the reduction of paid vacation time.

wages & benefits

Since distributive issues involve gains for one side and losses for the other, these issues lead to conflicts across the bargaining table. Determination of how distributive issues are resolved involves the exercise of bargaining power. The union, for example, tries to convince management to agree to its request for a higher wage by threatening to strike if management does not give in to this demand. Meanwhile, management threatens the union with the loss of income associated with such a strike and might also point out to the union that such a wage increase entails additional costs to the work force in the form of reductions in employment. In this way, the components of bargaining power, strike leverage, and elasticity of demand for labor emerge as the critical determinants of how distributive conflicts are resolved.

Distributive issues are at the center of the negotiation of a collective bargaining agreement since disagreement over the distribution of labor's product lies at the core of labor-management relations. Nevertheless, it would be a mistake for either students of collective bargaining or participants in the bargaining process to lose sight of the fact that there are other dimensions to bargaining in addition to distributive issues.

Integrative Bargaining

Integrative bargaining issues and processes are those in which a solution provides gains to both labor and management, leading to joint gain or win-win bargaining. Labor and management both gain when they resolve problems that are impeding productivity and organizational performance. If the productivity of the firm increases, for example, the employees can benefit in the form of higher compensation or shorter work hours while the firm can benefit in the form of greater profits.

productivity

There are numerous problems confronted at the workplace that provide the opportunity for integrative gains. Work is rarely performed in the most productive way possible: either cumbersome practices or outdated work rules often stand in the way of peak performance. Labor and management thus can improve firm performance by addressing such practices and either changing job classifications or seniority rules or in other ways creating procedures that promote high organizational performance.

The introduction of new technology often provides an avenue for integrative gains. Through the effective use of new technology productivity can increase, which can then provide rewards both to employees and the firm. Yet the mere introduction of new technology onto the shop floor or in the office does not lead readily to such productivity increases. Commonly technology works best if accompanied by changes in work practices—personnel levels might have to be reduced, training programs adopted, or reporting lines adjusted. Integrative bargaining would entail the negotiations surrounding how and to what extent these productivity-enhancing work rule changes are made as the new technology is introduced.

But why do the parties not automatically make integrative changes since such changes hold open the possibility of joint gain? In other words, why is integrative bargaining so difficult? The answer to this question is one of the key issues in industrial relations.

Why Integrative Bargaining Can Be So Difficult

Integrative bargaining is an ever-present and sometimes difficult component of the negotiations process for a number of reasons. For one thing, although integrative issues contain the possibility of providing joint gains to both sides, it is also true that the parties are simultaneously confronted with the question of how to divide up any joint gain. In effect, any integrative bargain also prompts the occurrence of distributive bargaining, and the difficulty in resolving this distributive issue can make integrative bargaining difficult.

Consider, for example, what happens when a new technology is introduced into a work site. If it is effectively introduced, the new technology provides the possibility of joint gains in the form of income to both employees and the firm. Yet, the involved parties cannot escape the fact that if productivity goes up when the new technology is implemented, it must then be decided how the increased income provided by that technology is divided. In this way, every integrative bargain prompts a distributive discussion. The problem for the bargaining parties is that it can be difficult for them to agree on how to resolve the distributive issue (namely, how to share the integrative gain). Thus, integrative solutions are sometimes blocked by labor and management's disagreement over how they would divide up the gains that result from problem resolution.

Integrative and Distributive Bargaining Involve Different Tactics

Integrative bargaining also can become difficult because the parties send confused signals and mixed messages to each other. This confusion springs from the fact that integrative and distributive bargaining entail very different tactics and negotiating styles. Exhibit 8–1 lists the different tactics used in distributive and integrative bargaining.

Remember, distributive bargaining concerns matters in which one side's gain is the other side's loss. To do well in such bargaining the negotiator typically finds it valuable to, among other things, overstate demands, withhold information, and project a stern and tough image. Effective integrative bargaining, on the other hand, involves first identifying and

EXHIBIT 8–1
Distributive versus Integrative Bargaining Tactics

	Distributive Tactics	Integrative Tactics
Issues	Many issues	Specific concerns
Positions	Overstate real position at outset—"demands"	Focus on objectives; no final positions
Use of information	Information is power; hold it close, use selectively	Share information openly; treat as data
Communication process	*Controlled*	*Open*
	Single spokesperson	Multiple voices
	Use of private caucuses to air internal differences and discuss responses	Use of subcommittees
Interpersonal style	*Hard bargaining*	*Problem solving*
	Focused on own goals and interests	Concern for mutual goals
	Short run; not concerned about long-term relations	Concerned about long-term relations
	Low trust	High trust

then solving problems. The tactics typically effective in such problem solving include open exchange of information, airing of multiple voices, and sharing of information. Distributive and integrative bargaining styles contrast sharply with each other.

The problem for both labor and management is that it is difficult to be effective at both distributive and integrative bargaining in the same negotiations. One side might set into a distributive bargaining mode just at the moment when the other side is ready for integrative problem solving. And when the latter party confronts hard distributive tactics, it might become discouraged about the possibility of integrative bargaining, making it difficult for such bargaining ever to occur.

Integrative bargaining also can be difficult because the problems that impede productivity are not always obvious to the two parties, even when they agree on how to divide up the possible joint gains. If this does not make negotiations hard enough, consider as well that there are two other subprocesses in the bargaining process.

Intraorganizational Bargaining

Intraorganizational bargaining occurs when there are different goals or preferences within either side, either the union or management. For example, intraorganizational bargaining arises when the members of the union (or the union negotiating team) have different preferences regarding what the union should strive for during negotiations. Senior union members may prefer that the union focus its negotiating strategy around attainment of better pensions, whereas younger union members may prefer up-front wage increases. Or, the craft workers in the union might be in favor of restricting the use of outside contractors to maintain machinery in the plant, whereas production workers might be concerned with having safer conditions on the line.

Management may also have different preferences or opinions about what is feasible in negotiations. Corporate management, for example, may favor strict adherence to the seniority policies used in other plants of the company, whereas local plant management may prefer negotiation of a seniority procedure that has never been tried elsewhere in the company.

Three years before the negotiations in question began, the teachers had engaged in a bitter strike. The board president and two other members of the current board were members of the board at the time of that strike and still bore extreme hostility toward the teachers. The other four members of the board held less antagonistic attitudes toward the teachers.

The board's professional negotiator was also a carryover from the strike. The relationship between him and the union was one of mutual and extreme distrust and antagonism. Thus, as the new negotiations got under way, the board and the teachers were still locked in a hostile relationship.

Shortly before negotiations began, the board had hired a new superintendent of schools. Repelled by the animosity between the teachers and the board, he sought to take a more conciliatory stance toward the union. Before long, bitter confrontations developed between the board's negotiator and the new superintendent.

During the summer months the superintendent held informal talks with the union president, and together they worked out a tentative agreement on a contract settlement, subject to board and union membership approval. The board refused to approve the agreement, partly because of objections by the board's negotiator. Throughout the course of the negotiations the superintendent tried to persuade the board to dismiss the negotiator.

Since these events took several months to transpire, the teachers pressured their union leaders into calling an impasse and began to engage in slowdowns and other forms of job actions short of a strike. During the months the superintendent and the negotiator were at loggerheads, each arranged separate meetings with the union representatives, one trying to work through a mediator and the other trying to keep the mediator out of the process. Meanwhile, both were lobbying members of the board to obtain the swing vote necessary to win the power struggle.

Obviously, no progress was made in negotiations until the internal dispute was resolved. The superintendent ultimately emerged as the victor in the power struggle, and the board dismissed its negotiator. The superintendent then brought in a new management negotiator with whom he could work, and a contract was successfully negotiated.

Intraorganizational conflict also can occur when one or both of the parties bring insufficient decision-making authority to the bargaining table. Nothing is more frustrating to negotiators than to realize they are engaging in what is called shadow boxing or **surface bargaining**—that is, bargaining opposite a representative who lacks the authority necessary to make commitments that will stick within his or her organization. Inadequate decision-making power or authority on the part of a negotiator greatly increases the probability of an impasse or a strike as the opponent turns to the strike to force the real decision makers to the bargaining table. This source of impasse is especially prevalent in the public sector or the quasi-public sector, such as not-for-profit hospitals.

Consider, for example, the severe intraorganizational conflict that appeared in the dispute between a teacher's union and a public school district, described in Box 8–1. This impasse was caused primarily by intramanagement conflicts. The union's only recourse was to call an impasse, bring in a mediator, and put pressure on the school board to resolve its internal differences and get on with the negotiations.

This example illustrates that intraorganizational conflicts are not solely a union phenomenon. It is true that the political structure of unions makes it more difficult for them than for most managements to resolve internal power struggles. Nonetheless, in firms where the locus of decision-making power is unclear or widely dispersed within management, open conflicts are also likely to occur and carry over into the negotiations process.

Intraorganizational conflict is common in the public sector because of its complex decision-making structures and numerous political constituencies.[4] Multiemployer bargaining structures in industries where there is wide variation in the goals or financial status of the employers is another likely environment for intramanagement conflicts.

Attitudinal Structuring

Negotiations often involve a lot of uncertainty. Uncertainty arises from the difficulties the parties face in anticipating how much strike power they possess and the complications involved in interpreting each other's intentions.

Negotiations also can be extremely emotional. The stakes involved are usually high, and the tactics often used in traditional negotiations—threats, bluffs, grandstanding for one's constituents, exaggerated anger—are hardly conducive to building rapport among the parties to the process. Add to these the fact that any single round of negotiations typically is part of a larger and longer-term power struggle between parties separated by an inherent conflict of interests. One can readily see why hostile attitudes can, and sometimes do, develop in a bargaining relationship and why they can constrain effective negotiations.

Consequently, **attitudinal structuring** (the degree of trust the respective sides feel or develop toward each other) is another subprocess within bargaining. If labor and management, for example, have a high degree of trust in one another, then it should be easier for the parties to engage in integrative bargaining since trust can facilitate the identification of problems (or solutions). In contrast, interpersonal mistrust can make it difficult to move from initial bargaining positions to compromise settlements. Mistrust hampers communications between the parties and can lead both parties to hold back on concessions they might otherwise be willing to make. Obviously, intense hostility can get in the way of serious discussion of the substantive merits of the issues.[5]

Labor and management can try to build trust by meeting prior to or during negotiations in forums that facilitate an open exchange of views and concerns. Here is where what is going on during the term of an agreement at the workplace and strategic levels of the relationship can make a big difference. If on an ongoing basis union leaders and managers are working together to build trust, share information, develop employee participation processes, and consult on critical issues, the trust that develops from these activities may carry over to the negotiations process. Alternatively, actions that demonstrate a lack of trust to the rank and file, union leaders, or managers during the term of a contract will likely carry over to influence negotiations as well.

Personality traits of negotiators also appear to play a role in trust building. Some personality traits, such as excessive authoritarianism, have been found to hinder the compromising necessary to bring about negotiated settlements.[6]

A recent study showed, for example, that the negotiators' "perspective-taking ability," that is, their ability to see the other party's point of view, enhances the likelihood of a negotiated agreement.[7] Those who are philosophically opposed to unions, however, or those who are opposed to the role managers play in a capitalistic society, may see bargaining issues as matters of great principle and thus find compromising difficult. Acceptance of the legitimacy of the other side's point of view can facilitate conflict resolution. Its absence in negotiations increases the probability of an impasse.

Management's Objectives

The formation of management's **wage objectives** (or targets) is a critical part of the negotiations process. Negotiators often have limits for bargaining, or the bottom-line terms they would accept short of taking a strike. The development of these wage targets is the heart of the internal management planning process that takes place before or during the early stages of negotiations.

Wages are important to management, but they are not the only critical issue addressed in a labor agreement. Yet the formation of management's targets for other bargaining issues occurs in a manner that is not very different from the formation of wage targets. Thus, the discussion that follows has general applicability.

Since top management is responsible for approving or authorizing any wage target in bargaining, the negotiating team must recommend targets that reflect top management's goals for the organization. To recommend too high a wage target risks rejection of the recommendations and the loss of influence that results from such a rejection. On the other hand, these targets play a pivotal role in the negotiations process once they are established because they indicate the negotiator's latitude for compromise.

Thus, the industrial relations staff has to develop bargaining targets that are realistic and achievable. The range of criteria that go into this decision-making process are discussed below.

The Union's Targets

Management must also take the union's preferences into account when setting targets for bargaining. Unless management is powerful enough to totally dominate bargaining, the management team will have to consider the potential acceptability of its wage offer to the union.

Unions will usually establish their own targets for wage bargaining. In setting those limits, union leaders employ two basic criteria for evaluating a proposed settlement: (1) the potential effects of the settlement on the real wages of the membership (the wage adjustment minus any increase in the cost of living), and (2) a comparison between the proposed settlement and settlements with other bargaining units or with other employees.

Comparisons with other units are important to unions for both economic and political reasons. Remember, the union's economic goal is to take wages out of competition. This leads unions to favor wage increases that maintain patterns. Union leaders also face pressure from their members to preserve "coercive comparisons" with the settlements achieved by other unions.[8] Rank-and-file union members often evaluate their leaders by comparing their own settlement to settlements achieved by leaders of other unions or granted by other employers.

Comparisons are especially relevant when one or more rival unions might potentially challenge another union for the right to represent a group of employees. This has been an important consideration in bargaining among mechanics in the airline industry in recent years since two different unions, the International Association of Machinists (IAM) and the Aircraft Mechanics Fraternal Association (AMFA) have been competing to represent these employees at various airlines.

Thus, the union tries to induce the firm to consider more than it might otherwise in wage setting. The union's bargaining power will determine the extent to which management actually takes into account the union's preferences.

Local Labor Market Comparisons *usually when union is weak.*

One factor an employer considers when setting their wage targets is the prevailing wage level in the **local labor market.** If the employer were to ignore the local labor market and allow wages inside the firm to fall low relative to wages at the other employment sites, high employee turnover might follow. Low wages also might produce a dissatisfied work force and difficulty in recruiting workers with the requisite ability to perform effectively. To set wages too high relative to the local labor market invites an excess of qualified job applicants and unnecessary costs.

Note this does not mean that the employer seeks to pay the lowest wage possible that will attract workers to a given job. Given a particular local labor market, the employer must choose the quality of employees it wishes to hire. The employer must decide if increasing the wage level will attract employees of sufficiently high quality and lower indirect personnel costs (such as training, turnover, and supervision).

Labor market comparisons are more likely to be used in bargaining relationships where the union is weak. Where unions are strong they use their bargaining power to do better than the local labor market and gain what they consider to be a fair wage.

Product Market Factors

Product market comparisons play an increasingly important role in management decision making. The ability of current or potentially new competitors to compete on the basis of lower labor costs has in fact been the dominant factor in management's drive to hold down or reduce wages, particularly of entry and low skill jobs. The threat of outsourcing this work has also been an important part of management's approach to negotiations in recent years.

The Firm's Ability to Pay

The effects of wage adjustments on the profits of the firm also influence management's wage target. Employers approaching the wage decision examine their **ability to pay** alternative wage increases. Ability-to-pay considerations are likely to be especially salient in small firms and in firms facing a weak union.

A union generally is reluctant to give a firm a lower settlement on ability-to-pay grounds unless the firm can demonstrate that a serious economic crisis would result otherwise. Union leaders and members often must be convinced that there would be sizable employment loss before they will agree to a low settlement. It took, for example, the threat of bankruptcy, along with government pressure, before the UAW agreed to give Chrysler wage concessions below the auto pattern in 1979. Ability-to-pay considerations have become more important in recent years. In response to heightened competitive pressures, management has preferred to shift away from externally driven wage criteria in favor of criteria that connect wages more closely to firm or worker performance. Thus, management has tried to shift away from factors such as wages in the industry or increases in the cost of living and toward the firm's ability to pay.

Internal Comparisons

Every negotiation is carefully watched by a firm's other employees. Management must consider how a wage settlement might influence the expectations and demands of other employees in the firm whether or not the other employees are represented by unions. Management, for example, often considers whether wage increases provided to unionized hourly workers will lead to pay increases for supervisors and other white-collar employees outside the bargaining unit. One reason management provides white-collar employees with pay increases is to weaken these employees' potential attraction to unionization.

The Dynamics of Management's Decision-Making Process

So far we have painted a rather static picture of management's decision making. Yet the actual process of decision making over the course of a bargaining cycle (from the prenegotiation planning stage to the signing of the final agreement) is a dynamic one. The process is replete with ambiguities over who has the authority to set policies, conflicts among decision makers over the appropriate weight to be attached to different goals, and power struggles among competing decision makers.

The process by which management establishes bargaining strategies involves extensive intraorganizational bargaining, which is every bit as intense as the bargaining between the union and management. Because the successful resolution of internal differences is a prerequisite to a smoothly functioning bargaining process, it is important to understand how firms prepare for negotiations.

To provide a more complete picture of how management prepares for collective bargaining, a typical case is described in Box 8–2.[9] This firm is preparing to negotiate a contract with the major bargaining unit in its largest manufacturing facility. The contract traditionally sets the pattern for the economic settlements with several smaller units at other locations.

Before negotiations (or very early in negotiations) the labor relations staff tries to predict as closely as possible what it will take to get a settlement. But ultimately the staff is at all times ready to revise its estimates based on new or better information about the union's position as the negotiations proceed.

The case in Box 8–2 illustrates the diversity of interests that exists in the different levels within any modern organization. It shows that the development of a company strategy for negotiations is a highly political process, one in which the different goals of various groups must ultimately be accommodated. Although the labor relations staff serves as a key participant in the development of the strategy, the concerns of operating management, financial staff, and other interest groups within the corporation are also integral to any final decision.

It is interesting to examine how preparations for traditional negotiations compare to preparation for an interest-based bargaining process. Box 8–3 draws on the experiences of the same firm in preparing for a recent round of interest-based bargaining. While much of the background research and information gathering is similar, some of this is done jointly with the union. In this case, the problem-solving processes that had been put in place in the company-union relationship at the workplace provided the foundation for taking a problem solving approach to negotiations as well.

Union and Worker Involvement in Negotiations

This section reviews the common procedures followed by unions and workers during the negotiation of a collective bargaining contract. This material parallels the discussion of the procedures used by management in preparing for negotiations described above.

INPUT FROM THE PLANTS

The first step in the process of preparing for negotiations takes place at the plant level. The plant labor relations staff holds meetings with plant supervisors to discuss problems experienced in administering the existing contract. From these discussions the staff puts together a list of suggested contract changes. At the same time, the staff also conducts a systematic review of the grievances that have arisen under the current contract and collects information on local labor market conditions and on the wages in other firms in the community.

The staff then holds a meeting with the plant manager who raises the industrial relations problems confronted in the plant. The plant's concerns are classified into two groups: those that are contractual problems, and those that should be addressed outside the negotiating process. In addition, the staff asks the plant manager to rank suggested contract changes on the basis of their potential for making a significant improvement in plant operations.

INPUT FROM HIGHER LEVELS OF THE FIRM

Next a series of meetings are held at the division level involving the division labor relations staff, operations management at the division level, and the corporate labor relations director and staff. From time to time outside industrial relations consultants also sit in on these division-level meetings. Here the concerns of the various plants are evaluated against two criteria: (1) the operational benefits expected from proposed contract changes, and (2) the likelihood the changes desired can be achieved in the negotiations process.

The corporate labor relations staff plays a vital role in these division-level discussions, since the expected benefits of different contractual changes can be a matter of dispute across the various plants. In addition, the division labor relations staff is responsible for carefully examining the contract language that exists in the various local agreements for inconsistencies or problems that could be removed by clauses that reflect corporate labor relations preferences. Sometimes the plant labor relations representatives object to changes suggested at the division level because they do not correspond to the priorities of the plant officials and because the existing "discrepancies" may be serving a useful purpose in the plant.

The corporate labor relations staff works closely with the vice president for finance to develop the wage targets. Information on plant labor costs, corporate earnings, and the long-term financial prospects of the company and the industry are built into the wage target the corporate staff ultimately recommends.

INPUT FROM RESEARCH

A *research subgroup* within the labor relations staff of the company also carries out background research that is used in management's preparations for negotiations. At least a year and a half before the opening of formal negotiations the research staff begins to prepare the background information necessary for developing the company's proposals.

The researchers use a data base on employee demographic characteristics and analyze personnel statistics such as turnover, absentee, and grievance rates. They also monitor internal union developments, specifically, union convention resolutions, union publications, and union leaders' statements about the upcoming negotiations. In addition, they survey plant managers for their views on their relations with the union and on the problems they would like to see addressed in the negotiations. The staff also consults plant labor relations staff members to obtain their suggestions. Note, this firm probably invests more resources and assigns more authority for bargaining preparation to its research staff than do most other corporations.

The research staff is ultimately responsible for putting together a summary report that goes to the vice president of industrial relations and the corporate director of compensation. These executives then work with the manager of the research and planning department to develop targets for bargaining.

THE FINAL STEPS IN MANAGEMENT'S PREPARATIONS

The final step in management's preparation for negotiations is a meeting involving the corporate labor relations staff, the chief executive officer, and the board of directors. At this meeting the corporate labor relations director presents for board approval the proposed wage targets and other proposed contract changes and the reasons for seeking the proposed changes. Sometimes this meeting does not take place until after the first

(continued)

negotiations session with the union. The industrial relations director might prefer waiting until then because it may be useful to hear from the union before making his recommendation to top management. This helps him identify both the relative importance the union is likely to place on pay issues and the intensity of the union's concern about other areas of the contract.

The industrial relations director described to us how he presents his recommendation to top management in this way:

I always number my proposed target settlements as proposed settlement target number 1. Someone once asked me what that meant. I said that this is what I think it will take to get a settlement but I number it because I may have to come back to you at some point with my proposed settlement number 2 or even my proposed settlement number 3, et cetera.

The Role of the Union Negotiating Committee

In negotiations with management the union is represented by a negotiating committee. The makeup of the **union negotiating committee** varies across unions, although it typically includes some union officers, support staff (such as members of the local or the national union's research staff, or both), and elected worker representatives. Often the leaders of the union's negotiating committee are the highest elected officers of the union covered by the collective bargaining agreement under negotiation. Some unions, such as local construction, hotel and restaurant, or trucking unions, tend to rely on hired business agents to lead their negotiations.

The negotiating committee will meet a number of times before the start of negotiations to formulate the union's list of demands and to begin to establish expectations regarding what the union can win in negotiations. Before these meetings the negotiating committee will solicit from union members their demands, either directly through membership meetings called to discuss the upcoming negotiations or in some cases through polls. In the UAW, for example, representatives elected from the local unions meet in a convention and vote on bargaining resolutions during preparations for companywide auto bargaining. Union members in the UAW are also consulted during the negotiation of plant contracts that supplement the companywide agreements.

A union negotiating committee typically also receives information and advice from the national union's research staff during its preparations for bargaining. The information provided frequently covers the financial performance of the company, forecasts the future performance of the company and the economy, and summarizes recent settlements in other unions or the pay improvements received by unorganized workers in the same city, firm, or industry.

Some unions, such as the Air Line Pilots Association (ALPA), carry out extensive research and analysis of economic developments in their industry and the financial situation of each company. Prior to entering negotiations, the ALPA research staff conducts extensive briefings with the bargaining committee at an airline and in some cases, such as at Continental Airlines, meets with company representatives to compare financial data and analysis. It is not uncommon for union and company research staff to request or share

The shift to a new approach to negotiations was a gradual and natural outgrowth of our employee involvement (EI) process. We took some steps in this direction in negotiations 10 years ago and more in our most recent round of bargaining. All of us—union and management representatives—have been training in the EI problem-solving tools and we essentially asked each other: Why can't we apply them in negotiations?

As in the past, we would keep a list of issues and problems that came up during the term of the agreement in a file and start preparations by reviewing this list and interviewing plant managers for their concerns. But this time, when we brought this material together and met with the top division executives, the director of industrial relations said he didn't want to take a laundry list of issues into negotiations only to discard some or many of them. Instead he asked his colleagues: "What are your critical problems? What are their root causes? What are the costs involved? If we can agree on these things, then let's go into negotiations and fix them."

Paring the list down and agreeing on what we needed to achieve to solve our problems (which were severe at that particular time) involved tough internal discussions and negotiations. Eventually, the chief executive officer had to decide on a couple of key points since these could conceivably affect the long-term future of the operations and, if we took the hardest line being advocated by some managers, would jeopardize the future of the labor-management relationship.

As a result, we brought about eight or nine issues to the table and the union only brought 15 or 16. In the past we would have both had a lot more.

We had much smaller bargaining committees than in the past as well. We had one representative each from legal, finance, manufacturing, and labor relations, along with the industrial relations director who chaired the committee.

We set up a big round table for bargaining, in a room complete with flip charts and all the other supports needed for brainstorming and problem solving. In the actual negotiations, from time to time we brought in specialists with expertise on particular issues such as the way the transfer language in the contract actually worked. Instead of simply exchanging proposals and working from each other's lists, we scheduled times to take up issues and problems. When we did so, we asked: Why is that a problem? Who's affected? What might we do about it? How would it affect things? Can we live with the solutions proposed?

We still had discipline at the table. We had chief spokespersons. In fact we got very upset and disappointed when at one point the process broke down. When we started talking about overtime, we had already done some joint staff work looking at some pilot programs we had started in a couple of settings to let the union handle how overtime is distributed. This is always a big problem and headache for management, and a costly issue. The staff had pretty much agreed privately to extend the pilot approach to the whole bargaining unit, but when the issue came up for discussion the manufacturing representative on our team said: "We'd never agree to that!" We read him the riot act later in private for springing this on us but it essentially killed discussion of this issue, and we never did get the job done on this issue.

As we got into the tough economic issues, bargaining took on more traditional features. These were very tough and the union leaders needed to be able to demonstrate to their constituents they squeezed us as hard as they could to get the best deal possible. We understood this.

Still, there was better communications, and we never worked past 8 P.M.

information from each other if for no other reason than to avoid debates over some of the basic facts that both need to prepare their respective teams for negotiations.

Many unions now use surveys, focus groups, and/or direct interviews with rank and file members to gather information on their concerns and priorities for negotiations. This serves as a two-way communications process. It both provides data on rank and file priorities and begins to engage the rank and file in the negotiations process, informing them of some of the issues that may come up. The UAW local union at the Saturn Corporation has developed what it calls a "one-on-one" approach to this process. The union recruits volunteers from its leadership and membership to interview every union member of the local prior to negotiations explicitly for this type of two-way communications. This is consistent with this union's emphasis on employee participation in decision making. As we will discuss below, it is also an important prerequisite for using an interest-based approach to negotiations.

Acquisition of Strike Authorization if at Impasse

If the union comes to an impasse with management during the negotiations and is considering going on strike over its unresolved disputes with management, two steps occur. In local contract negotiations the union's constitution typically requires the local to seek **strike authorization** from the national union. Strike approval is an important process because, among other things, it enables striking workers to receive strike benefits from the national union's strike fund.

A union considering a strike also typically will poll its members. The strike vote serves a dual purpose: it tells the union leadership whether the union's members support such an action, and it helps rally the workers around the purpose of the strike.

Contract Ratification

When an agreement is reached between the union's negotiating committee and management's representatives, the union proceeds through its **contract ratification** procedures. Here there is much variation in the exact procedures used by unions. Some unions first send a proposed agreement to a council made up of lower-level union officers. This council would include local union officers when a companywide agreement is negotiated (as in the steel and auto industries). Union constitutions typically also require that the workers covered by a negotiated agreement vote on any proposed settlement.

There are some notable exceptions to the normal pattern of union member votes over proposed contracts. For instance, until the 1970s, coal miners represented by the United Mine Workers did not have the right to vote on new contracts negotiated by their national union leaders. The same was true of Teamster union members covered under the master freight agreement until this was changed in 1987. But in the usual case workers must approve contract settlements (often by majority vote). This sort of voting provides a mechanism for participatory democracy in this critical aspect of union decision making.

Union Leaders' Roles in Shaping Strategies

The actual bargaining demands of unions reflect more than just an averaging of their members' preferences. Several factors combine to produce the complex process by which union leaders arrive at their bargaining objectives.

First, in addition to considering the preferences of their members, union leaders must evaluate objectives in light of the probability that they can be attained. Unrealistic goals must be discarded during prenegotiation planning sessions or early on in negotiations.

Second, individual union members have varying political influence within the union. Older or more skilled workers, for example, may be more politically influential than other members. Thus, the objectives ultimately selected may reflect some workers' goals more than others.

Third, union leaders must also be concerned about the long-run survival of the union and must take steps to preserve those interests. There is always the risk that union leaders will emphasize union security at the expense of member preferences.

Finally, it should be recognized that a central job for union leaders, like all leaders, is to lead! Union leaders must weigh strategic options, make decisions, and secure the ongoing support of their members for those decisions.

One of the keys to union leadership is effective internal communication. Union leaders need regular upward communication from the rank and file and from local union officers. Effective union leadership also requires that decision makers communicate their activities and decisions back to the members. Unions use such techniques as opinion surveys, satellite hookups, television advertising, and the Internet to communicate with their members. Indeed, the Internet is becoming a key resource in bargaining today. Union leaders are learning that if they do not develop skills in using this tool to communicate with members, rival groups within the union will do so. In one case ALPA found that the tentative wage agreement it had reached with Delta Airlines was criticized on a rival group's Web site before the union team even could describe its terms to union members! Thus, the role and means of communication within unions and in negotiations in general are changing rapidly in the age of the Internet.

The Cycle of Traditional Negotiations

Negotiations often proceed through a cycle in which the four subprocesses of bargaining emerge and interrelate.[10] A typical cycle for a traditional negotiations process is described below.

The Early Stages

In the initial stage of a traditional negotiation the parties present their opening proposals. This stage often involves a larger number of people than will be involved in the negotiations of the final agreement. The union, for example, may bring in representatives from various interest groups and levels of the union hierarchy. These people participate in developing the initial proposals and later become involved in securing ratification of any agreement. The involvement of all these different representatives can smooth any intraorganizational bargaining within the union.

The union then presents proposals that cover its entire range of concerns. Some of the proposals will be of critical importance and will be at the heart of the discussions as the strike deadline approaches. Some are important but may be traded off at the last minute. Some may be translated into more specific demands at a later stage of bargaining or may be issues to which the union will assign a high priority in some future round of negotiations. Other issues are of low priority and will be dropped as negotiations proceed into the serious decision-making stages.

The Presentation of a Laundry List

The presentation by the union of a **laundry list** of issues serves several purposes. Such a list allows union leaders to recognize different interest groups by at least mentioning their proposals. Some unrealistic demands will be aired, the problems underlying these demands can be explored, and the employer can then reject these demands. This process takes the pressure off union officers who might otherwise appear to have arbitrarily nixed some group's pet proposal. In a laundry list either side also could introduce issues that it hopes could be pursued in future negotiations.

Initially presenting a long list of proposals and inflated demands might also be useful at camouflaging the real priorities of the union. Or, a long list of proposals could assist integrative bargaining by facilitating trades across issues.

Employer Behavior in the Early Phase

Employer behavior at the outset of bargaining varies considerably. Sometimes the employer will present a set of proposals to counterbalance the union demands. At other times the employer will receive the union demands and promise a response at a future negotiating session. Many management representatives prefer to delay making any specific proposal on wages or other economic issues until well into the negotiations process. Because the wage issue can be emotional and divisive, management often tries to resolve nonwage issues first.

Management may also initially try to camouflage its bottom-line position, and it, too, may have unresolved internal differences at the start of negotiations. In some firms a decision on the bottom line is not made until after the union offers its initial proposals and gives some preliminary indication of its priorities.

In the early stages the speakers for each side will argue strongly and often emotionally for the objectives of their constituents, both to carry out their representational obligations and to determine how strongly the opponent feels about the issues at stake. It should be no surprise that these initial stages are the forum for a good deal of grandstanding by both parties (grandstanding that may be a part of intraorganizational bargaining).

The Middle Stages

The middle stages of negotiations involve more serious consideration of various proposals. The most important tasks performed in the middle stages of bargaining are (1) to develop an estimate of the relative priorities the other side attaches to the outstanding issues, (2) to estimate the likelihood that an agreement can be reached without a strike, and (3) to signal to the other side those issues that might be the subject of compromise at a later stage of the process.

Often the parties choose to divide the issues into economic and noneconomic issues. The separation of issues may facilitate problem resolution and integrative bargaining. It is at these intermediate stages that any obstacles to a settlement may begin to surface.

The Final Stages

The final stages of bargaining begin as the **strike deadline** approaches. At this point the process both heats up and speeds up. Off-the-record discussions of the issues may take place between two individuals or small groups of representatives from both sides, perhaps in conjunction with a mediator. These discussions serve several purposes: to save face in front of one's constituents; to allow a fuller clarification of each party's position; and to explore possible compromises.

The bargaining taking place at the table, in many cases, is only the formal presentation of proposals and counterproposals. At this point the negotiators have a better idea of their opponent's bottom-line positions and they may have private discussions over what it will take to reach a settlement.

Whether the real bargaining occurs at the table or in the back room is less important than are the factors that determine whether a settlement will be reached without an impasse. In these final stages before a strike deadline each party is seeking to convince the other of the credibility of its threats to strike. Each side also is trying to get the other side to change its bottom line to prevent a strike. And each party is trying to accurately predict the other side's real positions on the issues to avoid backing into an unnecessary strike. At this stage, therefore, usually only a small number of decision makers are involved in the process.

Even if the key bargainers may agree on how a bargaining settlement could be reached, agreement is not yet assured. Because of their inability to sell a settlement to their constituents, the agreement might still not be reached without calling an impasse (see Chapter 9).

Interest-Based Bargaining: An Alternative to Traditional Negotiations

The traditional approach to negotiations outlined above has often been criticized for its limited problem solving potential. The dominance of distributive issues and tactics, the overstating of demands, and tactical use and withholding of information have all been viewed by critics as ways traditional bargaining reinforces rather than overcomes arm's-length or adversarial tendencies in labor-management relations. As an alternative, a number of researchers, and a growing number of practitioners have suggested using **interest-based** or **mutual-gains** bargaining techniques.

Interest-based bargaining is essentially an effort to apply integrative bargaining principles from the Walton and McKersie model to the overall negotiations process. This approach to bargaining was first popularized by Fisher and Ury's best selling book on negotiations, *Getting to Yes*. In interest-based bargaining parties are encouraged and trained to (1) focus on their underlying interests, (2) generate options for satisfying these interests, (3) work together to gather data and share information needed to evaluate options, (4) evaluate the options against criteria that reflect their interests, and (5) choose options that maximize their mutual interests.

Consider how use of these principles alters the typical negotiations process described above. Instead of each party beginning bargaining with a laundry list of inflated demands, each separately produces a list of problems that need to be addressed in negotiations to address their core interests. In some cases, the parties may even frame the problems jointly by building on the reports of labor-management committees set up to collect data and study vexing problems such as safety and health hazards, health plan costs or quality, and so forth. A subcommittee might then be formed to collect further information needed to generate options for consideration by the full negotiating teams. Ideally, options are to be generated through use of brainstorming (a free-flowing discussion in which members of a group are encouraged to generate ideas without getting committed to a fixed position and without criticizing the ideas suggested by others). Analysis of the root causes of problems and extensive data sharing are also encouraged at this pre-bargaining or early stage of the negotiations process. As bargaining proceeds to a decision-making phase, standards or criteria are developed to evaluate options. The goal is to then choose options that do the best job of serving the interests of both parties.

In theory, an interest-based process does not differentiate between distributive and integrative issues. Instead, by focusing on basic interests and problems that lie in the way of achieving those interests, the parties attempt to use problem-solving or integrative strategies to address the full range of concerns each party brings to the table. However, experience has shown that some issues are harder to resolve through pure interest-based techniques since they do involve clear trade-offs. When such situations arise in interest-based negotiations, the parties may resort to more traditional tactics and thus mix the two approaches to negotiations.

Interest-based bargaining requires a high level of trust among the negotiators, and between the negotiators and their principals and constituents. Thus it is difficult to make this process work when attitudes in the larger relationship are hostile or where there are significant intraorganizational conflicts within one party or the other.

Since the development of these ideas in the early 1980s, a number of universities, private firms, and the Federal Mediation and Conciliation Service have developed interest-based bargaining training programs for labor and management negotiators. These have generated considerable interest in and experience with interest-based techniques. For example, 69 percent of the labor and management negotiators participating in a national survey carried out for FMCS in 1997 indicated they were aware of interest-based techniques, and fully 41 percent indicated they had used these techniques in negotiations.[11] About two-thirds (66 percent) said they preferred using interest-based techniques rather than traditional give and take bargaining. A follow-up national survey found that as of 2000, 57 percent of labor and management negotiators had made some use of interest based bargaining techniques. So it appears this newer problem-solving approach to negotiations has significant potential in the labor-management field. Indeed, this approach has been used with some success in settings as diverse as universities (the Harvard Clerical and Technical Workers Union and Harvard University and the University of Cincinnati and its faculty), in the telecommunications industry (Pacific Tel and the Communications Workers and Michigan Bell and the Communications Workers,) aerospace (Northrop Corporation and the United Auto Workers), health care (Kaiser Permanente and the Coalition of Kaiser Permanente Unions), airlines (various companies and unions), and in the public sector (over 50 school districts in Illinois and the Illinois Teachers' Association). Kaiser Permanente and its unions carried out interest-based negotiations using the structure of bargaining described in Chapter 7. This serves as the largest and most complex example of the use of this approach to negotiations carried out in the United States to date.

But case studies have shown that certain structural and political features of labor-management relations make it especially difficult to apply interest-based bargaining in this arena.[12] The biggest problem is how to deal with constituency pressures. The 2000 FMCS survey found that 20 percent of the parties using interest-based techniques experienced some internal backlash for doing so from constituents (within management or unions).[13] Negotiators need to demonstrate that they are pressing the other side hard to make concessions. The second biggest problem is a lack of trust between labor and management. A third is the perceived imbalance of power that many unions believe they face in dealing with employers. Because of these problems, most negotiations that use interest-based techniques end up with a mixture of interest-based and traditional negotiations. Indeed, as labor and management gain more experience with these new tools, they appear to be adapting them to fit the labor management setting and are more careful to use them only when the tools are appropriate for the organizations and the bargaining environment.

When should one consider using interest-based techniques and how should negotiators go about trying it out? Most experts agree that both negotiating teams need to be trained in these techniques well in advance of the start of negotiations. To overcome suspicion of constituents, some further recommend bringing rank-and-file union members and managers who are not on the negotiating team into the training, data gathering, and subcommittee deliberations. Often a specially trained *facilitator* (as opposed to a traditional mediator) is also brought in to coach and assist the parties in interest-based negotiations.

While the record of interest-based bargaining to date is still modest, and some cases of failure have been reported, it is clear that the growing complexity of the problems labor and management face are pressuring them to find better ways to produce "win-win" or mutual gains solutions. If the FMCS survey data are an indication, the growing knowledge and interest in these techniques will lead to further experimentation in the years ahead, and most likely both further development of these skills and refinements in the approach to fit the particular features of the collective bargaining structure and environment. If this is true, then future labor and management negotiators will need to master these techniques.

Strikes

In recent years, the number of strikes have declined, occurring in only about 5 percent of all labor-management negotiations. But in many negotiations, the *threat of a strike* continues to play a key role in motivating the parties to move toward an agreement. We explore the role of the strike and strike threat in this section.

How the Strike Threat Influences Negotiated Settlements

In negotiations the bargaining parties are unlikely to settle on terms that differ substantially from whatever terms they think would settle a strike if one were to occur. Consequently, strikes are an important determinant of both parties' bargaining power.

During negotiations both labor and management negotiators formulate expectations as to what might happen if the negotiations were to reach impasse and a strike were to follow. At the same time, both sides have a strong incentive to avoid a strike as each loses income during a strike.

During a strike workers give up forgone wages. They try to make up for those lost earnings by possibly taking a short-time job. Workers also turn to union strike benefits, the earnings of a spouse, or savings to support themselves and their families during a strike.

Firms lose forgone profits during a strike. They try to lessen the amount of profits lost through tactics such as bringing in replacement workers for the strikers, making sales out of any available inventories, or shifting production to an alternative site. The firm relies on assets or the earnings from other lines of business to meet any financial obligations (such as equipment expenses) during a strike. In service businesses such as airlines where business lost during a strike cannot be made up through inventory build up or post-strike deliveries, strikes are especially costly. This is one reason why more extensive efforts are made to avoid strikes in these settings, as we will see when we discuss dispute resolution procedures and proposals for reform in the airline industry in the next chapter.

EXHIBIT 8–2
The Hicks
Model of
Strikes

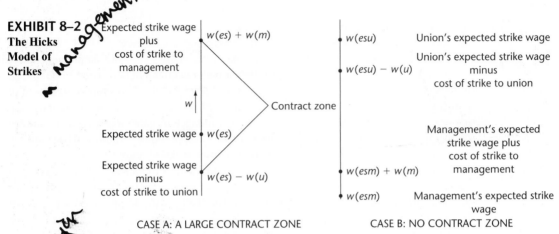

CASE A: A LARGE CONTRACT ZONE   CASE B: NO CONTRACT ZONE

The material below examines more closely the role played by the strike threat in the negotiations process and identifies the factors that lead to strikes.

The Hicks Model of Strikes

John R. Hicks developed a very insightful model to analyze the role played by strike leverage in shaping negotiated outcomes.[14] Exhibit 8–2 diagrams the **Hicks model of strikes.** To simplify the discussion, assume the parties are negotiating only over wages (or assume that all items in dispute can be reduced to monetary terms and represented by a simple wage).

In the Hicks model bargainers form an expectation of what they would eventually agree to if there was a strike. In case A in Exhibit 8–2, both parties expect that if there was a strike it would be ended with a wage settlement of *w(es)*. If a strike occurs, however, both labor and management will have to absorb income losses during the strike. Workers will forgo earnings during the strike, and management will lose profits because of the stoppage in production.

Cognizant of these potential income losses, *during the negotiations* the parties should be able to find a negotiated wage settlement that they prefer over the wage settlement they would end up with at the end of a strike, *w(es)*.

The income management would lose during a strike would amount to an hourly wage cost to management of *w(m)*. Given that they expect a strike to end with a wage of *w(es)*, management should be willing during negotiations to agree to a wage as high as the expected strike outcome plus the cost to management of the potential strike, or *w(es) + w(m)*.

Labor in this case also expects a strike to end with a wage of *w(es)*. The income workers would lose during a strike would amount to an hourly wage cost to labor of *w(u)*. The workers, *during negotiations,* therefore, should be willing to accept a wage as low as the expected strike outcome minus the hourly cost of the strike to labor, or *w(es) − w(u)*.

The difference between what management is willing to accept during negotiations and what labor is willing to accept during negotiations creates a **contract zone** of potential settlements. Both sides should prefer to reach settlements in the contract zone during negotiations to the alternative of taking a strike and ending up with the strike wage outcome and income losses during the strike.

It is, of course, possible for there not to be a contract zone. Case B in Exhibit 8–2 diagrams such a situation. In this case management expects a very low strike outcome of *w(esm)*, while the union expects a very high strike outcome of *w(esu)*. Even in the face of the expected strike costs, *w(m)* and *w(u)*, there is no contract zone because $w(esu) - w(u)$ is greater than $w(esm) + w(m)$.

The important point that Hicks noted is that, in this framework, there is *no* contract zone *only* if the parties have very different expectations of the strike outcome. The fact is that there is some true strike outcome. For labor and management to have divergent expectations from the strike outcome requires that one or both of the parties make **miscalculations** in their prediction of the strike outcome. One or both of the parties must be excessively optimistic regarding what it thinks will settle a strike for there not to be a contract zone.

Hicks was led to the conclusion that strikes occur only in the presence of miscalculation. The key point is that since a strike imposes costs on both sides, it should be less attractive than a negotiated settlement.

Strikes could also occur even if there is a contract zone, but in the Hicks framework this also requires miscalculation. Hicks argued that there may be situations where, even though a contract zone exists, the parties do not locate a settlement within the zone. This occurs because—through either previous bluffing or intransigence—the parties are unable to find the negotiated settlements they both would prefer over the strike outcome.

In the Hicks model negotiators have great latitude to further their side's interests. Given a particular contract zone it is in management's interest to reach a settlement at the lowest wage in the contract zone, and it is in labor's interest to reach the highest wage settlement in the contract zone.

Furthermore, during negotiations it is in each side's interest to attempt to change the other side's expectation of the strike outcome. Management would like to convince labor that the potential strike outcome is in fact a very low wage, and labor has an interest in convincing management that the potential strike outcome is a very high wage. The risk the parties face is that in their efforts to change the other side's expectation of the potential strike outcome, they might engage in tactics (such as bluffing or threats) that result in miscalculations, a strike, and the income losses associated with a strike.

Some of the Sources of Miscalculation

Note that the negotiators may hold expectations of the potential strike outcome that are different from those held by their constituents. Orley Ashenfelter and George Johnson posited that strikes occur because union members have unrealistic expectations.[15] They argued that management has accurate expectations of the strike outcome and so do union leaders, but union members are overly optimistic about what can be achieved in a strike. Under these conditions, strikes are a device to lower union members' expectations. Although it is difficult to justify why, of the three parties, union members alone carry unrealistic expectations, the Ashenfelter and Johnson framework highlights that strikes may occur when union members and leaders have diverging expectations of the strike outcome.

Hicks' model is a very useful starting point for analyzing the negotiations process. To build on his approach requires an understanding of the factors that influence the willingness and ability of either side to engage in a strike. These factors determine the wage the parties expect they will end up with at the end of a strike. Furthermore, the Hicks framework suggests the need to uncover those factors that lead either side to be overly optimistic about the potential strike outcome or in other ways to miscalculate during negotiations.

Behavioral Sources of Strikes

Behavioral factors such as the degree to which labor is integrated into the surrounding social community may be one source of miscalculation that leads to strikes. In a classic study Clark Kerr and Abraham Siegel analyzed strike data across countries and industries, finding that strike rates were consistently higher in certain industries, such as mining and longshoring.[16] The authors proposed that behavioral factors peculiar to certain industries were at least partly responsible for the higher strike rates. Workers in longshoring and mining often have their own subculture, they are distant from major population centers, and their work involves harsh physical labor. Kerr and Siegel argued that workers in these industries are comparatively poorly integrated into society and take out their frustrations and isolation by instigating relatively frequent strikes.

In Hicks' terminology, Kerr and Siegel identified a set of factors—social and geographic isolation—that contribute to the likelihood of miscalculation in bargaining. Note that Kerr and Siegel also emphasized that strike occurrence may have very little to do with the issues on the bargaining table.

Militancy as a Cause of Strikes

Strikes also may occur as a result of the militancy of the work force or union. Marxist theorists have noted that there is a strong statistical association between strike frequency rates and the business cycle. Over time (and across countries) strikes tend to occur more frequently during business upturns. This association is difficult to explain with the Hicks model, which predicts that wage settlements should be higher during business upturns, but not strike frequency.[17]

Marxist theorists instead argue that the procyclical movement in strike frequency demonstrates that conflict is a product of the bargaining power held by labor. This bargaining power model of strikes focuses on the fact that strikes are typically initiated by the union and the work force. Thus, during periods when the union's bargaining power is relatively weak, the union is less likely to press its demands and less likely to resort to a strike in seeking more favorable contract terms.[18]

The bargaining power thesis also recognizes that strikes are frequently initiated by workers on the shop floor who are upset by management's actions or by official union policy (these sorts of strikes often would be counted as unauthorized, or wildcat, strikes). Workers are less likely to engage in this sort of shop-floor action when labor markets are slack and workers fear the possibility of layoff.[19]

It is important to recognize that negotiations involve a large number of issues, that what would actually occur in a strike is highly uncertain, and that labor negotiations typically occur repeatedly between the same parties. These factors make it extremely difficult to predict the settlement point or causes of an impasse in any given negotiations.

Strike Activity

Exhibit 8–3 presents the record of strikes in the United States involving more than 1,000 workers since 1950.[20] These figures illustrate the wide variation that exists over time in the frequency of strikes. The number of strikes and lockouts annually between 1970 and 2006, for example, ranged from 14 to 381. Approximately two-thirds of all strikes are over negotiations of a new contract; the remaining one-third are (generally shorter) strikes called over other issues during the term of an agreement.[21]

Note that strikes occur infrequently. The total work time lost due to strikes has averaged well below one-half of 1 percent per year and was at an historic low in 2001 and 2002, before it began to rise somewhat. The low aggregate strike frequency reported in Exhibit 8–3 is a product of the fact that for any particular negotiations, the probability that a strike will result is low. For instance, in her analysis of a large sample of negotiations that involved manufacturing workers, Cynthia Gramm found that 13.8 percent of the negotiations involved a strike.[22] As mentioned earlier, a national FMCS survey found that strikes now occur in about 5 percent of all negotiations. The low frequency of strikes is consistent with Hick's prediction that both parties usually have strong incentives to avoid strikes. It also appears that the ability of unions to engage in a strike has declined in recent years, as a result of increased international and domestic competition and declining union coverage within and across industries, lending support to the bargaining power thesis noted above.

Whereas strikes in other periods seemed to provide a positive return to union members, strikes in recent years frequently appeared to be defensive weapons used only as a last resort by unions fighting for their continued existence. The strikes that did take place were often more hostile, violent, and emotional than the earlier strikes. Since strikes were so bitter they entailed greater costs to both sides, and, consequently, both labor and management had incentives to avoid their occurrence.

Many strikes in recent years occurred when labor and management could not agree on how to respond to the increasing cost of health care benefits. Many firms were seeking concessions in contract negotiations that would either require increased employee payments ("co-pays") to cover health care cost increases or reductions in health care benefits. Box 8–4 describes recent strikes in the grocery industry that centered on disputes concerning health benefits.

Even though for many unions in recent years the strike weapon had reduced potency, there were also some unions (and employees) who retained sizable strike leverage. NBA basketball players are one such group—their strike leverage derived from the fact that there were no substitutes for NBA superstars. An NBA players' strike in the fall of 1998 led to the cancellation of much of their season as players and owners squared off in a prolonged dispute that centered around the terms of the NBA's free agency system, and how the two sides would divide the expanding revenues of the NBA.

EXHIBIT 8–3
U.S. Work
Stoppages
Involving 1,000
Workers or
More

Source: www.bls
.gov/news.release/pdf/
wkstp.pdf

Year	Number of Work Stoppages*	Number of Workers Involved (000)	Days Idle during Month	
			Number (000)	Work Time Lost
1950	424	1,698	30,390	0.26%
1960	222	896	13,260	0.09
1965	268	999	15,140	0.10
1970	381	2,468	52,761	0.29
1975	235	965	17,563	0.09
1980	187	795	20,884	0.09
1981	145	729	16,908	0.07
1982	96	656	9,061	0.04
1983	81	909	17,461	0.08
1984	62	376	8,499	0.04
1985	54	324	7,079	0.03
1986	69	533	11,861	0.05
1987	46	174	4,481	0.02
1988	40	118	4,381	0.02
1989	51	452	16,996	0.07
1990	44	185	5,926	0.02
1991	40	392	4,584	0.02
1992	35	364	3,989	0.01
1993	35	182	3,981	0.01
1994	45	322	5,020	0.02
1995	31	192	5,771	0.02
1996	37	273	4,887	0.02
1997	29	339	4,497	0.01
1998	34	387	5,116	0.02
1999	17	73	1,996	0.01
2000	39	394	20,419	0.06
2001	29	99	1,151	<0.005
2002	19	46	660	<0.005
2003	14	129	4,091	0.01
2004	17	171	3,344	0.01
2005	22	100	1,736	0.01
2006	20	70	2,700	<0.005

*Includes strikes and lockouts lasting a full shift or longer.

Yet, in August 2002, baseball players and team owners settled contract negotiations without resorting to a strike, as described in Box 8–5. Apparently, both players and owners feared that a strike at that point would particularly upset fans and potentially lead to long-term damage to the game (and their own incomes). Fans had a strong negative reaction to the 1994 baseball strike, which had led to the cancellation of that year's World Series and in 2002 both sides feared even greater damaging effects if a strike occurred once again. The Commissioner of Baseball, Bud Selig, heralded the 2002 settlement as the start of a new relationship between players and owners, but whether that sort of optimism is warranted remains to be seen.

Strikes also can be initiated by management, in sports as in other sectors. This sort of impasse is referred to as a lockout. Box 8–6 describes the lockout that occurred in the National Hockey League (NHL), which led to the cancellation of the 2004–5 NHL season. As the box describes, the NHL players and team owners disagreed on how to set players salaries. NHL hockey finally resumed with the 2005–6 season after a salary cap and other new procedures were added to the NHL's collective bargaining agreement.

The Role of Striker Replacements

One of the most controversial strike issues is whether or not a firm hires temporary or permanent replacements when workers go on strike. Under our labor law, management has the right to hire temporary replacements and can hire permanent replacements if it notifies the union and the newly hired employees that it is doing so. One study found that hiring striker replacements increases the duration of strikes.[23] The threat of hiring permanent

Major League Baseball team owners and players (represented by the Major League Baseball Players Association) reached agreement on a new four-year labor agreement a few hours before a strike deadline set by the players on August 30, 2002. Since 1972, the eight contract negotiations between players and owners had produced five strikes and three lockouts. The previous negotiations, in 1994, led to cancellation of the season from August 12 on and cancellation of the 1994 World Series, all of which cost advertisers, ball clubs, and players millions in lost revenue.

The 2002–6 agreement includes greater revenue sharing of local revenue among baseball's 30 teams and a larger penalty for high payrolls, called a luxury tax, than the previous agreement had employed. The new agreement provides players with a form of employment security through a provision that ensures that no teams will be eliminated through the 2006 season (the owners had threatened to eliminate the Minnesota Twins and the Montreal Expos prior to the start of the 2002 season). The new agreement also provides for the testing of players for steroids for the first time.

Collective bargaining in baseball is noteworthy in that in this case it is the union that has pushed for increased reliance on the market to set players' salary while team owners want greater revenue sharing between teams (to promote competitive balance) and limited player movement (to constrain player salaries).

Players won free agency in 1975, which helped produce a rise in the average salary of baseball players from $51,501 in 1976 to $2.38 million in 2002. See Box 9–3 for a description of salary arbitration procedure used to set baseball players' salaries.

All teams will have to share 34 percent of their locally generated revenue in 2003, up from the 20 percent shared in 2002. Under the new agreement teams also will pay a luxury tax ranging from 17.5 percent to 40 percent of total player salaries above $117 million (in 2003). The luxury tax rate increases each year a team exceeds the tax threshold. The team most affected by the new revenue sharing formula and luxury tax is the New York Yankees, who paid $30 million in revenue sharing in 2002, and will have to pay approximately $15 million more than that in 2003 under the new formula. Plus, the Yankees, winners of four World Series since 1994, will have to pay roughly $9 million in luxury tax in 2003.

Explaining why players settled on the terms in the new agreement, Steve Kline, the St. Louis Cardinals' player representative said," It came down to us playing baseball or having our reputations and life ripped by the fans."

Sources: "Strike Averted: Negotiators Avoid Work Stoppage with Last-Minute Deal," http://sportsillstrated.cnn.com/baseball/news/2002/08/30/labor-friday/; and Murray Chase, "Last-Minute Deal in Baseball Talks Prevents a Strike," *New York Times,* August 31, 2002: A1 and D3.

---

replacements, therefore, is often taken as a signal of management's intent to bargain hard and even to eliminate the union if it goes on strike. This issue has achieved considerable visibility in recent years as big companies such as Continental Airlines, the Detroit News, International Paper, and Caterpillar all followed through on their threats to hire permanent replacements for striking workers and either eventually broke the strike or a decertification of the union occurred.

To try to eliminate this tactic, Democrats in Congress introduced legislation that would ban use of permanent replacements; however, the bill failed to overcome the opposition of the Republican majority. President Clinton then took action on his own by issuing an Executive Order restricting the use of permanent replacements, but this action was ruled unconstitutional by the Supreme Court, arguing that this was a legislative issue requiring Congressional action.

NHL Lockout in 2004 Leads to Cancellation of the Season

Box 8–6

On September 15, 2004, the commissioner of the National Hockey League (NHL), Garry Bettman, announced the beginning of a lockout of the NHL players that would later lead to the first American professional sports league ever to lose a complete season over a labor dispute. Time and time again it looked as if some sort of settlement would take place to enable the season to begin, and time and time again this failed to come to fruition because of one underlying question: Should the NHL institute a salary cap?

As early as February of 2004, it could be seen that there was trouble brewing between the National Hockey League Players' Association (NHLPA) and owners when a report (the "Levitt Study") was released to the public regarding the financial conditions of the league. The report claimed that due to exorbitant players' salaries— to which were attributed 75 percent of a team's total expenditures—nearly two-thirds of the franchises in the NHL lost a combined $273 million in the previous season, while the remaining franchises only averaged slightly greater than $5 million in profit.

Despite these facts, the Players' Association asserted that salary caps were not a necessity, but rather, were a way for owners to exploit the players. The Association contested the financial statements brought forth by the owners, claiming that the history of accounting practices in the NHL has not been air tight. Therefore, in opposition to a salary cap, the NHLPA pushed for a revenue-sharing plan among teams. The parties' inability to settle the salary issues was the key issue that led to the lockout in September 2004.

Although the players were still strongly opposed to the creation of a salary cap, on December 9, 2004— nearly three months into the lockout—the first true concessions were made when the NHLPA proposed a 24-percent reduction in player's salaries, among other cost reduction strategies. However, Bettman and the team owners denied this offer, as they claimed it only allowed for a temporary solution. The owners argued that projections showed that salary inflation of the current magnitude would resurface even before the new agreement would expire if this approach was to be ratified, thereby eliminating any real progress.

In February of 2005, the Players' Association finally agreed to a salary cap, although this did not immediately lead to a contract settlement. After the union proposed a $49 million cap ($3 million less than its first offer), the owners offered a cap of $42.5 million ($2.5 million more than their previous offer), and then neither side was willing to budge any further. As a result, the league then announced that the 2004–5 season was to be cancelled.

Over the next few months little changed, until July 22, 2005, 301 days after the lockout was called, when a new collective bargaining agreement was finally ratified. Not only was a salary cap instituted, which called for a maximum payroll of $39 million and a minimum payroll of $21.5 million, but many other salary changes were introduced. For example, the minimum entry level salary was raised from $185,000 to $450,000. In addition, the age for players to gain the right to unrestricted free agency was lowered to 27, and the league's total expenditure on player costs was not allowed to surpass 54 percent of hockey-related revenue. Moreover, other changes to the game were instituted, such as smaller goalie equipment, shoot-outs if there was a tie after an overtime period, and the elimination of the two-line offside.

Although many feel the owners won out in the end, can anyone be so sure? The lockout not only lost an entire season, but possibly the loyalty of a fan base that was already small in numbers when compared with the other major professional sports leagues. Nonetheless, there is hope for the future. At the onset of the new agreement, Bettman maintained, "Our foundation for the future is now in place . . . this [new collective bargaining agreement] signals a new era in our league and a new era in heightening competitive balance."

Sources: "NHL lockout talks end un deadlock," 02/05/05. *CNN.com,* February 5, 2005; "NHL cancel remainder of the season," 02/16/05. *CNN.com,* February 16, 2005; "NHL owners approve new deal," 07/22/05. *CBC News – CBC Sports,* July 22, 2005; "Back on the ice," 07/22/05. *CBC Sports Online,* July 22, 2005; "A 24 Per Cent Solution to the NHL Lockout?" 12/09/04. www.*proicehockey.about.com,* December 9, 2004; "The NHL Players' Association will not be swayed by catastrophic numbers," 02/13/04. www.*proicehockey.about. com,* February 13, 2004.

How frequently are threats of permanent replacements an issue in modern bargaining? The 1997 FMCS survey found that threats of permanent replacement were made in approximately 12 percent of the negotiations surveyed. This number declined somewhat in 2000 to approximately 10 percent. Replacement workers were actually used in about 29 percent of the strikes that occurred. Thus, while striker replacements are not a factor in most negotiations, they have sent a powerful message in a number of visible cases, and they are a factor in a significant number of negotiations where strikes are threatened and where strikes occur.

First Contract Negotiations

Another special concern of policy makers in recent years has been how to improve the process of first contract negotiations, that is, the first contract negotiated after a union wins certification in a new bargaining unit. Data from the FMCS show that approximately one-third of new bargaining units never reach a first contract agreement, thereby failing to deliver on the promise of collective bargaining for workers who voted for it. FMCS survey data further confirm that these negotiations, on average, experience a higher probability of a strike and a higher probability that striker replacements will be used than in ongoing bargaining relationships. Specifically, the FMCS study found strikes occurred in 9.5 percent of first contracts, compared to only 3.5 percent of contract renewal cases, and striker replacements were used in 31 percent of the cases where they were threatened, compared to only 9 percent of contract renewal negotiations in which this threat was made. Thus, first contract negotiations are hotly contested terrain, and one that warrants special attention of both policy makers and negotiators.

Indeed, the declining utility of strikes has led a number of unions to search for alternative ways to bring pressure on employers without risking the costs of a full-scale work stoppage. Box 8–7 describes how unionized pilots tried to use a strategy from the past: the work slowdown.

Public Pressure as an Alternative or Complement to a Strike

As unions have seen their traditional strike leverage decline as management has threatened the use of permanent replacements, outsourcing, or other tactics, some unions in recent years have used public pressure to strengthen their bargaining leverage. Exhibit 8–4 is a leaflet that NABET and the CWA, representing employees of the ABC Broadcasting Company (owned by the Disney Corporation), circulated in an effort to put pressure on Disney during contract negotiations.

In recent years both labor and management have recognized the growing importance of public opinion in the bargaining process, and especially in strike situations. After all, the public is often inconvenienced by or in many cases bears significant costs of strikes. The subway strike in New York City in 2005 is a perfect example of this. After only two days of picketing, the city's 35,000 mass transit workers returned to work following a public outcry (see Box 13–1). On the other side of the coin, the public backed the Teamsters–United Parcel Service strike of 1997. The fact that the majority of Americans in general, including large numbers of UPS customers, viewed the union's demands as reasonable played a substantial role in strengthening the resolve of the union. Similarly, insiders report that the fear of a strong negative media and sport fan reaction to another

Labor's difficulty in conducting successful strikes has led to the increased use of work slowdowns, but corporations and the courts have reacted as the following cases illustrate.

On March 15, 2001, the Supreme Court rejected a request by the Air Line Pilots Association (ALPA) to review the legality of a federal judge's injunction prohibiting work slowdowns by Delta Air Lines pilots. A dispute between Delta and its pilots began in late 2000 when the pilots, frustrated by a lack of progress in contract negotiations, decreased their requests for overtime, resulting in a large number of flight cancellations. Delta filed a lawsuit against the ALPA and over two hundred pilots, seeking an emergency injunction in order to stop the work slowdown. The Railway Labor Act, which governs airline labor relations, requires both parties to maintain the status quo during negotiations. In January of 2001, the Court of Appeals for the Seventh Circuit found an injunction necessary under the Railway Labor Act. The court decided that the union had a "duty to avoid interruption of commerce" and that the court had the obligation to force this duty, if necessary. The court prohibited ALPA and all pilots from issuing and engaging in a ban on working overtime or harassing pilots who chose to fly overtime.

One day later, on March 16, the Seventh Circuit decided that a federal district court erred in refusing to issue a preliminary injunction to compel the International Association of Machinists (IAM) to discourage its members from engaging in a work slowdown against United Airlines during a strike. United claimed that the IAM initiated an illegal work slowdown with 15,000 mechanics that resulted in the delay or cancellation of hundreds of flights. The union's motive was to gain bargaining leverage and pick up the pace in ongoing contract negotiations. The IAM argued that even if some mechanics engaged in a slowdown, there was insufficient evidence to prove that the union had authorized such actions. Judge William Hibbler of the U.S. District Court denied United's request for an injunction because he believed that United could stop the slowdown by disciplining individual employees. The Seventh Court reversed, concluding that the union was involved in the slow-down so management discipline of individual employees would not be very effective. The court based its decision on statistical evidence showing an increase in maintenance "write-up" calls for inspection and repair and an increase in flights delayed or cancelled due to mechanical problems. The court also scrutinized IAM letters and bulletins urging all employees to generate write-ups if they found something wrong on an aircraft. Some bulletins urged workers to "work safe," which United maintenance officials testified was a code word for a work slowdown. The court concluded that if either side unilaterally alters the status quo during negotiations, the courts have the right to issue an injunction to restore the status quo.

Although the Norris-LaGuardia Act generally prohibits injunctions against unions regarding labor disputes, the Supreme Court has ruled that specific provisions of the RLA take precedence over the more general provisions of the Norris-LaGuardia Act. Judge William Bauer of the Seventh Circuit wrote that in this case an injunction was the "only practical, effective means" to enforce the status quo and that a union "has the affirmative duty under the status quo provisions . . . to exert every reasonable effort to prevent or discourage a strike or a concerted work action like a slowdown in this case."

Sources: "Supreme Court Rejects Bid from Delta Pilots to Review Validity of Job Slowdown Injunctions," 05/15/01. *Daily Labor Report* 94, May 15, 2001: AA–2; and "Seventh Circuit Directs Preliminary Injunction Telling IAM to Discourage Slowdown at United," *Daily Labor Report* 52, March 16, 2001: AA–1.

possible strike in professional baseball played a key role in motivating the parties to reach an agrement in 2002 baseball negotiations. In a service-oriented economy and a media-intensive environment, collective bargaining is gradually becoming a much more public process than it had been in the past.

**EXHIBIT 8–4
Public Pressure
as a Bargaining
Tactic**

Reprinted with
permission.

Walt Disney Inc....

A "Family Company" That Hurts Working Families?

The Walt Disney Corporation likes to pass itself off as the world's most family-friendly company.

It's the company that brought you Mickey Mouse, Donald Duck, Aladdin, and The Lion King. It's a company that claims to be devoted to making America's children happy.

Disney – The Dark Side...

But a closer look at the world's largest entertainment company reveals that Disney's treatment of working families doesn't match its family-friendly image.

It turns out that the paraphernalia you'll see inside the Disney store today has been manufactured around the world by women and children working in sweatshops for just pennies an hour. In Haiti, for example, women sewing 101 Dalmations outfits which sell for $19.99 in the U.S. are paid *$12.20 per week— about $.06 for each garment.*

In the U.S. – No Sweatshops, Just Union-Busting

In the U.S., of course, it's harder for Disney to get away with sweatshop labor. But Disney shows little concern for the well-being and security of American workers who make the company successful.

Right now, 2,700 employees of ABC Television—which is owned by Disney—are negotiating for a new labor contract. Every company proposal so far seems designed to destroy the job security—and the family-supporting jobs—NABET-CWA workers have fought for over the years.

ABC wants to use new technology to eliminate union jobs. It wants to give work to non-union contractors making half the wages of union workers. It wants to increase the use of part-time workers who get no health or pension benefits.

In short, ABC-Disney seems intent on *busting our union and making it impossible for ABC workers to support their families.*

Why Union-Busting?

It can't be because ABC or Disney is struggling financially. Disney made $1.5 billion in profits last year; ABC's operating income was up 38% in the first three months of fiscal 1997, and four of ABC's five owned and operated stations are top-rated in their markets. Disney just gave its former President Mike Ovitz a $140 million buyout after 14 months, and its CEO, Michael Eisner, received a 10-year contract valued at nearly *$500 million dollars.*

It must be that the world's most family-friendly company actually cares more about the almighty dollar than it does about working families. That's something to think about when you shop at the Disney store today.

Let ABC-Disney Know...

American Families Think Union-Busting is Disgusting!

An informational message brought to you by the working families of NABET-CWA

The Role of Strategy in Negotiations and Strikes

To understand the course of negotiations and strikes it is necessary to consider the role played by management and union strategies. This provides another illustration of a point made throughout this book, that activities at one level of the industrial relations system interrelate with activities at other levels.

The Role of Management Strategies

Management strategies have a major effect on the negotiations process and on the strike record. For one thing, management's investment and product decisions affect bargaining power and negotiations strategies. For example, whether management chooses a low-cost, high-volume product strategy rather than a high-quality, high-innovation strategy shapes the extent to which the employer is concerned with lowering wage costs. In addition, a company's overall human resource strategy has an effect on negotiations, particularly, on employee attitudes. The history of bargaining airline industry provides a good illustration of these effects.

In Airlines Negotiations

Following the tragedy of September 11, 2001, the airline industry has seen enormous losses: four of the largest corporations in the industry have gone bankrupt, there have been layoffs in the tens of thousands, wage cuts totaling approximately $10 billion, and overall corporate losses of upwards of $30 billion. Moreover, the upsurge of gas prices in 2005 pushed even the most profitable of the national carriers deeper in debt and even caused many regional and point-to-point carriers, which had been much less susceptible to economic difficulties, to experience financial losses.

While all airlines have experienced severe economic pressures, the labor strategies adopted by the various airlines have differed across the carriers and also have evolved over time at a number of the carriers. Box 8–8 describes how Northwest Airlines ended up hiring replacement workers for striking mechanics and custodians. The bargaining power of the unions representing striking employees at Northwest were hurt when flight attendants and pilots decided not to honor their picket lines. At United Airlines mechanics in contrast agreed to sizeable concessions after a bankruptcy court ruled in favor of United Airline's plan that involved large wage and benefit cuts (see Box 8–9).

Meanwhile at American Airlines in May 2004, the company and the unions representing its employees negotiated a package of concessions that enabled the carrier to avoid declaring bankruptcy. First, senior management at American Airlines attempted to restructure by decreasing nonlabor costs, but in the end, American Airlines was forced to reduce its labor costs by nearly $2 billion—more than 20 percent of its total labor expenditures. By agreeing to these concessions the union representing American Airlines flight attendants opened itself up to a charge of unfair representation (see Box 8–10). When American Airlines faced another financial crisis and possible bankruptcy in 2005, the airline developed a new business plan. This time American Airline management did not base its cost savings plan on concessions from its workers and their unions. Instead, American Airlines CEO Gerard Arpey announced that he wished to bridge the gap between management, employees and unions. He wanted to allow for a supportive atmosphere where employee voice would

On August 20, 2005, the Aircraft Mechanics Fraternal Association (AMFA), which represents about 4,400 of Northwest Airlines' mechanics, custodians, and other employees, went on strike after the two opposing parties rejected the other's final offer contract proposals. The AMFA's final proposal, which would save $100 million annually by eliminating jobs, could not reach the $176 million that Northwest Airlines had hoped to cut. Northwest Airlines had already cut 5,000 jobs over the previous four years by outsourcing much of its operations, and hoped to take other measures that would assist in its attempt to compete with low-cost airlines and avoid bankruptcy. Skyrocketing fuel prices and increasing competitiveness of other airlines have put great pressure on Northwest since 2001.

Despite the AMFA's appeal to other unions for support, Northwest Airlines' two other major unions, the Professional Flight Attendants Association and the Airline Pilots Association, voted to not honor the picket lines by engaging in sympathy strikes. ALPA leaders announced that they would not honor the strike at all because it "was not in the best interests of NWA pilots." Officials from the PFAA, however, encouraged members to support the AMFA during off-duty time.

Initially, Northwest Airlines called in 1,900 temporary replacement workers to step in for the striking mechanics and custodians. Many of these replacement workers had been furloughed or laid off from other airlines, and still other tasks continued to be outsourced to third-party vendors. Despite the AMFA's claim that Northwest Airlines would suffer severe interruptions without experienced workers, flights continued to run without excessive delays or cancellations.

On September 13, 2005, two days after yet another failed negotiation with the AMFA, Northwest began hiring workers to *permanently* replace the striking mechanics. Despite these actions by management, AMFA officials continued to assure its members that the airline was incapable of running soundly with inexperienced replacement workers, and that the striking workers should not cross the picket lines.

Just one day later, Northwest Airlines filed Chapter 11 bankruptcy, saying that high fuel prices have increased its losses before it could adequately cut labor and other costs. The company said it would continue to run flights and maintain a competitive stance in the airline industry during its restructuring. In addition, it continued to work toward reaching an agreement with the AMFA.

Sources: Chris Isidore - "Northwest flies through strike." Article on *CNN Money:* http://money.cnn.com/2005/08/22/news/fortune500/northwest_strike/index.htm?cnn=yes; "Mechanics, Custodians Strike Northwest; Airline Uses Replacements to Keep Flying." *Daily Labor Report* 162, August 23, 2005: AA-1; "Northwest Starts Hiring Permanent Workers to Replace Striking Aircraft Mechanics." *Daily Labor Report* 177, September 14, 2005: A-8.

be great. As such, he pushed for managers to embrace the philosophy, "Involve before Deciding, Discuss before Implementing, Share before Announcing."

A more conciliatory approach has long characterized relations between Southwest Airlines and its employees and led to financial success, as Southwest Airlines was one of only two major airlines to report positive profits in 2005. The history, growth, and success of Southwest Airlines illustrates the links among competitive strategies, human resource policies, and labor negotiations. From its beginning as a small Texas regional carrier, Southwest emphasized creating a "family environment" at work, accepted unionization of its employees without a battle, and negotiated flexible work practices and relationships that supported the company's business model and strategy. That model calls for rapid turn-around of airplanes (turnaround refers to the time from when an airplane lands and then takes off with a new set of passengers). This requires that pilots, flight attendants, and all ground personnel work together in a highly coordinated and flexible fashion.

Roughly a year after the World Trade Center tragedy on September 11, 2001, United Airlines filed for Chapter 11 bankruptcy. In doing so, it was looking to cut nearly $1 billion in labor costs—on top of more than $2.5 billion in other cutbacks—to regain profitability and exit bankruptcy.

On January 28, 2005, the Aircraft Mechanics Fraternal Association (AMFA), which had overthrown the International Association of Machinists in mid-2003 as the representative of mechanics at United, rejected a proposal by the company that would have significantly decreased wages and benefits for up to five years. Three days later, a bankruptcy court ruled in favor of United, enacting a similar arrangement that would provide for wage and benefit reductions on a temporary basis—until May of 2005. As a result, it was feared that AMFA would call a strike. On February 1, 2005, though, AMFA declared that a strike would not be necessary, as the situation was too delicate and the wage cuts were only temporary. Therefore, there was still ample time to continue to bargain.

However, by May 16, 2005, AMFA was again threatened with the possibility of a court-ruled settlement. Instead of risking a mandatory agreement by a bankruptcy court that was heavily in favor of large corporations, AMFA signed a settlement agreeing to allow United to cut nearly 4 percent of employee base pay, reduce the number of paid holidays from ten to eight, and allow the outsourcing of specific functions.

Following this settlement, on February 1, 2006, United Airlines successfully returned from bankruptcy. This, nevertheless, came from an extreme sacrifice on the part of the union and the employees, who not only lost wages and benefits, but also lost billions of dollars after their stock holdings became worthless. Even so, union leaders are confident they can make strides in regaining what the employees lost now that United is unable to hide behind the "robes of bankruptcy." As Captain Mark Bathurst, of the Airline Pilots Association, noted, "no longer does the company have the ability to run to downtown Chicago to seek relief that it couldn't get through the normal process."

Sources: "Independent Union Replaces IAM as Representative of United Mechanics," 07/15/03. *Daily Labor Report,* July 15, 2003: A-8; "Bankruptcy Judge Imposes Temporary Wage Cuts on United Airlines' Mechanics," 02/02/05. *Daily Labor Report,* February 2, 2005: A-1; "United Reaches Tentative Pact with AMFA While Negotiations Intensify with Machinists," 05/18/05. *Daily Labor Report,* May 18, 2005: AA-1; "United Airlines Emerges from Bankruptcy Amid Challenging Climate for Carriers," 02/02/06. *Daily Labor Report,* February 2, 2006: A-14.

The favorable work environment that Southwest has created and sustained over more than a 20-year period has carried over to its labor negotiations. While on average it takes airline companies and their unions 17 months to negotiate a new agreement, Southwest has reached agreements in an average of 6 months time. Experts attribute a major part of the company's strong financial performance and its high customer satisfaction and quality ratings to synergies achieved among its business, work force, and labor relations strategies.[24]

Management's strategic initiatives altered the process of bargaining as well. To convince the work force that concessions were necessary, management introduced new communication tactics, some of which bypassed the traditional role unions played as an intermediary between management and workers. At American Airlines, for example, direct mailings outlining management's position to the employees played a critical role in labor negotiations at this company in recent years. Auto companies regularly use news broadcasts and analyses shown on video monitors on the shop floor to inform workers about industry developments.

In April of 2001, American Airlines acquired the assets of Trans World Airlines (TWA). In doing so, American decided to furlough all flight attendants who had been brought in through the acquisition of TWA, place them at the bottom of the seniority list (regardless of years of service), and eliminate their severance pay. At the same time, American Airlines failed to reveal that it had provided substantial benefits packages to top executives within the corporation.

At first, the Association of Professional Flight Attendants (APFA) fought against these actions. A few days later, however, the union decided to sign an agreement allowing American Airlines to take these measures, as it believed acting otherwise would lead the firm to bankruptcy.

Subsequently, flight attendants who had been hurt by these proceedings filed for an injunction against the furlough. They claimed that the union failed to justly represent them, that American Airlines had supported and assisted in these actions, and that American deceived them when it did not reveal pertinent information, such as the benefits packages top executives were to receive.

For the court to impose the injunction requested by disgruntled employees, the court needed evidence that the furlough would have caused permanent harm to the flight attendants. However, the court maintained that preventing the furlough could possibly lead American Airlines into bankruptcy, which would result in far more job losses than what had already been seen, in addition to the grounding of nearly 100 aircraft. As a result, on June 30, 2003, a federal judge denied the request for an injunction against the furlough.

Source: "Former TWA Flight Attendants Lose Bid to Halt Furloughs at American," 07/02/03. *Daily Labor Report,* July 2, 2003: AA-1.

On the West Coast Docks

As Box 8–11 describes, in fall 2002, a labor dispute involving shipping companies, port operators, and the longshoremen's union came to a head. In their collective bargaining relationship, West Coast shipping companies and port operators are represented by the Pacific Maritime Association (PMA) while dockworkers are represented by the International Longshore and Warehouse Union (ILWU). The two sides had been negotiating for months over renewal of their labor contract and were unable to reach agreement over the jurisdiction of new jobs that would be created through the introduction of new technology.

The dockworkers historically have held substantial bargaining leverage as management did not have easy recourse to strike replacements nor could management without great expense move the work (ship loading and unloading) to alternative production sites given technological constraints and worker solidarity across ports. Frustrated by the lack of progress in contract talks and claiming that workers were engaging in a work slowdown, in late September 2002, management imposed a lockout in an effort to strengthen their bargaining leverage.

Citing spreading economic costs from the closure of all West Coast ports, President Bush then asked the federal court to issue a Taft-Hartley injunction to end the work stoppage. The use of a lockout by shippers and port management seemed to be based on their hope that through the issuance of a Taft-Hartley injunction management would end up with a more palatable final settlement. Thus, in this case, management sought to gain bargaining power advantage through governmental intervention rather than through the more traditional sources of strike leverage or labor demand elasticity. This provides an interesting illustration of how adaptive management strategy can be.

U.S. District Judge William Alsup, responding to a request from President George Bush, on October 8, 2002, ordered the end of a management lockout at 29 ports from Seattle to San Diego.

The Pacific Maritime Association (PMA), representing shipping companies and port operators, had locked out dockworkers on September 27. A previous labor agreement covering dockworkers, represented by the International Longshore and Warehouse Union (ILWU), expired July 1, 2002, and had been extended to September 1. At the time it initiated the lockout, PMA accused the ILWU of engaging in a work slowdown that drastically cut productivity.

The negotiations for a new contract had become deadlocked over issues surrounding the implementation of new technology such as cargo-scanning computers. The ILWU wants jurisdiction over any new jobs that result from the new technology, but PMA has been unwilling to provide that guarantee. Instead, the PMA offered to increase longshoremen pay (from an average of $106,833 to $114,000), provide other health care and pension contract improvements, and guarantee that no current workers would lose their job due to the introduction of new technology. The ILWU worried that the future size of the work force and union, and the union's future bargaining leverage will be seriously reduced unless the union is granted jurisdiction over the new jobs. In the early 1960s when the ILWU and port operators negotiated a heralded mechanization agreement to cope with the introduction of containers, there were 100,000 West Coast dockworkers. In 2001, the West Coast ports handled over half the cargo that moved through U.S. ports with only 10,500 dockworkers.

Judge William Alsup acted under steps outlined in the Taft Hartley (Labor-Management Relations) Act (see Chapter 3). Under the national emergency dispute resolution procedures outlined in the Act, the federal courts are empowered to order an 80-day cooling-off period in the face of disputes that threaten the nation's health and safety. A court injunction requires the two sides to work under the terms of the previously expired contract while holding further negotiations supervised by a federal mediator. After 60 days, if no agreement is reached, federal fact-finders issue a report on the dispute. After that the National Labor Relations Board has 15 days to poll employees to see if a majority would accept management's final offer and another five days to count union votes. If the union membership rejects the offer, the union is free to strike. The U.S. Congress can then impose a settlement, but this authority rarely has been exercised.

Of the 35 national emergencies that have been settled under Taft-Hartley, 11 have involved dock strikes. The last time Taft-Hartley procedures were involved in a labor dispute was during a 1978 coal miner strike and in that situation, the courts refused to issue an injunction, as requested by President Carter, after concluding that a national emergency in fact did not prevail. The 2002 dock dispute is the first time a Taft-Hartley injunction has been sought in a lockout situation.

The dispute was settled in late November 2002 when port operators and the longshoremen reached agreement on a six-year collective bargaining agreement that provides gains to both labor and management. The new contract provides an 11 percent wage increase and large pension increases.

Under the agreement management gains the flexibility to introduce new technologies and the union maintains jurisdiction over marine clerk jobs, jobs the union feared would become nonunion. Existing clerks are guaranteed full-time work for the rest of their careers under the contract, but over time as clerks retire, fewer clerks positions will be available. An estimated 400 clerk positions will be affected by new technology and lost through attrition. An arbitration process was negotiated by the parties to settle anticipated differences over the assignment of new clerk jobs resulting from new technology.

Peter Hurtgen, director of the Federal Mediation and Conciliation Service, provided extensive mediation assistance to the parties that helped bring the settlement.

Sources: "ILWU Hails Proposed Pact with PMA Despite Member Concerns over Job Loss," *Daily Labor Report* 241, December 16, 2002: A6; "With Few Port Jobs at Issue, Economic Stakes Are Vast," *New York Times,* October 2, 2002: A20; and "Both Sides See Gains in Deal to End Port Labor Dispute," *New York Times,* November 25, 2002: A14.

The dispute was settled in late November 2002 when port operators and the longshoremen negotiated a six-year collective bargaining agreement that provides gains to both labor and management.

The Role of Union Strategies

The steel industry historically was characterized by "Big Steel" on one side and "Big Labor" on the other side given the oligopoly that prevailed on the company side and the extensive representation of the workforce by the United Steelworkers Union (USWA). In that era, collective bargaining was highly adversarial, with each side fighting viciously for their piece of the pie. With the rise of global trade, fewer barriers to foreign importation, and charges of the illegal "dumping" of steel by foreign competitors, the American steel industry has struggled, with the unionized integrated steel companies facing particularly intensive challenges (the nonunion U.S. mini-mills fared better in recent years). U.S. steel companies found that they were at a competitive disadvantage when it came to pricing in part they claimed due to the "legacy costs" associated with retiree pension and health care benefits (the latter were not common in other steel producing countries).

With these new challenges came new strategies, both from management and labor. By 2003, 37 companies filed for bankruptcy, including the second and third largest producers of steel, LTV Steel and Bethlehem Steel. In addition to allowing some firms to liquidate, the filing for Chapter 11 bankruptcy protection provided management with a way to reduce legacy costs and pension obligations.

While labor and management often engaged in intense fights over the legitimacy and consequences of bankruptcy declarations, on occasion they found themselves on the same side when they teamed up to lobby legislatures to help their cause. Specifically, the USWA worked with various corporations and successfully persuaded the Bush administration to impose strict tariffs on steel imports. Additionally, in recent years there has been a strong push toward transferring pension debt to the government's Pension Benefit Guaranty Corporation. The Bush Justice Department has waived antitrust laws to facilitate the conglomeration of the steel industry and in the process raised the profits of American steel companies.

At some of the steel companies a conciliatory relationship has emerged between labor and management in part as an outgrowth of joint regulatory lobbying and in some cases as a result of joint efforts at the workplace level to improve productivity. The productivity initiatives often involve some form of incentive pay and gain-sharing programs.

The Persistence of Historical Relationships

The dramatic reduction in passenger traffic and in revenues experienced by airlines in the aftermath of the September 11, 2001, terrorist attacks ushered in a new era in airline labor relations. All airline companies had to take quick and drastic steps to remain solvent, including large-scale layoffs, reconsideration of their underlying business models, pricing, network structures, and relationships with employees. Yet, a surprising degree of continuity in relationship patterns ensued at least in the first year following the attacks.

Southwest Airlines, for example, continued to stress the importance of good relations with its workforce and avoided immediate layoffs. It could do so because of its past financial success and its conservative financial management (it carried less debt than other major carriers). Continental Airlines, on the other hand, although having built up a positive employee and labor–management relationship in recent years, chose to lay off more than 10 percent of its workforce to cope with its large debts. Yet, Continental did so in a fashion that maintained good relations with its workers and their union leaders.

These interconnections between business strategies, union strategies, and collective bargaining can also be seen in other industries. Increases in health insurance costs, pensions, and the staggering expenses associated with legacy costs in the face of declining auto sales have forced the Big Three automotive companies—GM, Ford, and DaimlerChrysler—to focus on measures to reduce their workforces in the collective negotiations these companies carry out with the UAW. Collective bargaining became more of a process to reduce costs and the likelihood of corporate bankruptcy rather than a forum for employee or union gains.

At the Ford Motor Company "Guaranteed Employment Numbers" (GEN), in place since the mid-1980s, had allowed employees laid off due to plant closings to receive nearly 100 percent of their pay for the duration of the contract. After announcing plans to close multiple plants and cut up to 30,000 jobs in order to reverse ballooning losses, Ford sought alternatives to the GEN provisions (see Box 10–4). The 2003–2007 collective bargaining agreement between Ford and the UAW provides that any worker with at least one year of service in the company may voluntarily leave and either receive a lump sum payment of $100,000 or half of their annual salary and up to $15,000 a year in tuition assistance at an institution of higher learning in order to help change career paths. General Motors and DaimlerChrysler negotiated similar terms with the UAW.

Legacy costs associated with retirement benefits and pensions also became prominent collective bargaining issues. For example, the UAW allowed Ford to close 14 manufacturing facilities (26 percent capacity reduction by 2008) and eliminate up to 30,000 jobs, among other cost-saving measures. When Ford's profits declined further, even before the contract that introduced these terms had expired, in late 2005 Ford and the UAW raised drug co-payments in an effort to hold down retiree health care costs. With an 8 percent increase in annual health care costs, the UAW and the auto companies vowed to lobby Congress side-by-side in favor of a system of national (universal) health care coverage.

One of the most visible work stoppage of the past decade was the 15-day strike of the United Parcel Service (UPS) by its 185,000 Teamsters Union employees in August 1997 (see Chapter 10). This strike gained national attention in part because of its size (the largest number of workers on strike since the early 1980s) and in part because the public took a great interest in one of the key issues in the dispute, namely the union demand that UPS provide more full-time jobs to its many part-time workers. Over 60 percent of the bargaining unit was made up of part-time workers.

The public strongly supported the Teamsters' demand. Opinion polls conducted by CNN and others showed that the American public supported the striking workers rather than the company by a 2 to 1 margin (55 to 27 percent). The strike escalated to where the Secretary of Labor and the Director of the Federal Mediation and Conciliation Service engaged in four days of intensive round-the-clock mediation. The settlement achieved most of the union's demands—a commitment by UPS to move 10,000 part-time workers to full-time jobs and substantial pay increases for both part-time and full-time workers. This strike demonstrated the importance of public opinion can sometimes play in shaping the process and results of bargaining.

The memory of the 1997 negotiations had an impact on negotiation of the sucessor UPS–Teamsters collective bargaining agreement in 2002. This time the parties kept their negotiations largely out of the public eye. The union had built up its strike fund to demonstrate its willingness to strike if necessary, but the company was particularly eager to avoid another work stoppage. An agreement was reached that included a substantial wage increase and another commitment to convert part-time to full-time jobs just prior to the contract expiration date (see Box 10–3).

International Comparisons of Strike Activity

The United States is not alone in experiencing a declining trend in strike activity. The same is true in most industrialized countries that have a long history of collective bargaining. Even countries such as Australia and Ireland, which used to rival the United States as having the highest strike rates, have experienced marked declines in both the number of strikes and the overall amount of time lost due to strikes.

Strikes play different roles in various countries. In the United States strikes are tactical weapons wielded to induce employers to change their bargaining positions. Strikes in some European, South American, or Asian countries, however, often have political motives.

Strikes also vary in occurrence across countries depending on the degree of freedom trade unions have in the legal system. In some countries unions or strikes are outlawed, and it is not surprising that strike rates tend to be low in such countries. In some other countries unions are dominated by the government or play a part in the government through a union-led political party. These factors also affect strike frequency.

Summary

This chapter begins by analyzing the four subprocesses that make up negotiations. Distributive bargaining concerns issues in which the gain of one party is a loss to the other side. There is no possibility of joint gain with distributive issues.

Integrative bargaining, in contrast, involves issues in which it is possible for both sides to gain from the resolution of problems. The successful introduction of new technology, for example, can increase the profits received by management and the income received by the workforce. A number of factors can make the resolution of integrative issues difficult. The overuse of tactics oriented toward distributive bargaining can block an exchange of information and the identification of potential integrative solutions. In some cases the parties are not able to settle integrative issues because they do not agree on how to divide the gains

that would follow from integrative problem solving.

Intraorganizational bargaining arises from the differences in preferences that exist within either the union or management side. For the union it may be that union leaders have different views than the rank and file, or older union members may prefer a contract settlement that differs from what younger union members prefer. Plant versus corporate management differences are a frequent source of intraorganizational bargaining within management's ranks.

Attitudinal structuring concerns the extent to which trust exists between the union and management. It is trust that often facilitates the settlement of integrative issues. There are frequent other interrelationships across the four subprocesses of bargaining.

Traditional negotiations typically involve a complex cycle. Management engages in extensive preparation during the formation of its wage and other targets. Labor market data and other economic data are used by research staffs to prepare these targets. Similar preparations occur on the union side. Many unions engage in the polling of members to formulate their bargaining demands.

Recently, the search for a better way of negotiating has led to considerable use of interest-based or mutual-gains bargaining practices in an effort to extend problem solving or integrative bargaining across the entire range of negotiating issues. A strong majority of labor and management negotiators are aware of interest-based techniques, and many have tried them, suggesting that these techniques may become quite prominent features of collective bargaining in the future. To achieve their promised problem-solving potential, however, these techniques will need to be adapted and used skillfully to avoid the backlash of constituents.

There are a number of explanations as to why the parties in some cases reach an impasse and a strike occurs. The Hicks model emphasizes the role that miscalculation can play as the precipitator of a strike. Behavioral factors and worker militancy can also produce strikes.

The empirical record demonstrates the general infrequency of strikes in the United States and the especially low rates of strike occurrence over the previous twenty years. Recent events also illustrate the role played by management and union strategies as a factor that shapes negotiations and strikes.

At the other extreme, more parties are experienced with use of interest-based bargaining and problem-solving processes. Thus, at the moment, negotiations processes are moving in two opposite directions— toward more intensive, if less frequent, conflicts and toward greater problem solving.

Strikes represent one potential outcome to negotiations. The next chapter examines various techniques and procedures used to resolve strikes. The other potential (and more frequent) outcome to negotiations is a contract. After discussing impasse resolution in negotiations we will turn to a discussion of the common terms found in labor agreements.

Discussion Questions

1. Describe the four subprocesses of negotiations developed by Walton and McKersie.
2. What are the key aspects of the three stages in a typical negotiations cycle?
3. Describe the Hicks model of strikes.
4. Give some examples of how management strategy influenced the course of negotiations or strikes in the 1980s or 1990s.
5. How do traditional and interest-based bargaining differ?
6. When does interest-based bargaining work best? Under what conditions would you advise against its use?
7. Briefly describe some of the union strategies used in the steel, airline, and auto industries from the 1990s to the present.
8. What happened to the frequency of strikes in the United States from the early 1980s on and what explains this trend?

Related Web Sites

British Airways:
http://www.british-airways.com/lsp/newba/video/video.shtml

Continental Airlines:
http://www.flycontinental.com/corporate/cofacts/

Trans World Atlantic:
http://www.twa.com/about_twa/at_history.html

Amalgamated Transit Union (ATU):
http://www.cais.com/atu

Greyhound:
http://www.greyhound.com/Company/company.html

Bridgestone/Firestone:
http://www.bridgestone-firestone.com/wrld/wrldmain.htm

Airlines Pilots Association (ALPA):
http://www.alpa.org

Suggested Readings

Clark, Paul, John Delaney, and Ann Frost eds. *Collective Bargaining: Current Developments and Future Challenges* (Champaign, IL: Industrial Relations Research Association, 2003).

Fisher, Roger, and William Ury. *Getting to Yes: Negotiating Agreement without Giving In* (New York: Penguin Books, 1981).

Getman, Julius. *The Betrayal of Local 14a* (Ithaca, New York: ILR Press, 1998).

Juravich, Tom and Kate Bronfenbrenner. *Ravenswood: The Steelworkers' Victory and the Revival of American Labor* (Ithaca, New York: ILR Press, 1999).

Morse, Bruce. *How to Negotiate the Labor Agreement,* 10th ed. (Southfield, MI: Trends Publishing, 1984).

Rosenblum, Jonathan D. *Copper Crucible: How the Arizona Miners Strike of 1983 Recast Labor-Management Relations in America* (Ithaca, New York: ILR Press, 1995).

Walton, Richard E., and Robert B. McKersie. *A Behavioral Theory of Labor Negotiations* (New York: McGraw-Hill, 1965).

Walton, Richard E., Joel Cutcher-Gershenfeld, and Robert B. McKersie. *Strategic Negotiations: A Theory of Change in Labor-Management Relations* (Boston: Harvard Business School Press, 1994).

End Notes

1. See Edward Cohen-Rosenthal and Cynthia Burton, *Mutual Gains: A Guide to Union Management Cooperation* (Boston: Pitman, 1987); Roger Fisher and William Ury, *Getting to Yes* (Boston: Houghton Mifflin, 1981); and Richard E. Walton, Joel Cutcher-Gershenfeld, and Robert B. McKersie, *Strategic Negotiations: A Theory of Change in Labor-Management Relations* (Boston: Harvard Business School Press, 1994).

2. Richard E. Walton and Robert McKersie, *A Behavioral Theory of Labor Negotiations* (New York: McGraw-Hill, 1965).

3. It is, of course possible that there is some joint gain associated with a higher wage rate if labor productivity increases when wages are raised. This might result from the greater motivation workers feel when their pay goes up or from the better qualified workers the firm can recruit when it offers a higher wage. We ignore such considerations in the text discussion.

4. Thomas A. Kochan, George P. Huber, and L.L.Cummings,"DeterminantsofIntraorganizational Conflict in Collective Bargaining in the Public Sector," *Administrative Science Quarterly* 20 (March 1975): 10–23.

5. One empirical study found negotiator hostility to be a very strong predictor of public sector impasses, although it was not a strong predictor of strikes. See Thomas A. Kochan and Jean Baderschneider, "Dependence on Impasse Procedures: Police and Firefighters in New York State," *Industrial and Labor Relations Review* 31 (July 1978): 431–49.

6. For evidence on the role of personality traits in bargaining, see Jeffrey Z. Rubin and Bert T. Brown, "The Social Psychology of Bargaining and Negotiations," (New York: Academic Press, 1975), pp. 1583–96; and

Max Bazerman, *Judgement in Managerial Decision Making* (New York: John Wiley, 1986).

7. Margaret A. Neale and Max H. Bazerman, "The Role of Perspective-Taking Ability in Negotiating under Different Forms of Arbitration," *Industrial and Labor Relations Review* 36 (April 1983): 378–88.

8. Arthur M. Ross, *Trade Union Wage Policy* (Berkeley: University of California Press, 1948), pp. 45–74.

9. This case is a real firm we encountered in our field work. The firm preferred not to be identified by name.

10. This cycle is discussed in Carl M. Stevens, *Strategy and Collective Bargaining Negotiations,* (New York: McGraw-Hill, 1963), pp. 41–46.

11. The data in the FMCS survey discussed in this chapter are reported in Thomas A. Kochan and Joel Cutcher-Gershenfeld, "Final Report on the National Performance Review Survey for the Federal Mediation and Conciliation Service," MIT Sloan School of Management, June, 1997.

12. See for example, Ray A. Friedman, "Missing Ingredients in Mutual Gains Bargaining Theory," *The Negotiations Journal* 10 (1994): 265–80; Charles Heckscher and Livinia Hall, "Mutual Gain and Beyond: Two Levels of Intervention," *Negotiations Journal* 10 (1994): 235–45; and Ann Martin, "Interest Based Bargaining: What We're Learning, *Perspectives on Work* 2 (1997): 49–53.

13. Joel Cutcher Gershenfeld and Thomas A. Kochan, "Taking Stock of Collective Bargaining at the Turn of the Century," unpublished manuscript, MIT Sloan School of Management, 2002.

14. John R. Hicks, *The Theory of Wages* (New York: Macmillan, 1932), chapter 2.

15. Orley Ashenfelter and George E. Johnson, "Bargaining Theory, Trade Unions, and Industrial Strike Activity," *American Economic Review* 59 (March 1969): 35–49.

16. Clark Kerr and Abraham Siegel, "The Interindustry Propensity to Strike," in *Industrial Conflict,* ed. Arthur Kornhauser, Robert Dubin, and Arthur M. Ross (New York: McGraw-Hill, 1954), pp. 189–212.

17. Economists have also constructed models that involve "asymmetric information" to explain strike occurrence. These models rely on the notion that management knows the profitability of the firm, whereas the union must guess profitability and use wage offers to get the firm to reveal its true profitability. See, for example, Joseph S. Tracy, "An Investigation into the Determinants of U.S. Strike Activity," *American Economic Review* 76 (1986): 423–36.

18. Interindustry studies of strikes often yield results that support the bargaining power model of strikes. Specifically, these studies show that strikes are more frequent in industries with lower levels of unemployment, higher percentages of men in the work force, and a higher percentage of the work force organized. See David Britt and Omer Galle, "Structural Antecedents of the Shape of Strikes: A Comparative Analysis," *American Sociological Review* 39 (October 1974): 642–51.

19. For an interesting analysis of both contract strikes and strikes between contract negotiations that is consistent with a bargaining power model of strikes, see Sean Flaherty, "Contract Status and the Economic Determinants of Strike Activity," *Industrial Relations* 22 (Winter 1983): 20–33.

20. Strike activity can be measured in a variety of ways, depending on the purpose of the analysis including frequency, duration and breadth (size). For analysis of these issues see Robert N. Stern, "Methodolocial Issues in Quantitative Strike Analysis," *Industrial Relations* 17 (February 1978): 32–42.

21. Data on the total number of strikes and the number of strikes during negotiations and between contracts (not shown in Exhibit 8–3) can be found in *Handbook of Labor Statistics* (Washington, DC: Bureau of Labor Statistics, U.S. Department of Labor, various years). For a discussion of the procedures and difficulties involved in collecting and

compiling statistics on work stoppages, see *Handbook of Methods for Survey Studies, Bulletin 1910* (Washington, DC: Bureau of Labor Statistics, U.S. Department of Labor, 1976), chapter 27.

22. Cynthia L. Gramm, "The Determinants of Strike Incidence and Severity: A Micro-Level Study," *Industrial and Labor Relations Review* 39 (April 1986): 361–76.

23. John C. Schnell and Cynthia Gramm, "The Empirical Relations Between Employers' Striker Replacement Strategies and Strike Duration," *Industrial and Labor Relations Review* 47 (1994): 189–206.

24. Jody Hoffer Gittell, *The Southwest Way.* New York: McGraw-Hill, 2002.

Chapter 9

Dispute Resolution Procedures

When labor and management fail to reach agreement on a labor contract through a negotiated settlement, they may turn to a procedural technique to resolve the impasse. This chapter, still in the middle (functional) level of Exhibit 1–1, describes various dispute resolution techniques, shows how these techniques affect the negotiations process, and assesses how well the techniques perform in settling impasses.

The chapter first describes mediation, a process by which a third party tries to lead labor and management to a negotiated settlement through enhanced communication and recommendations. The discussion then turns to fact-finding, a more constraining procedure in which the third party makes their recommendations in a formal report. The next dispute procedure considered is interest arbitration where the parties are constrained to adhere to the decision of the third party, the arbitrator.[1]

As with our other aspects of collective bargaining, in the area of dispute resolution there are a number of new techniques and roles emerging. Some mediators are now using interest-based techniques to facilitate labor–management negotiations, consistent with the principles of interested-based bargaining as described in Chapter 8. We will describe this approach and contrast it to mediation of more traditional negotiations. This chapter finishes by discussing how new third-party roles are emerging to better respond to the environmental pressures that confront the parties and to improve labor-management relations.

Mediation

Mediation is the most widely used, yet the most informal, type of third-party intervention into collective bargaining. In **mediation** a neutral party assists the union and management negotiators in reaching a labor agreement. A mediator has no power to impose a settlement but, rather, acts as a facilitator for the bargaining parties.

Mediators keep the parties talking, they carry messages between the parties, and they make suggestions. Mediators must rely on their persuasion and communication skills to induce the parties to reach a voluntary agreement. A mediator's power is limited by the fact that he or she is an invited guest who can be asked to leave by either labor or management.

The Federal Mediation and Conciliation Service

The National Labor Relations Act specifies that the party proposing changes in a contract (usually the union) must notify the Federal Mediation and Conciliation Service (FMCS) at least 30 days before the start of a strike. The law does not require the parties to use mediation if they reach an impasse; yet the FMCS includes a staff of experienced mediators who are always ready to assist the negotiating parties if they are invited. Most states have state mediation and conciliation agencies that also make mediators available to negotiating parties. Both federal and state mediators are typically available free of charge.

FMCS annual reports estimate that approximately 15 to 20 percent of all cases in which 30-day strike notices were filed involved at least some informal (by telephone) type of mediation, and between 8 and 10 percent involved a formal mediation effort. The FMCS, the U.S. Secretary of Labor, other members of the President's cabinet, or the President is sometimes brought into the mediation process in important disputes or those designated as national emergencies, as defined by Title II of the Taft-Hartley Act. Mediation also arises frequently in hospital collective bargaining, as the 1974 amendments to the NLRA, which extended the act's coverage to private, nonprofit hospitals, specify that in those hospitals mediation has to take place before a legal strike can occur.

Mediation under the Railway Labor Act

The Railway Labor Act contains provisions for a mediation phase before a dispute can go to the next step of the impasse process. The staff mediators of the National Mediation Board, the administrative agency for the Railway Labor Act, serve as mediators in bargaining that occurs under the coverage of the Railway Labor Act.

Mediation in the Public Sector

Mediation is more commonly used in the public sector than in the private. Almost all of the bargaining statutes that cover state and local government employees call for mediation as the first phase of the impasse resolution process. In the state of New York, for example, on average, about 30 percent of all public-sector negotiations reach an impasse and required mediation. Other states have reported somewhat lower rates of reliance on mediation, but all states report rates that exceed the FMCS reported average for the private sector.

In the public sector mediation is the province of staff mediators employed by the various state agencies that administer the public employment bargaining statutes, and in some states it is the province of ad hoc, part-time mediators. These ad hoc mediators generally hold full-time posts as college professors, lawyers, or members of the clergy or in some occupation related to labor-management relations.

The Kinds of Disputes That Can Be Settled by Mediation

Mediation is most successful in addressing conflicts that arise from poor communications and misunderstandings caused, for instance, by one party or both becoming overcommitted to their bargaining positions or by a lack of experience on the part of the negotiators. Mediation is least successful, on the other hand, in resolving conflicts caused by the economic context of the dispute, such as the employer's inability to pay or major differences in the parties' expectations.

Where there is a wide divergence in the demands of labor and management, the mediation process is limited because here some form of outside pressure is necessary to induce the parties to make major changes in their bottom-line positions. Thus, the mediation process is best suited to helping the parties move marginally beyond their initial positions. Only in conjunction with some external pressure can mediation be expected to succeed in getting the parties to adjust their bottom lines and reach agreement when a large gap exists between them.

Disputes arising out of intraorganizational conflicts are also difficult to resolve through mediation. Consider again the example of the teacher dispute described in Box 8–1, which involved major internal conflicts within the school board's management. In that case one mediation session was held before the internal split was resolved, but little progress was made. After the session ended, the mediator was informed that the superintendent was going to try to get the board negotiator dismissed. For the next two months an internal power struggle ensued. The mediator kept in touch by telephone with all the parties (including, much to the dismay of the board's negotiator, the school superintendent), but no formal mediation session took place until the superintendent emerged as the victor of the internal battle and the board negotiator was replaced. Obviously, the mediator in this case had to walk a fine line in trying to convince management to resolve its internal conflicts so that negotiations could proceed.

The less the mediator becomes involved in trying to mediate disputes within one of the parties' organizations, the greater the likelihood that the mediator will be accepted by both parties and the more open the parties will be to the mediator. The difficulty for mediators is that the failure to resolve this sort of internal dispute can make it impossible to resolve the union–management dispute.

What Mediators Do

The ultimate objective of a mediator is to help the bargaining parties reach a settlement. Yet there is more to mediation than the final step that settles the contract. Mediation follows a continuously narrowing course as the mediator seeks to whittle away at the various issues in the dispute. Progress toward a settlement is possible without necessarily completely resolving any of the issues. In other words, progress has been made if the parties have succeeded in narrowing their differences over the open issues.

Mediation is also a device designed to help the parties "come clean without prejudice"— that is, to explore informally or off the record what would happen if they were to move away from their bottom-line positions. Mediators commonly undertake this exploratory effort to prevent the parties from miscalculating. Thus, one major function of mediation is to allow tacit bargaining to take place, either directly between the parties or indirectly by both parties' sharing confidential bargaining information with the mediator.[2]

The mediator also tries to prevent the parties from holding back on concessions they would be willing to make to avoid a strike. It is by no means an easy task for the mediator to identify what the resistance points of the parties are, since in most instances the negotiators are extremely wary of sharing this information openly with the mediator. Instead, the mediator must guess at the parties' positions from the statements they make and then try to get the parties to put forward their best offer.

What mediators do is influenced by whether the parties use traditional or interest-based strategies in negotiations. When negotiators use interest-based techniques, they expect mediators to be skilled facilitators of this type of process. The mediator must be good at generating options through brainstorming, knowing when to suggest formation of a subcommittee or other device for gathering additional information, and must be able to offer suggestions that are more than simple compromises of existing positions—he or she must help invent new options that satisfy both parties' interests. Most of all, the mediator needs to be alert to statements or actions by one party or the other that might indicate the process is reverting back to traditional positional bargaining and coach the parties in how to avoid this tendency. Finally, mediators must also be skilled teachers of these new approaches to negotiations and be sensitive to knowing when to recommend parties try out interest-based techniques. This must be done well before the start of a negotiations process since, as indicated in Chapter 8, most negotiators need to be trained in these techniques before they can use them successfully in actual bargaining.

The Traits of Successful Mediators

What are the traits of a good mediator? Perhaps the most critical requirement is that the mediator be acceptable to the parties. Because of the voluntary nature of this form of intervention, no mediator can function well without the trust of the parties.

Acceptability is also important because the mediator must obtain from the parties confidential bargaining information. This information, if used indiscriminately, could destroy a party's bargaining strategy. Although acceptability can be achieved by reputation, most experienced negotiators will be hesitant to divulge confidential bargaining information merely because the mediator has a good reputation. Thus, the early stages of most mediation efforts (when the mediator is not personally known to the parties) is often taken up with the mediator's attempts to establish his or her credibility.

Acceptability can also be lost as the process unfolds. When this occurs, a mediator may voluntarily withdraw from the case or the parties may seek other means of resolving the dispute.

The litany of desirable mediator traits often reads like a modified Boy or Girl Scout oath: A good mediator is trustworthy, helpful, friendly, intelligent, funny, knowledgeable about the substantive issues in question, and so on. Evidence suggests that nothing substitutes for experience as a quality that assists in a mediator's gaining of acceptance and in other ways promotes successful mediation. Mediation is an art that one must learn by trial and error through on-the-job training.[3]

What do managers and labor leaders think about the quality of mediators supplied by the FMCS? A national sample of FMCS's "customers" were asked to rate the mediator they used in their most recent case. The results are presented in Exhibit 9–1. Overall, FMCS's customers rate these mediators quite highly. Between 70 and 85 percent of the parties rated these federal mediators as either excellent or very good on their knowledge and expertise, acceptability, skill in handling negotiations, understanding of the issues, and trustworthiness with confidential information. Note, however, there is a consistent pattern of union representatives rating the mediators more favorably than management representatives. Other data in this survey were consistent with this pattern and suggested that management negotiators are more anxious for the mediators to deepen their knowledge of emerging issues in collective bargaining and industrial relations and would like to see the mediators accelerate the use of interest-based bargaining techniques more than their union counterparts. Thus, mediators, like their labor and management colleagues, are under pressure to change and learn new approaches to their occupation, and in turn assist the parties in updating and improving the process of collective bargaining. In doing so, they need to be aware

EXHIBIT 9–1
"Excellent" or
"Very Good"
Rating of
Mediator

of the different expectations that some labor and management representatives have for them and for the processes they bring to the bargaining table.

The novice mediator has a very difficult time breaking into the occupation. Fortunately, not every collective bargaining dispute constitutes a national emergency, and so novice mediators do obtain on-the-job training in some of the less complex disputes before taking on the challenge of a major case.

The Dynamics of Mediation in Traditional Bargaining

In a traditional bargaining process mediation, and the strategies of the mediator, often proceed through a cycle of different stages.[4]

The Initial Stage: Gaining Acceptability

During the initial stages of mediation the mediator is primarily concerned with achieving acceptability and identifying the issues in the dispute, the attitudinal climate between the parties, and the distribution of power within each negotiating team. The initial stages of mediation call for a relatively passive questioning and listening role on the part of the mediator. Normally the mediator will shuttle between the two negotiating teams to explore issues. Separate sessions with the mediator also give the parties an outlet for their pent-up emotions and frustrations.

In these stages the parties will often lash out at each other, exaggerate their differences, and try to convince the mediator of their own rationality and the unreasonableness of their opponent. It is in these early sessions that bonds of trust and credibility can be established between the mediator and the parties.

In short, in the early stage of mediation the parties are testing the mediator. Some of the same grandstanding that occurs in the early stages of the negotiating cycle is repeated at this point in mediation for the benefit of the newest entrant into the process.

The biggest challenges for the mediator at this stage are (1) to accurately diagnose the nature of the dispute and the obstacles to a settlement and (2) to get something started that will produce movement toward a final resolution. The mediator is often faced with the statement by one party that "we made the last move so the next move is up to them," only to proceed to the other side and hear the same thing. The mediator cannot let either party's hesitance to move first stop the process before it is given a chance. Neither party, in all likelihood, wants this to happen, or the mediator would not have been called in the first place.

The Middle Stage: Probing for Potential Compromises

Once the mediator overcomes this stalemate, the next step is to begin an exchange of proposals and test for potential areas of compromise. At this point it is crucial that the mediator have made an accurate diagnosis of the underlying sources of conflict. The mediator is now beginning to intervene more actively by trying to establish a framework for moving toward a settlement. If the mediator has misjudged the underlying difficulties and tries to push the parties toward a settlement prematurely, or in a way that does not overcome some of the major obstacles, his or her credibility can be lost. For example, a retired mediator once told the following story about one of his early experiences while mediating a strike on the West Coast between the International Longshoremen's and Warehousemen's Union and the Pacific Maritime Association:

> I started the mediation in the normal way, and the parties responded by discussing their differences in a serious fashion. I then broke the parties into separate caucuses. When I went to talk with the union team I found them playing cards. To my dismay, I could not convince them to stop playing cards and get down to the business of settling the strike. Instead, I was told to go back to my hotel room and that they would call me when they needed me. Later I learned that the major obstacle to a settlement in this case was a structural one—the longshoremen on the West Coast were waiting for the longshoremen on the East Coast to settle their contract so that they could then use it as a pattern for their own settlement.

During this second stage of the mediation process the mediator continues to probe to identify the priorities and bottom-line positions of the two parties. The mediator actively probes for possible acceptable solutions to the outstanding issues. Once the parties have begun to discuss specific proposals, the mediator attempts to determine whether their bottom-line positions are close enough. If they are, then the mediator presses for modifications that would yield an agreement.

The mediator's ability to estimate the parties' bottom-line positions is crucial at this stage, as is the timing. When the mediator judges the bottom-line positions to be close enough to push toward a settlement, he or she takes a more assertive role. The mediator can suggest compromises, push the parties to make compromises they earlier stated they would be unwilling to make, and, in general, try to close the gap between the parties. Engaging in such active tactics prematurely (that is, when the parties are still too far apart) damages the mediator's credibility and acceptability.

When conditions are not ripe for settlement, the mediator must hold back from overly aggressive tactics. When the situation is ripe, however, the mediator must take action or risk losing the opportunity to forge a settlement. The mediator's prior experience helps guide him or her in judging timing. At this point in the process the art in mediation comes to the fore.

The Final Stage: The Push to Compromise

As the pressure to reach a settlement builds and the mediator senses that the time for the final push toward resolution is at hand, the mediator becomes ever more aggressive. No longer passively listening to the parties' arguments and rationalizations, the mediator tries to get the parties to face reality and adjust their expectations. The mediator may push compromise solutions, while at the same time being careful to avoid becoming identified with a specific settlement point.

Overidentification with a solution that one or both parties rejects can limit the continued usefulness of the mediator. Thus, any compromises are proposed merely as recommendations.

The dynamics within each of the negotiating teams often change at this point as well. Frequently, team members will differ on the substantive issues. The mediator will often look to the professional negotiators on each team for help in dealing with the more militant team members. Sometimes the reverse is true as well: the negotiator will look to the mediator for help in calming a militant faction on the bargaining team.

These final-hour sessions often require that someone—the mediator, the professional negotiator, or both—convince the hard-liners that the best deal is at hand and that the final compromises necessary to reach a settlement should now be made. Again, the parties' confidence in the mediator is critical to the success of these final dynamics.

Sometimes the mediator is called on in these final stages to make what are called mediator proposals. Mediator proposals are riskier and more formal ventures than the many other suggestions a mediator will make during the course of an intervention. A mediator proposal is normally made only when both parties are close to a settlement and the mediator believes that by making the proposal the parties will come to agreement.

In some cases the mediator may make a proposal that the parties have already tacitly agreed to, but, for political or other reasons, they prefer not to offer themselves. Some mediators believe that a proposal should never be made unless the mediator is sure it will be acceptable to both parties.

The preceding description of the dynamics of mediation points out that mediators must be aggressive in pushing the parties toward a settlement—when the climate, timing, and pressures on the parties are right. The parties often prefer aggressive mediators, and the aggressiveness of the mediator has been shown to be related to the effectiveness of the mediation process.[5]

Mediation in Interest-Based Bargaining

We have already noted that the role of the mediator in interest-based processes takes on more of the role of an active facilitator, teacher, and coach than is the case in a traditional bargaining process. The cycle of negotiations is likely to be altered as well with less focus on the contract or strike deadline as the defining moment. Since training is required, the mediation process may begin well before the negotiations process starts. FMCS offers interest-based bargaining training to parties as part of what it refers to as "preventive mediation."

In Box 9–1 George Buckingham, one of the most experienced and successful interest-based mediators in the FMCS describes how and when he uses interest-based techniques to facilitate the bargaining process.

When is this approach likely to be most successful? FMCS Commissioner Buckingham suggests in one of two situations: (1) when the parties have other elements of a cooperative relationship already in place and want to take the next step by carrying problem solving into the bargaining process, or (2) where, if the parties don't solve a set of problems they face, there will be serious adverse consequences. In either case the key is to have some strong motivating factor that helps keep the process on course when the going gets tough.

Well before negotiations are scheduled to begin, I provide parties who express an interest or who we believe might be good candidates for an interest-based approach with a one and one-half hour informational briefing. We discuss factors to think about in deciding whether or not to use this approach. In the process of this discussion, I probe to see if there are any factors that would lead me to recommend against using the process, such as no evidence of cooperation in the relationship or a history of contract rejections by one side or the other.

If the parties agree to take the next step, we then hold a two-day required training session for all members of the union and employer negotiating committees. At the end of the training, we make a trilateral (union, employer, and mediator) decision on whether or not to go forward with the process.

The next step is to hold a prenegotiations meeting to agree on two sets of ground rules. The first set are *transitional* ground rules that outline what will happen if at some stage the interest-based process breaks down and the parties need to return to a more traditional process. This serves as a "road map" back to the traditional process and provides a safety valve for the parties. The second set are *process* ground rules. Here we deal with rules such as how we define consensus decision making, how we will deal with press releases, how and when information will be communicated to constituents, and so on.

Then we are ready for an exchange of issues using an interest-based format. This exchange takes the place of traditional exchange of proposals or the laundry list of demands. Each issue is framed as a question that cannot be answered in a yes or no fashion. For example, an issue might be framed as: "How can we accommodate employee needs to have greater time off for funerals and handle staffing needs effectively?" We also agree at this stage on the order to take issues up and on any information that needs to be obtained in order to discuss them. Bargaining dates are set at this time after giving adequate consideration to the time needed to collect the necessary data.

For the actual bargaining, we commit to participating in the first two sessions or until the first issue is settled, to returning when the economic issues are taken up, and to being present as the process is coming to an end.

What do I do in these sessions? My basic role is to facilitate the process, to keep the process on a problem solving track, and to make sure they lay out all the issues and problems and don't stray into a general discussion mode that will take them back to traditional positional bargaining. If, in the rare instance, I feel the need to make a substantive suggestion, I indicate that I am stepping out of my facilitating role to do so.

One of the hardest tasks the parties have is to agree on standards for evaluating options. I suggest three simple standards, but the parties are encouraged to develop their own as well. The three I use are: (1) Can we do it? (2) Does it convey benefits (related to their interests)? (3) Is it acceptable to the constituents?

The parties take up noneconomic issues first. Then, in perhaps about 35 to 40 percent of the cases, I find us using more traditional approaches to resolve the deep gut economic issues. But even here, when the interest-based process has been successful on the earlier issues, we generally find more of a problem-solving focus and willingness to listen to each other that is often absent in the final stages of a traditional negotiation. The parties are more apt to stay in an interest-based bargaining frame of mind.

Two big differences in my experience with this approach are that the contract deadline and the strike threat are not major factors. In only three out of 60 cases I've mediated in this way has a strike notice been issued, and then it was done to satisfy constituency needs rather than as a serious threat across the table. The overwhelming majority of cases have settled prior to the contract expiration date, while some have gone beyond the expiration with no serious repercussions. In only one occasion did I hold a mediation session beyond 8 P.M.

I like to use two criteria to judge whether the interest-based approach has been successful. The first is whether the parties use it again the next time. About 80 percent do so. The second is whether the number of relationship or noneconomic issues brought to negotiations decline the second time around. If interest-based bargaining is able to really solve problems the number of "relationship" or noneconomic" issues should go down.

Source: Interview with FMCS Commissioner George Buckingham, July 1997.

This dispute was resolved after one long night of mediation. The parties had been negotiating for over a year. A fact-finding report had been issued, and considerable progress had been made on economic issues. The major remaining unresolved issue was whether these employees [janitors, bus drivers, and cafeteria workers in a school district] would have binding grievance arbitration in their contract. . . . It was clear that the [school] Board was adamantly opposed to binding arbitration. . . . The [mediation] process was made more frustrating by the condescending attitude that the district administrators took toward the

members of the bargaining unit. Unfortunately, my role at this final step of the process was simply to get the union negotiators to face the reality that there was no way they could get an agreement containing binding arbitration. . . .

If I had let my own feelings toward the Board negotiating team surface during mediation, the process would have not only broken down but made it even harder for the parties to put this long and frustrating case behind them. Consequently, one walks away from this type of dispute with a lot of pent-up anger and frustration.

Effects on Settlements

What has been the track record for mediation in the private sector? The 1997 FMCS customer satisfaction survey provides some basic evidence on this. Mediation led to an agreement in 46 percent of the cases in which an FMCS mediator was involved in negotiations. In another 35 percent of these cases, the labor or management respondent indicated that mediation brought the parties closer together. Thus, in over 8 out of 10 cases, mediation had a positive effect on the process of reaching an agreement. Mediation was somewhat more successful in reaching agreements in bargaining units with fewer than 250 workers than those with more workers and somewhat more successful in cases with women negotiators than men. As another indicator of the acceptability and satisfaction with mediation, over 90 percent of FMCS's customers indicated they would use its mediation services again in the future whenever needed.

The Potential Tension between What Is Right and What Will Bring a Settlement

In theory the mediator is not supposed to be concerned with the substance of the outcome. Instead, the traditional view is that mediation works because the job of the mediator is simply to bring the parties to agreement. Yet there are definitely times when mediators have trouble accepting this principle. Consider, for example, the mediator in the case told in Box 9–2. Here, the mediator could not let his personal views of management's negotiating style get in the way of a settlement.

All mediators must struggle from time to time with the moral question of how far to compromise their personal values or perceptions of equity in attempting to fashion a contract settlement. The traditional answer to this question has been that the mediator's primary responsibility is to help the parties reach an agreement and to keep his or her values and preferences, or the values and preferences of the larger society, out of the process. According to this view, the mediator should not attempt to create a settlement that would be most consistent with "the public interest." The traditional view holds that the way the mediator best represents the public interest is by helping prevent or end an impasse.[6]

The moral dilemma is even more difficult to resolve if questions of individual rights are part of the settlement package preferred by one of the parties. Mediators will continue to struggle with this moral dilemma and decide how high a priority they are willing to put on the singular goal of achieving a settlement.[7]

Some mediators, especially those who favor the use of interest-based techniques, reject the traditional view. Instead they argue that an effective mediator will help the parties articulate their basic interests and then help steer the process to results that best serve their interests. Thus, in this view the substantive terms of the settlement are as important to the success of mediation as is a settlement per se. As labor and management get more conversant with interest-based processes, their expectations for the mediator and their indicators of success for both negotiations and for mediation are likely to likewise escalate.

Fact-Finding

Under **fact-finding** a third party (fact finder) is called in to study the issues that are in dispute between labor and management negotiators who have reached an impasse in their negotiations. After gathering facts the fact finder then makes a report or announcement that may be made public. The fact finder's report often includes recommendations of what the fact finder believes is an appropriate settlement of the impasse. Fact-finding is premised on the hope that the recommendations and a neutral report will bring sufficient pressure on the parties to induce them to accept the recommendations of the fact finder or to use them as the basis for a negotiated settlement.

Fact-finding is rarely used in the private sector (like mediation it is not required by the NLRA), but it is more commonly used in the public sector.[8] Fact-finding also has been used frequently in negotiations that are covered under the Railway Labor Act (the Railroad Mediation Board can call it into play). The national emergency dispute procedures of the NLRA also authorize the use of fact-finding as part of the process by which the President can call into action an emergency impasse resolution board.

The Performance of Fact-Finding

The record of fact-finding is mixed.[9] In most cases fact-finding recommendations do not generate the pressure needed to produce a settlement.[10]

Although the overall record of fact-finding has been less than spectacular, the procedure can make contributions to resolving certain types of disputes. It seems to be most useful as a supplement to mediation when one party is faced with internal differences and needs the recommendations of a neutral expert to overcome internal (intraorganizational) opposition to a settlement. Recall that the existence of internal differences was noted as a particularly difficult type of dispute for mediation to resolve.

Fact-finding also appears to work better with inexperienced than with experienced negotiators. This may explain why the effectiveness of fact-finding in the public sector seems to have declined over time. As the parties become more familiar with fact-finding and more adept at negotiating, they are apt to place less weight on the expert opinion of an outsider.

Fact-finding is less effective in overcoming serious disputes caused by a large gap between the expectations of one party and the bottom-line position of the other. The more experienced the parties, the less effective fact-finding will be in changing these expectations. On the other hand, as just noted, it can be a very useful device for one of the negotiators in convincing the rest of his or her constituents to face reality and reduce their expectations.

A Case of Fact-Finding

The following describes the use of fact-finding in a dispute between a teachers' union and a school district.

A neutral [person] first attempted to mediate the dispute but was discouraged by both the professional negotiators for each side. They explained that they knew what their differences were and that if it was up to them alone they could settle the dispute without the help of a neutral party. The problem was that the school board was unwilling to accept what both negotiators agreed was a reasonable salary settlement, and one faction within the union was unwilling to compromise on a contract-language issue. The mediator therefore agreed to proceed directly to fact-finding. In the course of the hearing, the two negotiators presented their cases in ways that made it clear to the fact finder what they tacitly agreed to, and, therefore, what they wanted the fact finder to recommend. The fact finder's recommendations closely followed these tacit resolutions. Both negotiators used the "neutral's recommendations" in selling the tacit agreement to their constituents.

Interest Arbitration

Interest arbitration involves the use of a third party (an arbitrator) who is empowered to impose a settlement in a contract dispute. In interest arbitration the arbitrator is setting the terms of the contract. Thus, interest arbitration is different from grievance (or rights) arbitration, in which an arbitrator is used to settle a dispute during the term or over the implementation of an existing contract (see Chapter 11).

Interest arbitration is not used very often in the private sector in the United States. The few exceptions in the private sector have been major league baseball (see Box 9–3), national emergency disputes under the Taft-Hartley or Railway Labor acts or cases in which the parties voluntarily submitted their disputes to arbitration. Interest arbitration has been used more frequently to settle impasses in public sector bargaining.

The NLRA gives labor and management the right to strike over impasses and thereby avoids the use of interest arbitration. Many proponents of collective bargaining in the private sector have long argued that the right to strike (and, hence, the absence of interest arbitration) was essential for the preservation of free collective bargaining.

As one scholar put it, over 35 years ago:

In the case against compulsory arbitration there are distinguished prosecutors galore, and the catalog of inevitable disasters runs the gamut from simple bad decisions to dislocation of the economic foundations of free enterprise. The division is not liberal/conservative, nor labor/management—there is no division. All the principal authorities are in agreement.[11]

In this view interest arbitration should be limited to cases of dire national emergency or to disputes in which the parties themselves decide it is in their interest to submit their dispute to a procedural substitute for the strike.

The Use of Interest Arbitration in the Public Sector

As the demand for public sector bargaining became more vocal, however, policy makers had to make a difficult choice: unions were calling for collective bargaining rights, while elected officials were reluctant to grant public employees the right to strike. Because of the general disfavor accorded interest arbitration, most states initially turned to fact-finding as a compromise between the "dual evils" of the right to strike and compulsory interest arbitration. Later, about half the states that had endorsed collective bargaining for public employees turned to some form of arbitration for resolving disputes between city governments and their police and fire fighters.

Since interest arbitration primarily has been used in the public sector, the public sector record reveals how interest arbitration works. This record is discussed below along with occasional reference to experience with arbitration in the private sector.

Types of Interest Arbitration

Exhibit 9–2 outlines the differences among the various forms of interest arbitration. The exhibit starts by differentiating between voluntary and compulsory arbitration. **Voluntary arbitration** is a dispute resolution system in which the parties agree to submit their differences to arbitration. **Compulsory arbitration** is a system in which law requires the parties to submit their unresolved differences to arbitration if they cannot reach a negotiated settlement on their own.

Another important distinction is the difference between conventional arbitration and final-offer arbitration. **Conventional arbitration** (which can be either voluntary or

EXHIBIT 9–2
The Terminology of Alternative Forms of Interest Arbitration

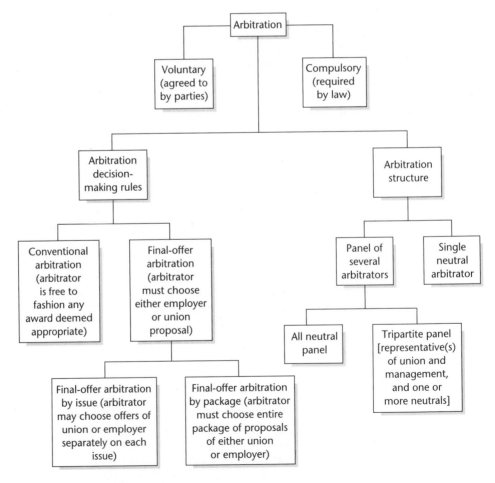

compulsory) is a dispute resolution process in which the arbitrator is free to fashion any award he or she deems appropriate. Although the conventional arbitration award may be a compromise between the proposals of the employer and those of the union, the arbitrator is also free to accept either party's proposals or, for that matter, to go below the employer's offer or above the union's (although that rarely happens).

In **final-offer arbitration** the arbitrator must choose either the employer's proposal or the union's; the arbitrator may not fashion his or her own compromise. As a further distinction, final-offer arbitration may be handled on a total package basis—that is, the arbitrator must choose the complete offer of the employer or of the union on all issues. Or final-offer arbitration can be handled on an issue-by-issue basis. The arbitrator, for example, might choose the employer's wage offer, the union's offer on health insurance, and the employer's offer on vacation days.[12]

There is yet another complication. The arbitrator can be an individual or a panel of individuals. Panels, in turn, can either be composed of all neutrals or can be tripartite. Tripartite panels are composed of one or more representatives of the employer, one or more representatives of the union, and one or more neutrals.

Debates over the Performance and Effects of Interest Arbitration

What does the use of interest arbitration do to the parties' ability to negotiate on their own? What kinds of settlements do arbitrators impose, and how do the arbitrators' settlements compare with the settlements labor and management reach on their own? Does interest arbitration actually prevent the occurrence of strikes? These questions are part of the controversy that surrounds the use of interest arbitration. The evidence on these issues is only summarized here because public sector experience with interest arbitration is examined in detail in Chapter 13.

Interest arbitration in the public sector has had a better record of preventing strikes than has fact-finding or bargaining without any impasse procedure. Although, obviously, no dispute resolution procedure, including interest arbitration, can prevent all strikes, interest arbitration appears to reduce the probability of strikes more than does fact-finding.

To date there is little evidence of excessive use of interest arbitration where it is available. The vast majority of disputes tend to be settled without resort to interest arbitration. Even in systems that have been followed for as long as 30 years, the rate of cases going to interest arbitration rarely exceeded 25 percent.[13]

The evidence of the effect of arbitration on contract terms is that arbitrators tend to impose settlements that are not very different from the settlements reached by parties bargaining where arbitration is not available as an impasse resolution procedure. The use of interest arbitration across a state (in settling public sector disputes) does appear to narrow the range of settlements by eliminating either extremely high or low settlements. The overall effect of interest arbitration on contract terms such as wage levels appears to be modest. Where an effect has been measured, arbitration tends to lead to wage levels that are 5–10 percent higher than wages in jurisdictions where arbitration is not available.

Voluntary Interest Arbitration in the Private Sector

A number of voluntary interest arbitration schemes have been used in the private sector in electrical construction, large construction projects (such as the Cape Canaveral space center and the Alaska pipeline projects), and newspapers.

Major League Baseball Salary Arbitration Procedure   **Box 9–3**

ELIGIBILITY

Any Player or Club may submit to salary arbitration with the consent of the other party. However, a player between three and six years of Major League service may submit to salary arbitration without the consent of the other party.

SELECTION OF ARBITRATOR

The Players Association and the Player Relations Committee shall annually select the arbitrators.

PROCEDURE

Within three days of salary arbitration submission, the Players Association and the Players Relations Committee exchange salary figures. The Player has the option of withdrawing within 7 days of the receipt of the Club's salary figure. And in the event the Club or Player reach a salary agreement before the arbitrator reaches his decision, the matter shall be withdrawn from arbitration.

TIMETABLE AND DECISION

The Player and the Club submit the salary figures to the arbitrator at the hearing. The arbitration hearing is held as soon as possible after submission and scheduled between February 1 and February 20. The arbitrator may render his decision on the day of the hearing, and shall make every effort to decide no later than 24 hours following the close of the hearing. Finally, the arbitrator is limited to awarding only one or the other of the two figures submitted.

CONDUCT OF HEARINGS

Each party is limited to one hour for initial presentation and a half-hour for rebuttal and submission. There are no continuances or adjournments.

CRITERIA

The criteria used in determining the Player's worth include the quality of the Player's contribution to his Club during the past season (including his overall performance, special qualities of leadership and public appeal), the length and consistency of his career contribution, the record of the Player's past compensation, comparative baseball salaries, the existence of any physical or mental defects on the part of the Player, and the recent performance record of the Club. In addition, any evidence relevant to these criteria may be submitted as evidence.

Source: Basic Agreement between the American and National League of Professional Baseball Clubs and the Major League Baseball Players Association, January 1, 1986.

The only significant private sector use of interest arbitration now occurs in major league baseball. As noted earlier, major league players and baseball club owners have, for a number of years, negotiated a master collective bargaining agreement. As stipulated in that master contract the salaries of individual players are determined through negotiations between each player and his respective club owner.

As Box 9–3 shows, the master agreement requires that a player's salary be set by an arbitrator if an impasse is reached between the player and the club owner in salary negotiations. The arbitrator is restricted to choosing either the final offer of the player or the team's owner. Terms and conditions of employment for baseball players other than salary are not subject to interest arbitration. Club owners became very dissatisfied with the use of arbitration in recent years and tried to eliminate it in negotiations and the strike of 1994; however, they were not successful on this point. Instead, the parties modified the procedure by agreeing to phase in the use of three neutral arbitrators per case rather than a single arbitrator. Reflecting an increase in the recent attention received by arbitration and other dispute resolution procedures, interest arbitration was introduced as a mandatory procedure to settle collective bargaining disputes in the agriculture industry in California, as Box 9–4 describes.

Voluntary interest arbitration has also been used on an ad hoc basis as a conflict resolution device of last resort. From time to time difficult strikes, such as disputes between

As one of the most essential industries in California, the agricultural industry had been under intense pressures to find a solution to a subpar collective bargaining system. Because of this, in 2002, a law was passed by the California legislature that created mandatory interest arbitration for cases where employers and unions in the agricultural industry were unable to come to a consensus while bargaining for an initial collective bargaining agreement. The law was quickly subject to legal challenge, although the challenge was ultimately denied.

Specifically, Hess Collection Winery, an agricultural employer in the Napa Valley, filed an appeal claiming that legislature had no authority to make such a law. In fact, it went as far as to say that mandatory interest arbitration solely in the agricultural sector of the economy seriously violated equal protection guarantees laid forth in the Constitution. As a result, the law was brought to the California Court of Appeals.

On July 5, 2006, because of the absolute need to efficiently reach an agreement in collective bargaining contracts in the industry and because the statute only applies to the initial bargaining offer, the Court of Appeals upheld the previous decision and deemed mandatory interest arbitration lawful because the court believed it to be constitutionally accurate. Justice Richard Sims of the appeals court stated that the law "bears a rational and conceivable relationship to a legitimate state purpose," and as such, it passes the constitutionality test and should therefore be allowed. Sims went on to say that "agricultural employees are in an especially unequal bargaining position with respect to their employers and that their health, safety, and welfare require special protection." Therefore, extra security must be awarded to them, and this law will help "protect the industry by promoting stability in agricultural employment."

Source: "California Court Upholds Constitutionality of State's Mandatory Interest Arbitration Law," 07/07/06. *Daily Labor Report*, July 7, 2006: AA-1.

the U.S. Postal Service and postal worker unions, have been resolved with an agreement to arbitrate.

In voluntary interest arbitration schemes the parties normally limit the discretion of the arbitrator. In baseball the arbitrator only rules on player salary (although other parts of the master baseball contract are subject to grievance arbitration).

The key to the negotiation of voluntary interest arbitration plans is that both parties must perceive benefits in agreeing to set aside the right to strike. Labor and management generally voluntarily accept interest arbitration only where strike costs are high.

Interest Arbitration Structure and Process

A wide array of choices is available for designing the structure of interest arbitration systems. These structural options determine the nature of the decision-making process in interest arbitration in important ways. In fact, the parties' choices of a particular structure reflects their fundamental views on the appropriate functions of an interest arbitration system. This section describes two divergent types of decision-making processes in interest arbitration and suggests how these are influenced by the structural design of the system.

A Combined Mediation-Arbitration Approach

The two decision-making processes available are (1) a mediation-arbitration process and (2) a judicial decision-making process. Advocates of the **mediation-arbitration** process view interest arbitration as an extension of the collective bargaining process in which the neutral arbitrator seeks to shape an award that is acceptable to the parties. Mediation-arbitration places a premium on using the interest arbitration proceeding as a forum for continued negotiations or mediation, albeit with the arbitrator holding the ultimate authority to decide on the contract.

Those advocating the mediation-arbitration approach claim that no system of interest arbitration can hope to survive for long unless it produces outcomes that are acceptable to the parties. They also argue that the parties should maintain maximum control over the discretion of the arbitrator and should participate in the decision-making process as much as possible in order to maximize the amount and accuracy of the information used by the arbitrator in making the final decision.

A Judicial Approach

The countervailing view of interest arbitration holds that the arbitrator should focus on the "facts" of the case. In this judicial approach the arbitrator adheres strictly to predetermined criteria and is not influenced by the bargaining power or preferences of the parties.

The Influence of Arbitration Structure

The structure of an interest arbitration system can influence which of these two types of decision-making processes will prevail. The following structural features all favor a mediation-arbitration process:

1. Selection of the arbitrator by the parties.
2. Use of a tripartite structure.
3. Use of private ad hoc arbitrators appointed on a case-by-case basis or arbitrators who serve as long as they remain mutually acceptable to both parties.
4. Use of decision-making criteria or standards that are flexible and can be assigned whatever weights are deemed appropriate to a given case.
5. Forms of judicial review of the arbitration award that scrutinize only the procedural aspects of the process and not the substantive merits of the arbitrator's decision.

The structural features favoring a judicial decision-making process, on the other hand, include selecting a single arbitrator (1) whose tenure for future cases is determined by someone other than the parties to the dispute, (2) who is required to apply predetermined weights to specified standards, and (3) whose decision can be reviewed by a court to determine whether the standards were appropriately applied in a given case.

Many state legislatures have been swayed by those favoring a mediation-arbitration process, and most public-sector interest arbitration systems have structural features favoring the mediation-arbitration approach. Whether the mediation-arbitration structure actually produces the outcomes predicted by its advocates—the greater acceptability of results and therefore its greater durability—remains a question for future research.

Nontraditional Dispute Resolution

The need for skilled third parties in conflict resolution and problem solving is not limited to the formal negotiations process. Indeed, in recent years a variety of new **dispute resolution** roles have emerged in settings where labor and management have been attempting to achieve fundamental changes in their bargaining relationships.

Neutrals, for example, are increasingly being called on to chair or facilitate labor-management committees, to serve as consultants to labor and management in quality-of-working-life programs, to facilitate the joint planning or design of a new plant or work system, or to work on other experimental projects designed to solve long-standing problems in a bargaining relationship. All of these roles require the skills of a labor mediator. In addition, however, these roles differ from traditional mediation or arbitration roles in several important ways.

First, most require that problems be addressed on an ongoing basis.[14] Often this requires that the parties first undergo a team-building effort to change their attitudes and to increase the level of trust they place in each other.

Second, these third parties must possess specialized knowledge of the substantive problems facing the parties. The third party is expected to be a consultant who brings technical expertise to bear on the problem and also is sensitive to the needs of both labor and management.

Third, the time horizon of the process tends to be very long. Whereas the traditional mediator is mainly concerned with achieving a settlement of the immediate impasse, third parties involved in these new roles must focus on the effects of any decision on the quality of the longer-term relationship.

The behavior of the parties to these new processes is also significantly different from traditional labor-management behavior. For example, to be successful, long-term problem solving requires the parties to share information more readily than they do in traditional collective bargaining.

In response to this growing demand, the FMCS has increased its emphasis on what it calls "preventive mediation," that is, programs designed to either train the parties in state-of-the-art labor-management practices or more direct facilitation of efforts to improve relations in particular industries or company-union pairs. In fact, the customer survey conducted by FMCS indicates that both business and labor representatives would prefer to see FMCS put significantly more resources into efforts to improve labor management relations outside of the formal bargaining process.

At the same time, however, the parties may still need to turn to the traditional mediation and arbitration processes. In short, effective conflict resolution and longer-term problem solving are both critical to the success of contemporary collective bargaining relationships.

Key Organizations and Agencies Involved in Impasse Resolution

The key organizations and agencies that are involved in the resolution of impasses are summarized below.

American Arbitration Association (AAA): A private nonprofit organization that facilitates the process of arbitration. The AAA maintains lists of arbitrators and also makes available facilities that can be used for arbitration hearings. The AAA offers a number of seminars to train young arbitrators and to keep experienced arbitrators informed about emerging developments. Much of the arbitration work performed by AAA arbitrators is grievance arbitration, but AAA arbitrators do also become involved in interest arbitration.

Federal Mediation and Conciliation Service (FMCS): An agency of the federal government mandated by the National Labor Relations Act. The NLRA requires the

FMCS be notified at least 30 days before a strike. The FMCS includes a staff of 250 mediators who offer their services to labor and management involved in impasses.

National Academy of Arbitrators (NAA): A professional society of experienced arbitrators. Most of the cases heard by NAA arbitrators are grievance arbitrations, although NAA members are involved in interest arbitration.

National Mediation Board (NMB): An administrative agency created by the Railway Labor Act. One of the functions of the board is to mediate disputes between labor and management that arise in the transportation industries covered by the Railway Labor Act.

State mediation and conciliation agencies: A variety of agencies exist at the state level to facilitate the mediation of labor impasses. In states that grant public employees bargaining rights, there frequently exists a separate agency concerned with the public sector bargaining impasses. In New York, for example, the Public Employment Relations Board (PERB) provides mediation assistance among its many functions.

Summary

This chapter describes the three major impasse resolution procedures—mediation, fact-finding, and interest arbitration. The use of these procedures has varied extensively. Mediation has been commonly used in both the private and public sectors. Fact-finding and interest arbitration, in contrast, have been used in the public sector, with only a few exceptions.

The procedures also vary in the degree to which they constrain the actions of labor and management. At one extreme is mediation, where the parties can, and sometimes do, either dismiss the mediator or ignore the advice given. At the other extreme is binding interest arbitration where the parties must follow the decision of the arbitrator.

The purpose of any impasse resolution procedure is to help the parties achieve a contract settlement that both labor and management find acceptable and a settlement that helps sustain a successful labor-management relationship. Good mediators, fact finders, and arbitrators understand the issues that divide labor and management and have the ability to offer creative solutions to these problems.

Discussion Questions

1. Describe the objectives of mediation.
2. What are the three stages that typically occur in a mediation?
3. Discuss some of the criticisms made of interest arbitration.
4. Contrast mediation-arbitration and judicial arbitration.

Related Web Sites

Federal Mediation and Conciliation Service (FMCS):
http://www.fmcs.gov

National Mediation Board (NMB):
http://nmb.gov/master.htm

National Arbitration Forum:
http://www.arb-forum.com/index.html

Suggested Readings

Cullen, Donald E. *National Emergency Disputes* (Ithaca: New York State School of Industrial and Labor Relations, Cornell University, 1968).

Goldberg, Stephen B., Eric D. Green, and Frank E. A. Sander. *Dispute Resolution* (Boston: Little, Brown, 1985).

Kolb, Deborah. *The Mediators* (Cambridge: MIT Press, 1982).

Pruitt, Dean G., and Jeffrey Z. Rubin. *Social Conflict: Escalation, Stalemate, and Settlement* (New York: Random House, 1986).

Rubin, Jeffrey Z. *Dynamics of Third-Party Intervention* (New York: Praeger, 1981).

End Notes

1. The parties are constrained to adhere to the decision in a binding arbitration procedure. As discussed below there is occasional use of nonbinding arbitration.

2. Carl M. Steven, *Strategy and Collective Bargaining Negotiation* (New York: McGraw-Hill, 1963), pp. 142–46.

3. One empirical study of mediation in the public sector did find a positive relationship between mediator experience (measured as the number of previous mediation cases) and the effectiveness of mediation, especially effectiveness in inducing movement toward settlement and in narrowing the number of issues open in the dispute. See Thomas A. Kochan and Todd Jick, "The Public Sector Mediation Process: A Theory and Empirical Examination," *Journal of Conflict Resolution* 22 (June 1978): 209–40.

4. For analysis of mediation strategies, see Kenneth Kressel, *Mediation: An Exploratory Survey* (Albany, NY: Association of Labor Mediation Agencies, 1972); and Deborah Kolb, *The Mediators* (Cambridge: MIT Press, 1982).

5. One study shows a positive effect for mediator aggressiveness and further noted that the more intense or difficult the dispute, the more aggressive the mediator tended to be. See Paul F. Gerhart and John E. Drotning, "Dispute Settlement and the Intensity of the Mediator," *Industrial Relations* 19 (1980): 352–59.

6. Eva Robbins, *A Guide for Labor Mediators* (Honolulu: Industrial Relations Center, University of Hawaii, 1976).

7. For a good discussion of this dilemma, see William E. Simkin, *Mediation and the Dynamics of Collective Bargaining* (Washington, DC: Bureau of National Affairs, 1971), pp. 34–40.

8. Fact-finding is the most common form of dispute resolution for occupations other than police or fire fighters in the public sector (for the latter, interest arbitration is most common).

9. Fact-finding boards were highly successful in inducing settlements over the years 1926–40; that record deteriorated somewhat during the 1940s, 1950s, and 1960s and then improved again in the 1970s and 1980s.

10. A review of the experience with fact-finding suggested that its effectiveness declined over time on most of the criteria listed above. See Craig A. Olson, "The Dynamics of Dispute Resolution," in *Public Sector Bargaining,* 2d ed., ed. Benjamin Aaron, James L. Stern, and Joyce M. Najita (Washington, DC: Bureau of National Affairs, 1988), pp. 160–88.

11. Orme Phelps, "Compulsory Arbitration: Some Perspectives," *Industrial and Labor Relations Review* 18 (October 1964): 8.

12. Some final-offer procedures allow the arbitrator to choose the recommendation of a fact finder involved in an earlier step of the process.

13. Mark Thompson and James Cairnie, "Compulsory Arbitration: The Case of British Columbia Teachers," *Industrial and Labor Relations Review* 27 (October 1973): 3–17.

14. Stephen B. Goldberg, Jeanne M. Brett, and William Ury, "A Study in Metamediation," unpublished manuscript, Evanston, IL, School of Law, Northwestern University, 1987.

Chapter 10

Contract Terms and Employment Outcomes

For those engaged in collective bargaining and those who are trying to understand its consequences, the impact of collective bargaining agreements on employment outcomes is of critical importance. This chapter continues the analysis of the middle (functional) tier of collective bargaining by examining the effects of collective bargaining on wages, fringe benefits, job security, and other bargaining outcomes. By comparing the wages, working conditions, and other employment conditions of union and nonunion employees, it is possible to estimate the average effects of collective bargaining. Then, by looking within the union sector, we can explore the considerable variation in union effects that reflect differences in the quality of the union–management relationship.

Another way of understanding the effects of unions and collective bargaining is to examine trends over time to see how labor and management have responded to the environmental pressures outlined in earlier chapters. The decline in unionization experienced in the past decade makes this an especially revealing and important source of information on the effects of collective bargaining and the implications of its decline for American workers, firms, and society.

Rather than provide an exhaustive analysis of all the different ways bargaining affects employment conditions, this chapter focuses on union effects that are either the most common or the most controversial.

Tracing the Effects of Union Wage Increases

The relationship between job outcomes and unionization is complex. Changes in wages, for example, set off second-order changes in other job outcomes. Some of these second-order changes move in the same direction as the wage effects, whereas others move in the opposite direction. On the one hand, for example, an increase in wages may result in a corresponding, automatic *roll up* in such **fringe benefits** as sick leave pay, vacation pay, pensions, and unemployment benefits. On the other hand, a wage or benefit increase may create pressures for the firm to hold down costs by tightening work rules or other practices.

EXHIBIT 10–1
The Consequences of Union Effects on Wages

In this way the primary direct effects of unions set off a chain reaction. Primary union effects lead to adjustments by management and consequences for employment conditions. Once management makes adjustments and employment conditions are altered, unions typically react and try to modify management adjustments. This leads to secondary union effects on employment outcomes.

Exhibit 10–1 diagrams the chain reaction set off when a union raises wages. (Similar chains can be traced for other employment conditions.) There are three stages in this chain reaction.

Stage 1: Primary Union Effects

The **primary union effects** are on the compensation received by their members. If unions did not raise wages, they would have a hard time attracting and keeping members. Thus, the primary union wage effect is positive. The critical analytic question concerns the size of this and other primary effects.

Stage 2: Management Adjustments

Management takes a number of actions in response to the union's primary wage effects. The central motivation for the employer is to try to recoup the costs associated with union-negotiated improvements in wages through productivity increases or other measures.

Increases in labor costs result in some combination of the following responses by the firm: (1) a reduction in the scale of output and employment; (2) an increase in the price of the product; or (3) a substitution of capital for labor—all mechanisms for raising the marginal productivity of labor. These managerial reactions may lead to either higher prices or reduced employment opportunities, both of which are costly to society. At the same time, it should be recognized that society might value the union's primary effects, namely, the higher wages received by those employees covered by the union contract.

It is also possible that after identifying ways to recoup the costs initially imposed by a union contract, management ends up with productivity that is higher than it was before the primary union effects. Sumner Slichter, in the 1940s, argued that such a shock effect was prevalent in management's response to early unionism.[1] Increases in wages, for example, may induce employees to quit less frequently and thereby reduce hiring and training costs to the firm. Higher wages also should attract better qualified workers for positions in the bargaining unit. In addition, improved wages might lead to employees who are more motivated and work harder.

Stage 3: Secondary Union Effects

If the employer reacts to a primary union effect by making at least some, if not all, of the adjustments discussed above, then employee welfare will be altered. The union might then take countervailing steps. This leads to **secondary union effects.**

If management responds to increased wage costs by reducing the number of jobs in the bargaining unit and increasing the pace of work, for example, the union may react to these changes in working conditions. The union might seek more elaborate job security language and stricter seniority rules in subsequent contract negotiations. The latter would represent secondary union effects on employment conditions.

Escape and Takeovers as Responses

These are all responses and reactions within the union-management relationship. However, in recent years two other avenues of response have been observed. One is what Walton, Cutcher-Gershenfeld, and McKersie describe as **escape.**[2] That is, when the option of finding a nonunion alternative location or way to get work previously done under a union contract is available, management may either threaten or use this option in response to union cost differentials. A second option observed in recent years is for an outside firm to take over or purchase the unionized operation and then to extract wage concessions using the threat to move the work to a lower-cost setting. In doing so, the new firm transfers some of the wage gains achieved by the union members to its shareholders. One study estimated that such takeovers have transferred approximately 8 percent of wages, or about half the average union wage premium from union members to shareholders.[3]

In this chapter we will focus on the effect of unions and management responses within collective bargaining. However, the escape and takeover options should be kept in mind since, increasingly, they may be options that employers use to evaluate whether or not to attempt to work within the bargaining relationship or search for an escape alternative.

Union Effects on Employment Conditions

union effects depend on bargaining power

The primary and secondary effects of unions on pay and working conditions depend on the union's bargaining power. The following sections review the empirical evidence regarding the magnitude of union effects on employment conditions.

Wages are of central importance to employees and employers. How do the earnings of union workers compare with what union workers would have earned if there had been no unions anywhere in the economy? This comparison is termed the **absolute union wage effect.** But because it is extremely difficult to estimate what employment conditions would have been in the absence of unions, most research has focused on assessing the relative union wage effect. The **relative union wage effect** compares the earnings of union and nonunion workers.[4]

The Empirical Evidence of Relative Union Wage Effects

Empirical studies indicate that the relative union wage effect averages 15 to 20 percent; that is, unionized workers earn roughly 15 to 20 percent more than nonunion workers.[5] Various studies also show that the wage effects of unions vary (1) over time, (2) over the course of the business cycle, (3) across occupations, (4) across industries, and (5) by workers' gender, race, education, and age.

Some of the key variations in union wage effects include the following:

1. Unions have a greater positive effect on the wages of blacks, and particularly black men, than on whites. There also is evidence that obtaining a union job and remaining on that job pays off more for black than for white youths.[6]

2. Unions reduce the effects of age and education on earnings. That is, unions increase the earnings of younger workers by raising the entry-level salaries on union jobs above what an inexperienced worker would be paid in a comparable nonunion job. At the upper end of the wage distribution, the effects of seniority provisions in union contracts protect older workers from wage erosion after they pass their peak productivity years.[7]

3. Unions have larger wage effects in some occupations. One study estimated the following union–nonunion pay differentials by occupation: laborers, 42 percent; transportation equipment operators, 38 percent; crafts workers, 19 percent; operatives, 18 percent; service workers, 15 percent; managers, 2 percent; clerical employees, 2 percent; and sales workers, 4 percent.[8]

4. Union wage effects also vary across industries. Union wages are relatively higher for white male, blue-collar workers: 43 percent in construction; 16 percent in transportation, communications, and utilities; 12 percent in nondurable goods manufacturing; and 9 percent in durable goods manufacturing.[9]

5. Unions reduce the white-collar/blue-collar wage differential in firms where blue-collar workers are organized. Unions also reduce intraindustry wage differentials by promoting wage standardization. The reduction in wage dispersion within an industry due to the presence of unions more than offsets the increase in earnings dispersion across industries, so that the net effect of unions is to reduce wage inequality among workers.[10]

6. Unions produce larger relative wage effects in less concentrated (less monopolistic) industries. This is because, even in the absence of unionization, highly concentrated industries would pay relatively high wages.[11]

Research Techniques

The following section discusses the techniques used by researchers to derive the findings discussed above. It may be of special interest to readers with statistical training. Statistical techniques and problems that are similar to those discussed below are involved in the analysis of union impacts on nonwage employment conditions as well.

The research technique most frequently used to measure relative union wage effects has been a regression analysis in which the wages of a pool of union and nonunion workers are used as the **dependent** (or outcome) **variable,** and the union status of each individual or group of workers is entered as an **independent** (or explanatory) **variable,** along with a series of controls for other determinants of wages.[12] The types of control variables normally included in these regression equations are (1) human capital or labor supply characteristics, such as worker age, education, experience, and training; (2) the region of the country; (3) worker race and gender (as measures of the effects of discrimination); (4) the industry and occupation; and (5) the size of the firm.

Several technical problems make it difficult to know if these estimates of the relative union effects provide a good approximation to the absolute effects of unions on employment conditions. The major problem in sorting out the net effects of unions is that union wages may spill over to the nonunion sector because to deter their employees from unionizing (the "threat" of unionization) nonunion employers may raise or, in the extreme case, match union-negotiated wage increases. The nonunion wage is therefore higher than it would be otherwise because of the **threat effect** of unionization. Thus, estimates of the relative union wage effect may understate the absolute effect of unions on wages because they do not fully account for the extent that union wages have spilled over to the nonunion sector.

On the other hand, by raising wages unions may induce unionized firms to cut back on employment. The workers displaced then seek employment in nonunion firms and industries. This **supply effect** results in lower wages for the nonunion workers. Thus, the supply effect leads to estimates of the relative union wage effect that may overstate the differential between union wages and the wages that would exist if there were no union. Researchers have not been able to identify whether the threat effects are larger than the supply effects of unions.

Another highly technical problem arises if union membership is influenced by wage levels.[13] Unions tend to organize high-wage industries or workers. As a result, the union coefficient in a single-stage regression equation captures both the effects of unions on wages (the true effect of interest here) and the effects of wages on unionization (that is, higher wage jobs attract more unionization). Estimates of the union's influence on wages may therefore be overstated or understated unless this reciprocal causality is accounted for.

Variation in Union Effects over Time

Union effects on wages and other employment conditions vary substantially over time. As with union growth there are both cyclical and structural factors.

The data show that unions have their largest relative wage effects during periods of recession because unions resist wage cuts whereas nonunion employees are not able to resist wage cutting during business downturns. As a result, unionized employees do relatively better than nonunion employees during business downturns. During business upturns, however, these relative wage effects decline.

The decline in unions in recent years, along with an overall decline in real wages, an increase in wage inequality, and a decline in the proportion of the work force covered by health insurance and pensions, has highlighted an important policy question: How much of these trends is due to the declining power and coverage of unions? While the time series data needed to fully address these questions are only now becoming available to researchers, the preliminary evidence is that union decline and changes in the structure of wage determination are important contributors to these trends, perhaps accounting for approximately 20 percent of the increase in the inequality of wages. More precise estimates of the size of these effects on declines in fringe benefit coverage will undoubtedly be forthcoming in the years ahead.

Shifts in Pay Bargaining Over Time

Union bargaining power varies over time, in part as a product of changes in the economy. The increased price competition from both international and domestic markets made it hard for unions to "take wages out of competition" from the mid-1980s on. This substantially weakened union bargaining power. As shown in Exhibit 10–2, from the mid-1980s on the rise in wages and salaries in the nonunion sector exceeded the increases occurring in the union sector. This occurred not only because of the pay moderation occurring in the union

EXHIBIT 10–2

Percentage Change in Employment Costs and Prices in the United States, 1985–2005

	1985	1986	1987	1988	1989	1990	1991	1992	1993	1994	1995	1996	1997	1998	1999	2000	2001	2002	2003	2004	2005
Employment costs (wages and salaries)																					
Union	3.3	2.5	2.0	2.7	2.6	3.5	3.6	3.4	2.9	2.9	2.6	2.6	2.6	3.1	2.8	3.0	3.9	4.1	2.8	2.8	2.2
Nonunion	4.9	4.0	3.4	3.6	3.7	4.7	3.8	3.5	3.1	2.8	2.9	3.5	3.7	4.2	3.5	4.3	3.7	3.2	2.9	2.5	2.4
Annual percentage change in the consumer price index	3.6	1.9	3.6	4.1	4.8	5.4	4.2	3.0	3.0	2.6	2.8	3.0	2.8	1.6	2.2	3.4	2.8	1.6	2.3	2.7	3.4

Sources: For employment costs (of private sector workers), www.bls.gov/ncs/ect/home.htm#overview "Employment Cost Index" for annual percentage change in the consumer price index, www.bls.gov/cpi/home.htm#tables "Annual Percentage Changes from 1913 to Present."

sector, another contributing factor was the large pay increases received by highly educated employees, many of whom worked in unorganized workplaces.

As large markets tightened in the late 1990s, especially in the hi-tech sector, highly educated employees gained substantial individual bargaining power. The tightening of labor markets from the mid-1990s through 2003, produced wage increase in both the union and nonunion sector that consistently and significantly exceeded increases occurring in the cost-of-living. To see this effect compare the wage increases in the first and second rows of Exhibit 10–2 with the annual increases in the consumer price index reported in row 3 for 1997 on through 2003. In 2004 and 2005, this pattern no longer held.

Union Effects on Wage Administration

A key aspect of wage administration is that union contracts tend to link worker wages to specific jobs and not to characteristics of the worker. Thus, while seniority is a strong guiding principle for worker transfers and other worker rights, it does not typically directly influence worker wages in the United States. The importance played by job characteristics as a determinant of worker wages is one reason why the U.S. labor movement has been labeled "job control" unionism.

Over the years, in addition to increasing wages, collective bargaining has introduced a number of innovations in the system of **wage administration.** Chief among these have been cost-of-living adjustments, deferred wage increases (sometimes referred to as **annual improvement factors), red circle wage rates** (stipulations that provide for rate retention to employees whose jobs are evaluated downward because of technological change), and **wage reopener** provisions (whereby the contract remains in force over several years, but wages are renegotiated at some specified point during the life of the agreement).

In some industries, such as steel, the union and the employers have jointly developed complex systems for evaluating jobs and establishing a more rational structure of wage rates. In many settings, the current trend is to consolidate jobs and reduce the number of different wage classifications in order to increase flexibility, encourage training, and pay for skills workers have rather than for the specific job to which they are assigned on a given day. These changes require not only adjustments in collective bargaining contracts but also considerable ongoing union and management joint effort to implement and fine tune these new plans during the term of an agreement.

In industries such as apparel, over the years unions and the employers have negotiated and administered complicated **wage incentive systems.** Historically, apparel industry unions provided technical advice to employers on how to structure jobs and set incentive rates.[14] In recent years, the pressures to respond to the combination of international competition for low-priced clothing and the need for rapid replenishment of stock by retailers has led clothing unions and some employers to move from individual jobs and incentives to various team-based work systems (called **modular production** in clothing).[15] At Levi-Strauss, for example, a joint union-management program was set up to assist individual plants in making this transition to a new work and compensation system.

Union Effects on Fringe Benefits

In general, unionized workers receive both a wider variety and a higher level of fringe benefits than nonunion workers—for a variety of reasons.[16] A focus by unions on fringe benefits is long-standing.

During World War II, the War Labor Board first sanctioned and then actively encouraged bargaining over fringe benefits as a means of holding down the size of the basic wage increase. Since then unions have fought to broaden the scope of fringe benefits included among the mandatory subjects of bargaining. In the 1948 Inland Steel case the NLRB ruled that pension and retirement issues belonged on the mandatory list of subjects.[17] By the late 1950s the board had added to the list issues such as health insurance, sick leave, supplementary unemployment benefits, vacations, and holidays, and since then these have become standard provisions in almost all collective bargaining agreements.

The Sources of Unions' Demands for Fringe Benefits

Union demands for improvements in fringe benefits derive from a number of factors. For one thing, union membership typically includes a disproportionately high number of older workers and workers with longer tenure who are likely to place a particularly high priority on pensions and life insurance benefits. Furthermore, the preferences of these older union members are likely to carry much weight in union decision making because older union members tend to have greater political influence within unions.

Union concern for certain fringe benefits also is a consequence of the fact that unionized employees exhibit low voluntary turnover (i.e., low quit rates). Since union members are likely to stay on their jobs for a longer time than do nonunion workers, they gain more from deferred benefits such as pension plans, vacation pay tied to seniority, early retirement, and disability retirement pay.

Employee demands for fringe benefits rise as employee income rises. Thus, as unions increase wages, their members will prefer to purchase additional fringe benefits over additional wage increases. This is compounded by the tax advantages associated with fringe benefits. Employees pay no income taxes on deferred benefits until they receive the benefits (if received as income, as in the case of a pension) and never pay tax on some benefits (such as medical care). Thus, workers will value an additional expenditure on fringe benefits more highly than the same expenditure on wages. This preference should increase as the wage level increases.

Trends in Fringe Benefit Provisions ~~union workers receive more fringe benefits~~

For all the reasons discussed above, unionized employees exhibit a strong preference for fringe benefits. Research shows that unionized workers on average receive (1) a wider range of fringe benefits and (2) a greater percentage of their total compensation in the form of fringe benefits than do nonunion employees.[18]

The vast majority of unionized workers receive a comprehensive package of fringe benefits. For example, health insurance benefits remain an integral part of nearly all collective bargaining contracts. Nearly all of current labor contracts provide insurance coverage for hospital visits (99 percent), doctor visits (96 percent) and prescription drugs (96 percent).[19] Moreover, although included in only 39 percent of union contracts in 2005, coverage of domestic partners as part of employee health benefits has been sharply increasing in the last several years.

Recent evidence indicates that the new jobs being created in the United States are less likely to provide health insurance and pension coverage than existing jobs. This is particularly true for less educated and lower wage earners.[20] While we cannot determine from the data available how much of this decline in coverage is due to the lack of union coverage in most of these new jobs, it undoubtedly is part of the explanation.

Within the unionized sector there have been major pressures to control health insurance costs. Surveys consistently show that this has been one of the top management bargaining objectives in recent years. As a result, many companies and unions have negotiated changes in their plans to encourage or require use of health maintenance organizations rather than individual doctors and to shift more of the costs of health insurance to workers by increasing deductibles or adding various types of copayment arrangements to existing plans. In addition, some unions and companies have set up joint committees to explore ways to reduce the costs of health insurance without lowering benefits.

Even in the face of these benefit cutbacks, union workers continue to receive more fringe benefits on average than do nonunion workers. For example, in 2005, retirement benefits were received by 85 percent of union members in the private sector, whereas only 46 percent of the nonunion workforce was granted this benefit.

As shown in Exhibit 10–3, since the 1950s retirement plans were the most costly fringe benefit provided by employers. Yet, the share of employer spending on health benefits rose dramatically after 1970 (see Exhibit 10–3) and this helped propel employer efforts to control health care spending.

Health care costs for most employers in 2006 increased between 6 and 10 percent. In response to these and prior benefit costs escalation unionized employers pressed to control health insurance costs. As a result, health care cost containment has become one of the top management bargaining objectives in recent years and will continue to play a large role in negotiations in the future.

Many companies and unions have negotiated changes in their plans to encourage or require the use of health maintenance organizations rather than individual doctors and to shift more of the costs of health insurance to workers by increasing deductibles or adding various types of employee co-payment arrangements to existing plans. Moreover, following

EXHIBIT 10–3

The Share of Employer Spending on Fringe Benefits, 1950–2004

Source: www.ebri.org/ pdf/EBRI_notes_12- 20053.pdf EBRI Notes Dec. 2005, Vol. 26, No. 12, pg. 5.

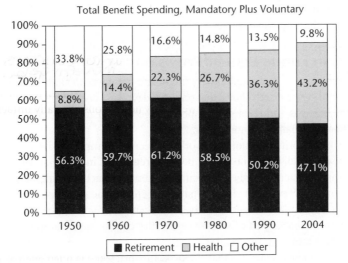

Total Benefit Spending, Mandatory Plus Voluntary

■ Retirement ☐ Health ☐ Other

the example of many airline and steel companies, firms are beginning to use bankruptcy court as a way around collective bargaining contracts if the union is unwilling to substantially cut health care costs. Delphi Corporation, the major supplier of parts to General Motors, threatened to use this method if a deal with the UAW failed to come to significantly lower wage and benefit costs.

Union Effects on Quit Rates *voice mechanism for wages and rules & conditions of work*

Research conducted by Freeman and Medoff and others shows that unionized establishments have significantly lower quit rates than nonunion establishments because they provide a voice mechanism through which employees can negotiate higher relative compensation and redress problems as an alternative to exit. Unions reduce the probability that workers will quit their jobs for two fundamental reasons. First, unions provide a voice mechanism through which workers gain higher compensation than they could earn in a similar nonunion job. Second, unions provide workers with a voice in determining an array of other rules and conditions of work, including policies that reduce pay inequality, grievance and arbitration procedures for appealing managerial decisions, "just cause" for discipline and discharge, and seniority clauses desired by workers. Thus, even after controlling for the union effects on wages, union establishments have been found to have lower quit rates. Quit rates in telecommunications establishments in 1998 ranged from 3.3 percent in unionized establishments (all had a grievance procedure) to 14.9 percent in nonunion establishments that had no formal complaint resolution procedure.[21]

A related stream of recent research has found that at the individual level, employee use of voice mechanisms is positively, not negatively, correlated with employee intent to quit and subsequent turnover. This research suggests that whereas quit rates may be lower in enterprises where stronger voice mechanisms are available, among enterprises that have similar voice mechanisms available to employees, greater usage of voice mechanisms appears to be associated with higher quit rates.

Union Effects on Work Rules

Employees are concerned with the difficulty and nature of their work at the same time that they are concerned with how much compensation they receive for performing that work. As a result, union effects extend beyond compensation. There are many **work rules** affecting matters such as the pace and difficulty of work that are of concern to unionized employees and, consequently, to unions. Below we review how unions generally influence some of the key work rules.

Protection from Arbitrary Treatment

Perhaps one of the most important effects of unions has been the protections they have secured for their members from arbitrary discipline, discharge, or denial of benefits. Unions pioneered the development of the principle of just cause for dismissal or discipline. Unions developed the grievance procedures ending in arbitration for adjudicating disputes over actions that violate the just-cause principle or some other term of the labor agreement. The installation of this system of industrial jurisprudence is often cited as one of the most distinct achievements of the U.S. collective bargaining system.

How does the union system of jurisprudence compare with practices in the nonunion sector? Although the number of nonunion grievance procedures has also swelled in recent years, most of them do not provide for binding arbitration by a neutral party.

Nonunion employees also receive some protection from statutory legal protections, although in most states (since state laws apply given the absence of federal law) these protections are limited. The primary statutory protections available to workers dismissed, denied benefits, or denied promotions are those prohibiting such actions on the basis of discrimination by race, gender, age, religion, disability, or support for union activity.

Seniority *benefit & competitive provisions*

Seniority plays a pivotal role in collective bargaining agreements, and the elaboration of **seniority rights** represents another important effect unions exert on employment conditions. Seniority rights are important to employees because they are used as a basis for allocating benefits and job opportunities to workers. Seniority rights are important to employers because they restrict the discretion they have in carrying out their personnel functions. And seniority is important to public officials as they administer equal employment opportunity labor policies.

Seniority is normally defined as the employee's length of service with the employer. In some cases, and for some purposes, it may be measured as the length of service in a particular department, job, or other subunit of the organization. Two types of seniority provisions commonly negotiated in collective bargaining agreements are benefit-status and competitive-status provisions. Benefit-status provisions tie increases in various economic benefits, such as vacations, pensions, supplementary unemployment pay, severance pay, and guaranteed annual wages, to the length of service with the employer. Competitive-status provisions make seniority a factor in personnel decisions, such as promotions, job assignments, layoffs, and transfers.

Seniority also plays a role in grievance arbitration. Most arbitrators will take the grievant's length of service into account in considering whether any disciplinary action taken against the worker was equitable, especially in light of a previously good personnel record.

As unionism developed in the United States, seniority emerged as an important bargaining goal of most unions as members viewed it as a means of curbing arbitrary treatment or favoritism in personnel decisions. Unions also came to support the notion that employees gain a property right to their jobs as their length of service increases. Accordingly, unions argued that those employees with the longest service should (1) be entitled to the most secure jobs, (2) have the first opportunity to bid for better jobs as they open up, and (3) be accorded some deference in scheduling vacations and accruing other benefits.

Frequency and Common Forms of Seniority Language

Seniority provisions are mentioned as a factor to be used in promotion decisions in 73 percent of the manufacturing and 57 percent of the nonmanufacturing agreements in the 1995 contract data base compiled by the Bureau of National Affairs (BNA). The lower percentage in the nonmanufacturing contracts is largely attributable to the relative absence of these provisions in the construction industry. Of those contracts mentioning seniority in the BNA study only 5 percent specified that it be the sole criterion governing promotions within the bargaining unit. It served as a determining factor, provided the employee was qualified, in 49 percent of the contracts; as a secondary factor considered only when other qualifying factors were equal, in 40 percent of the contracts; and as a consideration equal to other factors in fewer than 1 percent of the contracts.

Based on survey responses from about 400 firms Katharine Abraham and James Medoff concluded that over three-quarters of hourly unionized employees worked in settings in which seniority had an important independent role in the promotion process.[22] Interestingly, the authors also found that seniority was used frequently in the nonunion sector as well, though not to as great a degree as within unionized firms. Over half of both hourly, non-union employees and salaried, nonunion employees worked in settings in which seniority had an independent role in the promotion process.

The Pros and Cons of Seniority Provisions

Seniority provisions protect the security of high seniority workers' incomes and jobs by reducing the threat of layoff by increasing the chances of bumping (displacing a newer employee when a layoff occurs). Seniority provisions also play an important role in shaping the career prospects of workers.

Both the scope of the seniority unit and the weight assigned to seniority in promotions affect the range of possible paths for upward mobility and the probability that an individual worker will obtain a promotion. Together the scope of the seniority unit and the weight given to seniority determine the expected length of time required to move up in the organization.

Strong seniority provisions improve the promotion chances of workers with average to below-average ability and motivation. These provisions may serve to slow the career advancement of younger employees who possess higher than average ability and motivation. Thus, seniority does not necessarily benefit all employees equally.

Seniority provisions offer employers both advantages and disadvantages. By increasing the economic and job security of workers as their tenure increases, seniority provisions should help stabilize the work force and reduce the number of valued workers who leave the firm. They also may reduce psychological stress and increase older workers' satisfaction with their jobs. Furthermore, if experience contributes to improved job performance, the use of seniority should help keep the most productive workers within the organization.

Seniority provisions reduce managers' and workers' uncertainty about the ongoing makeup of the workforce. As a result, the employer can design jobs and training programs to ensure that job performance does improve with length of service, thereby simplifying the personnel function. Seniority provisions allow the employer to compute the probable movement of individual workers through different jobs in the organization over time.

All these benefits are greatest to those firms that have relatively routine and unchanging technologies in which individual worker differences have little effect on job performance. The more variable the technology and skill requirements, the greater the costs associated with strict adherence to seniority. In these cases employers will seek to limit both the scope of the seniority unit and the weight assigned to seniority in promotion decisions.

Strict adherence to seniority would entail large costs when jobs require great technical, professional, or artistic skill. It is hard to imagine, for example, seniority ever playing an important role in determining the starting lineup of a professional baseball team or the cast for a major motion picture.

The Importance of Seniority

This brief overview of the role of seniority provisions vividly illustrates why some see them as the heart of a collective bargaining agreement. Clearly, seniority provisions are among the most complex to negotiate and to modify as conditions change. The variations in the nature and strength of seniority provisions in union contracts attest to the ability of collective bargaining to fit a general principle to the specific circumstances of each bargaining pair.

Job and Income Security

In addition to its inherent importance to all workers, **job security** is of special concern to union members because of how management adjusts to unions' primary effects. As unions increase wages and other labor costs, they give employers reasons to make compensating adjustments in employment conditions that reduce employees' job security. An increase in labor costs, for example, leads firms to substitute technology for labor or to reduce the volume of production. Unions commonly respond to these adjustments by attempting to negotiate job and **income security** provisions that provide some protection from these adjustments or at least set rules about how the adjustment will be made (e.g., seniority rules regarding who gets laid off first if layoffs occur, limitations on management's right to contract out work).

Some security provisions make it more difficult or costly for the employer to substitute either nonunion labor or capital inputs for union work covered under the contract. The union may also try to negotiate additional paid time off to reduce the employment losses or require the hiring of additional workers.

Employers frequently oppose demands for job and income security provisions because they (1) increase labor costs, (2) reduce employers' ability to adjust labor costs to fluctuations in business conditions, and (3) limit managerial discretion and freedom.

The comprehensiveness of the job and income security protections that unionized workers achieve is a function of the bargaining power of the union. Bargaining over these issues represents the classic conflict over the workers' desire for security and the employer's desire for autonomy and flexibility.

Job Preservation

Some job security provisions are geared toward preserving jobs. One way unions try to preserve jobs is by negotiating **work-sharing** provisions that cut the workweek during periods of slack demand rather than allow the layoff of employees. This practice is found in 17 percent of all union contracts and in almost all apparel industry contracts.

One major disincentive to work sharing is that **unemployment benefits** in most states do not cover workers on a shortened workweek. In most states a complete layoff is necessary for unemployment eligibility, although a few states have experimented with providing unemployment compensation to workers affected by a reduction in work hours. Most contractual work-sharing agreements limit the time period during which this alternative can be used to forestall layoffs. Most also limit the number of hours that will be reduced before commencing layoffs.

Other types of work rule provisions that are geared to preserving jobs are restrictions on the following: supervisors' rights to do bargaining-unit work; transferring employees and filling vacancies; the ratio of apprentices to journeymen; management's right to change the pace of work; and the extent of subcontracting. Many of these provisions are desired by the union for their contribution to increased safety and other reasons in addition to their effects on job preservation. Note that management sometimes complains that these procedures lead to their retaining more workers than are needed to perform the work, or what is referred to as featherbedding.

Income Security during Temporary Layoffs

When sales turn down, firms commonly quickly try to reduce employment levels. This leads to layoffs that are temporary in duration if the laid-off workers are recalled when business improves. Temporary layoffs are a common occurrence in industries that produce durable goods such as automobiles or household appliances.

In the face of their experience with frequent layoffs over the post–World War period, unions in the United States developed a number of contractual provisions that address short-term layoffs. Many of these provisions provide income security rather than employment security.

The two major forms of income protection against short-term fluctuations in the demand for work are **supplementary unemployment benefit (SUB)** plans and guaranteed annual wage plans. The first major SUB plan to be negotiated was in the auto industry in 1955.[23] The United Auto Workers had originally sought a form of guaranteed annual income. Ford Motor Company, the target firm in that round of negotiations, countered with what has grown into the industry's SUB plan. The pattern set in the auto industry spread quickly.

Programs in Response to Permanent Job Loss

Not all workers are recalled when laid off. As a result, another important set of collective bargaining clauses deals with permanent job loss caused by either technological change or a plant shutdown. Here the provisions address both job preservation and income protection. They include interplant transfer rights or transfer rights to other jobs within the plant or organization; early notice of technological change, a plant shutdown, or both; and relocation allowances. For example, the 1999–2003 UAW collective bargaining agreements with General Motors, Ford, and Chrysler provided that each company would not close, nor partially or wholly sell, spin-off, consolidate or otherwise dispose of any plant or business unit during the life of the contract.

In the face of the substantial layoffs that occurred in many nonunion and unionized workplaces in the 1980s, Congress passed **The Worker Adjustment and Retraining Notification Act,** which took effect in February 1989. This law requires that employers provide advance notice to employees affected by plant closings: employers with 100 or more employees must give 60 days advance notice of plant shutdowns when they affect at least 50 workers at an employment site. In addition, the law contains a mass layoff provision, requiring advance notice in the case of layoffs that last more than six months and that affect 50 or more employees, 33 percent or more of the work force at a site, or more than 500 workers for any time frame.

Employment Security Initiatives

Responding to the same pressures that induced Congress to require advance notice of plant closings, a number of collective bargaining agreements in recent years provide enhanced employment security through a variety of mechanisms. These mechanisms include lifetime job guarantees to workers on the payroll as of a specified date. The auto and some other collective bargaining agreements provided for "job banks" to create employment or retraining alternatives for workers on layoff from their regular assignments. The unusual feature of these job banks is that workers receive full pay while in them even if the company fails to come up with a fitting work assignment.

The auto and a number of other agreements also increased the incentives for older workers to retire or quit. In these cases the companies hope that through attrition they can avoid the need to lay off workers and thereby avoid the high costs to the company for such layoffs imposed by clauses in their labor agreements. As Box 10–1 shows, unions were not immune from union pressures to provide income and other support to laid-off employees as unions too faced the need to downsize and reorganize.

Even unions have had to downsize and cope with the consequences. Box 10–1 reports on how the AFL-CIO negotiated new clauses in the contracts it has with unions representing its staff and professional employees. As the box reports, the AFL-CIO gained the right to lay off employees, but also agreed to discuss with employees and their union representatives ways to avoid layoffs, agreed to provide additional training, and banned the use of outside consultants to perform bargaining unit work.

One of the most hotly contested employment security issues of this decade involves the contracting out of work done by union members, or **outsourcing** as it is now commonly called. Outsourcing has become prevalent for three reasons: (1) the rise in availability of nonunion firms capable of doing many of the tasks performed by unionized workers, especially unionized workers in manufacturing firms, (2) the popularity of reengineering processes that dominated much of management thinking and actions, and (3) the general downsizing trends and the desire of many firms to focus on only the core activities over which the firm has a distinct competitive advantage in performing. Together or separately, these have led to considerable bargaining activity and in some cases considerable conflict. (See Box 10–2.)

Why the Emphasis on Employment Security

The dominance of employment security as an employee and union objective was hardly surprising in light of the extensive layoffs of recent years. Over most of the post–World War II period employment insecurity had taken the form of layoffs that were temporary, and most workers were eventually recalled from layoff. The unions' response had been to bargain for income maintenance via unemployment benefits supplemental to the state unemployment insurance programs.

Faced with the extensive economic restructuring of industries that began in the late 1970s, workers with substantial seniority could no longer assume they would be called back. For example, in the four recessions prior to 1990, 44 percent of those laid off were expected to get their job back when conditions improved. In the 1991–92 recession, this number declined to 14 percent. The other 86 percent were permanent job losers.[24] Plant shutdowns and the worldwide consolidation and technological updating of manufacturing facilities made recall less likely. Moreover, the average displaced worker could expect to experience about a 20 percent reduction in pay in whatever replacement job could be found. Since unionized workers, on average, have higher pay and more comprehensive benefits, they could expect to lose even more than that. As a result, workers and their unions shifted the bargaining agenda to demand greater protections against *permanent* job loss due to downsizing, restructuring, reengineering, or outsourcing.

The development of new work structures geared toward greater flexibility in the deployment of the workforce has also spurred interest in employment security. Traditionally, plants were organized along the conventional lines of occupations commonly found in the external labor market, lessening the difficulties associated with layoffs by making alternative employment more easily available. But as firms pushed for fewer classifications and more firm-specific training, workers sought assurances of employment continuity. Without such assurances they feared their specialized training would make them ill-equipped for jobs elsewhere.

Employment security programs also became attractive because the teamwork systems being simultaneously introduced in many settings were particularly effective if employees were highly trained and committed to their work. Both of those attributes can be encouraged by enhancing workers' employment security.

The Saturn-UAW agreement, for example guarantees employment security to 80 percent of the labor force. This was not only an inducement to GM workers from around the country to move to Tennessee to take the new jobs created at Saturn. It was also an important component of the overall human resource and work organization *system* implemented at Saturn. We will return to this point below when we discuss how the different contract terms combine to produce alternative systems of work organization and labor-management relations in American industry. In the face of rising gas prices and declining profits, the U.S. auto

With financial instability and uncertainty in the American automotive industry as gas prices rise and the sweeping success of SUVs begin the dwindle, the Big Three in recent years have found a need to begin to close plants down to reduce labor costs. However, union contracts make this extremely difficult to do. Since 1987, Ford Motor Corp. has had the Guaranteed Employment Numbers (GEN) program in place, which was set up to protect employees from plant closings by promising long-term pay and benefits if their jobs were lost due to closings. In light of the difficulties now facing Ford and the need to close plants down to save money, Ford has devised an agreement with the United Auto Workers to try to free them of the boundaries of the GEN program.

When Ford began closing plants in Edison, NJ, in early 2004, they attempted to solve the GEN problems by persuading employees to take advantage of five alternatives, four of which have been in place for years. The new alternative, known as the Educational Opportunity Program, offers laid-off employees the ability to gain a degree or certification from a four-year school, a two-year school, or a technical school with Ford paying up to $15,000 a year directly to that institution for a maximum of four years. In addition, the employee will be paid half of their yearly salary and full benefits until the education stage is completed. Following the conclusion of the educational period, no further benefits are offered and the person is no longer an employee of Ford.

Although this appears to be a viable option for those looking to advance their careers or delve into a new line of work, it has not proved extremely successful. To more quickly reduce its workforce, Ford then started encouraging employees to take advantage of the four other options available. For example, workers with 28–30 years of service were made eligible to receive 85 percent of yearly pay until they begin to receive postretirement benefits. Moreover, those with at least 30 years of service are eligible for full retirement benefits and $30,000 if they choose to voluntarily retire. In addition, if the Educational Opportunity Program does not appeal to an employee, Ford hopes that any employee with at least one year of service will take advantage of a $100,000 lump sum severance package by agreeing to leave the company without further benefits. Similarly, at GM, employees were offered up to $140,000 (approximately 2.5 years of pay) to voluntarily leave the company and forgo retiree heath care coverage.

Sources: "Laid-Off Ford Workers Offered Education Alternative to Jobs Program in Edison, Lorain," 01/23/06. *Daily Labor Report,* January 23, 2006: A-4; "Ford Could Extend Severance Incentives To UAW Workers at 14 Plants Slated to Close," 02/09/06. *Daily Labor Report,* February 9, 2006: A-2; Chris Isidore, "GM offers workers up to $140K to leave." March 22, 2006, CNNMoney.com.

companies sought to encourage early retirements through "buyouts" and other mechanisms to shrink their workforces as described in Box 10–3.

Nevertheless, employment security programs as comprehensive as those negotiated in the auto industry to date are included in only a few other collective bargaining agreements in this country. The interesting question is whether these recent developments toward enhancing employment security in return for greater flexibility in work organization will spread in the future.

It also remains to be seen exactly how the new employment security programs are implemented and what their implications are. Some programs provide employment guarantees to only a subset of the workforce, while others provide for the hiring of more temporary and part-time workers. As a result, these plans could engender intense political rivalries within unions—between those workers who have employment security and those who do not. It also will likely lead to a new round of union demands to either reduce the number of part-time workers or to improve their wages and employment conditions. This has been a major issue in negotiations between the Teamsters and UPS, a major package delivery firm. (See

On August 4, 1997, the Teamsters went on strike against United Parcel Service (UPS). The two major issues in the 15-day dispute revolved around wages and the increased use of part-time employees. Approximately 57 percent of the 185,000 UPS workers represented by the Teamsters were classified as part-time employees, defined as those working a weekly average of 35 hours or less. In the settlement agreement UPS agreed to create 10,000 new full-time positions from part-time jobs over the next four years. The parties also agreed upon a higher wage increase for part-time employees than for full-timers. The Teamsters' focus on part-time work allowed them to foster public support and to prompt national debate on the issue.

On July 15, 2002, UPS and the Teamsters reached an agreement on a six-year contract nearly two weeks before the expiration of the previous five-year contract. All employees received a $5 per hour increase over the term of the contract and part-time workers received an additional $1 per hour increase as "catch-up." The start rate will increase by 50 cents per hour for part-timers after the first 90 days of employment as well. Similar to the old contract, the new agreement calls for the creation of 10,000 new full-time jobs to lower the ratio between full-timers and part-timers. This will occur at a rate of 2,500 new positions in each of the last four years of the contract.

Part-timers constitute 58 percent of the 2002 UPS workforce and are paid significantly less than full-time workers. The average hourly rate of full-time workers at UPS is $22.10 while the average rate for part-timers is $10.72. The Teamster's goal is to lower the share of the part-time workforce at UPS to below 50 percent. Although the additional 10,000 full-time jobs provided for in the 2002–8 contract will increase the share of full-timers at UPS, full-time workers will still account for less than 50 percent of workers by the end of the new contract.

Sources: "Use of Part-Time Workers at UPS Underscores Thorny Workplace Issue," *Daily Labor Report,* August 8, 1997; "Use of Part-Time Workers Draws New Attention after UPS Strike," *Daily Labor Report,* September 11, 1997; and "UPS, Teamsters Agree on Six-Year Pact to Cover 230,000 Employees Nationwide," *Daily Labor Report* 137, July 17, 2002: AA–1.

Box 10–4.) It also remains to be seen whether employment security for some and exposure to the risks of outsourcing and use of part-time or contract workers for others results in greater worker acceptance of flexible work rules and a greater bond of commitment between the firm and its workforce or a more divisive workplace with two classes of workers.

Management's Response to Work Rules

The work rules provided in the traditional labor contract, grievance procedures, seniority rights, or job security, all limit the amount of discretion management exercises at the workplace. In response, traditionally, management has taken a number of actions to expand its discretion over work rules.

Management Rights Clauses

One conventional strategy management employs to limit the effects of restrictive work rules is to negotiate a management rights clause. Some **management rights** statements are simple, general statements such as, "The supervision, management, and control of the company's business, operations, and plants are exclusively the function of this company." The majority of the provisions, however, enumerated a specific list of rights reserved to management, as in the following example:

The rights to hire, promote, discharge or discipline for cause, and maintain the discipline and efficiency of employees are the sole responsibility of the corporation except that union members shall not be discriminated against as such. In addition, the products to be manufactured, the location of plants, the schedules of production, and the methods, processes, and means of manufacturing are solely and exclusively the responsibility of the corporation.

The obvious purpose of management rights clauses is to limit the territory of union influence and retain for management the freedom to run the organization. The traditional labor relations literature has articulated two views of the management rights concept; these are used by arbitrators and the courts in resolving disputes over contract interpretation. The reserved, or **residual, rights doctrine** takes the view that all rights not covered by a specific clause in the contract are retained by management. In contrast, the **implied obligations doctrine** assumes that the union recognition clause requires management to negotiate changes in terms and conditions of employment even in the absence of an express contract provision that covers the issue involved.

The Residual Rights Doctrine

The residual rights doctrine has been most popular among management practitioners. Those supporting this view argue that it derives logically from the property rights that stockholders (or the public, in a governmental organization) delegate to management. The supporters claim that neither union members nor their representatives are directly accountable to stockholders. This view holds that unions should not have a right to infringe on the ability of management to act on the owners' behalf, except in the case of an issue over which management has agreed to share its authority by way of specific contract language.

The Implied Obligations Doctrine

The residual rights doctrine has been challenged by labor relations scholars and arbitrators who support the implied obligations doctrine. This position is worth examining because some courts have used it as a rationale for limiting the firm's freedom to hire and fire at will.

Neil Chamberlain and James Kuhn, for example, proposed that while management may have a property right to allocate the resources needed to run the organization, the management of human resources requires the consent of the managed. They stated that workers are under no legal compulsion to cooperate with management.[25] Charles Killingsworth made a similar argument, noting that management's "right" to assert discretion over any subject is limited in a very practical way by its power to impose its will on employees. He noted that the residual rights doctrine is of little value as a legal principle because it ignores the power relationship between employer and employees.[26]

Productivity Bargaining

Over the years various approaches have been taken by management and labor to eliminate work rules that restrict changes that might improve productivity or become outmoded by technological change or changing ideas about how to best organize work. In the 1960s, for example, the concept of **productivity bargaining** was popular.[27] Productivity bargaining can take one of two forms: a one-time buyout of outmoded practices; or a long-term, joint union–management program for adjusting to technological change.

A highly publicized example of productivity bargaining occurred in 1960 when the Pacific Maritime Association, representing the west coast longshore industry, signed a Mechanization and Modernization Agreement with the International Longshoremen and Warehousemen's Union.[28] This agreement provided a $5 million productivity fund, wage and employment guarantees, and incentives for early retirement by high-seniority workers in return for an end to work rules that required multiple handling of goods and employment of more workers than needed as containerization swept through the docks.

In 1974 the International Typographical Union and the New York City newspapers negotiated an 11-year agreement that provided lifetime job security and early retirement incentives to typesetters in return for management's introduction of computerized technologies. The railroad industry also has periodically experienced productivity buyouts that involve quid pro quos exchanged for reductions in crew size.

The general focus of management's demands since the early 1980s has been to increase its flexibility in human resource management. This push has been particularly salient in management proposals for broader job classifications, greater managerial discretion in allocating overtime, more liberal subcontracting rights, and restrictions on voluntary transfers or other movements across jobs.

For many workers across industries, management's push for flexibility brought reductions in the number of job classifications and a lessening of the role seniority plays in job transfers and job assignments. Exhibit 10–4 outlines how the National Steel Company reduced the number of job classifications for craft workers in one of its plants, as part of a concessionary contract signed in 1986. This reclassification illustrates what has become one of the major issues in contemporary collective bargaining, namely, the reduction in job classifications.

As we will see below, all these management demands for increased flexibility reflect an effort to move, either through incremental steps or in a comprehensive fashion to an alternative to the traditional job control work system, namely one that stresses teamwork, flexibility, employee input in problem solving, and continuous quality improvement.

Alternative Work System: From Work Rules to Teamwork

From the 1980s on, one-time buyouts of specific work rules largely gave way to more comprehensive efforts to restructure work to enhance flexibility, teamwork, and continuous improvement in quality. These efforts reflect more of a sea-change in management thinking about work systems and human resource management than isolated efforts to change specific work rules. We will discuss these new systems and the forms of employee participation embedded within them in more detail in Chapter 12, however, it is useful to point out here how team-based work systems and their associated contract provisions differ from the more conventional work rules flowing from a job control model of union–management relations and the stakes involved in the choice between these two systems.

The detailed work rules covering job classifications, individual pay and/or incentive rates, promotion criteria, transfer rights, layoff procedures, and so on all are interrelated parts of the job control union–management system of industrial relations built up in the United States since the rise of mass production and the New Deal collective bargaining system was institutionalized. Together, these provisions and rules produced the uniformity, equitable treatment, clarity over rights and obligations, and stability that both management and labor needed to overcome the arbitrary and often inconsistent treatment workers experienced prior to unionization. In return for specific rights workers negotiated and wrote

EXHIBIT 10–4
A Draft of Job Unification of Trades and Crafts in a Steel Works

Source: Takahara Yamagami, "The Survival Strategy for the U.S. Steel Industry," master's thesis (Cambridge: Sloan School of Management, Massachusetts Institute of Technology, 1987).

NEW JOB CLASSIFICATION	EXISTING JOB CLASSIFICATION
Electrician	Motor inspector
	Wireman
	Electrical repairman
	Wireman leader
	Power repairman
	Tack welding function
Electronic technician	Instrument repairman
	Electronic repairman
Motor winder	Winder
Mechanic	Millwright
	Maintenance repairman
	Pipe fitter
	Rigger
	Welder
	Fitting fabricator
	Pipe repairman
	Roll shop machine repairman
	Maintenance repair layout man
	Sheeter
	Rigger leader
	System controller
	Rigger shop general layout man
	Weld shop equipment repairman
	General mechanic—rigger shop
	Layout man—dock
Crane repairman	Crane millwright
	Crane inspector
Refrigeration repairman	Refrigeration repairman
Machinist	Machinist
	Bearing repairman
Mobile equipment repairman	Mobile equipment mechanic
	Tractor repairman
Blacksmith	Blacksmith
	Forger

into collective bargaining agreements, management retained broad authority to manage its operations, protected as noted above by management rights' clauses. From the 1940s through the 1970s, unions and companies modified these provisions incrementally each time they renegotiated their contract to take account of changing conditions, new technologies, and so on. Over time, therefore, contracts became more lengthy and complex as new wage, fringe benefit, and work rule provisions were added.

As noted in the introduction to this chapter, managers adjusted to the detailed contracts by what Sumner Slichter and colleagues labeled the "shock effect," that is, the second stage of the three-stage model in Exhibit 10–1. By professionalizing the personnel and labor relations function and by taking advantage of the higher wages and benefits and the benefits that came with greater seniority (more vacation time, increasing pension benefits, etc.), turnover could be reduced and productivity improved. Over the 1940s through much of the 1970s, therefore, on average, both companies and workers did well under this type of labor management system. Productivity for the overall economy increased by an average

EXHIBIT 10–4
(*continued*)

NEW JOB CLASSIFICATION   EXISTING JOB CLASSIFICATION

Industrial carpenter —————————————— Carpenter
Painter
Decorative painter
Plasterer
Sign painter

Bricklayer ————————————————————— Bricklayer

Turbine and boiler —————————————— Turbine repairman
repairman — Boiler repairman

Roll turner ————————————————————— Roll turner

Electrical helper —————————————— Motor inspector helper
Wireman helper
Instrument repairman helper
Electronic repairman helper
Repairman helper (winder)
Repairman helper (yard)
Tractor repairman helper
Crane millwright helper
Power repairman helper

Mechanical helper —————————————— Millwright helper
Welder helper
Maintenance repairman
helper
Pipe fitter helper
Machinist helper
Blacksmith helper

Service helper —————————————— Carpenter helper
Painter helper
Bricklayer helper
Helper (roll shop)
Turbine and machine
repairman helper
Turbine repairman helper

of 3.2 percent during the 20 years following World War II, and workers' real wages tracked this rate of productivity improvement. Econometric studies using data from the 1970s in fact found that productivity was generally higher in union than nonunion establishments.[29] In short, American management had adjusted to the New Deal labor relations system and together labor and management professionals had made it work for the workers and shareholders they represented.

But the stability of this system began to first be challenged and then broken by developments from the mid-1970s that continue to be present today. One of these developments was the rise of nonunion human resource management systems discussed in Chapter 5 that did not implement as detailed set of work rules as found in union contract and that began to experiment with team-based work systems in some new worksites. Another development was the rise of international competition, especially competition from Japanese firms operating in Japan and, increasingly, head-to-head competition with Japanese firms such as Honda, Toyota, Nippon Denso, and others operating in the United States. The Japanese management and production systems also emphasized teamwork employee participation, training, and employment security but avoided detailed contractual work rules.

EXHIBIT 10–5
Quality and Productivity Comparison of Major Automobile Plants

Source: *ICL Technical Journal*, November 1988, p. 395.

	Productivity[1] (hrs/unit)	Quality[2] (defects/100 units)	Automation Level[3] (0:none)
Honda, Ohio	19.2	72.0	77.0
Nissan, Tenn.	24.5	70.0	89.2
NUMMI, Calif.	19.0	69.0	62.8
Toyota, Japan	15.6	63.0	79.6
GM, Mich.	33.7	137.4	100.0
GM, Mass.	34.2	116.5	7.3

[1]Productivity: standardized number of man-hours to weld, paint, and assemble a vehicle.
[2]Quality: defects attributable to assembly operations reported in first six months of ownership.
[3]Automation level: robotic applications/production rate, normalized to 100 for highest level in the group.

Over the course of the 1980s, case study and plant-to-plant comparisons began to show that these alternative work systems outperformed the traditional job control system on key indicators such as quality, productivity, and flexibility or ease of changing from one product to another. The evidence was clearest and most widely publicized in the auto industry, as illustrated in Exhibit 10–5. The data in this exhibit show the differences in quality and productivity between several traditional GM-UAW plants and the GM-Toyota joint venture plant known as the New United Motors Manufacturing Inc. (NUMMI).

By using the Toyota production system and a flexible team-based work system, extensive training, and a collaborative labor-management relationship, NUMMI was able to outperform by wide margins both low- and high-technology GM plants with traditional work systems and arms length labor-management relationships. NUMMI's unionized operations were also able to do as well, or in some cases, better, than the nonunion Japanese transplants opened up in the United States by Honda and Nissan, and its performance was nearly the same as the parent Toyota plant in Japan.[30]

These data became perhaps the most widely cited comparative performance statistics of the 1980s. Managers and union leaders, and academics all used them to discuss and debate their validity, their generalizability to other plants and industries, and their implications for the future of labor-management relations.

These data also sparked a wide range of experiments with new work systems both within the auto industry and in industries as diverse as apparel, steel, telecommunications, airlines, and others. It also sparked considerable research into the economic effects of these new work systems compared with the more traditional systems. By the mid-1990s, the evidence was quite convincing: These more flexible team-based systems in union or nonunion settings outperform the more traditional union or nonunion systems by achieving higher productivity and quality for their establishments.[31] These differences are also big enough to translate into significant profits for firms that are able to implement them fully. One study, for example, estimated that the difference between the "best" and "worst" work practices amounted to profits of $15,000 per employee.[32]

One finding from this research that makes introducing these changes difficult for labor and management is that changing one or two work practices does not have much effect on performance. Instead, the big effects are observed when the complete system of flexible job assignments, teamwork, training, and related human resource practices are implemented. This type of comprehensive change is difficult to achieve in an existing workplace that has built up traditional practices over a long period of time. Both workers and managers have equity stakes in preserving some of the existing practices. Thus we observe two features in contemporary work settings. Labor and management are engaged in continuous negotiations and experiments looking for ways to adapt some or all of these new practices in existing plants and work sites, often with mixed results. On the other hand, when a new plant or work site is opened, often management—and if given the opportunity, labor and management—will implement these flexible team systems from the outset. This was the case at GM's new Saturn Division. Boeing, Raytheon, Miller Brewing Company, and a number of other firms with high levels of unionization among their current employees have taken this approach and worked with their unions to design together the work systems in new facilities using state-of-the-art thinking and practices. Thus, we are likely to continue to see struggles to adapt new work systems in existing facilities for years to come and a gradual expansion of their coverage as new facilities come on line.

Safety and Health

Another important job outcome influenced by collective bargaining is the health and safety of the work force. Unions historically have used three interrelated strategies to improve safety and health conditions at the workplace: (1) supporting governmental regulations that mandate or encourage safe practices; (2) negotiating safety provisions into bargaining agreements; and (3) encouraging the formation of joint union–management safety and health committees at the plant level. The labor movement, for example, was the driving force behind passage of the Occupational Safety and Health Act (OSHA) of 1970. The number of safety provisions in bargaining agreements has expanded considerably since then, as has the number of safety and health committees in unionized plants.

Unions can affect safety and health at the workplace in two ways. First, they can demand a higher compensating wage differential for workers exposed to higher risks. Although the evidence is far from conclusive, there is some indication that unions have been successful in obtaining a positive wage differential for risky jobs. The differential, in turn, has both a direct effect and an indirect effect. The direct effect is obviously to compensate those workers who are exposed to risks. The indirect effect is to increase the employer's incentive to lower the risks on the job so as to avoid having to pay a compensating differential.

Second, unions can negotiate protections against job hazards, increased worker and supervisor training, and changes in the work environment that will eliminate the hazards. Whether these strategies are effective depends heavily on whether the parties have accurate information on the causes of injuries and occupational illnesses.

Exhibit 10–6 illustrates the range of safety and health provisions commonly found in collective bargaining agreements. A comparison of the percentages listed in this exhibit with comparable figures for earlier periods shows that all of these provisions became increasingly common over the last 35 years. For example, in 1970, 31 percent of the contracts in the Bureau of National Affairs (BNA) sample provided for safety and health committees; now that figure stands at 64 percent.

Unions also frequently negotiate general contractual provisions stating that the employer is responsible for making the work environment safe or that the employer agrees to comply with applicable safety laws (something employers presumably have to do whether the union contract requires it or not). This sort of language allows the union to use the contractual grievance procedure to process safety complaints. The alternative is for the union to rely solely on either a joint union–management committee or complaints to the Occupational Safety and Health Administration, which is responsible for administering and enforcing OSHA.

EXHIBIT 10–6
Incident
of Union–
Management
Relations Safety
Clauses in
Private-Sector
Collective
Bargaining
Contracts
Expiring
between
August 1997
and July 2007

Source: Bureau of
Labor Statistics,
*Monthly Labor
Review—Collective
Bargaining Agree-
ments: Safety and
Health Provisions, May
1998*, Table 6, p. 22.

Provision	Number of Contracts	Percent of Contracts
All contracts with safety and health provisions	433	100
Contracts with provisions for acknowledgment that the union will be held harmless in cases of employee safety and health problems	79	18
Furnishing of OSHA reports to the union	147	34
A labor–management safety and health Committee that is:		
Divisional	2	1
Local	219	50
National	56	13
A safety and health grievance procedure	101	23
Union cooperation with management on matters of safety and health	279	64
Authorization of a union representative to stop unsafe work	18	4
A union safety and health representative	22	5

In general, safety provisions were more common in manufacturing than in nonmanufacturing industries, and in all cases they were much more common in high-risk industries such
as mining. Thus the probability that these provisions will be included in contracts depends
partly on the magnitude of the risks found in the industry.

Summary

The presence of a union sets off a chain
reaction in a wide range of economic and
behavioral employment outcomes that affect
the goals of employees and employers. This
chapter presents a framework for tracing these
effects and summarizes the existing empirical
evidence. Estimates of the "average" effects of
collective bargaining must be interpreted with
caution because there is much variation across
and within union and nonunion workplaces.

The average effects of unions measured
by research are as follows.

1. Unions raise the wages of their members over those of comparable nonunion
   workers. The magnitude of this effect
   varies considerably over time and across
   occupations. The average wage effect is
   between 15 and 20 percent and is somewhat higher for nonwhites than for whites,
   for younger and older workers than for

workers in their prime working years, and
for blue-collar than white-collar workers.

2. A fundamental shift in the nature of wage
   setting in collective bargaining appears
   to have taken place in recent years that
   makes settlements more responsive to
   market forces. Union bargaining power
   is considerably weakened in this environment. The cumulative effects of these
   trends are to contribute to a decline in
   real wages, increased wage inequality,
   and a lower risk of inflation in response
   to lower unemployment.

3. Unions increase the range of fringe benefits available to workers and the level of
   benefits provided. Some of this effect is
   due to the built-in relationship between
   wages and those fringe benefits that are
   tied to the wage rate, while some is due
   to the direct effect that unions have on

benefits. Pressures to reduce benefit costs have shifted some of the costs to workers and produced significant savings in benefits some of which have been achieved through joint union–management efforts.

4. Unions have negotiated a wide range of job security provisions. The most prominent union effect on job security lies in the protection against arbitrary discharge or discipline afforded union members through the grievance arbitration provisions found in most private sector labor agreements. Unions have also increased the security of long-service employees through the seniority provisions in labor contracts. A minority of unions have been successful in negotiating income security provisions that supplement the state unemployment compensation system during short, temporary layoffs.

A smaller minority of unions have negotiated provisions that protect the income and job security of employees who are affected by permanent job loss resulting from technological change, outsourcing, or corporate restructuring. Again, the magnitude of these protections and benefits typically is set as a direct function of the worker's seniority. Recently some bargaining agreements have provided enhanced employment security in association with pay concessions or work reorganization.

5. Unions reduce turnover, primarily by increasing the value of the jobs held by union members over the value of the alternative jobs available in the external labor market. This effect increases directly with the seniority of the worker.

6. Historically, the average effect of unions, after management made adjustments to increased compensation costs, was to increase productivity. In more recent years, however, the development of more flexible, team-based work systems has led to pressures to introduce major changes in the traditional job control model of industrial relations. Where the full complement of team-based work systems is implemented, significant improvements in quality, productivity, and profitability have been realized. Now, and in the foreseeable future, there will continue to be considerable variability in work practices and work systems observed in American industry as union leaders and managers adapt to globalization and intensified economic pressures.

Discussion Questions

1. Wage increases set off a chain reaction. Describe the chain reaction.

2. Wages are of central importance to unions and their membership. Discuss some of the key variations in union relative wage effects.

3. Seniority is a vital issue in collective bargaining. Unions have argued that seniority protects against arbitrary treatment by the employer, but, with the advent of affirmative action, this has come under attack. It has been argued by some that seniority helps maintain, if not increase, the amount of racial discrimination in the workplace. Discuss the pros and cons of seniority systems.

4. How did management's response to work rules change from the 1980s on? What effects will this have on the future of industrial relations at the workplace?

5. Discuss how health insurance coverage has been affected by union decline.

6. Explain how outsourcing can threaten employment security and provide examples of union–management agreements that have reduced this threat.

7. How do team-based work systems and their associated contract provisions differ from the more conventional work rules flowing from a job control model of union–management relations?

Related Web Sites

Bureau of National Affairs (BNA):
http://www.bna.com/corp/index.html

Ford Motor Co.:
http://www.ford.com/corporate-info/index.html

Saturn:
http://www.saturn.com/company/index.html

Toyota:
http://www.toyota.com/welcome.html

Occupational Safety and Health Administration (OSHA):
http://www.osha.gov

United Parcel Service (UPS):
http://www.ups.com/about/story/html
http://teamster.org

Suggested Readings

Freeman, Richard B., and James L. Medoff. *What Do Unions Do?* (New York: Basic Books, 1984).

Hartman, Paul T. *Collective Bargaining and Productivity* (Berkeley: University of California Press, 1969).

Lewis, H. Gregg. *Union Relative Wage Effects: A Survey* (Chicago: University of Chicago Press, 1986).

Mishel, Lawrence, Jared Bernstein, and Sylvia Allegretto. *The State of Working America* (Ithaca, New York: ILR Press, 2007).

End Notes

1. Sumner Slichter, *Union Policies and Industrial Management* (Washington, DC: Brookings Institution, 1941).

2. Richard E. Walton, Joel Cutcher-Gershenfeld, and Robert E. McKersie, *Strategic Negotiations: A Theory of Change in Labor-Management Relations* (Boston: Harvard Business School Press, 1994).

3. Brian Becker, "Union Rents as a Source of Takeover Gains Among Target Shareholders," *Industrial and Labor Relations Review* 49 (October, 1995): 3–19.

4. H. Gregg Lewis, *Unionism and Relative Wages in the United States* (Chicago: University of Chicago Press, 1962).

5. Daniel Blanchflower, "The Effects of Unions on Wages in the U.S. and the U.K.," National Bureau of Economic Research Working Paper, Cambridge, MA, 1997.

6. Orley Ashenfelter, "Racial Discrimination and Trade Unionism," *Journal of Political Economy* 80 (May/June 1972): 435–64.

7. See, for example, George E. Johnson and Kenneth Youmans, "Union Relative Wage Effects by Age and Education," *Industrial and Labor Relations Review* 24 (January 1971): 171–79.

8. Farrell E. Bloch and Mark S. Kuskin, "Wage Determination in the Union and Nonunion Sectors," *Industrial and Labor Relations Review* 31 (January 1978): 183–92.

9. Orley Ashenfelter, "Union Relative Wage Effects: New Evidence and a Survey of Their Implications for Wage Inflation," in *Econometric Contributions to Public Policy,* ed. Richard Stone and William Peterson (New York: St. Martin's Press, 1978), pp. 31–60.

10. Richard B. Freeman, "Unionism and the Dispersion of Wages," *Industrial and Labor Relations Review* 34 (October 1980): 3–23; and Richard B. Freeman, "Union Wage Practices and Wage Dispersion within Establishments," *Industrial and Labor Relations Review* 36 (October 1982): 3–21.

11. James A. Dalton and E. J. Ford, Jr., "Concentration and Labor Earnings in Manufacturing and Utilities," *Industrial and Labor Relations Review* 31 (October 1977): 45–60.

12. See Lewis, *Unionism and Relative Wages;* and Richard B. Freeman and James L. Medoff, *What Do Unions Do?* (New York: Basic Books, 1984).

13. See, for example, Greg Duncan and Frank Stafford, "Do Union Members Receive Compensating Wage Differentials?" *American Economic Review* 70 (June 1980): 355–71; and John Abowd and Henry S. Farber, "Job

Queues and the Union Status of Workers," *Industrial and Labor Relations Review* 35 (April 1982): 354–67.

14. Mitchell Lokiec, *Productivity and Incentives* (Columbia, SC: Bobbin Publishing, 1977).

15. See John T. Dunlop and David Weil, "Diffusion and Performance of Modular Production in the U.S. Apparel Industry," *Industrial Relations* 35 (July 1996): 356–73.

16. The theoretical arguments and empirical evidence here draw heavily from Richard B. Freeman and James L. Medoff, *What Do Unions Do?* (New York: Basic Books, 1984), pp. 61–77.

17. *Inland Steel Co.* v. *NLRB,* 170 F. 2d 247 (1948).

18. See Freeman and Medoff, *What Do Unions Do?,* pp. 61–77.

19. See "Study Sees Health Care Costs Becoming Largest Portion of Employer Benefit Costs," 01/03/06. *Daily Labor Report,* January 3, 2006: A-8; "Union Companies' Health Costs Outpace Nonunion Firms' Costs, Dominate Bargaining," 08/30/05. *Daily Labor Report,* August 30, 2005: C-1; and "Rise in Benefit Costs Continues to Drive Increase in Competition for Labor Force," 10/31/03. *Daily Labor Report,* October 31, 2003: D-11.

20. Henry S. Farber, "The Incidence of Health and Pension Benefits in Old and New Jobs," Unpublished manuscript, Princeton University Industrial Relations Section, 1997. See also, Robert B. Reich, "The Unfinished Agenda," *Perspectives on Work* 1, no. 1 (1997): 26–29.

21. Rosemary Batt, Alexander Colvin, and Jeffrey Keefe, "Employee Voice, Human Resource Practices, and Quit Rates: Evidence From the Telecommunications Industry," *Industrial and Labor Relations Review* 55 (July 2002): 573–94. Analysis of individual level data on quit rates is provided in David Lewin and Richard Peterson, "Behavioral Outcomes of Grievance Activity," *Industrial Relations* 38 (October 199): 554–76.

22. Katharine G. Abraham and James L. Medoff, "Length of Service and Promotions

in Union and Nonunion Work Groups," *Industrial and Labor Relations Review* 38 (April 1985): 408–20.

23. For a good description and analysis of SUB plans, see Audrey Freedman, *Security Bargains Reconsidered: SUB, Severance Pay, Guaranteed Work* (New York: Conference Board, 1978).

24. *Factfinding Report,* Commission on the Future of Worker Management Relations (Washington, DC: U.S. Departments of Labor and Commerce, 1994), pp. 15–16.

25. Neil W. Chamberlain and James W. Kuhn, *Collective Bargaining,* 2d ed. (New York: McGraw-Hill, 1965), pp. 89–90.

26. Charles C. Killingsworth, "Management Rights Revisited," in *Arbitration and Social Change, Proceedings of the Twenty-Second Annual Meetings of the National Academy of Arbitrators,* ed. Gerald G. Somers (Washington, DC: Bureau of National Affairs, 1969), pp. 3–13.

27. See Robert B. McKersie and Lawrence C. Hunter, *Pay, Productivity and Collective Bargaining* (London: Macmillan, 1973).

28. Paul T. Hartman, *Collective Bargaining and Productivity: The Longshore Mechanization Agreement* (Berkeley: University of California Press, 1969).

29. For a summary of this evidence see Richard B. Freeman and James L. Medoff, *What Do Unions Do?* (New York: Basic Books, 1984).

30. For further discussion of these data, see John F. Krafcik, "World Class Manufacturing: An International Comparison of Automobile Assembly Plant Performance," *Sloan Management Review* 30 (1988): 41–52.

31. For a review of these studies see Casey Ichniowski, Thomas Kochan, David Levine, Craig Olsen, and George Strauss, "What Works at Work: Overview and Assessment," *Industrial Relations* 35 (July 1996): 299–333.

32. Mark Huselid, "The Impact of Human Resource Management Practices on Turnover, Productivity, and Corporate Financial Performance," *Academy of Management Journal* 38 (1995): 635–72.

Part 4

The Workplace Level of Industrial Relations

Chapter 11

Administering the Employment Relationship

Chapter 11 begins our examination of the workplace level of industrial relations, the third level of activities in Exhibit 1–1. The focus in this chapter is on the day-to-day employment relationship. In unionized settings this involves contract administration below the level of formal contract negotiations.

Collective bargaining agreements in the United States are elaborate and detailed documents. The existence of such extensive labor contracts contributed to the need for an orderly means for settling conflicts over interpretations of contract language.

Engrained in U.S. collective bargaining is the principle that "management acts and the union reacts," or, put another way, "it is management's job to manage and the union's job to grieve." This has led in unionized settings to reliance on grievance and arbitration procedures as mechanisms to resolve conflicts that arise at the workplace. The bulk of this chapter discusses how grievance and arbitration procedures operate.

In recent years in unionized settings, competitive environmental conditions and the increasingly complex needs of the labor force are giving rise to efforts to supplement formal contract administration procedures with more flexible mechanisms for resolving problems and conflict. Many large firms have established communication and informal complaint-handling processes for their nonunion employees, and increasingly they are instituting these for their unionized employees as well. Moreover, in recent years a number of parties have signed longer-term agreements, moving from the traditional three-year contract length to four-, five-, six-year, or even longer, collective bargaining agreements. This has increased the need to introduce procedures for continuous bargaining or other means of resolving problems and adjusting to circumstances that cannot be fully anticipated in negotiations. Thus, this chapter also considers some of the new less formal mechanisms that are being used to settle problems and adjust practices at the workplace.

The Grievance Procedure

The grievance procedure specifies a series of steps to be taken to resolve a worker's complaint that management has not followed the terms of the collective bargaining agreement. The steps found in a typical procedure are outlined in Box 11–1. Each succeeding step in

A. Employee-initiated grievance
   Step 1
   Employee discusses grievance or problem orally with supervisor.
   Union steward and employee may discuss problem orally with supervisor.
   Union steward and employee decide if (1) problem has been resolved or (2) if not resolved, whether a contract violation has occurred.
   Step 2
   Grievance is put in writing and submitted to production superintendent or other designated line manager.
   Steward and management representative meet and discuss grievance.
   Management's response is put in writing. A member of the industrial relations staff may be consulted at this stage.
   Step 3
   Grievance is appealed to top line management and industrial relations staff representatives.

Additional local or national union officers may become involved in discussions. Decision is put in writing.
   Step 4
   Union decides on whether to appeal unresolved grievance to arbitration according to procedures specified in its constitution and/or bylaws.
   Grievance is appealed to arbitration for binding decision.

B. Discharge grievance
   Procedure may begin at step 2 or step 3.
   Time limits between steps may be shorter to expedite the process.

C. Union or group grievance
   Union representative initiates grievance at step 1 or step 2 on behalf of the affected class of workers or union representatives.

the decision-making process involves a higher level of the union and management organizations. The final step in this and most grievance procedures involves a hearing of the dispute and a final binding judgment by an arbitrator (acting as the third party).

Most often the grievance procedure comes into play when an employee has a complaint about the actions taken by the supervisor. Below we trace how an employee complaint makes its way through the typical grievance procedure.

Step 1: Step 1 of the procedure outlined in Box 11–1 gives the employee and his or her supervisor the opportunity to resolve the employee's complaint by talking about the problem. The supervisor might be unaware that there is a problem, and oral discussion might quickly resolve the issue. At this point, the employee's union steward might assist the employee in bringing the issue to the attention of the supervisor.

Step 2: If the grievance (complaint) is not resolved in these discussions, the employee can choose to drop the matter or to proceed to step 2 where the grievance is put in writing. In step 2 the union steward meets with a management representative and management eventually writes a response. The process of writing the grievance and management's response down on paper gives the parties the opportunity to formally make their cases, and this often serves to clarify exactly what is in dispute. At this and the previous step many grievances are resolved or dropped by the grieving party.

Step 3: Step 3 in the grievance procedure involves top line management, industrial relations staff, local union officers, and possibly national union staff. The involvement of higher level union and management staff consumes valuable time and resources, and for this reason the decision to press a grievance to the third step is not usually taken lightly.

Step 4: If the grievance has not been resolved at earlier steps, in step 4 it can be appealed to arbitration for a binding decision. It is important to note that it is the union and not the employee that decides whether or not to appeal a grievance to arbitration. Court decisions gave unions this power on the grounds that it was the union that created and "owned" the grievance procedure. *arbitration*

The Reasons Why Grievances Are Filed

Employees commonly file a grievance when they think management is not fairly living up to the collective bargaining agreement. The grievance procedure provides a mechanism for workers to air their displeasure with management's actions, to change management's behavior, or to receive some form of compensation for management's actions.

Disagreements about employee discipline are a common source of grievances. Collective bargaining agreements commonly leave to management the right to discipline employees. Contracts often outline certain actions that can lead to discipline, such as repeated absenteeism or the failure to follow a direct order from a supervisor. An employee might file a grievance against a disciplinary action taken by management either because the employee contests management's claim that the employee did something wrong or because the employee believes too harsh a disciplinary action was imposed for whatever mistake was made by the employee.

When labor and management negotiate the collective bargaining contract, they try to cover the major issues and write language that will guide future behavior. Yet the contract does not specify what is to happen under all circumstances. It would be impossible and too costly for negotiators to write contractual language that covers any but the most common events. Thus the parties also turn to the grievance procedure as a way to resolve issues that are not explicitly covered by the labor contract.

Many collective bargaining agreements, for example, specify that supervisors are not allowed to perform work that is commonly performed by someone in the bargaining unit. Unions favor this clause as a way to preserve work for union members and to prevent management from circumventing the terms of the contract by moving work out of the bargaining unit. When new technology is introduced into a plant it often changes the duties performed by existing workers and adds new types of work. Is the new work still in the bargaining unit, or can it be performed by a supervisor? It would be extremely cumbersome for labor and management to include language in the labor agreement specifying in detail what is to happen in every such case. Instead, the parties use the grievance procedure to resolve disputes that arise over this issue.

Furthermore, at all workplaces things frequently happen that were never anticipated by the parties when they were negotiating the labor agreement. What form of compensation, for example, should workers receive if they are sent home after a power outage forces the closing of a plant in the middle of the day? Should employees be paid for a full day's work in such a case? Should the amount of compensation vary, depending on how much of the work day the employees worked before being sent home? If language was not included in the labor contract that covered this type of occurrence and employees were upset by the compensation management decided to provide, then the employees might turn to the grievance procedure to settle the matter.

The filing of grievances can also serve other purposes. For instance, grievances may be filed by employees as a way to demonstrate employee concern for issues that are not addressed in the collective bargaining agreement. For example, employees may be concerned about the long-term health effects from working with video displays and vent their concern by filing grievances over the issue. In these sorts of cases the grievance procedure can serve the valuable function of warning management about problems that might otherwise be ignored.

Employees and their union also might use the grievance procedure as a tactical pressure device. The filing of grievances over an issue can serve, for example, to rally employee interest in bringing the issue to the bargaining table in the next contract renewal negotiation. In this sort of case the union may know that the filing of grievances will not lead to immediate changes in management's behavior but will put pressure on management and thereby increase its bargaining leverage.

The Historical Evolution of Grievance Arbitration

Arbitration is the common device stipulated in labor contracts to resolve grievances that are not settled in earlier steps (see step 4 in Box 11–1). Arbitration is a quasi-judicial procedure in which a third party settles a dispute by issuing a binding judgment. The use of arbitration to settle grievances that arise during the term of a collective bargaining is referred to as grievance (or rights) arbitration.

Arbitration developed early in the U.S. industrial relations system. Arbitration of minor disputes over the interpretation of agreements, for example, was mentioned in the Industrial Commission Report of 1902. Before World War II grievance procedures ending in binding arbitration were common in the clothing and anthracite coal mining industries.

The Spread of Arbitration

It took the strong advocacy of the national War Labor Board (WLB) during World War II for grievance arbitration to become a common practice across unionized industries. In many of the thousands of disputes it handled, the board encouraged the parties to include an arbitration clause in their bargaining agreement, and in some cases the board required it.

Within a few years the Taft-Hartley Act embedded grievance arbitration in national labor policy. Section 203(d) of the act states: "Final adjustment by a method agreed upon by the parties is hereby declared to be the desirable method for settlement of grievance disputes arising out of the application or interpretation of an existing collective bargaining agreement."

Court Encouragement of Arbitration

A series of Supreme Court decisions known as the **Steelworkers' trilogy** encouraged the use of arbitration and insulated many arbitration awards from judicial review.[1] These cases also gave grievance arbitration its protected status and exalted image.[2]

The Steelworkers' trilogy decisions from 1960 are summarized in Box 11–2. These decisions provided that (1) the courts should rule only on questions about whether a dispute

Key Court and Administrative Decisions that Affect the Conduct of Grievance Arbitration

Box 11–2

Year	Case	Decision
1957	Textile Workers v. Lincoln Mills	Provided for court enforcement of arbitration awards.
1960	"Steelworkers' trilogy" 1. Steelworkers v. American Manufacturing Co., 363 US 564 (1960)	Court should determine only arbitrability, i.e., whether issue is covered by the contract, and should not decide the merits of a case. Doubts about arbitrability should be decided in favor of sending the case to arbitration.
	2. Steelworkers v. Warrior Gulf and Navigation Co., 363 US 574 (1960)	Disputes over contract terms are assumed to be arbitrable unless they are specifically excluded. Arbitration is viewed as the quid pro quo for giving up the right to strike during the term of the contract.
	3. Steelworkers v. Enterprise Wheel and Car Corp., 363 US 593 (1960)	Courts should not review the substantive merits of the arbitrator's decision as long as the arbitrator's award is based on the content of the agreement.
1970	Boys Markets, Inc. v. Retail Clerks, Local 770, 389 US 235 (1970)	Courts may issue an injunction against a union forcing it to refrain from violating a no-strike clause or where an issue is covered by an arbitration clause in the contract.
1971	Collyer Insulated Wire and Local Union 1098, 192 NLRB 837 (1971)	NLRB will defer to arbitration disputes in which the issue could be decided either through arbitration (because it is covered by a clause in the bargaining agreement) or by NLRB ruling (because it alleges an unfair labor practice).
1974	Alexander v. Gardner-Denver, 415 US 36 (1974)	Arbitrator's decision on a claim involving discrimination covered under Title VII of the Civil Rights Act does not preclude judicial review of the award, nor does it prevent the employee from pursuing legal remedies through federal agencies or the federal court. Courts will hear the case de novo and decide it on its merits and will give the arbitrator's decision whatever weight the court deems appropriate.
1976	Hines v. Anchor Motor Freight, Inc. 424 US 554 (1976) preceded by several other key cases, especially Steele v Louisville & Nashville R.R., 323 US 192 (1944), and Vaca v. Sipes, 386 US 171 (1967)	An arbitration award should not be sustained by the court when the union has violated its duty to represent the grievant fairly. Federal courts will entertain suits of this nature on the basis of Section 301 of Taft-Hartley.

(continued)

Year	Case	Decision
1983	*Bowen* v. *United States Postal Service,* 103 US (1983)	A union may be held liable for a portion of an award to an employee if the union has violated its duty of fair representation.
1984	Olin Corporation, 268 NLRB 86 (1984)	The NLRB expanded the Collyer doctrine of deferral to arbitration of disputes involving unfair labor practices. The NLRB will defer to an arbitrator's decision unless the arbitrator's award is "clearly repugnant" to the law. The NLRB retains the right to decide whether an arbitrator adequately considered the facts that would constitute an unfair labor practice.
1984	United Technologies, 268 NLRB 83 (1984)	The NLRB further expanded the Collyer doctrine of deferral to arbitration of disputes brought to the board before arbitration that both involve statutory rights and are covered by a collective bargaining contract.
1986	*AT&T Technologies* v. *Communications Workers,* Docket no. 84-1913, 7 April 1986	Courts, not arbitrators, should resolve disputes over arbitrability by examining the language found in the agreement giving rise to the issue.
1991	*Gilmer* v. *Interstate/Johnson Lane Corp.,* 500 US 20 (1991)	Statutory claims can be arbitrated without resort to the judicial forum. Arbitration of a statutory claim, however, does not forgo the substantive rights afforded by the statute.
1998	*Wright* v. *Universal Maritime Service Corp.,* 525 US 70 (1998)	A waiver of individual employee rights to bring discrimination charges in court included in a collective bargaining agreement must be clear and unmistakable in order to be enforceable.
2001	*Circuit City Stores* v. *Adams, 532* US 105 (2001)	According to the Federal Arbitration Act, employment disputes must be settled exclusively by final and binding arbitration if so dictated by the employment contract. Only interstate transportation workers are excluded. The courts and government must concede discretion to the arbitrator in such cases.
2002	*Equal Employment Opportunity Commission* v. *Waffle House, Inc.* 534 US 279 (2002)	Limits the decision in Circuit City. The EEOC still has the right to pursue judicial relief for victims of employment discrimination, even if the individuals signed an agreement to settle all disputes through binding arbitration with the employer, in certain cases.

can be arbitrated, they should resolve any doubts about such questions by ruling in favor of arbitration, and they should not consider the merits of the grievance when deciding whether the case can be arbitrated; (2) the parties should view arbitration as the quid pro quo for giving up the right to strike; and except for issues that are specifically excluded from the arbitration clause, all disputes arising out of contract administration should be resolved by arbitration; and (3) the courts should not review the substantive merits of an arbitration decision but should confine their review to whether due process procedures were followed or whether the arbitrator exceeded his or her authority.

Judicial Deference to Arbitration

The Steelworkers' trilogy cases established the principle that the courts would not review disputes that were arbitrable. Subsequent court decisions, summarized in Box 11–2, continued that basic principle and added some modifications. In the Collyer decision of 1971, for example, the court deferred to an arbitrator to decide if an employer had violated the obligation to bargain in good faith when it unilaterally changed certain wage rates and job duties. This gave to an arbitrator the responsibility to rule on an unfair labor practice issue. In the Olin decision of 1984 the courts substantially further broadened the deferral of other unfair labor practice issues to arbitration (also see the United Technologies decision of 1984). Some of the other key court cases summarized in Box 11–2 affected aspects of arbitration that do not involve **judicial deference to arbitration.**

For many unions and managers the grievance arbitration procedures have evolved from a clinical approach to a more judicial approach. The clinical approach had been advocated by the WLB and applied frequently during the early postwar years.[3] The **clinical approach** emphasizes mediation of disputes, informality of procedure, and arbitrator discretion in helping the parties develop a working relationship and consistent policies for interpreting and administering the contract.

In the 1950s, as the environment for collective bargaining became more structured and a body of past precedents emerged, the arbitrator's scope of discretion narrowed. As the parties themselves became more professional, they came to demand a more judicial approach to arbitration. The **judicial approach** is more formal and legalistic. The clinical model of arbitration may have filled a void in an otherwise unstructured environment, but as the parties formalized their internal policies, they turned to arbitrators only in disputes in which their differences were clearly defined by the contract and the precedents that had arisen.

Thus, modern grievance arbitration, though still considerably more informal than court proceedings, has become dependent on the use of formal rules of evidence, examination and cross-examination of witnesses, submission of written briefs and posthearing briefs, and written transcripts. It is the heavy formality of the grievance arbitration procedure that has led some of the parties to recently search for alternative dispute-resolution procedures, a subject we discuss in more detail later in this chapter and in the next chapter.

The Functions of Grievance Procedures and Arbitration

Grievance and arbitration procedures serve the needs of three separate constituencies— labor, management, and society.

Employee Interest in Due Process and Fairness

The grievance and arbitration procedures serve the interests of workers by delivering industrial justice and by protecting workers who use the procedure from recrimination for having exercised their rights. If workers lose confidence in the efficacy of these procedures, they may turn to other potentially more costly and disruptive mechanisms to provide due process. Thus management often agrees to grievance and arbitration procedures to provide employees with due process because of the costs to management of the alternatives.

Employer Interest in Labor Peace

Employers are also attracted to the grievance and arbitration procedures because they reduce the likelihood that disputes that occur during the term of a labor contract will lead to stoppages in production. In exchange for accepting third-party arbitration of grievances, management commonly gains union acceptance of a clause eliminating the union's right to conduct a strike over an issue that is covered by the grievance and arbitration clause. The labor contract between General Motors and the UAW, for example, contains the following language:

> During the life of this agreement, the Union will not cause or permit its members to cause, nor will any member of the Union take part in any sitdown, stay-in or slow-down, in any plant of the Corporation, or any curtailment of work or restriction of production or interference with the production of the Corporation. The Union will not cause or permit its members to cause nor will any member of the Union take part in any strike or stoppage of any of the Corporation's operations or picket any of the Corporation's plants or premises until all of the bargaining procedure as outlined in this Agreement has been exhausted, and in no case on which the Arbitrator shall have ruled. . . .[4]

The strong support of the Supreme Court for arbitration in the Steelworkers' trilogy was based in part on the role of the agreement to arbitrate grievances as the "quid pro quo" for the no-strike clause in contracts.

Some labor agreements exclude particular issues from coverage by the requirement to proceed to arbitration and allow the union to conduct a strike over unresolved grievances about these issues. **Production standards** (rules governing the pace of work) and health and safety issues are sometimes designated to be nonarbitrable. For health and safety disputes it may be impractical to require employees to follow management's orders and then wait for arbitration to settle disputes over the appropriateness and fairness of these orders. Thus some contracts allow workers to strike over health and safety issues.

Joint Interests in Continuity and Consistency

Another function served by the grievance and arbitration procedures is to address the common interests of labor and management. As Neil Chamberlain and James Kuhn noted, labor and management have a mutual interest in achieving continuity and consistency in the application of a collective bargaining agreement. They both also benefit from procedures that allow flexibility in addressing unforeseen developments and the unique needs of different groups and individuals.[5]

Finding the appropriate balance between uniformity and flexibility is a key challenge in administering the employment relationship. It is a particular challenge for grievance procedures and arbitration.

Society's Interest in Industrial Peace and Workplace Democracy

Grievance and arbitration procedures serve the interests of society by preserving industrial peace during the term of the contract, by keeping industrial disputes from overloading the courts or regulatory agencies, and by ensuring that unions and employers comply with public policies governing employment. As we will show, this set of public functions is becoming increasingly complex and difficult to carry out.

An additional public interest in supporting labor arbitration, articulated by the Supreme Court in the Steelworkers' trilogy of cases, follows from the idea that collective bargaining between labor and management establishes a form of democratic governance of the workplace. In this vision of workplace democracy, arbitration of grievances by neutral labor arbitrators serves a function similar to that of the courts in political democracy in providing independent adjudication of legal disputes. As Justice Douglas argued, ". . . the grievance machinery under a collective bargaining agreement is at the very heart of the system of industrial self-government. Arbitration is the means of solving the unforeseeable by molding a system of private law for all the problems which may arise and to provide for their solution in a way which will generally accord with the variant needs and desires of the parties."[6]

How Arbitration Works

The core of the arbitration procedure is a hearing in which the labor and management representatives present their positions on the issue in dispute to an arbitrator. At some point after this hearing, the arbitrator announces a judgment on the issue, a decision that is binding on the parties. Before the hearing the parties sometimes submit briefs to the arbitrator. Below are described each of the three components of arbitration—prehearing briefs, the hearing, and the arbitrator's decision.

The Components of Arbitration

Prehearing Briefs

The management and union representatives can submit **prehearing briefs** to the arbitrator before the arbitration hearing. In these briefs the parties can present their views of the issues, express their positions, and describe the evidence that supports their position. Briefs vary in length, sometimes amounting to long documents similar in form to legal briefs presented in legal cases.

In some cases the parties jointly present prehearing **stipulations** to the arbitrator. These stipulations tend to be shorter than a brief and focus more around the parties' statement of the issue in dispute and some of the key facts in the case. Briefs and stipulations can make it easier for the parties in the arbitration hearing to quickly focus on the evidence and issues in dispute.

The Arbitration Hearing

In the **arbitration hearing** the parties present their positions and evidence to support their cases. Hearings usually start with opening statements by union and management representatives. In disciplinary cases, management will commonly be asked to present their statement first.

The union and management representatives then present evidence to support their cases. Such evidence might include witnesses who observed particular events. If an employee is charged with committing an act that violates company policy, such as hitting a supervisor, for instance, management might call as a witness someone who saw the worker and supervisor interacting.

Critical to many arbitration hearings is evidence that documents past behavior, by either the employee or the company. As discussed below, the customs and past practices in the plant enter as important criteria in the arbitrator's decision process.

The hearing will typically end with closing statements by each side in which they summarize the key aspects of their case and their supporting evidence. The testimony given by witnesses or the other side during the hearing will sometimes lead the union or management representatives to alter their arguments during the course of the hearing. Thus it is not unusual for the parties' closing statements to focus on issues and evidence that differ substantially from the issues raised in the opening statements.

The hearing does not bring the presentation of evidence and arguments to a close. The parties can present their views in a posthearing brief, and they often do this in cases in which the issues in dispute are highly technical or complicated.

The Arbitrator's Decision

The arbitrator announces the **arbitrator's decision** sometime after the hearing. Some labor contracts stipulate time limits for these decisions. The arbitrator's decision can be written or oral and will vary, depending on the language in the labor agreement and the preferences of the arbitrator. Although arbitrators tend to follow similar procedures and look at similar kinds of evidence, the preferences of each arbitrator often play an important role in shaping their decisions.

In the decision the arbitrator commonly states the issues and facts in the case. The arbitrator also summarizes the contentions and claims made by the parties in the hearing or briefs. The arbitrator might discuss the merits of each side's evidence and claims. Of course, the most important part of the decision is the section that outlines the judgment reached by the arbitrator on the dispute. The arbitrator can uphold or deny the grievance and has substantial discretion in fashioning a remedy to the dispute.

In a grievance case in which a firm discharged an employee, for example, the arbitrator can deny the grievance and allow the discharge to stand, or the arbitrator can uphold the grievance and order the employer to reinstate the employee. If reinstatement is ordered, the arbitrator could order the company to pay the employee the full wages that have been lost due to the discharge. The arbitrator also could fashion a compromise settlement to such a case by ordering reinstatement but not ordering any back pay. Or, some other remedy might be ordered. The grievance-arbitration procedure grants to arbitrators substantial discretion to fashion any remedy the arbitrator believes is appropriate.

Arbitrators commonly see their task to be the resolution of the grievance. They do not commonly add substantial punitive penalties to their decisions. Thus, in the discharge case cited above, the best the employee could do is gain back the job, any back pay, and any lost rights (such as seniority lost while on discharge). The arbitrator would not assess a large punitive monetary penalty against the employer.

The Arbitrator's Decision Criteria

What does an arbitrator consider when deciding how to rule in a case? Below are outlined the criteria arbitrators commonly use in discipline and discharge cases. Discipline and discharge are used as the examples in part because these are frequent and important sources of grievances.

Discipline for Just Cause

Most labor agreements contain a clause stating that management has the right to **discipline** employees for **just cause**. Grievances over disciplinary actions arise so commonly in part because labor agreements rarely precisely define just cause.

In a discipline case the arbitrator must first decide if the employee actually carried out the act that management claims violates the labor agreement. If the arbitrator is convinced the act did not occur, then the grievance is upheld. In a case in which management alleges an employee hit a supervisor, for example, the arbitrator would rely on available evidence (possibly the testimony of eyewitnesses) to determine if the employee willfully did hit the supervisor. If the arbitrator concludes the act did occur (e.g., the supervisor was hit by the employee), the arbitrator must then decide if this act was a violation of the labor agreement.

Progressive Discipline

If the arbitrator concludes that the act did occur and it did violate the labor agreement, there remains the very important issue as to whether the discipline imposed by the company is appropriate. Arbitrators commonly require that management impose **progressive discipline**—namely, the penalties should increase in a stepwise fashion if there are repeated offenses. If an employee is absent once after a number of years of faithful service to the company, for example, an arbitrator is unlikely to uphold a penalty of discharge. Arbitrators will allow severe disciplinary penalties for repeated absences, however, and want those penalties to increase as the number of absences mount. The underlying principle is that discipline should be **corrective discipline** as well as punitive. Arbitrators commonly require that management take steps to assist employees in correcting their actions and performance. The common steps in progressive discipline are the issuance of an oral warning, suspension for some period of time, and then discharge. Needless to say, if the offense committed by the employee is so severe, such as destroying major company property, then the arbitrator might uphold immediate discharge.

The Importance of Past Practice

Arbitrators commonly rely heavily on the custom and **past practice** of management policy as a guide to decide grievance cases. If in the past employees in a firm have customarily been suspended for one week for their third unexcused absence, for example, an arbitrator would not allow a different disciplinary penalty on another employee for a similar offense unless there were extenuating circumstances. As a result, part of most arbitration hearings involves the union and management representative presenting their views regarding what past practice was for related cases. If a similar case has not arisen in the same firm, the parties (or the arbitrator) might turn to customary practice in another firm or industry to justify their actions.

The Impact of Public Policy Considerations in Arbitration

The role of the arbitrator is to interpret and decide grievances based on the collective bargaining agreement. The arbitrator's authority comes from the agreement and to the degree that his or her decision is based on factors going beyond the terms of the agreement, the decision lacks this authority. At the same time, events of the past two decades have raised concern about whether grievance and arbitration procedures are responsive to public policies that govern employee rights. Of chief concern is whether arbitration is useful in resolving claims of discrimination raised under the protection of Title VII of the Civil Rights Act. But the same concern also arises in claims that involve alleged violations of regulations on safety and health, wages and hours, pensions, disability benefits, workers' compensation, unemployment compensation, and many other regulations that may overlap or even conflict with the provisions of the collective bargaining agreement.

The arbitration community is divided over the issue whether arbitrators should consider the requirements of external laws when deciding grievances or instead confine their decisions to interpretations of the rights accorded by the bargaining agreement.[7] Those who advocate that the arbitrator stick to the bargaining agreement do so because they fear that considerations of external law will increase judicial scrutiny of arbitration decisions and that arbitrators may make erroneous interpretations of the law. They believe arbitration has not only been widely accepted as an institution by the parties but also assigned its protected status by the courts in the Steelworkers' trilogy precisely because arbitrators limit their decisions to issues in which they have special expertise. Thus, these advocates of minimal reference to external law are ready to trade off a reduced scope of jurisdiction in arbitration for protection of the status and autonomy that has been afforded labor arbitration since 1960.

Those who argue that arbitrators should play a more active role in resolving claims that involve public laws do so with full awareness that the arbitrator's role thereby shifts from one serving primarily the interests of the parties toward one serving public policies. The central arguments in favor of this new role are that arbitration is still cheaper, faster, and more efficient than the already overloaded judicial system. In this new role, it is argued, arbitration thus remains a useful procedure for resolving disputes that arise under collective bargaining.

Who Are the Arbitrators?

The people who serve as arbitrators usually have some expertise in industrial relations and the particularities of the industry in which the case arises. Some labor agreements provide for permanent arbitrators ("umpires") designated to handle all or some fraction of the grievances that arise during the term of a contract. The American Association of Arbitration (AAA) facilitates the process of arbitration. The AAA maintains an active list of arbitrators and can provide facilities for a hearing. A labor contract might stipulate that parties should turn to the AAA for a list of five arbitrators and then allow each side to cross off one name from the list to generate the arbitrator who will hear a particular case.

Some arbitrators work at arbitration as a full-time occupation. There are also many part-time arbitrators who are also industrial relations or law school professors. Box 11–3, provided by renown arbitrator Arnold Zack, describes who the arbitrators are and how someone can become an arbitrator.

Arnold Zack, Arbitrator and Former President, National Academy of Arbitrators

Virtually every collective bargaining agreement contains provisions for arbitration to resolve workplace disputes. The union agrees to continue to work while the case is being processed and the employer agrees to comply with the arbitrator's decision including remedy to make whole if awarded. Those agreements also provide the procedures for selecting arbitrators, usually by agreement on a single arbitrator or a revolving panel for the life of the parties' agreement or by utilizing the procedures of the American Arbitration Association or the Federal Mediation and Conciliation Service (FMCS) if the parties are unable to agree on an arbitrator for a pending case.

Although there are a couple of thousand individuals who offer their services, most arbitration is done by the 600 members of the National Academy of Arbitrators (NAA) who gain admission after having heard at least 50 cases in a five-year period. The shared concern over getting a decision that might make the employee whole and that conforms to the terms of the contract often leads disputants to wait many months for their preferred

choice among the more seasoned arbitrators, instead of trying newer less experienced arbitrators. This makes it challenging for new entrants to gain experience, and in turn, accounts for the rising average age of NAA arbitrators, which is now in the mid-60s.

While it is said that 90 percent of the cases are heard by 10 percent of the arbitrators, there are always new people breaking into the field. Parties want arbitrators with mature judgment and experience in labor-management relations that is not easy to acquire without working on the union or management side. But it is often difficult for partisans to gain acceptability unless they have somehow purged themselves of alleged bias by undertaking some time at a neutral position such as an academic, or working for a neutral government agency. Some newer arbitrators have come into the field by serving as interns with established arbitrators or from careers in government labor management agencies or as teachers of law, labor relations, economics, and psychology. Arbitration can hardly be an entry level occupation for one's career choice. Rather becoming an arbitrator is more a later-in-life happening as a reward for a career of fairness in whatever role an individual plays in the labor-management field. Don't give up your day job.

The Union's Decision to Go to Arbitration

Remember that it is the union, not the individual employee, that decides whether to appeal a grievance to arbitration. It is not a simple matter for the union to decide whether or not to press a grievance to arbitration. The use of arbitration is costly. The union might decide to drop the grievance if it believes the case is not winnable. Or, the union might drop the grievance even though it thinks it can win the case if the union concludes that the issue in dispute is small and insignificant (and not worth the effort). The union might also decide not to bring a grievance to arbitration if it believes the issue is very important and should be brought up at the next contract negotiations. In this situation the union might fear that winning the case in arbitration would diffuse the employee's concern needed to later press the union's case over the issue.

Or, the union might decide to proceed to arbitration even if it believes the case is not winnable, but the union officers feel an obligation to the grievant (maybe because the grievant loyally supported the union over the years) and cannot convince the employee to drop the issue. The union may also feel pressure to proceed to arbitration due to fear that the employee will file a legal claim contesting the union's decision not to go to arbitration. Although it is the union that makes the decision whether or not to appeal a grievance to arbitration, the union also owes a legal **duty of fair representation** to the individual employee in making this decision.

The Duty of Fair Representation

In 1944 the Supreme Court held that, in return for the rights of exclusive representation, the union has the duty to represent all members of the bargaining unit "without hostile discrimination, fairly, impartially, and in good faith."[8] Since then, the union's duty of fair representation has become an important issue.

Four related developments brought the issue of fair representation to the fore:

1. The stringency of the standards the courts have used to judge whether an employee has been fairly represented by the union.
2. The willingness of individual workers to bring claims against unions for failure to represent them fairly.
3. The rise in the number of court cases that deal with this issue.
4. The resulting reluctance of unions to drop grievances of questionable merit short of arbitration for fear of being sued for failure to represent the grievant fairly.

The U.S. Supreme Court has defined the duty of fair representation to prohibit "arbitrarily ignoring a meritorious grievance or processing it in a perfunctory manner"; fraud, deceit, or bad-faith conduct in the handling of a grievance; and refusal to handle a grievance out of personal hostility toward the grievant.[9]

In *Hines* v. *Anchor Motor Freight, Inc.* (see Box 11–2) the court ruled that both the employer and the union were liable for failure to handle fairly an employee representation case.[10] The case involved an employee whose discharge had been upheld in arbitration. After the arbitration award was rendered, new evidence was discovered that proved the employee was not guilty of the offense. Both parties were charged with having failed to fully investigate the facts of the case in the original procedure. Essentially, a charge of negligence was applied to both the union and the employer in this case.

In *Bowen* v. *United States Postal Service* the court went one step further by apportioning liability for back pay between a union and a company in a case in which an employee was reinstated after the union refused to take the case to arbitration.[11] The result was that the union was required to pay part of the employee's lost wages even though it was the employer's wrongful decision that had led to the employee being out of work.

Unfortunately, these various judicial efforts to clarify and specify the standards to be applied in duty of fair representation cases have not yielded unambiguous criteria for evaluating the union's performance. Box 11–4 extracts a comprehensive summary of the principles of the duty of fair representation. Although individual employees may sometimes feel that their union is not handling their grievances appropriately, there is also a danger that the threat of duty of fair representation cases may lead the union to take weak cases to arbitration instead of dropping the appeals. Taking unmeritorious cases to arbitration creates additional costs for the union and ultimately for individual union members whose dues provide the union with its source of finances to pay for arbitration hearings.

First, the individual employee has a right to have the clear and unquestioned terms of the collective agreement which have been made for his benefit followed and enforced until the agreement is properly amended.

Second, the individual employee has no right to insist on any particular interpretation of an ambiguous provision in a collective agreement, for the union must be free to settle a grievance in accordance with any reasonable interpretation thereof. The individual has a right, however, to be guaranteed that ambiguous provisions be applied consistently and that the provision mean the same when applied to him as when applied to other employees. Settlement of similar grievances on different terms is discriminatory and violates the union's duty to represent all employees equally.

Third, the union has no duty to carry every grievance to arbitration: it can sift out grievances that are trivial or lacking in merit. But the individual's right to equal treatment includes the right of equal access to the grievance procedure and arbitration for similar grievances of equal merit.

Fourth, settlement of grievances for improper motives such as personal hostility, political opposition, or racial prejudice constitutes bad faith regardless of the merits of the grievance.

Fifth, the individual employee has a right to have his grievance decided on its own merits. The union violates its duty to represent fairly when it trades an individual's meritorious grievance for the benefit of another individual or of the group.

Sixth, the union can make good-faith judgments in determining the merits of a grievance, but it owes the employees it represents the use of reasonable care and diligence both in investigating grievances in order to make that judgment and in processing and presenting grievances in their behalf.

Source: Clyde W. Summers, "The Individual Employee's Rights under the Collective Bargaining Agreement: What Constitutes Fair Representation?" in *The Duty of Fair Representation,* ed. Jean T. McKelvey (Ithaca: New York State School of Industrial and Labor Relations, Cornell University, 1977), pp. 82–83.

The Connections between Grievance Procedures and Other Aspects of the Labor-Management Relationship

In many ways the operation of the grievance procedure is closely linked to other aspects of the labor-management relationship. The next section considers some of these linkages.

Contract Bargaining versus Contract Administration

The administration of a collective bargaining agreement does not operate in isolation from the events that take place in the negotiations process. The behavior and attitudes of the parties during negotiations typically carry over into the administration of the contract, and vice versa. This is not surprising, because the same factors that increase the level of conflict and reduce the ability of the parties to settle without an impasse in negotiations also increase the level of antagonistic behavior during the course of administering the contract.

The attitudinal climate (i.e., the level of trust between the parties) often carries over directly from contract administration to contract negotiations. When a large backlog of unresolved grievances piles up and adds to a hostile atmosphere between the parties during the term of the agreement, the negotiations process becomes a convenient forum for venting these hostilities. Similarly, when the grievance procedure or an arbitration decision has failed to resolve a problem, one party or the other can be expected to place a demand on the negotiation table to remedy the situation. On the other hand, vague or inconsistent language

EXHIBIT 11–1
The Functions of a Workplace Industrial Relations System: Interrelationships and Outcomes

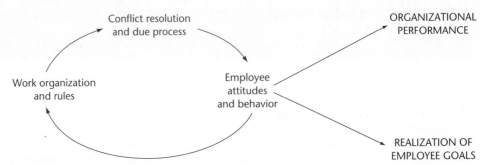

that was negotiated in a climate of distrust is likely to set the stage for conflict during the administration of the agreement.

The three basic functions served by any workplace industrial relations system are the following: conflict resolution and the assurance of due process; the supervision, motivation, and participation of individual workers; and the organization of work.[12] Exhibit 11–1 sketches the interrelationships among these three functions of workplace industrial relations and their effects on the performance of the firm and the fulfillment of workers' goals.

Researchers have found that cooperative attitudes between union and management officials increased the likelihood that grievances would be settled at the lower steps in the procedure.[13] Data from the auto industry show a positive correlation between the rate of grievances filed and two indicators of the intensity of conflict in local contract bargaining—namely, the number of issues introduced into the negotiations and the length of time taken to reach a contract settlement.[14]

A comparative study of the dynamics of grievance settlements in two auto plants further illustrates this point. In the plant that exhibited a highly adversarial relationship, grievance rates and rates of appeal to higher steps in the procedure followed the cycle of bargaining. That is, the union in this plant would save up grievances and file them just before the start of contract negotiations to use this stockpile as a lever in negotiations and to rally the rank and file in support of the union's contract demands. In contrast, no such politicization of the grievance process occurred in a comparable auto plant that had a history of cooperative labor–management relations.[15]

James Kuhn found that a lot of bargaining commonly occurs at the work group level outside the formal grievance procedure. Kuhn found that work groups can engage in **fractional bargaining**—that is, informal bargaining with the supervisor to modify or even to ignore provisions of the agreement that do not suit the group's particular needs.[16]

Mid-term or Continuous Bargaining

The average length of collective bargaining contracts appears to be increasing in the United States. Federal Mediation and Conciliation Service (FMCS) data suggest that the duration of nearly 40 percent of new agreements is more than three years. John Deere Inc., for example, entered into a six-year agreement with the UAW in 1997 that was renegotiated and renewed for another six years in 2003. To make this practice work, however, requires some means of addressing issues not anticipated in negotiations that arise during the term of the agreement. Several ways of doing so, in addition to the grievance procedure, have been developed.

One longstanding practice is for labor and management negotiators to meet periodically to explore issues and reach informal agreements that are perhaps codified as letters that supplement the bargaining agreement. These letters are in effect binding commitments—they can be enforced through the grievance procedure, but they are meant to be somewhat less permanent than formal contract language. Or in some cases the parties clarify how specific contract provisions will be interpreted or applied to different groups. Another practice, known as "continuous bargaining" is becoming more common. Box 11–5 describes a new provision in the BellSouth–CWA contract providing for continuous bargaining. The advantage of this approach is that it establishes clear guidelines over the timing, potential range of issues, and scope of authority or discretion for dealing with issues that come up during a long term contract. And it provides protection against erosion of contract provisions by individual supervisors or groups who see some contract provisions as a constraint in addressing production or service delivery problems. Instead of trying to get around the contract, these problems can be brought to the mid-term or continuous bargaining forum.

Many labor and management leaders now apply the use of the same interest-based principles used in contract negotiations to address problems that arise during the term of a collective bargaining agreement. This usually involves setting up some type of subcommittee or task force to study a problem and recommend a solution. More and more, the administration of labor agreements is blending with the use of these and other problem-solving processes and various types of employee and union–management participatory processes that will be discussed more fully in Chapter 12.

The Limits of Arbitration: Conflicts over Technological Change

Although arbitration is effective in resolving many workplace conflicts, technological change can produce problems that are difficult to resolve through the traditional arbitration mechanism. Changes in technology can render previous unit determination decisions obsolete by modifying how the work is performed, thereby raising the question whether the new jobs created should be excluded from the existing unit. Computer-aided design

Arbitrating over Technological Change   Box 11–6

THE ISSUE

Did the company violate the collective bargaining agreement when it assigned certain machining and fixturing work on robotics to nonbargaining unit personnel? If so, what shall be the remedy?

THE FACTS

The grievant and other bargaining unit personnel did fixturing work on production technology referred to as Robot No. 1. They did similar work for a while on Robots No. 2 and No. 3, but then this assignment stopped in 1984. In December 1983 the company formed a new department called Advanced Automation and Technology, and the fixturing work, what the company calls "development work," was given to nonbargaining unit engineering personnel assigned to the new department.

THE ARBITRATOR'S DISCUSSION

In establishing the Advanced Automation and Technology department, the company made a major change that affects the allocation of work that previously had been done by tool room personnel. . . . In a world of changing technology and methods specific duties and responsibilities may shift within an organization. The issue in this case arises because of a shift from earlier technology (that is rather standard and can be adapted in a straightforward manner by bargaining unit personnel) to new technology that requires considerable experimentation by engineers and technicians.

And so we have a situation where an organizational change has shifted the function of preparing production technology, but it is not clear whether the new skills and duties that are involved belong in the bargaining unit or elsewhere in the organization. *Given the grey area that is involved in this dispute, it would be desirable for the parties to establish principles to guide the allocation of work.*

THE ARBITRATOR'S DECISION

Given the fact that the union has not established conclusively that fixturing work for robotic technology belongs to the bargaining unit, it was not a violation of the collective bargaining agreement when the company assigned certain machining and fixturing work to nonbargaining unit personnel.

Nonetheless, given that the establishment of the Advanced Automation and Technology department represented a major decision with important consequences for the bargaining unit, . . . the parties are directed to negotiate in good faith over the effects of this change.

Source: Arbitration decision of Robert B. McKersie in the case of Northrup Corporation and United Auto Workers Local 1596, 1 July 1986. Adapted and used with permission of the arbitrator.

(CAD) serves as one example of just such a technological change. CAD can transfer drafting, model making, and other similar jobs from their traditional place within blue-collar production and maintenance units to the purview of design or manufacturing engineers, who traditionally have been either nonunion or in a separate engineers union and bargaining unit. In the aerospace industry, for instance, conflict has arisen over whether members of the machinists union or members of the professional engineers union should be given the work of maintaining the thousands of computers used in the firm.

Box 11–6 describes another technology-related dispute that was ultimately resolved by an arbitrator. In this case robots took over some of the tasks traditionally performed by blue-collar workers, and the issue was in part who should be given the job of bringing the robots on line and adapting their specifications to perform specific jobs.

This example illustrates an important feature of the structure of bargaining in the United States. Because so much rests on the definition of the boundary of the units, many fine legal distinctions have been drawn over the years. Labor and management often rely on these legalistic NLRB or arbitration rulings to modify the boundary to fit changing technologies or organizational practices.

As new technologies and new ways of organizing work are adopted, these issues will become more common. The parties will need to find better ways of resolving the issues than through arbitration or NLRB precedents. As the arbitrator quoted in Box 11–6 observed, it is generally preferable for the parties to develop their own principles for handling these issues as they arise, rather than to rely on an arbitrator to devise a viable solution after the fact.

The Japanese industrial relations system and some European systems may be better suited to respond to changing technologies than the U.S. system because they include both blue- and white-collar workers within the same union and the same election or bargaining unit. In Japan, for example, enterprise unions represent all blue- and white-collar workers within a single firm. In Germany most industrial unions include both the blue- and the white-collar workers employed within a company and an industry. In Great Britain, on the other hand, a tradition of not only separate blue- and white-collar unions but also a greater reliance on craft unions makes this problem potentially more troublesome than it is in our country. These issues are important because those industrial relations systems that make fine distinctions among election and bargaining units may be more likely than others to face difficulty in adapting to the new technologies now spreading across industries.

Evaluating the Performance of the Grievance System

One important question about the effectiveness of the negotiations process is whether the parties can avoid strikes and impasses. Similarly, an important criterion for evaluating grievance and arbitration procedures is whether the parties can avoid a heavy caseload. The advantages of settling disputes informally or at the step closest to the site where the problems arise are large.

In fact, although the United States has a tradition of very formal grievance systems in unionized settings, informal practices have emerged at the workplace. Most employee complaints are resolved informally before they become formal grievances. The study by Lewin and Peterson, for example, found that between 16 and 40 percent of the employees in the unionized organizations they studied reported having discussed (and resolved) with their supervisors a problem about their contractual rights.[17]

Yet low grievance rates may be due to the fact that the union is not aggressively enforcing the terms of the contract. For this reason, evaluation of the use of the grievance procedure should be accompanied by consideration of the reasons for low use.

Time and Costs of Settling Grievances

Two criteria commonly employed to evaluate grievance procedures are the time taken to settle claims and the costs associated with processing them through to arbitration. The original purpose in developing the procedures was to find an expeditious and inexpensive substitute for court procedures. Although still shorter than litigation, the time period required to resolve a grievance through arbitration has become substantial. In 2005, the average period between the request for an arbitrator and the award being issued was 401 days for arbitrations administered by the FMCS.[18] To this period must be added an average of 163 days between the grievance initially being filed and the request for arbitration. Although the average length of employment litigation cases remains longer, averaging 2–3 years, the idea of arbitration as a simple, expeditious procedure for resolving workplace disputes is being lost where grievances take over a year to be decided.

Similarly, costs of arbitration, while also generally cheaper than litigation, can be substantial. In 2005, the average total cost of hiring an arbitrator from the FMCS arbitrator list was $3,732.46, based on an average daily fee of $835.62 plus expenses and an average duration of 4 days for the hearing plus writing the award.[19] Yet, hiring an arbitrator is usually only one aspect of the entire cost of resolving a grievance-arbitration case. According to the National Labor Management Association, for a union to undertake all steps in a discharge arbitration case, it must account for the grievance process, staff time, cost of a transcript, hotels, and study time, as well as paying the arbitrator. The increasingly common use of lawyers as representatives at arbitration, particularly on the management side, further increases the cost of arbitration. This indicates that the modern grievance procedure may not be providing inexpensive due process as it was intended to. At the same time, court litigation to resolve an employment-related dispute can be extremely expensive and impractical for unions that have budget limitations. The fees to litigate an employment-related case typically exceed $10,000 (and in some cases by a large amount).

The Effects of Arbitration Decisions

Another important aspect of the evaluation of grievance and arbitration procedures is what happens after an arbitrator has reinstated a discharged employee. If the grievance procedure is effective in carrying out industrial justice, a worker unjustly discharged should be able to return to work and both perform well in the job and progress satisfactorily within the organization.

The procedure itself, however, may work against these results in several ways. First, the delays involved in processing a case through arbitration may lead a grievant who has been discharged to seek alternative employment; some reinstated employees therefore do not return to their former jobs. Second, reinstated employees are put back on their jobs frequently against the will of their employers, often to the dismay of their immediate supervisors, and sometimes to the dissatisfaction of their fellow workers. Some reinstated workers face hostility on their return to work. Even if management, supervisors, and fellow workers make a good faith effort to treat the reinstated employee fairly, the employee may distrust their intentions or lack the confidence to perform effectively. A number of studies suggest that reinstated employees do not fit back into the workplace.[20]

For example, one study showed that grievants in four firms, relative to a comparison group of employees who had not used the grievance procedure, later received lower job performance ratings, had lower probabilities of promotion, and were more likely to experience voluntary or involuntary turnover. Moreover, those grievants who had appealed their cases to the higher steps of the procedure later had more negative performance and promotion experiences than those who had settled at the lower steps. And those employees who had won their grievances—that is, whose grievances were found meritorious by either management or an arbitrator—had lower subsequent performance ratings than those whose grievances had been denied by management or an arbitrator. The same negative profile of aftereffects fit the supervisors of grievance filers. Relative to a comparison group, supervisors of grievance filers received lower performance ratings, were less likely to get promoted, and were more likely to experience involuntary turnover. This study suggests that grievance filers and their supervisors in the organizations studied faced considerable risk of retribution for using the procedure.[21]

An obvious implication of all this evidence is that both management and union representatives need to pay careful attention to what happens after a grievance is resolved.

Even in the face of the problem of retribution, the grievance procedures serve an important function as a common law of the shop. Management and union representatives often learn from grievance settlements and arbitration awards the appropriate interpretation of contract clauses and then adapt their behavior accordingly.[22]

In sum, the grievance and arbitration processes can have positive, learning effects or negative, retribution effects. Much depends on whether the management and labor representatives are committed to the goals the process was designed to foster.

Alternatives to the Grievance Procedure in the Union Sector

The costs and delays associated with the grievance procedure and arbitration have led labor and management to develop a number of innovative alternative procedures to cut down on excessive delays and costs. Among these alternatives are several minor modifications of existing practices, such as keeping grievances oral as far into the procedure as possible to promote informal resolution, tightening time allowances at various steps of the procedure, and agreeing that oral settlements or settlements at intermediate steps of the procedure will not serve in any way as precedential. Box 11–7 describes a well-known and successful oral settlement procedure.

Expedited Arbitration

Expedited arbitration is a type of grievance arbitration in which the parties agree to speed the resolution of disputes. Expedited procedures bypass steps in the normal grievance procedure and impose tight time limits. The specific features of expedited arbitration vary between contracts, but the following are some common components:

"Pre-hearing suggestions include (1) appointing a panel of arbitrators for the length of the contract rather than working through a new list of arbitrators each time an arbitration is scheduled; (2) appointing a permanent umpire [arbitrator] for a specific amount of time (one year of the life of the agreement, for example); (3) using pre-hearing briefs as a basis for stipulating facts and educating the arbitrator. Hearings may be expedited by substituting tape recordings for transcripts. Post-hearing expedition includes (1) setting a deadline for the award to be returned to the parties; (2) reducing or eliminating the number of citings for the arbitrator to research; and (3) setting a maximum on the length of one page for the award or establishing the maximum amount to be paid for the decision ahead of time."[23]

Labor, management, and arbitrators report positive results from expedited arbitration procedures. A six-year review of one expedited arbitration procedure—the Steelworkers' basic steel industry system—found that:

1. Oral resolution cut the cost of the average grievance arbitration case to roughly $55 per party.
2. More than half the grievances were resolved before arbitration.
3. The awards almost always conformed to the time limits specified (see Exhibit 11–2).

4. The procedure has spread to other Steelworkers contracts in the aluminum, can, copper, and metals industries.[24]

Expedited arbitration appears to be one viable strategy for reducing the costs and delays involved in many merely routine cases.

Grievance Mediation

Another innovation that has gained in popularity as a faster and less expensive alternative to arbitration is **grievance mediation**. In this procedure a neutral third party is asked to mediate a dispute. The process is typically highly informal, not involving written transcripts, briefs, attorneys, or written opinions. Rather, the mediator meets with the union and management and then often conducts a series of separate meetings with each party attempting to discern any underlying reasons for the grievance and possible points of compromise. The hope is that the mediator will be able to mediate settlements to many of the disputes and thereby reduce the frequency of arbitration. Although the decision of the mediator is not binding on the parties, one study has found that 80 percent of the grievance meditations are settled without the need for arbitration.[25]

A pioneering effort to use mediation to resolve grievances before they go to arbitration was developed and applied in the coal industry by William Ury, Jeanne Brett, and Stephen Goldberg.[26] These authors calculated that the average cost per arbitration case in the industry in 1985 was $1,300, whereas the average cost per mediation case was $309—a savings of roughly $1,000 per case. In addition, over the five-year period the average time lapse between the request for mediation and the resolution of the case was 19 days, a period considerably shorter than the average of 52 days required to schedule an arbitration hearing and receive a written award. But even further testimony to the value of grievance mediation can be found in the high levels of satisfaction with the procedure itself reported by the management and union representatives and the miners who took part in it.[27]

Although research supports the effectiveness of grievance mediation in resolving grievances quickly and at low cost, estimates suggest only about 3 percent of all contracts contain a mediation step in the grievance procedure. In a review of developments in this area, Peter Feuille argues that the reason for the lack of greater adoption of grievance mediation is the relative strength and robustness of the traditional grievance and arbitration process.[28] Indeed, the relative stability and enduring structure of grievance and arbitration procedures in unionized settings is a striking feature of American industrial relations given the many sweeping changes that have occurred in other areas in recent years.

Conflict Resolution in Nonunion Settings

The absence of a union does not eliminate the need for conflict resolution systems at the workplace. Nonunion employers also often find the need to perform this generic industrial relations function. Over recent decades, many employers have instituted complaint or appeal systems as well as other communication and conflict resolution procedures for their nonunion employees. These systems and procedures are often the only direct recourse available to nonunion employees who feel they have been treated unfairly in the workplace. However they are also often less consistent mechanisms for ensuring fair treatment and employee voice than union grievance procedures.

Reasons for Adopting Nonunion Grievance Procedures

As discussed earlier, in virtually all unionized settings grievance procedures are established to enforce jointly negotiated collective bargaining agreements with the strong encouragement of labor law statutes and court decisions. By contrast, in nonunion settings the establishment of a formal dispute resolution procedure is at the sole discretion of management. However in practice, many employers do choose to establish formal grievance procedures for complaints by nonunion. There are three major categories of reasons why employers chose to adopt nonunion grievance procedures.

First, employers may adopt nonunion grievance procedures as one part of a management strategy to improve the performance of their workforce. The absence of a union does not eliminate the need for conflict resolution systems in the workplace. According to Albert Hirschman's theory, employees who have no effective means to voice their discontent with any inequities they perceive may simply choose to exit the organization.[29] Such turnover can be very costly for employers, particularly for those following strategies, such as the human resource management pattern discussed in Chapter 5, that involve high levels of investment in the skills, training, and capability of their employees. To the degree that conflict resolution systems can reduce such costly turnover, there will be an incentive for employers to adopt them.

Second, employers may adopt nonunion grievance procedures as part of union avoidance strategies. The introduction of a union grievance procedure that allows the union to enforce the terms of the collective bargaining agreement and provide employees with due process is one of the major benefits of unionization that unions can offer in organizing campaigns. Research has shown that justice- and fairness-based arguments are particularly effective in organizing campaigns. To the degree that employers can provide employees with effective nonunion grievance procedures, this may reduce the desire for union representation and limit the strength of these arguments in an organizing campaign.

Third, employers may adopt nonunion grievance procedures to reduce the risk of litigation from employees. As discussed in Chapter 3, with the expansion of employment laws in recent decades, there has been a growth in the number of lawsuits filed by employees and an increase in the damages awarded against employers. Nonunion conflict resolution systems can help reduce the risk of litigation for employers by resolving workplace disputes before they turn into lawsuits. Effective grievance procedures may also help reduce the danger of lawsuits by allowing employers to identify more quickly managers who are engaging in improper or illegal actions toward employees and take appropriate corrective measures. Last, as will be discussed below, adoption of nonunion arbitration procedures can allow employers to avoid lawsuits entirely and substitute an arbitral forum for litigation to resolve employment law disputes.

Types of Nonunion Grievance Procedures

Union grievance procedures are very standard in structure, with multistep procedures culminating in binding arbitration being nearly universal in unionized settings. By contrast, there is wide variation in the incidence and structure of nonunion dispute resolution procedures. At least one-half or more of nonunion firms have formal grievance procedures, but conversely many continue to lack any procedures at all for the resolution of employee complaints or appeals. Among firms that have adopted nonunion procedures, the structure of these procedures varies widely.

The most basic type of procedure is the *open door* policy, under which employees are simply invited to bring their complaint or concern to a manager who will attempt to resolve it. More formal nonunion procedures for review of employee grievances often specify the person (often a supervisor or lower-level manager) to whom complaints can be brought and the person(s) (generally a higher-level manager) to whom the employee can appeal if they are unsatisfied with the initial manager's decision. More sophisticated systems like this may involve a committee or board of senior-level managers who will review and decide the employee's grievance and the opportunity for the employee to present his or her grievance in a more formal hearing. A common feature across these types of procedures, however, is that it is a manager or managers who are the final decision makers, not a third-party neutral as in union arbitration procedures.

Some nonunion firms have begun to adopt nonunion grievance procedures that feature nonmanagers as decision makers. Among these types of procedures are peer review panels, which use fellow employees as decision makers, and nonunion arbitration procedures, which use third-party neutral arbitrators. Both of these types of procedures will be discussed further below.

Data from the telecommunications industry reveal that in 1998 dispute resolution procedures appeared in the following frequencies across nonunion establishments: no formal procedure (49.5 percent); basic nonunion procedure (20.3 percent); management appeals board (10.8 percent); and peer review and/or binding arbitration (19.3 percent).[30]

- To give a personal and confidential hearing, to defuse rage, to provide a caring presence to those in grief about a dispute.

- To provide (and sometimes to receive) information on a one-to-one basis.

- To counsel people (confidentially) on how to help themselves, by helping to develop new options, by problem solving, by role playing.

- To conciliate (that is, to go between parties without bringing them face-to-face).

- To mediate by bringing parties together face-to-face.

- To investigate formally or informally, either with or without presenting recommendations.

- To arbitrate or adjudicate, although this is a rare function.

- To facilitate systems or procedural changes by recommending "generic" solutions, by upward feedback, internal memos, and "management consulting" with institutions, by public reports, by recommendations to legislatures, by supporting education and training.

The classic phrase describing most ombuds practitioners is "They may not make, or change, or set aside any law or policy or management decision; theirs is the power of reason and persuasion."

Source: Mary P. Rowe, "Notes on the Ombudsman in the United States, 1986," photocopy (Cambridge: Massachusetts Institute of Technology, 1986).

In addition to these formal procedures for appealing grievances, a number of employers have instituted a variety of alternative processes for resolving workplace conflict, including ombudsman offices, internal or external mediation, "speak up" programs, employee counseling services, and attitude surveys and related communications programs.

Ombudsman offices are an interesting alternative to traditional grievance procedures. The ombudsman is an individual employed by the organization to help resolve problems, complaints, or conflicts between or among employees, supervisors, and managers. Within the typical organizational chart, the ombudsman reports either directly to the office of the chief executive or to the head of the human resource management department, so as to remove him or her from the general management chain of command. Since the ombudsman's mandate is more open-ended than the mandate for a grievance procedure, ombudsmen play a more varied role in resolving conflicts and also often handle a broader range of issues than does the typical grievance procedure. Box 11–8 lists a range of functions the typical ombudsman might perform. Indeed, the flexibility and informality with which the ombudsman can approach this role is one of its distinct advantages.[31]

Integrated Conflict Management Systems

In recent years a trend has emerged toward the introduction of "integrated conflict management systems." An integrated conflict management system introduces a systematic approach to preventing, managing, and resolving conflict that focuses on the causes of conflict. The key features of an integrated conflict management system are provided in Box 11–9.

Many factors are contributing to the development of sophisticated conflict resolution procedures. Complaints by employees against supervisors, peer disputes, complaints of

An integrated conflict management system does the following:

- Encourages employees and managers to voice concerns and constructive dissent early;
- Integrates a collaborative problem-solving approach into the culture of the organization, encouraging direct negotiation between those involved in a dispute;
- Provides options for all types of problems for all people in the workplace;
- Coordinates a web of options and structures enabling problem solving across areas and functions;

- Aligns conflict management practices with each other and with the mission, vision, and values of the organization, thereby contributing significantly to internal culture transformation;
- Is understandable to all;
- Is flexible and user-friendly.

Source: "Designing Integrated Conflict Management Systems: Guidelines for Practitioners and Decision Makers in Organizations," Report prepared by The Society of Professionals in Dispute Resolution ADR in the Workplace Initiative, Institute for Conflict Resolution, ILR, Cornell University, 2002.

poor service by some part of an organization, or disagreements among work groups or teams are some of the reasons why organizations feel the need for systematic approaches to conflict resolution. In addition, disputes in the workplace now include complex problems concerning matters such as intellectual property, sexual harassment, and conflicts of interest.

Why Nonunion Employees Desire Complaint Procedures

Employees in nonunion firms seek complaint procedures in part because they desire a mechanism through which they might challenge discharge. Remember that in the absence of a collective bargaining agreement, U.S. courts have applied a doctrine called **employment at will.** The employment-at-will doctrine stipulates that both the employee and employer are free to end the employment relationship at any time, for any reason, and without liability, provided that the termination does not violate any statutory or constitutional provisions.

As discussed in Chapter 3, in recent years a number of state courts have loosened the application of the employment-at-will doctrine. Yet, even with the gradual expansion of nonunion complaint procedures and the courts' loosening of the employment-at-will doctrine, there is much controversy surrounding whether unorganized employees have an appropriate amount of due process. The importance of this as a public policy issue continues to grow as the percentage of the workforce represented by unions declines.

Differences between Union and Nonunion Grievance Procedures

Although both union and nonunion grievance procedures provide mechanisms for resolving workplace conflicts, there are also important general differences between the procedures found in union and nonunion workplaces. First, grievance procedures in unionized workplaces are created and operate under rules established in collective bargaining agreements jointly negotiated by the union and management. Nonunion grievance procedures are designed and adopted by management and apply the work rules unilaterally determined by the employer. Second, whereas the union represents the employee under a union grievance procedure, the employee typically must represent him- or herself under a nonunion grievance procedure. While a unionized employee may in some situations disagree with how the union handles his or her grievance, the nonunion employee acting on his or her own has the alternate problem of the lack of the expertise in grievance handling or negotiating power that union representation could have provided. Third, in most nonunion grievance procedures, it is management that makes the decisions, in contrast to the arbitrator who as a third-party neutral makes the final decision under virtually all union grievance procedures. Although in recent years some nonunion grievance procedures have included nonmanagerial decision makers such as arbitrators or peer employees, these types of procedures are only found in a minority of nonunion workplaces. Taken together, these differences indicate that the due process protections provided to employees in typical nonunion grievance procedures are substantially more limited than those in union grievance procedures.

Impact of Nonunion Grievance Procedures

Given the more limited due process protections in nonunion grievance procedures, it has long been recognized that employees are much less likely to use grievance procedures in nonunion than union workplaces. However, employees may be relatively more willing to use nonunion grievance procedures that do contain some due process protections. A study of employee usage of grievance procedures in the telecommunications industry found that rates of usage varied with the type of procedure. Grievance rates are often measured as the number of grievances filed annually per 100 workers. Looking just at grievances about discipline decisions, in unionized workplaces there was an average grievance rate of 5.3 for each 100 workers, whereas in workplaces with nonunion grievance procedures the average grievance rate was 2.0 per 100 workers. Among the nonunion workplaces, grievance rates were much higher where the procedure included nonmanagerial decision makers: 2.9 per 100 workers for procedures that included peer review and 3.2 per 100 workers for procedures that included arbitration versus only 1.3 per 100 workers for procedures that used only managers as decision makers.[32]

Critics of nonunion grievance systems argue that an important reason employees make lesser use of nonunion grievance procedures is because they fear reprisals. A study by David Lewin of the performance of grievance procedures in three high-technology, nonunion firms provides some support for these claims.[33] Lewin found that compared to employees who did not file grievances, grievance filers (and their supervisors) had lower performance ratings, lower promotion rates, and higher rates of turnover in the year after their use of the procedure. Survey responses from two of the firms indicated that approximately one-third of those who did not file grievances chose not to do so because they either feared reprisals or believed there was little chance their appeal would be successful. Thus, it appears the grievants in these nonunion firms exercised their right to use these procedures at considerable risk. If this pattern is at all representative of experiences in other firms, it supports some of the critics' arguments.

Peer Review and Union Avoidance

Conflict resolution systems in nonunion settings may serve important functions for employees and employers. These procedures can represent constructive additions to a modern industrial relations system, but they can also serve as a means of managerial control and union avoidance.

Evidence shows that in recent years a number of firms adopted peer review, a particular kind of complaint-resolution procedure, because it had the added virtue of being an effective union substitution device.[34] Under peer-review procedures, review panels or boards are established to hear and decide employee grievances.

The key feature of a peer-review procedure is that the majority of the members of the panel are peer employees of the grievant. The result is that this, "creates two important advantages for the use of peer-review panels as union substitution mechanisms. First, because a majority of the final decision makers in the procedure are no longer members of management, the panels promise greater neutrality in decision making. Second, because employees are involved in the procedure, there is some substitution for the representational function of the union in the workplace—albeit only a partial substitute, given that the panel members are not actually presenting the grievance on behalf of the employee."[35]

To the extent that the express purpose of having peer review and other complaint resolution procedures is one of union avoidance, the history of grievance procedures has taken an ironic twist: what started as a unique and highly acclaimed innovation designed to deliver due process to employees has been transformed into an employer strategy for reducing employees' chances of achieving union representation and acquiring a truly independent grievance procedure. Thus, like many other human resource management innovations that are driven at least in part by union avoidance motives, nonunion conflict resolution systems are a double-edged sword.

Nonunion Arbitration and Employment Laws

Use of arbitration as the final step in the procedure has long been a key feature of union grievance procedures. By contrast, until recently use of arbitration in nonunion grievance procedures was much rarer. This changed in the 1990s as employers began adopting arbitration procedures as an alternative to litigation through the courts for resolving claims by employees based on statutory employment laws.

Employment litigation costs increased dramatically in the 1960s, 70s, and 80s with the passage of various statutory protections, a shift in some state courts toward recognition of some common law protections against wrongful dismissal, and occasional high damage awards to plaintiffs in disputes over discrimination and other claims. This produced a strong desire by firms to reduce litigation costs and avoid court actions where possible.

The impetus for the use of arbitration as a mechanism to avoid the risks and costs of litigation came from a shift in the courts toward favoring arbitration as an alternative procedure for resolving statutory employment law claims. In its 1991 decision in *Gilmer* v. *Interstate/Johnson Lane,* 500 US 20 (1991), the United States Supreme Court held that a dispute based on a statutory employment right was subject to arbitration. Expanding upon the Gilmer decision, the courts have held that disputes involving a wide variety of employment rights, including racial, sexual, age, and disability-related charges of discrimination are subject to arbitration clauses included in the employment contracts of nonunion employers. More recently, the Supreme Court reaffirmed its support for arbitration with its decision in *Circuit City* v. *Adams* (see Box 11–10).

Employers that adopt arbitration procedures to resolve potential employment law claims typically require employees to sign an agreement to arbitrate potential legal claims against the employer as a mandatory term and condition of employment. The potential employee can choose not to sign the arbitration agreement, but the employer will then no longer

In *Circuit City Stores, Inc.* v. *Adams* (2001), the Supreme Court decided that all employment disputes must be settled with an arbitrator if so dictated by an employment contract. In 1995, Saint Clair Adams signed an employment application with Circuit City Stores stating that all disputes "relating to my application or candidacy for employment, employment and/or cessation from employment" will be settled "*exclusively* by final and binding *arbitration* before a neutral arbitrator." Adams was hired by the company shortly after. Two years later, he filed a lawsuit under California's Fair Employment Act in state court, alleging that he had been sexually harassed by three coworkers and faced retaliation for complaining about the harassment. Circuit City filed a petition in federal court to enforce the employment agreement signed by Adams and settle the dispute through binding arbitration. The district court granted the company's petition. The Ninth Circuit Court found the agreement unenforceable in 1999. However, the Supreme Court reversed the decision in 2001, reasoning that the Federal Arbitration Act (FAA) was designed so that the courts and other government agencies concede discretion to an expert in workplace affairs, the arbitrator. The court stated that only a small number of transportation workers, are exempted from binding arbitration under the FAA, although even these employees can be subject to state laws allowing for mandatory arbitration.

However, in 2002, when the case was remanded back to the Ninth Circuit Court, the court pointed out that under Section 2 of the FAA, an arbitration agreement "shall be valid, irrevocable, and enforceable, save upon such grounds that exist at law or equity for the revocation of any contract." The court said that general contract defenses such as fraud, duress, or unconscionability could invalidate an arbitration agreement. Procedural unconscionability, according to the court, examines the equality of bargaining power and disclosure while substantive unconscionability determines whether the terms of the contract are unduly harsh. Based on those criteria, the court found that the Circuit City's employment agreement was procedurally and substantively "unconscionable." The court decided that the company had more bargaining power than its employees and applicants, yet drafted the employment agreement itself and forced all employees to sign it. Also, since the employment agreement is a prerequisite to the actual start of employment, job applicants are not permitted to modify any of the terms in the agreement. Circuit City petitioned the Supreme Court again, claiming that the Ninth Circuit Court had relied on "generalized and abstract concerns about unequal bargaining power." The Supreme Court denied review of the case (certiorari) in June of 2002. This upheld the decision of the Ninth Circuit Court and allowed Adams' original lawsuit to proceed.

Sources: *Circuit City Stores, Inc.* v. *Adams,* 532 US 105; and "Supreme Court Denies Circuit City's Bid for Review on Second Trip to High Court." *Daily Labor Report,* June 4, 2002: AA–2.

offer the potential employee a job. For this reason, these procedures are often referred to as *mandatory arbitration*. Although mandatory arbitration is something the employer requires the employee to agree to in order to obtain employment, these contracts are still generally enforced by the courts, much as adhesive or "take-it-or-leave-it" contracts are enforced in many other areas (e.g., think of standard form rental car or apartment lease contracts).

In a more recent case, *Equal Employment Opportunity Commission (EEOC)* v. *Waffle House, Inc.* (2002), the Supreme Court limited somewhat the applicability of the Circuit City decision. The Supreme Court decided that the EEOC still has the right to pursue judicial relief for a victim of employment discrimination, even if the individual had signed a binding arbitration agreement with his employer. The EEOC can still seek relief such as backpay, reinstatement, and damages for victims of employment discrimination. Even in the face of this limitation, the *Gilmer* and *Circuit City* decisions are still having drastic effects on an employee's ability to dispute unfair work rules and treatment. Unless the

EEOC pursues discrimination-related cases on behalf of employees, which it only has the resources to do in a small percentage of cases, employees can be forced to settle an employment rights complaint through arbitration.

Mandatory arbitration spread rapidly in the wake of the *Gilmer* and *Circuit City* decisions. From being very rare before the 1990s, estimates suggest that by the mid-2000s around 15 percent or more of workplaces had mandatory arbitration procedures in place.[36] The practical significance of the enforcement of "mandatory arbitration" clauses is the diversion of employment rights disputes, including discrimination cases, into an employer-designed arbitration procedure. As a result, there has been much debate over mandatory arbitration procedures and various proposals to enhance their due process features.

Debates over Mandatory Arbitration

Advocates of mandatory arbitration argue that it provides a faster, more efficient mechanism for resolving employment law claims. They point to the lengthy delays and high costs of litigating employment claims through the courts and argue that arbitration provides a better, more accessible mechanism for resolving these claims for both employers and employees. Comparisons find that whereas the average employment discrimination case takes 709 days to be resolved in the federal court system, similar cases take an average of 383 days to resolve in arbitration.[37] For its advocates, the simplified procedures of arbitration are more appropriate for resolving routine employment law disputes, while retaining enough due process protections to ensure protection of the employee's statutory rights.[38]

Critics of mandatory arbitration argue that procedures are too much under the control of employers, suffer from potential bias of arbitrators, and move the adjudication of public employment law claims from the public forum of the courts to the private forum of arbitration. Since mandatory arbitration procedures are designed by employers and offered to potential employees on a take-it-or-leave-it basis, critics worry that procedures will include features systematically biasing them in favor of the employer, such as rules concerning who can serve as the arbitrator, limitations on access to information necessary to resolve the claim, and restrictions on how the employee can present his or her claim. In a colorful analogy, Katherine Stone described mandatory arbitration agreements as being a modern version of the "yellow-dog" contracts promising not to join unions that many employers used to require workers to sign until the practice was outlawed in the Norris-LaGuardia Act of 1932.[39] Another major concern of critics is that employers will have a systematic advantage in arbitration as arbitrators will tend to favor the employer in hopes of being selected to decide future claims. Research by Lisa Bingham has found evidence suggesting that there is a "repeat-player" bias in arbitration decisions in favor of employers, who are much more likely than employees to be involved in multiple cases, creating the potential for repeat business for the arbitrator.[40]

Due Process Models

While controversies and debates over the enforcement of mandatory arbitration procedures continue, there have also been efforts to establish models for what due process protections should be included in arbitration procedures used to resolve statutory claims. In 1994, the U.S. Department of Labor's Commission on the Future of Worker-Management Relations proposed a set of seven quality standards for fairness in nonunion arbitration:

a) A neutral arbitrator who knows the laws in question and understands the concerns of the parties;

b) A fair and simple method by which the employee can secure the necessary information to present the claim;

c) A fair method of cost-sharing between the employer and employee to ensure affordable access to the system;

d) The right to independent representation if the employee wants it;

e) A range of remedies equal to those available through litigation;

f) A written opinion by the arbitrator explaining the rationale for the result; and

g) Sufficient judicial review to ensure that the result is consistent with the governing laws.[41]

In 1995 a task force established by the American Bar Association's labor and employment law section, including representatives from both employer and employee side groups, developed a similar but more detailed "Due Process Protocol" for arbitration procedures designed to resolve statutory claims. Subsequently, the American Arbitration Association announced that it would follow procedures based on the recommendations contained in the Due Process Protocol in any employment arbitration cases it administers.[42] This is important because many employers decide that rather than developing an arbitration procedure entirely on their own, they will contract with the AAA to provide the arbitrators and run the arbitration hearings under its rules. The AAA estimates that by 2003 some 7 million workers were employed at companies for which the AAA provides employment arbitration services.[43]

Although the courts continue to enforce mandatory arbitration agreements, there is some evidence that they are beginning to expect higher standards of due process in arbitration procedures.[44] For example, courts have declined to enforce procedures that require employees to pay a sizable portion of arbitration costs that would serve as a barrier to employee access or procedures that require employees to go to arbitration while allowing the employer to retain the right to go to court (e.g., to enforce a noncompetition covenant signed by the employee).

Summary

Grievance procedures historically have been the centerpiece of the day-to-day administration of the collective bargaining agreement. The grievance procedure provides a mechanism to settle disputes that arise during the term of a collective bargaining agreement. The grievance procedure typically includes successive steps involving higher union and management officials. The union has the right to decide if it wishes to push any unsettled grievance to a higher step.

The grievance procedure has been hailed as one of the most innovative features of the U.S. industrial relations system. Its centrality was due in part to the understanding that it was "management's job to manage and the union's job to grieve."

Collective bargaining agreements in the United States are elaborate documents that often include highly detailed job descriptions. The existence of such elaborate labor contracts contributed to the need for an orderly means for settling conflicts over interpretations of contract language.

Binding arbitration by a third party is the common device used as the final step of grievance procedures. Arbitrators commonly consider past practice at the workpl intent of the parties during contract negotiations, and fairness in fashioning their awards. In discipline cases arbitrators generally require that progressive and corrective discipline be applied.

The centrality of the formal grievance and arbitration procedures is now being challenged by a number of recent developments. The need for greater adaptability and competitive pressures have led some unions and managements to simplify how conflicts are settled.

Furthermore, public laws that govern a broad spectrum of employment issues, such as equal employment opportunity, are challenging the exclusivity of the private arbitration system. The courts have granted employees the right to pursue complaints concerning these matters in the courts as well as through the grievance procedure.

The expansion of worker involvement in business and strategic decisions also has led labor and management to rely less on the grievance procedure to solve problems. An effective industrial relations system in union settings now must be more than simply a grievance procedure. To keep in step with the times, the system must combine the strengths of a well-functioning grievance procedure with mechanisms to informally solve problems and enhance communication.

The next chapter describes how worker and union participation programs have supplemented formal complaint procedures and led to major changes in workplace industrial relations in some locations.

Discussion Questions

1. Describe the typical steps followed in a grievance case.
2. Grievance procedures meet the needs of several groups. Name these groups and discuss how the grievance arbitration procedures help meet their respective needs.
3. Grievance arbitration procedures are often very costly and time-consuming. What are some of the alternatives to this process in the union sector?
4. Although nonunion firms do not usually have a formalized grievance process with binding arbitration, these firms must also contend with conflict resolution at the workplace. What are some of the techniques nonunion firms use to resolve conflict?
5. Nonunion firms are not required to have formal grievance procedures, but many do. What are some of the reasons that nonunion firms choose to adopt grievance procedures?
6. What are some of the arguments for and against mandatory arbitration of statutory employment law claims?

Related Web Sites

U.S. Steel Corporation (USX):
http://www.usx.com/ussteel/index.html

General information on binding arbitration:
http://www.frankgrin.com/arbit.html

Arbitration and mediation law information:
http://fedlaw.gsa.gov/legal89.htm

American Association of Arbitration:
http://www.adr.org

Suggested Readings

Elkouri, Frank, and Edna Asper Elkouri. *How Arbitration Works,* 5th ed. (Washington, DC: Bureau of National Affairs, 1997).

Institute for Conflict Resolution, *"Designing Integrated Conflict Management Systems: Guidelines for Practitioners and Decision Makers in Organizations,"* Report prepared by The Society of Professionals in Dispute Resolution ADR in the Workplace Initiative, ILR, Cornell University, 2002.

Kuhn, James W. *Bargaining and Grievance Settlement* (New York: Columbia University Press, 1961).

Lewin, David, and Richard Peterson. *The Modern Grievance Procedure in the American Economy* (New York: Quorum Books, 1988).

Lipsky, David B., Ronald L. Seeber, and Richard D. Fincher. *Emerging Systems for Managing Workplace Conflict* (San Francisco: John Wiley & Sons, 2003).

McKelvey, Jean T., ed. *The Changing Law of Fair Representation* (Ithaca, NY: ILR Press, 1985).

End Notes

1. For a good review of the historical development of court rulings on grievance procedures and arbitration, see Neil W. Chamberlain and James W. Kuhn, *Collective Bargaining,* 3d ed. (New York: McGraw-Hill, 1986), pp. 151–53.

2. For a more thorough review of the development of grievance arbitration, see Robben W. Fleming, *The Labor Arbitration Process* (Urbana: University of Illinois Press, 1964).

3. Charles C. Killingsworth and Saul Wallen, "Constraint and Variety in Arbitration Systems," in *Labor Arbitration-Perspectives and Problems: Proceedings of the National Academy of Arbitrators, 1964* (Washington, DC: Bureau of National Affairs, 1965), pp. 56–81.

4. "Agreement between General Motors Corporation and the UAW" (October 8, 1987), pp. 93–94.

5. Chamberlain and Kuhn, *Collective Bargaining,* pp. 151–53.

6. *United Steelworkers of America* v. *Warrior and Gulf Navigation*, 363 U.S. 547 at 581 (1960).

7. For a review of the different approaches, see David E. Feller, "The Impact of External Law upon Labor Arbitration," in *The Future of Labor Arbitration in America* (New York: American Arbitration Association, 1976), pp. 83–112; and David E. Feller, "The Coming End of Arbitration's Golden Age," in *Arbitration 1976: Proceedings of the 29th Annual Meeting of the National Academy of Arbitrators,* ed. Barbara D. Dennis and Gerald G. Somers (Washington, DC: Bureau of National Affairs, 1977), pp. 97–151.

8. *Steele* v. *Louisville & Nashville R.R. Co.,* 323 US 192 (1944).

9. *Vaca* v. *Sipes,* 386 US 171 (1967).

10. *Hines* v. *Anchor Motor Freight, Inc.,* 424 US 554 (1976).

11. *Bowen* v. *United States Postal Service,* 103 US (1983).

12. Harry C. Katz, Thomas A. Kochan, and Kenneth R. Gobeille, "Industrial Relations Performance, Economic Performance, and QWL Programs: An Interplant Analysis," *Industrial and Labor Relations Review* 37 (October 1983): 3–17.

13. James T. Turner and James W. Robinson, "A Pilot Study of the Validity of Grievance Settlement Rates as a Predictor of Union Management Relationships," *Journal of Industrial Relations* 14 (September 1972): 314–22.

14. Katz, Kochan, and Gobeille, "Industrial Relations Performance," pp. 8–9.

15. Nancy R. Mower, "The Labor-Management Relationship and Its Effects on Quality of Work Life," M.S. thesis (Cambridge: Massachusetts Institute of Technology, 1982).

16. James W. Kuhn, *Bargaining in Grievance Settlement* (New York: Columbia University Press, 1961).

17. David Lewin and Richard Peterson, *The Modern Grievance Procedure in the United States* (New York: Quorum Books, 1988).

18. Federal Mediation and Conciliation Service, Arbitration Statistics, Fiscal Year 2005.

19. Ibid.

20. Arthur M. Ross, "The Arbitration of Discharge Cases: What Happens After Reinstatement?" *Critical Issues in Arbitration: Proceedings of the Tenth Annual Meeting of the National Academy of Arbitrators,* 1956 (Washington DC: Bureau of National Affairs, 1957), pp. 21–56; and Robert C. Rodgers, I. B. Helburn, and John E. Hunter, "The Relationship of Seniority to Job Performance Following Reinstatement," *Academy of Management Journal* 29 (March 1986): 101–14.

21. Lewin and Peterson, *The Modern Grievance Procedure.*

22. Thomas R. Knight, "Feedback and Grievance Resolution," *Industrial and Labor Relations Review* 39 (July 1986): 585–98.

23. Nancy Kaufman, "The Idea of Expedited Arbitration Two Decades Later," *Arbitration Journal* (September 1991): 34–38.

24. John Zalusky, "Arbitration: Updating a Vital Process," *American Federationist* 83 (November 1976): 4.

25. Mediation Research & Education Project, Inc. "Grievance Mediation Found to Be Useful Alternative to Arbitration." Northwestern University Law School, 2002. www.mrep. org/cost_results.htm.

26. William L. Ury, Jeanne M. Brett, and Stephen B. Goldberg, *Getting Disputes Resolved: Designing Systems to Cut the Costs of Conflict* (San Francisco: Jossey-Bass, 1988).

27. Stephen B. Goldberg, "The Mediation of Grievances under a Collective Bargaining Contract: An Alternative to Arbitration," *Northwestern University Law Review* 77 (October 1982): 270–315.

28. Peter Feuille, "Grievance Mediation," Chapter 6 in Adrienne E. Eaton and Jeffrey H. Keefe, Editors, *Employment Dispute Resolution and Worker Rights in the Changing Workplace* (Champaign-Urbana, IL: Industrial Relations Research Association, 1999).

29. Albert O. Hirschman, *Exit, Voice, and Loyalty: Responses to Decline in Firms, Organizations, and States* (Cambridge, MA: Harvard University Press, 1971).

30. Alexander J.S. Colvin, 1999, *Citizens and Citadels: Dispute Resolution and the Governance of Employment Relations* (unpublished PhD dissertation, Cornell University).

31. David Lewin, 1997, "Workplace Dispute Resolution." In D. Lewin, D.J.B. Mitchell, and M.A. Zaidi (eds.), *The Human Resource Management Handbook, Part II* (Greenwich, CT: JAI Press), pp. 197–218.

32. Alexander J.S. Colvin, "The Dual Transformation of Workplace Dispute Resolution," *Industrial Relations* 42(4) (October 2003): 712–735.

33. David Lewin, "Conflict Resolution in High Technology Firms," in *Human Resource Management in High Technology,* ed. Archie Kleingartner and Cara Anderson (Lexington, MA: Lexington Books, 1987).

34. Alexander J.S. Colvin, "Institutional Pressures, Human Resource Strategies and the Rise of Nonunion Greivance Procedures." *Industrial & Labor Relations Review* 56(3) (April 2003): 375–392.

35. Ibid., 380.

36. Ibid.

37. Theodore Eisenberg and Elizabeth Hill. 2003. "Employment Arbitration and Litigation." *Dispute Resolution Journal* 58, pp. 44–55.

38. Samuel Estreicker, "Saturns for Rickshaws: The Stakes in the Debate over Predispute Employment Arbitration Agreements." *Ohio State Journal on Dispute Resolution* 16 (2001): 559–570.

39. Katherine V.W. Stone, "Mandatory Arbitration of Individual Employment Rights: The Yellow Dog Contract of the 1990's." *Denver University Law Review* 73 (1996): 1017–50.

40. Lisa B. Bingham, "Employment Arbitration: The Repeat Player Effect." *Employee Rights and Employment Policy Journal* 1 (1997): 189–220.

41. Commission on the Future of Worker-Management Relations (The Dunlop Commission), *Report and Recommendations,* Dec. 1994, Washington, DC: U.S. Department of Labor.

42. "Revised AAA Arbitration Procedures Reflect Due Process Task Force Scheme." 1996 *Daily Labor Report* 102 d6 (May 28, 1996).

43. Alison Grant, "Arbitration Replacing Litigation: Companies Want to Avoid Court as a Way to Resolve Workplace Issues," *Cleveland Plain Dealer* (Oct. 30, 2003), C1.

44. Michael Leroy and Peter Feuille. "Judicial Enforcement of Pre-Dispute Arbitration Agreements: Back to the Future." *Ohio State Journal on Dispute Resolution* 18(2) (2003): 249–341.

Chapter 12

Participatory Processes

Unionized industrial relations systems now face intense environmental pressures, including those arising from the lower costs found in many nonunion workplace systems in the United States and developing countries. Moreover, the United States, like other advanced societies, is in the midst of a transition from an industrial to a knowledge-based economy. A knowledge-based economy relies on human capital, worker skills, and commitment to add value to technology, financial resources, and other organizational assets. Taken together these developments are creating strong pressures on collective bargaining to adapt and better meet the needs and interests of contemporary workers and employers.

How well is collective bargaining doing in adapting to change? The 2000 FMCS national customer survey provides some provocative data on this question. Respondents were asked whether (and how fast) their bargaining relationships were changing. The answers provided by labor and management leaders were: 60 percent saw their relationships as stable and not changing, 6 percent saw them as getting worse, and about one-third saw them as improving. The majority of those that saw their relationships improving rated the pace of change as slow or very slow. Overall less than 10 percent of the respondents saw their relationships improving at a quick or very quick rate. Further analysis showed that those that were improving and moving toward more cooperative relationships were ones that had introduced workplace innovations, had some degree of information sharing or union–management consultation over at the strategic levels of their organizations, and used some aspects of interest-based bargaining in negotiations. Still, only a very small percentage (less than 10 percent of the total) fit this profile.

In this chapter we explore the experiences to date of efforts by unions and management representatives to introduce various joint change and improvement efforts into their bargaining relationships. The starting point for most of these efforts are participatory processes that involve individual workers and union representatives in decision making. In many cases these participatory processes provide informal mechanisms of worker involvement that are supplements or alternatives to the grievance and arbitration procedures.

Participatory processes often are linked to alterations in the organization of work that simplify work rules and increase flexibility in management of the workforce. In manufacturing settings participatory processes are also frequently introduced along with supply chain and production methods such as **just-in-time inventory systems** or **cell manufacturing.** Furthermore, a number of the participatory processes have now evolved to increase the participation of workers and unions in strategic business decisions.

The efforts to expand worker and union participation have had varying degrees of success. Some experiments flourished, whereas others failed and were followed by a return to traditional practices and bitter labor-management relations. Both examples of success and failure are reviewed in this chapter.

Participatory programs also have stirred much debate within the ranks of the labor movement. Supporters of the programs argue that they can provide the sort of industrial democracy unions have long sought although rarely achieved in the United States. Meanwhile, critics of the programs claim that they lead to co-opted workers and to the weakening, if not the demise, of union representation.

Thus, an understanding of participatory programs is of interest for a number of reasons. It is useful first to provide some historical perspective.

The Evolution of Worker and Union Participation

Much of the early efforts to create new mechanisms of worker and union involvement in decision making involved what are called quality of working life (or employee involvement) programs. **Quality of working life (QWL) programs** are oriented toward improving organizational performance and the working life of employees. These programs operate at the lowest level of industrial relations activity, namely, down on the shop floor through the involvement of groups of workers.

Early QWL—Limited Success

Efforts to spark interest in QWL programs expanded in the early 1970s. Many of these early QWL programs sought to address a perception that modern factories alienated workers by providing repetitive job tasks and few avenues through which employees could provide direct input into matters that affected their work lives. The highly publicized 1972 Work in America report tried to spark interest in QWL issues by calling for workplace reforms that would reduce worker alienation (what was sometimes referred to as "the blue-collar blues").[1]

Most of the early promotion of QWL programs was unsuccessful. For example, the federal government's National Commission on Productivity and Quality of Working Life tried hard to stimulate interest and experimentation but managed only to generate pilot projects in a handful of manufacturing firms and one coal mine. The commission was eventually disbanded after it received a negative evaluation by the federal government's General Accounting Office and lost its political support.[2]

The early programs also ran into much opposition from labor and management, for several reasons. First, because these programs were largely initiated from outside the organizations, labor and management did not see a clear need to change. Second, many labor leaders and industrial relations managers resisted change because they believed that the proposed alternatives questioned the basic assumptions of the traditional form of unionism and the process of collective bargaining. Professionals on both sides of the table were skeptical of claims by QWL advocates that increased problem solving and participation could replace contractual rules that had been carefully bargained over the years.

Third, labor and management representatives also feared that informal problem solving would threaten their roles and status. Many labor leaders believed that QWL was simply another in the long line of managerial tactics to undermine collective bargaining and further weaken unionism. Since most of the QWL experience before the 1970s had been in non-union firms and few of the advocates of QWL had much appreciation or understanding of unions, those fears were not unfounded.

Fourth, few line managers or top executives saw the bottom-line relevance of QWL. Instead, they tended to view QWL as a behavioral science fad that at most promised to improve job satisfaction and perhaps employee motivation. As we will see, this perspective was to change dramatically in the 1980s as line managers and an increasing number of top executives began to see participation and workplace innovations as keys to improving productivity and product quality.

The Rebirth of QWL in the 1980s

QWL was reborn in the 1980s as economic pressures intensified. Heightened economic pressure induced labor leaders and managers to find new ways to address their productivity, quality, and labor cost problems. By far most QWL efforts started out as narrow programs based on the premise that they be kept separate from collective bargaining issues and procedures. These narrow QWL programs were designed to increase individual and group problem solving around task-related issues.

Quality Circles

Quality circles (QCs) are an example of this narrow type of effort and the problems confronted by these narrow programs. In a typical QC program, the workers in one area of a plant met for one or two hours a week with their supervisor. Generally, higher management assigned QCs the task of identifying potential improvements in production and service delivery. The QC meetings were commonly held during normal work hours (the line might be stopped or meetings were added to the lunch hour), and workers were paid their normal hourly wage rate for their participation in these activities. (The latter was in contrast to how QCs operate in Japan where hourly workers typically attend QC meetings after work hours and are often not paid for their time.) Supervisors or other managers often played strong roles in the QC meetings. The supervisor, for example, might have led a discussion of statistical quality control techniques or taken the lead in listing priorities or communicating group recommendations to higher management.

Many companies initially reported large payouts from QC activities. For some companies scrap rates began to drop significantly after QCs were started up, and in others the groups were able to quickly identify methods for cost savings through changes in shop floor production processes.

The Limited Gains from Quality Circles

Over time the gains from QCs dissipated in company after company. At times workers became frustrated by, and in some cases stopped attending, QC meetings after management had rejected or ignored their suggestions and recommendations. In other cases workers continued to attend QC meetings but ran out of suggestions to offer because all their new suggestions required that changes be made in work rules or contractual clauses and these were deemed to be out of bounds to the QC. This latter problem arose because both management and the union typically defined QC activity as a supplement to normal collective bargaining. As a result, QCs were not normally authorized to address work rules, contractual issues, the nature of technology, or basic production methods. Other QWL efforts ran up against similar problems.

The Broadening of QC and QWL Programs

The most successful QC and QWL programs were those that eventually broadened to involve work rules, collective bargaining issues, and production methods (essentially all the things that initially had been kept separate from the participatory processes).[3] Unless this broadening occurred, the QWL change process was not able to address the important issues that affected economic performance and long-run employment security.

The Expansion of QWL at Xerox   *Xerox was generally accepting of unions*

Not all narrow QWL processes made that transition successfully. In fact, by the mid-1980s articles had begun appearing in management journals criticizing many firms for treating QCs as just another short-lived fad.[4] One QWL program that did succeed in broadening its focus involved Xerox Corporation and the Amalgamated Clothing and Textile Workers Union (ACTWU) in Rochester, New York. As summarized in Box 12–1, there was an iterative broadening of QWL at Xerox. At each successive stage the parties had to reaffirm their commitment to expanding the problem-solving process while at the same time resolving conflicts that occurred in negotiations and in day-to-day contract administration. The parties' ability to manage the tensions between problem solving and labor-management conflict was critical in this case, as in so many others.

For example, less than two years into the QWL process the program came under fire from rank-and-file workers when management shifted to a business and manufacturing strategy based on greater concern for cost controls. But instead of abandoning QWL, the parties began to use it to search for ways to cut costs and save jobs. The study team in the wiring harness area represented the first such effort. This study team suggested changes in work organization that required contractual changes, and thereby they created the need for the QWL process to be integrated into the collective bargaining process. The parties did this in their 1983 negotiations by agreeing to use the wiring harness study team experience as a model for how to handle similar subcontracting decisions in the future. In return for this and several other work rule and pay changes, management in 1983 agreed to a no-layoff provision.

As Box 12–1 indicates, over the 1980s and 1990s Xerox and the ACTWU (now UNITE-HERE) broadened their joint efforts to allow autonomous work groups in some areas, to plan a new work system for a new plant, and to establish decentralized "business area work groups" (teams that manage their unit's own affairs and tailor their participation and problem-solving processes).[5] Xerox won the prestigious Baldridge award for organizational excellence from the U.S. Commerce Department, and Xerox's participatory activities received much of the credit. Research also shows that the work areas in Xerox that had a greater intensity and wider range of cooperative activities had higher productivity and less scrap.[6]

Strategic Participation at Xerox

Several features of labor-management relations at the strategic level of Xerox helped increase the success of joint problem-solving efforts. Xerox has not resisted union organizing in its new facilities. In addition, top Xerox executives and ACTWU leaders meet

1980	QWL language put in collective bargaining agreement.	1985	Launch of Business Area Work Group concept at CMO.

1980 QWL language put in collective bargaining agreement.
Four joint Plant Advisory Committees and departmental steering committees established to create and support employee problem-solving groups.

1981 Over 90 problem-solving groups established. Outsourcing of 180 wiring harness jobs on hold pending analysis of joint Study-Action Team.

1982 Study-Action Team identifies over $3.2 million potential savings; jobs not subcontracted.
Over 150 problem-solving groups exist in seven facilities.
Massive layoffs of unionized and exempt personnel.
First semiautonomous work groups established on their own initiative.

1983 Contract includes no-layoff clause and mandated use of Study-Action Teams in all potential outsourcing situations, along with first-year wage freeze, copayment medical changes, and a restrictive absenteeism control program.
Strategic Planning Teams include the union to assess the future of the reprographic business.
QWL training made mandatory, polarizing the work force.
Study-Action Teams established in two additional areas, with work kept in-house in each case.

1984 Operating engineers' union withdraws from QWL in protest over issues of medical benefit changes.
QWL groups decline in New Building Operations; informal pre-shift meetings emerge in their place.
Study-Action Teams established in three areas, with work kept in-house in two cases.
Employee attitude survey in Components Manufacturing (CMO) prompts top-level reexamination of QWL.

1985 Launch of Business Area Work Group concept at CMO.
New plant built in Webster, New York, based on joint analysis and design team.

1986 Union supports flexible work assignments for hourly workers involved in new product development.
Contract extends no-layoff guarantee; modifies restrictive absenteeism program; establishes classification for hourly group leaders; and contemplates pilot study of gains sharing—all with a mixture of hard bargaining and problem solving.
Autonomous work groups increasingly established, prompted by early retirement of supervisors.

1992 Another three-year contract extends job security to the 650 workers hired during the previous three-year agreement. Lump sum, base pay, and COLA pay increases are provided in the new contract. A problem-solving bargaining style is used to negotiate the new contract. Prior to bargaining the new contract, labor and management agree to decentralize the factory complex in Webster, New York, so that all aspects of production are performed at one site.

1993 (May) Xerox and the ACTWU reach agreement to bring 300 jobs back into the United States (from Mexico and Asia) to a recently closed apparel factory in Utica, New York. The factory will perform simple assembly work and annual earnings on those jobs will range between $15,000 and $18,000 which is far below average earnings at the Webster Xerox complex. The company agrees to not oppose ACTWU organizing efforts at the Utica plant.

1993 (December) Xerox Chairman Paul Allaire shocks the ACTWU by announcing plans to cut 10,000 jobs (equivalent to 10 percent of the work force) through attrition, layoffs, and voluntary retirements in order to lower costs and increase productivity. Xerox's of

(continued)

earnings had declined in 1993 but were still positive and sizable.

1994   As an outgrowth of early contract talks, Xerox and the ACTWU negotiate a seven-year contract that provides job security and COLA but no base pay increases; allows the company to increase its use of temporary workers (up to 15 percent of the work force); and gives the company more flexibility in transfers and promotions.

2000–2002   Xerox lost market share, underwent restructuring, was charged with accounting irregularities, and outsourced most of its manufacturing.

Sources: Joel Cutcher-Gershenfeld, "New Path toward Organizational Effectiveness and Institutional Security: The Case of Xerox Corporation and the Amalgamated Clothing and Textile Workers Union," report to the Bureau of Labor Management Relations and Cooperative Programs, U.S. Department of Labor, 1987; and various issues of the *Daily Labor Report.*

periodically to share information and discuss long-range issues that affect the business. These discussions led to the agreement that brought 300 jobs back into the United States and into a closed apparel plant as mentioned in Box 12–1 in 1993. Thus, workplace QWL activities evolved in this case in an environment where strategic interactions reinforced worker and union shop floor participation.

The Limits of Participation

Events at Xerox at the start of the twenty-first century also illustrate the limits of participatory processes. These processes cannot override fundamental changes in market conditions or declines in the core business of a company caused by strategic mistakes. By 2000 Xerox had lost market share to other office technology and information system companies, underwent a failed restructuring of its sales and service operations, and was charged with accounting irregularities that further reduced earnings and financial reserves.

These developments put the survival of the firm at risk. As part of its response Xerox outsourced most of its manufacturing of low priced machines to Techtronics, a specialized manufacturing firm that operates mainly in China. The company continues at this point to maintain manufacturing operations in Rochester, New York, but employment there has been reduced by nearly 50 percent in recent years. Labor and management continue to promote employee participation and meet periodically to discuss the state of the business. While the extent and visibility of this longstanding partnership has been diminished by the declining fortunes of the company, efforts to work together and to negotiate adjustments have continued.

New Channels of Communication

The expansion of participation processes is often associated with the elaboration of new channels of communication between workers and supervisors. Often such communication is supplemented by expanded communication between union officers and higher management. The mutual growth forums at Ford Motor Company described in Box 12–2 illustrate how this can occur.

Both parties recognize that the need for change continues . . . and they must explore new methods of resolving their honest differences in orderly rational ways. . . . To provide such a new approach, to facilitate the process of continuing evolution and change, and to move the parties forward to new thresholds, Ford and the UAW have agreed to establish a Mutual Growth Forum that is intended to function—at both the local and national levels—as a highly visible new adjunct to the collective bargaining process.

"The forum does not replace collective bargaining, nor does it interfere in any way with the parties' grievance procedure. Rather, it provides a new framework designed to promote better Management-Union relations through better communications, systematic fact finding, and advance discussions of certain business developments that are of material interest and significance to the Union, the employees, and the Company."

Source: Letter of Understanding appended to the collective bargaining agreement between Ford Motor Company and the United Automobile, Aerospace and Agricultural Implement Workers of America (February 13, 1982).

Work Organization Restructuring—Links to QWL

As illustrated by the Xerox case, work reorganization became a central part of many participation processes. This occurred as a result of pressures for greater flexibility, higher quality, and lower costs. Yet altering work organization requires changing many of the practices that grew up under traditional collective bargaining. It is not surprising, therefore, that these changes do not come easily or without a great deal of internal debate within unions and companies.

Although there are many cases in which change is being introduced incrementally within existing work sites, the most significant examples of work organization restructuring are in new establishments or in ones that are being completely retrofitted with new technology or new products. In particular, examples can be found in most auto, steel, and other basic manufacturing firms, as they upgrade their facilities in an effort to be competitive with the newest nonunion and foreign producers in their industry. For example, the United Steelworkers and seven of the top eight steel firms created a series of industrywide joint training programs designed to diffuse knowledge and support for teamwork systems throughout their operations.[7]

It may be easier to see work restructuring when it occurs in a manufacturing site. Yet, now team and other new work systems are being used in many technical and service arenas. Box 12–3 describes how the labor–management partnership at Kaiser Permanente was used to jointly design and open a new hospital. The parties at Kaiser Permanente also have worked together to restructure and expand an optical laboratory in Northern California, another laboratory in Portland, Oregon, and a number of outpatient clinics in other locations. The telecommunications industry is another service-based industry where participation processes and team systems have appeared, for example, in customer service and network technician jobs.

Team-based management also has been introduced into elementary and secondary education. Although the development of new work systems is diffusing unevenly in these settings, technological and other pressures are leading to the spread of team systems of work among white-collar jobs.[8]

In early 1998, Kaiser Permanente (KP) decided it urgently needed to open a new hospital in Baldwin Park, California. Normally, it would take approximately two years to plan and open a new hospital of this size (approximately 240 beds). Top executives at KP determined that the new hospital needed to be brought on line before the next winter's flu season began in the late fall.

Because of the existence of the Kaiser Permanente Labor Management Partnership, a decision was made to give this problem to a joint task team made up of a broad cross-section of physicians, managers, nurses, technicians, and other employees who possessed expertise in how a new hospital could work. They were given a clean sheet of paper and urged to use the consensus-based principles built into the Partnership to design a hospital that all parties would experience as a positive working and healthcare environment. In April 1998, a labor–management team of more than 150 employees took up this task. They brought in those employees and managers from other medical centers who were considered leaders at their particular specialties. The parties engaged in training on problem solving and interest-based decision making, visited GM's Saturn and other innovative organizations to assess different models of joint participation and co-management, and

participated in what they called a five day "Blitz Week" of intensive discussions about how to design the flow of patient care.

The parties designed a hospital that focused on patient-centered care, so that much equipment was available at bedside rather than in specialized areas that required patient transport and coordination. For instance, telemetry units, often located only in critical care units, were installed in every room, making the hospital's capacity both greater and more flexible than many other hospitals. In the end they were successful in designing and opening an innovative, staffed, and well-designed, hospital in a virtually unheard of eight months. By opening in October, they beat the onslaught of the winter's flu season. Dr. Oliver Goldsmith, medical director for the Permanente Medical Group's Southern California region, remarked:

> This is probably the most significant venture we will do inside Kaiser Permanente over the next decade. It will serve as a building block for what lies ahead.

Source: Thomas A. Kochan, Susan Eaton, and Robert B. McKersie, "The Kaiser Permanente Labor Management Partnership: The First Five Years," unpublished manuscript, MIT Sloan School of Management, 2002.

The Links between Teamwork, Participation, and Work Restructuring

Teamwork systems require a fundamental reorganization of workplace relations because they replace multiple and narrow job classifications with jobs that are broader in scope, that involve workers in making discretionary judgments, and that require investments in training. Typically, work teams do their own inspections since they must take responsibility for quality performance. In some cases the teams also do their own scheduling, task assignment, certification of workers' skill levels, material handling, housekeeping, and routine repair work. Team and other participatory meetings also provide a forum for the sharing of information on financial performance and business matters.

In some auto plants under a pay-for-knowledge plan workers are required to be proficient at two different jobs in the work area. If the workers can perform five different jobs in their work area, they receive 30 cents more per hour; they receive another 30 cents more per hour if they can perform eight different jobs in their work area and another 30 cents per hour if they are proficient at all the jobs in their work area. Under pay-for-knowledge schemes workers are paid their skill rate each day regardless of whether they are actually assigned to a job that requires the use of their level of skill.

New Roles for Supervisors

Traditional supervisors often are replaced with team leaders who are sometimes, but not always, members of the bargaining unit rather than members of the first line of management. In some cases, such as the Saturn Corporation, union and nonunion team leaders are paired as "partners" who share responsibility for managing and supporting work teams. When this occurs the number of traditional supervisors is reduced proportionately (or more). The evidence is that these types of team-based supervisory relationships work best when the partners share a common view of their goals and responsibilities and share equally in managing both the people and production-related duties.[9]

The Expansion to Co-Management

In some team plants there exists a top "administrative" team, which includes the plant manager and the chairman of the local union's bargaining committee, giving the union access to a broad array of financial and other strategic information as a matter of course and a significant role in the governance of the organization. One key to the success of this type of arrangement is local union participation in the initial design of the plant's new organizational structure.

Managing the Overlap between Participation, Work Restructuring, and Collective Bargaining

As participatory processes expand and become meshed in work restructuring, a union that represents workers at such a site faces a challenge regarding how to manage and coordinate the overlap. On the one hand, unions are tempted to try to maintain a clear and sharp separation between participatory activities and collective bargaining procedures and issues. Drawing such a separation can help the union leadership, particularly when a participatory program has just begun and some workers (or union officers) remain skeptical of the program's objectives and implications. One way the parties try to accomplish this separation, for example, is through the adoption of a rule declaring that during team meetings workers cannot raise issues that are normally dealt with through the grievance procedure or the collective bargaining agreement.

Although separating participatory processes and collective bargaining issues might make sense in this early phase, over time if the participatory process matures, the line between collective bargaining and participatory process blurs. In the Xerox case described in Box 12–1, for example, in their effort to lower production costs the wire harness study team began to make recommendations that altered job descriptions and transfer rights.

The same separation principle was followed in the initial stages of the Kaiser Permanente partnership, however, the parties quickly realized that they needed to bring collective bargaining into their joint efforts. The triggering event was a strike in Portland, Oregon. Labor and management leaders recognized that they could not sustain their partnership efforts if each time a local union and management negotiated a labor agreement they did so in a traditional fashion with the potential of a strike. Both the Xerox and Kaiser Permanente cases illustrate a general point: some way of integrating contract negotiations with ongoing participation and partnership processes must be found if the joint effort is to be sustained for any length of time.

Changes in Contractual Procedures that Emerge from Participation

As unions and workers participate more directly in decisions, labor and management often find that the formal procedures outlined in the labor agreement become less important. In some firms as team meetings begin to tackle serious issues they become a forum for workers to air complaints. The parties then make alterations that might otherwise be processed through the grievance procedure.

As an illustration of modification of the grievance procedure, Box 12–4 describes how the Dayton Power and Light Company and the Utility Workers Union radically altered the language governing the resolution of grievances. The language described in this box grew out of a broad transformation that occurred in the relationship between Dayton Power management and their union and work force. In 1986 labor and management at Dayton Power replaced their 114-page labor agreement with a "Compact" that was only 13 pages long. In that compact the issue resolution procedures outlined in Box 12–4 replaced the traditional four-step grievance procedure previously used at the firm.

The three-year compact adopted in 1986 (and renewed in 1989) at Dayton Power also introduced a no-layoff clause and a new incentive pay system that paid workers bonuses if the performance of their work area exceeded a target. A 1993–1998 contract extended the no-layoff language for another six years. This contract provided lump-sum wage increases in lieu of base wage increases and also established separate lower wage scales for new hires.[10] All these contractual changes were accompanied by a shift in the management of the company that decentralized authority into service areas. Events at Dayton Power illustrate how increased worker and union participation can be linked to changes in the labor agreement and managerial practices.

An Issue for Unions: How Far to Go in Lessening Formal Rules and Procedures

The unions at the sites described above want to allow the participatory process to evolve and to produce the very kind of innovations that can lead to improved cost competitiveness and employment security. Yet the unions also do not want to abandon the important roles that remain for the grievance procedure and formal negotiations.

How then can a union maintain a proper balance between direct worker involvement in decisions and the union's representation responsibilities? The answer seems to lie in a shift in union and union officer roles. The union must allow participation to proceed, but must continuously coordinate and oversee this process and the connections to collective bargaining. This requires that union committee persons, for example, stay in tune with what transpires in any team meetings in their jurisdiction. The union also should discuss the participatory programs at union meetings and report about any role the union plays in participatory activities in the union newsletter and other official communication channels.

A number of cases show that if the union ignores or maintains an arm's-length distance to a participatory process, at some point a confrontation develops or the participatory process withers. This may be just the outcome a union opposed to participation wants, but for unions that support participation, it can be an unfortunate development.

The following language appears in the 1989–1993 collective bargaining agreement of the Dayton Power and Light Company and the Utility Workers Union of America, Local 175. This language appears in the section of the contract entitled "issue resolution." This language replaces the traditional four-step grievance procedure outlined in previous labor agreements between these parties.

The success of our mutual relations under this agreement depends on our commitment to address issues in a fair and responsible way. It is a matter of trust. It is the method we have chosen to avoid an agreement of rigid and unnecessary detail which hinders both management freedom and employee opportunity. Through mutual pledges to approach concerns in a problem-solving manner, we have established the following procedures for issues which arise among us.

A. *Unlimited Referral*—There is no limit on the nature of issues which may be referred to this process by employees, the Union, or the Company. The process will be used to advance positive ideas as well as to examine perceived wrongs. The only qualifications are that the affected person(s) certify the issue as a responsible one of genuine concern and thereafter participate first hand in its resolution. Employees will be paid scheduled rates for work time required for issue resolution. Union representatives may participate as they choose in any phase of issue resolution.

B. *Procedure*—An issue should be addressed promptly between the affected person and those with the resources and authority to resolve the issue. The initiator and responder have the responsibility for introducing the issue constructively, for identifying the necessary participants and resources for the resolution of the issue, and any further necessary interaction to resolve the issue.

If not resolved within twenty (20) days, the issue will be jointly defined in writing and referred to the appropriate management and Union personnel to review the process/issue before the issue may be referred to mediation.

C. *Mediation*—The Mediation Panel will be composed of a Union representative, a Company representative and a neutral Umpire. No issue shall be referred to arbitration until the neutral Umpire and one other panel member certify they have failed to handle the matter satisfactorily.

D. *Arbitration*—Upon failure of mediation, the neutral Umpire shall reconvene the panel as arbitrators and conduct such hearing as is required, with the Umpire serving as the neutral Arbitrator. The Arbitrators shall have no power to add to or subtract from or modify the terms of this agreement. The Arbitration Panel shall announce their decision or resolution as speedily as possible in writing, and it shall be binding upon the parties. The parties shall bear their own costs of mediation and arbitration. The neutral Umpire's fee will be split equally between the Union and the Company.

E. *Discharge Cases*—Employee discharge cases shall be referred directly to the appropriate Company officer, and may be subject to mediation upon mutual agreement. The mediation Umpire shall not serve as a discharge Arbitrator. Arbitrators for discharge cases will normally be selected through the Federal Mediation and Conciliation Service.

Source: *The Compact,* Local 175, UWUA, AFL-CIO and the Dayton Power and Light Company, November 1, 1989, pp. 5–6.

New Union Roles

Union oversight and coordination of participatory processes can be assisted through joint steering committees or planning boards. In addition, individuals who serve in the role of facilitators in joint activities play a critical role in mediating any tensions that arise. Some of the best facilitators are former union officers as these people tend to be well respected by the work force and adept at fashioning compromises. The net result is the creation of a complex set of committees and new jobs (e.g., facilitators) that serve to bridge and coordinate participation, work restructuring, and collective bargaining. The simultaneous expansion of so many joint activities has combined to bring a restructuring of the job responsibilities of union representatives. In many unionized settings, union officers now spend as much (or even more) of their time in joint activities than they do in traditional arm's-length activities characterized by opposing labor–management interests.

This trend has led to changes in job titles and job funding. With the expansion of joint activities, there are many more union jobs in which the jobholder's responsibility is to function as a facilitator. Many of these positions are funded out of jointly managed funds.

At the same time, union leaders run considerable political risks and put the joint effort at risk as well if they become so involved in managing their participatory process that they lose sight of their responsibilities to represent member interests in grievance handling or other day-to-day developments. In essence a new role for union leaders is developing that requires them to balance their different responsibilities. Box 12–5 summarizes the nature of the balancing act that Saul Rubinstein identified in his studies of the changing role of local union leaders. The union's coordinating role (and balancing act) becomes ever more important where the participatory process evolves to the point that it includes strategic business issues.

The Expansion of Joint Activities

As participatory programs expand to include discussion of work organization, they become one among a growing number of joint activities operating in contemporary unionized settings. Other joint activities commonly in existence in unionized settings include employee assistance programs (alcohol and drug abuse counseling and assistance), health and safety committees, absentee programs, training and education activities, and community service programs. These programs are all joint as each is administered (and often funded) by both union and management representatives.

In service industries such as hotels or hospitals where multiemployer bargaining structures exist, these joint efforts often cut across employers. Two of the more innovative examples are the San Francisco Hotel Association and the Hotel and Restaurant Employees Union and Local 1199 of the Service Employees International Union and the New York City League of Voluntary Hospitals. Both of these efforts are funded out of allocations negotiated in collective bargaining. They provide a wide range of services relevant to the workers and their families in these bargaining units, including immigration assistance, child care, and job-related education and training.

Many of these joint programs started long before the expansion of participatory processes. Nevertheless, the economic and social pressures that are leading to an expansion in participatory processes also are prompting the expansion of other joint programs. Absentee programs, for example, also are expanding because of cost-control pressures.

How widespread are these joint efforts at the workplace? Data from the 1999 FMCS national customer survey provide some estimates. Labor and management representatives reported that approximately 26 percent of their relationships have some employee involvement, quality improvement, or team-based work system initiatives underway.[11]

Worker and Union Participation in Strategic Decisions

In some plants worker or union involvement in strategic issues comes about through formal committees such as the administrative team described earlier. In other cases workers and union officers are drawn into strategic issues on a gradual and informal basis. An example of this evolutionary expansion in roles occurs in a number of auto plants where workers and union representatives now sit on planning committees that operate at the plant level. These committees have the task of developing modifications in work rules and other manufacturing practices to keep work in the plant (and avoid outsourcing) or to help the plant win bids on new work.

In order to keep or win new business, these committees typically develop methods to reduce costs and improve product quality and customer services. Like the joint design teams at Kaiser Permanente, these committees are drawn into strategic issues as the participants gained access to financial and operating information that previously had only been available to plant management as part of efforts to develop cost-reduction strategies.

The Effects of Downsizing and Outsourcing Pressures: Heightened Concern for Employment Security

Experiences with **downsizing** and the threat that companies will outsource even more work abroad or to lower cost (and often nonunion) domestic production sites led many unions to increase their involvement in business issues. In addition, these concerns led unions to bargain for explicit employment security clauses as part of agreements that included participation programs as well as contractual concessions on pay or work rules. In the face of union concerns about declining membership, a number of agreements that promoted joint labor and management partnerships also provided for employer neutrality during union organizing campaigns and, in some cases, even card check union recognition procedures that avoided the need for representation elections. The agreements at SBC and Ford, described earlier in Chapter 6, are examples of partnership agreements that include union organizing concessions by management. Still, as will be noted on the next page, these labor–management efforts are often not able to override the pressures of international competition.

The Sources of Failure

Joint processes seldom last forever. Many fail in their early stages because either management or union leaders are unable to make the organizational and role adjustments needed to integrate joint efforts with collective bargaining, ongoing labor–management relations, or operational decisions that in the past were made solely by supervisors or middle managers. Some joint processes that have been successful for a number of years lose support when their initial management and/or labor champions and supporters retire or leave their organizations. Other joint processes, such as those at Xerox and Levi-Strauss, eventually fall victim to fundamental changes in markets or business strategies that lie beyond the influence of the joint effort. The recognition that participatory processes are vulnerable to business decisions traditionally under the control of top management is one of the reasons that some labor leaders have pressed to gain a voice in strategic management decision making.

Strategic involvement by workers or unions historically has been rare in the United States because it goes against the grain of the core principle that "management manages and unions grieve." This principle has been central to the traditional American collective bargaining system. It is only in recent years that this principle has been challenged. Some labor leaders have come to believe that effective representation of their members' long-run interests requires influencing managerial decisions before they are made rather than only addressing the effects of these decisions after the fact through collective bargaining.

How widespread is strategic involvement at the present time? The FMCS survey provides a good estimate. Approximately 35 percent of union and management respondents indicated that they had some form of "partnership to promote joint approaches for addressing strategic business issues such as new technology or products, things management has historically done alone."[12] While this is a rather general definition of strategic involvement, the data suggest that a sizable number of labor and management representatives are exploring ways to engage each other at the strategic level of their relationship.

The Types of Strategic Involvement

The mildest form of strategic interaction is that of information sharing and prior consultation between management and labor, as illustrated by the periodic meetings described above between Ford executives and union officials. More significant forms are represented by the plants described earlier where the union leader is formally included in the plant manager's administrative staff and attends management staff meetings.

Another form of involvement comes in joint strategic planning of new facilities or in implementing other major organizational changes. The governance structure of the Saturn Corporation, a subsidiary of General Motors, exhibits many of these features (see Box 12–6). What is noteworthy at Saturn is the extent to which the union (UAW) plays a role in business and strategic decisions in the plant. The local officers of the UAW at Saturn participate in a wide range of issues, including choosing parts suppliers (and considering how much union representation at these suppliers versus cost and product quality attri-butes should count in the choice process). Employees and union officers at Saturn also have had a role in planning which technologies are used in the plant complex and in decisions on how to configure the car assembly process.

ORGANIZATIONAL STRUCTURE OF SATURN:

Strategic Advisory Committee
*Does long-range planning. Consists of Saturn president and
his staff and top UAW advisor*
Manufacturing Advisory Committee
*Oversees Saturn complex. Includes company and elected union
representatives and specialists in engineering, marketing, etc.*
Business Unit
*Coordinates plant-level operations. Made up of company
representatives, elected union adviser, and specialists*
Work Unit Module
Groups of three to six work units led by a company "work unit advisor"
Work Units
Teams of 6 to 15 workers led by an elected UAW "counselor"

KEY INDUSTRIAL RELATIONS PRINCIPLES:

- Team forms of work organization with few job classifications
- Performance-based bonuses with all employees paid normal earnings on a salaried basis
- 80 percent of the workforce protected against layoffs except in case of "catastrophic" events
- Worker and union participation in decision making

Source: Memorandum of Agreement between Saturn Corporation and UAW (Detroit: General Motors Corporation, July 1985).

Worker and Union Voice in Twenty-first Century Corporations

The crisis in corporate confidence that emerged in the early years of the twenty-first century out of the accounting and executive compensation scandals in companies such as Enron, Tyco, Polaroid, Adelphi Communications, raised questions about the role that employees and their union representatives should play in corporate governance. Many employees absorbed significant losses from these scandals through lost jobs and lost retirement savings. Whether the reforms that follow in the years ahead will include an increased role for employees in monitoring top management practices and give employees a more direct voice in corporate governance remains to be seen. Given the growing importance of knowledge, skills, and human capital as a source of competitive advantage to modern corporations, this issue is likely to feature prominently in debates over the roles of employees in the twenty-first century corporation.

The Debate Surrounding Participatory Programs

There is much debate within the ranks of workers, unionists, and academicians over the nature and consequences of participatory programs. Critics of these programs argue that they do not lead to real increases in the extent of worker or union involvement in decisions.

Instead, the critics claim that the participatory programs are used by management to increase the pace and difficulty of work. These critics claim, for example, that team systems are used to put peer pressure on workers and remove the independent voice provided through union representation. To them teams and other participatory programs are part of **management by stress.**[13] The critics also argue that participatory programs are designed as a halfway house in the transition from union representation to nonunion operation.

The proponents of participatory processes see things differently. They admit that the pressure of heightened international and nonunion competition has led to increases in work pace and many pay concessions. But the proponents claim that increased worker and union participation in decision making can lead to both cost reductions and improvements in employment security, as well as more interesting work. To the proponents of participation, if a union becomes forcefully involved in a participatory process (possibly through the joint committees discussed above), the union can gain greater involvement in the very issues that are of critical importance to workers. What better way for the union to carry out its historic mission of representing workers' interests than to be involved in work restructuring and the strategic business decisions that shape workers' lives, say the proponents.

At the workplace level, the debates about participation often were not based on abstract issues, but rather dealt with very practical matters. At the Saturn complex, for example, workers argued about the role of the grievance procedure and seniority rights with some workers preferring to go back to more traditional practices. These debates extended upward in the UAW and at GM with the top officers of the union and company seeking to reign in Saturn's innovative spirit and integrate it more tightly back into the GM organizational structure and management system. By the turn of the century Saturn had evolved into a hybrid organization that maintained many of its original design principles, but operated within the small car division and structure of its parent corporation.

Although the AFL-CIO had long maintained a neutral position in these debates over work restructuring, in 1994 the federation finally came down on the side favoring expansion of partnership relationships with the statement summarized in Box 12–7.

There also continues to be extensive debate concerning whether the NLRA should be modified to spur employee involvement processes. Some of this debate has focused around the TEAM Act described in Box 12–8. It may be impossible to resolve this and other debates about participation through abstract argumentation. The test will come as participatory processes and work restructuring evolve. In the end, workers and unions will learn whether the critics or proponents are correct as a result of what they experience.

Assessing the Effects of Participatory Processes

Management seems convinced that participatory processes and work organization reforms can contribute significantly to improved productivity and product quality and service, and a number of unionists are coming to a similar judgment.

Research shows that the narrowly defined QC types of QWL programs have only small positive effects on product quality and negligible effects on productivity.[14] It is also clear that complex political dynamics and conflicts commonly emerge throughout the evolution of participatory programs and these sometimes lead unions to withdraw their support for the programs.[15]

Studies also show that the auto plants with the highest productivity and product quality are not those with the most advanced technology, but, rather, they are those that integrate their human resource strategy with their production processes.[16] Companies that tried to solve their productivity problems by focusing on technology alone tended to perform poorly, as GM did in the 1980s. In contrast, many of the best performing plants found ways to link the "humanware" and the "hardware" components of technology tightly together.[17]

Research also shows that the participatory programs are often accompanied by work rule changes. Consistent with the integration argument discussed above, evidence suggests that the biggest payouts to work rule changes occur where workers are simultaneously increasing their involvement in decision making.[18] Evidence from airlines and hospitals suggests that the same positive effects on productivity and customer service can be achieved when workplace participation is linked with flexible work rules and positive union–management relationships in negotiations.[19]

Eileen Appelbaum led a research team that conducted detailed analysis of the impacts that high performance work practices (i.e., teams, participation, and task broadening) exert on economic performance and worker outcomes in the apparel, steel, and medical instruments industry.[20] The research shows that plant performance on average was increased by work reorganization that gave workers the opportunity to gather information, participate in decisions, and intervene in work practices. The researchers also found that high performance work systems generally enhance workers' levels of organizational commitment and job satisfaction. Analyzing data from a national sample of establishments, Paul Osterman found that while high performance work practices spread substantially in the 1990s, those

On December 16, 1992, the National Labor Relations Board (NLRB) ruled that the employee action committees set up by Electromation, Inc. were equivalent to employer-dominated labor organizations. The Board concluded that the Indiana-based electronics company "hand-picked, dominated, and supported the committees" thereby imposing its own unilateral form of collective bargaining.

Five committees had been set up by Electromation management in response to employee concerns over an attendance bonus program and wage issues. Supervisors and managers served on the committees and discussed conditions of employment. A few months after the action committees had been established, the International Brotherhood of Teamsters (IBT) held a representation election at the company, at which time the company claimed to have no knowledge of an organizing effort and disbanded the action committees until after the election, which the union lost. The Board found that the committees were a labor organization because they served the purpose of dealing with the employer over conditions of employment. A clear distinction was made in the Board's opinion between lawful committees set up to address productivity and efficiency problems and those concerned with grievances, labor disputes, wages, pay, hours, or working conditions. The latter are illegal under the National Labor Relations Act (NLRA).

Although the Board acknowledged that the Electromation decision did not deem all employee participation programs illegal, many have voiced concern over the future of such programs. Soon after the decision was issued, Congressman Steve Gunderson (R–WI), backed by a number of probusiness groups and the Republican Party, introduced the Teamwork for Employees and Managers (TEAM) Act. The Act proposes to amend section 8 (a)(2) of the NLRA by adding a provision that gives management more leeway in establishing employee involvement groups. Supporters feel that employers in nonunion settings need greater latitude, in the face of increasingly horizontal organizational structures, in involving employees in business decisions and opening up lines of communication. The AFL-CIO is strongly opposed to the TEAM Act, arguing that the amendment opens the door for "sham" unions and poses a great threat to the future of union organizing.

The Act was approved by the Senate Labor and Human Resources Committee in March of 1997 but no further action has been taken. President Clinton vetoed a similar bill in 1996.

Amendments to the Act have been proposed, such as the addition of a clause prohibiting the use of employee involvement programs to impede workers' efforts to organize. The AFL-CIO continues to show discontent, however, and remains concerned over the issue of who gets to select the workers who participate in involvement committees. The AFL also points out that while the proposed bill would prohibit the creation of teams once 30 percent of employees had signed a union election petition, teams could still be formed so long as the organizing activity was not the motivating factor for establishment. The labor community finds this unacceptable.

The TEAM Act remains a priority issue for the Republican Party and many probusiness groups.

Sources: Various articles taken from *Daily Labor Report,* 1992–1997.

practices led to less than rosy outcomes for workers. Osterman found that high performance work systems introduced in the 1990s did not reduce layoffs nor did they lead to pay gains for workers.[21]

Yet we must be extremely careful not to overgeneralize from the small number of research studies in this area. Furthermore, research must be careful to isolate the effects of participation from the many other changes that often are occurring simultaneously, such as the introduction of new technology. Clearly, further research is needed to reach definitive conclusions on the effects of worker and union participation.

Board Representation and Employee Ownership

Union Representation on a Company's Board of Directors

Formal representation on the board of directors of a company is another way unions have achieved involvement in strategic business decisions. Starting with the addition of a UAW representative to Chrysler's board as part of the federal government's loan guarantees in 1980, a number of firms added union representatives to their boards in return for union concessions in other areas of the contract. In all of these cases the union in question represented a significant number of the firm's employees at the time board representation was granted.

Employee participation on the board of Rath Packing Company was not successful as Rath eventually went out of business, which ended the experiment with employee board representation. Nevertheless, Rath is an interesting case because it illustrates some of the complex dynamics associated with union representation on a company board and the difficulties board representation poses for union leadership. In the Rath case a former union officer at one point became the chief executive of the company and in that role had difficulty convincing workers at Rath of the need for subsequent pay and other concessions. Eastern Airlines at one stage also experienced a period of union representation on its board, eventually went out of business, and has some parallels to the Rath case.

It would be wrong to conclude from Rath or Eastern Airlines that board representation is doomed to fail. But we do know that union influence on the employer's board of directors ultimately will require new communication and managerial skills and technical knowledge on the part of the worker representatives.

The evidence suggests that board membership by unions or employees on its own does not yield substantial payouts for workers or employers. To have lasting, positive results, this initiative has to be linked to the changes in collective bargaining and at the workplace that are discussed in other parts of this chapter.

Employee Ownership

A more radical form of workplace participation is that which follows after employees purchase a business from their employer. In some cases employee buyouts occurred in the face of impending plant shutdowns. Overcoming their initial skepticism about **employee ownership,** unions in recent years have in a number of cases promoted employee ownership as a way to improve employee job security. The employee buyout of United Airlines, through an employee stock ownership plan (ESOP), produced the largest employee-owned company in the United States. Yet, as Box 12–9 describes, it is not clear that employee ownership of United Airlines has had significant positive effects on either employee morale or corporate performance.

The Views of the Labor Movement toward Employee Ownership

As in the case of codetermination, the labor movement traditionally has for the most part been unenthusiastic about employee ownership as a means of averting threatened plant shutdowns. The objections raised typically mention both economic and organizational concerns. The union leaders' chief organizational concern is that their members' perceived need for the union will wither away under an employee-owned firm, since the

On July 12, 1994, United Airlines became the largest employee-owned company in the United States. The employee stock ownership plan (ESOP) was formulated by top management, directors, and union leaders. Under the terms of the agreement certain United employee groups will give up $4.9 billion in wages and work rule changes over nearly six years in return for 55 percent equity stake in the company.

The ESOP emerged from a fiscal crisis facing United. United realized that it had to either implement a large-scale downsizing effort eliminating many jobs or create a new cost eliminating relationship with its workers.

It is not clear that employee ownership had positive effects on employee morale or corporate performance at United Airlines. In the aftermath of the September 11, 2001, terrorist attacks, airlines struggled to cope with greatly reduced passenger volumes and additional security expenses. After suffering $4 billion in losses from the spring of 2001 through the fall of 2002, United Airlines filed for bankruptcy in early December 2002. This filing came after the Air Transportation Stabilization Board

(created by the U.S. Congress after September 11 to help U.S. airlines) rejected the company's bid for $1.8 billion in federal loan guarantees. In preparing its application to the Stabilization Board, United had received pledges of support for $5.2 billion in concessions from its five labor unions and an internal group representing salaried and management personnel. United kept flying after filing for bankruptcy and pledged to use the bankruptcy process to restructure and recover.

United Airline's unions stated that they were disappointed, but not surprised, by the bankruptcy filing. Leaders of the Airline Pilots Association (ALPA), which represents 9,000 pilots at United, pledged their support for an orderly bankruptcy process and prepared for negotiations with the company and the courts. Analysts speculated that United Airlines' employee owners would have little to show for their investments if, and when, the airline emerges from bankruptcy.

Source: "United Airlines Finally Files for Bankruptcy; Imposes Immediate Management Pay Cuts," *Daily Labor Report* 237, December 10, 2002:B1.

employees would essentially be bargaining against themselves. Yet, as in the United case described above, unions recently have viewed employee ownership as a potentially favorable alternative.

One of the reasons unions have changed their views about employee ownership is that the empirical evidence shows that member support for a union involved in an employee-owned firm has remained strong in nearly all the cases reported. Several studies have examined the effects of employee ownership on workers' attitudes toward their union and on the union as a bargaining organization.[22]

The major conclusions to emerge from these case studies are that (1) the majority of employees still believe there is a strong need for union representation; (2) the role of the union changes in that it becomes a quasi-partner in making some of the strategic decisions the union would not have made under its former status; (3) the collective bargaining process remains an important decision-making forum within the organization; (4) the majority of blue-collar workers still prefer to see the bargaining process handle the traditional issues of wages and fringe benefits; and (5) new forums for decision making outside of collective bargaining often arise.

The major economic reasons for union leaders' opposition to employee takeovers are that the ventures create pressures to cut wages and fringe benefits in order to save jobs. Union leaders are also concerned with the effects any concessions at the plants would have on wage levels in other unionized firms in the industry.

Union leaders worry that employee takeovers encourage worker investments in the oldest, least profitable, and least-likely-to-succeed plants in private industry. The leaders argue that if the plant could be made profitable, either the existing employer would not want to pull out or other forms of private capital could be attracted to take over the plant and save the jobs. Nevertheless, many unions have become convinced that through appropriate safeguards and diligence they can prevent these harmful occurrences from surfacing in employee-owned firms. The bottom line still is that unions support employee ownership as a way to save jobs.[23]

As to whether employee-owned firms also promote industrial democracy, the jury is still out. Although more democratic decision-making methods and structures have developed in some employee-owned firms, a traditional division of labor between managers and line workers still remained in many employee-owned firms. And the workers continued to perceive this division as legitimate and necessary to the success of the enterprise. At the same time, however, the evidence shows the majority of blue-collar and white-collar workers wished they had had more influence over decisions that affected their jobs than they were given under the employee-owned firms.[24]

The Impact of Worker Ownership on Economic Performance

Finally, an extremely interesting and important question is whether worker-owned firms outperform other firms.[25] The available evidence from other sites suggests that firm performance improves in those employee-owned firms in which employee involvement in decisions is broadened.[26]

Employee ownership appears to work best in small firms where the workforce is relatively stable and committed to the community and to the organization, and where the workers are skilled enough to be able to improve plant productivity and economic performance through higher motivation and higher levels of individual and group performance.

Participation through Industrywide Labor–Management Committees

In some highly competitive industries that involve numerous employers and a single union or a small number of unions, industrywide **labor–management committees** historically were used to discuss problems of mutual interest. Those committees represented early efforts by unions to participate in issues of broad (strategic) concern outside of formal collective bargaining processes.

The Textile Industry Case

In the men's clothing industry the Tailored Clothing Technology Corporation (TC 2) program has been under way since 1980.[27] This project represents a dramatic example of a union's (the Amalgamated Clothing and Textile Workers Union, ACTWU) becoming involved at a very early and basic stage in a research and development effort to mechanize production to help stem the flow of imported goods. In contrast, most unions in the United States limit their involvement with new technology to its consequences—that is, they seek to address technology only after management has made the strategic decision to introduce it.

The ACTWU and the International Ladies' Garment Workers' Union (both now part of UNITE-HERE) have been involved in strategic matters throughout the history of the garment and textile industries. These industries are characterized by having many small employers and substantial ease of market entry (and also substantial involuntary exit). The union has historically served as a stabilizing force in the organized portions of these industries. During the early 1900s, for example, the unions provided technical assistance in running many of the small shops on a modern basis.[28] By doing this they were able to transform what otherwise would have been a proliferation of sweatshops into enterprises capable of providing a living wage and acceptable working conditions.

A labor–management committee also has been at work in the men and boys tailored clothing (suits and sport coats) industry. The committee was formed after the 1987 contract negotiations had reached an impasse over the question of whether to allow unionized firms to import garments from abroad in addition to manufacturing in the United States. A joint committee worked on this issue for two years with the help of an outside facilitator and a grant from the Federal Mediation and Conciliation Service.

An agreement eventually was reached that provided for an experimental program in which firms were allowed to import a fraction of their production in return for employment guarantees and a commitment to reinvest in their U.S. manufacturing facilities. The committee is now working on new approaches to recruitment, training, compensation, and the organization of work. Thus, the long tradition of union-management cooperation continues in this industry despite (or perhaps because of) the intense international competition that faces the parties.

Industrywide committees are often far removed from the attitudes and behaviors of individual employers, local union officials, and rank-and-file workers. Consequently, their efforts to introduce employee and union participation change must be supplemented with efforts at the workplace level. The committees can be very useful, however, in drawing links between participation and formal bargaining processes.

Summary

Although efforts to achieve change and improvements in labor management relations through participatory processes represent a departure from the traditional collective bargaining system, experience suggests that they cannot operate in isolation from collective bargaining. Collective bargaining reforms seem to work best when they are associated with consistent changes across all three levels of industrial relations activity; that is, workplace changes must be reinforced by changes at the collective bargaining and strategic levels, and the same is true for changes at the other two levels.

The ultimate success of employee involvement processes and other workplace reform efforts depends on the ability of the organization to reinforce and sustain high levels of trust. That trust, in turn, depends heavily on the extent to which the strategies and events unfolding at the higher levels of the industrial relations system are consistent with and linked to the development of greater trust at the workplace.

To achieve tangible rewards, the expansion of worker participatory programs and the introduction of new forms of work organization have often been accompanied by changes in the contract terms negotiated in collective bargaining. The expansion of shop-floor worker participation has also been spurred by increased worker and union involvement in strategic issues. This involvement is critical because it both assures the unions that worker participation is not a step toward the demise of union representation and helps convince workers and the union that enhanced employment security will follow.

But expansion of the process to the strategic level of decision making does not occur easily or automatically. Management tends to closely guard its control over issues that have traditionally been viewed as its prerogatives. Thus a strong union presence and active union support for the process are essential. Nonunion firms and firms with weak unions are unlikely to develop or sustain a full form of worker participation.

Strategic involvement by employees or unions still occurs in isolated cases and probably will diffuse only gradually. Significant internal debate and conflict within management and labor ranks still exists over the wisdom of taking on these new roles. Opponents within the labor movement cite fears that unions will be co-opted into supporting managerially controlled and potentially unpopular decisions. These critics believe that union independence will be compromised and rank-and-file dissent will grow. And managers who are not committed to allowing workers or unions greater participation in strategic decisions may be an even more formidable barrier.

Only in crisis settings or settings in which unions have both the strength and the desire to demand greater involvement in managerial issues has participation extended beyond a single issue or a short period of time. Furthermore, union involvement at the strategic level has generally emerged only in settings in which unions already represent a large percentage of the firm's workforce.

It is difficult to confidently make predictions about the future course of increased union and worker involvement in business decisions. In some cases when labor and management confronted tough economic and political problems participation programs that began with much fanfare faded as acrimonious conflict returned to labor–management relations. At the same time, at a number of sites, extensive employee and union involvement has survived over the last 20 years, even in the face of difficult economic pressures that tested the resolve of labor and management.

Piecemeal programs are often short lived. Yet, participatory processes that changed the roles of workers and managers and institutionalized these new roles in concrete practices have proven successful. The growing number of deep participatory relationships such as Saturn, Kaiser Permanente, San Francisco Hotels, and New York City Hospitals suggest that in a number of firms labor and management in this country are fundamentally changing the nature of collective bargaining.

Discussion Questions

1. Give a brief overview of how participatory programs evolved in the union sector from the 1970s on.

2. Participatory programs provide challenges to unions and their leaders. Discuss how unions might be able to manage the overlapping roles of participation, work restructuring, and collective bargaining.

3. Participatory programs have been the subject of much debate. Briefly describe this debate.

4. How do labor leaders and unions generally view employee ownership?

Related Web Sites

Kaiser Permanente:
http://www.kptx.org/background.html

Amalgamated Clothing and Textile Worker Union (ACTWU) & Union of Needletrades, Industrial and Textile Employees (UNITE):
http://www.uniteunion.org/whatisunite/unionisborn/unionis born.html

http://www.ilr.cornell.edu/lib/bookshelf/Hottopics/UNITE/UNITE_Merger/KeyEvents_ILGWU.html

National Commission on Production and Quality of Life:
http://fatty.law.cornell.edu/uscode/15/ch51.html

Suggested Readings

Appelbaum, Eileen, Thomas Bailey, Peter Berg, and Arne L. Kalleberg, *Manufacturing Advantage: Why High Performance Work Systems Pay Off* (Ithaca, NY: ILR Press, 2000).

Bluestone, Barry, and Irving Bluestone. *Negotiating the Future* (New York, Basic Books, 1992)

Cooke, William N. *Labor-Management Cooperation: New Partnerships or Going in Circles?* (Kalamazoo, MI: W. E. Upjohn Institute for Employment Research, 1990).

Klingel, Sally, and Ann Martin, eds. *A Fighting Chance: New Strategies to Save Jobs and Reduce Costs* (Ithaca, NY: ILR Press, 1989).

Kochan, Thomas A., Harry C. Katz, and Robert B. McKersie. *The Transformation of American Industrial Relations* 2d ed. (Ithaca, NY: ILR Press, 1994).

Whyte, William Foote, Tove Helland Hammer, Christopher B. Meek, Reed Nelson, and Robert N. Stern. *Worker Participation and Ownership: Cooperative Strategies for Strengthening Local Economies* (Ithaca, NY: ILR Press, 1983).

End Notes

1. *Work in America*, A Report of a Special Task Force to the Secretary of Health, Education and Welfare (Cambridge, MA: MIT Press, 1973).

2. "GAO Report Finds Productivity Center's Accomplishments Limited," *Daily Labor Report* 103, May 26, 1978, pp. A5–A6.

3. Thomas A. Kochan, Harry C. Katz, and Robert B. McKersie, *The Transformation of American Industrial Relations*, 2d ed. (Ithaca, NY: ILR Press, 1994), pp. 62–65.

4. See, for example, Edward E. Lawler III and Susan Mohrman, "Quality Circles after the Fad," *Harvard Business Review* 63 (January–February 1985): 64–71.

5. For a full case study of events at Xerox, see Joel Cutcher-Gershenfeld, "New Path toward Organizational Effectiveness and Institutional Security: The Case of Xerox Corporation and the Amalgamated Clothing and Textile Workers Union," report to the Bureau of Labor Management Relations and Cooperative Programs, U.S. Department of Labor, 1987.

6. See Joel Cutcher-Gershenfeld, "The Impact on Economic Performance of a Transformation in Workplace Relations," *Industrial and Labor Relations Review* 44 (January 1991): 241–60.

7. "Steelmakers Want To Make Teamwork an Institution," *BusinessWeek,* May 11, 1987, p. 84.

8. See Stephen R. Barley, "Technology as an Occasion for Structuring: Evidence from Observations of CT Scanners and the Social Order of Radiology Departments," *Administrative Science Quarterly* 31 (March 1986): 78–108.

9. Saul A. Rubinstein, "The Impact of Co-Management on Quality Performance: The Case of the Saturn Corporation," *Industrial and Labor Relations Review* 53 (January 2000): 197–218.

10. The 1993–1998 contract between Dayton Power and the Utility Workers Union is described in *Daily Labor Report,* Bureau of National Affairs, December 29, 1993, p. D–5.

11. Thomas A. Kochan and Joel Cutcher-Gershenfeld, "Taking Stock: Collective Bargaining at the Turn of the Century," unpublished manuscript, MIT Sloan School of Management, July 2002.

12. Ibid.

13. The term *management by stress* is used by Mike Parker and Jane Slaughter in *Choosing Sides: Unions and the Team Concept* (Boston: South End Press, 1988). Also see Guillermo J. Grenier, *Inhuman Relations: Quality Circles and Anti-Unionism in American Industry* (Philadelphia: Temple University Press, 1988).

14. See, for example, Harry C. Katz, Thomas A. Kochan, and Kenneth R. Gobeille, "Industrial Relations Performance, Economic Performance, and QWL Programs: An Interplant Analysis," *Industrial and Labor Relations Review* 37 (October 1983): 3–17; and Peter Cappelli and David Neumark, "Do 'High-Performance' Work Practices

Improve Establishment-Level Outcomes?" *Industrial and Labor Relations Review* 54 (July 2001): 737–75.

15. Paul S. Goodman, *Assessing Organizational Change: The Rushton Quality of Work Experiment* (New York: Wiley-Interscience, 1979).

16. John Paul MacDuffie and John F. Krafcik, "Flexible Production Systems and Manufacturing Performance," in *Transforming Organizations* ed. Thomas A. Kochan and Michael Useem (New York: Oxford University Press, 1991).

17. Haruo Shimada and John Paul MacDuffie, "Industrial Relations and Humanware," Sloan School of Management Working Paper (Cambridge: Massachusetts Institute of Technology, 1987).

18. Harry C. Katz, Thomas A. Kochan, and Jeffrey H. Keefe, "Industrial Relations and Productivity in the U.S. Automobile Industry," *Brookings Papers on Economic Activity,* vol. 3, 1987, pp. 685–715, and Cutcher-Gershenfeld, "The Impact on Economic Performance."

19. Jody Gittell, Kittell, Andrew vonNordenflycht, and Thomas A. Kochan, "Mutual Gains or Zero Sum: The Effects of Labor Relations on Performance in the Airline Industry," working paper, MIT Sloan School of Management, 2002.

20. Eileen, Appelbaum, Thomas Bailey, Peter Berg, and Arne L. Kalleberg, *Manufacturing Advantage: Why High Performance Work Systems Pay Off* (Ithaca, NY: ILR Press, 2000).

21. Paul Osterman, "Work Re-organization in an Era of Restructuring: Trends in Diffusion and Effects on Employee Welfare," *Industrial and Labor Relations Review* 53 (January 2000): 179–96.

22. See, for example, Joseph Blasi, *Employee Ownership: Revolution or Ripoff?* (Cambridge, MA: Ballinger, 1988).

23. Tove Hammer and Robert Stern, "Democracy in Work Organizations," unpublished manuscript, NYSSILR, 1983.

24. Tove H. Hammer and Robert N. Stern, "Employee Ownership: Implications for the Organizational Distribution of Power," *Academy of Management Journal* 23 (March 1980): 78–100.

25. One of the difficulties in answering this question is that worker-owned firms may tend to be those that were already in poor health when the employees bought them. Thus, to succeed in identifying the independent influence of worker ownership, researchers need to control fully for the influence of other factors that influence organizational performance, but this is very hard to do.

26. Conte and Tannenbaum examined 98 U.S. and Canadian firms whose employees held substantial amounts of their employer's stock shares and found a strong relationship between the amount of equity held by nonmanagerial employees and company profit levels. See Michael Conte and Arnold Tannenbaum, "Employee-owned Companies: Is the Difference Measurable?" *Monthly Labor Review* (July 1978): 23–28.

27. See Kochan, Katz and McKersie, *The Transformation,* pp. 187–89.

28. See Jesse Thomas Carpenter, *Competition and Collective Bargaining in the Needle Trades, 1960–1967* (Ithaca: New York State School of Industrial and Labor Relations, Cornell University, 1972); and Steven Fraser, "Dress Rehearsal for the New Deal: Shop Floor Insurgents, Political Elites, and Industrial Democracy," in *Working Class America,* ed. Michael A. Frisch and Daniel J. Walkowitz (Urbana: University of Illinois Press, 1983), pp. 212–55.

Part

Special Topics

5

13

Collective Bargaining in the Public Sector

Collective bargaining has spread rapidly in the public sector since the early 1960s, to the point that, today, 36.2 percent of federal, state, and local government employees are represented by a union. This alone makes the public sector experience worthy of a separate chapter in this book—especially at a time when, each year, a smaller fraction of private sector employees have union representation.

This chapter applies the general framework developed in the previous chapters to examine industrial relations in the public sector. It is important to recognize at the outset, however, that the public sector is a special case of bargaining and employment practice. Government is not just an employer and a provider of services, but a provider of public services, and as such the public sector bargaining system must be particularly responsive to the demands of the public.

There has been much debate about the appropriate legal regulation of public sector collective bargaining. Some analysts have argued that the unique nature of government as an employer makes collective bargaining, as traditionally practiced in the private sector, inappropriate for the public sector. Other observers would allow the traditional type of collective bargaining, but in a shape and form adapted to meet the special circumstances of the public sector.

The first section of this chapter examines the historical phases through which public sector bargaining has passed. The following sections review the practice and outcomes of public sector bargaining and consider how bargaining in the public sector actually compares with bargaining in the private sector. The text then considers on normative grounds whether the legal regulation of public sector unions should be different from that of private sector bargaining.

The Evolution of Public Sector Collective Bargaining

The percentage of all federal, state, and local government employees who were members of unions underwent dramatic growth in the 1960s and early 1970s, rising from 12.8 in 1960 to 20.6 in 1974. Other public employees had joined associations, such as the National Education Association, many of which also engaged in collective bargaining by the 1970s.

EXHIBIT 13–1
Public Sector Union Membership, 2005*

Source: Data are taken from Courtney D. Gifford, *Directory of U.S. Labor Organizations,* 2005 Edition (Washington, DC: Bureau of National Affairs, 2005), Part III.

Teachers	
Education Association; National (Ind.)	2,679,396
Teachers; American Federation of (AFL-CIO)	816,300
University Professors; American Association of (Ind.)	43,183
State and Local Government	
State, County and Municipal Employees; American Federation of (AFL-CIO)	1,350,000
Police; Fraternal Order of (Ind.) (1998)	261,551
Postal Service	
Postal Workers Union; American (AFL-CIO)	239,147
Letter Carriers; National Association of (AFL-CIO)	290,109
Federal Government	
Government Employees; American Federation of (AFL-CIO)	204,282
Treasury Employees Union; National (Ind.)	77,806

*Data for all independent organizations are estimates for 2001 taken from *Directory of U.S. Labor Organizations,* 2001 Edition, pp. 41–63.

By 1974, 37.7 percent of all public employees were members of a bargaining organization (whether it was a union or an association that engaged in collective bargaining).[1] Exhibit 13–1 shows the estimated public sector membership of unions whose membership predominantly is employed in the public sector.

The 1960s and Early 1970s: The Era of Growth

Factors that contributed to the expansion of public sector unionism in the 1960s and 1970s included the growth in government budgets throughout the 1960s and early 1970s, the example of civil disobedience set by civil rights and other groups in the 1960s, and the passage of laws favorable to public sector collective bargaining.

The Mid- and Late 1970s: The Taxpayers' Revolt

The economic environment for public sector bargaining, however, tightened sharply in the mid-1970s as a consequence of slowdowns in the economy and in response to a conservative political tide that questioned the value of many government expenditures. A number of state and local governments had begun to face major fiscal problems. Moreover, taxpayer resistance to public expenditures created a backlash against public employees and reduced the political influence of public sector employee organizations.

New York City, the prime example of the fiscal crises of the cities in the 1970s, hovered on the brink of bankruptcy for several years. Eventually, the city accepted an emergency financial control board composed of representatives of the state government, private sector, unions, and the federal government. Between 1974 and 1979 the number of employees on the city payroll declined through a combination of layoffs and attrition.[2]

Other cities faced similar fiscal crises.[3] In the fall of 1975 voters in San Francisco altered municipal procedures in a number of ways to the detriment of city employees.[4] Wage and pension-setting procedures were modified, and city craft workers received pay cuts that averaged $2,000 and went as high as $4,500 annually for some workers. Those craft workers then went on strike but were resoundingly defeated, returning to work a month later under management's salary terms.

New York's and San Francisco's financial problems received tremendous national attention and helped fuel taxpayer resistance to further growth in public budgets. As a result, nine states adopted new tax or spending limitations. The most widely publicized example, California's Proposition 13, was approved by the voters in 1979. This constitutional amendment limited property taxes to 1 percent of the real market value and tax increases to 2 percent per year.[5]

Although public sector employers may have grown more resistant to union demands in the mid- and late 1970s, they did not aggressively try to remove their unions. In this way, the institutions of collective bargaining in the public sector have exhibited much more stability than have their counterparts in the private sector.

The Early 1980s: The PATCO Strike

The one important exception to union stability in the public sector was the Professional Air Traffic Controllers Organization (PATCO). In August 1981 PATCO led its members on a strike. The controllers wanted their employer, the federal government, to increase their wages and benefits. President Reagan then fired the strikers on the grounds they had violated a no-strike clause in their employment contract. The government called in military controllers who, along with supervisors and some controllers who crossed picket lines, kept the air traffic system functioning (though limits were imposed on certain flights).

The Federal Labor Relations Authority eventually decertified the union. (In 1987 the new controllers voted in a new union.) Some analysts argue that the firing of the controllers had enormous ramifications by legitimizing a hard line in bargaining by other public and private sector employers. During the Clinton Administration the strikers were offered their jobs back and a few of them returned to work.

The Mid- and Late 1980s: Institutional Stability and Some Gains

The firing of PATCO strikers may have contributed to the wave of concessionary bargaining that occurred in the private sector in the 1980s. Nevertheless, it is important to note that public sector collective bargaining underwent a relatively calm period in the 1980s. In part, this stability resulted from the absence of extreme economic pressures. Public sector unions did not face international competition, and the growth of alternative nonunion suppliers was modest in the public sector in comparison with what confronted many private sector unions.

Furthermore, public sector management did not use strategic business actions or in other ways exert pressure for radical changes in the process of collective bargaining to the extent that occurred in the private sector. Team systems of work and new forms of direct communication between supervisors and workers, for example, were diffused in the public sector much less widely than in the private sector.

By the mid-1980s, the political tide had begun to turn back in favor of the public sector. Some politicians and observers were claiming that cutbacks in government spending had gone too far.

At the same time, public attention was turning to the problems in American primary and secondary education. Many newspaper editorials argued that weaknesses in the nation's schools, particularly in comparison with Japanese schools, were contributing to American trade and competitive problems. The Carnegie Commission, among others, issued reports charging that public education was inadequate and that part of the solution lay in upgrading the salary and status of public school teachers.[6] Evidence in support of that charge came from the fact that school districts were having difficulty recruiting science and math teachers because of competition from the computer industry.

All these factors added strength to the claims of public employee unions, especially the teachers unions. These pressures also spurred experimentation in industrial relations practices. As discussed in more detail at the end of this chapter, extensive employee and union participation in business decisions began to surface in the public schools by the late 1980s.

Reinventing Government: To the Present

From the 1990s on, the public sector has come under intense pressure to improve its performance and in the process shrink its size. Some of the calls for government reforms arose from formal reviews or commissions, which often called for a "reinvention" of the public employment system to address alleged bureaucratization and inefficiencies. Interestingly, a number of these performance reviews concluded that reform programs should empower the public sector work force through partnerships with unions. In the words of a Task Force of the U.S. Secretary of Labor, "From school house to fire house, a growing number of state and local governments are forming cooperative workplace partnerships in an effort to transform their public agencies into flexible, customer-responsive organizations better equipped to serve citizens."[7] The Task Force goes on to observe that work restructuring in the public sector has "major parallels" to efforts underway in the private sector.

At the same time, calls for reinventing government also often came along with efforts to downsize the public sector payroll through a privatization of service provision (a public sector version of the increased outsourcing that was occurring in this period in the private sector). Simultaneously there were efforts to shift responsibilities downward from the federal level to states and localities. While endorsing calls to empower employees and enhance joint partnerships, public sector unions also struggled to defend the interests of their members against the harmful consequences that often followed in various cost-cutting approaches.

To summarize, the 1960s witnessed rapid expansion in public sector union membership and militancy. But in the mid-1970s a taxpayers' revolt emerged and slowed the gains of public employee unions. Then in the mid-1980s teachers and other public employee groups benefited from public concerns over the adequacy of public services and saw their bargaining power rebound. Since the 1990s calls to reinvent the public sector led to diverse strategies that ranged from downsizing and privatization to efforts to bring empowerment and a quality focus to public service provision.

Public employees and unions, like their private sector counterparts, have felt the effects of changing environmental pressures. But the environmental pressures and the changes that emerged within public sector collective bargaining were different in some ways from events in the private sector. In contrast to the private sector, generally there has been substantial continuity and stability in the process of public sector collective bargaining over the last 35 years.

The Legal Regulation of Public Sector Unionism

Federal, state, and local government employees are all excluded from coverage under the NLRA. Separate legal regulations govern collective bargaining in each of these sectors. Exhibit 13–2 reports the percentages of federal, state, and local government employees

EXHIBIT 13–2
Percentages of
Workers
Unionized in
the Public and
Private Sectors
in the United
States, 2006

Sector	Percentage
Private sector	7.4
Public sector	36.2
Federal	28.4
State	30.2
Local	41.9

Source: "Union
Membership Rates
Dropped in 2006 to 12
Percent; Manufacturing
Leads the Way," *Daily
Labor Report* 17,
January 26, 2007: D-1.

that are unionized. Collective bargaining coverage exceeds union membership in jurisdictions where there are employees covered by a collective bargaining agreement who are not members of a union, a situation that is much less common in the private sector. Note, the exhibit shows how much higher the level of unionization has become in the public sector as compared with the private sector.

Federal Employees

Federal employees received the rights to unionize and to negotiate over employment conditions other than wages or fringe benefits through Executive Order 10988, signed by President Kennedy in 1962. This order was subsequently extended by President Nixon in Executive Order 11491.

In 1970, as part of its effort to reform the postal service, however, Congress provided postal employees the right to engage in collective bargaining over wages, hours, and working conditions.

In 1978 Congress replaced the executive orders of Presidents Kennedy and Nixon with the first comprehensive federal law providing collective bargaining rights to federal employees. This law was part of a broad reform of civil service procedures and policies. Title VII of this law (Public Law 95-454) protects the rights to organize and to bargain collectively on conditions of employment. The law continues to exclude pay and fringe benefits from the scope of bargaining.

Collective bargaining in the federal sector is now regulated by the Federal Labor Relations Authority. Responsibility for impasse resolution is vested in the Federal Services Impasse Panel. The panel may use mediation, fact-finding, or arbitration to resolve disputes. The right to strike is prohibited.

State and Local Government Employees

As of 2006, all but nine states had legislation that provides at least some of their state or local government employees with the rights to organize and to bargain collectively. Exhibit 13–3 lists these states by the type of coverage provided. Of the 41 states, 24 have passed comprehensive laws that cover a number of occupational groups; the others that have not yet enacted public sector bargaining laws are primarily in the south.

Comprehensive collective bargaining laws for state and local employees were first passed in a number of states during the late 1960s and the early 1970s. In the 1980s, on the other hand, only two states, Illinois and Ohio, passed such comprehensive laws and in the 1990s only New Mexico did the same thing. Instead, the recent years have been witness to a number of revisions to the laws that were passed in earlier years. Those amendments expanded the scope of collective bargaining to new issues, covered new employee groups,

EXHIBIT 13–3
State Public Employees Collective Bargaining Laws

Source: *Government Employee Relations Report* (Washington, DC: Bureau of National Affairs, various years); *Public Sector Bargaining* (Washington, DC: Bureau of National Affairs, 1988), Chap. 6; and *Public Sector Employment in a Time of Transition* (Industrial Relations Research Association Series, 1996), Chap. 1.

Coverage	States
All-inclusive laws	Florida, Hawaii, Iowa, Massachusetts, Minnesota,[*] Montana, New Hampshire, New Jersey, New York, Oregon, New Mexico,[†] South Dakota
All employees, separate laws	Alaska, California, Connecticut, Delaware, Illinois, Kansas, Maine, Nebraska, Pennsylvania, Rhode Island, Vermont, Wisconsin
Some employees covered	
Teachers	Indiana, Maryland, Tennessee, North Dakota and Utah
Police and fire fighters	Kentucky,[‡] Texas[¶]
Fire fighters	Wyoming, Alabama
Police, fire fighters, and public school employees	Oklahoma, Nevada
All but state civil service	Michigan, Washington
Fire fighters and teachers	Georgia, Idaho
All but teachers and police	Missouri[§]
All but judicial	Ohio
No laws	Arizona, Arkansas, Colorado, Louisiana, Mississippi, North Carolina, South Carolina, Virginia, West Virginia

[*]Excludes employees in charitable hospitals.
[†]This category also includes the District of Columbia.
[‡]Qualified for certain cities.
[¶]Conditional on municipal vote.
[§]By Executive Order.

strengthened the agencies charged with administration of the laws, or modified the dispute resolution procedures.

The Diffusion of State Bargaining Laws

Public sector bargaining laws were passed earliest and are most comprehensive in those states with liberal political histories, high levels of expenditures per capita on government services, and above-average growth in personal income between 1960 and 1970.[8] States with public sector laws also tend to be those with a relatively high percentage of their private sector employees unionized.

The pattern of legal enactment experienced in the public sector conforms to the hypothesis that public policy reflects the existing political balance of power and social norms. Legal enactment does not appear to make up for power imbalances. That is, laws that provide bargaining rights were passed where government expenditures were already relatively high and where labor had the greatest influence. Similar laws have not yet been passed in the states where wages are lower and the unions are weaker.

Variations in the political effectiveness of occupational groups also influence the nature of the laws that govern different groups within each state. Police and fire fighters, for example, tend to have the most comprehensive statutes and to have impasse resolution procedures that end in arbitration rather than in mediation or fact-finding. Teachers also fare better than other local employees in the majority of states. State government employees tend to have the least comprehensive forms of collective bargaining rights and impasse procedures.

Public sector unions can exert influence even in the absence of the right to bargain. For instance, public sector unions already operate effectively as associations representing professional employee interests in some states that lack collective bargaining laws (e.g., the NEA in North Carolina), and often work in alliance with major professional associations such as the National Association of Social Workers, and the American Speech, Hearing and Language Association. Other examples of this are the locals of the CWA in Mississippi and the SEIU in Georgia that represent corrections officers and blue-collar units in state agencies and operate much like typical unions (representing workers in the context of civil service regulations), even though in the absence of state collective bargaining law these local unions are relegated to minority status.[9]

Studies of public sector union growth suggest that the state bargaining laws accelerated unionization. States that enacted laws had relatively large increases in unionization in the ensuing years. Furthermore, the more favorable the laws were to unions, the greater the growth of unionization. At the same time, however, the passage of laws favorable to public sector unions and collective bargaining appears to have been partially caused by the presence of unions that grew before the laws. Thus union growth and legal regulation of public sector bargaining appear to have a complicated interrelationship.[10] Public sector unions have had some success in recent years using political action to expand union coverage at state and local levels. An example is the extension of bargaining rights to home healthcare workers under public sector laws in California and Pennsylvania in response to campaigns by SEIU and AFSCME. In California unions first secured legislation in the early 1990s that authorized counties to create authorities to administer home care programs, a step that would essentially transform home care workers from individual contractors to local government employees. Over the past 10 years the unions have persuaded several populous counties to establish these new agencies, and have won representation elections to represent a majority of the state's 180,000 home care workers.[11]

Legal Regulation of the Right to Strike

No state provides public employees with the right to strike equivalent to that specified by the NLRA for private sector workers. Nevertheless, some states do provide a limited right to strike.[12] Colorado, for example, permits strikes by all public sector employees while Pennsylvania has a more limited right to strike that permits strikes by nonuniformed employees if they do not endanger the public health, safety, or welfare of its citizens.

At the same time, some states do not allow any public sector strikes, and some impose harsh penalties on public sector strikers. In New York, for example, the **Taylor Law** provides a "two for one" penalty under which a striking employee is penalized one day's pay for each strike day, which is in addition to the day's pay the employee loses while striking. Under the Taylor Law, the struck employer is responsible for collecting the monetary penalty and also keeps the money raised by the strike penalty. Box 13–1 describes how Taylor Law penalties were imposed on New York City transit workers when those workers went out on strike in 2005.

The Frequency of Strikes

New York is not the only state where public sector strikes sometimes occur even in the face of state laws that make those strikes illegal. In fact, while the highest strike rates appear in states where public sector workers have the right to strike, high strike rates also appear in states that ban strikes including Michigan, Oklahoma, Washington, and Virginia.[13] At the same time, strike penalties, when they are enforced, do appear to affect the frequency of strikes. A sharp decline occurred in the total number of public sector strikes after 1980,

On December 19, 2005, two private bus lines servicing New York City went on strike; the next day, employees of the MTA Bus Company and the NYC Transit subway and bus operations followed suit. The commencement of the strike, called by TWU Local 100 President Roger Toussaint, was preceded by two months of unsuccessful collective bargaining efforts between the union and the Metropolitan Transportation Authority (MTA).

Because the 35,000 New York City transit workers fall under the jurisdiction of the Taylor Law, strikers were subject to fiscal penalties in the amount of two days pay for each day of the strike. Strikers, however, held out for three days before returning to their jobs. The workers went on strike over the MTA's refusal to grant increases to hourly wages, improved health plans, a change to disciplinary proceedings, and a stronger pension plan. The MTA, which had a $1 million budget surplus at the time, claimed that projected future budget deficits made it impossible to meet the union's demands. Instead, the MTA offered a one-time lump sum bonus as a means to share the current surplus with employees, in exchange for reductions in hourly wage hikes from 10½ percent to 8 percent.

The strike shut down the city's subway and bus system, the largest in the nation, serving more than 7 million people a day. Additionally, the timing of the strike stressed the city economically, as it prevented not only individuals attempting to get to work but also affected the city's residents and tourists during the peak holiday shopping season. The city had not experienced a strike such as this since 1980.

When the strike stated an emergency hearing was held before Brooklyn Supreme Court Justice Theodore Jones, who had already issued a preliminary injunction on December 13, 2005, almost a week before the commencement of the strike. The injunction was intended to serve as a deterrent of potential walk-outs, work stoppages, slow-downs, or any other effort to interrupt the normal service of city transportation. On December 20, Judge Jones found the transit strikers to be in contempt of his prior orders. He imposed a $1 million fine for each day of the strike.

The State of New York Public Employment Relations Board (PERB) provided a team of mediators to help resolve the issue. According to the mediators' suggestions, transit employees returned to work after three days on strike. On December 27, 2005 the TWU membership voted against ratification of the tentative agreement. A petition for interest arbitration was filed on January 25, 2006. Members of the interest arbitration panel were then appointed by both the MTA and the TWU. On April 18, 2006, 71 percent of the membership voted in favor of the contract they had previously rejected, but the MTA said that in the face of the strike it was no longer bound to the terms of that tentative contract. The arbitration panel later issued an award that closely followed the terms in the tentative agreement that had been reached earlier.

Sources: "New York City Transit Union Ends Subway, Bus Strike After Three Days." *Daily Labor Report,* December 27, 2005, http://www.pubs.bna.com; "Strike by TWU Local Shuts Down New York City Subway, Bus System," *Daily Labor Report,* December 21, 2005, http://pubs.bna.com; "Tentative Agreement Reached on Pact for New York City Subway, Bus Workers," *Daily Labor Report,* December 29, 2005, http://pubs.bna.com; and "Transit Union Approves Contract That It Rejected Before," *New York Times,* April 19, 2006, http://www.nytimes.com.

however, there were some signs that labor conflicts were being diverted into other channels such as into the grievance procedure.

The types of employees involved also appear to affect the propensity to strike. Teachers in large districts, for example, are more likely to strike than are teachers in small districts. Strike propensities also vary substantially across other public sector occupations.[14]

The Bargaining Rights of Supervisors

The bargaining rights of supervisors differ substantially in the public and private sectors. Most state laws do not exclude public sector supervisors from collective bargaining, which diametrically opposes the Taft-Hartley restrictions on supervisor union involvement in the private sector. Some state laws do require supervisors to form separate bargaining units from rank-and-file employees, however.

Why are public sector supervisors treated differently? Unlike in the private sector, where supervisors are assumed to have the authority to make independent judgments on critical personnel functions, in the public sector many of those functions are often handled by a civil service commission. Moreover, there are many more levels of supervisors in the public sector hierarchies, and many individuals with the title of supervisor do not serve as bona fide supervisors.[15] Some have also argued that there exists a community of interests between supervisors and their subordinates in the public sector. Although not everyone agrees that public sector supervisors should be treated differently, to date the law has evolved differently in the public sector.

Calls for Federal Legislation Affecting State and Local Employees

The failure of the remaining states to provide collective bargaining rights for public employees has spurred calls for federal legislation to extend bargaining rights to all public employees. Movement on this issue has been blocked by two obstacles. The most formidable is the constitutional question whether the federal government has the authority to mandate collective bargaining legislation that covers state and local employees.[16] A second major obstacle has been the inability of various labor unions to agree on the form the legislation should take. Three different approaches for federal regulation of public sector collective bargaining have been advocated:

1. A simple extension of the National Labor Relations Act and the jurisdiction of the National Labor Relations Board to cover state and local employees.
2. Special comprehensive legislation that takes into account the unique characteristics of public employees.
3. A minimum-standards law of collective bargaining rights for state and local employees, with the specific form of the legislation left to the states.

Like its private sector counterpart, public sector collective bargaining is influenced not only by collective bargaining legislation, but also by other regulations in state and federal statutes. Chief among these are the laws, outlined previously, that govern taxation. Also important are civil service laws and procedures. One of the more difficult issues that has arisen in the public sector, as collective bargaining has spread, is how to resolve conflict between the rights provided public employees in collective bargaining statutes and the provisions of other laws.

Differences in the Bargaining Process between the Public and Private Sectors

The more public sector employees are able and willing to sustain a strike and the less employers are willing and able to withstand a strike, the greater will be the bargaining power held by these employees. Furthermore, public sector employees will have greater bargaining power the less employment drops over the long run in response to an increase in labor costs. These are the same conditions that influence bargaining power in the private sector. Thus in the public sector bargaining power is determined by the same basic set of factors as it is in the private sector.

But what about the level of bargaining power held on average by public and private sector unions. Does unionism or the right to strike give public employees excessive power? Are there differences in the way collective bargaining occurs in the public and private sectors that produce vastly different outcomes in the two sectors?

To resolve whether public sector unions have more power than private sector unions, it is necessary to consider how environmental factors influence union bargaining power. As in the private sector, this requires analysis of Marshall's conditions and the trade-off between wages and employment (the elasticity of demand for labor).

How Marshall's Conditions Operate in the Public Sector

Alfred Marshall's first condition states that employees have more bargaining power (face a smaller reduction in employment from an increase in wages) when it is difficult for management to substitute other factors of production for employees. On this score public employees, on average, should have more bargaining power than private employees do. It is difficult, for example, to substitute machines for public employees that provide many public services. Machines would be hard-pressed to substitute for public school teachers or police and fire fighters.

Some substitution of capital for labor is feasible even for public services: computers can at least partially substitute for teachers, police can acquire more cars and other equipment, and fire fighters can use more and better equipment. Nevertheless, public employees probably gain some advantage due to the relative difficulty to substitute other factors for employees.

Marshall's second condition concerns the price elasticity of demand for the final good. Here again public employees, on average, should have an advantage over most private employees. Government is typically the sole provider of a public good or service. A public employer cannot typically go out of business or move to some other area to escape higher labor costs. As a result, the demand for many public goods is relatively price inelastic.[17] This makes public employment relatively insensitive to increases in wages.

Marshall's third condition concerns what happens to the price of substitute factors of production if the demand for them increases. Here there is no clear difference between the public and private sectors.

With regard to the fourth Marshallian condition, the importance of being unimportant, public employees are likely to be at a disadvantage. In most cases, labor costs make up a substantial share of total production costs. The ratio of labor to total costs varies in the public sector from a high of around 90 percent in police and fire departments to a low of between 60 and 70 percent in education and other public services. This means that wage increases have a significant effect on total increases in government budgets. Labor costs are a prime target for cost-cutting efforts when the public demands lower taxes and expenditure levels. In the long run, then, the high percentage of labor costs to total costs may act as a major impediment to public employee union power.

On net, Marshall's conditions predict that the demand for public services is relatively price-inelastic so that increases in labor costs should lead to relatively small declines in employment.

Shifts in the Demand for Public Services

Marshall's conditions concern the responsiveness of employment to price (wage) changes in the short run when other environmental influences on bargaining power are constant. The bargaining power held by public employees after the mid-1970s and then again in recent years, however, was limited by the fact that environmental pressures were building. Tax revenues were declining in some jurisdictions, and the public expressed a reduced demand for many public services. These pressures led to cutbacks in government expenditures. The decline in the public's demand for government services was, in part, a product of the public's reaction to the advance in relative earnings public employees had received earlier.

The taxpayers' revolt was to some extent a delayed "price effect." The public had reduced its demand for public services in response to the rising cost of those services. Thus, the long-run demand for labor in the public sector is much more elastic than the short-run demand for labor.[18] It just takes a while for politicians to reduce employment levels significantly in response to wage increases.

Strike Leverage—Public versus Private

The strike leverage of public employees is influenced by their ability and willingness to sustain income losses as a result of a strike. Just as in the private sector, striking employees in the public sector rely on alternative sources of income, such as temporary jobs or the earnings of other members of the household. The critical factor that confronts public employees is the high penalty they face if they choose to strike.

In the private sector the employer's willingness to continue a strike is heavily influenced by the firm's ability and willingness to sustain the income losses that result from the shutdown in production and sales during the strike. In the public sector income is not necessarily tied to sales and production. Public agencies typically collect revenue through taxes and do not charge explicitly for services.[19] Thus, during a strike the public employer generally continues to receive revenue and consequently is not under pressure to agree to the strikers' demands as a result of fears of potential bankruptcy. Nor do public agencies typically face competitors who may continue to produce during a strike and thereby strip the struck employer of customers. This absence of a link between strikes and employer revenues clearly works in favor of public employers during strike situations.

The public employer may not lose income during a strike, but a strike can certainly anger the employer's constituents, namely, the public. The public is sometimes hard-pressed to do without certain public services, such as police and fire protection, education, and hospital services. These can be called essential services. Few substitutes for these services can be made available quickly, and the absence of these services can create hardships and, in some cases, health risks to the public.

Public services vary substantially in the degree to which they are essential. Police and fire protection may well be essential services, but do city clerks and engineers provide essential services? Parents may vocally complain when schools are closed by striking teachers, but when social workers strike do cities or states hear any public outcry?

Moreover, how the public reacts to strikes varies significantly over time. In the late 1960s and early 1970s public agencies frequently did not resist the demands of striking public employees. Yet in the mid- and late 1970s and then again in the 1990s taxpayers often seemed eager to confront striking public employees as part of efforts to lower taxes and the cost of government. The public's willingness to sustain public sector strikes seems to sway with political and economic winds.

Financial Sources of Governments

To fully appreciate the special pressures that arise in public sector bargaining, it is important to understand the sources of revenue on which public employers rely. In 1993, local governments generated 55 percent of their revenue from their own sources, much of that came from property and other taxes. An additional 30 percent of local government revenues were federally funded.[20] The amount of federal aid to states and local governments has fluctuated over the past few decades. The amount of federal aid grew considerably in the 1970s reaching a high of 32 percent of local revenues in 1975. Ten years later, however, that percentage fell to 29 percent and then gradually rose again.

In 1997 federal legislation shifted direct regulation of the welfare system from the federal government to the states and this had significant impacts on state and local government finances. This shift in the nation's AFDC programs was linked to efforts to devolve federal responsibilities and to calls to enhance the work requirements within the welfare system. As states began to assume greater responsibility for management of the welfare system and in the process impose more stringent work requirements on welfare recipients, collective bargaining issues surfaced. One such issue was whether welfare recipients who now worked would be eligible for unionization. Public sector unions have begun to target these recipients as an organizing target.

Beyond direct tax-based sources of revenues, local and state officials can generate funds from user charges and borrowing. In addition to the limits imposed by the credit and debt capital markets, the revenue-generating capacity of local government is constrained by (1) the size of the tax base in the community, (2) the willingness of the public to tax itself, and (3) constitutional or other legal limitations on the amount of taxes local governments raise.

Public Sector Bargaining Structures

Key aspects of bargaining structure are the degree of centralization in employer interests in the formal bargaining structure and the breadth or scope of employee interests included in bargaining units.

The Degree of Centralization

Collective bargaining in the public sector is highly decentralized. Almost all bargaining is done on a single-employer basis, that is, with a particular government or agency. There are a few isolated examples of formal multiemployer bargaining.

A number of factors have contributed to the continuation of decentralized bargaining in local governments. The diverse financial conditions that exist in local governments make both employers and unions hesitant to consolidate bargaining units.[21] Another pressure that limits centralized bargaining is that local governments like decision-making autonomy.

Nonetheless, information sharing and informal coordination do occur across state and local governments. As public sector bargaining has grown, so has the number of organizations of labor relations professionals in the public sector. These groups share information and conduct surveys to assist one another in the conduct of their separate negotiations.[22]

In some states, such as New York, school districts are organized into area associations that correspond to county or comparable regional subdivisions. Many of these associations

In January of 2001, the New York State Supreme Court ruled that the city's schools were inadequate and seriously underfinanced. The court reasoned that the state had not fulfilled its obligation under New York's Constitution to provide "a sound, basic education" for its children. The state's system for apportioning billions of dollars a year, based on political dealings and esoteric mathematical formulas was, according to the judgment, incomprehensible and unconstitutional. Furthermore, the Supreme Court ordered the New York State legislature to formulate a more straightforward and fair method of school financing. Since under such a new system New York City's schools could receive up to $1 billion more a year in state school aid, New York City officials whom have long campaigned for increased state funds to combat the city's poor education system, cheered the court's decision. Advocates for other urban schools systems interpreted the court's decision as support for their efforts to file similar lawsuits in their own states.

However, in June of 2002, a panel of the Appellate Division of the Supreme Court overruled the Court's earlier decision and argued that the state was not constitutionally obliged to provide anything more than a middle-school-level education. The Appellate Division's decision stated that the state's school system was constitutionally required to prepare students only for the lowest level jobs. The Division's majority decision stated that, "Society needs workers in all levels of jobs, the majority of which may very well be low level." To support its decision the Appellate Division cited the state's contention that only an 8th grade education is needed to understand jury instruction, and newspaper coverage of political campaigns is written anywhere from a 6th-grade to an 11th-grade level. The Appellate Division also found as unpersuasive evidence that New York City schools offer an inadequate education. The court reasoned that the presence of teachers with poor qualifications, overcrowded schools, outdated computers, poor physical conditions, and a lack of libraries did not prove that an acceptable minimum education was not being provided.

The Campaign for Fiscal Equity, the plaintiff in the lawsuit, appealed to New York State's highest court, the Court of Appeals. The Court of Appeals eventually ruled for the plaintiffs and ordered the state of New York to substantially increase its funding of the New York City schools.

Source: Richard Perez-Pena, "Court Reverses Finance Ruling on City Schools," *New York Times,* June 6, 2002:A–1.

pool the funds of member school districts and hire a single labor relations professional to represent them. This practice has produced pattern following as the professional negotiators developed consistent policies and contract provisions across the various school districts. And, because the teachers unions in these districts also normally rely on only a small number of business agents, the professional negotiators on both sides of the table in any given geographic region tend to be the same people.

There is some recent movement toward greater centralization in the financing of public education. If this continues, it may lead to greater centralization in teacher bargaining. The pressure for centralization in school financing comes from courts ruling that the existing heavy reliance on local property taxes to fund public education violates state constitutions. Box 13–2 describes one such court decision on New York school financing. In recent years a number of state governments have shifted toward state sales or income taxes to replace the local property tax. As a result, public school financing is becoming more centralized and may become substantially more centralized if the court decisions described in Box 13–2 spread. As school financing becomes more centralized it is likely that school collective bargaining structures will also eventually become more centralized. Imagine how awkward it would be if bargaining over public school teacher contracts continued on a local school district basis in states in which most of the revenues funding the schools come from the state government. This is an issue worth watching in the future.

The Scope of Bargaining Units

Bargaining in the public sector tends to follow occupational lines more than is the case in the private sector. A city government is likely to have separate bargaining units for police officers, fire fighters, blue-collar workers (either in one citywide unit or separate departmentwide units), and various professional groups. Public schools tend to have separate units for teachers, clerical and secretarial employees, bus drivers and maintenance employees, and school principals.

The rivalries that separate police and fire fighters in many cities effectively limit the potential for coalition bargaining with these two groups. Nevertheless, in the vast majority of municipal governments, the wages and fringe benefits of police and fire fighters are tied to each other through pay parity or pattern following.

State governments also tend to have a relatively large number of occupational or departmental groups. There has been a recent trend to consolidate some of these units into large, statewide units.[23]

Management Structure in the Public Sector

In the public sector managerial authority and responsibility are widely shared. As a result, collective bargaining in the public sector is multilateral and not bilateral as it is in the private sector.

Consider the typical elementary (or secondary) public school district. Each of the following groups has some managerial role to play in any collective bargaining that exists between the school district and its employees: the district superintendent, the professional industrial relations administrators who report to the superintendent, the elected school board, the mayor of the city in which the district resides, the citizens who approve school tax measures and elect the school board, the parent groups active in the community (including the PTA), the state legislature and the state governor who regulate state educational aid, the state education department officials who regulate school programs, the federal education department officials who regulate school expenditures and school programs, and possibly other parties.

Not only is managerial authority divided among a number of actors, but also there tend to be substantial differences in the goals of the various public sector managers. This arises because public sector organizations usually lack a clear hierarchy of decision makers to facilitate internal conflict resolution. Conflicts between the mayor and the city council, for example, are as likely to occur in collective bargaining as they are over other political issues. The consequence is that the internal conflicts within management's ranks frequently spill over into the formal negotiations process.[24]

Given this complex array of managerial interests and the diffusion of power, the role of the management negotiator in the public sector is a difficult one. Like the representative of any employer, the management negotiator must serve in the dual capacity of (1) coordinating internal organizational interests and (2) representing the organization in its dealings with the union. The more internal diversity there is and the more power is shared among different individuals, the more difficult the internal coordination role becomes.

When unions have considerable access to elected officials, the management negotiator may find it particularly difficult to hold elected officials together as a united management team.

In November 1998, 2,500 teachers in the Jersey City (New Jersey) public schools conducted a five-day strike, which brought substantial disruption to the 32,000-student district. Disorder occurred when on the first day of the strike the school district tried to continue to operate the schools with only 200 substitute teachers. As *The New York Times* reported, ". . . students at many of the schools began hurling bottles and bricks, turning over desks and computers, pulling fire alarms and even assaulting each other." Classes at the city's five high schools were then cancelled and the elementary schools met for the duration of the strike on a limited schedule."

Settlement of the strike was spurred by a court order fining the teachers' union $100,000 a day and providing that if teachers did not return to work they could be fired. Typical of the fact that public sector disputes often involve a broad array of issues, in the strike pay was not the central issue in contention. Rather, teachers were particularly

upset about a new evaluation system being introduced into the district. Teachers complained that under the new system evaluators could arrive unannounced into their classrooms and teachers had no chance to respond to the evaluations. Under the settlement, teachers would meet with evaluators before the evaluations to discuss what is expected of them. Another key issue in dispute was the length of the school day.

In addition to the role played by the courts, the multilateral nature of public sector labor relations was illustrated in this strike by the fact that the settlement could not be implemented until it was approved by the New Jersey State Commissioner of Education because the district has been under state control since 1989 due to poor performance.

Source: Maria Newman, *The New York Times,* November 11, 1998, p. B–9.

The Negotiations Process in the Face of Multilateral Bargaining

Multilateral bargaining is a negotiations process that includes more than two distinct parties. In multilateral bargaining no clear dichotomy exists between the union and the management organization. Multilateral bargaining leads to novel bargaining techniques. One frequently observed union tactic in public sector negotiations, for example, is the "end run," in which union officials try to sidestep the formal management negotiating team and take their proposals before an alternative group—city council representatives, school board officials, or even the city or state legislature. As illustrated in Box 13–3, local public sector disputes often involve the courts or higher level governmental officials who have a stake in the issues under dispute. In the recent New Jersey public school strike court-ordered fines helped induce settlement, but even that settlement could not be implemented until it was approved by state officials.

Still another form of multilateral negotiations occurs when a decision-making group rejects a negotiated agreement and refuses to implement it. Civil service commissions, school boards, or city councils, for example, often must ratify the final agreement. At the ratification stage constituent political pressures may come to bear on officials to change the terms and conditions of the bargain.

Yet another example of multilateralism arises when community interest groups become involved in the negotiations process. As the scope of bargaining in teacher negotiations expands to deal, for example, with issues of student discipline, the curriculum, or the welfare of minority interests, community groups step up their involvement in negotiations.

Multilateral bargaining also has emerged in jurisdictions that face fiscal crises. In these cases state and federal authorities, public employee pension managers, and private sector business leaders all have usually demanded some say in negotiated outcomes in return for their financial support.

A Case Study of Multilateral Bargaining: AFSCME and the State Government of Wisconsin

The presence of multilateral bargaining is nicely illustrated by the events that surrounded a strike of state employees in Wisconsin. The previous contract had been settled through an end run around the management negotiators, in an agreement worked out in consultations between Wisconsin's governor and Jerry Wurf, then president of the American Federation of State, County and Municipal Employees (AFSCME). The memory of this end run carried over to the next contract negotiations.

These negotiations were further complicated by an agreement between the parties to open negotiations to the public. Moreover, in the early negotiations sessions, which were characterized by much verbal sparring but little substantive negotiating, the union negotiators repeatedly protested that the management negotiators lacked adequate authority to bargain. In the background of the formal negotiations was a highly complex political situation. An interim governor took office at about the time the contract expired. Supervising the management negotiating team were the Secretary of the Department of Administration, the governor, and a bipartisan committee of the state legislature. The negotiators, therefore, were reporting to a set of administrative and elected officials who were separated by a long history of interparty rivalry over who should control the course of labor negotiations.

Thus most of the sources of impasse that we discussed earlier were factors in this dispute. The parties had a history of difficult bargaining. In previous negotiations the governor and other political officials who were not present in formal negotiations usually had become involved as the negotiations process heated up. The decision-making structure on the management side was highly complex, with power shared among a number of competing political and administrative officials. Furthermore, intense political rivalries and differences existed among these management officials. The union and management negotiators distrusted each other, and the membership and union officers displayed a willingness to engage in militant action from the start of the negotiations. The fact that the bargaining unit covered employees in all parts of the state ensured that this dispute would become a major political issue statewide. Thus the presence of all these potential sources of impasse indicated that bargaining would be difficult.

The dispute was settled only after the following sequence of events.

1. The state employees went on strike for 15 days, during which time the governor declared a state of emergency, called out the National Guard, and transferred physically and mentally handicapped patients from state to private institutions.
2. A court injunction was issued against the strikers.
3. An ad hoc, out-of-state mediator was brought in.
4. The governor and national officials from AFSCME entered the negotiations process.
5. The Joint Legislative Committee on Labor rejected a settlement that had brought the employees back to work.

6. Further negotiations and mediation efforts among the governor, representatives of the legislative committee, and the union took place.
7. The negotiated strike settlement was modified and approved by the legislature.
8. The state attorney general pursued contempt-of-court proceedings against the striking workers over the objections of the governor.

This case provides a good illustration of how diverse political pressures can affect the course of public sector collective bargaining.

The Effects of Public Sector Bargaining on Outcomes

Studies of collective bargaining in the public sector have found the following effects. (You may want to contrast these with the private sector bargaining outcomes described in Chapter 10.)

Wage and Other Compensation Outcomes

Although the magnitudes of the estimates on wages and costs vary across the studies, the vast majority of the studies have found a wage differential between unionized and non-unionized public employees.[25] These estimates also indicate, however, that the wage effects of collective bargaining in the public sector are not greater than the effects of collective bargaining in the private sector. The public sector union-nonunion wage differential is typically in the range of 5 to 15 percent. That is, unions do not appear to exert a stronger effect on the wages of public employees than they do on the wages of private employees.

There also is evidence that collective bargaining has had a positive effect on selected fringe benefits of public employees. Unionism leads to higher pension benefits, fewer hours and days worked, and increased time off with pay.[26] The large pension increases won by unions suggest that the simple wage differential seriously underestimates the compensation effects of bargaining.

The Dynamics of Union Effects on Pay

Historical or **longitudinal data** also reveal that unions have raised relative earnings and point out some interesting dynamics in union wage effects.

The Effects on Public Sector Budgets

Did the increases in expenditures on employees' salaries and benefits result in major budgetary reallocations from other areas? Evidence comparing employment in union and nonunion cities suggests that public sector unionism raises or at least does not lower employment in the public sector. Apparently public sector unions are able to lobby for greater government expenditures to eliminate any employment displacement caused by higher earnings.[27]

Union Effects on Public Administration

There is little doubt that collective bargaining has had a profound effect on both the process and the substance of personnel administration in public employment. As in the private sector, collective bargaining has increased the formalization of personnel practices and reduced the discretion of management in matters of discipline and discharge, promotions, transfers, and work assignments.[28]

Case studies of both successful productivity improvement programs and of resistance by public sector unions to changes in work rules have been reported. There have been a few cases of successful labor-management committees in the public sector.

Studies find that the effect of collective bargaining on the quality of public services is influenced by how well management adapts to the presence of the union.[29] As in the private sector, the effects of public sector unions and collective bargaining on the economic performance of the employer depend on the effectiveness of the relationship between the union and the employer.

The Use of Interest Arbitration

Some form of **interest arbitration,** arbitration that determines contract terms, is available in 22 states for the resolution of impasses in negotiations between state or local governments and at least some of their employees. Police and fire fighters are the groups most frequently covered by the procedure. There is a wide variety of forms of interest arbitration, including conventional, final offer, and various combinations of mediation, fact-finding, and interest arbitration.

Box 13–4 describes a recent interest arbitration case concerning the pay of New York City police officers (the NYPD). In this case, as in other public sector disputes, pattern bargaining and ability to pay were key issues. What made this case unusual was the significant role played by recruitment and retention issues in the arbitrator's decision.

Does Interest Arbitration Adversely Affect Collective Bargaining?

There is much controversy in the industrial relations community over the long-term consequences of binding interest arbitration.[30] Some claim that interest arbitration violates the spirit of free collective bargaining. Interest arbitration also has been criticized on the grounds that the availability of these procedures reduces the parties' incentive to bargain, thus imposing a *chilling effect* on the negotiations process. The parties avoid making compromises they might otherwise be willing to make because they fear the fact finder or arbitrator will split the difference between their stated positions.

A management negotiator, for example, may believe that it is better to go into fact-finding or interest arbitration offering only 4 percent when management would actually be willing to offer 6 percent to avoid a strike or impasse. By going in at 4 percent, the negotiator may increase the probability that the arbitrator (fact finder) will award (recommend) 6 percent. Put differently, if the negotiator were to enter the procedure offering 6 percent, this may increase the probability that the recommendation or award will be for something greater than this amount. The same rationale, it is argued, drives the union negotiator. Thus, the bargaining process is chilled: each party tends to hold back concessions rather than lay its best offer on the table.

These procedures also may suffer from overuse even in the absence of a chilling effect if they are not as economically costly as the strike. Remember, it is the income losses suffered during a strike that spur the parties to negotiate a settlement. Third-party procedures may lead to lower income losses.[31]

Furthermore, use of interest arbitration may serve political objectives for the union or management negotiators by allowing them to pass the blame on to the arbitrator. Parties

A three-person arbitration panel awarded New York City's 24,000 police officers retroactive raises totaling 11.75 percent for the July 2000 to July 2002 period. Leaders of the Patrolmen's Benevolent Association (PBA), who represent patrol officers in the NYPD, hailed the award, even tough the raises were well below the 21.9 percent increases the union had sought. Other unions within the "uniform forces coalition," representing city employees such as sanitation and corrections officers, earlier had negotiated a contract with the City providing an 11.75 percent wage increase over a 30-month period. The PBA said the arbitration award was significant because it broke the city's long-standing tradition of pattern bargaining. The arbitrator justified the pattern deviating wage increase (11.75 percent over 24 rather than 30 months) on the grounds that the NYPD suffered a recruitment and retention crisis.

Mayor Michael Bloomberg criticized the arbitration award, favoring instead a pact that would have raised police officer pay by 14 percent and increased the number of tours (shifts) each officer was required to work (and shortened the regular work day). He criticized the union and arbitrators for failing to link the pay increase to working time changes. Interestingly, the PBA had expressed a willingness to consider work time changes, but the union wanted to lengthen police officer's work day, and claimed that this method of altering working hours would lead to more significant productivity increases.

N.Y. City teachers, who by law are not subject to arbitration, had reached a settlement with the City in the spring of 2002 that provided 16–22 percent wage increases, in a contract that followed the recommendations of a fact-finding board and included a 20-minute per day increase in teachers' work time.

The IAFF, the union representing firefighters, had reached an agreement with the City that followed along the lines of the uniform coalition pattern in August 2001 and were just about to vote on the contract when the World Trade Center terrorist attack took place, killing a large number of firefighters. In November 2002, firefighters and the City of New York negotiated a settlement to their 2000–2002 collective bargaining agreement on terms that were identical to the police arbitration award.

Meanwhile, N.Y. City and its employee unions now must negotiate collective bargaining agreements to cover the period from July 2002 on. These negotiations, whenever they take place, will be heavily influenced by the budget problems facing N.Y. City.

An interest arbitration panel settled disputes between the PBA and the City of New York over contracts covering uniformed patrol officers in the NYPD again in 2004. In an award covering the 2002–4 period arbitrator Eric Schmertz awarded the patrol officers wage increases of 5 percent in each of two years, amounts that exceeded the significantly lower settlement the city had negotiated months before with DC 37, which represented a variety of administrative and other positions in city government including social workers. In his award Aribtrator Schmertz lowered the starting pay of patrol officers. The latter became the focus of press attention when the number of applicants to the Police Department subsequently declined. The City and the PBA once again reached impasse in their negotiations concerning the 2004–6 collective bargaining agreement, in part due to differences regarding how to respond to the new hire shortfall, and their dispute will be presented to an interest arbitration panel.

Sources: "Arbitration Panel Gives 11.7% Raises to City's Officers," *The New York Times* (September 5, 2002): A1; and "They'll Take It: Pay Award May Seem Disappointing But the Police Union Likes It Anyway," *New York Times* (September 5, 2002): B4.

faced with difficult internal conflicts may prefer to pass the buck to the fact finder or arbitrator and let themselves off the hook.[32] There is also the worry that these procedures would favor one side or the other. This would occur if the arbitrators make awards that are different from what the parties would end up with if interest arbitration were not available as an alternative.

There is also concern that these procedures are inherently conservative and that they favor the party that seeks the fewest deviations from the status quo. Thus some fear that the presence of these procedures stifles innovation in bargaining or new breakthroughs in contract terms. In recent years, there has been concern that arbitrators are ill suited to fashion major changes in collective bargaining agreements involving work rule changes, the restructuring of fringe benefit packages, work reorganization, and changes in the roles of labor and management.

Evidence on the Effects of Interest Arbitration

Most negotiations that occur where interest arbitration is available are settled without the use of arbitration. One comprehensive study found that in states where it is available, interest arbitration is used in between 6 and 29 percent of negotiations.[33] The variance in usage across states is partially a function of the different forms of arbitration used. **Final-offer arbitration,** where the arbitrator must choose between the parties' final offers, for example, appears to produce lower usage rates than does conventional arbitration. Is the usage of arbitration unusually high? The evidence shows that it is not. The rate of interest arbitration usage cited above is in the same range of the frequency of strikes in the private sector.[34]

Even though the overall usage of interest arbitration is not high, it is still possible that particular bargaining units become addicted to the procedure once they use it. Is this "narcotic effect" evident? To answer this question, researchers have analyzed the experience of the individual bargaining units over successive rounds of negotiations. The data suggest that the existence of interest arbitration does not erode bargaining to the point that even a substantial majority of bargaining units become dependent on the procedure. But larger units with the most complex bargaining relationships are more likely to rely heavily on the procedures.[35] The evidence consistently shows that in those states where interest arbitration is available, strikes occur less frequently than in states where arbitration is not available.[36] At the same time, the data show that even in states that require interest arbitration, strikes sometimes do occur.

The Impacts of Interest Arbitration on Contractual Outcomes

Numerous analysts have studied the effects of interest arbitration on bargaining outcomes. A number of researchers have found that the availability of interest arbitration has led to slightly higher wage settlements and more favorable nonwage contract terms.[37] In some states there is also evidence of less variation in collective bargaining outcomes across municipalities that make interest arbitration available although this leveling effect of interest arbitration has not been found in some other states.

Judgments about the appropriateness of interest arbitration should take into consideration these contract effects and the lower incidence of strikes that results from the availability of interest arbitration noted earlier. To date, the public generally appears to be satisfied with the use of interest arbitration, particularly for police and firefighters, as an alternative to the right to strike.

Participatory Programs and Work Restructuring in Public Schools

Under pressure to lower costs and improve service quality a number of public sector sites in recent years turned to work restructuring and participatory programs. Many bold experiments were initiated in elementary or secondary public schools.[38] Developments in the public schools are examined below. Particular emphasis is placed on comparing public sector experience to what has been transpiring in the private sector (described in Chapter 12).

The History of School Reforms

Many school districts began to alter the roles and responsibilities of teachers, principals, and district administrators. There were a proliferation of programs under names such as school improvement teams, lead (or master) teachers programs, school-based management, site-based management, and many others.

Reforms came in response to pressures to improve the education of students. In 1983 a well-publicized report by the Carnegie Commission, *A Nation at Risk,* argued that weaknesses in elementary and secondary schools were contributing to America's economic problems by producing a poorly trained work force. Public schools were also facing heightened social problems, including alarming rates of drug dependence among youth, reports of frequent illiteracy among high school graduates, and high school truancy rates. All of this was occurring in a fiscal environment in which state governments and the public were expressing reservations about making substantially larger contributions to the public schools. President Bush devised a plan to overhaul the nation's education system with greater federal involvement. President Clinton embellished upon and enacted these plans.

In 1994, the perception that Japan and Germany were more economically competitive because they had better trained workers, combined with the deteriorating state of the nation's public schools, prompted President Clinton to propose a host of educational reforms.[39] The Goals 2000: Educate America Act and the Improving America's Schools Act (IASA) are two of the many that were passed. These acts lay out curriculum frameworks to help schools comply with newly formed national education standards. The other major areas covered are appropriation of increased federal funds to schools, better training for teachers, parental and community involvement in education, adult literacy, and drugs and violence in schools. While public concern over educational quality remains high, there is much debate concerning whether a new role for federal standards should be introduced.

Education has historically been viewed as a local matter in the United States, with the federal government in the backdrop protecting civil rights and aiding the poor. With the enactment of new laws the American education system has taken a different turn. National standards and increased federal involvement no longer allow education to be a purely local matter. School employees are now under pressure to improve learning and lower costs. Federal aid eases some of the burden but districts compete against each other for small allowances. This pressure to improve productivity and lower costs parallels the experience of employees in many private sector firms.

The "Low-Cost–Hierarchical" School Reform Strategy

As in the private sector, there was a wide divergence of opinion over what was the appropriate way to restructure schools. At one extreme were those who claimed that what was needed were tighter controls over classroom activities and stricter adherence to hierarchical lines of authority among school employees. The notion here was that tighter controls and greater standardization would lead to greater work effort by teachers and other employees and stronger discipline in the classroom.

A number of techniques were advocated in this strategy. There was support for stricter and more frequent testing of teachers. Others recommended greater use of merit pay that

The Houston Independent School District Board of Education voted unanimously on January 12, 2006, to adopt a performance-based pay system in its schools. Houston, with over 200,000 students, is the largest district in the country to implement such a pay plan.

Instead of granting traditional pay raises, the pay program would allow up to half of the teachers in the district the chance to earn up to $3,000 extra per year, $1,000 for each of three aspects: (1) the school's overall performance compared with 40 other schools of comparable demographics throughout the state; (2) individual student attainment on two separate achievement tests as compared to that of other students in the district; and (3) individual student achievement on the Texas Assessment of Knowledge and Skills test, which compares students to others across the state.

The Houston Federation of Teachers has spoken out strongly against the implementation of this new pay system. The Federation of Teachers believes the new pay plan does not account for teachers in areas such as art and music, and that the teachers are being forced to accept the plan. Instead of basing pay on test scores, the teachers union argues that an increase in the base pay of teachers is more appropriate, as Houston's teacher starting salary is one of the lowest among districts in the area.

Sources: "Houston to Tie Teachers' Pay to Test Scores," 01/12/06. CNN.com, January 12, 2006; and "Houston Ties Teachers' Pay to Test Scores," 01/13/06. nytimes.com, January 13, 2006.

would reward higher performing teachers with monetary incentives. In recent years there have been attempts to link teacher pay to student performance. Box 13–5 describes how performance-based pay was introduced into the Houston School District in 2006. Some argued that school management needed to take a harder line in collective bargaining with teacher unions. A hard line was recommended to gain concessions in contractual work rules that would increase the hours of work and give school administrators more flexibility in teacher allocations (promotions, transfers, and classroom assignments).

In many ways this strategy was the public schools counterpart to the low-cost business strategy pursued by some private sector firms. This strategy relied on greater control by administrators and less participation in decisions by teachers and support employees.

A "Decentralization-Participation" School Reform Strategy

At the other extreme was a strategy that relied on decentralizing decision-making authority within school systems. Decentralization would provide teachers and support staff with greater participation in decisions.

Advocates of this strategy argued that involving teachers more extensively in decisions would improve the quality of education. The hope was (and is) that with decentralization and participation teachers would be freed to innovate in classroom instruction and respond to student needs quickly. Even within the decentralization-participation strategy there was much diversity in the techniques being tried.

School Improvement Teams

Some school districts introduced school improvement teams with a committee of 10 to 15 members that typically included a principal and some teachers, parents, and support staff who would meet for a few hours each week to work on specific tasks. In some cases the principal would run the team meetings.[40] A team might study how guidance services might be better provided to students or might focus on the problems that surround the introduction of a new reading program in a specific school.

School improvement teams are analogous to the quality circle programs initiated in many private firms over the previous 15 years. As one would expect, school improvement teams faced problems and limitations that were similar to those experienced by private sector quality circle programs. Teachers on the improvement teams, for example, sometimes deferred to the authority of the principal or became frustrated when suggestions offered by teachers were later turned down by higher levels of school district administration.

School improvement teams sometimes were constrained by the myriad of regulations that surround public education. If an improvement team wanted to extensively restructure work rules in order to address a problem, for example, it could be constrained by district, state, or collective bargaining policies and rules.

Lead Teacher Programs

Lead (or master) **teacher programs** were often part of the decentralization-participation strategy. The goal here was to allow experienced and committed senior teachers to serve as mentors and role models for younger teachers. In addition, lead teacher programs provided a mechanism through which financial incentives could be provided to superior teachers. The latter was a way to cope with the fact that typically teacher salary schedules are stringently based on seniority with no mechanism allowed for rewarding meritorious performance.[41] Lead teachers performed the following activities: clinical supervision support, teaching demonstration classes, reviewing curriculum options, analyzing student test data and attendance records, and facilitating communication between teachers and administrators.

School-Based Management

An extreme reform adopted in some school districts was school-based management. School-based management typically included teams (either school- or building-based) composed of teachers, administrators, parents, students, and local community leaders. The range of issues such teams become involved in has included curriculum, teaching strategies, the hiring of administrators, professional development, discipline, and school schedules. The objective here is to give the teams at the school or building level latitude over the use of resources, budgeting, and time. At the core of school-based management is getting teachers directly involved in making decisions on scheduling, redeploying teachers, or teaching methods.

School-based management (and related reforms) attempt to create more flexibility in school systems that are otherwise constrained by regulations and rules. In some cases it is the state regulations that are most constraining. In North Carolina, for example, state school aid had been provided in 76 line items. Before 1987 schools were not allowed to transfer funds from one line item to another regardless of local priorities or needs.[42] School-based management experiments in North Carolina proceeded only after the state legislature agreed to waive fund transfer limitations for districts engaged in the reform process.

In some other cases it is the collectively bargained rules that must be altered to facilitate school-based management reforms. Some school-based teams, for example, developed new schedules that put some of the curriculum in large classrooms and thereby freed up teacher time for one-on-one student-teacher interaction. To implement this change the teachers unions would have to waive the contractual limitations on class size that are included in many teacher collective bargaining agreements.

Even in the face of the tensions between school reforms and participatory processes, the national teachers unions (particularly the American Federation of Teachers) have generally supported participatory restructuring. Yet there is much diversity in the stance taken by local teachers unions toward participatory processes.[43]

The Problems Inhibiting New Efforts

Since participatory programs in the public schools are so similar to participatory programs adopted in the private sector, it is not surprising that many of the same problems arise. Many school-based management programs, for example, have been inhibited by principals or district administrators who are reluctant to give up control and allow teachers or parents greater input into decisions. In this way principals and administrators are expressing the same fears as those exhibited by supervisors and top executives in the private sector.

The school-based management and related reforms also create a critical issue concerning the relationship between collective bargaining and participatory processes. What is the role left for a contractual grievance procedure when a teacher can turn to a building-level team to solve a workplace problem? Can a sharp dividing line be drawn between the collective bargaining process and participatory processes? What will the role of the teachers union be if school-based teams take on extensive decision-making authority? These issues will be central to the evolution of participatory programs in the public schools and, interestingly, have clear parallels to the issues that are emerging in private sector participatory programs.

Accountability Programs

A number of school reforms, whatever their strategic focus, include efforts to establish greater **accountability** for educational attainment. Accountability programs focus on the generation and monitoring of data on student progress (test scores), student attendance, or teacher performance. The pressure for closer accountability derives in part from the public's concern over the quality of education and the apparently relatively poor educational attainment of U.S. school-age children.

The implementation of accountability programs arises in some districts as an outgrowth of the expansion of participatory processes. With the weakening of formal hierarchies between teachers and administrators, school districts are turning toward accountability measures to assess teacher performance.

The Effects of School Reforms on School Outcomes

Which of the school reform strategies lead to concrete improvements in student performance, and what are the costs (or savings) produced by various reforms?[44] Unfortunately, there is very little hard evidence about whether or how school reforms affect educational quality. In part, the lack of knowledge stems from the fact that the reforms have not been around long enough to demonstrate effects. In addition, complexities in the educational process make it extremely difficult to measure the effects of even long-lasting programs.

Assessing the payouts from school reforms remains one of the critical challenges for the future. It is also important to note that unionization and collective bargaining are likely to remain a central part of public education whatever the course of school reforms.

Normative Premises

How should industrial relations in the public sector be legally regulated? American labor law is governed by the premise that in the private sector (1) an inherent conflict of interests exists between employees and employers and (2) workers should have the right to pursue their interests through a union if they so choose. Furthermore, there is a strong preference for the process of free collective bargaining in which labor and management are given the opportunity to resolve their problems without extensive third-party interference.

Yet government differs from a private sector employer because, although government officials have traditional managerial responsibilities, the government is elected by the public. The public thereby has a dual role to play in public sector industrial relations. The public acts at the same time as citizens who regulate the provision of public services and as consumers of public services (paying for the public services as taxpayers). The problem for public policy is how to maintain the rights of employees to influence their employment conditions, through collective bargaining if they so desire, while maintaining citizens' rights to influence governmental action.

Criticisms of Public Sector Bargaining

Harry Wellington and Ralph Winter, among others, have taken the extreme position that government's primary responsibility—to represent the public interest—makes collective bargaining inappropriate for the public sector.[45] Critics of public sector bargaining also claim that if labor unions are granted the rights to exclusive representation and negotiations, they will achieve undue political power.

The Virtues of Public Sector Bargaining

We believe these positions ignore employee interests and inaccurately assess the actual effects of public sector collective bargaining. It is our view that public employees, like private sector employees, have an inherent right to participate in the determination of their working conditions. Why should the mere fact that an employee works for the government strip that employee of the right to influence employment conditions through collective bargaining?

Furthermore, the charge that collective bargaining leads to a perverse distortion of governmental decision making is not supported by the facts. The evidence discussed in this chapter shows that public sector unions have had a modest impact on employee pay and other working conditions. In fact, where they exist, public sector unions influence governmental decision making as but one among the many interest groups participating in this process. Public employee representation seems to enhance rather than detract from the process of representative democracy. Our argument does not necessarily imply that public sector collective bargaining rights should be identical to those in the private sector. Because a variety of interest groups are affected by governmental decisions their diverse interests must be taken into account in the collective bargaining process. Public policy must balance these objectives.

Summary

The questions in this chapter are as follows: (1) Has collective bargaining increased the political access and influence of public sector employees? (2) Has the strike proved to be a strong source of power in the public sector? (3) Have dispute resolution procedures, particularly binding interest arbitration, led to outcomes injurious to the public welfare? Early fears that public sector bargaining would tip the balance of power in favor of the unions have proved to be overly simplistic.

There has been a diverse range of experience in public sector bargaining. Cities, for example, developed various responses to public employee unions. There also were major shifts over time in the public's reaction to public employee demands and unionism. Wide differences also have appeared in the economic power of police, fire fighters, teachers, and other public employees. Therefore, it is inappropriate to generalize across public sector collective bargaining experiences.

Unionism in the public sector does not appear to warp the democratic process. The evidence also suggests that the strike has not consistently proven to be a one-sided source of union power. Furthermore, analysis of wage effects finds that the union–nonunion wage differential does not appear to be larger in the public sector than in the private sector.

Public sector unions do appear to have raised some fringe benefits substantially and to have increased the total amount of governmental expenditures and employment. Yet these effects are hardly significant enough to warrant any call for a dismantling of public sector bargaining. Finally, there is no evidence that the presence of interest arbitration has seriously perverted the collective bargaining process in the public sector.

Work restructuring and participatory programs have emerged as a central issue in the public sector, particularly in the face of recent calls to reinvent government and efforts to privatize or devolve public service provision. Here, as in the private sector, there are a variety of experiments under way. Many similarities prevail in the problems that arise in public and private sector restructuring including issues surrounding the relationship between participatory processes and collective bargaining. Furthermore, at this point we have little hard evidence on the effects reforms exert on educational outcomes.

What are the long-term consequences of a system that relies heavily on both third-party neutrals and outside advocates? What are the long-term effects of a system whose outcomes depend more on public choices and political decisions than on the direct constraints of the economic market? These are issues that will continue to be debated as experience unfolds. At the very least, the emergence of public sector bargaining has stimulated thought and analysis around these questions. In doing so it has opened the door to new ways of thinking about how collective bargaining can be adapted to new environments.

The high levels of union representation that exist in the public sector contrast ever more with developments in the private sector. Whether labor-management relations diverge even more so between these sectors in the future is an issue worthy of careful attention.

Discussion Questions

1. What factors contributed to the growth of public sector unions and public sector collective bargaining in the 1960s?

2. There is debate over whether public sector unions have more power than those in the private sector. Evaluate the power

of public employee unions in terms of Marshall's Conditions.

3. Describe the structure of most public sector collective bargaining.

4. Discuss the pros and cons of giving public sector employees the right to strike.

5. To what extent do you think the lessons about union and employee empowerment learned from the private sector carry over to the public sector?

6. Describe the reforms that have taken place in public education since the 1990s. Discuss the reasons for these reforms.

Related Web Sites

American Federation of Teachers (AFT):
http://www.aft.org//index.htm

PATCO:
http://members.aol.com/Tjnga/patco.html
http://members.aol.com/fsepulveda/PATCO/Patco.htm

Federal Labor Relations Authority:
http://fedbbs.access.gpo.gov/flra01.htm

Carnegie Commission, *A Nation at Risk:*
http://www.ncrel.org/sdrs/areas/issues/content/cntareas/science/sc3risk.htm

Suggested Readings

Belman, Dale; Morley Gunderson; and Douglas Hyatt eds. *Public Sector Employment* (Madison, WI: IRRA, 1996)

Freeman, Richard B. "Unionism Comes to the Public Sector," *Journal of Economic Literature* 24 (March 1986): 41–86.

Lewin, David; Peter Feuille; Thomas A. Kochan; and John T. Delaney. *Public Sector Labor Relations: Analysis and Readings,*

3d ed. (Lexington, MA: Lexington Books, 1987).

U.S. Department of Labor, *Working Together for Public Service,* Report of the U.S. Secretary of Labor's Task Force on Excellence in State and Local Government through Labor–Management Cooperation, Washington, DC, May 1996.

End Notes

1. Public employee union membership figures are traced in John F. Burton, Jr., and Terry Thomason, "The Extent of Collective Bargaining in the Public Sector," in *Public-Sector Bargaining,* 2d ed., ed. Benjamin Aaron, Joyce M. Najita, and James L. Stern (Washington, DC: Bureau of National Affairs, 1988), pp. 1–51; and Richard B. Freeman, "Through Public Sector Eyes: Employee Attitudes toward Public Sector Labor Relations in the U.S." in *Public Sector Employment,* ed. D. Belman, M. Gunderson, and D. Hyatt, (Madison: IRRA, 1994) pp. 59–84.

2. See Joan P. Weitzman, "The Effect of Economic Restraints on Public Sector Collective Bargaining: The Lessons from New York City," in *Government Labor*

Relations: Trends and Information for the Future, ed. Hugh D. Jascourt (Oak Park, IL: Moore, 1979), pp. 334–46.

3. We trace the broad wage trends in the public sector in more detail later in this chapter.

4. The events in San Francisco are analyzed in Harry C. Katz, "Municipal Pay Determination: The Case of San Francisco," *Industrial Relations* 18 (Winter 1979): 44–59.

5. For a description of Proposition 13 and the measures adopted in the other eight states, see "COPE Charts Impact of States' Spending and Tax Limitations," *Government Employee Relations Report* 812, May 28, 1979, pp. 14–17.

6. See Carnegie Forum on Education and the Economy, *A Nation Prepared: Teachers for*

the Twenty-First Century (Washington, DC: Carnegie Foundation, 1986).

7. U.S. Department of Labor, *Working Together for Public Service,* Report of the U.S. Secretary of Labor's Task Force on Excellence in State and Local Government through Labor–Management Cooperation, Washington, DC, May 1996.

8. Thomas A. Kochan, "Correlates of State Public Employee Bargaining Laws," *Industrial Relations* 12 (October 1973): 322–37.

9. Richard W. Hurd and Sharon Pinnock, "Public Sector Unions: Will They Thrive or Struggle to Survive?" *Journal of Labor Research,* forthcoming.

10. It is difficult to identify statistically the independent influence the law exerted on union growth. It is possible that passage of a law favorable to public sector unions was a reflection of factors that would have spurred the growth of unions even if the law had not been passed. See Gregory Saltzman, "Bargaining Laws as a Cause and Consequence of the Growth of Teacher Unionism," *Industrial and Labor Relations Review* 38 (April 1985): 335–51. Other studies are reviewed in Richard B. Freeman, "Unionism Comes to the Public Sector," *Journal of Economic Literature* 24 (March 1986):42–86.

11. Hurd and Pinnock, "Public Sector Unions: Will They Thrive or Struggle to Survive?"

12. A comprehensive summary of public sector strike experience is found in Robert Hebdon, "Public Sector Dispute Resolution in Transition," in Belman, Gunderson, and Hyatt, *Public Sector Employment,* pp. 85–126. Also see Craig A. Olson, "Dispute Resolution in the Public Sector," in *Public-Sector Bargaining,* 2d ed., ed. Benjamin Aaron, Joyce M. Najita, and James Stern (Washington, DC: Bureau of National Affairs, 1988), pp. 160–88.

13. See Casey Ichniowski, "Arbitration and Police Bargaining: Prescriptions for the Blue Flu," *Industrial Relations* 21 (Spring 1982): 149; and Hebdon, "Public Sector Dispute Resolution in Transition," p. 93.

14. Ibid., pp. 94–96.

15. Stephen L. Hayford and Anthony V. Sinicropi, "Bargaining Rights Status of Public Sector Supervisors," *Industrial Relations* 15 (February 1976): 44–61.

16. The issue of federal jurisdiction arose in *Joe G. Garcia v. San Antonio Metropolitan Transit Authority et al.,* 105 US 1005 (1985), and National *League of Cities* v. *Usery,* 426 US (1976).

17. One early study (and many later studies) concluded that, on average, the demand for labor in the public sector was more inelastic than the demand for labor in the private sector. See Orley Ashenfelter and Ronald G. Ehrenberg, "The Demand for Labor in the Public Sector," in *Labor in the Public and Non-Profit Sectors,* ed. Daniel S. Hamermesh (Princeton: Princeton University Press, 1975), pp. 55–78.

18. Robert J. Thornton, "The Elasticity of Demand for Public School Teachers," *Industrial Relations* 18 (Winter 1979): 86–91.

19. There are some exceptions to this, such as the tolls collected on roads and fees collected at parks.

20. These data are from *Facts and Figures on Government Finance,* 3d ed. (Washington, DC: Tax Foundation, 1997), table F–19.

21. The ups and downs of coordinated bargaining across various unions in New York City are traced in David Lewin and Mary McCormick, "Coalition Bargaining in Municipal Government: New York City in the 1970s," *Industrial and Labor Relations Review* 34 (July 1981): 175–90.

22. Peter Feuille, Hervey Juris, Ralph Jones, and Michael Jay Jedel, "Multi-Employer Negotiations among Local Governments," in *Public Sector Labor Relations: Analysis and Readings,* 3d ed., ed. David Lewin, Peter Feuille, Thomas A. Kochan, and John T. Delaney (Lexington, MA: Lexington Books, 1987), pp. 110–13.

23. Some cities have consolidated their bargaining units. As mentioned in Chapter 4, between 1967 and 1977 New York City reduced the number of its bargaining units from 400 to just under 100.

24. Thomas A. Kochan, "City Government Bargaining: A Path Analysis," *Industrial Relations* 14 (February 1975): 90–101.

25. For a review of these studies see Freeman, "Unionism Comes." Also see David Lewin, Peter Feuille, Thomas A. Kochan, and John T. Delaney, "The Impact of Unions on Public Sector Wages," in *Public Sector Labor Relations,* pp. 397–405.

26. Ibid.

27. See ibid. These studies of union effects on expenditures had difficulty detecting whether higher government expenditures are caused by the same factors that cause public sector unions to grow or by the unions themselves.

28. See David T. Stanley, *Managing Local Government under Union Pressure* (Washington, DC: Brookings Institution, 1972); Hervey Juris and Peter Feuille, *Police Unionism* (Lexington, MA: D.C. Heath, 1973), pp. 125–50; Lorraine McDonnell and Anthony Pascal, *Organized Teachers in American Schools* (Santa Monica, CA: Rand Corporation, 1978), pp. 75–82; George Sulzer, *The Impact of Labor-Management Relations upon Selected Federal Personnel Policies and Practices* (Washington, DC: Superintendent of Documents, 1979).

29. See McDonnell and Pascal, *Organized Teachers;* and Sulzer, *The Impact of Labor-Management Relations.* For an analysis of the consequences of technological change, see David Lewin, "Technological Service," in *Workers, Managers and Technological Change: Emerging Patterns of Labor Relations,* ed. Daniel B. Cornfield (New York: Plenum, 1986), pp. 281–309.

30. Carl M. Stevens, "Is Compulsory Arbitration Compatible with Collective Bargaining?" *Industrial Relations* 5 (February 1966): 38–52.

31. The costs associated with arbitration include the costs of the uncertainty associated with guessing what the arbitrator will do and any direct costs (such as fees) associated with use of the procedure. See Henry S. Farber and Harry C. Katz, "Interest Arbitration, Outcomes and the Incentive to Bargain," *Industrial and Labor Relations Review* 55 (October 1979): 55–63.

32. One study that compared the causes of impasses under arbitration and the causes of strikes found, for example, that internal political and attitudinal sources of conflict were more important in causing impasses than in causing strikes. Thomas A. Kochan, Mordehai Mironi, Ronald G. Ehrenberg, Jean Baderschneider, and Todd Jick, *Dispute Resolution under Factfinding and Arbitration* (New York: American Arbitration Association, 1979), pp. 99–111.

33. Richard A. Lester, *Labor Arbitration in State and Local Government: An Examination of Experiences in Eight States and New York City* (Princeton, NJ: Princeton, 1984); and Olson, "Dispute Resolution."

34. Cynthia Gramm, "The Determinants of Strike Incidence and Severity: A Micro-Level Study," *Industrial and Labor Relations Review* 39 (April 1988): 361–76.

35. For conflicting conclusions on whether arbitration induces a narcotic effect, see Thomas A. Kochan and Jean Baderschneider, "Dependence on Impasse Procedures: Police and Firefighters in New York State," *Industrial and Labor Relations Review* 31 (July 1978): 431–39; and Richard J. Butler and Ronald G. Ehrenberg, "Estimating the Narcotic Effect of Public Sector Impasse Procedures," *Industrial and Labor Relations Review* 35 (October 1981): 3–20.

36. See Olson, "Dispute Resolution."

37. For example, Craig A. Olson, in "The Impact of Arbitration on the Wages of Firefighters," *Industrial Relations* 19 (Fall 1980): 325–39, found that arbitration leads to higher firefighter compensation. Peter Feuille, John Thomas Delaney, and Wallace Hendricks, in "The Impact of Interest Arbitration on Police Contracts," *Industrial Relations* 24 (Spring 1985): 161–81, found that the availability of arbitration improves the earnings and other contract provisions of police. A few studies showed that interest arbitration had no effect on salaries. David E. Bloom, in "Collective Bargaining,

Compulsory Arbitration, and Salary Settlements in the Public Sector: The Case of New Jersey's Municipal Police Officers," *Journal of Labor Research* 2 (Fall 1981): 369–84, found no salary effects of arbitration in New Jersey.

38. Samuel B. Bacharach, ed., *Education Reform: Making Sense of It All* (Boston: Allyn & Bacon, 1990), p. B–10

39. See "New Education Legislation Defines Federal Role in Nation's Classrooms," *The New York Times,* March 30, 1994; and *A Nation at Risk, National Commission on Excellence in Education, A Report to the Secretary of Education,* U.S. Department of Education, April 1983.

40. The principal's role is in some ways comparable to that of the supervisor in a private sector firm. One important difference between the private and public sectors is that in many school districts principals and other administrators are represented by a union. Remember, the public sector is not covered by the NLRA (and the Taft-Hartley amendments).

41. The controversy that surrounds merit pay is discussed in Samuel B. Bacharach, David B. Lipsky, and Joseph B. Shedd, *Paying for Better Teaching: Merit Pay and Its Alternatives* (Ithaca, NY: Organizational Analysis and Practice, 1984).

42. See "North Carolina's Lead Teacher/Restructured School Pilot Project: An Interim Report," Public School Forum of North Carolina, The Forum (Spring 1988): 1–15.

43. See Bureau of Labor-Management Relations and Cooperative Programs, U.S. Department of Labor, "Participatory Leadership: School and the Workplace," Report 138 (Washington, DC: GPO, 1990).

44. Skepticism about the payout from school-based management is expressed in Betty Malen, Rodney T. Ogawa, and Jennifer Kranz, "Unfilled Promises," *The School Administrator* (February 1990), pp. 3–32 and 53–60.

45. This argument can be found in Harry H. Wellington and Ralph K. Winter, Jr., *The Unions and the Cities* (Washington, DC: Brookings Institution, 1971).

Chapter

14

International and Comparative Industrial Relations

An excellent way to gain perspective on one's own industrial relations system is to compare it with systems found in other countries.

The U.S. industrial relations system is unique in many ways. The United States, for example, has one of the lowest rates of unionization of any advanced democratic economy, and its rate of unionization has fallen faster in the past 30 years than that of any other industrialized country in the world. Furthermore, American management opposes unions more strongly than managers in most other countries. In addition, unions in the United States are less closely tied to political parties than are their counterparts in Europe, Australia, and many developing countries.

Other differences between industrial relations in the United States and practices elsewhere are noted throughout this chapter. Through a comparative perspective it is possible to assess whether there are any features of the industrial relations systems in other countries that should be imported and applied in the United States. This question is now on the minds of many industrial relations practitioners in the United States.

There are other reasons why an international focus on industrial relations practice is important. The U.S. economy is becoming more international as exports and imports make up a larger share of total gross national product. The **trade deficit** has emerged as a critical policy issue particularly in light of the negotiation of a number of regional trade pacts in recent years. Further expansion of exports from and imports into the United States is likely in the future, in part due to the U.S. Congress' recent extension of "fast track" authority to President Bush as described in Box 14–1.

Exhibit 14–1 presents statistics on the U.S. trade deficit and trade flows. As a result of increased trade U.S. managers and unionists are more frequently exposed to and involved in the industrial relations practices of other nations. The globalization of the economy requires a globalization of our understanding of industrial relations.

The three-tiered framework is used in this chapter to study industrial relations in countries other than the United States. A comparative assessment of industrial relations should take account of the substantial institutional differences that exist across countries. However,

On July 27, 2002, the House of Representatives voted 215 to 212 to approve a trade package that gives President Bush the authority to negotiate trade deals that cannot be changed by Congress, only ratified or rejected, otherwise known as fast track authority. President Bush actively supported ratification of the agreement, even making a rare appearance on Capitol Hill to lobby Republicans personally for the package. The trade negotiating authority had substantial support in the Senate where it passed easily. The negotiating power that President Bush has won was held by five earlier presidents, but had expired in 1994.

Bush expects that approval of the fast track legislation will facilitate the process of negotiating trade treaties with other countries. The United States is currently negotiating treaties with Canada, Mexico, and 31 other countries in the Western Hemisphere in the proposed Free Trade Area of the Americas. The negotiating parties have a goal of reaching an agreement by 2005. Democrats and Republicans were divided on the issue. Republicans said that the measure would bring more economic growth and lower consumer prices. Democrats, however, fear that the bill will increase the number of job losses from trade, especially in textile and manufacturing industries.

The bill created some benefits for American workers. These benefits were added in part to get votes from moderate Democrats in support of the bill. The Trade Adjustment Assistance program, created under NAFTA, was extended by the fast track bill. (See a later section of this chapter for a description of NAFTA.) Under this program workers who lose their jobs because of shifts in imports and exports or as a result of a company moving its productions overseas can receive cash assistance and job training benefits for up to two years after discharge. The new trade package also created a program of subsidized health insurance for workers who lose their jobs because of foreign competition. The government must pay 65 percent of the health insurance for displaced workers in the form of refundable tax credits.

However, many Democrats still argued that it is difficult to determine which workers would be displaced by globalization and would therefore be eligible for assistance. Also, the tax credits do not guarantee that displaced workers would be able to afford coverage anyway. Minority Leader Richard Gephardt expressed disapproval for the bill, saying that it failed to "enhance human rights, reaffirm workers rights and promote environmental legislation."

Organized labor has strongly opposed trade promotion authority as well and criticizes the assistance to displaced workers as insignificant. AFL-CIO President John Sweeney said the agreement will cause more job loss to nations "where corporations routinely exploit child labor, workers' rights, and the environment."

Sources: "Bush Hails Vote in House Backing Trade Legislation," *New York Times,* July 28, 2002; and "Bush Signs Major Trade Legislation Renewing Trade Promotion Authority," *Daily Labor Report* 152, August 7, 2002: AA-1.

the wide diversity in industrial relations practices around the globe makes it infeasible to present even a cursory examination of all of them. As a framework for an international perspective, then, this chapter examines in detail the key features of the industrial relations systems in Germany and Japan.[1]

This chapter includes a focus on Germany and Japan for a number of reasons. First, these countries have had strong economic growth over the last 40 years, and they now play very important roles in world trade.[2] Second, this economic success has drawn attention to their industrial relations practices as some analysts argue that these industrial relations systems caused their high economic growth. The industrial relations systems in Japan and Germany are widely discussed as models that might be appropriate for other countries. Third, Japan and Germany warrant special attention because their industrial relations practices are so different—both from each other and from the practices that exist in the United States. Thus they nicely illustrate the diversity that exists in industrial relations.

EXHIBIT 14–1
United States Imports and Exports, 1930–2004

Sources: Data on exports and imports from *Statistical Abstracts of the United States* (Washington, DC: U.S. Department of Commerce): 1961 ed., table 1195; 1990 ed., table 216; 1996 ed., table 1308; 2001 ed., table 1306 and 646; 2006 ed., table 656 and 1288. GNP data from *Statistical Abstract of the United States* (Washington, DC: U.S. Department of Commerce): 1990 ed., table 690; 1996 ed., table 691; 2001 ed., table 1297; 2006 ed., table 656.

Years	Exports as Share of GNP (%)	Imports as Share of GNP (%)	Balance of Trade (Exports-Imports) ($ Billion)
1930	5.2%	4.3%	1.0
1935	4.5	4.3	.1
1940	5.3	3.6	1.7
1945	7.6	4.8	6.0
1950	5.0	4.2	2.3
1955	5.5	4.4	4.4
1960	5.6	4.5	5.7
1965	3.8	3.0	5.3
1970	4.2	3.9	3.4
1975	6.7	6.2	10.8
1980	8.1	9.0	−19.6
1985	5.3	8.6	−117.7
1990	6.5	8.5	−101.7
1995	7.6	10.2	−158.7
2001	7.2	12.1	−436.1
2002	6.6	11.0	−471.6
2003	6.6	11.4	−532.4
2004	7.0	12.5	−650.9

This chapter also considers the key international industrial relations issues that have emerged in recent years—the effects of firms that operate in more than one country (multinationals), the integration of the European Union, the formation of a North American trading bloc, and the role of labor in the political democratization that has been occurring in countries such as Poland and Korea. The final section of this chapter examines whether it is feasible to import the industrial relations practices of other countries into the United States.

Industrial Relations in Germany

The distinguishing feature of industrial relations in Germany is the presence of **codetermination**.[3] Codetermination procedures are mandated by German federal law and apply to all enterprises in the country whether or not employees in those enterprises belong to unions.

Codetermination

There are two key parts to German codetermination: employee representation on company boards and works councils.[4] Codetermination provides a parallel form of representation to employees that is in addition to the union representation available to German workers. At the same time, although codetermination and collective bargaining procedures are formally distinct forms of worker representation, there are many close connections between the operation of these two channels of representation and the individuals involved in each.

Board Representation

German federal law mandates that employees elect representatives to the **supervisory boards** of all German companies.[5] The number of representatives elected to the supervisory board by employees varies by the size of the firm and the industry (special provisions cover the coal and steel industries). Exhibit 14–2 describes the various codetermination requirements and the number of employees affected by these procedures. To understand the implications of these procedures it is helpful to examine the nature of German company board structure.

German firms have a two-tiered board structure. The supervisory board (*Aufsichtsrat*) is the higher ranked board and has the responsibility to control managerial performance and appoint top managers. The lower managing board (*Vorstund*) runs the firm on a day-to-day basis and implements most managerial decisions.

Employee representatives to the supervisory board are elected proportionately from the ranks of blue- and white-collar employees. The law also reserves two or three (depending on the size of the board) of the supervisory board seats for union delegates. In impasse situations, the chair of the supervisory board (the chair is nominated by shareholders) can vote to break the tie. Employee representatives on the supervisory board often run on slates associated with particular unions and are often active in unions (and frequently are union officials).

The consequences of employee representation on supervisory boards varies across companies and is sometimes hard to detect. Some analysts claim that employee board representation has provided a major contribution to the low strike frequency that has been characteristic of the German industrial relations system over the post–World War II period (discussed below).

Wolfgang Streeck, for example, documented how employee representation on the Volkswagen board influenced that company's expansion into the United States. In that case employee and union involvement did not stop the company from making a major investment outside Germany, but it did alter the timing and scale of the investment.[6] In general, representation on the supervisory board appears to provide employees and unions a meaningful amount of access to and involvement in the formation of strategic business decisions.

EXHIBIT 14–2
Codetermination Rights in Germany

Source: *Sueddeutsche Zeitung,* February 27, 1979.

Form of Codetermination	Sector	No. of Employees Covered (millions)
Full parity codetermination in supervisory boards and a labor director in management board; works councils	Coal and steel industries	0.6
Counterbalancing parity in supervisory boards; works councils	Large companies with more than 2,000 employees	4.1
One-third of seats for employee representatives in supervisory boards; works councils	Smaller and medium-sized companies	0.9
Works councils	Other private enterprises with more than five employees	9.4
Personnel councils	Public service	3.6
No institutionalized workers' participation	Private enterprises with less than five employees	3.0

Works Councils

The second major component of the German codetermination structure is the works councils mandated by federal law for all private enterprises with more than five employees. Works councils have many rights to information, consultation, and codetermination. The 1972 Works Constitution Act, for example, authorized works councils to be involved in the resolution of all of the following:

Discipline

Daily working hours and breaks

Temporary short-time or overtime work

The setting of job piece rates

Pay systems

Suggestion schemes

Holiday schedules

Monitoring of employee performance

Safety regulations

Welfare services in the establishment

Administration of housing for employees

Works councils also codetermine any changes in the pace of work or the working environment. In the event of any major operational changes in the enterprise, the law requires that the works council and the employer negotiate over the change. If management wants to lay off employees it must negotiate with the works council and reach agreement (specified in a "social plan") on the factors that determine who gets laid off and the compensation arrangements for those who are laid off.

The works councilors are elected by all employees in a firm regardless of union affiliation. Nevertheless, works councilors usually cooperate closely with union officers or hold union office themselves. Works councils cannot call a strike, but they can sue management in a case of a breach of contractual rights.

Union Representation and Structure

Unions also play an important role in the German industrial relations system. Unions represented 25 percent of the German workforce in 2004 (see Exhibit 14–3), and union membership (as a fraction of the workforce) has been steady since 1960.[7] After German reunification in 1990, unions based in the former West Germany extended their jurisdiction to the former East Germany. While economic transformations and the bankruptcy of many firms has weakened unions in the eastern parts of unified Germany, at the same time, unions have played a key role in the restructuring of this region.

German unions provide representation through the negotiation of collective bargaining agreements and typically are actively involved in the codetermination processes, in some cases through the union activists or officers that serve either as employee representatives on a supervisory board or as works councilors.

German unions also are generally active in political and social life and issues. The largest federation of German unions, the Deutscher Gewerkschaftsbund (DGB), is closely aligned to the Social Democratic Party (SPD).[8]

EXHIBIT 14–3
Economic and Labor Data from the Countries of the European Union, 2004

Country	Labor Force Participation Rate (a) (%)	Unemployment Rate (b) (%)	Per Capita GDP (c) ($)	Unionization Rate (d) (%)	Hourly Compensation Cost in Manufacturing (e) ($)
Austria	71.6	4.7	27,920	37	25.38
Belgium	64.3	7.7	26,730	56	27.73
Cyprus					
Czech Republic	70.4	7.8	5,240	27	4.71
Denmark	79.4	5.5	34,890	74	32.18
Estonia			3,360		
Finland	74.1	9.1	24,790	76	27.17
France	68.2	9.3	26,300	10	21.13
Germany	71.3	9.4	28,280	25	29.91
Greece	63.8	9.1	11,640	27	
Hungary	60.6	5.9	4,510	20	
Ireland	68	4.5	17,790	38	19.14
Italy	61.6	8.7	20,170	35	18.35
Latvia			2,430		
Lithuania			2,260		
Luxembourg	65.3	2.6	45,360	34	23.11
Malta			8,650		
Netherlands	76.4	3.6	25,830	23	26.84
Poland	64.2	20	3,590	15	
Portugal	72	6.8	11,010	24	6.23
Slovakia	70	17.6	3,680	36	
Slovenia			9,840		
Spain	68.5	11.4	14,490	15	14.96
Sweden	78.9	5.8	26,210	79	25.18
United Kingdom	76.6	4.9	20,870	31	20.37

a) Data are from *OECD Employment Outlook, June 2004,* Organisation for Economic Cooperation and Development, Paris, Table B.
b) Data are from *OECD Employment Outlook, June 2004,* Organisation for Economic Cooperation and Development, Paris, Table B.
c) Data are from *World Labour Report, 2000,* International Labour Office, Geneva, Table 5.
d) Data are from *OECD Employment Outlook,* June 2004, Organisation for Economic Cooperation and Development, Paris, Table 3.3.
e) Data are from U.S. Department of Labor, Bureau of Labor Statistics, November 2004, Table 2.

Collective Bargaining in Germany

Collective bargaining in Germany is generally highly centralized. Most collective agreements are reached at the industry or regional level. The most important unions in the private sector represent workers in one or more industries. IG Metall, for example, represents workers in the metal working industries.[9] Recently a super union, Verdi, representing workers throughout the service sector, was formed through the amalgamation of a number of private and public sector unions (see Box 14–2).

German labor law does not give unions exclusive representation rights. More than one union can (and often does) represent employees at a work site, even among employees who perform similar jobs.

Employers are commonly represented by an employer association in industry or in regional collective bargaining.[10] Once an agreement is reached between a union and

On March 17, 2001, more than one thousand delegates from Germany's five service-sector unions voted to dissolve the structures in their respective organizations and merge into one of the world's largest labor organizations. The new organization, which has a total membership of 3 million, is called the United Services Producers, or Verdi in German. Verdi will consist of workers from the Public Services and Transportation Union (OTV), German Salaried Employees Union (DAG), German Postal Employees Union (DPG), Retail, Banking, and Insurance (HBV), and Media Union (IG Medien).

The Verdi founders hope that the merger will create a united front to combat new problems the labor movement faces in Germany. The goal is that Verdi will create a stronger position for the former unions to combat problems such as declining membership levels, tariff negotiations that would create foreign competition, and even accusations that the union's inflexibility is to blame for the country's high unemployment rate. The new super union also wants to counteract the growing lobbying efforts of business interests that want to restructure employment markets and weaken the role of unions.

Sources: "Merger of German Labor Groups Would Create World's Largest Union," *Daily Labor Report,* 250, December 29, 2000:A-3 and "Merger of German Service Unions Creates 3-Million Member Union," *Daily Labor Report,* 54, March 20, 2001:A-4.

an industry association over wages and other basic employment terms, these terms are extended by law to other employees and firms in that industry. Distinctions between unionized and nonunionized workers are not allowed in collective bargaining agreements.

There are often "ordinary" collective bargaining agreements that last only one year and include pay in their terms. These ordinary agreements are signed under "framework" agreements that last for a number of years. Plant-level negotiations between the works council and management typically supplement the industry agreements.

In recent years, there has been some movement toward more decentralized collective bargaining in Germany. This has come about, for example, when firms in the eastern region refused to honor terms in a master industry-level collective bargaining agreement. Even in the western region there has also been a growing tendency for firm-level deviations ("concessions") in firms that face job losses and threatened closure. And yet, even in the face of these pressures, the German collective bargaining system remains relatively centralized.

Strike Rates in Germany

Over the post–World War II period, Germany has had a lower strike frequency than the other major industrialized countries.[11] A number of hypotheses explain why this may be so. Some analysts argue that the low strike rate is a product of the conflict mediation accomplished through the codetermination system. Others say that it is possible that German workers and employers strove particularly hard to avoid strikes during this period because of their fear that strikes could bring a return to the social instability and turmoil that had occurred before the rise to power of Adolf Hitler and the Nazis. It could also be that the low strike rate is a product of the economic success of the German economy over the last 30 years as much as it is a cause of that success. At the same time strikes do occur in Germany.

For example, there was also a bitter series of strikes in the 1990s centered on whether companies in the eastern region of Germany would maintain their commitments to scheduled wage increases that brought the pay of workers in the eastern region up closer to that earned by German workers in the western region.[12] Although initially refusing to honor these scheduled increases, employers eventually backed down although individual firms have in some cases failed to pay the wage rates agreed to in the industry-level collective bargaining agreements.[13]

Vocational and Apprenticeship Training

Supporting German labor management relations is a very strong vocational and **apprenticeship training** system. High school-aged youth must choose among three educational tracks around age 16: a college-bound program, an apprenticeship vocational school program, or a general education program.

Two-thirds of high school graduates who do not go on to college enter the labor force as graduates of a vocational educational program. The apprenticeship programs in the vocational schools are overseen by a joint business-labor group that sets the qualifications for each occupational program. This system of training and certification provides German employers with a highly skilled labor force and is often cited as one of the key sources of Germany's economic success.

In summary, the German model of industrial relations stresses formal, legally mandated structures for worker representation and training; codetermination, board representation, works councils, apprenticeship training, and the extension of collective bargaining terms across all the firms in an industry. Through these formal structures, German unions and employers have achieved high levels of wages and social benefits, strong productivity performance, flexibility in the use of human resources, and low rates of strike activity.

Given the relative success of the German model, it is not surprising that its major features were extended by law to what was formerly East Germany as part of German reunification. Although the modernization of eastern Germany has been very costly and led to high unemployment, it is noteworthy that this transition occurred without significant opposition from either management or labor. This too attests to the high level of acceptance by German society of unions and the codetermination system.

Industrial Relations in Japan

Enterprise Unionism

The distinguishing feature of Japanese industrial relations is the central role of enterprise unions.[14] Enterprise unions in Japan represent both the white- and blue-collar employees of a firm, regardless of occupation and includes management staff. Of the firm's full-time employees, only the higher level managers do not belong to the enterprise unions. Thus foremen and line workers belong to the same enterprise union, and foremen often play a very active role in union affairs. Newly acquired employees to the firm (other than managers) automatically become union members and pay dues to the enterprise union through a dues check-off system.

Union and Employer Federations

The enterprise unions commonly are associated with industry union federations, which are, in turn, affiliated with union confederations.[15] Employers commonly belong to counterpart federations, the employer federations. Both union and employer federations provide advice and engage in political lobbying but do not become directly involved in enterprise-level collective bargaining.

Although industrial, craft, or general unions are rare in Japan, some important exceptions do exist. Furthermore, while most collective bargaining occurs at the enterprise level (between an enterprise union and the management of a firm), industry-level collective bargaining does occur in private railways, bus services, textiles, and some other cases.

The Lifetime Employment Principle

Japanese firms, particularly the large ones, tend to hire new employees upon their graduation from school (high school graduation for blue-collar workers and university graduation for managers), and the employees stay employed with that firm until they reach retirement age. This is **lifetime employment.** To avoid laying off "permanent" employees during business downturns, Japanese firms transfer workers across work areas and sometimes into training. If a large firm faces extreme financial difficulties it might also shift some of its work force to other firms in its **trading group.** The trading groups are firms linked together through either common owners or close business connections.[16] These employees are in effect loaned across companies and return to their original firm if it recovers.

The internal movement of permanent employees within and across firms is facilitated by the fact that workers receive extensive training and often rotate across jobs in a work area (or across work areas) during their work careers. This, like many of the other industrial relations practices in Japan, leads employees to strongly identify their personal interests with those of the firm.

Japanese firms can fulfill their promise to avoid laying off "permanent" employees because they also employ large numbers of workers on a part-time or temporary basis. These workers then fall outside the lifetime employment system.

In addition, workers retire relatively early in Japanese firms. Traditionally the average retirement age was 55; today it has risen to a mean of 64 in the face of declines in the number of new workers entering the Japanese workforce.

Many employees promoted to supervisory and/or management were previously union members and some were union leaders. Furthermore, the movement between union and management careers can go both ways. When conducting an interview with a vice-president of the Honda Motor Workers Union a few years ago, one of the authors was struck to discover that this person had at one point been a manager at Honda and after serving in a management personnel staff job had decided to run for union office. This practice is not uncommon.[17]

Lifetime employment is not guaranteed through a contractual clause or any other binding agreement between Japanese firms and their workers or unions. Rather, firms promise to try to avoid layoffs. Firms do lay off workers if they are faced by extreme financial pressures, however. This informal arrangement is typical of Japanese industrial relations. Few of the distinguishing features of the Japanese system are the products of legal requirements, nor do they appear in formal contractual language. Instead, Japanese practices are shaped heavily by norms and customs that have built up over the years.

The enterprise union system just described is typical of large firms in Japan; by some estimates it covers one-third of the Japanese work force. But this system is found to a lesser extent in small and medium-sized firms, even though smaller firms often serve as supplier or subcontractor to a large firm.[18] Wages, for example, are typically 15 to 30 percent lower in the small firms, and there is less employment security.

Pay Determination in Japan

Most pay agreements are set in annual negotiations that occur between a firm and the enterprise union. Many pay negotiations occur in the spring as part of the annual national spring offensive (Shunto). In this offensive enterprise unions and managements consider guidelines issued by their respective union and employer associations and give special attention to wage settlements reached in negotiations at a handful of key firms.

Workers typically are paid on a salary basis. Workers also commonly receive annual bonuses that are on the order of five months' salary, although the exact size of the annual bonus varies somewhat in response to the firm's financial performance and management's assessment of individual worker performance.

Workers' pay grades are heavily influenced by an individual's seniority with the firm. **Seniority-based pay** in combination with the lifetime employment system produces a pay system with a heavy role for age. Thus workers who perform identical jobs can receive pay rates that vary significantly as a function of their age and performance appraisal.

Performance Appraisal

The fact that blue-collar workers receive regular performance appraisals (many workers are assessed twice a year) is another important feature of Japanese industrial relations. In a given year a worker who receives a top performance evaluation can receive up to a 10 percent larger pay increase than a worker who receives a poor performance appraisal. Over a worker's career these appraisal-based pay differences can add up and produce sizable differences in pay levels across employees. A worker's promotion and career path will also be heavily influenced by the cumulative effects of performance appraisals.

In the United States, in contrast, while many nonunion firms regularly appraise the performance of their employees, it is rare for blue-collar workers to undergo performance appraisals in traditional unionized settings.

Broad Job Definitions

Jobs in Japan tend to be defined relatively broadly on the shop floor even for blue-collar workers. Such broad job definitions go along with the practice of rotating workers across tasks and the provision of substantial training to the workforce. In addition, the strong links between pay rates and worker age and individual performance lessen the role exercised by job task in pay determination. Some analysts argue that the breadth of job definitions contributes significantly to the flexibility in the Japanese production system.[19]

The Role of Consultation in Japanese Industrial Relations

The labor relations system in Japan relies heavily on informal **consultation** between labor and management to settle disputes. Grievance and arbitration procedures are often included in enterprise-level collective bargaining agreements, but these procedures are rarely used. Instead, grievances are typically settled through consultation at the work shop level. In addition, consultation over broader issues commonly occurs in labor-management committees that operate at the plant and company level. Workers also have input into shop floor production issues through the quality circles that often meet regularly.[20]

Union strength in these labor-management discussions is directly related to their membership and independence from management influence. One of the troubling issues confronting Japanese unions is declining membership. Union density in Japan stood at around

35 percent of the labor force from the early 1950s on through 1973. Since then, union membership (as a percentage of the workforce) has fallen to 19.2 percent as of 2004 (it was 31 percent in 1980). Some analysts wonder if this decline is an inevitable product of enterprise unionism.

Debates continue about the extent to which enterprise unions are truly independent from management influence. This arises as an issue not only because of the enterprise nature of union structure but also because of the heavy role played by labor-management consultation in the Japanese system. Critics see in this consultation the co-optation of independent unionism, whereas others see an industrial relations system that successfully mediates conflict as it provides gains in the form of high levels of employee commitment, economic growth, pay, and employment security.

Industrial Relations in Multinational Firms

A **multinational firm** engages in economic activity in more than one country. Over the last 50 years multinational firms have expanded greatly, to the point that they now assert a major influence on world commerce and the conduct of industrial relations in nearly every country.[21] This section considers why and the extent to which industrial relations in a multinational firm is different from that in a firm that operates solely in one country.

The framework developed in earlier parts of this book can be used to understand how industrial relations works in a multinational firm. The basic nature of the conflict between labor and management and the logic of how the environment affects the bargaining process and bargaining outcomes is not fundamentally altered because a firm operates in more than one country. Furthermore, it also makes sense to distinguish between strategic, middle, and workplace levels of industrial relations in multinational firms just as we can in firms that are solely "domestic." Thus, the three-tiered framework applies to multinational firms.

Problems Created by Multinationals for Management and Labor

A firm's operation in more than one country does add pressures to the conduct of industrial relations. The most important factors are the extensive cultural, legal, and institutional differences that multinational firms face and the bargaining power advantages that multinational operation provides to management.

For management, the key decision that emerges from the diverse political and social institutions that they face in different countries is how much to centralize the direction of industrial relations. At one extreme, industrial relations management can be centralized in the corporate offices of the multinational. Alternatively, local management in each country in which the multinational operates can be allowed to independently direct industrial relations.

For labor, the key problem created by multinationals is responding to the bargaining power advantage that management gains from its ability to shift production and capital across country boundaries in the multinational firm.

The Pressure of Diversity

The management of a multinational enterprise confronts cultural, legal, and institutional diversity. Cultural diversity arises from the fact that workers in different countries often view work differently, attach different meanings to work, and place different demands on their unions.[22]

Of course, management in any firm faces some diversity across workers in their culture and attitudes toward work. Some workers are concerned most about their pensions, whereas others may be most concerned about their current income and pay little attention to deferred compensation. Some workers have strong work ethics and would like to work on their own, whereas others may need constant supervision. The extent of this cultural diversity widens, however, as the firm crosses national boundaries. As a result, for example, compensation policies that work in one country may be inappropriate in another. Or, communication and motivation techniques that succeed in one culture will fail in another.[23]

There is also wide diversity in the legal regulation of industrial relations and employment conditions and the institutions shaping industrial relations across countries. In some countries, for example, national laws recognize workers' rights to form unions and carry out strikes; in other countries unions are outlawed or dominated by the government. In some countries the national government extensively regulates the substance of employment conditions. Commonly in Europe, for example, national governments stipulate employee rights to challenge dismissal (and government labor courts hear such cases), whereas, as we have discussed, in the United States in the nonunion sector employment at will is the rule.

The labor movement also differs markedly in its ideology and form across countries. In European countries, for example, labor unions are often affiliated with a particular political party. In France, the two most important unions and their political affiliations are, respectively, the CGT (affiliated with the Communist Party) and the CFDT (affiliated with the Socialist Party). By contrast, in the United States (and some other countries) unions are not formally linked to any political party.

Furthermore, the structure of unions differs markedly across countries. In Germany, for example, IG Metall represents workers across firms in metal working industries such as auto, steel, machine tools, and electronics. In contrast, in Canada (as in the United States) there are a variety of craft and industrial unions and only a few unions (such as the Teamsters and SEIU) that include workers from a number of industries.[24]

The Degree of Industrial Relations Centralization

The presence of so much diversity in culture, law, and institutions poses control and coordination problems for the multinational firm. Management's problem is how to pursue companywide objectives through industrial relations policies in the face of all the diversity that arises across the multinational firm.

Traditionally, multinational firms responded to this problem by maintaining a high degree of local control (decentralization) in the direction of industrial relations.[25] Analysts of multinational firms, in fact, generally conclude that the administration of industrial relations is more decentralized than other management functions such as finance or marketing.

Multinationals found that there were substantial benefits to be gained from the decentralization of industrial relations. These benefits include the ability to respond flexibly to the diversity discussed above. By allowing local managers in each country to fashion industrial relations policies, these managers could create policies and procedures that fit with local conditions and events.

In recent years, however, multinational firms have begun to increase the central control and administration of industrial relations. Centralization of a corporate function has always had the advantage of providing consistency and scale economies. Yet diversity in local environments overwhelmed these advantages in the past.

Why then the switch to more centralized control? The explanation appears to lie in the fact that multinational firms are becoming more global in their strategies and organizational form.[26] The emergence of global firms leads management to strive to integrate their internal operations and policies. If production across national boundaries is integrated, for example, it makes less sense for the multinational firm to maintain wide variation in industrial relations policies. The opening of trade through mechanisms such as the European Union, the North American Free Trade Agreement, and the formation of other regional trading blocs provides further impetus to corporate globalization.

This trend provides another illustration of one of the central themes of this book—namely, that managements are increasingly striving to link industrial relations more closely to business strategy. Increased globalization induces multinational firms to first develop particular business strategies and then align their production and industrial relations systems with those business strategies. This is not very different from the pressures at work in domestic firms. The special dilemma for industrial relations managers in the multinationals, however, is that culture, law, and institutions retain much of their international diversity at the same time that globalization has increased the premium on coordination and centralization.

The Power Advantage Provided to Management by Multinational Operation

The expansion of economic activity across national boundaries poses a bargaining power disadvantage for workers and unions. Multinational operation allows management to shift production and capital across national borders and raises the competitive pressures facing the work force. The concepts discussed earlier in this book illustrate how this can happen.

If faced by a strike in their operations in one country, management can gain a bargaining power advantage from multinational operation if it can turn to alternative production facilities in other countries or substitute workers in other countries for those out on strike. In many ways, the expansion of the firm across multinational boundaries is an extension of the same forces that were at work in early industrialization. As John Commons noted, the expansion of markets in early industrialization created "competitive menaces" for workers and weakened the bargaining leverage of unions.

Multinational operation confronts workers with new competitive menaces. Imagine, for example, the pressures faced by high-paid western European (or North American) workers because multinational firms operating in their countries can shift production to countries in which workers receive hourly wages that are a fraction of those received in western Europe and where environmental and other social regulations are weaker, what European unionists refer to as "social dumping."

The primary way a union could counter the advantages management gains from the expansion of markets is to expand the union's jurisdiction so it is coextensive with the boundaries of the multinational. If this were accomplished, the resulting **multinational unionism** would be better able to remove competition across workers in the different locations in which the multinational operates.

Multinational Unionism

In the United States at the start of the twentieth century unions expanded their jurisdiction by shifting from local or regional unions to become national unions.[27] How successful have unions been at following a similar strategy and becoming multinational? This section examines that issue.

The expansion of firms across national boundaries creates strong incentives for unions to expand their jurisdiction across national boundaries and create multinational unions. Even though there are some examples of multinational unions or at least the coordination of policies of national unions, overall, their occurrence has been infrequent.[28] Let us consider why this has been so and then look at some counterexamples.

The Difficulties Unions Face

Unions have found it difficult to become multinational because of the wide diversity that exists across countries in culture, law, and institutions as discussed above.[29] It is difficult enough for a union operating in one country to maintain cohesion and solidarity across its members. When the economic and cultural differences, communication difficulties, and fears that exist across workers in different countries are added on top of the normal problems, the maintenance of solidarity becomes a nearly insurmountable problem.

Consider the problems that multinational operation in less developed as well as highly industrialized countries creates for union solidarity. Workers in a less developed country, who earn low wages and face few employment alternatives, are generally very reluctant to support the bargaining demands of their high-wage counterparts in developed countries. There are strong short-run incentives for the workers in these two countries to view each other as competitors.

Furthermore, imagine how hard it is for a union to communicate to its members if those members speak a variety of languages. Indeed, the managers in a multinational firm typically have a lot of awareness of company objectives and worldwide activities, whereas workers and unions, in contrast, are often hard-pressed to gain information about such activities.[30]

The merger of independent unions across national borders has not been a solution to multinational pressures. The merger of independent unions is difficult enough even within a single country where there are strong bargaining power advantages to be gained. Even greater impediments exist for such a merger if it were to involve two unions based in different countries that represent workers at the same multinational firm.

It is most likely that the structure of two unions that might consider merging would not be similar even if the workers were employed by the same firm. Autoworkers in the United States, for example, are represented by an industrial union (UAW), whereas autoworkers in Germany belong to a union that spans industries (IG Metall). Similar problems exist even if the two unions were to merely coordinate their bargaining demands.

Examples of Multinational Unionism

Even in the face of the many impediments to international solidarity and coordination that confront unions, some multinational unionism has followed the expansion of multinational firms. There are, for example, a number of **international trade secretariats** that provide information to member unions and coordinate activities across national borders. These secretariats are autonomous agencies that cover particular industries or groups of industries. The International Metalworkers Federation, one of the most active of these secretariats, includes members from many less developed as well as highly industrialized nations. Among its many activities, it issues research reports to its members.

Many of the secretariats have a close working relationship with the International Federation of Free Trade Unions (ICFTU). The ICFTU includes affiliated unions that represent 48 million workers around the world. The ICFTU includes non-Communist unions.

The World Federation of Trade Unions (WRTU) at one time represented 134 million workers in the Communist unions that were affiliated with it.[31] Nevertheless, the political differences that traditionally separated these federations and many of their member unions have impeded coordination across these and other union federations.

The global expansion of trade is leading unions around the world to communicate more extensively with unions in other countries. Box 14–3 describes a global network recently formed involving 20 unions that represent employees at the various international operations of the International Paper Company. As multinational corporations expand it is only natural to expect further expansion of union networks. A key challenge for unions is whether increased cross-national communications and company networks will lead to the formation of cross-national unions.

There also are some cases in which unions in different countries have coordinated their response to the actions taken by a particular multinational firm. Box 14–4 describes how the Communications Workers of America helped Mexican unions win representation rights at Maxi-Switch, a computer keyboard manufacturer that has plants in Mexico. This case also is interesting as it involved complaint procedures established as part of the North American Free Trade Agreement discussed more fully on the following pages.

The Expansion of International Trade Through Trade Pacts

Expanded trade has been spurred in recent years through efforts to integrate European markets through the formation of the **European Union (EU),** through the negotiation of the **North American Free Trade Agreement (NAFTA)** linking Canada, the United States, and Mexico, and other regional trade pacts. The next section discusses these developments as they are both important in their own right and informative of the issues involved in multinational unionism.

NAFTA

NAFTA, which took effect in January 1994, removes tariffs and other trade barriers among the United States, Mexico, and Canada over a 15-year period. Both the passage and the continuing effects of NAFTA have been extremely controversial. NAFTA has been widely criticized by labor unions who claim that Mexico's low wages cause many U.S. firms to relocate south of the border. Meanwhile, environmentalists worry that companies flee south in order to take advantage of weak pollution controls and lax enforcement of environmental regulations. Presidents Clinton and Bush, the American business community, and many economists, on the other side of this debate, support NAFTA on grounds that it provides gains through trade to all three countries. Furthermore, NAFTA supporters claim that it will help integrate Mexico more fully into the world economy and thereby address Mexico's social problems and their spillover effects on the United States (such as high immigration and the drug trade).

To address its critics, side agreements were added to NAFTA concerning the environment and labor rights. The labor side agreements create National Administrative Offices authorized to investigate public charges that one of the NAFTA countries is not enforcing its own labor laws. Box 14–5 describes the first test case of the NAFTA labor protections. (Also see the description of events involving union organizing and Maxi-Switch described in Boxes 14–4, 14–5, and 14–6.)

NAFTA also includes a "Transitional Adjustment Assistance" (TAA) program to provide training to workers who lose their jobs because of the trade pact. In 2005, the U.S. Department of Labor certified $165 million for NAFTA-TAA benefits.[32] Economist Lori Kletzer estimates that NAFTA import-related job loss accounted for 24 to 27 percent (1,238,593 workers) of the jobs lost in manufacturing in the United States over the 1993–1999 period.[33]

On September 12, 1994, a group of Mexican workers told a U.S. panel that they and coworkers were harassed and eventually fired because of their union activity at "maquiladora" plants in northern Mexico near the U.S. border operated by Honeywell Inc. and General Electric Company. These allegations formed the first test case of the labor protections in the North American Free Trade Agreement (NAFTA). Under the NAFTA side accord, each country (the United States, Canada, and Mexico) created its own National Administrative Office responsible for, among other things, investigating public charges that one of the NAFTA countries did not enforce its own labor laws. Furthermore, public complaints must relate to the government's efforts to enforce its labor laws, not to a particular company's labor practices.

Officials from Honeywell and GE did not testify at the hearing but in prepared statements dismissed the unions' complaints, calling the allegations another effort to undermine NAFTA. The main participants at the hearing were the Mexican workers themselves, who described workplaces characterized by repression, fear, and retaliation against workers who supported union activities. Ofelia Sanchez, a 23-year-old worker at Honeywell's plant, for example, said she was fired after she refused to give company officials the names of other workers supporting the union organizing drive. She also detailed how workers were not adequately protected against the toxic chemicals they used, and how some were forced to work faster and longer than they physically could.

In October 1994, the U.S. National Administrative Office found that there was no evidence to show that Mexico failed to enforce its labor laws when dealing with Honeywell Inc. and the General Electric Corporation. The review was not "aimed primarily at determining whether or not the two companies . . . may have acted in violation of Mexican labor law," but rather to "gather as much information as possible to better understand and publically report on" the Mexican government's promotion, compliance, and effective enforcement of its labor law in accordance with NAFTA.

Sources: This account draws heavily from, "NAFTA Labor Protections Put to First Test as Mexican Workers Tell U.S. About Firings," *Daily Labor Report,* Bureau of National Affairs, no. 175, September 13, 1994, pp. A–12–14; and "NAO Closes Complaints Against Honeywell, GE," *Daily Labor Report,* Bureau of National Affairs, no. 197, October 14, 1994, p. AA–1.

Labor unions complain that this assistance program fails to meet the needs of the much larger number of workers harmfully affected by NAFTA, while critics argue that many assisted workers lost their jobs for reasons that had nothing to do with NAFTA or trade. Needless to say, there is much continuing debate in the United States regarding the effects of NAFTA on workers and the U.S. and Mexican economies.

Even in the face of debate about the effects of NAFTA, in the fall of 2002, Congress extended "fast track" trade negotiating authority to President George Bush. As Box 14–1 points out, the new fast track authorization included additional trade adjustment and retraining assistance to workers displaced by imports.

The International Labor Rights Movement

A variety of organizations and activities seeking to protect international labor rights have been spurred in recent years by concerns about the effects of globalization. Labor rights activists worry that globalization will set off a downward spiral in labor and social conditions. On university campuses these concerns have been manifest in student protests concerning global sweatshops and the working conditions in factories in developing countries.

Union Organizing in Mexico's Maquiladora Industry

Box 14–6

An independent union in Mexico has set the precedent for collective bargaining rights for the maquiladora industry by organizing a plant in Mexico City called Kukdong de Mexico. The new independent union is the Sindicato de Trabajadores de la Empresa Mex Mode. Kukdong, which supplies clothing for Nike and Reebok, had been pressured by international labor groups because of its failure to allow its employees to organize. Labor rights groups, such as the Workers Rights Consortium, also accused the plant of mistreating its workers by providing substandard food and bathroom facilities, physically abusing workers, employing children, and paying wages below the minimum. To symbolize a change in the plant's practices, its name has been changed to Mex Mode.

Mex Mode, the first to be organized in its industry, is a maquiladora, or an export-oriented manufacturing and assembly plant located near the U.S border for easy access to the U.S. market. Scott Nova, director of the Workers Rights Consortium, said that the newly negotiated contract had small economic gains for workers. However, he said the symbolic effect was more important, noting that "the key factor is the creation and recognition of the independent union."

Although unions have long been key players in labor relations in Mexico, labor activists hope the new union will be different from previous ones. Before the certification of this union, Mex Mode was represented by a "traditional" union known as the CROC or, in English, the Revolutionary Worker and Peasant Confederation. Like other traditional unions, the CROC had worked closely with Mexico's former ruling party, the Institutional Revolutionary Party, and was known for routinely negotiating with management and the government to install low-wage "protection contracts" that did not represent workers. Activists claimed that the CROC presence at the former Kukdong plant was part of a government policy aimed at attracting and keeping foreign investment.

One activist said he hoped that recognition of an independent union would be a "watershed" event for Mexico that would lead to the formation of independent unions throughout the maquiladora industry. However, a major obstacle in the process may be a lack of political will for change, even though laws give workers the right to organize.

Source: "Certification of Independent Labor Union at Maquiladora May Set Mexican Precedent," *Daily Labor Report* 190, November 3, 2001:A-11.

As Box 14–7 describes, two consortiums involving unions, employers, and nongovernmental organizations seek to monitor and improve global labor standards in the apparel industry. Also increasing in prominence are "fair" trade initiatives on coffee and other consumer goods oriented on providing a fair return to producers in order to support decent work and other activities focused on limiting child labor and strengthening unionism in developing countries. U.S. unions also have sought to improve international labor standards and conditions by influencing U.S. trade practices. Box 14–8 describes the efforts of the AFL-CIO to challenge China's labor practices.

Collective bargaining based efforts as well as political channels increasingly are being used by U.S. unions have to improve the employment and working conditions of American workers through reductions in offshore outsourcing. Box 14–9 reviews two such efforts, one that focuses on organizing companies whose business is providing outsourced service work, while the other effort involves negotiating the return of previously outsourced work to the United States. Interestingly, both of the examples cited in Box 14–9 involve service work, highlighting the recent controversies surrounding the location of service work.

The European Union

The European Union (EU), previously referred to as the **European Economic Community,** is the most ambitious effort to create a common regional market.[34] The integration of Europe (or steps made toward integration even if full integration is not accomplished) will have major consequences on industrial relations, and industrial relations issues likely will influence the form of integration. This section reviews the history of **European integration** and the industrial relations issues spurred by integration.

The Goals of Integration

A union of countries across Europe was first established by Belgium, France, West Germany, Italy, Luxembourg, and the Netherlands as the European Economic Community. In 1992, the European affiliate countries officially transitioned into existence as the European Union. Currently, the EU consists of 25 member countries. It serves as a governmental organization that unites countries across Europe, providing common law, currency, health and economic policy, and defense. It serves as a legislative body, whose powers are dictated by treaties signed by the individual member states. Most recently, it has transitioned from a primary focus on trade to an economic and political affiliation among its member states. Beyond its affiliate countries, it retains close associations with a number of overseas territories such as Greenland, the Isle of Man, the Azores, and Madeira.

The European Union continues to evolve to meet the needs of its current membership and those hoping to gain admission. Of primary focus are issues regarding structure, constitution, policy, procedure, and membership. A treaty instating a constitution has already been adopted by the heads of states. However, a constitution will not be implemented without the ratification of individual member states.

The next structural change to the European Union included the addition of Romania and Bulgaria on January 1, 2007. The addition of these two countries brought membership to a total of 27 participating countries. In coming years, the EU will monitor its ability to represent its current member states before agreeing to the acceptance of any new member states.

A central goal of European integration is to eliminate trade barriers across the 25 member states of the European Union and to allow the free movement of workers, products, and investments across national borders. Economic integration will remove explicit trade restrictions and tariffs and create greater standardization in government regulations over such matters as products and taxes. Labor relations and other employment laws and policies, now vastly different across the 25 countries, are to be "harmonized" in accordance with directives and regulations issued by the bodies governing the European Union.[35] With the signing of the Maastricht Treaty in the early 1990s, the goal of integration was extended to include full monetary union through the creation of a common currency.

For both labor and management, harmonization could bring a host of costs and benefits.[36] Because so much is at stake, there already has been much disagreement over the exact content and form of labor harmonization. To date, there has been only modest progress by the EU in specifying how and around what standard industrial relations will be integrated, and it is likely that this will continue to be the focus of much debate and controversy in the years ahead.

Preintegration Structure of Industrial Relations in the EU

The regulation of industrial relations and employment conditions varies widely across the 25 EU member nations. The labor movements in the countries also vary substantially in their ideological orientation, organizational structure, and strength.

Unionization rates of the 25 countries were presented in Exhibit 14–3. Compared with the United States, many of the EU nations are highly unionized, yet, as these figures show, there is wide variation. For example, France has a unionization rate of 10 percent, whereas 79 percent of the Swedish and 74 percent of the Denmark work forces are unionized.

Living standards and hourly labor rates also differ markedly across the countries, as reported in Exhibit 14–3. Germany's hourly manufacturing compensation costs ($29.91), for example, are substantially greater than those in the Czech Republic ($4.71) and Portugal ($6.23). It is these wage differences that are at the root of the labor movement's fears that European integration could lead to a lowering of labor standards in Germany and other high-wage countries.

There also are substantial differences in the industrial relations laws and practices in the 25 nations. In Germany, for example (as discussed earlier in this chapter), federal law mandates an elaborate system of works councils and employee representation on corporate boards (also required in Luxembourg and Denmark). In Ireland, in contrast, there are no formal legal requirements for works councils or employee representation on corporate boards.[37]

The structure of union representation also varies substantially across countries. In Spain, for example, unions within a single industry tend to be divided along political lines (this is also characteristic of France). In Germany, Belgium, and Denmark unions often span industries.

EU Regulation of the "Social Dimension"

There has been heated debate among representatives from the 25 nations and between labor and management over what is often referred to as the **social dimension** of European integration.[38] The social dimension includes the regulations, directives, and possible eventual laws that will govern employment and industrial relations policies in the 25 EU countries. The EU already has adopted a variety of health and safety standards, provisions to encourage labor mobility across national borders, provisions promoting gender equality, and special commissions to address these issues.

A major event in European regulation of the social dimension was the issuance of a **Social Charter** in May 1989. Box 14–10 lists the basic topics addressed by the Social Charter. The charter includes giving workers the right to form and join unions and the ability to resort to collective action (i.e., strikes) in the event of conflicts of interests (this right is presently mandated by law by many, but not all, of the EU countries). The Social Charter is a declaration of principles without legal force and leaves it up to member countries to develop specific policies. The charter extends an apparent retreat by the EU from strict harmonization of labor standards and the avoidance of central regulation of industrial relations issues.

Directives that address worker rights in the event of layoffs, employer bankruptcies, or the sale or merger of a company have been adopted by the EU. These directives require member nations to change their laws, if necessary, to conform to the intent of the directive.[39] In 1994, a directive was accepted that promotes Europeanwide works councils in multinational corporations that operate in more than one member country. These councils do not possess any formal powers, but do provide a forum for an exchange of views and "social dialogue." A number of European works councils are now in operation, including councils at a number of American-based multinationals.[40]

Other directives have been proposed and hotly debated, reflecting the differences of opinion that persist across countries and between labor and management.[41] The exact terms of regulation of the social dimension that emerges from integration of the EU market remain to be seen. Furthermore, the implementation of directives, charters, or other regulations will be heavily influenced by subsequent actions taken by governments within the respective countries, as well as by the actions taken by unions and managements.

Labor's Concerns about Integration

Unions are particularly worried that the harmonization of labor standards will bring a lowering of labor standards. In this way European unions are reflecting fears similar to those held by American trade unionists as they confronted the expansion of markets, transportation, and communication systems across the United States at the start of the 20th century. As Commons and others pointed out, unions' fears of the competition created by expanding markets are well founded.

At the same time, the heightened trade and associated economic development that may follow from market integration could provide benefits to labor. Large gains may be received by workers and unions in the countries that currently have lower labor standards if integration leads to greater investments in those countries.

The steps being taken to centrally regulate industrial relations in the integrated market also provide the possibility of union gains. Through European integration and the creation of a strong oversight regulation provided by the EU, unions might be able to raise labor standards to levels they were unable to otherwise accomplish. This is the primary reason why, for example, the British unions favor European integration. Many of the directives (adopted or proposed) and the Social Charter extend aspects of the employee and union representation now provided in Germany to countries that have not on their own seen fit to extend such rights.

So, it is not clear that unions (or workers) will necessarily lose from market integration. Much depends on how market integration is regulated.

Management Concerns over European Integration

Managements operating in either one country or multinationally stand to benefit from the reduction in trade restrictions that will come with market integration.[42] In the preintegration economic system, multinational corporations confront a myriad of regulations and a variety of industrial relations practices in the countries in which they operate. Market integration, therefore, could greatly simplify the management of industrial relations across the EU countries. Integration also could greatly increase the flexibility within corporate operations by easing the movement of people and operations across national boundaries. European managers see the formation of a European union as offering their firms more strategic options as to where to locate and what business and labor relations strategies to pursue. They hope this will bring increased managerial discretion.

At the same time, management in Europe (and in multinationals headquartered outside of Europe) are worried about the possible restrictions and heightened labor costs that might follow from increased EU regulation of industrial relations. Management's fears here are the reciprocal of the labor worries discussed above.

Management would like to have greater freedom to move workers and capital, in part to achieve greater flexibility and to take advantage of the lower costs found in some of the EU countries. Yet the integration of markets simultaneously has created a centralized regulatory process that might give unions and workers bargaining leverage to counter management's moves. Management's worry and the union's hope is that EU centralized regulation accomplishes what in other situations is attained by labor through collective negotiations between an individual employer and a union.

This explains some of the motivation for management to oppose the Vredling Directive and many others of the proposals being debated. Management generally prefers that the regulation of industrial relations and employment conditions be left to the member nations or to the parties at the firm level and that centralized regulations be avoided.

Industrial Relations in Developing Countries

Even with the diversity in the industrial relations practices and institutions found in the United States, Japan, and the EU countries, there are still many similarities among them. In all these countries, for instance, national laws give workers the right to join unions, and these unions have the right to strike.[43] Furthermore, although the exact terms of union–government and union–management relations vary across the countries, in all the countries labor unions are independent from government or management dominance. Unions are independent in the sense that they generally exercise free will and conduct democratic elections to determine union leadership and union policies.

Workers and labor unions do not possess such rights in countries that lack democratic governments and political pluralism. In these countries, in contrast, workers are denied the right to join unions. If unions exist at all, they are typically dominated by the government and/or employers. Yet history suggests that the outlawing or dominance of independent trade unions does not eliminate labor conflict, and in some ways only postpones and intensifies it. In the end, all countries are forced to wrestle with how to structure industrial relations in a manner that provides workers with enough representation at least to satisfy those workers while also maintaining social stability and economic growth.

In the 1980s and 1990s these issues came to the fore as **democratization** movements arose in many developing countries. The next sections review developments in Poland and Korea, countries with very different cultures and histories. At the same time, these two countries nicely illustrate how the labor movement and industrial relations issues are at the center of the democratization processes.

Industrial Relations and Political Change in Poland

In July 1980 the Polish government announced steep price increases in basic foodstuffs for the third time in a 10-year period. In 1980, as in 1970 and 1976, workers responded with protests, but unlike the previous two occasions, the strikers did not return to work after the government agreed to repeal the price increases. Rather, the workers at the Lenin Shipyard, under the leadership of Lech Walesa, demanded the right to establish a free and independent trade union. After a two-week sit-in strike and intensive public negotiations, the trade union **Solidarity** was born.

Throughout the remainder of 1980 and 1981, the government came under increasing pressure from the Soviet Union and elements of the Communist Party to erode the power of Solidarity. The union, in turn, persisted in its attempts to enforce the spirit of the Gdansk accords, and at its national congress in August 1981 went one step further by supporting the cause of free trade unionism throughout the socialist bloc. The months after the congress were marked by a further deterioration of the Polish economy and growing tension between the trade union and the government. The crisis of authority culminated in the imposition of martial law, the imprisonment of Solidarity leaders, and the repeal of the union's legal mandate.

In the years that followed martial law, the government's attempts to implement economic reform were undermined by the absence of a social accord. Refusing to allow the emergence of consultative institutions, yet recognizing the need for societal consensus, the government decided to hold a popular referendum in the fall of 1987 to legitimate its economic reform program. Despite the government campaign, the proposed referendum was voted down.

Without a comprehensive program for restructuring the Polish economy, it was only a matter of time before a restive work force would once again attempt to organize. Indeed, in the spring and summer after the failed referendum, workers in a number of key industrial establishments went on strike. Despite the determination of the striking workers, the government did not yield to their demands. Finally, after the intervention of Lech Walesa, the strikers returned to work with the understanding that the relegalization of Solidarity would be Walesa's central demand at the upcoming "roundtable" discussions.

After a number of false starts, Solidarity and government representatives finally began the roundtable talks in February 1989, and two months later an accord was reached. Under the terms of the roundtable agreement, Solidarity was allowed to register as a trade union, and a new constitution was to be introduced that included the establishment of a democratically elected Senate and a restructured parliament. In June 1989 Solidarity candidates were swept into office, paving the way for Poland's transition to a market economy. Then in December 1990 Lech Walesa won a landslide victory in Poland's first direct presidential elections.

Severe challenges then confronted the Polish economy and Poland's political leadership. By 1991 it was clear that Poland's transition to a market economy would involve severe economic dislocation. The unemployment rate was rising and industrial output was falling. Solidarity also faced challenges as it attempted to work with a government whose rise to power was the result of support received from the trade union movement. Solidarity has subsequently been torn between its desire to provide political leadership while remaining independent of the government in a new pluralistic Poland.

In recent years, Solidarity has had a difficult time formulating a new strategy. In the first years of the transition, the trade union leadership initially supported a fiscally conservative macroeconomic program that resulted in severe economic dislocation. At the same time, the union had an ambivalent view of its own role in firm governance. Prior to a firm's privatization, Solidarity used its influence to help ensure that employees receive an economic stake in the firm. After a firm's privatization, Solidarity was less sure of its new role and tended to cede broad managerial prerogatives to new owners.

As privatization spread more and more workers have come to face greater economic uncertainty and reduced voice in firms, and as a result many employees withdrew their support from Solidarity. The result has been a fragmentation of the Solidarity movement.

In recent years the key economic problem facing the Polish economy has been high unemployment. This created particularly difficult problems for the new left-wing government that came to power following parliamentary elections in 2001. The government offered various proposals for amendments to the Labor Code, which seek to reduce labor costs and make labor law more flexible.

A number of differences of opinion have emerged between the two largest trade union organizations, NSZZ 'Soldarno' and OPZZ, in the debates over labor law reforms. Negotiations over the changes to the labor code are being conducted in the re-invigorated Tripartite Commission, which includes the main national employers' and employees' organizations and the government. The Commission, created in 1993, had virtually ceased to function from 1996–2001 due to disagreements between the two main union organizations.

While overall the strike rate declined dramatically from 1995 on, this was largely due to trade union weakness. With a few exceptions, vibrant and militant unions only now appear in the public sector. Over the past 20 years, trade union density in Poland dropped from 80 percent of the workforce to 15 percent in 2004.[44]

Industrial Relations and Political Change in Korea

Trade unions in Korea have not attained the status and strong political role acquired by Solidarity. Rather, Korea is struggling with the issue of how far to democraticize its political system and the role that trade unions and collective bargaining will play in Korean society.

The post–World War II history of Korea is marked by authoritarian rule by governments in league with the military. Nevertheless, periodically, violent political protests have erupted to challenge that rule.[45] Labor unions have played leading roles in those political protests. Collective bargaining has taken hold in a number of large firms such as Hyundai and Lucky Goldstar, but is much weaker in small and medium-sized firms.[46]

Korea has experienced periodic violent labor protests. The first major wave of labor protests occurred in the middle of 1987 after the ruling Democratic Justice's Party presidential candidate (and eventual victor in a subsequent election), Roh Tae-Woo, pledged his support for popular elections to determine a new president of the Republic of Korea. The subsequent democratization process unleashed popular protests and demands among Koreans, particularly within the trade union movement.

A massive strike wave followed, along with a rapid rise in union membership and a wage explosion. On May 2, 1990, for example, there were violent protests in the port city of Ulsan when 30,000 workers from affiliated Hyundai companies held rallies at work sites to protest a massive police raid that had occurred earlier on strikers at the Hyundai Heavy Industries Company.

Worker protests were in part directed at existing trade unions and union leaders. There was an array of unions affiliated with the Korean Federation of Trade Unions. Yet protesting workers opposed the complicity that had existed between these unions and the government and employers. Protesting workers not only demanded higher wages and better working conditions but also sought procedures that would allow the emergence of unions that were independent from government and managerial dominance. Some new unions sprang up in response to these demands, such as Chunnohyop, a new federation of independent unions, even though the government did not recognize their legitimacy.

The protest wave cooled down in the early 1990s but then another wave of labor protest occurred in early 1997. This wave of protest was spurred by government efforts to change Korea's labor laws so as to introduce more flexibility into the labor market and address international competitive problems that had begun to surface in Korea.

It should be kept in mind that although Korea's growth rate was slowing below the extreme highly rates experienced in the 1970s and 1980s, often in the range of 15 percent growth per year, in the mid-1990s Korea's economy was still growing at rates that were quite respectable (at around 7 percent per year) when compared with the growth being experienced in the United States and many European economies (3 percent per year or less). Nevertheless, the Korean business community was feeling increased international competitive pressure and felt constrained by Korea's labor laws. These laws made it difficult for firms to lay off workers and enabled striking workers to subsequently often receive full back pay for any wages lost during a strike. Meanwhile, the Korean labor movement wanted to establish the right of workers to join officially recognized unions that did not belong to the government-sanctioned trade union confederation and wanted to improve employment conditions, especially those in small and medium-sized firms.

Labor protests erupted in January 1997 after a secret session of the National Assembly (held without the opposition elected members of the opposition parties and with the support of the President of Korea) imposed a harsh bill that among other things made it easier for firms to lay-off employees. A three-week strike wave followed with strikes concentrated in the large firms including Hyundai Motor Car Company. The strike wave cooled and was followed by months of often behind-the-scene negotiations, which led to a new labor law bill that was adopted in March 1997 with the support of the opposition and government political parties.[47]

Then a financial crisis, which had started in Thailand and Indonesia and spread to other parts of Asia in the summer of 1997, also engulfed Korea. After the collapse of a number of major firms and banks, the Korean currency (the won) collapsed. A rescue package involving $57 billion in loans was eventually provided by the International Monetary Fund (with United States backing), but only after the Korean government agreed to radically change the country's economic policies and labor laws. A key labor issue was the allowance of layoffs. Initially, Korean unions were unwilling to allow layoffs and threatened to conduct national protest strikes. The unions relented after negotiations held in a new Tripartite Commission produced other "compromise" industrial relations changes, including legalization of collective bargaining for public school teachers and the creation of an unemployment fund.

The successful completion of these Tripartite negotiations and the eventual easing of Korea's international debt and currency crisis was aided by the election of President Kim Dae-jung in December 1997. Kim had been jailed for many years as a political dissident and during those years had the strong support of labor unions. It appeared that only Kim was able to guarantee to unions that their concerns would be heard and that workers would be fairly compensated if, and when, the Korean economy recovered. In that way, political democratization was intimately linked to industrial relations changes and broader economic events in Korea.

By 2000 the Korean economy was growing again at a solid rate. However, much instability remained in the country's industrial-relations system. Unions were bitter about the fact that workers had to bear substantial costs during the 1997–99 economic crisis in the form of layoffs and pay cuts. Even in the face of the recent economic recovery, there was a significant increase in the amount of nonregular (i.e., temporary) employment.[48] Nonregular employees lacked employment security and fringe benefits and they typically received substantially lower wages as compared to regular employees. A number of nonregular employees, including many in the banking industry, previously worked as regular employees, but after being laid off they were rehired as nonregular employees by the same firm, even though they continued to carry out many of the same job duties.

To enhance their bargaining leverage, a number of Korean unions are seeking industry-wide bargaining. In the banking industry, the first industrywide collective bargaining agreement was signed in 2001. Yet, it remains to be seen if this trend toward more centralized collective bargaining grows and whether it actually enhances union leverage.

Similarities in the Issues in Poland and Korea

What is similar about events in Poland and Korea? Poland was attempting to radically transform its economy through the introduction of markets and incentives. At the same time, Poland was creating new democratic institutions to replace those that had been Communist dominated.

Meanwhile, Korea approached the issue of how to structure and stabilize industrial relations from a very different political and economic history. In Korea it was autocratic and military rule that had previously dominated and controlled the labor movement. Furthermore, Korea had undergone enormous economic growth since 1960. It was not confronted with the issue of creating a market economy.

Yet in both Poland and Korea, as in many other developing countries, how to create and sustain more democratic and stable industrial relations were major political and economic issues. In both countries, in the long run the suppression of industrial relations and independent unionism proved to be neither socially stable nor economically productive.

Comparative Economic and Industrial Relations Performance

There are long-standing debates as to whether any particular economic system outperforms other systems and the contribution that industrial relations makes to economic performance. These debates ebb and flow with the ups and downs of various countries' economic fortunes. In the 1980s, reflecting Japan's strong economic and export growth, a number of analysts heralded the Japanese economic system. A related claim was that the Japanese industrial relations system played a key role in that economic success by stimulating employee loyalty and problem solving. The German economic and industrial relations system also received much praise in the 1980s, the latter was cheered on the grounds that the codetermination system facilitated skill development and conflict resolution.

In the 1990s this debate shifted in response to the strong economic performance, particularly the price stability and employment growth, which appeared in the United States. The U.S. economic system then began to receive praise for its flexibility and promotion of entrepreneurialism. As the unemployment rate dropped to historic lows in the late 1990s, some analysts claimed that traditional internal labor markets had been replaced by "boundaryless" careers (i.e., frequent job changes).[49] Furthermore, the tightening of labor markets led to accelerated wage growth, particularly among highly skilled employees such as software programmers and high-tech engineers.

The debate on comparative economic system performance shifted yet again after the bursting of the dot.com bubble in the spring of 2000 and the emergence of corporate financial scandals involving Enron, Worldcom, and other major U.S. corporations. Criticisms surfaced concerning whether the market and financially oriented U.S. economic system gave too much authority to corporate owners and top executives and provided too limited a role to representatives of the public and employees. While unionism served to check executive authority in other countries, the U.S. labor movement appeared to be too weak to serve that role. Whether unionism or some other form of employee voice will rise to fill this void in the United States is an open question (and subject to further discussion in the final chapter of this book).

Summary

There are substantial differences in the way industrial relations are practiced in Germany, Japan, and the United States. In the United States collective bargaining is relatively decentralized and the written collective bargaining agreement plays a central role. The American collective bargaining system is also noteworthy for its heavy reliance on grievance and arbitration procedures.

In Germany, by contrast, codetermination procedures are central. These procedures provide employees with parallel representation from unions and works councils. Collective bargaining in Germany usually occurs on a regional or industrial basis and produces annual labor agreements.

In Japan, enterprise unions are dominant, and these unions represent both blue- and white-collar employees in a firm. Disputes tend to be settled and information exchanged through a variety of consultative procedures. Worker seniority and the economic performance of the firm influence worker earnings, and annual bonuses are an important share of worker compensation.

Yet, even in the face of these country differences there are some common trends across countries. In most of the countries mentioned in this chapter, there is movement to more decentralized collective bargaining.

In addition, the expansion of team systems of work organization, often associated with the adoption of just-in-time and other "lean" production techniques, is common in many countries. Interest in international comparisons of management and labor practices is currently at an all-time high. Interest has been spurred in part by the expansion of multinational firms and the expansion of regional trading blocs. The process of collective bargaining and the determinants of bargaining power do not change fundamentally as a firm moves multinational. Yet unions generally see their bargaining leverage weakened as firms expand production across country borders. It remains to be seen how well high-wage countries are able to protect their high employment standards in the face of heightened international trade.

All countries must wrestle with the issue of how to structure industrial relations. Where collective bargaining and unions flourished in the past, the pressures of globalization are raising questions about the future viability of these institutions. Meanwhile, countries that lack stable industrial relations due to continuing labor suppression must face the fact that free and independent labor movements have been central to the development of democracy throughout history.

Discussion Questions

1. Briefly describe how codetermination works in Germany.

2. Describe three significant ways industrial relations in Japan differ from industrial relations in the United States.

3. What are some of the factors that make it difficult for unions to coordinate their efforts across national borders?

4. Why are some unionists worried about European integration? What are some of management's concerns about European integration?

5. Do you think NAFTA is a good idea? How would your views change if you were a trade union leader? A business executive?

6. What role did unions play in the democratization of Korea and Poland? What are the implications for public policy in developing or developed countries of the links between unions and democratization?

Related Web Sites

Volkswagen:
http://www.vw.com/vwworld/history.htm

International Federation of Free Trade Unions (ICFTU):
http://signet.com.sg/ ~icftu/welcome.htm

Japan Institute of Labor:
http://www.jil.go.jp/bulletin/index.htm

North American Free Trade Agreement (NAFTA):
http://www.nafta.net/naftagre.htm

Maxi-Switch:
http://www.maxiswitch.com/index.htm

European Union (EU):
http://europa.eu.int/en/eu.html

Hyundai Motor Car Co.:
http://www.hyundai.com/inside/index.htm

International Labor Organization:
www.ilo.org

Paperworkers union:
www.paceunion.org

Quadrtech case:
www.iue-cwa.org/quadrtech.htm

Workers Rights Consortium:
www.workersrights.org

Fair Labor Association:
www.fairlabor.org

Suggested Readings

Bamber, Greg J., and Russell D. Lansbury, eds. *International and Comparative Industrial Relations,* 4th ed. (London: Allen & Unwin, 2002).

Berghahn, Volker R., and Detlev Karsten. *Industrial Relations in West Germany* (Oxford: Berg Publisher, 1987).

Cole, Robert E. *Japanese Blue Collar* (Berkeley and Los Angeles: University of California Press, 1971).

Cusumano, Michael. *The Japanese Automobile Industry* (Cambridge, MA: Harvard University Press, 1986).

Flanagan, Robert J., and Arnold R. Weber, eds. *Bargaining without Boundaries* (Chicago: University of Chicago Press, 1974).

Gladwin, Thomas N., and Ingo Walter. *Multinationals under Fire* (New York: Wiley, 1980).

Katz, Harry C., and Owen Darbishire. *Converging Divergences: Worldwide Changes in Employment Systems* (Ithaca, New York: ILR Press, 2000).

End Notes

1. Throughout this chapter we refer to Germany even though some of the history recounted refers to the history of West Germany. With the unification of Germany, the national laws of West Germany were extended to what was previously East Germany, including laws about industrial relations. Needless to say, unification has brought substantial changes to industrial relations practices and institutions in what was formerly East Germany.

2. From 1960 to 1980 the annual rate of growth in productivity in manufacturing in the United States, Germany, and Japan was, respectively, 2.7, 5.4, and 9.4 percent. See Patricia Capdevielle and Donato Alvarez, "International Comparisons of Trends in Productivity and Labor Costs," *Monthly Labor Review* 104 (December 1981), p. 16.

3. This section draws heavily from Friedrich Fuerstenberg, "Industrial Relations in the Federal Republic of Germany," in

International and Comparative Industrial Relations, ed. Greg J. Bamber and Russell D. Lansbury (London: Allen & Unwin, 1987), pp. 165–86.

4. The major federal laws establishing the codetermination structure were the Codetermination Acts of 1951 and 1976. At the same time, there were long historical traditions to this system. Works councils were first established by law in 1916, in industries that were important for the economy in the First World War, and they became obligatory under the Works Council Act of 1920. See Fuerstenberg, "Industrial Relations in the Federal Republic of Germany," for more on this history.

5. Supervisory boards generally meet four times a year.

6. Volkswagen initially planned to open an American car assembly plant and stamping facility right at the time when layoffs were spreading within German auto plants. The union at Volkswagen became involved in this decision through board representation and opposed the initial plans. Volkswagen then reduced the scale of its investment and delayed the project. See Wolfgang Streeck, *Industrial Relations in West Germany* (New York: St. Martin's Press, 1984).

7. These figures refer to union membership in West Germany alone. Union membership as a fraction of the work force since 1950 in a number of countries is reported in "Appendix," table A–17, p. 257 in Greg J. Bamber and Russell D. Lansbury, *International and Comparative Industrial Relations.*

8. The DGB had 17 affiliated unions with 7,745,000 members as of 1983.

9. In 1983, IG Metall had 2,536,000 members.

10. The Confederation of German Employers' Associations (BDA) is the employer counterpart to the DGB. It includes 46 branch employer federations that engage in collective bargaining. One important exception is the negotiation of a companywide collective bargaining agreement at Volkswagen. This is because of the special financial and legal status held by Volkswagen. See Streeck, *Industrial Relations in West Germany.*

11. Comparative strike data are reported in "Appendix: Comparative International Data" in Greg J. Bamber and Russell D. Lansbury, *International and Comparative Industrial Relations,* table A–19, p. 258. Trade unions are required by law to poll their members, and before they call a strike, at least 75 percent of the members must vote for a strike.

12. Working time flexibility also has become a major issue in Germany and a number of works councils have negotiated agreements that allow workers to "bank" hours.

13. The labor dimension of German unification is analyzed in Lowell Turner, *Fighting for Partnership* (Ithaca, NY: Cornell University Press, 1998).

14. Enterprise unions are 94.9 percent of all trade unions in Japan and represent 85.6 percent of organized employees.

15. In 1982 labor federations in the private sector joined together to form Zenminrokyo (Japanese Private Sector Trade Union Council). Then in 1989 most private and public sector unions became affiliated with the new Rengo (Japanese Trade Union Confederation). See *Labor-Management Relations in Japan* (Tokyo: Japan Institute of Labor, 1990), p. 19, figure 2.

16. In earlier years these trading groups formed the zaibatsu that were outlawed after World War II.

17. It remains to be seen if this sort of career movement continues in the future. It may not, due to the professionalization of managerial training and career development.

18. The modern day extension of the traditional zaibatsu system often links large and small firms together into close business relations. For example, upon their retirement from the large "parent" firm, senior executives often then move on to serve as executives of one of the smaller firms in the same group.

19. See Michael J. Piore and Charles F. Sabel, *The Second Industrial Divide* (New York: Basic Books, 1984).

20. An informative account of life on the shop floor in Japan is provided in Robert E. Cole, *Japanese Blue Collar* (Berkeley and Los Angeles: University of California Press, 1971).

21. On the growth of multinationals and the particular issues they pose, see Thomas N. Gladwin and Ingo Walters, *Multinationals under Fire* (New York: Wiley, 1980).

22. See Jan H. Katz, "Cultural Issues in International Business," *Handbook of International Business,* ed. Ingo Walter (New York: Wiley, 1988), pp. 11–1—11–17.

23. Ibid.

24. The member local unions within the Teamsters and SEIU are craft or industrial rather than multiindustrial like IG Metall.

25. See Duane Kujawa, "Labor Relations of U.S. Multinationals Abroad," in *Labor Relations in Advanced Industrial Societies: Issues and Problems,* ed. Benjamin Martin and Everett M. Kassalow (New York: Carnegie Endowment for Peace, 1980), pp. 15–17.

26. See Alfred D. Chandler, Jr., "The Evolution of Modern Global Competition," in *Competition in Global Industries,* ed. Michael E. Porter (Cambridge, MA: Harvard Business School Press, 1986), pp. 405–48.

27. See Lloyd Ulman, *The Rise of the National Trade Union* (Cambridge, MA: Harvard University Press, 1958).

28. A study of 134 U.S.-based multinational firms found that only 10 percent of them had ever experienced labor actions taken against them across national frontiers. See David C. Hershfield, *The Multinational Union Challenges the Multinational Company* (New York: The Conference Board, 1975), p. 12.

29. See Lloyd Ulman, "The Rise of the International Union," in *Bargaining without Boundaries,* ed. Robert J. Flanagan and Arnold R. Weber (Chicago: University of Chicago Press, 1974), pp. 37–69.

30. For a discussion of unions' and workers' lack of information about the multinationals they bargain with, see Richard Prosten and Raymond MacDonald, "A Union View of the Multinational Problem," in *Labor Relations in Advanced Industrial Societies: Issues and Problems,* ed. Benjamin Martin and Everett M. Kassalow (New York: Carnegie Endowment for Peace, 1980), p. 8.

31. Enormous changes occurred in the WRTU after democratization occurred in eastern Europe. Another important international union federation is the World Confederation of Labor (WCL), which includes Christian unions, representing 15 million workers worldwide.

32. Lori Kletzer, "Globalization and American Job Loss," *Perspectives on Work* 6, 2002: 28–30.

33. Ibid., p.29.

34. The EU countries are listed in Exhibit 14–3.

35. The governance structure of the European Union includes a legislative, executive, and judicial branch. The European Commission is the executive branch and proposes legislation to the Council of Europe, which sends all successful legislation to the Council of Ministers for preliminary approval. The Council then sends the legislation to the European Parliament and the Economic and Social Committee for their reactions. Each nation's representatives to the European Parliament are elected directly, and representation is proportional to a nation's population. If the Council enacts legislation, it is then sent to the 15 EU member nations for implementation. The Court of Justice enforces any treaties. For further details, see James B. Dworkin and Barbara A. Lee, "The Implications of Europe 1992," in *The Future of Industrial Relations,* ed. Harry C. Katz (Ithaca, NY: Institute of Collective Bargaining, 1991).

36. It should be noted that EU legislative enactments would not replace national industrial relations laws or practices. EU legislative enactments refer to firm-level industrial relations only, and, thus, within the subsidiary levels of a firm, national enactments would apply. At the same time, policies within firms would surely be significantly affected by any EU regulations of firm policies.

37. A number of other EU countries require works councils. See Dworkin and Lee, "The Implications of Europe 1992."

38. A nice overview of the evolution of EU labor policies is provided in Hans Slomp, *Between Bargaining and Politics* (Westport: Praeger, 1996), pp.115–26.

39. For example, directive 75/129, adopted in 1975, requires the employer to consult workers through their representatives, with the goal of reaching agreement on ways to avoid layoffs or methods to either reduce the number of workers affected or the consequences of layoff. See Dworkin and Lee, "The Implications of Europe 1992," pp. 9–10.

40. See "EWCs State of Play," *European Industrial Relations Review* 280, May 1997, pp. 14–16.

41. Conservative Party leaders Margaret Thatcher and John Major long led U.K. opposition to the social charter. However, shortly after Tony Blair was elected Prime Minister in 1997, he pledged British support for the social charter.

42. Note that all firms do not necessarily benefit from expanded trade. Some companies will lose the protections provided by government regulations or suffer when confronted by greater direct competition from firms in other EU countries.

43. This is true with regard to private sector unions.

44. "Poland-Industrial Relations Background," *European Industrial Relations Review* 307, August 1999: 22–27. Also see various reports covering industrial rela-tions in Poland posted on the European Industrial Relations Observatory On-Line at www.eiro.eurofound.ie/2002/06/InBrief/PL0206101N.html.

45. In 1960 trade unions played a leading part in the violent protests that culminated in the fall of the government, under Syngman Rhee. In 1980 violent protests again swept the country as workers demanded worker and union rights as well as improved wages and working conditions. See Russell Lansbury and John Zappala, "Korean Industrial Relations in Transition: The Relevance of Australian Experience," unpublished paper, Department of Industrial Relations, University of Sydney, Australia, 1990.

46. See Mario F. Bognonno and Sookon Kim, "Collective Bargaining in Korea," *Papers and Proceedings of the 34th Annual Meeting,* (Madison, WI: Industrial Relations Research Association, 1982), pp. 193–201.

47. See Kim Yong-bom, "House Passes New Labor Reform Bills," *Korea Times,* March 11, 1997, pp. 1, 3, and 9.

48. See Wonduck Lee and Joohee Lee, "Will the Model of Uncoordinated Decentralization Persist? Changes in Korean Industrial Relations after the Financial Crisis," in H. Katz, W. Lee, and J. Lee eds., *The New Structure of Labor Relations: Tripartism and Decentralization* (Ithaca, NY: ILR and Cornell University Press, 2003).

49. For debates about whether job mobility and instability has increased in the United States, see Peter Cappelli, *The New Deal at Work* (Boston: Harvard Business School Press, 1999); Sanford M. Jacoby, "Are Career Jobs Headed for Extinction?' *California Management Review* 42 (Fall 1999): 123–45; and Paul Osterman, *Securing Prosperity* (New York: Oxford University Press, 1999).

15

The Future of U.S. Labor Policy and Industrial Relations

This book has traced how changes in the environment are challenging many traditional collective bargaining practices in the United States. In recent years there has been much experimentation in industrial relations among a significant number of companies and unions. At the same time, conflicts emerged between a number of unions and employers, and the nation experienced a significant decline in union representation.

Which of these two developments will dominate labor-management relations in the future? Will experiments with new forms of worker participation and new work systems and labor–management partnerships diffuse and become the foundation for a new model of U.S. industrial relations? Or will unionism continue to decline and experimentation with new industrial relations practices halt as labor and management remain locked in a stalemate over the future of national labor policy?

Or, will the profound changes occurring in the work force, the nature of work, the role of the corporation, and the relationship between work and family life result in broader changes in employment and regulatory policies that reshape the industrial relations system of the twenty-first century? These are some of the key questions facing policymakers and industrial relations professionals today and, therefore, we take them up in this final chapter. In doing so, we identify some different paths that industrial relations might take in the years ahead, and we lay out our own views on these questions.

When considering future possibilities it is necessary to examine the various channels through which the government can influence the conduct of collective bargaining. The most important federal statute affecting collective bargaining is the National Labor Relations Act. Government labor policy includes administration of this statute and other statutes dealing with collective bargaining such as the Railway Labor Act.

The nation's labor policy is also shaped by an array of regulations that govern employment conditions, training, and other aspects of the labor market. Industrial relations and employment conditions also are affected by economic and social policies. The social security system, for example, affects worker earnings and retirement decisions.

EXHIBIT 15–1
Selected
Components of
National Labor
Policies

(A) **General Economic and Social Policies**	(B) **Labor Relations Policies**	(C) **Employment and Human Resource Policies**

Aggregate monetary and
  fiscal policies
	Railway Labor Act	Wage and hour legislation (e.g.,
		  Fair Labor Standards Act,
		  Davis-Bacon Act)

Incomes policies	Norris-LaGuardia Act	Equal employment opportunity
		  laws, regulations, and
		  enforcement efforts

Trade policies	Wagner Act	Occupational Safety and Health Act
Immigration policies	Taft-Hartley Act	Employee Retirement Income Security Act
Antitrust policies	Landrum-Griffin Act	Unemployment insurance system

Regulation of multinational
  corporations
	Civil Service Reform Act of
	  1978, Title VII
		Social security system

Environmental protection
  policies
	Postal Reorganization Act of
	  1970, Public Law 91-375
		Workers' compensation system

National health insurance
  proposals
	"Little Wagner acts" at
	  state level
		Job Training Partnership Act and
		  related employment
		  adjustment programs

Energy policies	State employee bargaining
	  laws and policies
		Programs to improve labor–
		  management cooperation

Productivity improvement and capital formation policies		Family and Medical Leave Policies

Industry regulatory policies
  (hospitals, transportation, etc.)
		Living Wage and State Minimum
		  Wage Policies

Welfare policies		
Corporate Governance Regulations		

Thus, national labor policy, defined broadly, includes general economic and social policies, labor relations policies, and employment and human resource policies. Exhibit 15–1 outlines the key components of our current national labor policy.

The History of Government-Promoted Labor–Management Dialogue

There have been very few successful efforts at national-level dialogue and debate over national labor policies in the history of the country. The major previous efforts and their results are reviewed below.

National-Level Committees

A number of national labor–management committees have tried to change industrial relations practices. At the turn of the century, for example, various national investigative commissions examined labor conditions and problems. Industrial relations commissions issued reports in 1880, 1902, and 1915. The 1915 commission, for example, cited the absence of industrial democracy and inadequate working conditions as two of the most serious social problems of the time. The reports of these commissions were used as background material by those who wrote the New Deal labor legislation in the 1930s.

Other labor–management committees were created during wartime. Both Presidents Woodrow Wilson and Franklin Roosevelt created national war labor boards to promote labor peace and wage stability during World Wars I and II, respectively. These boards were generally successful in fulfilling their mandate during the course of the wars. Both, however, failed to keep labor and management working together at the national level after the wars. In 1945, for example, following the end of World War II, President Truman called labor and management representatives together in a national conference to try to work out principles for continuing the cooperation achieved during the war. But efforts to reach an accord broke down over labor's demand for a commitment to union security and management's demand for some stated limit on the scope of labor's influence over employment issues.

While every President from the 1930s through the 1960s established one or more top-level labor–management advisory committees to deal with various issues, this tradition was abandoned in the 1970s, and not renewed. Instead, several private national level committees have been formed in recent years.

Some of the committees that functioned with government encouragement continued to meet privately after the public effort dissolved. For example the top-level committee that functioned when John Dunlop was Secretary of Labor in 1974–75 continued to meet under private auspices with Dunlop as chairman for years after he left office. This group discussed various labor policy issues other than collective bargaining problems. Their view has been that collective bargaining issues are best discussed at more decentralized levels between the parties that are directly involved. Bargaining issues, they believed, are too controversial to be settled through national labor-management dialogue.

In 1985, Malcolm Lovell, a former Undersecretary of Labor, established the Collective Bargaining Forum composed of top union and corporate leaders. This group, which continues to meet today, discusses long-term strategies for improving collective bargaining. Excerpts from one of the Forum's reports is contained in Box 15–1.

The record shows little direct effect of national forums on the practice of collective bargaining. A number of factors have made it difficult to change labor–management relations through national level dialogue in the United States. Such inhibiting factors include the highly decentralized structure of U.S. collective bargaining; the absence of a unified strategic view within either the labor movement or the business community over labor issues, and in some cases deep-seated ideological disagreements between labor and business leaders over labor policy. On the other hand, these forums build personal and professional relationships among top-level business and labor leaders that can be drawn on to address problems or respond to national crises. Thus, the absence of any functioning national dialogue forums may limit the nation's capacity to mobilize broad-based support if needed in the future.

Local and Regional Government Dialogue Efforts

There have also been a number of efforts to promote labor–management dialogue at local and regional levels of the country. These labor–management committees usually include labor and management representatives and key community politicians. Almost all have been started under the active leadership of one individual.[1] The Jamestown, New York, committee, for example, developed largely out of the efforts of the former mayor of the city.

In 1988, the Collective Bargaining Forum (an informal working group of major union and corporate leaders) adopted a statement of principles. The statement includes the following:

> We recognize that the institution of collective bargaining is an integral part of American economic life. We recognize that unions cannot be expected to expand their work with management to improve the economic performance of domestic enterprises and to help those firms adopt to technological, market, and other changes, if they are not accepted by employers and public policy makers as having a legitimate and valued role in the strategic decisions of the enterprise and in public policy making. It was also clear to us that employers need to expand their cooperative efforts with unions to revitalize U.S. industry and retain and expand opportunities for secure well-paid jobs for American workers. . . . The Forum, therefore urges adherence to the following principles:
>
> Acceptance in practice by American management both of the legitimacy of unions and a broader role for worker and union participation.
>
> Acceptance in practice by American unions of their responsibility to work with management to improve the economic performance of their enterprises, in ways that serve the interests of workers, consumers, stockholders, and society.
>
> Encouragement of a public policy which assures choice, free from any coercion, in determining whether to be represented by a union and which is conducive to labor-management relations based on mutual respect and trust at all levels.
>
> Acceptance by American corporations of employment security, the continuity of employment for its work force, as a major policy objective that will figure as importantly in the planning process as product development, marketing, and capital requirements.

The Forum also developed a *Compact* covering procedures needed to put its principles into practice. This compact suggests a new set of obligations and responsibilities that transcend and expand traditional collective bargaining relationships. The *Compact* states, "Our purpose is to formulate standards or 'rules of the game' with respect to certain fundamental aspects of the relationship." The *Compact* suggests standards for governing joint efforts to improve the economic performance of U.S. enterprises: acceptance of unions within companies and in American society; the promotion of employment security, worker participation, and empowerment; improved conflict resolution; diffusion of innovations in labor management relations; and development of common positions on public policy issues.

Source: Labor–Management Commitment: A Compact for Change, Views from the Collective Bargaining Forum. Distributed by the U.S. Department of Labor, Bureau of Labor Management Relations and Cooperative Programs, Report No. 141, 1991.

Area (local or regional) committees have tended to grow out of an economic crisis, such as plant closings. This was the motivation in Jamestown. In a few communities, such as Toledo, Ohio, the initial stimulus was a high number of strikes.

Area committees have mobilized community resources to attract new business and encouraged local educational institutions to respond better to industrial needs. Area committees also have attracted federal and state economic development funds. Area committees, however, rarely have been able to convince employers or local unions to change collective bargaining practices. Recommendations of area committees for collective bargaining are often resisted by plant-level managers and union officers on the grounds that they interfere unwarrantedly with the prerogatives of these individuals. Involvement in civic affairs has, however, proven to be a useful network-building activity for local union and management leaders. Relationships developed through involvement in community affairs have helped many union leaders to build coalitions with immigrant groups, religious leaders, and elected officials that have supported organizing campaigns and bargaining processes.

The Limits and Contributions of Labor–Management Dialogue

Our participation in a variety of national and area labor–management committees has left us with ambivalent feelings about their potential contributions. None of these efforts seems to be producing reforms sufficient to stem job losses or slow declines in union membership; none have changed the attitudes of employers who are ideologically opposed to unionization; none have produced a new coherent strategy to foster employee participation; and none have produced a consensus over changes in national labor policy. They have, however, been helpful in solving specific problems and building trust among leaders who otherwise might not know each other. The decline in the number of these network-building forums, therefore, is another worrisome development in U.S. industrial relations.

Labor Policy Reform Efforts

As discussed in Chapter 3, American labor law does not change often or easily. The National Labor Relations Act was only passed as one of the last major reform efforts of the New Deal. It took the deep economic and social crisis of the Great Depression and the fear that American style capitalism might be at risk to build the political support necessary to pass that legislation. Then in 1947 in response to a wave of strikes, the Taft-Hartley amendments to the NLRA were passed to rebalance power by limiting the use of secondary boycotts, closed shop clauses, and other actions deemed to be unfair union bargaining practices. A series of widely publicized union corruption scandals then produced the Landrum Griffin Act in 1959.

Efforts to update or amend labor law in the absence of a deep crisis atmosphere have been largely unsuccessful. For example, in 1977 the Carter Administration failed in an effort to pass labor law reforms aimed at stiffening the penalties on employers that violate worker rights in organizing campaigns. As a result, there has been a general stalemate in efforts to reform and update national labor policy that dates back at least 30 years to the failed effort to enact labor law reform in 1978.

The Dunlop Commission

An attempt was made to resolve the long-standing impasse over labor policy when the Clinton Administration first took office in 1993. A national-level Commission on the Future of Worker Management Relations (known as the Dunlop Commission, since former Labor Secretary John T. Dunlop chaired the Commission) was established to recommend ways to update national labor policies in ways that would enhance the nation's competitiveness and improve workers' standards of living.

The Commission was charged with answering the following questions

1. What (if any) new methods or institutions should be encouraged, or required, to enhance workplace productivity through labor–management cooperation and employee participation?
2. What (if any) changes should be made in the present legal framework and practices of collective bargaining to enhance cooperative behavior, improve productivity, and reduce conflict and delay?
3. What (if anything) should be done to increase the extent to which workplace problems are directly resolved by the parties themselves, rather than through recourse to state and federal courts and government regulatory bodies?[2]

EXHIBIT 15–2
**Recommenda-
tions of the
Dunlop
Commission**

Source: Final Report
and Recommendations
of the Commission on
the Future of Worker
Management Relations
(Washington, DC:
Government Printing
Office, January 1995).

Facilitate growth of employee involvement by clarifying Section 8(a)(2) of the NLRA.
Continue the ban on company unions.
Reduce the scope of supervisory and managerial exclusions from NLRA coverage.
Authorize use of prehire agreements when an employer opens new operations.
Hold union representation elections before legal challenges to bargaining units are heard.
Use court injunctions to remedy discrimination against workers in organizing campaigns.
Use mediation and when necessary arbitration to resolve disputes over first contracts.
Expand union access to employees during the organizing process.
Encourage adoption of alternative dispute resolution (ADR) programs within enterprises.
Support voluntary use of arbitration for resolving disputes over statutory rights.
Require arbitration systems to meet specific quality and due process standards.
Encourage employee participation in the development/administration of ADR systems.
Forbid agreements making use of arbitration for statutory disputes a condition of employment.
Simplify and standard the legal definitions of "employee," and "independent contractor."
Use an economic realities test to separate independent contractors from employees.
Use an economic realities test to determine who is the employer of contingent workers.
Expand "single" and "joint" employer definitions of who is responsible for labor law violations.
Expand use of negotiated rule making in developing new workplace regulations.
Promote self-regulation of workplaces where high quality ADR systems are in place.
Create national and local forums for ongoing labor–management learning and dialogue.

The Commission issued two reports: (1) a *Fact Finding Report* in which it reviewed the current state of labor management relations and arrayed the evidence presented to it on these questions, and (2) a *Final Report and Recommendations* outlining its proposal for reform. Exhibit 15–2 summarizes the major recommendations in the report.

The recommendations, however, gained no support from business, labor, or government officials. Why was this the case? Two reasons can be suggested.

First, the recommendations sought to find a compromise within the existing framework of the National Labor Relations Act that would be acceptable to both business and labor. Essentially the compromise was to loosen the constraints on employee participation in non-union settings (something of great interest and concern to the business community) and to strengthen the protection of workers seeking to organize a union. The evidence contained in the Commissioned Findings of Fact documented the need for both of these changes. But neither labor nor business were willing to make these compromises in their positions.

Second, the shift in control of the Congress from a Democratic to a Republican majority that occurred in November 1994 in the midst of the Commission's work ended any hope for realizing a change in labor policy. This shift in political power further polarized the positions of both business and labor. Labor leaders made the judgment that they could not get the Republican Congress to seriously consider any changes in labor law that might benefit workers or unions and therefore preferred the status quo. Business leaders concluded they could go to Republicans in Congress directly and lobby only for those changes in labor law it favored (such as the TEAM Act) and therefore preferred to see the Commission's recommendations ignored.

The key conclusion that appears to be warranted from this experience is that there is "no compromise deal" to be found that would be acceptable to labor and management within the existing structure of labor law. Thus, neither leaders in Congress nor in the

Clinton Administration demonstrate an interest or willingness to take up these issues on their own in the face of the ongoing labor–business stalemate. In fact, the issues appear to once again fallen off the national agenda altogether, along with most other employment policy issues.[3]

Alternative Directions for Future National Labor Policy

If major reforms in collective bargaining do not come from the normal policymaking processes of government, nor from labor–management committees, one might reasonably ask from where, if at all, will these changes come?

One answer to this question is that changes must now, as in the past, come from outside the interest-group structure that reinforces the current system. Recall that the ideas behind the New Deal industrial relations system came from the institutional economists who studied labor problems for over 30 years before passage of the Wagner Act. It may be, therefore, that we are in a similar situation. The logjam over labor policy will require ideas that, in the short run, may not be acceptable to either (or certainly not to both) labor or management but that need to be developed and put forward now to structure the debates that will take place over labor policy at some point in the future.

There are three possible strategic directions for future national labor policy. One approach would continue the labor policies of the last 20 years. The emphasis would be on further deregulation of product markets and reliance on the market to determine employment conditions. This strategy would emphasize the policies shown in column A of Exhibit 15–1 and deemphasize the policies in columns B and C.

Alternatively, the strategy could focus on the policies in column B in Exhibit 15–1 and marginally reform the National Labor Relations Act by either attempting to revive the deliberations started in the Dunlop Commission in hopes of identifying some other marginally different set of compromises than those the Commission proposed.

A third policy approach would recognize that much more fundamental changes in national policies are needed and see labor policy reform as part of a broad effort to rebuild the social contract at work. By reframing the policy debate in this way and broadening who was involved in the debate, labor policy discussions might be able to escape their past label as "special interest politics." A broad policy debate has the potential to address the fading belief in the American Dream, a dream that had held that each generation should experience an improved standard of living.

The three policy approaches are discussed in more detail below.

Strategy 1: Reliance on Deregulation and the Market

One strategy for national labor policy would involve extension of the deregulation wave that began in the late 1970s. The primary objective of deregulation is to increase product market competition.

- The federal government has been reducing regulation of the labor market since the mid-1970s, and the first policy approach would further limit federal regulations. From 1960 to 1975, for example, the number of employment regulations administered by the U.S. Department of Labor tripled.[4] Except for the Family and Medical Leave Act passed in 1993 and the advanced notice requirement for plant closing passed in 1989, no major new labor regulations were enacted since 1975 when the deregulation era began.

Furthermore, over the last 20 years the benefit levels in many social welfare and employment programs were either frozen, reduced, or conservatively enforced.[5] The federal budget for employment and training activities, for example, was cut substantially. The number of Occupational Safety and Health Administration employees was reduced by 25 percent in the early 1980s alone. Welfare benefits were dramatically altered by placing lifetime limits on the length of time individuals would qualify, implementing work requirements, and eliminating benefits for many immigrants. Thus, under this first policy approach benefit cuts or freezes such as these would continue to be enacted.

The Case for Further Deregulation

Why not extend the deregulation policies pursued over the last 25 years and allow market forces even freer rein to determine employment conditions? The basic argument in favor of product market deregulation and limited labor market regulation is twofold. First, market forces are extremely efficient in allocating labor. Efficiency derives, in part, from the pressure the market puts on labor and management to maximize profits.

Second, if market pressures are blocked, inefficient practices can persist. Society not only bears the cost of the output forgone while resources are misallocated, but often must help the parties absorb the costs of later adjustments to market pressures. Some would argue that the decline in the competitiveness of the U.S. steel industry illustrates the inertia that can set in when management and labor believe that their actions will be protected from market forces.[6]

Even if one does not like the outcomes generated by market forces, it is not clear that appropriate alternative policies can be successfully designed or implemented. This also recommends limited regulation of product and labor markets.

Criticisms of a Market and Deregulation Policy Approach

Reliance on market forces and a deregulation policy approach presumes that the market will lead to outcomes that society finds acceptable. Recently, attention has focused on the limited health care benefits provided to employees at Wal-Mart and accusations that in many other ways, Wal-Mart has taken advantage of its market power (see Box 15–2). Critics worry that an unregulated market will lead to a "Wal-Martization" of the United States employment system.

Normative arguments against reliance on the market alone to determine employment conditions were effectively articulated in the early years of this century by institutional economists of the Wisconsin School. The institutionalists stressed that labor is more than an economic commodity and that conflicts of interest between employees and employers are inherent and enduring. Put simply, competitive labor markets may leave too many workers in a weak bargaining position with their employers and give workers too little job security.

For these reasons the early institutional economists supported policies designed to allow workers to accumulate "property rights" in their jobs. The institutionalists believed that such a policy would be equitable. Moreover, if the workplace is to reflect the democratic values of the broader society, the institutionalists argued that employees should have a chance to influence managerial decisions that affect employment conditions.

Employment Law and Labor Relations Issues at Wal-Mart

Box 15–2

A California jury forced Wal-Mart to write a check for $172 million, to be split by 116,000 Wal-Mart Inc. employees who were forced to work through their allotted 30-minute, unpaid meal breaks. The world's largest retailer owes these individuals $57 million in wages for missed meal periods, in addition to $115 million in punitive damages. After review of Wal-Mart Inc.'s documentation, it was ruled that corporate leaders have been aware of the situation since 1998 and have taken steps to conceal the issue. Wal-Mart has since invested in new technology to alert cashiers of their meal breaks and automatically shut down registers if employees do not leave on break after a certain period of time.

The December 22, 2005, ruling is not the first to address denial of rest and meal breaks to Wal-Mart employees, nor is this the only issue for which Wal-Mart has found itself in the news or court. A Missouri court also ruled in favor of employees after hearing testimony and reviewing evidence of Wal-Mart managers knowingly requiring employees to work after they clocked out, not allowing employees to leave the store premises until the doors were unlocked by management, and forcing employees to miss scheduled breaks. Evidence included the training of a manager to systematically eliminate rest breaks and meals from time records, without needing authorization by a supervisor or employee.

Wal-Mart also found itself in the news in January 2006 as in Maryland a bill won approval in the state House of Delegates to force Wal-Mart to spend more on employee health care. The bill requires companies with more than 10,000 employees to spend a minimum of 8 percent of payroll on health insurance benefits. It provides these companies with the option of paying this sum into state low-income health insurance funds as well.

Wal-Mart also encountered legal difficulties concerning the hiring and working conditions of undocumented workers at its facilities. A raid of 21 Wal-Mart stores in 2003 had resulted in the arrest of 250 undocumented immigrant workers by the Department of Homeland Security's Bureau of Immigration and Customs Enforcement. Wal-Mart may face both civil and criminal penalties for their failure to abide by U.S. immigration law.

Despite these numerous employment law disputes, Wal-Mart employees continue to vote against union representation in the United States. In February 2005, tire and lube employees in a Loveland, Colorado, Wal-Mart voted 17–1 against representation by the United Food and Commercial Workers Local 7. Two weeks before this event, a similar department in a New Castle, Pennsylvania, Wal-Mart voted against UFCW representation 17–0.

Although no Wal-Mart employees in the United States are organized, this is not the case in Wal-Mart stores in other parts of the world. Many employees in South American and British Wal-Mart sites are unionized, and every Wal-Mart Supercenter in Germany is organized. The Quebec Labour Relations Board also certified the United Food and Commercial Workers of Canada to represent a Wal-Mart Canada site on August 2, 2004.

Similarly, Wal-Mart locations in China have recently become unionized. Prior to 2004, Wal-Mart China had issued statements asserting the futility of unions in its stores because of the openness of direct channels between management and workers. However, in late 2004, Wal-Mart China granted employees union rights and, facing threats from the government-backed All-China Federation of Trade Unions (ACFTA), on August 9, 2006, Wal-Mart announced that labor unions in all 60 of its stores throughout China would be permitted without backlash to employees. Chinese Unions differ significantly from those in the United States, as they traditionally work closely with management and rarely press for higher wages. Since officially allowing unions, Wal-Mart China has openly cooperated with the ACFTA by attempting to jointly set up unions within each of its stores.

Sources: "Association for Wal-Mart Employees Provides Information, Services Clearinghouse." *Daily Labor Report,* November 6, 2005, http://ippubs.bna.com; "Jury Rules Wal-Mart Must Pay $172 Million Over Meal Breaks." *The New York Times,* December 23, 2005, http:www.nytimes.com; "Maryland OKs Wal-Mart health care bill." CNNMoney, January 13, 2006, http://cnnmoney.com; "Missouri Court Certifies Large Class in Case Claiming Wal-Mart Forced Off-the-Clock Work." *Daily Labor Report,* November 3, 2005, http://ippubs.bna.com; and "Official Union Set Up in China at Wal-Mart," *The New York Times,* July 31, 2006, http:www.nytimes.com.

The Potential Consequences of Further Declines in Union Membership

One might also worry what would happen if union representation continues to shrink. If union decline continues, management's abuse of its power might eventually produce an even more adversarial form of collective bargaining and costly conflict.

Moreover, as unions decline, they may lose the capacity to innovate as their members and leaders see their security erode. A lack of union innovativeness could, in turn, reinforce employers' resolve to avoid unions. Thus, further union decline might create a reinforcing cycle of intensified conflict, reduced innovation, and declining competitiveness. The conflicts that emerged between companies like Bridgestone, Eastern Airlines, International Paper, or Caterpillar and their unions illustrate this scenario.

We may now be witnessing some of the longer term economic and social effects of union decline. Concerns over stagnant or declining real wages, increased wage inequality, and the stresses that long hours of work inflicted on workers and their families are gaining national attention. Is union weakness part of the explanation for these trends? Most analysts believe it is a part, although how big a part, and whether a resurgence of unionism would be able to address these issues effectively, remain open to debate.

Most of the debates over the consequences of union decline focus on economic issues similar to the above discussion. But unions are also an important institution in a democratic society. The absence of a strong voice for workers in community or national affairs leaves a void that diminishes the quality of political discourse and narrows the range of options considered seriously on critical economic and social policy issues.

Costs to Workers of Adjusting to Economic Changes

Any future labor policy will have to address the fact that union membership is heavily concentrated in the oldest and most mature sectors of the economy and those most exposed to international competition. Those sectors will undoubtedly continue to reduce employment levels and shift large numbers of workers across jobs and occupations. Employment adjustments will occur in these mature sectors as a consequence of new labor-saving technology, the development of new products, the adoption of new business strategies, and the shift of jobs to lower cost countries.

Many of the jobs being eliminated in mature industries are high-wage jobs held by union members. Older workers displaced from these jobs are not well trained to fill any of the new high-skilled jobs being created. A painful transition confronts those displaced older workers who have to accept low-wage jobs. Market forces alone may not fully smooth these adjustment processes.[7]

What Will Be the U.S. Comparative Advantage in World Trade: Low Wages or High Skills?

The events that followed deregulation of the airline and telecommunications industries suggest that deregulation may greatly reduce workers' power to resist management's efforts to minimize labor costs and/or avoid unionization. Deregulated industries have experienced widespread pay and work rule concessions, reduced employment security, and difficulties sustaining innovations in labor–management relationships. Once product market competition increased after deregulation, management often found it easier to cut labor costs by creating new lower cost nonunion organizations or outsourcing work rather than compete through managerial reforms and labor–management innovations.

If the government were to promote further deregulation, then the minimization of labor costs might spread as a business strategy. Yet labor cost minimization may in the long run be self-defeating as American firms that compete on the basis of labor costs may not fare well in world trade. The problem is that workers in newly industrializing countries receive very low wages. U.S. firms may be unable (or unwilling) to keep wages low enough to compete through low costs with firms in developing countries.

American firms, however, might be more successful if they pursued the comparative advantages derived from high technology, worker knowledge and commitment, and product innovativeness. Few dispute that the comparative advantage of the U.S. economy lies in its high-technology, high-quality products and in its ability to adapt rapidly. These traits require skilled employees who are strongly committed to their employers. Thus, reducing labor costs may help save some jobs in the short run, but in the long run the U.S. economy and workers' interest may be better served if employers invest in the quality of their human resources. Yet, it does not appear that market forces alone will adequately push employers toward a high-skills human resource strategy.

All the reasons discussed in this section suggest the need to supplement the market with labor policies. But what should the policies be? Here, there is much debate. Below are sketched two alternative strategies.

Strategy 2: Modest Reforms within the Current Collective Bargaining System

A second alternative for future labor policy is to actively support the types of modest reforms of traditional collective bargaining and labor law as embodied in the Dunlop Commission recommendations. This would require, among other things, marginally reforming the NLRA and its administration. The reforms would make it more difficult for employers to oppose union-organizing efforts and make it easier for unions to achieve first contracts after they win a representation election. Restrictions on employee participation in nonunion settings might be relaxed. Alternative dispute resolution procedures might be encouraged to help reduce the backlogs in enforcement of employment laws and to provide access to speedy and equitable enforcement of these laws. A bill to do so has been gaining considerable momentum among Democrats in the U.S. Congress in recent years. The bill, entitled the Employee Free Choice Act, would increase penalties for violating workers' rights during organizing campaigns, allow for union recognition by showing a majority of workers have signed union authorization cards, and provide for arbitration of first contracts if a voluntary agreement cannot be reached. There is also some discussion in Congress around packaging this bill with Republican-backed bills that would loosen constraints on various forms of employee participation. Neither of these approaches yet has gained sufficient support to overcome a threatened veto by the President.

Following in the New Deal tradition, the focus of this strategy would be on procedural rules that specify the rights of the parties and place limits on each party's rights to use power. This policy approach is based on the belief that the parties can use collective bargaining and employee participation to promote their long-term interests without imposing undue costs on society.

But there is no reason to believe that this policy approach would be any more acceptable or successful today or in the future than it was in 1995 when the Dunlop Commission issued its recommendations. Moreover, it may not be flexible enough to address the full range of

EXHIBIT 15–3
Elements in a
New Industrial
Relations
System

> **Strategic Level**
>
> Information sharing between management and workers.
> Worker and union participation and representation.
> Cross-functional consultations.
> Integration of industrial relations with business and technology strategies.
>
> **Functional Level**
>
> Contingent compensation.
> Employment continuity and security.
> Strong commitment to training and development.
>
> **Workplace Level**
>
> Employee participation.
> Flexible work organization.
> Grievance procedures with communication and due process supplements.

employment settings found in the economy today. It may, therefore, be time to propose a broader, and more comprehensive approach to labor and employment policy that opens up new avenues for employee representation, participation in decisions, and encourages workers and employers to resolve problems and conflicts efficiently and equitably, and lowers the costs of mobility for workers as they move across jobs or in and out of the paid labor force at different points in their careers and family lives. A new industrial relations system might better meet today's economic pressures.

Strategy 3: A New Industrial Relations System

We believe it is time to open up labor law and related employment policies to a period of active experimentation and learning that, over time, can create the type of new industrial relations system summarized in Exhibit 15–3. Industrial relations innovation along these lines could provide valuable improvements in productivity and living standards while providing equitable due process.

Workplace industrial relations in the new system would feature employee participation in workplace decisions, flexibility in the organization of work, and extensive informal communication between labor and management. The goal is to develop trust and avoid the low trust–high conflict cycle often found in traditional collective bargaining relationships. Another major goal of the workplace system is to increase flexibility by moving away from detailed contractual provisions and narrow job descriptions. At the same time, workplace procedures should facilitate employee input into decisions and due process.

At the middle level of the new industrial relations system gains-sharing, profit-sharing, and employee stock ownership arrangements would be encouraged. The parties must be careful, however, not to let the shift to these "contingent" compensation procedures erode workers' standards of living. The goal here is to make wages responsive to current economic conditions and to give employees an economic stake in their enterprise. Employee training and career development also would be encouraged at the middle level. Employment and income security programs can contribute toward this end.

At the strategic level, the new system would break with the principle that it is management's job to manage the enterprise and the union's job solely to negotiate over the effects of management actions. Instead, the new system would encourage information sharing and consultation between management and worker representatives. No single form of worker involvement at the strategic level is anticipated, in keeping with the variety of mechanisms already being developed by labor and management, however, the policy would encourage and support consultative bodies made up of union and nonrepresented employees as well as employee representation on boards of directors.

These reforms would do more than just improve labor–management relations. Elected employee representatives would bring another independent voice to corporate governance and a new transparency to human resource practices and policy formation. This could exert positive benefits on issues ranging from executive compensation to organizational design. These reforms would complement those recently enacted into law designed to bring more transparency and accountability to managerial fiscal behavior following the disclosure of corporate accounting and executive misconduct.

In the new system, the exclusive representation provided by unions to workers in a bargaining unit would be modified. Employee-management councils that provide representation to a cross-section of blue- and white-collar workers would be allowed. The parties would be encouraged to create consultation procedures involving employees from a variety of occupations. These consultative procedures could supplement formal negotiations for those employee groups that choose to be represented by a union for the purposes of collective bargaining.

In addition, unions, professional associations, and other organizations would be encouraged to develop a broad range of labor market services for individuals not covered by formal collective bargaining and those who work in various contingent, networked, independent contractor, or part-time arrangements. Labor market information, training and education, pension, health insurance, supplemental unemployment insurance, legal representation, technical advice and services on issues such as occupational safety and health might all be possible services provided by the "full service" unions of tomorrow. The objective here would be to create the incentives and opportunity for a variety of new labor market organizations and institutions to emerge to meet the changing needs of workers not tied to traditional ongoing employment relationships at a single or fixed workplace. These labor market institutions would help lower the costs of mobility to workers who have to find new jobs in the wake of corporate failures, restructuring, or layoffs. By building this type of institutional infrastructure, labor market policies could then move in the long run to wean benefits from their corporate focus by making pensions, heath insurance, and other leave benefits portable.

The complete features of this new system cannot yet be found in any employment relationship or occupational setting in the United States. Yet, each of the features of the new system is currently used somewhere in both union and nonunion firms or by various occupational groups. The new system builds on these experiences and brings together some of the reform proposals that have been advocated in recent years.

Beyond Labor Law: The Need to Integrate Labor, Economic, and Social Policies

Implementing and diffusing a new industrial relations system will require the active support of federal and state policy makers and significant shifts in the strategies of management and labor. Below are outlined steps the government, labor, and management could take to encourage spread of the new industrial relations system.

Government Strategies

Major reform of the NLRA is necessary to achieve the new industrial relations system envisioned in Exhibit 15–2. Industrial relations over the past decade has included frequent employer unfair labor practices, weak remedies for unfair labor practice violations, and low rates of union success (and long delays) in achieving first contracts. Respect for the NLRB should be reestablished. Furthermore, employees should be assured of their right to decide whether or not they want to be represented by a union, and the form of that representation, without employer interference.

Current policy encourages the parties to begin worker representation in an adversarial proceeding with the hope that eventually their relationship will mature and become more cooperative. A more affirmative policy that promotes participatory industrial relations is necessary.

Other legal constraints on the participation by employees, supervisors, and middle managers in decision making should be removed, regardless of whether a union is present or not. As long as employees have the freedom to decide whether or not to be represented by a union, employee participation should be deregulated and allowed to take whatever form best suits the problems and circumstances of the parties involved. The restriction of bargaining rights for supervisors contained in the law is outmoded. So too are efforts to draw a clear line of demarcation between exempt and nonexempt employees. These restrictions conflict with the contemporary decentralization of managerial decision making. Without reform of the law, first-line supervisors and middle managers are in an untenable predicament. On the one hand, changes in technology and personnel policies have reduced the power and status of supervisors and given rank-and-file employees more influence. On the other hand, supervisors remain unprotected by the law if they engage in collective efforts to improve their employment conditions.

Given their precarious position, it is not surprising that supervisors so often find ways to block workplace innovations. This resistance to change is likely to continue unless supervisors are involved more meaningfully in the change process.

Likewise, constraints on the "mandatory" and "permissible" scope of bargaining no longer make sense. Strategic business decisions have serious consequences for employment and income security. Effective employee representation, therefore, requires employee participation in strategic business decision making at an early stage of the process.

Changes in Other Government Policies

The diffusion of the new industrial relations system should be accompanied by changes in other federal economic and social policies. An extensive employment and training policy, for example, is needed to assist workers transitioning across employers or occupations. The unemployment compensation system should be altered to cover a higher percentage of the unemployed and encourage the acquisition of new skills. Pension portability needs to be encouraged. Other employment regulations should be modified to reduce the costs of worker mobility and to eliminate artificial distinctions between the definition of an employee, independent contractor, or a consultant. Anyone who works should be entitled to the basic protections provided by labor and employment laws, regardless of whether they are labeled employees, independent contractors, or temporary workers.

Macroeconomic policies should promote economic expansion and productivity growth. Support for basic education and research should be increased in the United States in light of the support given to such activities by our economic competitors.

Given the increased interdependence between work and family life that comes with the rise in labor force participation of women and the work requirements that are now part of our welfare policies, issues of family and medical leave take on increased importance. The United States is the only advanced industrial economy and democracy that does not presently offer some form of paid leave to attend to family needs. There is much debate over the future of the Family and Medical Leave Act. Employers find it too inflexible, cumbersome to administer, and difficult to integrate with existing leave policies. Family advocates criticize the Act for only covering about 55 percent of the labor force (companies with 50 or fewer employees are excluded) and for only providing *unpaid* leave.

One option for addressing both concerns is to establish minimum and flexible standards for paid leave that apply more broadly, but can be linked to existing leave policies offered by employers. Many companies do this already, especially in unionized settings where the parties have negotiated leave policies suited specifically to the needs of their particular work force and business settings. As discussed in prior chapters, a number of unions and companies have established jointly funded and managed programs to support child care, elder care, and related family services. These are all ways to address the changing demographic profile and increased work–family interdependence that characterizes today's labor markets. Clearly, these issues will be front and center in any future debates over how to modernize American labor and employment law to catch up with the changing workforce and changing nature of work.

State and Local Government Policies

The sustained impasse in labor policy at the national level has led to increased calls for and increased action at the local and state government level. This is consistent with the history of innovation in social and labor policy in the United States. Most of what was introduced into federal law in the 1930s such as unemployment insurance, workers' compensation, wage and hour protections, and even some aspects of collective bargaining law, were developed earlier and tested in states such as Wisconsin, New York, and Massachusetts.

Today we see a similar trend. The enactment of "living wage" ordinances in over 50 communities is one example. California enacted the first paid family leave act in 2004 and similar bills are being debated in many other states. States took the lead in developing the basic changes included in national welfare reform. Public sector labor relations statutes are another example of the importance of state-level labor policy. Given the ongoing national stalemate over labor policy, we are likely to see an increase in efforts to enact changes at the state and local level. These initiatives should service as laboratories for experimentation and learning that can inform national policy debates at some point in the future.

Government policy alone, however, cannot spark changes in industrial relations. The diffusion of a new industrial relations system requires the active support of management and labor.

Management Values and Strategies

U.S. managers will influence the diffusion of reforms in industrial relations through their values and their business strategies. In a new industrial relations system, management will have to accept a broad role for unions and workers in strategic decision making. Yet, opposition to unions is a deep-seated value of many U.S. managers. This is a significant barrier to the diffusion of a new system of industrial relations.

If management adheres to this oppositional view of unionism, efforts to unionize new groups of employees will be highly adversarial. Unions probably will lose a majority of these contests and fail to achieve contracts in a significant number of the representation elections they do win. This will further discredit NLRA procedures in the eyes of workers and union representatives. In cases in which unions do achieve recognition through an adversarial contest, the adversarial relationship likely will carry over to the subsequent bargaining relationship.

At the workplace level this hostile climate will strengthen the position of those union leaders who favor traditional adversarial relationships with management. Distrust will inhibit the flexibility and participation necessary for the new system of industrial relations.

The Role of Business Strategies

Not all business strategies are equally compatible with the industrial relations reforms proposed in Exhibit 15–2. Business competition based on low labor costs undermines worker trust, flexibility, and adaptability. Yet, because unions have difficulty in taking wages out of competition, many firms now are tempted to pursue a low-wage business strategy. The distrust that develops in firms that pursue low-wage strategies makes participatory practices impossible.

Business strategies that move work to different locations in response to variations in labor costs also are incompatible with a new system of industrial relations. A low-cost production strategy can divert management's attention away from the need to develop other comparative advantages. Firms that focus on low-cost strategies tend to give too little attention to the development of advantages based on technology, labor skills, and product innovation.

Other business strategies that limit worker trust also need to be avoided if industrial relations innovations are to take hold. The buying and selling of productive assets as mere short-run financial instruments without attending to the employment consequences borne by those actions have negative effects. Thus, corporate takeovers that meet only short-term corporate objectives have dysfunctional consequences on industrial relations. Corporate financial maneuvers should either be limited by public policy or required to provide compensation to the affected work force.

Technological Strategies

Technological strategies that maintain managerial control and maximize labor savings lead to deskilled and unmotivated workers. These technological strategies limit the opportunity for organizational learning and improvement.

More consistent with new industrial relations practices is a "socio-technical" approach to new technology. Socio-technical policies use technology to decentralize decision making in organizations and upgrade worker skills. The upgrading of skills occurs by broadening job tasks and blurring traditional distinctions between white- and blue-collar work. Thus, as with business strategy, U.S. management should follow technological strategies that reinforce the diffusion of industrial relations reforms.

Is it likely that a majority of U.S. managers quickly will adopt values and strategies that support the diffusion of a new industrial relations system? If history is any guide, the answer is clearly no. Most managers are likely to prefer either traditional practices or incremental change. Yet, with international and domestic competition increasing, technology changing rapidly, and worker aspirations intensifying, the need grows for extensive changes in industrial relations. Economic pressures, and pressures from government and unions, may eventually induce management to make major changes.

Broader Corporate Reforms

Confidence in American corporations and their top executives fell to historic low points in the wake of the scandals uncovered in recent years. Restoring this confidence has to be a high priority for the nation and its economy. This may well require providing employees with more opportunities to monitor and contribute to corporate governance and managerial strategies and behaviors. This becomes even more critical, if as many believe, human capital and knowledge are becoming increasingly important sources of competitive advantage in modern corporations.

To gain value from employees' knowledge will require rebuilding employees' trust. This will, in turn, require that employees understand the risks they are taking in joining or staying with a particular firm. Thus, the future of industrial relations and the nature of employee participation and voice that emerges out of this historic set of developments could have a profound effect on the future of industrial relations.

Union Strategies

Labor leaders face a similar strategic choice regarding whether to support the diffusion of a new system of industrial relations. At present the leaders of the U.S. labor movement generally support worker participation and union–management partnerships but they have not developed an explicit or clear and visible strategy for promoting these initiatives. The reluctance of union leaders to strongly support participation in managerial decision making stems, in part, from leaders' fears that they will be co-opted. Union leaders worry that increased participation will lead them to support management's goals at the expense of their members' interests.

Union leaders will have to reassess their views and become more visible champions of these innovations if industrial reforms are to diffuse. Without the strong support of the labor movement, it is difficult for management to take the risks associated with the introduction of new practices. Visible support from union leaders is also necessary to convince public policy officials, rank-and-file workers, and the public that a new industrial relations system is possible. Even union leaders' passive acceptance of new practices is unlikely to suffice.

If they do become more heavily involved in strategic business issues, union leaders will have to become more expert in communicating with their members about their participation. Otherwise, members will remain suspicious of union leaders' new roles. Furthermore, union leaders will have to match increased participation in business decisions with increased member participation in internal union affairs.

Why should labor leaders embrace a new industrial relations system and adopt the new roles it requires of them? The answer to this question is quite simple: Union leaders have to do so if they are to represent the interests of their current members effectively and organize new members. Failure to do so will likely lead to further union decline in members and influence, or at best perhaps a leveling off of members. Continuation of its current strategies will relegate labor to playing a marginal rather than a central role in economic and social affairs.

The scope of industrial relations activity has broadened in recent years to involve more activities above and below the level of traditional collective bargaining. Strategic decisions made at the top of corporations and interactions at the workplace are now as important as the negotiations process. Union leaders, therefore, have to acquire the ability to influence decisions made at the strategic and workplace levels as well as in collective bargaining negotiations. If they do not, their influence over the future of industrial relations will continue to decline. But most importantly, unions, professional associations, or other organizations need to find ways of recruiting and representing the full range of participants in the modern labor force. These new representational approaches should not require participants to risk their jobs, engage in highly adversarial conflicts with employers, or depend on garnering a majority of their peers in a specific bargaining unit in order to gain the services, opportunities, and representation they need to succeed in today's labor markets.

Broader Experiments: New Models of Employee Representation?

The inability of unions to reverse membership declines even in the face of increasing resources devoted to traditional organizing strategies, workers' increased uncertainty over job security, and changing labor force demographics that produce more demands for part-time work, movement in and out of the labor force to attend to education and family needs, and changes in retirement patterns all are posing challenges to the traditional industrial model that is characteristic of many U.S. unions. As a result, craft and professional union models that support worker mobility may become increasingly important in the future since they are not tied to a specific workplace and may not be as dependent on exclusive representation and formal collective bargaining rights as are industrial unions.

To support labor mobility, unions will need to develop new capabilities and new structures. These are needed to satisfy workers' needs for lifelong learning and skill retraining, information on job opportunities, and continuous benefit coverage. This, in turn, would require unions to recruit members and maintain their membership over the full course of their careers and to modify union structures to allow movement across union jurisdictions and organizations over workers' careers.

One might envision unions of the future as networks that provide a range of representational services and benefits. Whether or not such broadscale experimentation with this type of network strategy occurs in U.S. unions is an open question. If it does not, substitute organizations that provide these services are likely to continue to expand and fill these needs.

Will the current debates over corporate reform trigger regulatory reforms that introduce new rights for participation and voice for employees? This was the case in the 1930s when the reforms that created the Security and Exchange Commission to regulate investor rights were followed by enactment of the NLRA. Whether history will repeat itself cannot be known at this time. If it does, we may witness more profound changes in American industrial relations policy and practice than would be predicted by the past two decades of policy stalemate.

Summary

This book began by presenting a normative perspective on work and employment relations and a broad framework for analyzing industrial relations. The text then explored how the strategic choices of the parties interact with environmental conditions to shape industrial relations. It seems appropriate, therefore, that this final chapter poses the strategic choices now faced by labor, management, and governmental decision makers regarding the future of industrial relations.

The field of industrial relations has a heritage of close connections between research, teaching, public policy, and private practice. The fostering of this tradition would help the parties address the challenges that now face industrial relations.

Discussion Questions

1. What are some of the key components of the current U.S. national labor policy?

2. What are the lessons of the Dunlop Commission for future efforts to reform labor policy?

3. Briefly outline the deregulation-market approach to national labor policy. Discuss some of the strengths and weaknesses of this approach.

4. Describe the key features of the new labor policy advocated by the authors.

5. How could the government encourage the diffusion of the new industrial relations system recommended by the authors if it chooses to do so?

6. What do you think are the most important issues that need to be dealt with through future labor policy?

Related Web Sites

Dunlop Commission & Commission on Future of Worker Management:
http://www.ilr.cornell.edu/library/ e_archives/Dunlop/
http://garnet.berkeley.edu:3333/. labor/.files/.archive/.dunlop/ labnotesdun.html

U.S. Department of Labor:
http://www.dol.gov

Suggested Readings

Heckscher, Charles C. *The New Unionism* (Ithaca, NY: ILR Press, 1996).

Kochan, Thomas A. *Restoring the American Dream: A Working Families Agenda for America* (Cambridge, MA: MIT Press, 2005).

Kochan, Thomas A., Harry C. Katz, and Robert B. McKersie. *The Transformation of American Industrial Relations* (Ithaca, NY: ILR Press, 1994).

Osterman, Paul, Thomas A. Kochan, Richard M. Locke, and Michael J. Piore. *Working in America: A Blueprint for the New Labor Market* (Cambridge, MA: MIT Press, 2001).

Piore, Michael J., and Charles F. Sabel. *The Second Industrial Divide* (New York: Basic Books, 1984).

Stern, Andy. *A Country That Works* (New York: Free Press, 2006).

End Notes

1. Joel Cutcher-Gershenfeld, "The Emergence of Community Labor–Management Cooperatives," in *Industrial Democracy: Strategies for Community Revitalization.* ed. Warner Woodworth, Christopher Meek, and William Foote Whyte (Beverly Hills, CA: Sage, 1985), pp. 99–120.

2. *Fact Finding Report,* Commission on the Future of Worker Management Relations

(Washington, DC: U.S. Departments of Commerce and Labor, May, 1994), p. xi.

3. For a discussion of the difficulty in getting labor and employment policy issues considered by national leaders see Robert B. Reich, *Locked in the Cabinet* (New York: Simon and Schuster, 1997).

4. John T. Dunlop, "The Limits of Legal Compulsion," *Labor Law Journal* 27 (February 1976): 67.

5. Data on changes in the funding and administration of labor policies during the Reagan administration years are found in Sar A. Levitan, Peter E. Carlson, and Isaac Shapiro, *Protecting American Workers: An Assessment of Government Programs.* (Washington, DC: Bureau of National Affairs, 1986).

6. For a discussion of the decline of the steel industry, see Robert W. Crandall, *The U.S. Steel Industry in Recurrent Crisis* (Washington, DC: Brookings Institution, 1981). For a historical analysis of labor relations in the steel industry through the mid-1980s, see John Hoerr, *And the Wolf Finally Came* (New York: Praeger, 1987).

7. Paul Osterman, *Employment Futures* (New York and Oxford: Oxford University Press, 1988).

Appendix A

Private Sector Mock Bargaining Exercise

The following materials provide the basic data for a mock exercise in collective bargaining in the private sector. The exercise involves the D. G. Barnhouse Company and the union representing Barnhouse's blue-collar employees, the United Metal Products Workers. Both the company and union names, as well as the material and data, are fictitious.

The students should divide into company and union negotiating teams. Three members per side are recommended. The roles on the union bargaining committee include a representative from the national union, the president of the local union, and a senior employee who is a shop steward in the local union. The roles on the management bargaining committee include the company director of industrial relations, the company director of production, and a general supervisor.

All negotiators should receive the materials that follow. There are also additional company and union supplemental materials available in the Instructor's Manual for the text. Negotiators should receive *either* company *or* union supplemental materials.

The task confronting the negotiators is to bargain a new contract covering Barnhouse's unionized employees. A copy of the expiring agreement and other pertinent data are included in the materials that follow.

After reading the materials, students should meet with their team before bargaining to formulate their team's demands and any strategy they may choose to follow in negotiations. Students may want to consult other collective bargaining agreements available in a library or sources of economic data. The U.S. Department of Labor, Bureau of Labor Statistics, publishes a number of economic reports on a regular basis. The Bureau of National Affairs publishes a number of reports tracing recent collective bargaining agreements.

Bargaining between D. G. Barnhouse Co., Inc. and the United Metal Products Workers

At the turn of the 20th century, Mr. Donald Grayson Barnhouse, a highly skilled lathe craftsman, opened a small shop in which he made specialty machine tools. Based on very little financial capital—he had only about $1,000 available from savings and small personal loans—but a great deal of entrepreneurial stamina, he scraped together enough used tools to open his shop on the outskirts of Grandville, Illinois. After 10 years in operation, D. G. Barnhouse had gained a steady enough business to support himself and his small family, but had been able to take on only one apprenticed employee.

By 1915, however, Barnhouse's luck began to turn as small auto companies began to be built in the general vicinity of Grandville. His company, D. G. Barnhouse Co., Inc., had developed a reputation for quality, which soon led nascent area auto companies to buy tools from him. Thus, D. G. Barnhouse Co. (DGB) began to be looked on as one of the foremost suppliers to the auto industry.

By the mid-1920s DGB began diversifying into several new kinds of lathes, which came to be in higher and higher demand as the decade progressed. These were now produced in the machine tool plant DGB had built up over the previous decade. DGB had also maintained the older plant, in which primarily auto parts were produced. DGB's success led Barnhouse to allow the company to go public in order to capitalize on a rapidly expanding market. The capital thus generated was put to use in a new shop devoted solely to the production of machine tools.

The business suffered during the depression years, but managed to survive. During World War II the company did very well. After the war, however, the firm's growth became sporadic. Attempts to diversify into a greater variety of industrial products were not uniformly successful. By the late 1950s, DGB was making profits but not at a high rate.

In 1958, D. G. Barnhouse III took over from his father as President and Chief Executive Officer. Under the new leadership, the company's strategy shifted to place greater emphasis on research and development, as well as diversification and expansion into new markets. The company grew rapidly throughout the 1960s and early 1970s as a combined result of the new leadership and the growth conditions in the international economy during that period. The employees at the Grandville plant gained respectable wage and benefit increases annually, and the company itself was able to sustain a reasonable profit margin.

By the mid-1970s a new plant was opened in nearby Newton, Indiana, a relatively rural area that offered low-cost labor. This plant finished and assembled several types of low-cost machine tools. It employed 90 women and 60 men; the employees, who were not unionized, fell into five job classifications from production and assembly workers to a single general mechanic for the maintenance crew. (Blue-collar employment in the Grandville plant numbered 500 at the time.)

Recently, it became time again to consider a new strategic direction for DGB. Under current consideration was the possibility of investing in new automated manufacturing equipment, which would allow for a total workforce reduction in the Grandville plant of about 10 percent. Alternately, the new equipment could be installed in the Newton plant, while the older Grandville plant could slowly be phased out. This option would entail moving some of the existing Grandville plant equipment to Newton and increasing the number of employees at the newer plant.

Labor Relations at D. G. Barnhouse Co., Inc.

The Barnhouse family had always played an active role in directing the company's labor relations. The company carefully protected senior employees against shifting economic conditions. During the depression, several skilled employees were given jobs sweeping the floors of the Grandville plant in order to avoid layoffs. The firm's employees were granted life insurance pensions and hospitalization insurance long before these became standard benefits even in unionized companies. It was partly as a result of these long-standing policies that the Steelworkers, the Machinists, and the Auto Workers had been unable to unionize DGB's employees throughout the 1930s.

After World War II the company used overtime work and subcontracting to keep the number of employees low and steady. Then, in the early 1960s, as business picked up for the company, workers were put on a seven-day work schedule, and morale was severely strained. As a result, the employees of DGB decided to form a union of their own, with substantial encouragement from several first-line supervisors, and with the help of a local of the United Metal Products Workers of America (UMP). The company was certain that this effort at unionization simply reflected the work of a handful of "radicals," and was therefore taken completely by surprise when the National Labor Relations Board representation election resulted in a substantial majority in favor of unionization.

Even before the union had been voted in, DGB had generally paid wages more or less equal to those paid in competing unionized plants in the area. It had regularly participated in industrywide wage surveys in order to keep appraised of the going rates. But, at the same time, DGB had always been reluctant to grant long-term or automatic cost-of-living increases, or to appear to be following the bargaining pattern set in any particular industry. This aversion to automatic wage/benefit increases and to following pattern bargains was reflected in the contracts negotiated with the union until the early 1980s. But in 1982 DGB for the first time, and quite reluctantly, negotiated a cost-of-living clause in its contract with the UMP.

With respect to fringe benefits, DGB has always been relatively liberal. The life insurance plan provides at least two years' pay, as well as double indemnity, with the company paying half of the premium. DGB also pays for half of its employees' Blue Cross Blue Shield insurance. The company's policy has always been to pay regular employees half-pay during periods of sick leave.

The company's pension plan currently provides retiring employees with 2 percent of average earnings based on the last five years of service for each year of service up to 30 years. The company contributes half the cost of the pension. The combined weekly employee contribution for pension and insurance (life and health) is $50.00.

The 2006 Contract

The 2006 contract was difficult to negotiate, since the union was quite unhappy about lagging wages and benefits and because the company was facing very difficult market conditions. The union was unable to gain anything approaching workers' demands. By a 400 to 80 vote (with 20 members not voting), the membership rejected a contract with the following general features:

1. An hourly pay raise of 12 cents to unskilled and 18 cents to skilled workers.
2. A modest cost-of-living (COLA) clause.
3. An agreement to study ways of upgrading the pension plan.
4. An agreement to consider modifications in work rules and job and pay classifications.

After another unsuccessful week of negotiations, the workers began a strike. But three days later, all of the skilled workers and some of the unskilled employees went back to work voluntarily, and DGB was operating at close to full capacity again. Finally, a one-year agreement was signed on June 30, 2006.

The Aftermath

After the strike, all of the employees at DGB were very discontented. Old divisions between skill groups flared up. Unskilled workers were angry with both the company and their union. All the workers began to feel it was time for some sort of change.

Two months after the abortive strike, a young drill press operator named Bill White challenged and narrowly defeated the incumbent local union president, on the basis of a campaign emphasizing the need for more worker input into plant operations and control over technology and investment. The younger workers were in general pleased with White's approach, but the older employees (with less fear of losing their jobs) were not so sanguine, particularly since White seemed to be uninterested in pension plan improvements.

All the workers shared a certain nervousness about their jobs, however, due to increasing publicity about automation in machine tool plants, and about sluggish demand for machine tools themselves. DGB had done nothing to allay the employees' fears of replacement by robots, or about layoffs.

The Community

Grandville, Illinois, has about 160,000 inhabitants. The nearest large city is Detroit. The working population numbers about 70,000 of which fully 10 percent are unemployed. The unemployment rate is significantly higher for minorities and women. Some of the unemployed population secure a nominal income from the sale of small farm produce.

Aside from the Grandville plant of DGB, there are nine organized firms in the city. Their products, unions and employee statistics are shown below:

Company	Principal Products	Union	No. of Employees
1	Hoists	United Steel Workers	315
2	Pumps	Machinists (IAM)	712
3	Controls	Machinists (IAM)	342
4	Electronics	IUE	2,498
5	Truck bodies	Allied Industrial Workers	2,902
6	Metal parts	UAW	1,240
7	Structural steel	Iron Workers	1,198
8	Bakery	Bakery Workers	202
9	Trucking	Teamsters	79

Building construction employees are also extensively organized in Grandville. No other company is organized by the UMP. The largest of a number of unorganized plants manufactures office equipment and employs about 1,000 people. This group of workers has been subject to three unsuccessful organization drives over the last decade.

The Upcoming Negotiations

Employee recommendations as to the substance of the union's position in the upcoming negotiations were being considered by the UMP local leadership. The union had already notified DGB that it wished to renegotiate the contract and that a list of proposals would be sent to the company when the negotiations were to begin. Donald Grayson Barnhouse III responded that the company's counterproposals would be sent to the union as soon as he had received their negotiating demands.

> It is the responsibility of the union and management bargaining teams to formulate their bargaining strategies, to put priorities or weights on various items, to develop specific changes in contract language to implement various proposals, to decide what compromises to make, and to decide what will constitute an acceptable agreement.

Collective Bargaining Agreement

Parties to the Agreement

This Agreement, made and entered into this 30th day of June 2006, is made by and between D. G. Barnhouse Co., Incorporated, of Illinois, hereinafter called the "Company," and Local 245 International Union, United Metal Products, Machinery and Related Equipment Workers of America, hereinafter called the "Union."

Article I

Intent and Purpose

Section 1—The parties hereto intend and propose herein to set forth and comply with an agreement concerning pay rates, work hours, and employment conditions, and to set procedures for the prompt and equitable adjustment of alleged grievances.

Section 2—The Company shall in no way discriminate against any employee on the grounds of membership in or affiliation with the Union.

Article II

Recognition

Section 1—The Company recognizes the Union as the sole and exclusive bargaining agent representing the employees in the Grandville, Illinois, plant of the Company for the purpose of collective bargaining with respect to rates of pay, wages, hours of work, and other conditions of employment.

Section 2—The term "Employees" for the purpose of this Agreement shall mean all of the employees of the Company except office employees, foremen, watchmen and guards, timekeepers, and supervisors who have and exercise the authority to recommend the hiring, promoting, discharge, disciplining of employees, or otherwise effecting changes in the status of employees.

Article III

Strikes and Lockouts

Section 1—The Company agrees there shall be no lockout of its employees and the Union agrees that neither it nor any of its members shall cause, permit, or take part in any strike during the term of this Agreement.

Article IV

Hours of Work

Section 1—The normal work hours for all employees shall be eight (8) per day and forty (40) per week and, for production employees, shall be limited to the period of Monday to Friday (both days included).

Section 2—Hours worked in addition to the normal work hours shall be according to the following schedule: forty (40) to forty-five (45) shall be limited to five (5) days; over forty-five (45) to fifty-five (55) hours shall be limited to five and one-half (5 1/2) days; over fifty-five (55) to sixty (60) hours shall be limited to six (6) days. All other work schedules shall be mutually approved by the Company and the Union.

Section 3—All time worked by an employee in excess of eight (8) hours in any one day and forty hours (40) hours in any one week and all time worked on Saturday shall be paid for at the time and one-half rate; provided, however, employees shall not receive time and one-half for Saturday as such if they were absent during the week except for one of the following reasons: sickness, accident or death in the family, jury duty or subpoena to court. In cases when employees were absent due to one of the above reasons, they shall turn in a slip stating the reason for that absence, not later than Saturday of the week in which they were absent. All time worked on Sunday shall be paid for at the double time rate.

Section 4—The company will attempt to distribute overtime as equitably as possible among affected employees; and shall allow union officials to verify same.

Section 5—The Company shall allow Union Bargaining Committee members first priority for working the first shift; and when feasible employees with the greatest seniority within their job classifications shall be granted second priority to work the first shift, and those next in seniority, the second shift. Further, once an employee exercises seniority rights to obtain a transfer from one shift to another, he/she shall not return to the original shift until a period of six (6) months after the transfer shall have elapsed.

Section 6—All employees shall be granted two (2) fifteen- (15-) minute rest periods, at a time to be mutually agreed upon by the Company and the Union, and with pay at their hourly base rate. Smoking, other than during rest periods, is prohibited, and then only in the designated places.

Section 7—Employees shall not be absent from work without permission, except for good and sufficient reason, and must, except in an emergency, get word to the Company no later than three (3) hours after the scheduled starting time, when s/he cannot work.

Section 8—Penalty for violation of Section 7 of this Article will be:

1st Offense—Caution by foreman and a written report to Union and Personnel Department.

2nd Offense—One day suspension without pay.

3rd Offense—Two days suspension without pay.

4th Offense—Cause for dismissal.

Article V

Wages

Section 1—The rates for all employees shall be in accordance with the "Rate Classification of Jobs," which shall be appended hereto as Exhibit 1 and made a part of this Agreement.

Section 2—All employees shall receive a cost-of-living adjustment in pay, as of the first of January 2007, of one (1) cent per hour for each 0.3-point rise in the U.S. Bureau of Labor Statistics All-Cities Consumer Price Index for the period covering January 2006 through December 2006. However, if the Consumer Price Index declines to levels below those of January 2006, there shall be no pay reduction.

Section 3—Newly hired employees with less than thirty (30) days of employment to their credit shall be considered probationary employees: provided, however, the Company may request an extension of the probationary period not to exceed thirty (30) days for employees whose qualifications or capabilities are in doubt. Any employee remaining in the service of the Company beyond his/her probationary period shall automatically receive an increase of five (5) cents per hour and continuing every fourth (4th) week thereafter, until the minimum of his/her classification is reached.

Section 4—Any employee who is placed in his/her regular occupation after a layoff or transfer for reasons beyond his/her control shall be paid the wage rate applicable at the time of the layoff or transfer, plus or minus any general wage increases or decreases effective during that period.

Section 5—Except for the above provisions, no employee's wage rate shall be changed except by mutual agreement between the Company and the Union.

Article VI

Seniority, Layoffs, and Rehiring

Section 1—The Company shall notify the Union at such time as any newly hired employees who have completed their probationary period will have worked for thirty (30) days.

Section 2—An employee's seniority rights shall be measured on a plantwide and departmental basis, starting from the first day or hour worked. If, however, an employee is hired after having quit voluntarily or after having been duly discharged, that employee's seniority will be measured as of the time of rehiring.

With respect to the scheduled hours of work per week, the Company shall conform with the following provisions:

A. The hours of work shall be reduced to forty (40) hours a week before any such employees are laid off.

B. The schedule of hours per week may be increased from between forty (40) to forty-five (45) inclusive without any employee being called back.

C. The schedule of hours per week may be increased to over forty-five (45) for a maximum period of four (4) weeks, after which time enough employees who have been laid off will be recalled in order to revert to a maximum forty-five (45) hour work week.

Section 3—In the event of a layoff, employees with the least plantwide seniority will be laid off first, and employees with the most seniority will be retained, subject to their ability to perform the available work without being trained.

Section 4—In the event that workers shall be recalled after having been laid off, the last to have been laid off shall be the first to be recalled, as per the conditions noted in Section 2 of this Article, above. Any laid off employees shall accrue seniority, to be credited after his/her return to work, for a grace period of up to three (3) months. However, no employee shall surpass any other employee in seniority solely as a result of the provisions of Section 2 of this Article, above. An employee shall be considered to have quit voluntarily if he/she does not return to work within five (5) days of receiving notification of recall by registered letter to his/her last known address by the Company.

Section 5—On any layoff or return to work the Company shall notify the Union and the employee affected not less than two (2) working days before such layoff or return to work is effected. Any grievances involving such layoff or return to work shall be submitted to the Company no later than five (5) working days after the Company has given due notice of the fact.

Section 6—The Company shall post an updated seniority list on all bulletin boards at the workplace, shall furnish the Union with such lists, and shall consider such lists to be a matter of mutual approval with the Union. Such lists will include the names, hiring dates, and seniority positions, on a plantwide departmental basis, of all employees.

Section 7—In case of layoff, the president of the Union shall have seniority over all other employees during his/her term of office, regardless of length of service with the company.

Article VII

Discharge

Section 1—If the Company discharges an employee, such action will be taken for good and sufficient reason, and shall be taken after notifying the Union Bargaining Committee of the action and reasons therefore. If investigation of such an action leads the Union to conclude that the employee affected was discharged unfairly, that employee shall have the right to lodge a grievance against the Company in accordance with the grievance procedure established in Article XII of this document.

Article VIII

New Jobs, Transfers, Promotion, and Merit Rating

Section 1—The Company shall notify the Union president when any vacancy or a new job of any occupation occurs which is under the jurisdiction of the Union, and which results in the need for additional help in the department affected. Such notification shall include a statement of the required job qualifications, of the approximate wage rate, and of any other pertinent information. Upon receipt of such notification, the Union will post the job opening on the designated bulletin board(s), after which time interested applicants shall submit written bids to the Company's Personnel Office. Any such jobs shall be awarded on the basis of seniority when the qualifications of applicants are approximately equal.

Section 2—All employees accepting promotion or transfer shall be granted a reasonable period of time for training, during which time they shall receive no less pay than the minimum established in Exhibit 1. Any higher rate of pay shall be determined on the basis of experience, application and general qualifications for the job in question, at the time of the employee's reclassification.

Section 3—With the exception of trainees, each employee on rate ranges shall be considered for merit a raise six (6) months after employment in his/her classification, and at six (6) month intervals thereafter until he/she reaches the maximum rate in the classification. Trainees shall receive merit consideration six (6) months after completion of the ninety (90) day training period. Foremen shall submit written reports of all employees' progress to the Personnel Department at six (6) month intervals, with copies of such reports being furnished at the time of their receipt to the president of the Union.

Article IX

Military Service

Section 1—When an employee with seniority is called or volunteers for service in any of the armed forces of the United States, he shall, upon termination of such service, be restored to his former position, or to a position of similar status and pay; provided, however, that he has received honorable discharge, is physically and mentally competent, notifies the Company of his intention to return to work at least ninety (90) days prior to his discharge, and reports for work not more than ninety (90) days after release from service; and provided further, that the Company's circumstances have not been changed so as to make it impossible or unreasonable to do so.

Section 2—Any employee who is rehired in accordance with the provisions of this Article shall advance in seniority in the same manner as though he had remained in the Company's service.

Article X

Vacations

Section 1—All employees shall receive a vacation with pay in accordance with the following schedule:

A. All employees with between six (6) months and one (1) year service at the start of the vacation period shall receive a one (1) week vacation with forty (40) hours straight time pay, provided they have worked at least 125 hours in each month following the month in which they were employed. The latter provision with respect to the number of hours worked per month may be modified upon mutual agreement between the Union Bargaining Committee and the Company.

B. Vacation for all other employees shall be computed from the following table: All employees will receive vacation according to the following criteria, in which the time of service is to be measured at the start of the vacation period. More than one (1) but less than ten (10) years of service—two (2) weeks vacation with eighty (80) hours straight time pay; more than ten (10) but less than twenty (20) years' service—three (3) weeks vacation with one hundred twenty (120) hours straight time pay; more than twenty (20) years' service—four (4) weeks vacation with one-hundred sixty (160) hours straight time pay.

Section 2—Employees voluntarily terminating their service to the Company shall receive vacation pay earned during the previous year at the time of separation. Vacation pay earned the current year shall be paid not later than March of the following year.

Section 3—The vacation period shall be the first two (2) weeks in August, at which time the plant shall shut down; provided, however, that when August 1 occurs later in the week than Wednesday, the vacation period shall start the following Monday.

Section 4—Upon request, any employee with ten (10) to twenty (20) years of service shall be granted a fourth week of unpaid vacation. Employees with twenty (20) or more years of service shall be granted a fifth week of unpaid vacation. For these additional weeks, eligible employees will have the right to select their vacation dates on the basis of seniority provided it does not interfere with the operation of the business.

Section 5—Employees are not permitted to postpone their vacations from one year to another or to omit vacations and draw pay allowance in lieu thereof.

Article XI

Holidays

Section 1—The following days shall be considered work holidays:

New Year's Day
Memorial Day
The Fourth of July
Labor Day
Thanksgiving Day
Christmas Eve
Christmas Day

The Union shall be able to determine one further floating work holiday per year.

Section 2—When employees perform no work on a holiday, as defined in Section 1, above, they shall receive eight (8) hours pay at their base rate for each such holiday, unless such a holiday occurs on a day not regularly scheduled for work, and unless an employee has not completed his/her probationary period with the Company as of the date of such a holiday.

A. Employees shall receive pay for each holiday not worked, as outlined above, if they worked the scheduled work days immediately before and immediately after the holiday. If the schedule of work hours exceeds fifty (50) hours per week at the time of a holiday, an employee shall receive holiday pay in accordance with the above provisions if he/she has worked at least 80 percent of the scheduled hours on the scheduled work days immediately preceding and immediately following the holiday. An employee is also qualified for holiday pay if his/her failure to work on the days immediately preceding and following the holiday is caused by any of the following:

1. The employee is excused from working because he/she is ill;
2. The employee is injured in the plant;
3. The employee suffers a death in his/her family;
4. The employee must serve on a jury or attend court pursuant to subpoena;
5. The employee becomes a parent.

B. Any employee required to work on a holiday shall be paid at his/her straight time hourly rate for all hours actually worked plus straight time at his/her hourly rate for eight (8) hours.

Article XII

Grievance Procedure

In the event any employee feels that he/she has a just complaint or grievance with respect to any employer-employee matter, an earnest effort shall be made by the parties thereto to settle such differences at the earliest time and in the following manner:

A. Between the aggrieved employee and his or her foreman or between the Department Steward and the foreman.
B. If no satisfactory agreement is reached, the matter in dispute shall be referred in writing to the president of the Union, and the Bargaining Committee shall then bring the matter to the attention of the duly designated representative of the Company.
C. If no satisfactory agreement is reached by the Union and the Company representatives, the matter in dispute may be referred by either party to the American Arbitration Association for final and binding arbitration by an arbitrator to be designated by the Association. The proceedings shall be conducted in accordance with the rules of the Association.

Article XIII

Insurance and Pensions

The Company will continue in effect the existing insurance covering death and accidental death or dismemberment of full-time regular employees and hospitalization and surgical care of regular full-time employees, except as the terms and conditions of such insurance may be altered by the carrier.

The Company will also continue in effect the existing Pension Plan. (See Exhibit 3.)

Article XIV

Union Business

Section 1—Any employee who is a member of the Union and who may be called upon to transact Union business, shall, upon application to the proper representatives of the Company and the Union, be allowed to leave work for sufficient time to transact such business or to attend such meetings as may be necessary.

Section 2—Any member of the Union who may be elected or appointed to any office in the Union that requires a leave of absence shall, at the expiration of such term of office, be reinstated to his/her former or equivalent position, including all rights previously held, provided that the Company's circumstances had not changed so as to make it impossible or unreasonable to do so.

Section 3—The Union shall be allowed to collect dues, sign membership application cards, ballot for Union officers and distribute the regular monthly Union publications after working hours on Company property.

Section 4—The Company shall install and maintain bulletin boards for the Union in places mutually agreed upon by both parties. No material shall be posted thereon except that pertaining to the activities and business of the Union.

Article XV

Duration of Agreement

This Agreement shall be effective July 1, 2006. It shall remain in full force and effect from July 1, 2006 to and including June 30, 2007, and thereafter it shall be automatically renewed from time to time for further periods of one (1) year unless either party at least sixty (60) days prior to June 30, 2007, or any subsequent expiration date, serves on the other party written notice of its desire to amend or terminate the Agreement.

If the notice given is one expressing an election to terminate, then the Agreement shall expire upon such ensuing expiration date. If the notice given is one expressing a desire to amend the Agreement, the party serving such notice to amend shall, within thirty (30) days from the date of such notice to amend is served, transmit to the other party in writing the amendments proposed for negotiation and mutual agreement. If the party upon whom such notice to amend is served desires to amend the Agreement, it shall be no later than ten (10) days after receipt of such notice to amend serve written notice to that effect on the other party; and within thirty (30) days from the date its notice is served shall transmit to the other party in writing the amendments it proposes for negotiation and mutual agreement.

Negotiations between the parties on the amendments so proposed shall begin as soon as possible after the above mentioned notices have been given, but pending consummation of an Agreement on the proposed amendments, the terms and conditions of the old Agreement shall continue in effect.

IN WITNESS WHEREOF, we hereunto set our hands at Fort Jefferson, Indiana, on this 30th day of June 2006.

(Signed)

Company: _____

D. G. Barnhouse Co., Incorporated
D. G. Barnhouse III, President

Union: _____

U.M.P. LOCAL 245
William White, President
James LaPierre, Secretary

Background Data

EXHIBIT 1
Rate
Classification
of Jobs

Labor Grade	Job Title	Rate Range (per hour)
1	Tool and Die Maker	$15.25–$18.10
2	Machinist	$14.96–$17.30
	All Around Mechanical Inspector	
	Plant Electrician	
	Plant Mechanic	
3	Machine Specialist	$14.49–$16.91
	Gauge Inspector	
4	Tool Grinder	$14.40–$16.81
5	Electrician	$14.03–$16.61
6	Carpenter	$13.39–$16.54
7	All Around Instrument Assembler	$13.39–$16.54
8	Mechanical Inspector	$13.39–$16.54
	All Around Mechanical Assembler	
9	Turret Lathe Operator	$13.29–$16.24
	Engine Lathe Operator	
	Handscrew Machine Operator	
	Milling Machine Operator	
10	Drill Press Operator	$12.29–$15.90
	Final Assembler	
11	Set-up	$11.81–$15.26
	Welder (Tool Room)	
	Grinder Operator	
12	Production Tester	$11.81–$15.26
13	Instrument Assembler	$11.73–$14.95
	Production Inspector	
14	Shear Operator	$11.64–$14.86
15	Resolver Assembler	$11.47–$14.66
	Punch Press Operator	
16	Outside Truck Driver	$11.33–$14.58
17	Expeditor, Machine Shop	$11.26–$14.40
	Shipper and Receiver	
	Painter	
	Storekeeper	
	Expeditor, Assembly	
18	Fireman	$11.14–$14.20
	Expeditor, Tooling	
	Subassembler	
19	Oiler	$10.89–$13.73
	Bonding and Spraying	
	Tool Keeper	
20	Power Trucker	$10.43–$13.89
	Timekeeper	
	Bonding	
	Store Clerk	
21	Groundskeeper	
	Basic Assembler	
	Routine Assembler	
22	Sweeper	
	Assembler	

EXHIBIT 2
Distribution Table

Job Grade	Number of Current Employees
1	5
2	10
3	11
4	17
5	22
6	26
7	30
8	34
9	36
10	36
11	39
12	38
13	35
14	32
15	32
16	29
17	26
18	14
19	10
20	6
21	7
22	5
Total	500

EXHIBIT 3

Illinois First Life Insurance Co., Life Insurance and Retirement Benefit Agreement Summary

The employees covered under this agreement include all full-time employees of the Company; new employees become eligible after the probationary period of employment, or immediately if they are over 55 years old. At the option of the Company, employees can remain insured after layoff or become reinsured upon rehiring but with no credit given for the period during which they were not insured.

Life Insurance

In case of the death of an employee, except by suicide or while serving in the Armed Forces, the beneficiary will receive a death benefit of double the annual salary of the employee, i.e., 2,080 times the employee's last base hourly wage rate. Upon proof that death occurred as a result of accidental injury on the job, this benefit will be doubled. The employee can change his/her beneficiary by notifying the Company in writing. If he/she dies with no beneficiary on record, the benefit will be paid to his/her estate. The beneficiary may elect to be paid the benefit in equal installments of an amount determined by the insurer and based on the age of the beneficiary.

If an employee terminates his/her employment with the Company, he/she may automatically purchase from the insurer insurance providing coverage up to the level of that in force at the time of such termination at the insurer's individual premium rates.

Pensions

Upon retirement at age 65 or later eligible employees with at least 10 years of service with the Company will receive pension benefits monthly for life of 2 percent of the average monthly base wage during the 60 months prior to retirement, multiplied by the number of years of service (up to 30), and reduced by 20 percent of the amount the employee would normally receive under the Social Security Act.

Employees with more than 10 years of service who terminate employment with the Company before retirement will receive pensions as per the above, calculated on the basis of the 60-month period prior to termination.

Premiums

The total weekly premium will be paid within 7 days of the end of each calendar week of coverage. Interest will start to accrue on unpaid premiums of the 8th day after the end of the calendar week of coverage. After 26 weeks of failure to pay premiums the agreements will be terminated as outlined below.

If the Company pays less than the full premium per employee, it must collect the balance from the employees and pay the full premium to the insurer. Employees working full time will pay no more than 50 percent of the premium. Employees on layoff or Company-approved leaves of absence can pay up to 100 percent of the premium. All employees within each of these categories will pay the same percentage of the premium.

Employees who have contributed as above and who terminate employment with the Company can receive a refund for their payments with 6 percent annually compounded interest, after which point they lose all rights of future retirement benefits.

Funding

The insurer will apply the premiums received to the purchase of term life insurance and permanent annuity coverage sufficient to provide the stipulated benefits for service credited to covered employees before or after the date of the agreement, as appropriate.

Administration

The Company will be responsible for maintaining records for each covered employee, showing the following data on the employee: name and current address; date of birth; name and address of beneficiary; current base hourly rate; number of years and months of credited service both before the date of the agreement and after the date of the agreement; wages received during the preceding sixty (60) month period; and amount and date of each employee contribution to pension coverage premiums.

These records will be available to the Insurer for inspection or audit at any reasonable time.

Upon notification from the Company of the death of a covered employee, the Insurer will be responsible for making payment of the death benefit to the beneficiary.

The Insurer will be responsible for regular payment of retirement benefits to retiring employees upon Company notification of retirement by a covered employee or upon notification by a terminated employee with vested retirement benefits. The Insurer will not be responsible for payment of that portion of a benefit which results from the employee's service to the Company prior to the date of the agreement and/or for which the Company has not paid sufficient premiums.

Upon notification from the Company within seven (7) days of the termination of a covered employee, the Insurer will be responsible for notifying the employee of his options, if applicable, to receive refund of pension benefit premiums, if any, with interest, or, if eligible, to vest his or her rights to future retirement benefits under the plan, and to convert to a regular individual life insurance policy available from the Insurer.

Within thirty (30) days of the end of each calendar year or other Company-designated fiscal period, the Insurer will provide the Company with the following information: premiums paid by the Company and by employees during the year for current coverage; premiums paid during the year for coverage prior to the agreement date; contingent liability for unpaid premiums for prior coverage; interest paid on late premiums for current coverage and premiums for prior coverage; interest on premiums for prior coverage which has accrued and has not been paid; and other appropriate information.

Applicable Law

The terms of this plan are governed by the laws of the State of Illinois.

The Company is responsible for securing approval for the agreement from the Internal Revenue Service.

Termination

The plan may be terminated by either party on any anniversary date, provided that at least sixty (60) days written notice has been given and received. The agreement will terminate automatically if at any time there are fewer than one hundred (100) covered employees.

Upon termination of the agreement, all covered employees will be given the options normally provided, as if they had terminated employment with the Company.

The Insurer will not be released by termination of this agreement from the responsibilities (1) to continue paying retirement benefits to those who have already retired and (2) to initiate retirement benefits to those employees with a vested right to retirement benefits at the date of such termination.

For the Insurer:

/s/ James Gordon
CEO

Illinois Cooperative Life Insurance Co.

June 30, 2006

For the Company:

/s/ D. G. Barnhouse III
President

D. G. Barnhouse Co., Inc.

EXHIBIT 4
Exercise
Background
Statistics

*Source: Actual data,
U.S. Department of
Labor, Bureau of
Labor Statistics,
various years.

TABLE 1*
Consumer Price Index
(All-Cities Index, 1984 = 100)

January 1997	159.1
January 1998	161.6
January 1999	164.3
January 2000	168.8
January 2001	175.1
January 2002	177.1
January 2003	181.7
January 2004	185.2
January 2005	190.7
January 2006	198.3

TABLE 2

D. G. Barnhouse Co., Inc.
Statement of Financial Position

	Last Year	Two Years Ago
Current Assets		
Cash	$ 1,450,258	$ 1,378,516
Accounts receivable (net)	$ 3,784,345	$ 4,869,781
Inventory	$15,050,351	$14,634,726
Other	$ 180,633	$ 130,621
Total current assets	$20,465,587	$21,013,645
Fixed Assets		
Investments (at cost)	$ 142,615	$ 142,615
Plant, property, and equipment	$24,526,289	$26,263,725
Less: Accumulated depreciation	$14,971,181	$14,730,806
Plant, property, and equipment (net)	$12,555,108	$11,532,919
Total fixed assets	$12,697,723	$11,675,534
Other Assets		
Intangible assets (net)	$ 195,560	$ 205,818
Deferred charges	$ 341,498	$ 383,980
Total other assets	$ 592,058	$ 589,798
Total Assets	$33,710,366	$33,278,978
Liabilities and Equities		
Current Liabilities	$ 1,617,038	$ 1,143,994
Accounts payable	$ 2,766,125	$ 3,995,625
Notes payable	$ 438,361	$ 627,491
Accrued expenses	$ 12,324	$ 626,546
Accrued taxes payable	$ 930,215	$ 919,350
Total current liabilities	$ 5,864,063	$ 7,260,506
(Net working capital)	$14,601,524	$13,753,139
Total Liabilities	$ 5,864,063	$ 7,260,506

(continued)

TABLE 2
(continued)

Shareholder Equity

Common stock (par value $1.00) (5,800,000 shares authorized and issued)	$ 833,750	$ 833,750
Less: Treasure stock (200,000 shares)	$ 28,750	$ 28,750
Common stock outstanding (5,600,000 shares)	$ 8,050,000	$ 8,050,000
Retaining earnings	$19,796,304	$17,968,470
Total shareholder equity (per common share)	$27,546,304	$26,018,470
Total Liabilities and Equities	$33,710,367	$33,278,977

TABLE 3

D. G. Barnhouse Co., Inc.
Statement of Income and Retained Earnings

	Last Year	Two Years Ago
Income Statement		
Net sales	$ 38,224,783	$ 38,782,026
Cost of goods sold	$ 27,529,484	$ 26,616,109
Gross profit on sales	$(10,695,299)	$(12,165,918)
Selling and administrative expense	$ 5,942,501	$ 7,600,770
Net operating profit	$ 4,752,798	$ 4,565,148
Other income and expense		
Income	$ 13,721	$ 76,600
Expense	$ 167,800	$ 219,106
Net other expenses	$ 154,079	$ 142,506
Net income before taxes	$ 4,598,719	$ 4,422,641
Income tax expense	$ 2,207,385	$ 2,122,868
Net income (per common share)	$ 2,391,334	$ 2,299,774
Retained Earnings Statement		
Retained Earnings, beginning of year	$ 17,968,470	$ 16,232,196
Net income for the period	$ 2,391,334	$ 2,299,774
Less: Dividends paid	$ 563,500	$ 563,500
Retained earnings, end of year	$ 19,796,304	$ 17,968,470

TABLE 4
Statement of Sources and Uses of Funds
(Last Year)

Sources of Funds

Net earnings for the period	$ 2,391,334
Depreciation	$ 240,375
Decrease in intangible assets and deferred charges	$ 42,740
Total	$ 2,674,449

Uses of Funds

Increase in working capital	$ 848,385
Property, plant, equipment additions	$ 1,262,564
Cash dividends paid	$ 563,500
Total	$ 2,674,449

Analysis of Increase in Working Capital

Increase (Decrease) in current assets

Cash	$ 71,741
Accounts receivable	$(1,085,436)
Inventory	$ 415,625
Other current assets	$ 50,012
	$ 548,059

Decrease (Increase) in current liabilities

Accounts payable	$ (473,044)
Notes payable	$ 1,187,000
Accrued expenses	$ 149,130
Accrued taxes payable	$ 554,223
Other current liabilities	$ (20,865)
	$ 1,396,444
Net increase in working capital	$ 848,385

TABLE 5

D. G. Barnhouse Co., Inc.
Quarterly Sales and Earnings per Share Record
(Sales in $ Million; Earnings and Dividends in $)

Quarter	Last Year	2 Years Ago	3 Years Ago	4 Years Ago	5 Years Ago	6 Years Ago
First	$10.64	$10.69	$8.69	$7.09	$6.40	$6.34
Second	$ 9.78	$10.48	$7.75	$7.23	$5.09	$6.99
Third	$ 9.40	$ 9.36	$7.93	$6.91	$6.74	$6.88
Fourth	$ 8.41	$ 8.25	$7.11	$6.71	$6.61	$6.29
Earnings/share	$ 0.41	$ 0.40	$0.38	$0.40	$0.05	$0.25
Dividends/share	$ 0.11	$ 0.11	$0.11	$0.11	$0.11	$0.11

TABLE 6

**D. G. Barnhouse Co., Inc.
Employee Age Groups**

Age	Number of Current Employees
Under 30	164
30–39	112
40–49	90
50–59	73
Over 60	61
Total	500

TABLE 7

**D. G. Barnhouse Co., Inc.
Seniority List**

Term of Service	Number of Current Employees
0–2 years	71
3–9 years	160
10–14 years	49
15–20 years	122
Over 20 years	98
Total	500

Appendix B

Public Sector Mock Bargaining Exercise

The following materials provide the basic data for a mock exercise in the public sector. The exercise involves negotiations between Queen City and a police association representing police officers employed by the city, the Queen City Police Association. (Both the city and union names, as well as the material and data, are fictitious.)

The students should divide into union and management teams. Three students per team are preferred. The roles on the union bargaining committee include the union president and chief negotiator, the union attorney, and the union secretary-treasurer. The roles on the management bargaining team include the director of labor relations and chief negotiator, an assistant city attorney, and a deputy police commissioner. More union and management roles may be added if desired.

The task confronting the negotiators is to bargain a new contract covering the police officers. A copy of the current police contract and other pertinent data are provided at the end of the case. The material below presents background material to the police negotiations.

Bargaining between Queen City, New York, and the Queen City Police Association (Ind.)

Background

Queen City is an aging central city of about 350,000 (2006 estimate) located in upstate New York, and is the center of a standard metropolitan statistical area (SMSA) of more than one million people. The city's job base is in heavy manufacturing, but the area has become steadily less attractive to employers because of obsolete plants and equipment, high taxes, high labor costs, and the like. As a result, many of them have moved away, taking thousands of jobs with them. This job decline is reflected in the SMSA's high unemployment rate (9.0 percent in 2006). The hardest-hit part of the area has been Queen City itself.

Note: Peter Feuille developed this exercise and we are grateful for his permission to use it. An earlier version of the exercise appears in David Lewin, Peter Feuille, Thomas A. Kochan, and John T. Delaney, *Public Sector Labor Relations: Analysis and Readings,* 3d ed. (Lexington, MA: Lexington Books, 1987): 597–617.

The city has been losing population for years (in 1950 it had 560,000 residents), and it is no secret that most of the city's emigrants are middle-class white people, fleeing what they perceive as unsafe streets, poor schools, and high taxes. Over the past two decades there has been an influx of black people and Puerto Ricans, to the point where African Americans currently make up about 25 percent of the city's population and Hispanics about 10 percent. As a result of a variety of pressures, the tax roll has not grown in recent years.

The city government is organized on a strong-mayor basis (that is, the mayor has appointive, budgetary, and veto powers over the city council), with the city council consisting of 15 seats elected on a ward basis. The mayor and the council members serve four-year terms, with half of the council up for election every two years. The elections are partisan, and the city is solidly Democratic (the mayor and 13 of the 15 council incumbents are Democrats). The mayor is not only the dominant elected official but also the local strongman in the Democratic party—the closest thing Queen City has to a political boss. As a result, the council tends to pass what the mayor wants and to reject what he doesn't want. The annual budget approval process provides the best example of the mayor's hegemony.

City finances strongly reflect the city's weak economic situation. The 2006 city budget totals $350 million (the city school district has its own budget, and the school district has been similarly hit by stagnating revenues and increasing costs), and the city expects that its 2007 budget will require even more money. The current budget includes about $175 million in county- and state-collected revenues of various kinds and about $80 million in federal revenue, so the city has become the fiscal handmaiden of higher level governments. With stagnating local revenues and increasing costs (the city's population decline has not been matched by a similar decline in the demand for city services, especially police and fire services), each year is a struggle to break even.

Next year promises to be tough because of the state's own financial problems and proclaimed inability to increase the amount of aid to local governments. City officials are constantly trying to persuade Queen County to assume various city functions (and, of course, their associated costs); but, given that county government is largely Republican, the usual response is negative. The city has reached the constitutional ceiling on its property tax (taxes equal to 2 percent of the full value of city property), which means that in coming years only minimal additional revenues can be derived from this source. Because of very strong voter resistance to higher taxes (New York citizens on a per capita basis pay among the highest state and local taxes in the nation), city officials are reluctant to increase property taxes and do not dare institute a city sales or income tax (the latter two taxes would need enabling legislation from Albany). For 2007 the city's best estimate is that it will have 2 percent more money to spend on services and functions that it now provides. Labor costs account for about 70 percent of the city budget.

The city government employs about 5,300 people (down from 6,500 in 1980), most of whom are in one of five bargaining units. The independent Queen City Police Association represents the patrol officers and communications operators in the police department; the International Association of Fire Fighters, AFL-CIO, represents the uniformed, non-supervisory employees in the fire department; the American Federation of State, County, and Municipal Employees, AFL-CIO, represents most of the city's blue-collar employees (the majority of whom are in the public works and parks departments); the independent Queen City Civil Service Association represents most of the city's white-collar employees (who are scattered across virtually all city departments); and the Queen City Building and Construction Trades Council, AFL-CIO, represents the various craft classifications (electrician, carpenter, plumber, and so on).

The city has a reputation as a union town because of the high incidence of unionization in the private sector. Although this union influence contributed to the early and solid organization of the city's employees, and although some private sector union officials play important roles in local politics, it is not entirely clear how this union context has directly benefitted city employees. Except for special cases, the city has not done any general hiring in the past several years, and municipal employee ranks have been thinned by attrition. City officials contemplate actual layoffs, but in recent years layoffs have not been necessary.

The city's director of labor relations (DLR) heads the city's Office of Labor Relations and is responsible for the negotiation and administration of contracts with all the city unions. He is appointed by and serves at the pleasure of the mayor, and he currently enjoys the mayor's complete confidence. He receives policy (that is, maximum dollar limit) guidance from the mayor and has been able to convince the mayor and the council to shut off union end runs on matters within the scope of bargaining. The DLR also maintains good relations with city department heads and works closely with them on contract language questions so that city labor contracts will not unduly limit managerial prerogatives. The city's collective bargaining takes place under the aegis of New York's Taylor Law (except as expressly modified for the purposes of this case) and the state Public Employment Relations Board's (PERB) decisions regarding the interpretation of the Taylor Law.

The Queen City Police Department is one of the most important of the city's departments. The police budget for 2006 totals about $74 million, of which almost 50 percent goes for labor costs (including fringes, which average about 50 percent of salaries). The average 2006 salary (excluding fringes) in the entire department is about $29,000, and the department consists of about 1,050 sworn officers and about 125 civilian employees, with the civilians employed in a wide variety of jobs (clerical, custodial, mechanical, administrative, communications, and so forth). The police bargaining unit consists of 800 patrol officers (including detectives) and 40 communications officers (COs). The COs are civilians, but they wear uniforms and some of them eventually become patrol officers.

The department is directed by the police commissioner, who is appointed by and serves at the pleasure of the mayor. The department is divided into 10 police precincts, each with its own stationhouse. Patrol officers assigned to regular patrol duty work out of the various station houses. Most patrol officers and COs work rotating shifts, which rotate every three months. The police department has the usual big city problems of poverty, police-minority group friction, and increasing violence (much of which is associated with drug trade).

A recent incident stirred much controversy and antagonism between the police force (who are mostly white males) and community groups representing the black community. A white patrol officer shot a 15-year-old black youth after stopping the youth for questioning. The officer claimed the youth had reached into his pocket as if to go for a gun. Community groups saw this as another in a long series of police actions in which excessive force was used against the black community. These groups demanded the creation of a public review board to investigate this and other police actions. After an investigation directed by the police chief, the police officer in question was exonerated and the mayor pledged to study the possibility of a public review board.

The police union consists of two occupational groups, the patrol officers and the COs. The patrol officers naturally look down on the COs because of the latter's civilian status—they have no arrest powers and carry no weapons. The COs are in the unit, however, because there is some measurable "community of interest" across the two groups and because the union leadership wants the COs there in case of a strike so that the police communications processes will be disrupted and there will be fewer personnel available for management to use during the stoppage.

The union's membership (which includes 98 percent of the eligibles) is divided along the usual lines: age and seniority (the older officers are interested in pensions; the younger ones are interested in wages and, more recently, job security), duties (the street patrol officers, or the "combatants," sneer at the desk jockeys, or "noncombatants," in headquarters), and so on. There is—for a police union—the usual rank-and-file militance to get "more" and get it yesterday.

The parties negotiated 5 percent pay increases each year in the current two-year contract covering 2005 and 2006. Because these pay raises lagged behind increases in some other New York cities, the union and its members are looking for a nice catch-up increase. In addition, the younger and shorter service officers, concerned over possible layoffs, are looking for job security protection in this year's contract as well as the usual bundle of cash and other benefits.

Currently there is police and fire pay parity—not contractually, but as a result of a long-standing political custom. As a result, pay increases negotiated by one public safety group are given to the other group. In some years the police settle first, and in other years the fire fighters are the pacesetters. Neither group has settled yet for 2007, and each group is keeping a sharp eye on the other.

The city also is engaged in negotiations with all the other unions representing municipal employees. Each of these unions is jockeying for position while keeping an eye on what is going on with the other groups.

Union Demands

After careful evaluation of membership desires, the police union leadership has formulated the following package of contract demands to be submitted to management. They are listed in no particular order of importance, though the weights bargainers may choose to attach to them should reflect the facts of the case. To facilitate cost calculations, background information is provided for some of these demands. The union wants:

1. In light of police salaries elsewhere and increases in inflation, a 12 percent pay increase at all steps for patrol officers and communications operators.
2. The city to pay the entire cost of the family Blue Cross-Blue Shield-major medical coverage. The city already pays the employees' premium and most of the family premium. The current employee-only premium is $1,200 per year; the current family premium is $2,400 per year ($1,200 additional). Blue Cross benefits are the same across all city groups. Premiums have increased about 5 percent annually during the past three years. About 80 percent of the members have family coverage, and about 20 percent have single coverage. The health insurance plan covers all city employees.
3. The mayor and the police chief to go on record opposed to any sort of public review board of police actions. If such a board were to be created, the police want to be guaranteed that they and their representatives will be provided equal participation in any such board.

4. An increase in life insurance coverage from $25,000 to $40,000, and the city to continue to pay the full premium. Premiums currently are $80 per year per employee; the premium for $40,000 coverage would be $120 per year per employee. Police and fire fighters receive the same life insurance benefits, but other city employees receive from $5,000 to $10,000 less coverage, depending on the unit.

5. A dental insurance plan covering each employee and his or her family. Premiums are $125 per year for single coverage and $300 per year ($175 additional) for family coverage. No other city group has dental insurance.

6. A 10 percent shift premium for all hours worked between the hours of 6 p.m. and 6 a.m. No other city group receives such a premium. Approximately 50 percent of all police hours are worked between 6 p.m. and 6 a.m.

7. An increase in annual longevity pay for patrol officers as follows: from the present $300 to $600 after 10 years' service and $900 after 15 years' service; from the present $600 to $1,200 after 20 years' service and $1,500 after 25 years' service. For COs, increases will be from $150 to $300 after 10 years' service, to $450 after 15 years' service, to $600 after 20 years' service, and to $750 after 25 years' service. Fire fighters receive the same longevity pay as police; other city employees receive lesser amounts depending on the unit.

8. An increase in sick leave accrual to 18 days per year of service (or one and one-half days per month), including the first year, with the maximum accrual increased to 300 days. Whenever an employee is terminated for any reason, the employee shall receive a cash payment equal to the value of all accrued sick leave.

9. An increase in the uniform allowance to $450 for patrol officers and $225 for COs.

10. Four more paid holidays (Martin Luther King's birthday, Washington's birthday, Lincoln's birthday, and the day after Thanksgiving). Other city employees receive the same number of holidays the police currently receive. All officers are given one day's pay for each holiday. Officers who work on a holiday receive the one day's holiday pay just mentioned plus time-and-one-half for working on that day.

11. An increase in vacation time to three weeks after five years, four weeks after 10 years, five weeks after 15 years, and six weeks after 20 years. At present all city employees, including police, receive the same amount of vacation.

12. An increase in the standby pay rate as follows: 60 percent of the employee's straight time hourly pay rate for the first eight hours; $35 for each 12-hour period (or fraction) thereafter. In an average week approximately 15 officers will be required to stand by for one shift (eight hours) each.

13. A new Section 2.3 to be added to Article II that will establish an agency shop. About 98 percent of the unit already belong to the union, but union leaders believe that everyone should help pay for the costs of collective bargaining services.

14. Section 5.6 (Civil Service) to be deleted and replaced by a new section: "Just Cause. No disciplinary action shall be taken against any member of the bargaining unit except for just cause." In 1998 seven major disciplinary cases were processed and discipline was levied by the police commissioner according to departmental and civil service regulations. Two of these cases involved discharges (for on-the-job misconduct), and both cases have been appealed to court (with the association's assistance).

15. A no-layoff clause.

16. A requirement that seniority be the determining factor in layoffs, work assignments, transfers, vacation selection, and holiday scheduling. As a result of long-standing custom, seniority is currently used on a de facto basis for vacation selection and holiday scheduling, but this is not a contractual requirement. As in any large city police department, there is the usual griping that many personnel decisions are made according to favoritism and political criteria. Also as usual, there is little hard evidence to support these complaints.

17. A one-year contract expiring on June 30, 2008.

> These union demands are not listed in any particular order of importance beyond the facts presented in the case. It is the responsibility of the union bargaining team to gather supporting evidence, to put priorities or weights on various items, to develop specific contract language to implement various proposals, to develop justifications for its demands, to decide what compromises to make, and to decide what will constitute a minimum acceptable agreement.

Employer Demands

In collective bargaining the employer typically spends much time responding to union demands. However, as a result of problems that have arisen during the life of the existing contract and because of the city's fiscal constraints, the city has formulated the following demands. The city wants:

1. In light of the city's finances and the modest rate of inflation, no increase in pay during 2007, a 2 percent salary increase on January 1, 2008, and another 2 percent on January 1, 2009, and no increase in any fringe benefit at any time. Considering how fringe benefit increases spread to other city bargaining units, the city is especially eager to avoid benefit increases.

2. A reduction in the off-duty court appearance pay minimum guarantee to one hour. About 100 officers per week make off-duty court appearances, and the city estimates that about 50 percent of them complete their appearances in less than three hours.

3. Sick leave accrual to remain the same; however, there shall be no payment to terminated or retired officers.

4. The definition of a grievance to be changed so that everything beyond the comma in Section 5.1 is deleted. During 2006, about 300 step 1 grievances were filed, and five of these went all the way to arbitration. The association won three cases (overtime pay, court appearance pay, and standby pay), and the city won two (sick leave pay at termination, association representation at a step 1 grievance meeting). All five of the arbitration cases involved contractual interpretation disputes, but about one-quarter of the step 1 grievances did not. The city does not want to process city or department rules complaints through the grievance procedure, and it notes that these matters can be processed through the existing civil service appeals procedure.

5. Deletion of the phrase "or at least reasonably close to these time limits" in the second sentence of Section 5.4.

6. Insertion of the following sentence into Article VI so that the second sentence in that article reads: "The Association agrees that if any such activity occurs, the Association and its officers and agents shall work as speedily and diligently as possible for the complete cessation of any such activity." There have been no strikes in the department's history, but at contract negotiation time there are periodic rumblings from some officers about "showing the city we mean business."

7. The elimination of communications operators from the bargaining unit so that the unit will be limited to police patrol officers.

8. A three-year contract expiring on June 30, 2010.

> These employer demands are not presented in any particular order of importance. It is the responsibility of the management bargaining team to gather supporting evidence, to put priorities or weights on various items, to develop specific contract language to implement various proposals, to develop justifications for its proposals, to respond to union demands, to decide what compromises to make, and to decide what will constitute an acceptable agreement.

Impasse Resolution

If no agreement is reached by the end of the time set aside for direct negotiations, there are a variety of methods for resolving the impasse: mediation, fact-finding, some form of arbitration, or strike. In light of the increasing use of compulsory arbitration to resolve police and fire fighter bargaining impasses, it would be useful and instructive to have any impasse in this case be resolved by the following arbitration procedures. If two or more negotiations arenas exist, it may be particularly instructive to use two or three of the following methods in order to see what impact the different procedures have on the bargaining process.

Final-Offer Arbitration with Package Selection

If the two sides do not reach full and complete agreement by the end of the time set aside for negotiations, then all unresolved items shall be submitted directly to final-offer arbitration. Specifically, at the next class session, each party shall submit to the arbitrator (the instructor or instructor's designee) and to the other party a written list of all unresolved items and its final offer on each of those items. Each party shall concurrently submit a list of all items, if any, that have been agreed on in direct negotiations. The arbitration hearing shall commence promptly at the beginning of the class period and shall be heard by the single arbitrator with full powers to issue a binding decision.

Each side shall have 20 minutes to present its case and an additional five minutes for rebuttal, and each side shall be responsible for developing and presenting justifications for its final offer. The arbitrator's decision shall be final and binding upon the parties. The decision, together with accompanying explanation, shall be delivered orally to the parties before the end of the class period.

The arbitrator shall be limited in his or her decision to choosing the most reasonable final offer. The arbitrator shall not compromise or alter *in any way* the final offer s/he selects. The arbitrator shall make her/his selection decision on an entire package basis (that is, s/he shall *not* make separate selection decisions on each issue), and her/his selection, together with any previously agreed-on items, shall constitute the new collective bargaining agreement between the parties. In making her/his determination of the most reasonable offer, the arbitrator shall be guided by the arbitration criteria listed at the end of this section.

Nothing in the foregoing shall preclude the parties from requesting a recess during the arbitration hearing in order to resume direct negotiations, nor shall it preclude the arbitrator from recessing the hearing and ordering the parties to resume direct negotiations if the arbitrator believes that such resumption of negotiations may be helpful in resolving the impasse. Similarly, nothing in the foregoing shall limit the arbitrator from rendering any mediation assistance to the parties if the arbitrator believes such assistance will be helpful in resolving the impasse. (Time constraints, however, will limit the amount of additional negotiation or mediation activities during the arbitration session.)

Final-Offer Arbitration with Issue-by-Issue Selection

Everything is the same as stated in the preceding section, with the important exception that the arbitrator will make a separate "most reasonable" selection decision on each issue in dispute.

Conventional Arbitration

In reaching a decision, the arbitrator shall take into consideration the following:

1. Comparisons of the wages, hours, and conditions of employment of the employees involved in the arbitration proceeding with the wages, hours, and conditions of employment of other employees performing similar services or requiring similar skills under similar working conditions in public employment in comparable communities.
2. The interests and welfare of the public and the financial ability of the public employer to pay.
3. The average consumer prices for goods and services in the area, commonly known as the cost of living.
4. The overall compensation currently received by the employees, including direct wages, vacations and other excused time, insurance and pensions, medical and hospitalization benefits, the continuity and stability of employment, and all other benefits received.
5. Changes in any of the foregoing circumstances during the preceding negotiations or during the arbitration proceedings.
6. Such other factors, not confined to the foregoing, that are normally or traditionally taken into consideration in the determination of wages, hours, and conditions of employment through collective bargaining, fact-finding, or arbitration in public employment.

Post-Exercise Analysis

The instructor and the students will find it profitable to spend all or most of a class period analyzing the negotiation and impasse resolution experiences of the various bargaining teams (whether or not they go to arbitration). The students probably will have numerous questions about various facts of the negotiation and impasse processes, and the instructor should have a variety of constructively critical comments to make about how the students tried to obtain a favorable contract.

Background Data

Tables 1 through 4 provide background information for this exercise.

TABLE 1
Queen City Budget, 2006

Revenues

Local	
Property taxes	$102,732,500
Licenses and permits	$ 3,516,500
Parking meters	$ 3,120,000
Fines and forfeitures	$ 4,615,000
Interest	$ 1,690,000
Other local	$ 7,124,000
County and state distributions	
Sales taxes	$ 91,780,000
Gasoline taxes	$ 6,110,000
State aid	$130,149,500
Federal revenues	
Shared revenue	$ 23,270,000
Housing and community development	$ 66,144,000
Other federal	$ 15,658,500
Total Revenues	**$455,910,000**

Appropriations

Police department	$ 74,295,000
Fire department	$ 54,093,000
Public works and sanitation department	$ 78,975,000
Parks and recreation department	$ 15,177,500
Finance and accounting department	$ 6,506,500
City auditor	$ 1,924,000
Total Departments	**$230,971,000**

Appropriations

City's share of special districts	
School	$ 11,284,000
Sewers	$ 20,624,500
Public health	$ 8,027,500
Public housing	$104,650,000
General administration	$ 79,417,000
Reserve	$ 936,000
Total Appropriations	**$455,910,000**

TABLE 2
New York Comparability Information for Patrol Officers, 2006*

		Longevity Pay		Health Insurance (percentage paid by employer)		Dental Insurance (percentage paid by employer)	
City (population)	Maximum Salary	Maximum Amount	No. Years to Maximum	Employee	Family	Employee	Family
Rockville (250,000)	$36,790	$1,300	28	100%	100%	100%	50%
Swinton (180,000)	35,750	1,040	20	100	90	100	0
York (200,000)	35,620	1,560	30	100	100	75	0
Albert (110,000)	34,710	975	25	100	95	Not provided	
Queen View (50,000)	33,800	780	20	100	80	Not provided	
Queen Woods (60,000)	35,620	780	20	100	90	Not provided	
Queen Falls (85,000)	35,100	1,170	25	100	100	100	0

			Sick Leave			
	Annual Clothing Allowance	Term Life Insurance Coverage	No. Days per Year	No. Days Maximum Accrual	Night Shift Premium	No. of Paid Holidays
Rockville	$676	$50,700	12	180	None	12
Swinton	541	33,800	12	150	33c/hr.	11
York	592	42,250	12	120	35%	12
Albert	676	33,800	15	200	None	11
Queen View	507	25,350	10	125	None	11
Queen Woods	549	33,800	12	140	None	10
Queen Falls	541	33,800	12	160	None	10

*Over the years the City and the Association have relied heavily on these New York cities for comparison purposes. Queen View, Queen Woods, and Queen Falls are suburbs of Queen City; the other cities are located in upstate New York. None of these cities have negotiated or arbitrated their 2007 contracts. From time to time, the City and the Association also look at similar size cities in other states.

TABLE 3
Queen City Police Salary History

Year	Step D Patrol Officer	Step D Communication Operator
1996	$23,400	$17,940
1997	24,570	19,110
1998	26,130	20,540
1999	27,170	21,450
2000	28,080	22,100
2001	28,990	22,880
2002	29,900	23,660
2003	30,875	24,440
2004	31,980	25,285
2005	33,540	25,675
2006	35,230	27,625

TABLE 4
Police Bargaining Unit
Seniority Distribution

Years of Service*	Number of Employees
26 or more	90
20–25	160
15–19	230
10–14	225
5–9	100
4	12
3	10
2	8
1	5
Probationary	0

*Within each years-of-service category, employees are distributed on a linear basis.

Agreement between Queen City, New York, and the Queen City Police Association

July 1, 2005 through June 30, 2007

Parties to the Agreement

This Agreement is entered into by and between Queen City, New York (hereinafter called the "City"), and the Queen City Police Association (hereinafter called the "Association").

Article I

Recognition and Representation

The City recognizes the Association as the sole and exclusive bargaining agent with respect to wages, hours, and other conditions of employment for employees classified as Police Patrol Officer and Communications Operator.

Article II

Check-off

Section 2.1—Check-off Association Dues

Upon receipt of a signed authorization from an employee in the form set forth by the City, the City agrees for the duration of this Agreement to deduct from such employee's pay uniform monthly Association dues. The Association will notify the City in writing of the amount of the uniform dues to be deducted. Deductions shall be made on the second City payday of each month and shall be remitted, together with an itemized statement, to the

Treasurer of the Association by the 15th day of the month following the month in which the deduction is made.

Section 2.2—Indemnification

The Association shall indemnify the City and hold it harmless against any and all claims, demands, suits, or other forms of liability that may arise out of, or by reason of, any action taken by the City for the purpose of complying with the provisions of this Article.

Article III

No-Discrimination

Section 3.1—General

Neither the City nor the Association shall discriminate against any employees because of race, creed, color, national origin, sex, or Association activity.

Section 3.2—Job Transfer

The City will not use job transfer as a form of disciplinary action. Violations of this section will be subject to the grievance procedure.

Article IV

Management Rights

The City shall retain the sole right and authority to operate and direct the affairs of the City and the Police Department in all its various aspects, including, but not limited to, all rights and authority exercised by the City prior to the execution of this Agreement. Among the rights retained is the City's right to determine its mission and set standards of service offered to the public; to direct the working forces; to plan, direct, control and determine the operations or services to be conducted in or at the Police Department or by employees of the City; to assign or transfer employees; to hire, promote, demote, suspend, discipline, or discharge for cause, or relieve employees due to lack of work or for other legitimate reasons; to make and enforce reasonable rules and regulations; to change methods, equipment, or facilities; provided, however, that the exercise of any of the above rights shall not conflict with any of the provisions of this Agreement.

Article V

Grievance Procedures

Section 5.1—Definition of Grievance

A grievance is a difference of opinion between an employee or the Association and the City with respect to the meaning or application of the express terms of this Agreement, or with respect to inequitable application of the Personnel Rules of the City or with respect to inequitable application of the Rules of the Police Department.

Section 5.2—Association Representation

The Association shall appoint an Employee Committee of not more than three members to attend grievance meetings scheduled pursuant to Steps 3 and 4. The Association may appoint three Stewards, one from each shift (who may be the same persons selected for the Employee Committee), to participate in the grievance procedure to the extent set forth in Step 1 and Step 2 of the grievance procedure. The Association shall notify the Director of Labor Relations in writing of the names of employees serving on the Employee Committee and as Stewards. One representative of the Executive Board of the Association and/or the Association's legal counsel shall have the right to participate in Steps 3, 4, and 5 of the grievance procedure.

Section 5.3—Grievance Procedure

Recognizing that grievances should be raised and settled promptly, a grievance must be raised within seven (7) calendar days of the occurrence of the event giving rise to the grievance. A grievance shall be processed as follows:

Step 1—Verbal to Immediate Supervisor: By discussion between the employee, accompanied by the Steward, if the employee so desires, and the employee's immediate supervisor. The immediate supervisor shall answer verbally within seven (7) calendar days of this discussion.

Step 2—Appeal to Captain: If the grievance is not settled in Step 1, the Association may, within seven (7) calendar days following receipt of the immediate supervisor's answer, file a written grievance signed by the employee and her/his Steward on a form provided by the City setting forth the nature of the grievance and the contract provision(s) involved. The Captain shall give a written answer in seven (7) calendar days after receipt of the written grievance.

Step 3—Appeal to the Police Commissioner: If the grievance is not settled in Step 2 and the Association decides to appeal, the Association shall, within seven (7) calendar days from receipt of the Step 2 answer, appeal in writing to the Police Commissioner. The Employer Committee and the Commissioner will discuss the grievance at a mutually agreeable time. If no agreement is reached in such discussion, the Commissioner will give an answer in writing within seven (7) days of the discussion. The City may join the Step 3 and Step 4 meetings if it so desires, by having in attendance both the Commissioner and the Director of Labor Relations or the Director's designee.

Step 4—Appeal to Director of Labor Relations: If the grievance is not settled in Step 3 and the Association decides to appeal, the Association shall, within seven (7) calendar days after receipt of the Step 3 answer, file a written appeal to the Director of Labor Relations. A meeting between the Director, or his/her designee, and the Employee Committee will be held at a mutually agreeable time. If no settlement is reached at such meeting, the Director, or the designee, shall give an answer in writing within ten (10) calendar days of the meeting.

Step 5—Arbitration: If the grievance is not settled in accordance with the foregoing procedure, the Association may refer the grievance to arbitration by giving written notice to the director of Labor Relations within twenty-one (21) calendar days after receipt of the City's answer in Step 4. The parties shall attempt to agree upon an arbitrator promptly. In the event the parties are unable to agree upon an arbitrator, they shall jointly request the Federal Mediation and Conciliation Service to submit a panel of five arbitrators. The Association shall strike one name and the City shall strike one name; then the Association shall strike another name, and the City shall strike another name, and the person whose name remains shall be the arbitrator; provided that either party, before striking any names, shall have the right to reject one panel of arbitrators. The arbitrator shall be notified of the selection by a joint letter from the City and the Association requesting that he/she set a time and a place for hearing, subject to the availability of the City and Association representative. The arbitrator shall have no right to amend, modify, nullify, ignore, add to, or subtract from the provisions of this Agreement. The arbitrator shall consider and decide only the specific issue submitted, whose decision shall be based solely upon his/her interpretation of the meaning or application of the terms of this Agreement to the facts of the grievance presented. The decision of the arbitrator shall be final and binding. The costs of the arbitration, including the fee and expenses of the arbitrator, shall be divided equally between the City and the Association.

Section 5.4—Time Limits

No grievance shall be entertained or processed unless it is filed within the time limits set forth in Section 5.3. If a grievance is not appealed within the time limits for appeal set forth above, or at least reasonably close to the time limits, it shall be deemed settled on the basis of the last answer of the City, provided that the parties may agree to extend any time limits. If the City fails to provide an answer within the time limits so provided, the Association may immediately appeal to the next Step.

Section 5.5—Investigation and Discussion

All grievance discussions and investigations shall take place in a manner that does not interfere with City operations.

Section 5.6—Civil Service

It is understood that matters subject to Civil Service, such as promotion, discharge, and disciplinary suspension of seven days or more, are not subject to this grievance procedure. However, in the event a permanent employee is discharged or suspended for seven days or more, the Association may request a meeting to discuss said discharge or suspension prior to institution of a Civil Service appeal. Upon receipt of such request, the City will meet promptly at Step 3 or Step 4 for this purpose.

Article VI

No Strikes–No Lockouts

The Association, its officers and agents, and the employees covered by this Agreement agree not to instigate, promote, sponsor, engage in, or condone any strike, slowdown, concerted stoppage of work, or any other intentional interruption of operations. Any or all employees who violate any of the provisions of this Article may be discharged or otherwise disciplined by the City. The city will not lock out any employees during the term of this Agreement as a result of a labor dispute with the Association.

Article VII

Wages and Benefits

Section 7.1—Salary Schedules

The salary schedule and longevity pay effective from July 1, 2005, through June 30, 2006, and from July 1, 2006 through June 30, 2007, is attached hereto as Exhibit 1.

Section 7.2—Fringe Benefits

The fringe benefits in effect during the term of this Agreement shall be as follows:

A. Holidays shall be as follows:

New Year's Day	Veteran's Day
Good Friday	Thanksgiving
Memorial Day	Christmas Eve
Fourth of July	Christmas
Labor Day	New Year's Eve

B. Vacation shall be accrued at the following rates:

Recruitment through sixth year	2 weeks
Seventh through fourteenth year	3 weeks
Fifteenth and later years	4 weeks

C. Uniform allowance: The City shall provide annual uniform allowances as follows:

Patrol Officers	$350
Communications Operators	$175

In the administration of the foregoing uniform allowance, the City will not set any dollar limit on any authorized item.

D. Group Insurance. The City's term life insurance program ($25,000 coverage per employee) shall be continued in effect for the term of this Agreement, and the City's 100 percent contribution shall continue. The City's Blue Cross/Blue Shield-major medical program (single and family coverage) shall be continued in effect for the term of this agreement. For the term of this Agreement, the city shall pay the entire cost of "employee only" Blue Cross/Blue Shield or major medical coverage. As of January 1, 2006, the employee's monthly contribution for "family" Blue Cross/Blue Shield or major medical coverage shall be $8.00.

E. Retiree Blue Cross/Blue Shield or Major Medical Coverage. An employee who retires on or after January 1, 2006, and is eligible for an immediate pension under the New York Police pension fund, may elect "employee only" or "family" coverage under the City's Blue Cross/Blue Shield or major medical program by paying the entire group premium cost, which may increase from time to time, by means of deduction from the pensioner's pension check.

F. Sick Leave. The City's sick leave plan shall be continued in effect for the term of this Agreement (accrual of six days for the first full year of employment and 12 days for subsequent full years of employment), with the maximum accrual increased to 150 days. Whenever an employee with ten years or more of service is terminated for any reason, the employee shall receive one of the following, whichever is greater: (1) payment of all sick days accrued in excess of 50 days (to a maximum of 25 days pay), or (2) the current four-week special retirement allowance for employees who retire with eligibility for current pension benefits.

Section 7.3—Overtime Pay for Emergency Duty

A Patrol Officer shall receive time and one-half his regular straight-time hourly rate when ordered to report for overtime emergency duty or when ordered to remain on the job for overtime emergency duty. A Patrol Officer will not receive overtime pay for any work during his regular working hours.

Section 7.4—Off-Duty Court Appearance Pay

A Patrol Officer shall receive time and one-half his/her regular straight-time hourly rate for required court appearances during his off-duty hours. Patrol Officers shall be guaranteed three hours at the time and one-half rate for each separate off-duty court appearance or actual time spent, whichever is greater.

Section 7.5—Emergency Standby Pay

Whenever the City places an employee on emergency standby, the employee shall receive standby pay as follows: (1) for the first four hours, 30 percent of the employee's straight-time hourly rate, and (2) for each 12-hour period thereafter, or fraction thereof, $15.00.

Article VIII

Termination and Legality Clauses

Section 8.1—Savings

If any provision of this Agreement is subsequently declared by legislative or judicial authority to be unlawful, unenforceable, or not in accordance with applicable statutes or ordinances, all other provisions of this Agreement shall remain in full force and effect for the duration of this Agreement.

Section 8.2—Entire Agreement

This Agreement constitutes the entire agreement between the parties and concludes collective bargaining on any subject, whether included in this Agreement or not, for the term of this Agreement.

Section 8.3—Term

This Agreement shall become effective July 1, 2005, and shall terminate at 11:59 P.M. on June 30, 2007. Not earlier than Jan. 1, 2007, and not later than April 30, 2007, either the City or the Association may give written notice to the other party by registered or certified mail of its desire to negotiate modifications to this Agreement, said modifications to be effective July 1, 2007.

Queen City	Queen City Police Association

EXHIBIT 1

Annual Salary
Schedule and
Longevity Pay,
Queen City,
New York

TABLE 1
Salary Schedule
(Annual salaries)

Step	Patrol Officers	Communications Operators
Effective July 1, 2005, through June 30, 2006		
A (Probationary)	$28,600	$21,710
B	28,925	22,360
C	30,550	23,985
D	33,540	25,675
Effective July 1, 2006, through June 30, 2007		
A (Probationary)	$28,860	$21,970
B	30,745	23,920
C	32,500	25,610
D	35,230	27,625

Note: On the annual anniversary date of his or her employment, each employee shall
advance one step until Step D is reached.

After completing the specified years of service, each employee shall receive an annual
longevity stipend as follows:

TABLE 2
Longevity Pay
Effective July 1, 2005, through June 30, 2007

	Patrol Officer	Communications Operators
After 10 years	$390	$195
After 20 years	$780	$390

Appendix C

Grievance Arbitration Exercises

Case 1

In the Matter of Arbitration between
International Brotherhood
of Electrical Workers, AFL-CIO, Local 400,
        –and–
ABC Wire Making Company

The Issue

At the outset of the hearing the parties stipulated the issue to be as follows:

> Was the company's decision to hire Mitchell Carey as a primary operator of the dual-head
> extruder in violation of Article 10, Section 1(d) of the collective bargaining agreement?
> If so, what shall be the remedy?

The Facts

On September 26, 2006, the company posted job openings for three shifts for the position
of Grade 3 Dual-Head Extruder/Primary Operator. Two employees bid for and were placed
in these positions. The company then sought applicants from outside the company for the
third position and hired Mr. Mitchell Carey. On October 28, the day after Mr. Carey began
work, the union filed a grievance claiming the company violated Article 10, Section 1(d) of
the collective bargaining agreement by not offering the job to Mr. Michael Seiss, the most
senior maintenance mechanic who was on layoff status at that time.

Article 10.1(d) reads as follows:

> If the job is not filled by (a), (b), or (c) above, the Company may select from the callback list
> the employee who, in their opinion, is the best qualified for that job; and if, in their opinion,
> no one is qualified, the Company may hire a new employee.

The union agrees that the company properly followed the procedures called for in paragraphs (a), (b), and (c) of Section 1 of Article 10. Therefore, the dispute focuses on the company's application of paragraph (d).

The Union's Arguments

Michael Seiss testified that he has worked for the company as a maintenance mechanic for eight years. As part of this job he has had responsibility for maintaining, repairing, setting up, and installing machinery in the plant. He also testified that he has done this work on machine #802—the dual-head extruder. While Mr. Seiss testified that he has not set up or run this particular machine by himself, he said that he has set the dies and heat temperature controls and has observed the extruder in operation. It is his belief that he could run this machine. Mr. Seiss also indicated that he was on layoff from September 2006 to February 2007 and would have taken the dual-head extruder operator job if it had been offered to him.

The union argues that maintenance mechanics are qualified to do the job in question and that the company should call back any employee who is qualified for this job before hiring from the outside. Therefore, the union requests that Mr. Seiss be made whole for lost wages and benefits from October 27, 2006, to the time of his recall in February 2007.

The Company's Argument

The company argues that the job of extruder operator requires a more complex level of skill and expertise than do other machine operator jobs in the plant. A letter of agreement on skill progression rates contained in the collective bargaining agreement is cited as evidence for the high level of skill required. That letter provides for a pay rate increase of 20 cents per hour for each year of experience in this job title.

The company's central argument is that Article 10, Section 1(d) indicates that the company may, but is not required to, recall an employee from the callback list after it has complied with the procedures outlined in paragraphs (a), (b), and (c). It stresses that the word "may" in paragraph (d) should be taken for its plain meaning, particularly since it contrasts with the words "shall" in paragraphs (a) and (b) and "will" in paragraph (c). Thus, the company argues that it had the discretion to decide whether any current employees were qualified to perform the job of extruder operator.

The company further argues that it did not act in an unreasonable or arbitrary fashion in deciding that Mr. Seiss's experience as a maintenance mechanic did not qualify him to operate the dual-head extruder. As noted in the letter of agreement cited above, the dual-head extruder job is critical to the plant's operations and, in the company's opinion, requires a higher level of skill and expertise than the other machine jobs in the plant. Mr. John Reilly, Director of Human Resources, testified that he and the company's personnel manager reviewed the employees on layoff status and concluded that, in their opinion, none was qualified for this position or could do the job without extensive training. The company also notes that Mr. Seiss had never run nor been trained on this machine. The company rejects the view that he was qualified to operate this machine because he had worked on it in his capacity as a maintenance mechanic. The company further notes that Article 9, Section 2 of the collective bargaining agreement states: "to be qualified, an employee must be able to perform the job without assistance. . . ."

Questions for Discussion

1. What is the company's contractual responsibility in this case?
2. Who has the burden of proof of the current employee's (Mr. Seiss's) ability or inability to perform the vacant job?
3. Assume you are the arbitrator. What would you decide?
4. Assume you were brought in as a human resource consultant to the company and the union following this case. What changes in practices would you recommend to avoid disputes like this in the future?

Case 2

In the Matter of Arbitration between
American Federation of Teachers Union, Local 3000,
                         –and–
Homer City School System

The Issue

The parties stipulated the issue in this case as follows:

> Did the school administration have just cause to reprimand teacher Joseph O'Connell? If not, what shall be the remedy?

The Facts

Mr. O'Connell is a white, male gym teacher at Homer City High School. Before classes started on the morning of February 7, 2007, he was assigned to supervise one end of the third-floor corridor until homeroom period began. While performing his duties, Mr. O'Connell noticed a seventh-grade African-American male student in the hall near his locker. Mr. O'Connell instructed the student to go to his homeroom; however, the student said he had permission from his homeroom teacher to go to his locker and walked away. Several minutes later Mr. O'Connell again saw the student in the hall and again instructed him to go to his homeroom, but the student did not do so. A third time Mr. O'Connell instructed the student to return to his homeroom, but the student ran down an adjacent stairway instead.

Mr. O'Connell then encountered the student in the corridor near the stairwell. A verbal confrontation occurred and, Mr. O'Connell testified, the student pushed Mr. O'Connell and shouted obscenities at him. Mr. O'Connell then told the student to go to the office with him. As they approached the top of a set of stairs, the student swung his arm around as if to hit Mr. O'Connell, whereupon Mr. O'Connell grabbed the student from behind and lifted him off the ground to restrain him.

Mr. Steven Smith, another teacher whose duty post was at the other end of the hall, testified that he ran to the scene in response to the noise he heard. Mr. Smith asked Mr. O'Connell to release the student and told the student to go to the office with him. The student did so. The student was subsequently suspended for his actions.

There were no witnesses to the interaction between Mr. O'Connell and the student before Mr. Smith's arrival.

Mr. Michael Rogers, the principal of Homer City High School, testified that he was not at the school on the day of the incident. When he returned to school he reviewed the reports of the incident prepared by his staff and by Mr. Smith and Mr. O'Connell. He also received a letter from the student's mother that was critical of Mr. O'Connell's behavior and demanded that appropriate disciplinary action be taken against him. She also requested a meeting with Mr. Rogers and said she would bring along a prominent local attorney who was formerly associated with the U.S. Office of Civil Rights. This meeting was held on February 10, 2007. Mr. Rogers also met with Mr. O'Connell to discuss the incident.

On March 7th Mr. Rogers wrote a letter to Mr. O'Connell stating, in part:

> I originally accepted your description of the incident. Nevertheless, I am concerned about the use of unnecessary force on your part in handling the situation. My review of all of the statements submitted leads me to conclude that you did indeed use excessive force in dealing with [the student]. You state that [he] threatened you physically and that you felt it necessary to restrain him by clamping him in a bear hug and physically carrying him to the office. I find that your decision to use physical force to restrain [the student] was an unnecessary and inappropriate overreaction.
>
> Since we have spoken on previous occasions about your handling of incidents involving minority students, I have decided to forward my summary of this matter to the Deputy Superintendent/Operations for review and possible further disciplinary action.
>
> A copy of this memorandum has been placed in your personnel folder.

A hearing to review this matter was subsequently conducted by Mr. Richard Hortoy, assistant superintendent of the school system, at which the student, his mother, his attorney, Mr. O'Connell, and appropriate school and union representatives were present. Thereafter Mr. Hortoy and the other school representatives are called the "school administration."

After the hearing, in a letter to Mr. O'Connell, Mr. Hortoy reported the following decision:

> Based on the testimony presented at the hearing, the School administration determined that you did overreact by using unnecessary physical force in a situation that should have been addressed via appropriate school channels. . . . Please be advised that this letter is a written reprimand of poor judgment in handling a difficult situation. The use of excessive physical force in a similar type of situation will result in further disciplinary action, suspension, or dismissal. This letter will be placed in your personnel file.

Mr. O'Connell subsequently filed a grievance claiming that both the Rogers and the Hortoy letters constituted discipline without just cause as required in Article VI, Section B of the collective bargaining agreement. That clause states:

> Any discipline in relation to collective bargaining unit members shall be for just cause.

The Union's Argument

The union begins its argument by noting that there were no direct witnesses to most of the incident. Only the teacher and the student involved were present.

The school principal testified that he had expressed his concern to Mr. O'Connell about Mr. O'Connell's excessive use of force in similar incidents with minority students. However, on this point the union argues that the administration failed to abide by its written rules governing the conduct of disciplinary hearings and issuance of discipline by failing to follow the progressive discipline procedures outlined in the school superintendent's personnel policies. No record of these conversations was ever made or placed in Mr. O'Connell's personnel file.

The School Administration's Argument

The school administration argues that the Management Rights clause of the collective bargaining agreement gives it the right to set and apply disciplinary rules and policies. An arbitrator should only set aside the administration's judgment in disciplinary cases involving the use of physical force if it can be shown that the administration acted in bad faith or in an arbitrary, discriminatory, or capricious manner. Since the administration acted in this case after a careful review of the facts and the conduct of a hearing, its judgment that Mr. O'Connell did use excessive force should stand.

The school administration also argues that while it does have a policy of progressive discipline, it may impose a more severe penalty and skip the oral warning for a first offense when the incident in question is serious in nature. Use of physical force against a student fits this description.

The administration further argues that the sheer differences in physical size and strength between the teacher and the student indicate that the teacher was in no physical danger and therefore his use of a bear hug to restrain the student was a clear overreaction.

Finally, the administration argues that Mr. O'Connell had available and was aware of other, more appropriate alternatives for dealing with the student's actions. He could have asked for Mr. Smith or some other teacher to assist him after the verbal threats were made by the student. Or, Mr. O'Connell could have referred the issue to Ms. Wickett, the assistant principal in charge at the time of the incident.

Questions for Discussion

1. Who has the burden of proof in this case?
2. What relevance, if any, would you give to the fact that the teacher was a large, muscular, white gym teacher and the student was a seventh-grade African-American?
3. What relevance, if any, would you give to the school administration's claim that this teacher had similar cases of excessive force with minority students in the past that had not resulted in disciplinary action?
4. If you were the arbitrator, what would you decide in this case? If you decide Mr. O'Connell was unjustly disciplined, what remedy would you require? If you decide that the school administration acted properly in its discipline Mr. O'Connell, what, if any, advice would you give to the student's parent?
5. If you were the principal in this school, what would you do to avoid a repetition of this type of case in the future between students and faculty?

Case 3

In the Matter of Arbitration between
Minnesota Mining & Manufacturing Co. (3M)
             –and–
Oil, Chemical & Atomic Workers
International Union, Local 6–75

The Issue

The parties stipulated the issue in this case as follows:

> Has the company violated the collective bargaining agreement by following a practice of not using bargaining unit employees to repair personal computers?

The Facts

This grievance was brought by the Oil, Chemical & Atomic Workers International Union, Local 6–75 on behalf of the grievant, Terry Begley, and members of the bargaining unit. The grievant is a systems control technician employed by the Minnesota Mining & Manufacturing Co. (3M), and the union is his sole representative.

The union and the company are parties to a collective bargaining agreement. Article 2.01 in the agreement recognizes the union as the exclusive bargaining agent for all hourly paid employees designated in the bargaining unit. The unit includes all production and maintenance employees, including service control technicians. Furthermore, Article 8.17(c) provides that "Supervisory and other salaried employees will not perform the work of hourly production employees except in cases of emergency." The union argues that the company has violated the contract by giving to salaried employees bargaining unit work that should have been performed by service control technicians.

Two years ago the company purchased 4,000 desktop personal computers. Salaried repair technicians, who are not members of the bargaining unit, were given the responsibility for repairing those personal computers. The company claims that this assignment is a logical extension of its longstanding practice of having salaried repair technicians repair all of the company's office equipment.

The union disagrees and notes that systems control technicians, who are members of the bargaining unit, have historically repaired and maintained equipment associated with the operation, maintenance, and process control of the manufacturing processes. Because this has included working regularly with computers, the introduction of personal computers simply expanded the work that should have been made available to members of the bargaining unit. Furthermore, the union argues that denying service control technicians this work threatens their job security, for as computerization becomes more prevalent, bargaining unit members will be denied the opportunity to keep pace with changing technology. Therefore, the union submits that the company should be directed to assign the work of repairing and maintaining personal computers and ancillary equipment to the systems control technicians.

The Union's Argument

The evidence that members of the bargaining unit are qualified to perform the work in question is compelling. The union presented evidence that service control technicians have extensive training, both to obtain their positions and under a continuing on-the-job training program. Part of that continued training includes work with computers.

Personal computers are electronic devices that serve a purpose similar to the equipment for which service control technicians have always been responsible. Furthermore, bargaining unit members are qualified to service personal computers.

The union rejects the company's argument that the contested work is not bargaining unit work because it involves office rather than production equipment. The evidence shows that bargaining unit members already work extensively in offices, where they perform a variety of tasks in nonproduction areas. For example, service control technicians are responsible for lighting, for the entire heating and cooling system, and for the physical furniture.

The company claims that bargaining unit members cannot work on personal computers because they might gain access to confidential information. Service control technicians, however, are already entering the premises for other reasons; there is no reason to suspect their work with personal computers.

Finally, the union submits that service control technicians must be given the opportunity to grow with their craft. Assigning the repair and maintenance of personal computers and ancillary equipment to service control technicians would be a logical extension of work that they are presently performing and for which they are well qualified. Denying them that right threatens to render them obsolete in the future operations of 3M.

The Company's Argument

The company submits that by this grievance the union seeks to gain for bargaining unit members work that is not rightfully theirs. First, the company argues that the contract does not prohibit the assignment of this work to non-bargaining unit members; rather, it expressly provides this right to the company in Article 4, the Management Rights clause. Thus, the contract clearly supports management's actions in this case.

Second, the company submits that the contested work is properly assigned to non-bargaining unit, salaried employees. The company has never asked or directed office equipment repair workers to perform bargaining unit work, and service control technicians have never been responsible for repairing desktop personal computers. The salaried persons who presently perform this work are highly skilled in a number of areas for which bargaining unit members are limited by experience and training. They are cross-trained with respect to both types of equipment and product lines. Service control technicians are not expected to have that expertise. Furthermore, the nature of the contested work makes it ill-suited for assignment to bargaining unit members. The union should not be in a position to gain access to information that relates directly to the management of the company.

Finally, the company is puzzled that the union is alarmed at the possibility that technology may someday eliminate the position of service control technician, when it is technology that created that position in the first place. The company notes that no service control technician has been laid off or had hours reduced as the result of the introduction of personal computers at 3M. In fact, the position of service control technician is one of the more secure jobs at the company.

Questions for Discussion

1. If you were the arbitrator, what would you decide in this case?
2. What responsibilities should the company have to provide career opportunities to workers like service control technicians who are the highest paid members of the bargaining unit?
3. If a company offers training and promotional opportunities to jobs outside of the bargaining unit, should workers have the opportunity to carry over their union membership and coverage under collective bargaining? What would our labor law say in this case? What would good human resource management practice suggest?

   4. How should a company and a union handle cases like this? Is arbitration the best option? If you were the arbitrator in this case, what alternative ways might you suggest for handling such issues in the future?

Case 4

Productivity Bargaining for Meter Readers: A Mediation/Arbitration Process

In 2007 negotiations between Central City Electric Utility Inc. and the Utility Workers Union reached a settlement on a new contract on all items *except* the proposed revision of the work standards that govern meter readers. The parties were attempting to achieve a significant overhaul of work standards that had been in place since 1979. Because of the complexity of the issues involved, the parties agreed to establish a joint study committee to work on this issue for six months following the ratification of the other terms of the agreement.

   If the study committee failed to reach an agreement on new, updated standards, the parties agreed to refer the issue to a mediator. If mediation failed to resolve the issue, the issue would be submitted to arbitration. Both parties wanted to reach an acceptable solution on their own or, if necessary, with the help of a mediator and avoid arbitration. Arbitration was viewed by both sides as undesirable since the issues were extremely complicated. The parties estimated it might take up to 20 days of hearings to "educate" the arbitrator sufficiently to receive an informed decision.

   Despite good faith efforts on everyone's part, the joint study committee failed to make any significant progress. Therefore, a mediator was brought in with the understanding that the mediator would arbitrate the dispute if necessary.

Background

The current Meter Route Evaluation Program was developed by a management consulting firm in the mid-1970s and agreed to by the parties in negotiations in 1979. This program continued in existence to the present and consists of the following key features:

> Each meter route is composed of a measured eight-hour work day made up of six and one-half hours of field time and one and one-half hours of paperwork and processing time. Meter readers report for work in the morning and turn in the *prior* day's readings at that time. They then proceed into the field and are free to go home without reporting back to the company office whenever they finish their allotted number of meters.

Travel time and other adjustments for walking time are built into the schedule. Although the meter routes were originally established to require an average of 6.5 hours to complete, a number of improvements in technology and worker-initiated "shortcuts" have reduced the actual time required by most meter readers. Recent data collected by the company suggest that, on average, readers are finishing their routes in 4.5 hours.

   Over the 20-plus years the existing system was in place, a number of changes were introduced in the technology and process of meter reading. The most important of these, the use of electronic meter-reading devices called "itrons," was first introduced in 2004 and had spread across the system by 2007. Itrons allow many of the reader's tabulations and reporting tasks that had been done manually to now be done electronically. The itron is also fitted with a clock that provides management with significant additional information and allows for close monitoring of the reader's work practices and workday. Data are collected, for example, on such things as reader identity, car mileage, number of meters assigned, number read, number skipped (for example, because nobody is home), number not read, time the itron is energized, time of first and last read, and time between reads. In addition, the reader can enter valuable discrepancy data or any other notes on observations made during the time in the field that might be helpful to improving or changing routes or other operating procedures.

These data are used for a variety of management and control systems and are fed into a computer program that is used for setting and modifying routes to equalize workloads within the allotted field time.

A bargaining unit member is responsible for setting and adjusting the routes under the direction of a nonbargaining unit manager. Both the manager and the union member who sets the routes sit on their respective bargaining teams for the contract negotiations and therefore both serve as "expert resources" and are available for consultation in joint and/or separate sessions. Since they work closely together, these two individuals, as with most members of the union and management bargaining teams, appear to have good working relationships.

Future Technological Changes

While the itron represents the current stage of technology, new electronic devices are being developed that can be mounted on poles or in some cases on the meters themselves that would eliminate the need for meter readers altogether. Depending on the rate of capital investment by the company, these new devices could cover a majority of the meter readers' current work in 10 years. No significant introduction of this future wave of technology is likely to occur, however, for at least three to five years.

Pressures for Upgrading the Work Standards

Management is pressing hard to update the existing work standards for the following reasons:

1. Itron-generated reports disclose that the actual work time required by the readers to complete their routes has declined to an average of 4.5 hours.
2. The company realizes that it could significantly reduce its read-bill cycle (time between when a meter is read, a bill is sent to the customer, and a payment is received) if the meter readings were returned at the end of the workday rather than the following morning.
3. A 20-company comparison of comparable utilities showed that Central City had:

   A. The *highest* meter-reading expense per customer

   B. The smallest number of meters per route

   C. Average wage rates that were 25.8 percent above the mean for the 20 companies.

Given that the existing work standards and work rules were designed for an older technology and now produce the highest costs and lowest productivity in a group of 20 comparable firms, it was clear to all parties that some productivity improvements needed to be introduced into the system. The question, however, was what changes?

Management's Proposals

The company proposed the following changes:

1. Each worker would report twice a day—once in the morning and once at the end of his/her route when the itron would be returned to begin immediate processing and billing.
2. It was estimated that it should now take workers one-half hour less each day to complete existing routes due to the greater efficiency of the itron.
3. In light of the 30 minutes saved by the itron, the number of meters to be read per person per day would be increased from the current level of 240 to 300. Management's specific proposal when the study committee broke off deliberations was for a 25 percent increase in productivity, but management also indicated this number was not a firm demand and could be reduced if the overall settlement promised continuous future productivity increases rather than only a one-time improvement.

The Union's Position

The union did not offer a concrete alternative proposal but put a general offer of a 4 percent increase in the number of meters to be read by each worker on the table during the joint study process. The union leaders realized that further compromise from this number would be needed to get a settlement. But the union members were adamantly opposed to management's demand that they report back to the company office at the end of the day with their itron since that would eliminate their "incentive"—that is, the ability to go home as soon as they finished their last read. They understood management's desire for getting the billing out sooner but wondered if there wasn't some other way to accomplish this while preserving their freedom to go home when finished. Moreover, they suspected that management's real motive was to get them back to the office to "hassle" them if they got done "too early." Union negotiators also expressed a concern that this "speed-up" proposed by management was just the first in what would prove to be a continuous speed-up in work standards with no benefit to the workers.

Mediation

When he was selected, the mediator phoned the chief spokesmen for the union and the company bargaining teams to get some background information. Both the union and company negotiators indicated a strong hope that a mediated settlement could be achieved, thereby avoiding a costly, lengthy, and possibly unworkable arbitration award.

The mediator was warned by management that its team was under intense pressure to achieve significant productivity improvements from and greater accountability of the meter readers. Top management was frustrated by the comparative cost and productivity numbers presented above. Management was determined to get the data in at the end of the day to reduce its billing cycle and wanted the workers to report back to the office as a further check on the actual times required to complete different routes.

Although the union recognized the validity of management's case for improvements, there were serious internal differences among young and old union members. Furthermore, a change in union leadership was about to occur as the current president took over his new office as president of the state AFL-CIO. Another member of the bargaining team was to take office as union president. This new president was obviously not interested in accepting an unpopular new agreement as his first act in office!

After listening to a briefing by the union and management negotiating teams, the mediator offered the following preliminary comments:

1. It seems both sides have perverse incentives here. Workers are being asked to accept higher workloads now with no apparent monetary rewards. Moreover, under the current system there are no further incentives for workers to identify additional ways to improve productivity and lower costs.

2. Given that workers don't help find ways to improve productivity under the current system, the incentive increases for management to accelerate the timetable for investing in new technology that will eventually eliminate the meter readers' jobs.

3. The parties have no joint process in place for planning for the introduction of the new technology or for the retraining or transfer of current readers to other jobs in the bargaining unit or the company. Yet the parties do share workday schedule data—a union member manages the schedules with a management supervisor.

At a break the mediator described the problem to himself (as mediators are prone to do from time to time) as follows:

> Here I'm faced with a really complex, outdated system that needs fundamental overhaul and parties that face a lot of internal politics. Their working relationship, however, seems quite good. Moreover, we have on the teams the two best technical experts who know how the system works and clearly have more knowledge than I do about what alternatives might work and how different changes will play out in practice. Somehow I've got to tap and use this joint expertise to find a solution.
>
> Furthermore, there must be a way to create an ongoing structure and compensation arrangement that gives both parties an incentive to plan for the future and to produce *continuous* performance improvements rather than just a *one-time* jump from the results of these negotiations. But to do this we must give the meter readers themselves some incentive to participate with management in the benefits of productivity improvement and to overcome their fear of a continuous speed-up ending in the elimination of their jobs!

Questions for Discussion

1. If you were the mediator, how might you go about helping the parties find a solution? For example, would you spend most of your time working with the parties in separate sessions by shuttling ideas and proposals back and forth between the labor and management teams? Or would you work jointly with both sides in a common session?

2. As mediator, how might you draw out the expertise of the union and management technical experts who work with the key data as part of their jobs? Would a subcommittee be advisable? What guidelines should the subcommittee work under?

3. If mediation failed and you were the arbitrator, what would you decide? How would you increase the chances that your decision was workable and equitable?

Glossary

Ability to pay   Management's financial ability to meet union demands, which is determined by company earnings and assets.

Absolute union wage effect   A measure of how much union workers earn above what those workers would earn if there were no unions.

Accountability   Programs in the public schools that assess how well teachers are meeting school and student goals.

Accretion clause   A clause in a labor contract providing that any new plant not previously represented by a union will be automatically added to the bargaining unit.

Affirmative action   Programs aimed at alleviating past discrimination by giving discriminated workers preference over others in the hiring or promotion process.

AFL-CIO   A federation of national labor unions formed through the merger of the American Federation of Labor and the Congress of Industrial Organizations in 1955, with the goal of promoting the political objectives of the labor movement and assisting the member unions in their collective bargaining activities.

AFL-CIO Committee on the Evolution of Work   A committee created by the AFL-CIO in 1984 to meet, study, and debate alternative union organizing, bargaining, and political strategies. The committee has focused on how changes in the nature of work and demographic composition of the work force create the need for new union strategies.

AFL-CIO Organizing Institute   An institute created by the AFL-CIO in 1989 to engage in the recruitment and training of new organizers; it also provides affiliated unions with strategic planning and analysis concerning organizing campaigns.

Age Discrimination in Employment Act   Federal legislation passed in 1967 prohibiting discrimination in employment against older workers over the age of 40.

Agency shop   A contract clause providing that members of the bargaining unit must pay dues to the union covering the cost of union representation (but individuals do not necessarily have to become members of the union).

Aid to Families with Dependent Children (AFDC)   Federally created, but recently shifted to states, AFDC is a welfare program aimed at helping low income families with children by providing income and housing assistance.

American Arbitration Association (AAA)   A private nonprofit organization that facilitates the arbitration process by maintaining lists of arbitrators and making available facilities for arbitration hearings.

American Federation of Labor (AFL)   A federation of national labor unions founded by Samuel Gompers in 1886 with the goal of organizing craft workers into exclusive unions to achieve improved wages and working conditions and to protect the status of the trade through collective bargaining.

Americans with Disabilities Act   Federal legislation passed in 1990 prohibiting discrimination in employment based on disabilities.

Annual improvement factor   Annual wage increases in auto and other multiyear labor contracts usually equal to 3 percent per year in addition to cost-of-living increases.

Antitrust legislation   Legislation against trusts and monopoly applied to unions in the early part of the 20th century.

Apprenticeship program   A formal system of training and certification to obtain skilled workers.

Arbitration   A procedure used to settle impasses in which a third party (the arbitrator) makes a binding decision.

Arbitration hearing   A stage of the arbitration procedure when both parties present their positions and evidence to support their cases, usually initiated with opening statements by the union and management representatives.

Arbitrator's decision   The ruling of an arbitrator given either orally or in written form. If written, the decision typically includes a summary of the issues, facts, and claims made by the parties and the arbitrator's resolution of the grievance.

Attitudinal structuring   The degree of trust that exists in a relationship between management and labor.

Authorization cards   Cards signed by unorganized employees declaring their interest in unionization. Before the NLRB can schedule an election, a minimum of 30 percent of the election unit must sign authorization cards.

Bargaining in good faith   A characteristic of collective bargaining that is required of labor and management by the National Labor Relations Act. This has been interpreted to occur when the employer and the representative of the employees meet at reasonable times and exhibit both give and take.

Bargaining outcomes   The results of the negotiations process (the rights and obligations of management and labor) codified in the collective bargaining agreement.

Bargaining power   The ability of either party (management or labor) to achieve its goals. The parties are affected by the total bargaining power held by labor and management in a particular situation and their respective relative bargaining power.

Bargaining power model of strikes   A model that views strikes as a product of the militance of the union and workforce. During periods when the union's bargaining power is weak, the union is less likely to resort to a strike.

Bargaining structure   The scope of employees and employers covered or affected by the terms of a collective bargaining agreement, both formal and informal, centralized or decentralized.

Bargaining unit   The workers or jobs formally covered by a collective bargaining agreement.

Behavioral strike model   A model that views strikes as determined by the extent to which workers are integrated into society.

Board of directors   The top governing board of a company.

Boulwarism   A hard-line management strategy for regaining the initiative in bargaining used by General Electric in the 1950s. Under this strategy management polled workers to determine their interests, and then made one final offer in negotiations that reflected the financial condition of the firm and the results of the workers' surveys.

Broad bargaining unit   A bargaining unit that includes a number of skill types of employees. The broadest unit is an industrial unit including all the unionized employees in a plant (skilled and unskilled).

Bureaucratic pattern   A nonunion industrial relations pattern characterized by highly formalized procedures, detailed job classifications, and job evaluation schemes.

Business agent   An individual who operates as the chief administrative officer of a local union by directing the local contract negotiations and handling grievances.

Business cycle   Fluctuations in national output and unemployment. The U.S. economy historically has experienced sizable, although usually short, business cycles.

Business necessity   A defense to employment discrimination claims of disparate impact in which the employer can prove that a policy or practice that unintentionally operates to disadvantage some group of employees defined by prohibited grounds (i.e., race, sex, religion, etc.) is justified as a reasonable job related requirement.

Business strategies   High-level management decisions that involve matters such as investments, the sourcing of supplies, and production strategies.

Business unionism   The philosophy of the AFL and the dominant philosophy of U.S. trade unions in which business unions focus on practical objectives, such as improvements in wages and employment conditions, and eschew concern for broad political change.

Captive audience speech   A speech during a management-led meeting on company time and on company facilities during a representation election campaign used to dissuade employees from voting for the union.

Cell manufacturing   A production technique where teams of employees direct the operation of a group of machines.

Centralized bargaining structure   Bargaining that covers all the plants of a company and, in the extreme case, all the companies in an industry with the same collective bargaining agreement.

Chilling effect   A result that occurs when labor and management avoid making compromises they might otherwise be willing to make because they believe the fact finder or arbitrator will split the difference between their final positions.

Civil Rights Act   Federal legislation passed in 1965 that requires equal pay for equal work and disallows discrimination based on race, sex, color, or creed.

Civil Rights Act of 1991   An amendment to Title VII of the Civil Rights Act of 1964 strengthening protections against discrimination, including allowing for jury trials and awards for pain and suffering and punitive damages.

Clayton Act   Federal legislation passed in 1914, which declares that human labor is not an article of commerce.

Clinical approach   An approach to arbitration taken by arbitrators or the courts. Emphasizes the mediation of disputes, informality of procedure, and arbitrator discretion in helping the parties develop a working relationship.

Closed shop   A contractual clause providing that individuals must be a member of the union in order to be eligible for hire into the bargaining unit.

Coalition bargaining   Bargaining that occurs when the unions that represent different groups of employees in a company coordinate their bargaining against that company.

Codetermination   Employee representation on boards of directors and in works councils. This system is mandated by federal law in Germany.

Collective bargaining   A mechanism for organized groups of workers and their employers to resolve conflicting interests and to pursue agreement over common interests.

Collective bargaining agreement   The results of labor-management negotiations codified in written form.

Committee on Political Education (COPE)   A committee in the AFL-CIO concerned with educating union members on political issues and lobbying for union-supported legislative and political programs.

Common law   Court decisions that stand until they are overturned by a higher court or altered by legislation.

Commonwealth* v. *Hunt Case   A landmark case of 1842 that broke the courts from the criminal conspiracy doctrine by ruling that unions had a right to exist but that prohibited them from using coercive pressures to achieve their goals.

Competitive menaces   A term coined by John Commons to refer to the pressures employees faced from market expansion and industrialization. Commons argued that workers formed unions to counteract the effects of competitive menaces such as child, prison, or immigrant labor.

Compulsory arbitration   A dispute resolution procedure in which both parties are required to adhere to the settlement imposed by an arbitrator if they are unable to reach a negotiated settlement on their own.

Concessionary bargaining   The negotiation of pay freezes, pay cuts, rollbacks, or work rule changes that occurred frequently in the 1980s.

Conflict   A situation that arises from a difference in economic interests between workers and employers.

Conflict pattern   An unstable industrial relations union pattern under which labor and management are engaged in a struggle over basic rights.

Congress of Industrial Organizations (CIO)   A federation of national labor unions formed in 1938 with the goal of promoting industrial unionism.

Construction Industry Stabilization Committee   A tripartite group that reviewed wage increases and used its authority to reject increases it found were out of line in an attempt to control wage inflation in the construction industry in the 1970s.

Consultation   Informal meetings between labor and management to settle disputes.

Contract administration   The day-to-day implementation and application of the labor contract. The processing of grievances is a central activity here.

Contract ratification   A vote by union members to reject or approve the settlement of a negotiated contract.

Contract zone   The potential contract settlements created by the overlap between what management and labor are willing to accept during negotiations.

Conventional arbitration   A dispute resolution procedure in which the arbitrator is free to fashion any award he or she deems appropriate.

Cordwainers' case   A landmark case of 1806 in which the court ruled that efforts by unions or other combinations of workers to raise wages were illegal and that unions were "criminal conspiracies."

Corporate campaigns   An aggressive tactic by unions designed to increase the probability of organizing new workers by bringing public, financial, and political pressures on management.

Corrective discipline   Penalties that increase incrementally in severity to give employees the opportunity to reform their behavior; usually a part of progressive discipline.

Cost-of-living adjustment (COLA)   Increases in worker earnings based on increases in inflation.

Covenant of good faith and fair dealing   An exception to the employment at will rule recognized in a few states, making dismissals illegal where they violate a term implied into the employment contract that the employer will not unfairly or deceptively deprive the employee of the benefits of the contract, such as a dismissal to prevent the employee from collecting a bonus due to be collected for work already successfully performed.

Craft unions   Unions organized on the basis of skill or trade.

Criminal conspiracy doctrine   An early view adopted by the courts that labor unions per se were illegal.

Cross-sectional   Data from different individuals or firms (or other observations) at a given point in time.

Cyclical factors   Union growth factors influenced by the state of the economy.

Danbury Hatters case   A landmark antitrust case of 1908 in which the U.S. Supreme Court ruled that unions were covered under the Sherman Antitrust Act.

Davis-Bacon procedures   Procedures that pay workers on government-funded projects wages equal to those prevailing in union contracts in the area.

Decentralized bargaining structure   Bargaining that involves either a single or few plants in a firm.

Decertification election   A vote by employees in a bargaining unit to determine whether they desire to maintain their existing union representation.

Deindustrialization   The loss of manufacturing jobs and the industrial base of the U.S. economy.

Demand for labor   The quantity of labor employed by a firm or industry at various prices of labor.

Democratization   The spread of political democracy in countries that were previously governed by totalitarianism or dictatorship.

Demographic context   The factors in the environment that influence collective bargaining, such as the racial and sexual composition and educational attainment of the workforce.

Dependency ratio   The number of people not in the labor force compared to the number in the labor force.

Dependent variable   The outcome caused (explained) by various independent variables.

Deregulation   The elimination of federal laws that stipulate how firms in an industry should price their services and that restrict the entry of firms into an industry.

Deskilling   The lowering of the skills required in jobs.

Discipline   The punishment given an employee for not abiding by an organization's rules.

Disparate impact   Illegal discrimination in employment where a policy or practice that is neutral on its face operates to disadvantage some group of employees defined by race, sex, religion, or other prohibited grounds.

Disparate treatment   Illegal discrimination in employment where an employee is intentionally being treated differently because of his or her race, sex, religion, or other prohibited grounds.

Dispute resolution   The process by which labor and management settle their differences (i.e., arbitration, fact-finding, or mediation).

Distribution of income   The extent to which income is distributed evenly in a country.

Distributive bargaining   A win-lose bargaining process in which one side's gains are the other side's losses: also termed zero-sum gain bargaining.

Double-breasting   The existence of separate union and nonunion divisions within a single firm.

Downsizing   Plant shutdowns, worldwide consolidation, and technological updating of manufacturing facilities created a decline in the size of the required labor force for the average firm, displacing workers from their jobs.

Drive system   A workplace in which the supervisor exercises much control over the workforce, deciding matters such as discipline, hiring, firing, and pay setting.

Dual image of trade unions   Simultaneous skepticism of the political activities of trade unions and support for the social benefits of collective bargaining activities by U.S. workers.

Due process   Procedures that give employees the opportunity to redress managerial policies with which they disagree.

Dunlop Commission   Created to recommend whether changes in the practice of industrial relations in the areas of labor-management cooperation, employee participation, and workplace governance should lead to changes in labor laws and regulations to stimulate a better and more efficient working environment in the United States.

Duty of fair representation   The responsibility of unions to represent all members of the bargaining unit fairly and impartially.

Economic context   The economic factors of the environment that influence the bargaining process and bargaining outcomes such as the unemployment rate, the growth in the economy, and the rate of inflation.

Elasticity of demand   The degree to which the demand for a good or input changes when its price changes.

Election unit   The group of employees the National Labor Relations Board determines is eligible to vote in a union representation election.

Employee   The individuals (blue- and white-collar) who work for a firm or organization.

Employee ownership   A form of worker ownership in which employees of a firm also own a sizable share of the firm.

Employee Retirement Income Security Act (ERISA)   Federal legislation passed in 1974 that specifies minimum standards for pensions concerning matters such as funding, vesting, and the disclosure of information.

Employee stock ownership plan (ESOP) A form of worker ownership in which workers, encouraged by favorable federal tax laws, buy company stock.

Employer The firm or organization that makes decisions about employment practices and the production of goods and services.

Employer election neutrality A situation in which the employer neither supports nor opposes the union's efforts to organize a plant or company.

Employer federation A group of employers who join together to pursue their mutual interests. These federations typically provide member firms with advice and engage in political lobbying.

Employment at will A doctrine stipulating that employers are free to discharge employees without liability and due process, provided that the termination does not violate statutory or constitutional provisions.

Employment stabilization Management's use of extensive measures such as transfers, overtime cutbacks, and reductions in subcontracting to avoid layoffs during business downturns.

Enterprise union A union whose membership includes both the blue- and white-collar workers from only one company. Most Japanese unions are structured in this fashion.

Equal employment opportunity Programs aimed at providing equal wages for equal work and hiring and promotion decisions that are made without concern for an individual's race, sex, creed, or religion.

Escape A union avoidance strategy by management. Escape consists of finding, or threatening to find a non-union alternative location or a nonunion workforce to do the work that was previously done under a union contract.

European Economic Community (EEC) An organization of 12 European nations that regulated trade and political relations among them.

European integration The process of accomplishing the EEC's goal of eliminating explicit trade restrictions and standardizing government regulations over labor, product, and tax matters by December 31, 1992.

European Union (EU) Previously known as the European Economic Community, the 15 members of the EU will remove explicit trade restrictions and tariffs to create greater stabilization in government regulations over employment practices, products, taxes, and a common currency.

Exclusive jurisdiction The right for only one union to represent a designated group of workers.

Executive Order 10988 An order issued by President John F. Kennedy in 1962 that extended collective bargaining rights to federal government employees.

Exempt employees Employees who are not subject to the wage and hours provisions of the Fair Labor Standards Act, most commonly managers and professionals, and who are as a result not entitled to overtime pay.

Expansionary policy Political and economic policy, usually either monetary or fiscal in form, aimed at increasing economic growth in order to allow the reemployment of any workers displaced by inflationary wage increases.

Expedited arbitration A type of grievance arbitration procedure in which the parties agree to speed the resolution of disputes by bypassing some of the steps in the normal grievance procedure and adhering to tight time limits.

External environment The key dimensions (economic, law and public policy, demography, social attitudes, and technology) that set the context for collective bargaining and strongly influence the bargaining process and bargaining outcomes.

Facilitator An individual who seeks to create compromises in disputes between quarreling parties.

Fact-finding The process through which a neutral party analyzes and then conveys the facts of a labor-management dispute. Used frequently in the public sector, but rarely employed in the private sector.

Federal Mediation and Conciliation Service (FMCS) A federal agency that provides mediation services.

Final-offer arbitration A form of binding interest arbitration in which the arbitrator must select as the settlement the final offer of either the union or management.

Fiscal policy The tax and expenditure decisions of the federal government that affect the national output of goods and services.

Formal bargaining structure The bargaining unit (employees and employers) that is bound by the terms of a collective bargaining agreement.

Fractional bargaining The extension of bargaining down to the work group and shop floor level, where supervisors and workers often negotiate unwritten agreements or ignore certain provisions of the contract.

Free collective bargaining The negotiation and enforcement of labor agreements by the parties directly affected by those agreements with minimal government intervention.

Fringe benefit Compensation that supplements wages, such as a pension or health insurance.

Functional level The middle tier of industrial relations activity that involves the negotiation and administration of a collective bargaining agreement.

Gain sharing A contingent compensation system that distributes earnings to employees as a function of output or profits.

Government Local, state, and federal agencies that carry out legislative and executive duties.

Grievance A complaint by an employee (or union) that management is inaccurately or unfairly implementing the labor contract.

Grievance administration The processing and resolution of grievances by labor and management.

Grievance arbitration The final step in most grievance procedures in which a neutral third party is selected to resolve the dispute.

Grievance mediation A type of mediation in which a third party is selected to function as both mediator and arbitrator with the goal of mediating settlements to grievances, thereby reducing the frequency of arbitrations.

Harmonization The process of bringing greater standardization in the regulations, laws, and practices of the member nations of the EEC.

Haymarket affair An outburst of violence that occurred in Chicago in 1886 after a lockout of workers at the McCormick Harvester Works plant.

Hicks model of strikes A model developed by John R. Hicks that argues that strikes occur as a result of miscalculations by labor and/or management.

High-tech paradox The surprising finding that plants with the highest technology are not the most productive; generally these plants fail to effectively integrate new technologies and manufacturing practices with innovative industrial relations practices.

Home-based work The performance of employment tasks at home.

Homestead strike A strike in 1892 involving the Carnegie Steel Company and the Amalgamated Association of Iron, Steel, and Tin Workers that turned violent when striking workers tried to prevent replacement workers from entering the facility and fought with private security guards.

Hostile environment Illegal harassment of a sexual nature in the workplace that is so severe and pervasive as to change the terms and conditions of employment, even if not premised on threats relating to preserving or receiving job benefits.

Hot cargo clause A clause requiring that unionized employees in a firm not engaged directly in a labor dispute not handle goods from a company that is engaged directly in a strike.

Human relations movement A school of thought in the 1920s and 1930s that maintained that worker satisfaction would result in higher productivity and stressed the social significance of work and work groups.

Human resource management pattern A nonunion industrial relations pattern that includes policies such as career development, team forms of work organization, skill-based pay, and elaborate communication and complaint procedures.

Illegal subjects of bargaining Topics that may not be lawfully included in contractual negotiations, such as a racially discriminating clause, as stipulated by the NLRA.

Impasse The point in negotiations where no compromise appears achievable and a strike or lockout is imminent.

Impasse resolution Efforts including arbitration, fact-finding, and mediation that are used to resolve a dispute between labor and management.

Implied contract A contract that a court finds is implied to exist between an individual nonunion employee and an employer based on the statements or conduct of the parties.

Implied obligations doctrine The view that while management may have a property right to allocate the resources needed for the proper functioning of the organization, workers should have due process rights. This argument has been used by critics of employment at will.

Income security Programs that provide income support to laid-off workers provided through a collective bargaining agreement.

Incomes policies Direct efforts by the government to limit wage increases that have been adopted in some countries during periods of inflation.

Indentured servants An employment arrangement that prevailed in the colonial period in the United States under which passage to the colonies was gained by individuals in exchange for their services for a specified number of years.

Independent variable The manipulated or control variables that explain why a particular outcome occurred (i.e., the variables that cause an outcome).

Industrial relations A broad interdisciplinary field of study that encompasses all aspects of the employment relationship.

Industrial unions Unions that represent workers across a number of different skill levels.

Industrial Workers of the World (IWW) A union active in the early 20th century that supported direct action to improve working conditions and the creation of an independent political party to work for the overthrow of capitalism and the establishment of a cooperative commonwealth.

Industrialization The process of technological change and industrial development that brought forth economic expansion and modernization.

Inelastic A lack of responsiveness in demand (or supply) to price.

Informal bargaining structure The employees or employers who, even though they are not a direct party, are affected by the results of a collective bargaining agreement.

Institutional economists Individuals who reject the view that labor can be viewed and analyzed as a commodity. These economists study the role that history, politics, and conflict play in the determination of employment conditions.

Integrative bargaining A win-win bargaining process in which solutions to problems provide gains to both labor and management.

Interest arbitration The binding determination of a collective bargaining agreement by a third party called into play after labor and management have reached impasse, rarely used in the private sector but used extensively in the public sector.

Interest-based bargaining A form of integrative bargaining whereby labor and management jointly frame and solve issues in order to reach solutions that provide gains to both sides.

International trade secretariat An autonomous agency that provides information to member unions and coordinates union activities across national borders.

Intraindustry pattern bargaining The informal spillover of contract terms across firms in an industry.

Intraorganizational bargaining The presence of differing interests within the union and/or management.

Jawboning The attempt by government officials to convince labor and/or management to voluntarily settle on low contract terms so as to assist efforts to lower inflation.

Job classification A description of the skills needed for and responsibilities of a particular job as formally stated in a contract or personnel manual.

Job control unionism Unionism characterized by detailed and complex contracts that outline workers' rights and job obligations.

Job definition The breadth and responsibilities of a job.

Job security A clause in collective bargaining agreements that provides employment or income protection to workers affected by layoffs or plant closings.

Joint steering committee An employer-employee committee with the goal of coordinating participation, work restructuring, and collective bargaining activities.

Jones and Laughlin case A landmark Supreme Court case of 1937 that established the constitutionality of the National Labor Relations Act.

Judicial approach A formal and legalistic style of arbitration that has the arbitrator act like a judge and not like a mediator.

Judicial deference to arbitration The view established in the Steelworkers' trilogy cases that the courts would only review arbitrable disputes in exceptional circumstances.

Just cause The issue of whether management had legitimate reasons to take actions, especially whether management acted appropriately and fairly in disciplining an employee.

Just-in-time inventory system A system in which the firm maintains few inventories on hand and relies on suppliers for frequent deliveries. One of the central features of Japanese production systems.

Knights of Labor One of the most important early national labor movements in the United States. It organized workers on a city-by-city basis across crafts in the period 1860 to 1890 under the philosophy that all workers had common interests regardless of skill or occupation.

Labor A term used to refer to employees and the unions that represent them.

Labor law reform Legislation introduced into congress to impose harsher penalties on firms that violate labor laws and in other ways limit managerial efforts to defeat union-organizing campaigns.

Labor–management committee A group of workers (and possibly union representatives) who meet with management in an effort to resolve problems and improve organizational performance outside of formal collective bargaining.

Labor–management cooperation Efforts by labor and management to jointly solve problems (i.e., pursue integrative bargaining). Often involves work restructuring and participation processes.

Labor–management dialogue An effort to open communication channels between management and labor to solve mutual problems.

Labor–Management Relations Act (*see* Taft-Hartley Act)

Labor–Management Reporting and Disclosure Act (Landrum-Griffin Act) Amendments to the National Labor Relations Act, passed in 1959, that established reporting and disclosure requirements for union finances, specified the rights of individual union members, and imposed a duty on union leaders to represent their members' interests in a fair manner.

Labor relations staff The management personnel with responsibility for handling union-organizing attempts, negotiations, contract administration, and litigation with regard to union activity.

Laboratory conditions The notion that workers should be free to judge whether they want union representation in an environment free of coercion and misinformation.

Laundry list (of issues) A long list of proposals and inflated demands used by labor at the start of negotiations.

Lead teacher program A program that uses experienced committed senior school teachers as mentors and role models for younger teachers.

Lifetime employment The practice common to Japanese firms of employing employees from the time they finish school until they reach retirement age.

Litigation The legal term for the process of presenting and arguing a case in a court of law.

Lloyd-Follette Act Federal legislation passed in 1912 that provided postal employees with the right to organize.

Local labor market The employment opportunities within a specific geographic area.

Local union A branch of a national union often confined to a specific plant or geographic area.

Lockout The initiative an employer takes to close operations (and lay off employees) after an impasse is reached in contract negotiations.

Locus of power The amount of power workers and the union exert in society. Labor's power in national political affairs is a major component.

Longitudinal data Historical data that track individuals or some other observations over time.

Management A term used to refer to the individuals responsible for promoting the goals of employers and their organizations. Encompasses owners and shareholders of an organization, top executives, line managers, and industrial relations and human resource staff professionals.

Management by stress The argument that Japanese management techniques pressure workers to work exceedingly fast and under the strain of continuous peer and managerial oversight.

Management rights Contractual language or understandings that give management the right to take certain actions unfettered by contractual restrictions.

Mandatory subjects of bargaining Topics required in contractual negotiations, such as wages and other conditions of employment, as stipulated by the NLRA.

Marshall's Conditions Four factors that influence the elasticity of labor demand: the degree to which labor can be replaced by technology; the demand elasticity of the final product; the elasticity of supply of nonlabor factors of production; and the share of labor costs in total costs.

Means-ends doctrine The decision of the courts in *Commonwealth* v. *Hunt* to assess whether unions had abused their power or violated the constitutional rights of workers or employers through their actions rather than to conclude that unions per se were illegal.

Mediation A voluntary form of intervention in labor-management disputes whose objective is to help the parties reach a settlement. Mediators only make suggestions as their advice is not binding.

Mediation-arbitration An impasse resolution procedure in which a third party first tries to mediate a settlement and then acts as the arbitrator if mediation fails.

Microelectronic technology Technology that uses computers or microprocessors in its circuits or components.

Miscalculation   Labor contract negotiations in which either labor or management is excessively optimistic regarding what will settle or result from a strike.

Modular production   A new form of team-based work systems used in the clothing and other industries that is replacing the traditional individual jobs and incentive work system.

Molly Maguires   A militant society of Irish mine workers formed to aid striking miners' resistance to wage cuts.

Monetary policy   The amount of money in circulation and the interest rate; used by the federal government to influence economic growth. Monetary policy is set by the Federal Treasury Department and the Federal Reserve Bank.

Multilateral bargaining   Collective bargaining in which there are many individuals who have some managerial responsibility and input into management's decisions. This form of bargaining is common in the public sector.

Multinational firm   A firm or organization that engages in economic activity in more than one country.

Multinational unionism   Union jurisdiction or coordination that spans national boundaries.

Multiple interests   An industrial relations perspective that recognizes the diversity of goals and conflicts across the parties involved in the employment relationship.

Mutual-gains bargaining   See Interest-based bargaining.

Narrow bargaining unit   A bargaining unit that includes employees of only one occupational or skill type, such as a union that only represents police.

National Academy of Arbitrators (NAA)   A professional society of experienced arbitrators.

National emergency dispute   A strike or lockout that emerges from a negotiation impasse in a major industry and which causes major disruptions to the national economy. The NLRA outlines special procedures to be followed to resolve such disputes.

National Industrial Recovery Act (NIRA)   Federal legislation passed in 1933 that included language giving employees the right to organize into unions.

National Labor Relations Act (NLRA)   Federal legislation passed in 1935 that became the basic law governing private sector collective bargaining and unions in the United States. The purpose of the act is to promote the orderly and peaceful recognition of unions and the use

of collective bargaining as a means for establishing the terms and conditions of employment.

National Labor Relations Board (NLRB)   Five members appointed by the President and confirmed by the Senate who oversee representation and election questions, and investigate unfair labor practice charges and issue complaints over such charges.

National Mediation Board (NMB)   A board authorized by a 1934 amendment to the Railway Labor Act to conduct representation elections and to mediate disputes that arise during negotiations covered by the act.

National Trade Union   An effort in the 1830s to bring separate unions together into one organization to promote the interests of all workers.

National union   The national level of a union; the most powerful union body in the U.S. labor movement.

Negotiations process   The efforts by labor and management to resolve conflicts, typically involving tactics, strategies, and counterstrategies, until they reach a collective bargaining agreement.

New Deal   A series of governmental programs designed by President Franklin D. Roosevelt during the great depression to bolster citizens' purchasing power and to assist workers with economic hardships.

New Deal industrial relations system   Industrial relations activities characterized by managerial initiative and prerogatives at the strategic level, a central role for the grievance procedure at the middle level, and job control at the workplace level.

New Deal pattern   The traditional union employment pattern in the United States characterized by highly detailed and formal labor contracts, grievance arbitration, seniority rights, detailed job classifications, and standardized pay.

New industrial relations system   An industrial relations system that features employee participation in strategic and workplace decisions, flexibility in the organization of work, and extensive informal communication between labor and management.

Normative argument   An argument based on ethics or morals.

Norris-LaGuardia Act   Federal legislation passed in 1932 that outlawed yellow-dog contracts and endorsed workers' rights to form unions.

North American Free Trade Agreement (NAFTA)   Effective January 1994, NAFTA removes tariffs and other trade barriers across the United States, Mexico, and Canada over a 15-year period for the purpose of stimulating trade.

Occupational Safety and Health Act   Federal legislation passed in 1970 that required employer compliance with safety and health standards. Administration of the act is in the hands of the U.S. Department of Labor.

Ombudsman   An individual selected (typically by management) to mediate workplace complaints or conflicts as an alternative to the traditional grievance procedure.

Open shop movement   A movement that sought to discourage unionization through company-controlled unions and the expansion of pensions, welfare, and profit-sharing programs.

Organizational change   Efforts to reshape relationships between workers and managers through trust building or changes in work assignments.

Organizers   Individuals who rally employee support in favor of union representation during an election campaign.

Organizing model   A model of union representation which focuses a substantial share of the union's activity and resources on organizing through actively involving union members in the organizing process and in the internal operation of the union.

Outsourcing   When management contracts out work previously done by union members to nonunion workers in order to lower its labor and production costs.

Participatory pattern   A union pattern of industrial relations characterized by contingent compensation systems, team forms of work organization, employment security programs, and direct participation by workers and unions in strategic and workplace decision making.

Part-time   Working less than a 40-hour week.

Past practice   Customary policies or methods. Arbitrators often give much weight to past practice in deciding grievances.

Paternalistic pattern   A nonunion industrial relations pattern in which personnel policies are informally administered with substantial managerial discretion.

Pattern bargaining   The imitation of collective bargaining settlements by parties not directly involved in the initial negotiations.

Pay-for-knowledge   A step-increase form of compensation in which workers receive additional pay based on the number of different jobs (or skills) they are proficient at in the work area. Workers are paid their skill rate each day regardless of whether they are actually assigned to a job that requires the use of all of those skills.

Performance appraisal   An evaluation of the productivity and the contribution of an employee through formal evaluative techniques.

Permissible subjects of bargaining   Contractual issues the parties may discuss but which are not mandatory subjects, as stipulated by the NLRA.

Positional bargaining   A traditional form of collective bargaining that emphasizes distributive issues where there is direct conflict of interests between the positions of both sides. Labor and management are adversaries attempting to win concessions at some expense to other side.

Pregnancy Discrimination Act   An amendment to Title VII of the Civil Rights Act of 1964, passed in 1978, which provides that discrimination based on pregnancy is a type of sex discrimination.

Prehearing briefs   Statements presented to the arbitrator before an arbitration hearing in which the parties present their views of the issues, express their positions, and describe the evidence that supports their position.

Primary union effects   The extent to which a union is able to raise worker compensation through contract negotiations.

Private sector   Firms that are privately owned and employment opportunities within those firms (i.e., not in the public sector).

Product market   The firms that compete against one another in the sale or production of a good.

Production standard   Rules for or expectations about the pace of work, such as the speed of an assembly line.

Productivity   The ability to create goods and services; formally measured as a ratio of output to inputs.

Productivity bargaining   Bargaining concerned with improving output and performance through the removal of inefficient practices. Often involves a one-time buyout of outmoded practices to facilitate the efficient operation of new technology.

Professional employee   An employee engaged in work that consistently involves the exercise of discretion and judgment.

Profit sharing   Compensation awarded employees based on the profits of the firm (a form of contingent compensation).

Progressive discipline   Penalties that increase in a stepwise fashion after repeated offenses by an employee, such as the issuance of an oral warning, suspension, and then discharge.

Public policy exception   An exception to the employment at will rule making dismissals illegal where the reason for firing the employee violates a strong public policy, such as where the employee is dismissed for refusing to commit a crime.

Public sector Organizations and jobs that are part of the government (i.e., not in the private sector).

Pullman strike A strike by the American Labor Union led by Eugene Debs in the early 1890s against wage cuts. Federal troops were sent to enforce a court injunction against the striking workers on the grounds that they were impeding the delivery of mail and interstate commerce.

Quality circle (QC) A group of workers and their supervisors who meet with the purpose of solving production problems.

Quality of working life (QWL) program Activities oriented toward improving organizational performance and the working life of employees. QWL activities can include small work group meetings, labor-management committees, study teams, and the discussion of business plans.

Quid pro quo Illegal sexual harassment in which an employee is subject to sexually related demands based on threats relating to preserving or receiving job benefits.

Railway Labor Act The first federal law (passed in 1926) to endorse the process of collective bargaining in the private sector. The act provides railway employees with the rights to organize and to bargain collectively and was amended to include airline employees.

Rank-and-file members The membership of a union.

Recognition strikes An organizing tactic of unions in the 1930s and earlier in which workers supporting the union go on strike until the employer agrees to recognize the union as the representative of the worker.

Red circle wage rates Wage rates that cannot be downgraded in the aftermath of technological change or other organizational restructuring.

Relative bargaining power The amount of power held by labor or management in a particular situation in relation to the power held by the other side. This is heavily influenced by strike leverage and the elasticity of demand for labor.

Relative union wage effect A comparison of the earnings of union and nonunion workers given the presence of the union. Nonunion earnings are measured without considering what they would be if there were no unions.

Representation election A vote by employees in an election unit to determine whether a union is desired.

Representation gap The difference between the number of people currently represented by unions and the number of people who desire representation.

Residual rights doctrine The view that unions should not have a right to infringe on the ability of management to act on the owners' behalf, except in the case of an issue over which management has agreed to share its authority by way of specific contract language.

Restructuring Management's development of new work structures geared toward achieving greater flexibility in the deployment of the workforce.

Right-to-work laws Laws that make it illegal to require employees to join unions as a condition of employment (i.e., a union shop is not allowed). The Taft-Hartley Act allows states to pass such a law.

School-based management Reforms in the public schools that give teachers broader responsibilities. In some of the reforms parents and other community groups are drawn into decision processes.

Scientific management A school of thought developed by Frederick Taylor in the early part of the 20th century that blends economic incentives and industrial engineering methods. Scientific management advocates argued that appropriate task designs and wage systems could eliminate the sources of conflict between workers and employers.

Scope of bargaining The breadth of issues discussed in labor negotiations.

Secondary boycott An effort by a union to exert bargaining leverage on a firm by convincing customers to boycott stores that sell the firm's products or employees in other firms not to handle the products of the original firm.

Secondary union effects The extent to which a firm alters work rules and other practices to counteract the measures the firm took in response to the higher wages negotiated by the union. For example, firms often alter employment practices by increasing the pace of work.

Seniority-based pay A pay system in which wages increase with employee tenure, used widely in Japan.

Seniority rights The use of an employee's length of service to allocate benefits or job opportunities.

Service sector Jobs that produce some sort of service rather than a tangible good. Service workers include retail clerks, social workers, teachers, and the like.

Servicing model The traditional model of union representation that focuses on contract negotiation, contract administration, and the provision of various services to union members.

Sherman Antitrust Act   Federal legislation passed in 1890 that originally was intended to limit the power of business trusts, but which was applied to unions in the early part of the 20th century.

Shock effect   Improvements in the performance of the enterprise spurred by management's efforts to pay for the gains won by a union.

Shop steward   An employee who serves as the union representative who provides union services at the shop floor level when a grievance or other dispute arises.

Sit-down strike   Where the workers occupy the factory and refuse to leave the premises in an effort to pressure management. Used in the mid-1930s but later ruled illegal.

Skill (knowledge)-based pay   A wage system that provides greater pay (often in step increases) as a worker becomes competent in more skills and jobs.

Social Charter   A declaration of principles concerning worker rights issued by the EU. The charter favors giving workers the rights to form unions and to collectively bargain.

Social context   Social factors such as public attitudes toward and the public's image of unions that are a part of the environment influencing the bargaining process.

Social dimension   The regulations, directives, and laws that govern employment and industrial relations policies in the EU.

Social technical approach   The use of technology to decentralize decision making in organizations and to upgrade worker skills by broadening job tasks.

Solidarity   A Polish labor union led by Lech Walesa. The initial goals of Solidarity, in 1980, were to improve the wages and employment conditions of shipyard workers. Solidarity eventually became a broad social movement and Walesa was elected president of Poland.

Southern strategy   The construction of auto plants in the south by General Motors in the 1970s and the initial operation of these plants on a nonunion basis.

Spring Wage Offensive   The annual setting of wages in a handful of key firms in the spring in Japan. These settlements set a wage pattern that is followed by many enterprise unions.

State mediation and conciliation agencies   Various agencies that exist at the state level to facilitate the mediation of labor impasses.

Steelworkers' trilogy   A series of Supreme Court decisions (the first appeared in 1960) that elevated the status

and role of grievance arbitration. The decisions limited court review of arbitration.

Stipulation   A joint presentation by labor and management made before an arbitration hearing that out-lines the areas of agreement and makes it easier for the arbitration hearing to focus on the evidence and the dispute.

Strategic involvement   Participation by workers and/or a union in high-level business decisions such as product planning, sourcing, investment, and other broad issues.

Strategic level   The top tier of industrial relations activity that involves both managerial and union strategies and structures. At this level are shaped the goals that exert long-run influences on collective bargaining.

Strike authorization   A vote by union members expressing their support for a strike.

Strike deadline   The date at which a collective bargaining contract expires and a strike can start if a settlement is not reached.

Strike leverage   The degree to which labor or management is willing and able to sustain a strike.

Structural factors   Historical, political, and social factors that influence union growth.

Subprocesses of bargaining   The various aspects involved in the negotiation of any collective bargaining agreement. The subprocesses include distributive bargaining, integrative bargaining, intraorganizational bargaining, and attitudinal structuring.

Substantive regulation   Direct government regulation of employment conditions, such as a minimum wage law.

Supervisor   An employee who has authority, in the interest of the employer, to hire, transfer, suspend, lay off, recall, promote, discharge , assign, reward, or discipline other employees if such authority is not merely routine or clerical in nature, but requires the use of independent judgment.

Supervisory board   A committee of individuals who control managerial performance and appoint top managers in German firms.

Supplementary unemployment benefit (SUB)   Income protection negotiated by some unions to provide benefits during temporary layoffs that supplement unemployment insurance. In some industries, such as the auto industry, SUB benefits (in combination with unemployment insurance) can provide 95 percent of the take-home pay for up to three years.

Supply effect   The lowering of the wages of nonunion workers because of employment reductions in the union sector (and subsequent labor market crowding in the nonunion sector) caused by union-negotiated wage increases.

Surface bargaining   Bargaining opposite a representative who lacks the authority necessary to make commitments that will stick within the organization. Also known as shadow boxing.

Taft-Hartley Act (Labor Management Relations Act)   Amendments to the National Labor Relations Act, passed in 1947, that were designed to strengthen management's power by eliminating unions' rights to conduct secondary boycotts and outlining unfair labor practices by unions and rules governing a union's obligation to bargain in good faith.

Taylor Law   Legislation that regulates public sector bargaining in New York State. Deters strikes through a penalty whereby a striking public employee is penalized one day's pay for each strike day in addition to the day's pay the employee loses while striking.

Team form of work organization   A system in which workers are organized into work groups and perform a broader than normal set of tasks. In some teams workers perform material handling, inspection and repair duties, and budget and planning tasks.

Technological context   Technological factors in the environment that influence the bargaining process and bargaining outcomes. Important factors include the extent of new technology and the degree to which technology either leads to labor displacement or requires high- versus low-skilled employees.

Texas and New Orleans Railroad Company **v.** *Brotherhood of Railway and Steamship Clerks Case*   A landmark U.S. Supreme Court case of 1930 that upheld the constitutionality of the Railway Labor Act. This ruling marked the first time the Court had recognized the authority of the government to protect the rights of workers to organize into unions and to collectively bargain.

Threat effect   The fact that non-union employers improve wages and other employment conditions in order to deter their employees from unionizing.

Title VII of the Civil Rights Act of 1964   Federal legislation passed in 1964 making illegal discrimination in employment on the basis of race, color, religion, sex and national origin.

Total bargaining power   The total amount of power held by labor and management in a particular situation. This is determined by the economic profit (economic rents) available to both sides, which is affected by factors such as the extent of market competition facing the firm or the state of the economy and level of demand for the products produced by the firm.

Trade deficit   The amount by which a country's imports exceed its exports.

Trading group   The existence of strong connections (often financially based) between Japanese companies.

Transfer rights   Employee prerogatives that influence how or whether they can transfer to other jobs within the plant or organization.

Two-tiered wage agreements   Wage settlements that decrease the pay rates of future hires while they maintain or increase the pay rates of existing employees.

Unemployment benefits   Payments provided to laid-off workers through unemployment insurance systems. Federal legislation guides these systems, but the level and duration of unemployment benefits is regulated and varies by state governments The unemployment system is funded by employer tax contributions.

Unfair labor practice by employer   An action by an employer that interferes with or coerces employees or unions in their NLRA rights.

Unfair labor practice by union   An action by a union that interferes with or coerces union members or employers in their NLRA rights.

Union decertification   An election in which unionized workers vote on whether to terminate their union representation.

Union democracy   The extent to which union members influence union decisions and finances in an open and democratic manner.

Union density   The extent of union membership in a particular workforce. This is usually measured as the percentage of the relevant workforce that belongs to a union or is covered by a union contract.

Union federation   A coalition of unions that usually provides advice and engages in political lobbying but does not become directly involved in collective bargaining.

Union jurisdiction   The workers represented by a union. U.S. unions follow a practice of exclusive jurisdiction.

Union merger   The consolidation of two unions, usually intended to gain efficiencies, coordinate bargaining, and reduce rivalry.

Union negotiating committee   The union officers, staff, and members who participate in negotiations. This committee usually prepares for negotiations by meeting a number of times before the start of negotiations to formulate the union's list of demands and to form expectations about what the union can win.

Union Privilege Program A subsidiary of the AFL-CIO that promotes associate unionism and the provision of consumer benefits (such as credit cards) to members.

Union security A clause in collective bargaining agreements that provides either a union shop or an agency shop.

Union shop A contractual clause providing that all members of the bargaining unit as a condition of employment must be dues-paying members of the union.

Union suppression A management strategy to actively resist union organizing through threats or employee intimidation.

U.S. Department of Labor (DOL) A federal agency that serves as advisor to the President on labor issues, conducts research and collects data on labor matters, and oversees the administration of many labor policies.

Utopian movements An 1800s social movement that favored the creation of communities of workers, citizens, and consumers who would work and advance together in an effort to avoid the dehumanizing effects of the factory system.

Voluntary arbitration A dispute resolution procedure in which both parties agree voluntarily to submit a dispute to arbitration. The arbitrator's decision may or may not be binding on the parties.

Voluntary recognition An employer's voluntarily recognizing that a union may provide representation for their employees without the occurrence of a representation election. The employer can do this when presented with authorization cards signed by at least 50 percent of the election unit.

Wage administration The implementation of wages and wage adjustments on a daily basis.

Wage and price controls Direct efforts by the government to restrain wage and price increases, for example, through a wage and price freeze. Some governments have turned to these policies during periods of high inflation.

Wage-employment trade-off The extent to which a wage increase leads to declines in employment. This trade-off is determined by the elasticity of demand for labor.

Wage incentive systems The payment of wages based in part on piece rates or some other measure of individual worker performance.

Wage objectives The wages that management or the union desire to achieve through negotiations.

Wage–price guideposts Advisory or voluntary limits unions and management negotiators are asked to observe in their wage settlements by the federal government.

Wage reopener A stipulation through which the contract remains in force over several years, but wages are renegotiated at some specified point during the life of the agreement.

War Labor Board A government board created in both World Wars I and II with the purpose of reducing impediments to war production created by labor strife. The boards encouraged union recognition and pattern bargaining and strongly discouraged strikes.

Welfare capitalism Personnel practices such as job ladders, pensions, and various insurance benefits introduced by management with the hope that these would lead employees to shun unionism.

Welfare plans Employer provided health insurance and other benefit plans regulated under the Employee Retirement Income Security Act (ERISA).

Whipsawing Union whipsawing occurs when a union negotiates a bargain at one plant or company and then puts pressure on the next plant or company to equal or surpass the contract terms negotiated at the first site. Employer whipsawing occurs when management wins concessions in one plant or company and then tries to use this as a pattern for concessions in other plants or companies by threatening noncompliant unions with plant closings.

Wildcat strike A strike by a union that is not sanctioned by the national union. These strikes are typically illegal in U.S. collective bargaining agreements. Unions commonly gave up the right to wildcat strike in exchange for the arbitration-grievance system.

Work restructuring Rearranging the duties and the responsibilities of jobs or workers in an effort to improve organizational performance. The introduction of work teams, reductions in the number of job classifications, and the broadening of worker duties are forms of work restructuring.

Work rules Language or understandings that guide the way work is done and influence matters such as the pace and difficulty of work or the number and scope of job classifications.

Worker Adjustment and Retraining Notification Act (S2527) Federal legislation passed in 1989 that requires employers to provide advance notice to employees affected by plant closings.

Workingmen's political parties Parties that attempted to establish political coalitions to advance labor's interests active in the 19th century.

Workplace level The lower tier of industrial relations activity that involves worker-supervisor relations, employee attitudes, and other shop floor issues.

Works council A committee of employees that is given the right to discuss a variety of personnel matters and other powers through federal legislation in Germany. Works councils are a major feature of the German codetermination system.

Work-sharing Contractual provisions geared toward preserving jobs by cutting the workweek during output declines rather than by instigating employee layoffs.

Yellow-dog contract An agreement between employee and employer stating that the employee will neither join nor participate in union activities as a condition of employment. Such contracts were outlawed by the Norris-LaGuardia Act.

Name Index

Subject Index